Lecture Notes in Computer Science 15375

Founding Editors

Gerhard Goos
Juris Hartmanis

The series Lecture Notes in Computer Science (LNCS), including its subseries Lecture Notes in Artificial Intelligence (LNAI) and Lecture Notes in Bioinformatics (LNBI), has established itself as a medium for the publication of new developments in computer science and information technology research, teaching, and education.

LNCS enjoys close cooperation with the computer science R & D community, the series counts many renowned academics among its volume editors and paper authors, and collaborates with prestigious societies. Its mission is to serve this international community by providing an invaluable service, mainly focused on the publication of conference and workshop proceedings and postproceedings. LNCS commenced publication in 1973.

Adela Coman · Simona Vasilache ·
Fiona Fui-Hoon Nah · Keng Leng Siau ·
June Wei · George Margetis
Editors

HCI International 2024 – Late Breaking Papers

26th International Conference on
Human-Computer Interaction, HCII 2024
Washington, DC, USA, June 29 – July 4, 2024
Proceedings, Part II

Springer

Editors

Adela Coman
University of Bucharest
Bucharest, Romania

Simona Vasilache
University of Tsukuba
Tsukuba, Japan

Fiona Fui-Hoon Nah
City University of Hong Kong
Kowloon Tong, Hong Kong

Keng Leng Siau
City University of Hong Kong
Kowloon Tong, Hong Kong

June Wei
University of West Florida
Pensacola, FL, USA

George Margetis
Foundation for Research
and Technology – Hellas (FORTH)
Heraklion, Crete, Greece

ISSN 0302-9743   ISSN 1611-3349 (electronic)
Lecture Notes in Computer Science
ISBN 978-3-031-76805-7   ISBN 978-3-031-76806-4 (eBook)
https://doi.org/10.1007/978-3-031-76806-4

This Springer imprint is published by the registered company Springer Nature Switzerland AG
The registered company address is: Gewerbestrasse 11, 6330 Cham, Switzerland

If disposing of this product, please recycle the paper.

Foreword

This year we celebrate 40 years since the establishment of the HCI International (HCII) Conference, which has been a hub for presenting groundbreaking research and novel ideas and collaboration for people from all over the world.

The HCII conference was founded in 1984 by Prof. Gavriel Salvendy (Purdue University, USA, Tsinghua University, P.R. China, and University of Central Florida, USA) and the first event of the series, "1st USA-Japan Conference on Human-Computer Interaction", was held in Honolulu, Hawaii, USA, 18–20 August. Since then, HCI International is held jointly with several Thematic Areas and Affiliated Conferences, with each one under the auspices of a distinguished international Program Board and under one management and one registration. Twenty-six HCI International Conferences have been organized so far (every two years until 2013, and annually thereafter).

Over the years, this conference has served as a platform for scholars, researchers, industry experts and students to exchange ideas, connect, and address challenges in the ever-evolving HCI field. Throughout these 40 years, the conference has evolved itself, adapting to new technologies and emerging trends, while staying committed to its core mission of advancing knowledge and driving change.

As we celebrate this milestone anniversary, we reflect on the contributions of its founding members and appreciate the commitment of its current and past Affiliated Conference Program Board Chairs and members. We are also thankful to all past conference attendees who have shaped this community into what it is today.

The 26th International Conference on Human-Computer Interaction, HCI International 2024 (HCII 2024), was held as a 'hybrid' event at the Washington Hilton Hotel, Washington, DC, USA, during 29 June – 4 July 2024. It incorporated the 21 thematic areas and affiliated conferences listed below.

A total of 5108 individuals from academia, research institutes, industry, and government agencies from 85 countries submitted contributions, and 1271 papers and 309 posters were included in the volumes of the proceedings that were published just before the start of the conference. Additionally, 222 papers and 104 posters were included in the volumes of the proceedings published after the conference, as "Late Breaking Work". The contributions thoroughly cover the entire field of human-computer interaction, addressing major advances in knowledge and effective use of computers in a variety of application areas. These papers provide academics, researchers, engineers, scientists, practitioners and students with state-of-the-art information on the most recent advances in HCI. The volumes constituting the full set of the HCII 2024 conference proceedings are listed on the following pages.

I would like to thank the Program Board Chairs and the members of the Program Boards of all thematic areas and affiliated conferences for their contribution towards the high scientific quality and overall success of the HCI International 2024 conference. Their manifold support in terms of paper reviewing (single-blind review process, with a minimum of two reviews per submission), session organization and their willingness to act as goodwill ambassadors for the conference is most highly appreciated.

This conference would not have been possible without the continuous and unwavering support and advice of Gavriel Salvendy, founder, General Chair Emeritus, and Scientific Advisor. For his outstanding efforts, I would like to express my sincere appreciation to Abbas Moallem, Communications Chair and Editor of HCI International News.

September 2024   Constantine Stephanidis

HCI International 2024 Thematic Areas
and Affiliated Conferences

- HCI: Human-Computer Interaction Thematic Area
- HIMI: Human Interface and the Management of Information Thematic Area
- EPCE: 21st International Conference on Engineering Psychology and Cognitive Ergonomics
- AC: 18th International Conference on Augmented Cognition
- UAHCI: 18th International Conference on Universal Access in Human-Computer Interaction
- CCD: 16th International Conference on Cross-Cultural Design
- SCSM: 16th International Conference on Social Computing and Social Media
- VAMR: 16th International Conference on Virtual, Augmented and Mixed Reality
- DHM: 15th International Conference on Digital Human Modeling & Applications in Health, Safety, Ergonomics & Risk Management
- DUXU: 13th International Conference on Design, User Experience and Usability
- C&C: 12th International Conference on Culture and Computing
- DAPI: 12th International Conference on Distributed, Ambient and Pervasive Interactions
- HCIBGO: 11th International Conference on HCI in Business, Government and Organizations
- LCT: 11th International Conference on Learning and Collaboration Technologies
- ITAP: 10th International Conference on Human Aspects of IT for the Aged Population
- AIS: 6th International Conference on Adaptive Instructional Systems
- HCI-CPT: 6th International Conference on HCI for Cybersecurity, Privacy and Trust
- HCI-Games: 6th International Conference on HCI in Games
- MobiTAS: 6th International Conference on HCI in Mobility, Transport and Automotive Systems
- AI-HCI: 5th International Conference on Artificial Intelligence in HCI
- MOBILE: 5th International Conference on Human-Centered Design, Operation and Evaluation of Mobile Communications

Conference Proceedings – Full List of Volumes

1. LNCS 14684, Human-Computer Interaction: Part I, edited by Masaaki Kurosu and Ayako Hashizume
2. LNCS 14685, Human-Computer Interaction: Part II, edited by Masaaki Kurosu and Ayako Hashizume
3. LNCS 14686, Human-Computer Interaction: Part III, edited by Masaaki Kurosu and Ayako Hashizume
4. LNCS 14687, Human-Computer Interaction: Part IV, edited by Masaaki Kurosu and Ayako Hashizume
5. LNCS 14688, Human-Computer Interaction: Part V, edited by Masaaki Kurosu and Ayako Hashizume
6. LNCS 14689, Human Interface and the Management of Information: Part I, edited by Hirohiko Mori and Yumi Asahi
7. LNCS 14690, Human Interface and the Management of Information: Part II, edited by Hirohiko Mori and Yumi Asahi
8. LNCS 14691, Human Interface and the Management of Information: Part III, edited by Hirohiko Mori and Yumi Asahi
9. LNAI 14692, Engineering Psychology and Cognitive Ergonomics: Part I, edited by Don Harris and Wen-Chin Li
10. LNAI 14693, Engineering Psychology and Cognitive Ergonomics: Part II, edited by Don Harris and Wen-Chin Li
11. LNAI 14694, Augmented Cognition: Part I, edited by Dylan D. Schmorrow and Cali M. Fidopiastis
12. LNAI 14695, Augmented Cognition: Part II, edited by Dylan D. Schmorrow and Cali M. Fidopiastis
13. LNCS 14696, Universal Access in Human-Computer Interaction: Part I, edited by Margherita Antona and Constantine Stephanidis
14. LNCS 14697, Universal Access in Human-Computer Interaction: Part II, edited by Margherita Antona and Constantine Stephanidis
15. LNCS 14698, Universal Access in Human-Computer Interaction: Part III, edited by Margherita Antona and Constantine Stephanidis
16. LNCS 14699, Cross-Cultural Design: Part I, edited by Pei-Luen Patrick Rau
17. LNCS 14700, Cross-Cultural Design: Part II, edited by Pei-Luen Patrick Rau
18. LNCS 14701, Cross-Cultural Design: Part III, edited by Pei-Luen Patrick Rau
19. LNCS 14702, Cross-Cultural Design: Part IV, edited by Pei-Luen Patrick Rau
20. LNCS 14703, Social Computing and Social Media: Part I, edited by Adela Coman and Simona Vasilache
21. LNCS 14704, Social Computing and Social Media: Part II, edited by Adela Coman and Simona Vasilache
22. LNCS 14705, Social Computing and Social Media: Part III, edited by Adela Coman and Simona Vasilache

https://2024.hci.international/proceedings

26th International Conference on Human-Computer Interaction (HCII 2024)

The full list with the Program Board Chairs and the members of the Program Boards of all thematic areas and affiliated conferences of HCII2024 is available online at:

http://www.hci.international/board-members-2024.php

HCI International 2025 Conference

The 27th International Conference on Human-Computer Interaction, HCI International 2025, will be held jointly with the affiliated conferences at the Swedish Exhibition & Congress Centre and Gothia Towers Hotel, Gothenburg, Sweden, June 22–27, 2025. It will cover a broad spectrum of themes related to Human-Computer Interaction, including theoretical issues, methods, tools, processes, and case studies in HCI design, as well as novel interaction techniques, interfaces, and applications. The proceedings will be published by Springer. More information is available on the conference website: https://2025.hci.international/.

General Chair
Prof. Constantine Stephanidis
University of Crete and ICS-FORTH
Heraklion, Crete, Greece
Email: general_chair@2025.hci.international

https://2025.hci.international/

Contents – Part II

Interacting with Chatbots
and Generative AI

Exploring the Dynamics of ChatGPT Adoption Among College Students: A Comprehensive Analysis

Raina Dhaka[✉]

Underwood International College, Yonsei University, Seoul, South Korea
`raina001@yonsei.ac.kr`

Abstract. ChatGPT is an example of how generative artificial intelligence services have become essential to our everyday lives and work-related activities. However, there has been much discussion about their widespread adoption, especially in relation to their use in educational settings. Concerns have been expressed by educators about the growing dependence of students on ChatGPT for learning, with some using it carelessly to complete assignments. Nevertheless, there is a dearth of both a thorough understanding and practical solutions for dealing with this phenomenon. The purpose of this study is to investigate the rationale and approaches used by college students to utilize ChatGPT for academic purposes and daily usage. We intend to investigate how thirteen college students perceive generative AI, specifically ChatGPT, how they incorporate it into their assignment processes, and what concerns and recommendations they have for improvement. We did this through semi-structured interviews. Building on these discoveries, our research suggests design principles and significant implications to guide the responsible and beneficial integration of generative AI—including ChatGPT—in educational settings.

Keywords: Generative AI · ChatGPT · Educational Settings

1 Introduction

With the rise of services like ChatGPT, generative artificial intelligence (AI) has become an ever-present force reshaping both our personal and professional spheres [7]. Though there have been some controversies surrounding this rise in popularity, one of the most important one's centers on the widespread use of ChatGPT in educational settings [11]. Drawn in by the potential of generative AI, students are using ChatGPT and other similar tools more frequently as learning tools, but some are using them carelessly for things like finishing assignments [5]. Teachers are raising concerns about this new trend and how it might affect academic integrity and the educational process as a whole [8]. Even though this problem is becoming more widely recognized, it is still difficult to pinpoint the motivation behind and methods by which college students are using ChatGPT. Lack of specific knowledge and workable solutions to these problems impedes the creation of responsible and beneficial frameworks for the integration of generative AI in educational settings, even as educational institutions struggle with this technological revolution [10].

A. Coman et al. (Eds.): HCII 2024, LNCS 15375, pp. 3–12, 2025.
https://doi.org/10.1007/978-3-031-76806-4_1

Our study intends to perform a thorough investigation of the motivations and strategies underlying college students' use of ChatGPT in academic settings in order to close this knowledge gap. We aim to explore how thirteen college students perceive generative AI, with a particular focus on ChatGPT, and the subtle ways in which they use it to accomplish assignments through semi-structured interviews. Furthermore, through documenting their issues and recommendations for enhancement, we hope to provide significant perspectives that can guide the development of upcoming instructional strategies utilizing generative AI technologies. The results of this study have the potential to clarify the existing situation and provide useful suggestions and design principles for the appropriate use of Chat GPT and related technologies in the classroom.

2 Related Works

Significant changes have occurred worldwide, especially in educational institutions, since the release of ChatGPT, a well-known generative AI language service. Students were interviewed for a study by the New York Times [9] in order to learn more about their first impressions of ChatGPT. The results showed a range of viewpoints. While some students expressed skepticism about the tool because they thought it had flaws and inconsistencies, others saw it as a potential spark for creative learning. This study provides a starting point for investigating the various reactions that students have to ChatGPT.

Teachers' reactions to students using ChatGPT were complex. According to the Harvard Crimson article [3], some educators have embraced the tool because they recognize its potential to speed up tasks and improve comprehension. In keeping with the development of internet integration into education, the article also highlights the necessity for educators to mentor students in the moral use of ChatGPT. This offers insightful information about how students, teachers, and developing AI technologies interact dynamically.

Due to ChatGPT's user-friendliness, there have been cases of abuse, raising regulatory issues. The Technology Review [6] published by MIT explores the fallout from unethical behavior and the subsequent limitations that states, colleges, and universities in the US, Australia, and the UK impose. The essay emphasizes the need for a reasonable approach to regulation, taking into account both ChatGPT's possible advantages and disadvantages.

Susan D'Agostino's observations offer an important viewpoint on how educators handled the difficulties that ChatGPT presented [4]. Instructors changed their methods, creating assignments that were more complex than what AI tools could handle. This section describes the tactics teachers use to preserve the integrity of the learning process while utilizing ChatGPT's benefits.

By presenting ChatGPT's viewpoint on ethics and regulations, Sophie Bushwick and Madhusree Mukerjee's paper [2] presents a novel viewpoint. The article accepts that the tool has shortcomings and argues in favor of transparent disclosure and a regulatory agency monitoring its use. This source aids in the comprehension of the possible ramifications and ethical aspects of using large language models like ChatGPT in educational settings.

Based on observations from a number of articles, the general idea is that incorporating AI tools such as ChatGPT into the classroom requires careful consideration. Although these tools are beneficial for learning and increasing task efficiency, their misuse highlights the need for careful and thoughtful integration. This compilation of relevant works establishes the groundwork for a thorough grasp of ChatGPT's diverse effects in educational settings.

The above-mentioned studies and articles present a range of viewpoints regarding ChatGPT's effects in learning environments. Students' opinions range from acceptance of its potential for creative learning to skepticism over its alleged shortcomings. Teachers respond in a variety of ways, praising the tool's advantages but stressing the need of assisting students in using it morally. Misused cases give rise to regulatory concerns, which in turn lead to calls for balanced regulation that takes both benefits and drawbacks into account. Instructors' modify assignments to preserve the integrity of learning, a phenomenon known as educational redesign. Even ChatGPT admits to having flaws and is in favor of open disclosure and government regulation. The collection as a whole highlights the necessity of integrating AI tools into education with caution, taking into account both their advantages and ethical ramifications. Expanding upon the understandings obtained from different viewpoints regarding ChatGPT's influence in learning environments, our goal is to carry out an extensive survey to collect a range of viewpoints from students. The purpose is to learn about their experiences with ChatGPT and to investigate their opinions regarding the moral issues raised by its use. By doing this, we hope to find recurring themes, issues, and possible advantages that students may perceive. We will also examine potential approaches and resolutions for dealing with ethical issues, taking cues from the differing opinions expressed in the body of current literature, regulatory conversations, and educator responses.

3 Methodology

To understand how university students' using ChatGPT, we conducted a semistructured interview. The study protocol was reviewed and approved by the IRB of our institution.

3.1 Participants

Our main goal in selecting interview candidates was to make sure that a wide range of academic majors—including Creative Technology Management, Culture Design Management, International Studies, Business, and Economics—were represented. The goal was to assemble a diverse group that represented a range of nationalities and academic specialties. Consequently, we were able to successfully recruit students from a variety of backgrounds, including South Korea, the United States, Russia, India, the Netherlands, and the Philippines. We purposefully put recruitment notices on campus bulletin boards to draw in possible participants. Concurrently, we utilized a snowball sampling method to take advantage of current relationships and increase our presence among the student body. Students who had previously used ChatGPT, either occasionally or frequently as part of their regular activities, were among the selection criteria. It's interesting to note that a large number of the students who were hired mentioned combining ChatGPT with different generative AI tools. We were able to successfully recruit 13 participants in total, 9 of whom were female and 4 of whom were male, and whose ages ranged from 19 to 24. Despite the fact that the participants came from a range of countries, it was noteworthy that they were all very proficient in English. With this deliberate diversity in our participant pool, we hope to enhance the insights gained from the interviews and promote a thorough grasp of the experiences and viewpoints surrounding students' use of ChatGPT (Table 1).

Table 1. Participants Information

Participant #	Age	Sex	Major
P1	22	F	Technology management
P2	21	F	Technology management
P3	23	F	Information science
P4	20	F	Technology management
P5	23	M	Business
P6	22	F	Culture and design
P7	19	M	Technology management
P8	20	F	Economics
P9	21	M	Technology management
P10	24	M	Culture and design
P11	21	F	Information science
P12	21	F	Information science
P13	20	F	Information science

3.2 Interview and Analysis Procedure

The purpose of the interview was to get the participants' opinions on ChatGPT and other AI-related technologies. Notably, the students' responses varied greatly, indicating a range of comfort levels and attitudes. A few students answered with some discretion and showed hesitation in their answers. Conversely, some people provided in-depth analysis and demonstrated sincere interest in ChatGPT and other AI technologies.

One noteworthy finding was that a considerable proportion of the respondents tended to identify Generative AI primarily with ChatGPT. As a result, their understanding of AI as a whole was somewhat limited because they primarily associated AI with ChatGPT and related tools. This narrow viewpoint might affect how well they comprehend the larger field of artificial intelligence technologies. During the interviews, additional details surfaced, such as the fact that certain students answered questions with a sense of urgency. It's interesting to note that people who replied fast tended to think better of ChatGPT. On the other hand, individuals who had lengthier interviews were inclined to speak candidly about their worries and previous ChatGPT experiences. The contrast in response styles offers important information about the wide range of perspectives and backgrounds that participants in the ChatGPT and AI technology discussion brought to the table. All of these interviews were recorded and were transcribed for further analysis.

In continuation, a qualitative technique was used in the research methodology to examine and understand the information contained in the transcripts of interviews. During the data collection phase, all interviews were taped to guarantee accurate documentation. The recorded files were then transcribed to produce a large textual dataset that could be analyzed. The main technique for exploring qualitative data was thematic analysis [1]. This method is frequently applied to reveal insights, patterns, and meanings in textual data, especially when it comes to transcripts of interviews. All members of the research team read over every line in the transcribed scripts as the first step in the analysis process. The aim was to acquaint oneself with the subject matter and acquire a thorough comprehension of the interview results. Important sections of every line were then found and noted for additional examination. The group used highlighting, incorporating pertinent summaries or keywords to encapsulate the main ideas of the highlighted material. The next stage was to identify more general themes that revolved around these highlighted lines. The research team's cooperative conversations made it easier to find recurrent themes and overarching ideas in the dataset.

Team members had to go over the themes that had been identified and go back over the transcribed scripts in order to make any necessary revisions during the iterative analysis process. This iterative procedure persisted until all researchers arrived at a consensus, guaranteeing a thorough examination of the data. Three major themes that captured key patterns, meanings, and insights found in the interview transcripts were identified as the thematic analysis's final product.

4   Findings

Through the analysis, we induced three major topics on students using ChatGPT, main reasons why they use Chat GPT, their perception of Chat GPT, and their concerns about it.

4.1   The Main Reasons of Using Chat GPT

We observed various reasons provided by users. P1 emphasized that their main motivation was to save time and organize information, highlighting ChatGPT's effectiveness in gathering and condensing information from online sources. P3 provided an example of a recreational use case in which they used ChatGPT to write creatively and produce humorous content. P6 highlighted the model's ability to come up with original essay titles and help with coding, especially in Python. P8 demonstrated ChatGPT's ability to close knowledge gaps by using it for project guidance and idea generation in assignments. When given unclear assignments, P9 turned to ChatGPT for group idea generation and brainstorming. P10, who prioritized time management, utilized ChatGPT to accelerate assignments during periods of indecision, acknowledging its function in furnishing prompt resolutions. P5 demonstrated ChatGPT's versatility by using it for personal and design work, expanding its use beyond the classroom. In order to reduce the risk of plagiarism, P11 called attention to ethical issues, stressing the significance of avoiding direct copying and recommending the use of paraphrasing tools. The Perspectives collectively provided a nuanced understanding of ChatGPT's multifarious utility, which included considerations for ethical content creation, creative endeavors, and academic support.

4.2 Perception

The interviewees shared their experiences with ChatGPT from a variety of angles for the second section of the analysis, "Students' Perception of Using Chat-GPT," emphasizing the wide range of uses and viewpoints for the AI tool. The users—identified by labels like P3, P4, P5, etc.—share information about their experiences using ChatGPT for the first time, alternate applications of generative AI, their level of AI comprehension, and the factors that influenced their decision to use ChatGPT.

For example, P3 describes how she first learned about ChatGPT from a friend who used it to make funny stories. Later, the user investigated ChatGPT's usefulness for educational purposes, but stressed the value of human verification and advised against relying solely on the tool's results. P4 considers their experience, which began when AI tools were introduced in a class and was progressively integrated into assignments. The user notes ChatGPT's flexibility, emphasizing how it can be used to generate code and create images for design purposes. Users generally agree that AI technology is evolving, with P3 expressing difficulties in keeping up with the quick changes and advancements in the industry. Although P10 first admits to using ChatGPT only for homework, the user observes that ChatGPT's responses have improved over time, demonstrating the model's capacity for learning and adaptation.

P3 raises doubts regarding the veracity of the information produced by ChatGPT and highlights the necessity for users to double-check the information. P8 agrees, emphasizing the need to exercise caution when relying solely on ChatGPT and recommending a careful examination of its results to ensure accuracy. A number of users talk about their experiences using different AI tools; P10, for example, mentions using BARD in addition to ChatGPT to get more scholarly answers. P8, who views ChatGPT as a tool to supplement current skills, expresses the opinion that it is an enhancer rather than an enabler.

4.3 Concerns with Using ChatGPT

Concerns with Using ChatGPT', the third section of the analysis, discusses viewpoints and worries about students' use of ChatGPT. Like in the case of P1 shows doubt about completely relying on ChatGPT, stressing the necessity to confirm and double-check its answers to guarantee accuracy. P12 echoes similar thoughts when he draws a comparison between ChatGPT and Wikipedia and stresses the significance of verifying information gleaned from the tool independently.

A noteworthy apprehension expressed by numerous users is the possibility of plagiarism. P5 emphasizes how artificial intelligence (AI)-generated content could have a long-term negative influence on academic integrity and diminish the value of human labor. P3 highlights the necessity of human labor in group projects, arguing that the authenticity of the work is compromised by total reliance on ChatGPT. P4 and P11 talk about their worries about getting detected for plagiarism by software and how they protect themselves from it by paraphrasing and using other paraphrasing tools. Some users admit that the possibility of penalties or dangers from getting caught could have affected their choice to use ChatGPT. P6 and P12 voice concerns about using the tool; P12 specifically mentions researching alternatives because they are afraid of getting caught. Some, like P8 and P10, however, say they would keep using ChatGPT regardless, showing that they are willing to modify their strategy rather than stop using it entirely.

The ethical issues surrounding ChatGPT use are also covered in the conversation. P3 and P13 emphasize the significance of following academic rules and argue for stronger rules against copying and pasting entire assignments. P5 recommends using AI detectors, especially in research papers, to differentiate between content generated by AI and content created by humans. P11 suggests laws that target unethical content specifically, as opposed to limiting usage in general. Divergent views arise about the necessity of regulations. Some users, like P6 and P10, emphasize personal responsibility and the tool's potential as a learning aid, suggesting that strict policies banning ChatGPT might not be necessary. However, P8 acknowledges that AI is inevitable and proposes a middle ground for policies to more effectively incorporate AI into daily life. P12 concludes by offering an intriguing viewpoint on referencing ChatGPT responses and drawing comparisons to picture watermarking. By offering an approach to acknowledging AI assistance that is akin to citing sources, this proposal may allay worries about authenticity and transparency when using AI-generated content.

5 Discussion

The analysis of user experiences provided a thorough picture of ChatGPT's flexibility and adaptability, highlighting its vast range of features. A recurring theme among users is their gratitude for ChatGPT as a productive time-saver. They specifically mention how helpful it is for organizing information, summarizing content, and helping with coding and idea generation. Another common use case is academic support, which includes idea generation, task creation, and learning about difficult subjects. Though they acknowledge the model's usefulness, users also express conscious awareness of ethical concerns, particularly with regard to plagiarism. Users emphasize that ChatGPT-generated content should be used as a starting point for improvement rather than being directly copied, while also highlighting the importance of responsible use. Users incorporate ChatGPT into a variety of contexts outside of academia, including design work, trip planning, and general organization, demonstrating its adaptability.

Users express mixed feelings about ChatGPT, pointing out its advantages and disadvantages, as well as questions about its legitimacy and the need for human verification. However, they also recognize the platform's potential for growth in the future. Users discuss their experiences using different AI tools, which reflects a growing curiosity about experimenting with various technologies for a range of uses. All of the testimonies point to the complicated environment that surrounds ChatGPT use. Users emphasize trust and verification as key themes, expressing a need for independent validation and caution. Concerns about academic integrity and plagiarism are common, and users strongly disagree with using ChatGPT-generated content directly for assignments. Decisionmaking is influenced by users' fear of plagiarism detection tools, which makes them take preventative steps like paraphrasing to avoid attention.

Users prioritize ethical considerations, placing a high value on creativity and adherence to academic guidelines. Diverse perspectives exist regarding regulation, spanning from promoting a fair and impartial strategy that acknowledges the incorporation of AI in everyday life to demanding stringent guidelines in educational environments. They argue over whether ChatGPT should be allowed as an educational tool or subject to regulation to avoid overuse. To address concerns about accountability, suggestions include acknowledging AI assistance in a manner similar to citing sources. References and transparency are suggested as potential fixes. These testimonials shed light on the complex issues surrounding ChatGPT use by collectively highlighting responsible usage, ethical reflections, concerns about accuracy and plagiarism, and diverse viewpoints on regulation and integration into educational practices.

The research's conclusions, which came from speaking with college students, provide insightful information about ChatGPT's diverse role in education. Students use ChatGPT for a variety of reasons, from time-saving and information organization to help with coding and creative writing. Their opinions of the tool differ, with worries about accuracy and moral use countering considerations for its adaptability and potential as a teaching tool.

Simultaneously, we can see that responses from the literature review offer an expanded framework by enumerating previous research on ChatGPT. Examined are the opinions of students, educators' responses, legal concerns, methods for educational redesign, and the tool's own moral position. This review of the literature provides a starting point for comprehending the intricacies involved in integrating ChatGPT into learning environments.

5.1 Design Implications or Suggestions

Based on the findings, we suggest design implications for students' using Chat GPT in academic settings.

– Transparent Attribution: Acknowledge AI Assistance in Content Creation: Establish a policy that motivates students to openly acknowledge the use of generative AI in content creation—such as ChatGPT. To ensure correct acknowledgment of AI contributions, this may entail adding a standard attribution statement for content generated by AI.
– Guidelines for Ethical Content: Stress Appropriate Usage in Academic Work: Clearly define the rules for the moral application of generative AI in academic projects. Teach students the value of using AI tools responsibly, highlighting the necessity of using AI-generated content as a springboard for improvement as opposed to submitting it directly. This can entail incorporating moral issues into codes of academic integrity.
– Curriculum Integration: Include Artificial Intelligence Literacy: Incorporate curriculum modules on AI literacy to improve students' comprehension of generative AI technologies. Encourage students to use tools like ChatGPT responsibly by educating them about their features and limitations. To ensure that students have a comprehensive understanding of AI's role in academia, this could entail offering specialized workshops, courses, or instructional materials.

– Collaborative Learning Environments: Encourage Ethics in AI Group Discussions: Students should be encouraged to have candid conversations about the moral ramifications of applying generative AI to group projects. Provide a forum where students can exchange insights, worries, and best practices about using AI. This cooperative strategy can aid in the development of a community that works together to overcome the difficulties presented by generative AI in educational environments.

6   Limitations and Future Work

This study offers insightful information about students' opinions and worries about using this AI tool. Although the content is informative, there are a few limitations to take into account when interpreting the results: First, even though participants discuss the necessity of regulation, the research does not go into great detail about the precise regulations they have in mind. A more thorough analysis of the recommendations made by participants regarding ChatGPT regulation would offer useful information about possible governance structures. Second, the lack of viewpoints from educators with knowledge or experience incorporating ChatGPT into educational settings is another significant limitation. When it comes to integrating AI tools like ChatGPT in online learning environments or classrooms, educators are essential. Their viewpoints may offer insightful information about the possible advantages, difficulties, and moral issues unique to educational settings. Incorporating feedback and perspectives from educators would be necessary for a more thorough understanding of the tool's educational impact and to enable a more comprehensive evaluation of ChatGPT's role in educational settings.

Further research on ChatGPT may pursue various paths to augment our comprehension of user viewpoints. First, utilizing quantitative techniques like experiments or surveys could yield numerical understandings of Preferences and experiences. A longitudinal study might also be able to document how attitudes change over time and in reaction to new technology. The impact of cultural backgrounds on user attitudes could be clarified by conducting cross-cultural analyses. A more comprehensive viewpoint might be obtained by examining participants' opinions on regulation in greater detail and contrasting ChatGPT with other AI tools. Interventions in education that tackle issues of plagiarism and investigate how AI tools affect learning and creativity may prove beneficial. Finally, investigating cooperative AI solutions for group projects could assist in resolving issues related to impartiality and copying in shared work settings. These approaches seek to inform the creation of responsible guidelines and policies and advance a more nuanced understanding of the use of AI tools.

7   Conclusion

In general, a thorough investigation of college students' use of ChatGPT in learning environments has been conducted by this study. Through the use of semistructured interviews, the research has shed light on the various reasons, complex views, and justifiable worries related to the use of generative AI—specifically, ChatGPT—in academic settings. The results highlight ChatGPT's flexibility, making it a useful tool for students in both personal and academic contexts. It also has the potential to be used as an additional learning resource and save a significant amount of time. Nonetheless, the research has raised important concerns about moral application, possible plagiarism, and the necessity of clear crediting. The research's recommendations support design principles that can direct the responsible integration of ChatGPT into educational environments. These guidelines include defining ethical content guidelines, integrating AI literacy modules into curricula, highlighting transparent attribution practices, and encouraging cooperative settings for candid conversations about ethical issues. While offering insightful information, it is important to recognize that the research has certain limitations. The need for a balanced understanding of ChatGPT's impact in educational settings is highlighted by the potential bias towards emphasizing the negative aspects and difficulties, as well as the lack of educator perspectives. Subsequent investigations may examine quantitative approaches, cross-cultural evaluations, and remediation tactics targeted at resolving plagiarism issues. To put it simply, this study adds a great deal to the current conversation about the appropriate use of AI in education. The research findings have yielded useful recommendations that will assist educators, policymakers, and technologists in incorporating generative AI, like ChatGPT, into educational settings in a more deliberate and morally sound manner. These realizations help us navigate the rapidly changing field of AI technologies and provide the groundwork for developing frameworks that support ethical and advantageous AI integration in the educational setting.

References

1. Virginia Braun and Victoria Clarke. Thematic analysis. American Psycholoical Association (2012)
2. Bushwick, S.: Chatgpt explains why AIS like CHATGPT should be regulated (2023). https://www.scientificamerican.com/article/chatgpt-explains-why-ais-like-chatgpt-should-be-regulated1/
3. Weil, S.E., Duffy,H.: CHATGPT, cheating and the future of education: Magazine: the Harvard Crimson (2023). https://www.thecrimson.com/article/2023/2/23/chatgpt-scrut/
4. D'Agostino, S.: CHATGPT Sparks debate on how to design student assignments now (2023). https://www.insidehighered.com/news/2023/01/31/chatgpt-sparks-debate-how-design-student-assignments-now
5. Fyfe, P.: How to cheat on your final paper: assigning AI for student writing. AI Soc. **38**, 4, 1395ś1405 (2023)
6. Heaven, W.D.: CHATGPT is going to change education, not destroy it (2023). https://www.technologyreview.com/2023/04/06/1071059/chatgpt-change-not-destroy-education-openai/
7. Lee, H.: The rise of ChatGPT: exploring its potential in medical education. Anatomical Sciences Education (2023)
8. Nazaretsky, T., Ariely, M., Cukurova, M., Alexandron, G.: Teachers' trust in AI-powered educational technology and a professional development program to improve it. British J. Educ. Technol. **53**, 4, 914ś931 (2022)
9. Network, T.L.: What students are saying about chatgpt (2023). https://www.nytimes.com/2023/02/02/learning/students-chatgpt.html
10. Roll, I., Wylie, R.: Evolution and revolution in artificial intelligence in education. Int. J. Artific. Intell. Educ. **26**, 582ś599 (2016)
11. Tyson, J.: Shortcomings of ChatGPT. J. Chem. Educ. **100**, 8, 3098ś3101 (2023)

Optimizing Style Guide Prompts for Enhanced ChatGPT-4 Performance in Translation and Summarization Tasks

Zidian Guo[✉]

Middlebury Institute of International Studies at Monterey, Monterey, CA 93940, USA
zidiang@middlebury.edu

Abstract. This study delves into optimizing the performance of ChatGPT, in the realm of translation and summarization tasks, with a focus on the effective use of style guides. Conducted in November and December 2023, the research employed the latest version of ChatGPT to explore its capabilities and limitations in style guide adaptation. The study investigates how the design of prompts, incorporation of examples, complexity of instructions, and style guide format influence ChatGPT's ability to comprehend and accurately translate and summarize content. Results show that it is critical to align examples with instructions in style guide prompts for effective AI comprehension and performance. It is imperative that every element detailed in the instructions be vividly illustrated in the corresponding examples, ensuring cohesive functionality. Moreover, the research introduced a mixed approach to divide style guides by leveraging both attachments and prompts. It experimented with a customized spreadsheet designed for AI. The study employed confusion matrices as a quantitative tool to measure ChatGPT's performances with and without the approach. The results show that the mixed approach augmented the True Positives (TP) count from 44 to 95 out of 120 points that need to be edited according to style guides, and elevated the Recall rate from 36.67% to 79.10%, which underscores the effectiveness of the mixed approach in enhancing ChatGPT's adherence to prescribed style guides.

Keywords: Style Guide Adaptation · Prompt Engineering · AI-assisted translation

1 Introduction

Historically, Neural Machine Translation (NMT) has played a pivotal role in breaking language barriers, yet it has faced limitations in handling complex linguistic tasks that require adherence to specific style guides. The emergence of Large Language Models (LLMs) like ChatGPT has opened new frontiers in this area, offering enhanced capabilities in understanding and generating text in a customized style.

The study thus delves into the relationship between the design of prompts and style guides and their impact on ChatGPT performance. Through empirical findings, the research investigates how the structuring of instructions, the integration of examples,

A. Coman et al. (Eds.): HCII 2024, LNCS 15375, pp. 13–24, 2025.
https://doi.org/10.1007/978-3-031-76806-4_2

the complexity of prompts, and the format of style guides influence artificial intelligence (AI)'s ability to accurately translate content. The experiment was carried out in November and December 2023, utilizing the subscribed version of ChatGPT-4, which represents the most advanced iteration of the model. The aim was to delve into the capabilities of this cutting-edge technology, exploring its potential and limitations at the forefront of AI development.

The tasks assigned to ChatGPT in this experiment is to translate and summarize an English news article into a Chinese news brief, with format and language handled according to style guides. Materials used for this research, including example texts, glossary, and style guides, are derived from the newsletter production team of the Institute for AI International Governance of Tsinghua University (I-AIIG).

The task involves a blend of translation and summarization. ChatGPT is required to distill extensive English texts, often running into thousands of words, into concise Chinese newsletters comprising only a few hundred characters. It used to be a challenging process for linguists, as human linguists must navigate through a dense landscape of specialized terminologies and jargons, which in our case, constitute a significant portion of the language used, far exceeding the typical frequency in the general domain. At the I-AIIG, the intricate translation and summarization tasks are meticulously executed by a team of skilled human linguists equipped with translation technology, and subject matter experts who bring specialized knowledge in the subject matter field. Together, they ensure the precision and appropriateness of language and terminology used.

The inherent complexity of this work is evident in the time-consuming and demanding nature of the process. Such a specialized task demands detailed guidelines on restructuring information and translating terminologies and proper nouns, which forms the bedrock for the AI style guide learning and adaptation experiments.

Upon the background, this research seeks to answer a pivotal question: How can we optimize prompt and style guide design to maximize the translation and localization capabilities of AI language models? The findings and methodologies presented here aim to contribute to the field of AI-assisted translation and localization, offering insights into creating more efficient and effective AI interactions in these domains.

2 Methodology

The dataset needed for the experiments comprises style guides designed by me for the I-AIIG, and example texts sourced from the institute. For data analysis, the study employs the confusion matrices to measure and compare ChatGPT's performance upon different strategies. The matrix is divided into four parts:

TP (True Positives: Instances Correctly Predicted as Positive). In this study, TP refers to the amount of instances of correct editing conducted by ChatGPT according to style guides;

FN (False Negatives: Instances Incorrectly Predicted as Negative. In this study, FN refers to the number of instances where ChatGPT fails to make a necessary edit according to the style guide. For example, if the style guide dictates a specific format for dates, and ChatGPT fails to format a date accordingly, this would be a FN.

TN (True Negatives: Instances Correctly Predicted as Negative). In this study and in the localization industry, where style guides must always be complied with, the concept of TN is essentially non-existent, and the data is calculated as 0.

FP (False Positives: Instances Incorrectly Predicted as Positive). In this study, FP refers to the amount of incorrect or unnecessary editing made by ChatGPT (Table 1).

Table 1. The Confusion Matrix

		True Values	
		True	False
Predic-tion	True	TP Correct result	FP Unexpected result
	False	FN Missing result	TN Coorext absence of result

With the four data points, the study may calculate the Precision, Recall, and F1-score metrics.

Precision measures the accuracy of positive predictions. It is the ratio of true positives to the sum of true and false positives.

$$Precision = TP(TP + FP) \qquad (1)$$

Recall measures the fraction of positives that were correctly identified. It is the ratio of true positives to the sum of true positives and false negatives. By the nature of the study's design, Recall becomes the most relevant metric, as it directly measures the proportion of correct edits made by ChatGPT out of all the edits that should have been made according to the style guides.

$$Recall = TP(TP + FN) \qquad (2)$$

F1-Score: This is the harmonic mean of precision and recall, providing a balance between them. It's particularly useful when the class distribution is imbalanced.

$$F1 \, Score = 2(Precision \, Recall/Precision + Recall) \qquad (3)$$

The evaluation of ChatGPT's performance was based on the adherence to style guides, focusing on both the direct interpretation of instructions and the application of examples provided in the guides.

In the pursuit of a rigorous and comprehensive evaluation of ChatGPT's adherence to style guides in translation and summarization tasks, this study incorporates human evaluation.

3 Results

3.1 Style Guides Delivery by Prompting

To prompt style guides to ChatGPT essentially constitute a list of guidelines akin to those found in traditional linguistic style guide documents. The key distinction lies in presenting these instructions in positive and complete sentences to facilitate ChatGPT's comprehension; this is crucial as negative phrasing can impede ChatGPT's adherence to instructions.

In the initial phase of this experiment, the prompt did not fully demonstrate all the mentioned style guidelines. For instance, only the guideline pertaining to date formatting was exemplified. The initial expectation was for ChatGPT to learn how to translate and edit through the instructions and grasp the construction of a newsletter from the example, thereby enabling the two elements to work in tandem. The prompt was crafted as follows to test this hypothesis:

Prompt 1. I am going to assign you a translation and summarization task from English to Chinese. I need you to learn from style guides and examples.

- Stye Guide:

  1. All kinds of text should be summarized into only one paragraph
  2. Put the title in a pair of []
  3. Start the text with date under the format of "x月y日"
  4. Removes the press, the publishing time of the source text, any metadata about the illustration, and jumps to the body.
  5. When you encounter an English name, leave it in English.
  6. Terminology: Provide their Chinese translation with the English term. Put the English term outside the quotation marks. E.g., "持久参与理论" (Persistent Engagement Theory).
  7. Abbreviations: Include the full English name followed by the abbreviation in parentheses. E.g., 国防创新小组(Defense Innovation Unit,简称DIU).
  8. Book/Article Titles: Provide their Chinese translation with the English term. Put the English term outside the Chinese book title marks. Example:《在线安全法案》(Online Safety Bill).

- Examples:

  [Meta推出生成式人工智能语音模型Voicebox]
  6月23日,Meta推出生成式人工智能语音模型Voicebox,该模型可利用长度仅为两秒的音频样本和附带文本生成不同风格的语音。Voicebox可以根据文本及语音匹配对应的风格,也可用于编辑音频,如消除狗叫声或远处汽车喇叭的背景噪音。其编辑过程的工作原理是重新生成被噪音打断的语音部分,从而无需重新录制整段音频。Voicebox为多语言模型,可以生成包括英语、法语、德语、西班牙语、波兰语和葡萄牙语在内的六种语言。即使音频样本和附带文本使用不同的语言,Voicebox也可以生成不同语言的版本。不过,考虑到模型可能会被恶意使用,该模型暂不公开发布。

- Text to be edited:

UK Treasury drops plans for Royal Mint NFT

The United Kingdom has shelved plans to launch a government-backed "NFT for Britain," which was initially proposed by crypto-friendly Prime Minister Rishi Sunak.

While serving as chancellor of the Exchequer, the equivalent of a chief financial minister, Sunak asked the Royal Mint in April 2022 to create an "NFT for Britain" as part of the government's "ambition to make the UK a global hub for crypto-asset technology and investment."

The project was meant to be launched by the summer of 2022, but has ultimately failed to meet the deadline.

Asked by the chair of the Treasury Select Committee whether there was still a plan for the Royal Mint to issue a nonfungible token on March 27, Economic Secretary of the Treasury Andrew Griffith noted that:

"In consultation with HM Treasury, the Royal Mint is not proceeding with the launch of a Non-Fungible Token at this time but will keep this proposal under review."

Harriet Baldwin, the chair of the Treasury Select Committee who posed the question in Parliament, was later quoted in a March 26 BBC report as saying:

"We have not yet seen a lot of evidence that our constituents should be putting their money in these speculative tokens unless they are prepared to lose all their money."

"So perhaps that is why the Royal Mint has made this decision in conjunction with the Treasury," she added.

The NFT for Britain concept ultimately appears to be quite vague, as the Royal Mint and Treasury haven't elaborated on what the NFTs would do and how they would be used.

At the time of the initial announcement, it was simply stated that more details would be announced "soon," while opponents of the plan, such as Labor MP and Shadow Chancellor Rachel Reeves, questioned Sunak's priorities.

"The country is facing a severe cost of living crisis made worse by this chancellor's choices. This is his priority right now. Hopeless," she said last year.[1]

However, ChatGPT did not adhere to the instructions regarding neither newsletter format nor proper nouns. Instead of creating a concise news brief, it expanded the English news into several paragraphs and translated English names into Chinese, contrary to the style guide's requirements. Additionally, ChatGPT did not provide full names for abbreviations as required. This pattern of non-compliance with the style guide was consistent across multiple new chats (Fig. 1).

In response to these insights, the example was redesigned to incorporate each element mentioned in the style guide instructions and initiated a new chat with ChatGPT. The revised prompt was crafted as follows: (the text to be edited, similar to the above, are omitted for brevity.)

Prompt 2. I am going to assign you a translation and summarization task from English to Chinese. I need you to learn from style guides and examples.

---

[1] Text to be edited: Brian Quarmby, "UK Treasury drops plans for Royal Mint NFT." Cointelegraph, 28 March. 2023, https://cointelegraph.com/news/uk-treasury-drops-plans-for-royal-mint-nft.

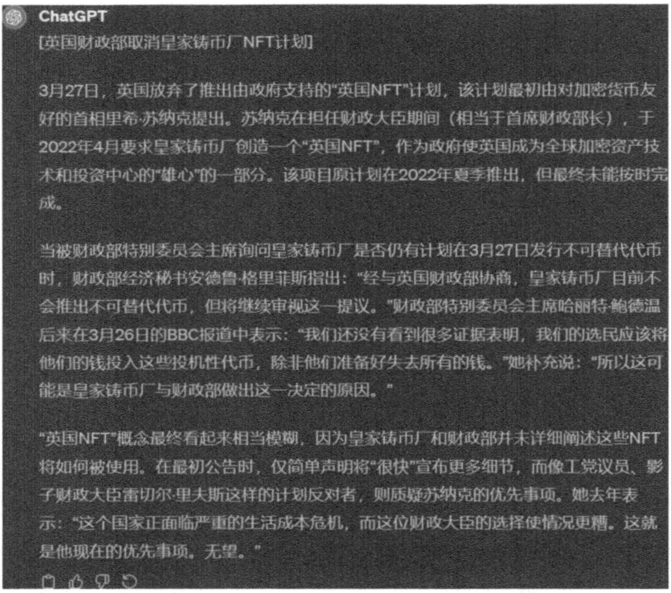

ChatGPT

[英国财政部取消皇家铸币厂NFT计划]

3月27日，英国放弃了推出由政府支持的“英国NFT”计划，该计划最初由对加密货币友好的首相里希·苏纳克提出。苏纳克在担任财政大臣期间（相当于首席财政部长），于2022年4月要求皇家铸币厂创造一个“英国NFT”，作为政府使英国成为全球加密资产技术和投资中心的“雄心”的一部分。该项目原计划在2022年夏季推出，但最终未能按时完成。

当被财政部特别委员会主席询问皇家铸币厂是否仍有计划在3月27日发行不可替代代币时，财政部经济秘书安德鲁·格里菲斯指出：“经与英国财政部协商，皇家铸币厂目前不会推出不可替代代币，但将继续审视这一提议。”财政部特别委员会主席哈丽特·鲍德温后来在3月26日的BBC报道中表示：“我们还没有看到很多证据表明，我们的选民应该将他们的钱投入这些投机性代币，除非他们准备好失去所有的钱。”她补充说：“所以这可能是皇家铸币厂与财政部做出这一决定的原因。”

“英国NFT”概念最终看起来相当模糊，因为皇家铸币厂和财政部并未详细阐述这些NFT将如何被使用。在最初公告时，仅简单声明将“很快”宣布更多细节，而像工党议员、影子财政大臣雷切尔·里夫斯这样的计划反对者，则质疑苏纳克的优先事项。她去年表示：“这个国家正面临严重的生活成本危机，而这位财政大臣的选择使情况更糟。这就是他现在的优先事项。无望。”

Fig. 1. ChatGPT’s response when instructions and examples were not aligned[2]

- Stye Guide:

  1. All kinds of text should be summarized into only one paragraph
  2. Put the title in a pair of []
  3. Start the text with date under the format of “x月y日”
  4. Removes the press, the publishing time of the source text, any metadata about the illustration, and jumps to the body.
  5. When you encounter an English name, leave it in English.
  6. Terminology: Provide their Chinese translation with the English term. Put the English term outside the quotation marks. E.g., “持久参与理论” (Persistent Engagement Theory).
  7. Abbreviations: Include the full English name followed by the abbreviation in parentheses. E.g., 国防创新小组(Defense Innovation Unit,简称DIU).
  8. Book/Article Titles: Provide their Chinese translation with the English term. Put the English term outside the Chinese book title marks. Example:《在线安全法案》(Online Safety Bill).

- Examples:

  「人工智能辅助抗癌药物研发」

  3月27日,《化学科学》(Chemical Science) 上发表的一篇论文指出,Insilico 医药公司的科学家使用 DeepMind 公司开发的人工智能工具 AlphaFold 预测蛋白质的结构, 加速治疗肝细胞癌药物的研发。该研究由诺贝尔奖获得者 Michael

[2] https://chat.openai.com/share/4b41a10c-ad28-4299-88b0-66812ac13e52.

Levitt、英矽智能创始人兼首席执行官 Alex Zhavoronkov 领导,"多伦多大学加速联盟" (Toronto Acceleration Consortium)参与研发。肝细胞癌 (Hepatocellular carcinoma cancer,简称HCC)是最为常见的癌症。这项研究为制药公司进入临床试验阶段提供了概念证明。与此同时,Insilico公司正在研究如何使用人工智能来简化该药物的临床试验阶段。

- Text to be edited:

This adjustment led to a notable improvement in ChatGPT's performance. The AI model accurately rendered proper nouns and abbreviations in accordance with the style guide, affirming the importance of aligning instructions with examples (Fig. 2).

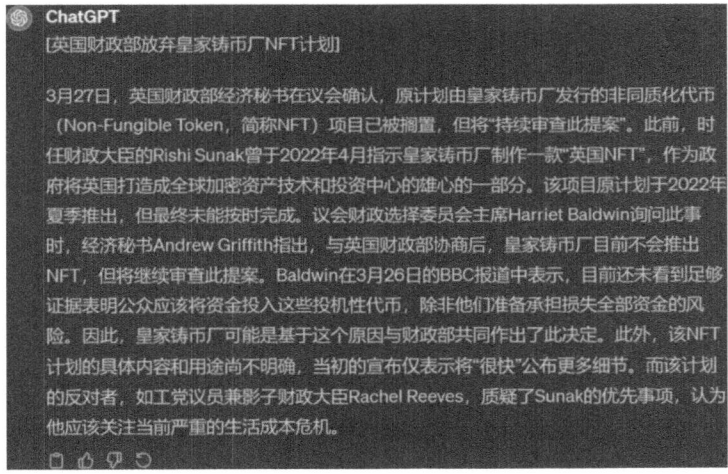

Fig. 2. ChatGPT's response when instructions and examples were aligned[3]

A key observation is the need for a strong alignment between the instructions and the examples. The examples must not only reflect but also encompass all aspects of the style guides as outlined in the instructions. This overlap is essential; any disconnect between the two can result in confusion for the AI model, leading to inconsistent or irrelevant content generation. ChatGPT, typically not soliciting clarifications, may struggle in such scenarios.

It is demonstrated that a harmonious alignment between examples and instructions is imperative. It is essential that all elements outlined in the instructions are explicitly demonstrated in the accompanying examples, ensuring that they function cohesively. The experiments highlighted that providing either examples or instructions in isolation is inadequate, as each alone leads to suboptimal performance by ChatGPT. Thus, the synergy of both examples and instructions is crucial for ChatGPT to deliver accurate and effective results.

---

[3] https://chat.openai.com/share/5d16abfa-5cdf-4ded-b45b-cd743d724701.

3.2   Style Guides Delivery by Both Prompting and Attachment

In the prior experiments, it has been evident that ChatGPT struggled with handling abbreviations, even after multiple attempts to rephrase the prompt in various ways. According to the style guide, linguists must provide the full English name followed by the Chinese translation of each abbreviation upon its first appearance in the text. For instance, the first appearance of 'DIU' should be translated into:

国防创新小组 (Defense Innovation Unit, 简称DIU)

Chinese	English Full	English
Translation	Name	Abbreviation

It is assumed this particular aspect of the style guide poses a significant challenge for ChatGPT because the task requires not just editing, but also an intuitive capacity to conduct research or reference its database to deduce the full name of an abbreviation based on the context. Such complexity appears to exceed ChatGPT's computational capabilities when it has to comply with many other instructions. This difficulty has proven to be an insightful revelation about ChatGPT's functional limits and serves as a critical point of reference.

To address this, this research experimented with a mixed approach, leveraging both prompting and attachment to deliver a style guide to the AI model. The approach is an integration of a style guide prompt and a glossary attachment, wherein the translation of abbreviations was pre-prepared by human linguists in accordance with the style guide.

In this approach, the glossary is structured in a manner that deviates from conventional formats. Traditionally, a glossary would present a column of source-language terminology directly paired with its target-language equivalent, accompanied by other metadata in specific data categories [1]. However, in this instance, the glossary serves as a ready-to-use reference for ChatGPT to efficiently 'copy and paste' the pre-edited translation of abbreviations. Below is a screenshot of a part of the glossary (Fig. 3):

For the purposes of this experiment, ChatGPT was provided with a glossary attachment containing 672 abbreviations. The task was for ChatGPT to reference this glossary during translation and summarization tasks, while concurrently adhering to the other requirements set forth in the style guide. With the glossary attachment, the style guide prompt excludes all the terminology-related instructions, which simplifies the prompt. The new prompt is:

Prompt 3.   I am going to assign you a translation and summarization task, please adhere to instructions below.

● Format instruction:

   1. Summarize the article into only one paragraph
   2. Put the title in a pair of []
   3. Start the text with date under the format of "x月y日"
   4. Remove the press, the publishing time of the source text, any metadata about the illustration, and jump to the body.

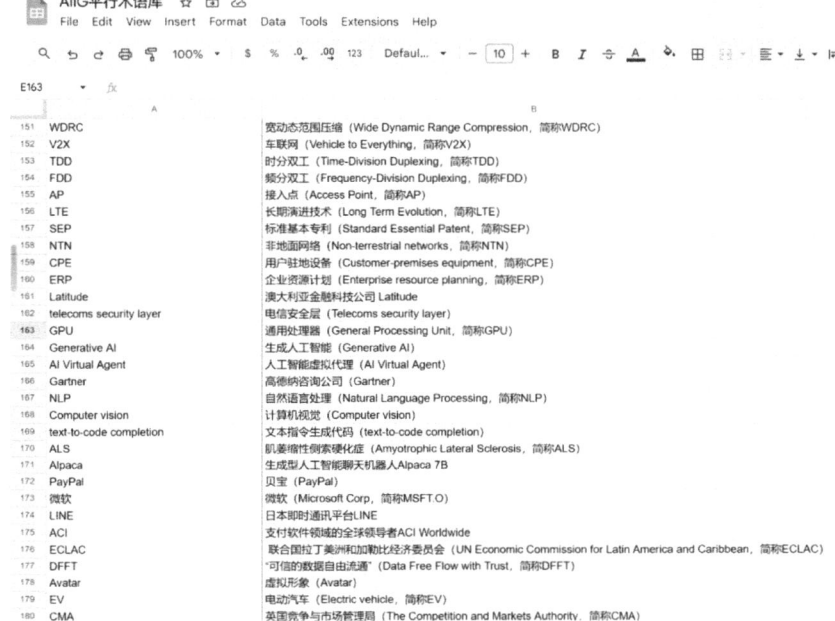

Fig. 3. A ready-to-use abbreviation glossary designed according to style guides[4]

5. When you encounter an English name, leave it in English.

- Format Examples:

「人工智能辅助抗癌药物研发」

3月27日，《化学科学》（Chemical Science）上发表的一篇论文指出，Insilico医药公司的科学家使用DeepMind公司开发的人工智能工具AlphaFold预测蛋白质的结构，加速治疗肝细胞癌药物的研发。该研究由诺贝尔奖获得者Michael Levitt、英矽智能创始人兼首席执行官Alex Zhavoronkov领导，"多伦多大学加速联盟"（Toronto Acceleration Consortium）参与研发。肝细胞癌（Hepatocellular carcinoma cancer，简称HCC）是最为常见的癌症。这项研究为制药公司进入临床试验阶段提供了概念证明。与此同时，Insilico公司正在研究如何使用人工智能来简化该药物的临床试验阶段。

- Terminology instruction:

1. Refer to the glossary to find translation, copy and paste the entire cell content

---

[4] AIIG Parallel Abbreviation Glossary. https://docs.google.com/spreadsheets/d/149oi5R9AQwb d4x0DIbminnB9FEStSy4r_APiMgQaFY8/edit?usp=sharing.

2. When translation is not found in the glossary, leave it in English
3. Use the full translation only for the first time when a term appears

• Text to be edited:

The new approach has demonstrated remarkable efficacy in optimizing ChatGPT's performance. ChatGPT operated as a proficient linguist in terms of editing, but it also effectively searched for abbreviations within the attached glossary and applied the correct translations.

To further test the effectiveness of the technique, 18 English texts are prepared for the experiment. Among them, there are 120 points that need to be edited according to the style guides. A comparison is conducted between ChatGPT's performance with and without the mixed approach, which utilize Prompt 3 and Prompt 2 respectively. The output is based on human evaluation, utilizing the confusion matrix, rounding figures to two decimal places. The testing results are describes on Table 2:

Table 2. Comparison of ChatGPT's performance upon different prompting techniques

	With the mixed approach	With prompting only
TP	95	44
TN	0	0
FP	0	0
FN	25	76
Precision	100%	100%
Recall	79.10%	36.67%
F1-Score	1.59	0.74

Without using the mixed approach, the Recall score is significantly lower. This can be attributed to the absence of a terminology attachment, which results in lengthier style guides. In such instances, ChatGPT exhibited a propensity to overlook certain items within the prompts. Notably, in the experiments conducted without the glossary attachment, ChatGPT frequently failed to adhere to the style guide regarding paragraph structuring, often unable to confine its output to a single paragraph as required. Furthermore, the lack of a terminology reference impeded ChatGPT's ability to accurately explain abbreviations or to provide the correct full English names. These shortcomings were pivotal in contributing to a reduced count of TP, as they directly impacted the AI's adherence to specified style guides.

It reflects that employing a mixed approach yields two primary advantages. Firstly, it facilitates enhanced control over terminology translation, thereby significantly improving the accuracy and consistency in technical translation. Secondly, the approach leveraging both instructions and attachments effectively shortens the length of prompts, consequently reducing the computational load on the model. By extracting the most challenging aspects from ChatGPT's workload, the model could apply its computational capabilities to efficiently execute certain translation and editing tasks based on the style guides. Converting the most complex tasks into simpler 'copy and paste' operations for ChatGPT not only prevents it from grappling with the more demanding aspects but also significantly enhances overall work efficiency.

4 Discussions

The findings of the mixed approach using both prompting and attachment, have significant implications for the field of technical translation, particularly in contexts where extensive terminology management and rigorous post-translation editing and proofreading are crucial. In the past, the processes of translation and summarization at the newsletter production team of the I-AIIG were heavily reliant on human linguists and a strict translation-editing-proofreading workflow. However, with well-engineered prompts and AI-targeted attachment, ChatGPT can assist humans for the complicated task and automate a great translation and editing parts of the workflow. The enhancement of the model's compliance with style guides may greatly reduce the time and effort required for proofreading.

With the terminological adaptability and style guide adaptability, LLMs may allow people to adapt glossaries and style guides for more complex tasks, such as cross-language summarization and editing, which have wide-ranging implications in the language service industry.

Additionally, the findings of aligning instructions and examples, and the mixed approach conclusively highlights how AI models process information differently from human linguists. This divergence in processing information necessitates a reevaluation of traditional style guide designs.

Traditional style guides emphasize aspects such as branding elements and language usage [2]. They operate under the assumption that human linguists can intuitively and flexibly draw on additional referential materials and make context-specific decisions. In contrast, LLMs process information with a greater emphasis on the precision of prompts [3]. A crucial distinction is that LLMs cannot access external materials beyond what is explicitly provided to them. This inherent limitation in contextual understanding and flexibility necessitates a more comprehensive approach in prompt design.

The difference in information process pattern between AI and human is also reflected in the mixed approach proposed in this research. Instructions like 'search for terminology translation in the extensive file' are not typically the most efficient method for human translators. Yet, it proves to be a highly effective strategy for simplifying the task for ChatGPT. The principle could be effectively adapted to various other scenarios, in which relevant reference materials tailored to the specific requirements of language service projects are provided to ChatGPT. Such a practice could be exceptionally advantageous in processes such as pre-translation checks and Machine Translation Post-Editing (MTPE).

One of the primary constraints of this study is its focus on the English-Chinese language pair. The findings might not be entirely representative of ChatGPT's performance across other language pairs. The research revolves around the terminology aspect of style guides, which may not be directly transferable to other translation tasks that do not prioritize terminological accuracy to the same extent. Consequently, the glossary design approach proposed in this experiment may have limited applicability outside technical translation scenarios.

5 Conclusions

This research has embarked on optimizing AI performance in translation and summarization tasks, specifically focusing on the adaptation and utilization of style guides with ChatGPT. A core revelation of this study is the critical role of the alignment between instructions and examples in enhancing AI comprehension. It demonstrates that both components must work in unison for ChatGPT to deliver accurate and effective results. This insight not only enhances our understanding of AI's learning mechanisms but also highlights the fundamental differences in information processing between AI models and human translators.

A notable finding of the study is a mixed approach, breaking down style guides into attachments and prompts. The creation of a custom spreadsheet specifically designed for AI reflects an effective strategy. The implementation of the approach escalated the Recall score from 36.67% to 79.10%, which underscores its efficacy in enhancing ChatGPT's performance in adhering to style guides.

It shows that adapting methods to overcome ChatGPT's disadvantages in dealing with long and complicated prompts can lead to more effective outcomes. Future research could concentrate on determining the most effective way to structure materials for optimal AI comprehension and performance, and expand their scope to include language pairs beyond Chinese-English, as well as exploring domains other than technical translation. Such endeavors have the potential to set new standards for AI-targeted style guides, contributing significantly to the evolving field of AI-assisted language services. By innovating in the customization of style guides and prompts to align more closely with AI capabilities, this work aims to enhance human expertise through the augmentation of AI tools.

References

1. ISO/TC 37/SC 2: ISO 30042:2019 Management of terminology resources: TermBase eXchange (TBX). ISO (2019)
2. WIKIPEDIA, The Free Encyclopedia, Style Guide
3. https://en.wikipedia.org/wiki/Style_guide#References

Use of ChatGPT in the Classrooms of a Junior Highschool Science to Invoke Ability of Questioning

Kieko Ido[1], Katsuhiro Goto[2], Miu Yamada[1], and Shu Matsuura[1]([⊠])

[1] Tokyo Gakugei University, 4-1-1 Nukuikita, Koganei 184-8501, Tokyo, Japan
shum00@u-gakugei.ac.jp

[2] Shibuya Ward Shibuya Honmachi Gakuen, 4-3-1 Honmachi, Shibuya 151-0071, Tokyo, Japan

Abstract. We attempted a science lesson that encourages middle school students to ask their own questions through ChatGPT. First, in a literacy session, students experienced the merits and demerits of ChatGPT by having the teacher ask questions to ChatGPT on their behalf about what they wanted to ask the AI. Next, as an introduction to the sound unit, a hands-on session was conducted in which the students themselves asked questions to ChatGPT while experiencing the experimental manipulation. Finally, a reflection session was conducted in which feedback comments by ChatGPT on the students' questioning of ChatGPT were presented to the students.

During the hands-on session, most students asked a single question, similar to a web search, where the search term was submitted once. A few students, however, repeated the question around 10 times. In the process of repeating the dialogue, questions that led to scientific inquiry emerged, such as how and why the phenomenon is the way it is. The most common reason for students' desire to repeat the question was that the dialogue helped them understand what they wanted to ask. A large number of students in the reflection sessions were positively receptive to the assessments from the ChatGPT.

These results suggest that a generative AI that responds to students' questions individually can be a learning partner for learning to ignite questioning and thinking, provided that appropriate literacy education is provided.

Keywords: Questioning · ChatGPT · Science Education

1 Introduction

ChatGPT, the prototype of which was released to the public on November 30, 2022, was able to generate convincing text based on LLM in response to users' utterances and requests and reached 100 million users in just two months.

For educators, it is expected to be very useful in developing teaching materials, responding to individual questions from students, and facilitating group work, and it is also expected to bring about significant changes in the way teachers work and in individual and school-based learning [1–4]. Responsible implementation of technology in educational use is required [5]. Questions are currently being raised about whether the role of the teacher can be replaced by a generative AI [6], and the advantages and disadvantages that ChatGPT brings are being actively examined [7, 8]. On the other hand, many attempts to utilize ChatGPT in the classroom have been initiated.

Japan's Ministry of Education, Culture, Sports, Science and Technology (MEXT) published "Tentative Guidelines for the Use of Generative AI in the Primary and Secondary Education Stage" [9] on July 4, 2023, calling for specific attention from educational institutions. In order not to exclude the potential of generative AI and to provide practical examples of how to take advantage of its benefits in both education and academic affairs, MEXT has called for applications of pilot schools for the use of generative AI throughout Japan, and each school has started its own project [10].

In Japan, the new Courses of Study was fully implemented in the 2020 school year for elementary schools, the 2021 school year for junior high schools, and the 2022 school year for senior high schools. These Courses of Study place emphasis on developing the qualities and abilities of students that will enable them to cope with a changing society. In particular, it supports the evaluation and development of students from the three perspectives of "knowledge and skills," "thinking, judgment, and expression," and "attitude toward independent learning".

A feature of ChatGPT regarding interaction with humans is that it attempts to generate AI utterances intended by humans by asking questions using natural language. This is in contrast to conventional web search, which acquires information from search terms and examines the context of related URLs.

When learning in the classroom, students and teachers talk to each other. The teacher asks questions of the students, and the students respond. However, thinking for oneself begins with asking questions. The first notable characteristic of ChatGPT is that it is a "system for people to ask questions". The second characteristic is that it generates corresponding "human natural language responses" from a large-scale language model to human questions.

Furthermore, on January 26, 2021, Japan's Central Council for Education compiled a report entitled "Toward the Construction of '2021 Japanese-Style School Education': Realization of Individual Optimal Learning and Collaborative Learning that Draws Out the Potential of All Children" (Report). In order to develop the qualities and abilities of students based on the new curriculum guidelines, it is required to make maximum use of ICT to improve classes to realize "independent, interactive, and deep learning" by integrating and enhancing "individualized learning" and "collaborative learning" more than ever before. ChatGPT gives spoken words that are in line with the user's questions, so the individuality of the dialogue can be high. It is expected to enhance individualized learning by cultivating the skills and abilities to use ChatGPT.

The individualized nature of learning in ChatGPT may help to reduce the participation gap among children.

Furthermore, Eloundou et al. extensively examined white-collar work affected by ChatGPT, but noted that work using scientific inquiry and critical thinking was not affected [11]. When ChatGPT is used in science education, there is a possible risk of making the knowledge authoritative [12]. The process of forming a hypothesis based on measured facts about a substance and testing it inductively through experiments and observations, and the process of making critical decisions based on certain arguments must be done by humans, and such qualities and abilities need to be acquired as generic abilities in school education [13]. Cultivating these qualities and abilities in science education and making use of AI in this process will be important in the future symbiosis between AI and humans.

Objective. In this study, as an introduction to a unit on sound in junior high school science classes, participants experience manipulating tuning forks and use ChatGPT to deepen their understanding of what they came up with through their experiences. The purpose of this study is to clarify how questions develop through dialogue with ChatGPT, and to propose how ChatGPT can be used in the school classroom.

2   Methods

The educational practices in this study were conducted in four first-grade classes at a public junior high school. The practice consisted of the following three sessions.

1. Literacy session (in-class): A media literacy session to learn about the features and problems of ChatGPT.
2. Hands-on session (in-class): A session to introduce a unit on sound, in which students can freely manipulate tuning forks and other devices while asking questions to ChatGPT themselves.
3. Reflection session (outside of class): In response to the students' questions to Chat-GPT in the hands-on session, we had ChatGPT generate comments on the students' questioning and provide feedback to them. Students who read the feedback were asked to write their thoughts on the ChatGPT comments. This session took place at an optional time outside of class time.

2.1   Literacy Session

First, in July 2023, a lesson on the merits and demerits of ChatGPT as a familiar AI was conducted as a media literacy education, as shown in Table 1. In the literacy session, the teacher represented the students' opinions and other input into ChatGPT; in Step 1.4, two of the four classes projected the browser screen of ChatGPT to view the teacher's input and ChatGPT's responses as text.

The other two classes spoke to the communication robot Sota ver. 1.26.1 (Social Talker, Vstone Co., Ltd.) Intel Edison Developer Edition [14]. The development environment is Vstone Co.'s VstoneMagic ver. 1.0.6390.17171. Conversations between Sota and humans were carried out using Vstone's speech-to-text conversion cloud and connected to ChatGPT using the GPT-3.5 turbo API.

The browser screen was the visual while the robot was the auditory interface, but students were attentive to both mediums.

The purpose of this session was to (1) raise awareness of media literacy and the merits and demerits of AI, and in parallel, (2) experience the deepening of thinking through a series of questions. We did not make (1) and (2) completely independent but attempted to ignite the thinking in (2) by actually finding hallucinations and by being exposed to information about the dangers of AI.

Table 1. Media literacy lesson plan.

Step	Activity Type	Topic
1.1	Teacher presents	Advanced information utilization skills are required. We must judge the reliability of information for ourselves
1.2	Asks students to speak	Where and how is AI around you helping you?
1.3	Asks students to fill out a questionnaire of their opinions (Questionnaire 1.1)	"If you had an AI (robot) that could have a conversation and answer anything you wanted, what would you want to ask it?" The survey will be conducted using Forms on Google for Education's Classroom to share about the following questions
1.4	The teacher asks the AI the students' questions on behalf of the students	The teacher collects what students want to ask ChatGPT (or to Sota, a robot that speaks ChatGPT) and ask ChatGPT to answer each question. Hallucination is also checked
1.5	The teacher presents a video	Explanation of ChatGPT's terms of use and precautions, watching a video about the dangers of AI
1.6	The teacher inputs students' opinions into ChatGPT browser	Activity in which students who raised their hands take turns to develop a dialogue with the AI about the dangers of AI
1.7	Questionnaire 1.2	Have you extended your own ideas by interacting with AI?
1.8	Summary statement	Students think about the human ability of questioning to derive AI intelligence and to think critically. To use AI effectively, it is important to improve one's own "ability to ask questions"

2.2 Hands-On Session

Experiment and ChatGPT Input. In September 2023, a class was conducted using ChatGPT in the lesson steps shown in Table 2 as an introduction to the sound lesson unit. Students were divided into groups of 4 students each in the laboratory. First, the students were shown how to use ChatGPT from their own PCs. Next, the students were placed with the instruments, mainly tuning forks and resonators, and some instruments were placed on a table in the center of the room so that they could manipulate them at their discretion. In class step 2.3, the teacher demonstrated the phenomena of sound resonance and buzzing, followed by a demonstration in which the students asked ChatGPT about the mechanism of the phenomena. After that, as the core activity of Step 2.4, the students were free to conduct their experiments and input their questions into ChatGPT.

Table 2. Hands-on session plan.

Step	Activity Type	Topic
2.1	Teacher Presentation	Classroom uses AI to enable students to articulate their concerns after seeing a demonstration of an experiment using a tuning fork
2.2	Student starts PC and launches ChatGPT	Students log in to Google for Education's Classroom to share data. Each group logs into ChatGPT from their respective browsers using their assigned account
2.3	Students start their "New chat" and prepare to type. Students watch and learn from the teacher's demonstration	The teacher's demonstration includes tuning fork resonance, tactile experience of vibrations, visualization of vibrations through water waves by placing the tuning fork in water, generating sound waves by combining different frequencies, and bone conduction experiments The teacher also demonstrates how to ask questions to ChatGPT based on the experimental demonstration: "What is a tuning fork?" "Please explain in a way that a middle school student could understand."
2.4	Students are free to interact with ChatGPT and manipulate the tuning fork. The time limit is approximately 10 min	Tuning forks were distributed to students' desks, and tuning forks and water tanks were placed in the center of the classroom to encourage students to freely conduct experiments or interact with ChatGPT. There was a lot of conversation among the students
2.5	Students share their chats (about 5 min)	Group members introduced their own chats to each other
2.6	Allow some of the students to present their dialogues to the entire class	The teacher selected particularly interesting chats from the students' questions and presented them to the entire class. The evolution of questions and answers featuring engaging content, as well as the deepening of dialogue content, was noted

(continued)

Table 2. (*continued*)

Step	Activity Type	Topic
2.7	Summary statement	It is humans who bring out the power of AI; utilizing AI can extend human capabilities
2.8	Questionnaire 2	Students were asked to copy their dialogues. Also, survey questionnaires on their use of ChatGPT and their motivation and thinking skills were conducted
after class 3.1	Students receive individual comments generated by ChatGPT at a later date	Have ChatGPT evaluate each student's interaction with ChatGPT and provide individual feedback to the student
3.2	Students submit their thoughts on the individual comments as a final survey	Students submit their thoughts on the ChatGPT feedback

In-Class Surveys for Students. Table 3 summarizes the questions asked in Questionnaire 1.1 in the literacy session (step 1.3 for in-class opinion sharing) and Questionnaire 1.2 in step 1.7 and Questionnaire 2 in step 2.8 in the sound learning session.

Table 3. Questionnaire Content.

Lesson	Survey	Questions	Question Type
Media literacy	Questionnaire 1.1	Do you know about ChatGPT?	5 L.S
		Have you ever used ChatGPT?	5 L. S
		If you had a robot that could have a conversation and answer everything, what would you want to talk about? Enter what you would like to discuss or what questions you would like to ask	free-text entry
	Questionnaire 1.2	Did your interactions with ChatGPT broaden or deepen your thinking or give you new ideas? Please describe your impressions in detail	free-text entry
Introduction of Sound	Questionnaire 2	Satisfied with ChatGPT's first answer?	5 L. S

(*continued*)

Table 3. (*continued*)

Lesson	Survey	Questions	Question Type
		Could you ask ChatGPT the question again?	5 L. S
		What made you want to ask the question again? 1. The teacher's instruction 2. What I wanted to understand became clear 3. I was exploring it for reference 4. I found an appropriate word to ask a question 5. Other	choice type
		Does sharing your dialogue with ChatGPT with your friends help you to create your own ideas?	5 L. S
		Did you find other students' interaction with ChatGPT interesting and engaging?	5 L. S

L. S. (Likert Scales.)

Analysis of Interaction with ChatGPT. We are interested in whether questions can be elicited by using ChatGPT in addition to the experimental experience in science. Experiments and observations are optional. Therefore, we are interested in whether the behavior of the students is linked to the experiment and the chat. The video was fixed at the side of the teaching table, away from the students, and care was taken to avoid overloading the students with attention. Only about four students were able to see the behavior within the angle of view.

The students' question input was classified into the nine question types and two request types shown in Table 4, and the transition of question types as the dialogue unfolded was examined.

Table 4. Question Type Classification.

	Type symbols	Meaning	Example
Question type	What_is_it	Questioning definition, meaning, and existence. What is it in the end?	What is Sound?
	What_happens	What will happen? What will happen?	What happens if you put a tuning fork in your mouth?

(continued)

Table 4. (*continued*)

	Type symbols	Meaning	Example
	What_else	Other. What else	Does it resonate with any object other than a tuning fork?
	Who_does_it	Who did/does it	Who invented the tuning fork?
	How_it_works	How does it work? Ask how it works	How does a tuning fork produce sound?
	How_is_it_done	How is it done? Question the process and methods	How is the resonance used around us?
	Why_does_it_do	Why is this so? Question the cause, purpose, and rationale	Why does it vibrate?
	Is_it_possible	Consider the possibilities	Is there a sound you can't hear?
	is_related_to	Consider the relationship	How does the pitch of the sound relate to the frequency?"
request type	Make_it_more	Change the degree	Explain more simply
	Make_it_fit	Make it fit something	Explain so that middle school students can understand

2.3   Reflection Session

Table 5. Evaluation Feedback on Student Speech by ChatGPT

evaluation point of view	(computer) prompt to ChatGPT
Evaluation of your learning attitude	The text below is a dialogue in which ChatGPT answers the User's questions; please compliment the User's attitude of having questions
Evaluation of your interests and ideas	The text below is a dialogue in which ChatGPT is answering User's questions, please rate User's questions qualitatively in terms of depth of interest in "sound" and "tuning fork", uniqueness of ideas, and creativity
ChatGPT's idea of "Questions to Further Extend Learning"	The text below is a dialogue in which ChatGPT answers the User's question, and in order to encourage the User to come up with new ideas, please provide one interesting and original example of a question related to the User's question. The question should be related to "sound" or "tuning fork"

After class, we had ChatGPT individually evaluate the students' questions submitted by the students and provided this evaluation text as feedback from the AI to each student. The prompts for the three perspectives are shown in Table 5.

Students' comments on this feedback from the AI were collected as the final questionnaire. The question text is as follows. "Please feel free to tell us anything about your thoughts on the feedback you saw from ChatGPT!".

3   Results and Discussions

3.1   Literacy Session

Figure 1 shows the results of the initial questionnaire 1.1 in Media Literacy on whether ChatGPT is known. As the figure shows, 42.1% of all students indicated that they are familiar well or familiar with ChatGPT, making it a known medium for first-year middle school students. In addition, 9.8% of students indicated that they use ChatGPT very often or often, indicating that it is already familiar to the students. This indicates that ChatGPT is already becoming a familiar AI tool for middle school students.

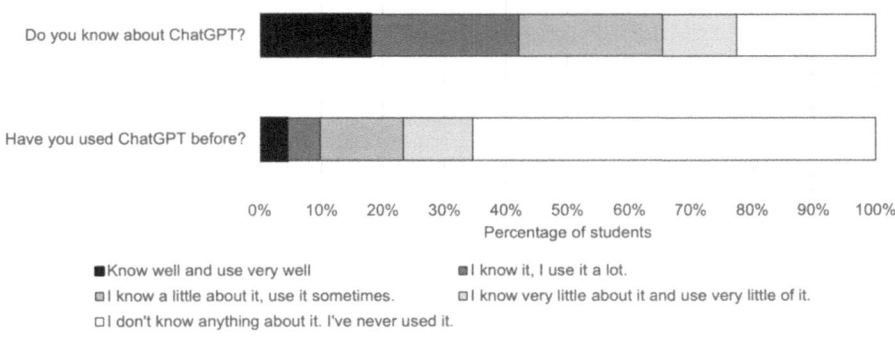

Fig. 1. Results of Likert-scale Questionnaire 1.1 on ChatGPT.

Next, Fig. 2 shows the top five most frequent results of categorizing the free-response statements about what they would like to discuss or ask AI in Questionnaire 1.1. Along with general questions, many students want to ask questions about their own lives. The result implies that they are positioning and accepting AI in the aspect of their life feelings. Students may be more interested in whether it is useful in their daily lives than in resources such as scientific knowledge.

The media literacy class surveyed the merits and demerits of ChatGPT, but also students became interested in its interactivity. The immediate follow-up questionnaire1.2 asked students about their perspectives on learning with ChatGPT, whether they expanded their thinking or gained new ideas. The results are shown in Fig. 3. One of the main features of ChatGPT as a teaching material is that it is a system in which learners ask questions, and it is expected that the process of dialogue will deepen the

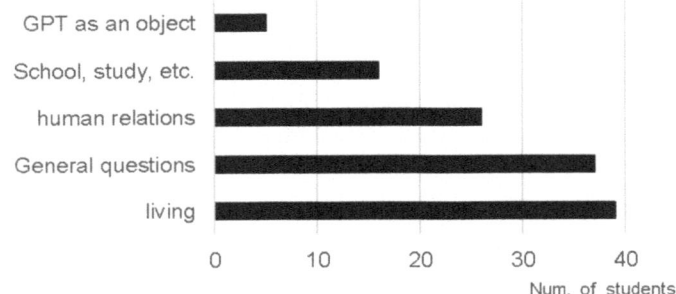

Fig. 2. Results of the free statement of Questionnaire 1.1 on ChatGPT.

learners' thinking. In Questionnaire 1.2, there were many comments that students have a perception of their self-image toward AI. This tendency was almost the same whether they used ChatGPT visually in a browser or aurally in a robot conversation. Going beyond seeing AI as an object to be used, imagining the relationship between AI and humans may be a step toward a symbiotic relationship between AI and humans. Table 6 shows examples of actual student opinions categorized as "Recognizing one's attitude toward AI."

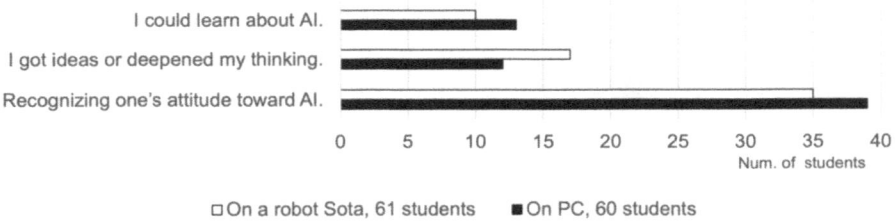

Fig. 3. A classification of answers whether the students extended their thinking on ChatGPT.

Table 6. Examples of students' opinions classified as recognizing one's attitudes toward AI

Opinions (excerpts#)	Relationship
ChatGPT's answer is not necessarily a justified decision, but it is trying to enrich human life	AI and the human way of life
AI can make bad decisions and hurt people, so we should not leave everything to AI	AI and humans who tend to depend on it
There are many conveniences,,, but we use AI with good judgment	AI functions and humans make decisions

(continued)

Table 6. (*continued*)

Opinions (excerpts#)	Relationship
If we interact with AI while recognizing its quirks, we will get good opinions	AI and humans who recognize AI quirks
If something advanced is created, humans may be lumbered with it	Artifacts and overwhelmed humans
AI can tell us what we don't know, but we should not overuse it and lose our own sensitivity	AI and humans losing sensitivity
AI is useful, but there is a danger of losing the ability to think for oneself	AI and thoughtless humans
AI technology will develop, and AI will become more active than humans	AI and humans losing their raison d'etre
AI will be integral to our future	AI and the humans who make it indispensable
AI only mimics human behavior patterns, so the threat lies in human malice or ignorance。	AI imitating humans and human malice or ignorance
It is important to be responsible in your own use of AI	AI and the responsibility of humans who use it
A person in a high position, powerful people, should seriously consider whether AI, which is useful but also dangerous, can be integrated into daily life	Powerful people who overwhelmingly prioritize profit in spite of the danger

#Opinion statements were shortened and reformed so as not to change the meaning

3.2 Hands-On Session

In the "sound" introduction class shown in Table 2, after the teacher demonstrated Chat-GPT in step 2.3, the students were allowed to freely operate the apparatus and interact with ChatGPT as step 2.4. Figure 4 shows the time course of instrument manipulation and chat for 12 students in total in three classes, displayed as black and white rectangles. The time course was shown horizontally.

st represents an individual student. The horizontal length of the black-and-white rectangle represents the duration of time. The total duration of the activity was approximately 10 min (indicated by the arrows), and an alarm was sounded in the classroom at the end of the activity. The horizontal right direction shows the time elapsed.

In Class 1, all group members spent 10 min in step 2.4 only for chatting. In Class 2, one group member spent only for chatting, while the other members began to operate the equipment later. Since group members talked to each other and advised each other on the operation of PCs and equipment, it is assumed that the effect of induction among members is also included. In the Class 3, all members of the group started by operating the instruments, and one of them spent a long time on the experimental experience. Under a class design that allows diverse learning styles and shares what was learned and

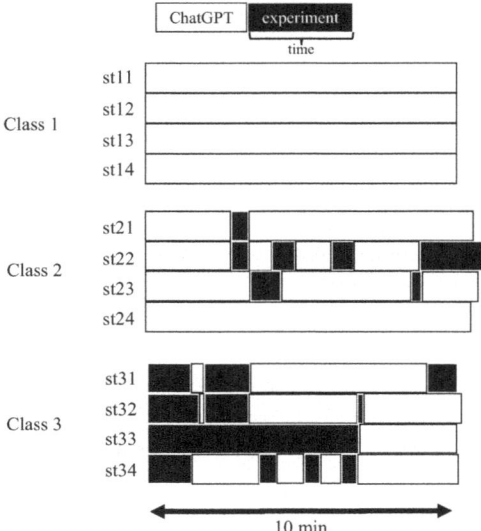

Fig. 4. Time course of student instrument manipulation (in black) and ChatGPT input (in white).

how it was learned in the next step, it may be effective as a method of learning utilization to trigger diverse behaviors while meeting the objectives.

Figure 5 shows the results of the questionnaire about the time of sharing Chat in step 2.5 and 2.6. Most of the students were interested in sharing Chat among friends (89.4%), and most of the positive responses indicated that sharing was useful in creating their own ideas (86.0%), and the expressions on the students' faces in the actual step 2.5 and 2.6 situations showed a high level of interest.

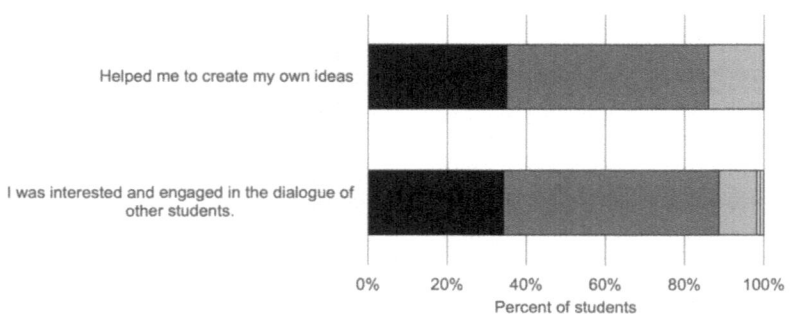

■Very much so. ■I think so. ▣Can't say either way ▢Not so much. ▢Not at all.

Fig. 5. On sharing the dialogue with ChatGPT with other students.

The results of Questionnaire 2, conducted after sharing the dialogue with ChatGPT in the sound introduction class, are shown in Figs. 6 and 7. Figure 6 shows that students generally had a satisfactory understanding of the explanation provided by ChatGPT when they read it. However, 77.2% of the students indicated that they would have liked to ask further questions.

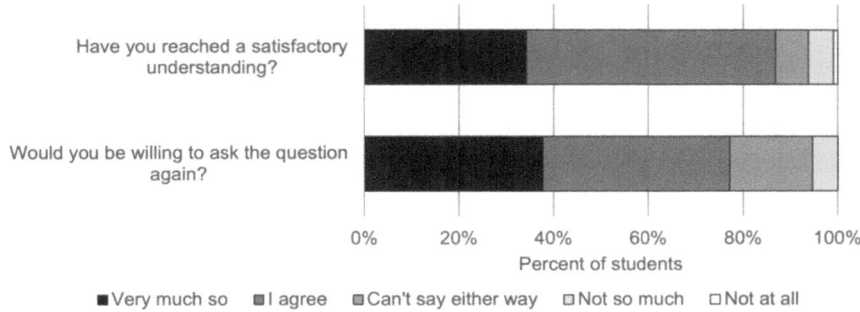

Fig. 6. About whether the students were satisfied with the answers to the ChatGPT and would like to ask further questions.

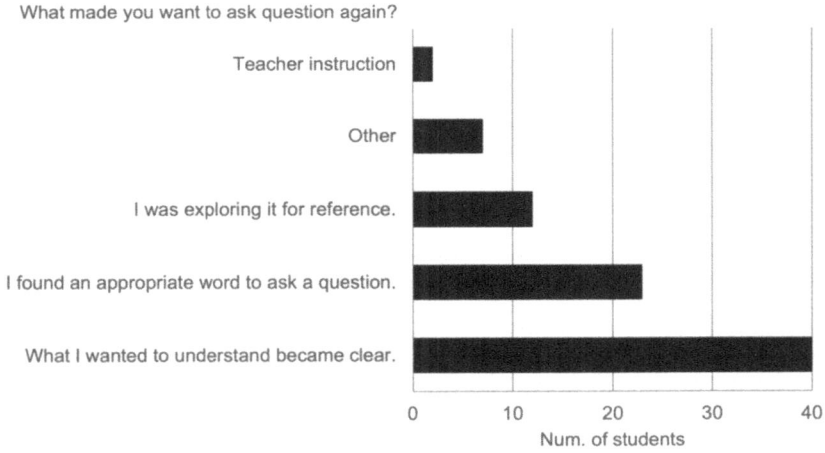

Fig. 7. Why students wanted to ask ChatGPT again.

The most common reason for wanting to ask more questions, as shown in Fig. 7, was that "what I wanted to understand became clear" (47.6% of students), followed by "I found an appropriate word to ask a question" (27.4%). In other words, the initial explanation by ChatGPT positioned what they wanted to know and gave them an idea of how to develop the question again. The fact that the appropriate words were known also meant that the students found keywords to ask questions. It is also to connect an ambiguous question to a clear one and be motivated to solve it. These can help the questioner, who has not clarified the question, to think about it.

From the above, it was confirmed that the series of lesson designs of experiment presentation, manipulation of the experimental apparatus and ChatGPT, and sharing the dialogue with ChatGPT among students are something that students can actively participate in.

3.3   Analysis of Conversations with ChatGPT

As shown in Fig. 8, the most frequent dialogue with ChatGPT was a single interaction with one question and one response. Many questions seemed equivalent to a web search, such as "What is a tuning fork?" (typically, what_is_it type in Table 4). While many students had few experiences conversing with AI (Fig. 1), they regularly searched for information on the web. The number of dialogues including more than 6 questions was small, but we also found a maximum of 13 dialogues (Fig. 8).

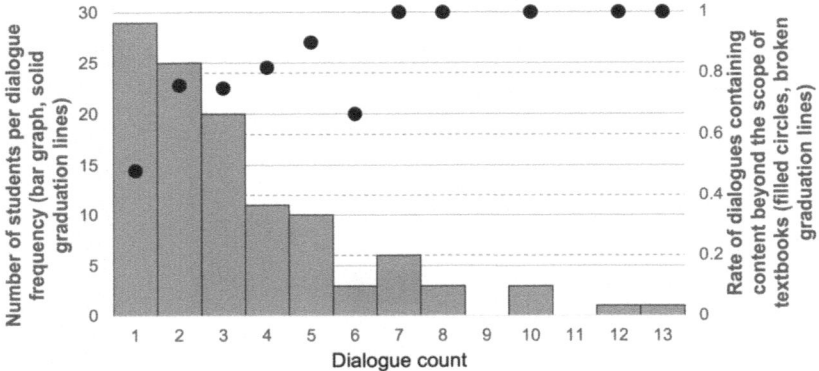

Fig. 8. Distribution of dialogue repetitions and rate of dialogues with content beyond the scope of textbook.

Figure 8 also shows, for each dialogue count case, the percentage of questions in which the dialogue content went beyond what was written in the textbook. Although there were a small number of cases with numerous repetitions of dialogues, the dialogues that took place more than seven times always included questions that went beyond what was written in the textbooks. Even when the number of dialogues was less than five, content beyond the textbook appeared in about 67.4% of the dialogues. This may be due to the wide range of content explained in the ChatGPT, the fact that the students' interests were easily broadened, and the fact that the students themselves connected the questions.

In addition, in this practice, the teacher is conducting a demonstration experiment. Therefore, while students are stimulated by the teacher's demonstration, the content of their questions may also be limited to the scope of the demonstration. Figure 9 compares the number of times per student that questions about the content of the demonstration experiment and questions about phenomena other than the demonstration experiment were asked. While there is a large percentage of questions about the demonstrated experiment, there are also around one reference per student to phenomena other than the demonstrated phenomenon. While it is important to gain many insights from real phenomena in the process of exploration, this practice is also meaningful to broaden the image of a new field of study as an introductory process.

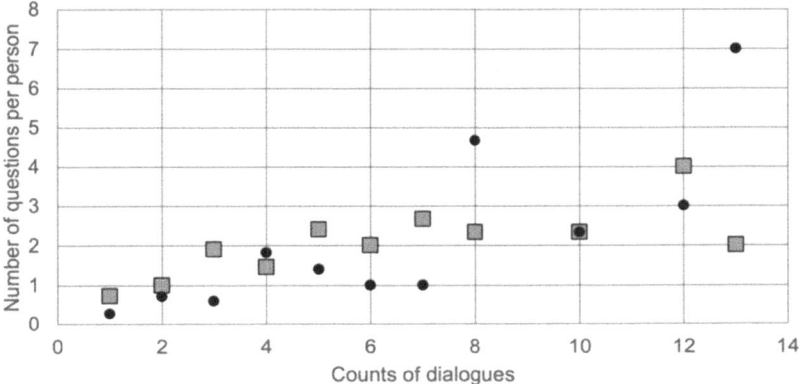

Fig. 9. Comparison of the number of dialogs about performed experiments and the number of questions about non-performed phenomena at each number of dialogs.

As described above, we believe that it is useful to incorporate interactive activities with a generative AI as a strategy for a "free exploratory introduction class" that expands knowledge and interests based on demonstrative experiments and real-life experiences.

We now turn to the distribution and transitions of student question types (Table 4).

Figure 10 shows the percentage of question types by the number of dialogues; the What_is_it type was prevalent throughout the entire number of dialogues. The question types that appeared more frequently among students with fewer dialogues were What_is_it, Why_does_it_do, and How_does_it_work. These types of questions were also frequent in the first and second dialogues, and their percentages decreased with the number of dialogues. It is possible that not many students were strongly interested in the explanation of the mechanism. On the other hand, "What_happens" and "How_is_it_done," which are questions related to the occurrence of the event, tended to increase with the number of dialogues after the third dialogue, suggesting a high level of interest in the occurrence of the event itself.

Furthermore, we focus on the transition of question types as the dialogue progresses. Figure 11 shows the transition of question types from the first to the fourth dialogue session, as indicated by the arrows. The thickness of the arrows is proportional to the number of students who showed the transition. The three main question types, What_is_it, Why_does_it_do, and How_does_it_work diverged frequently to different question types, but on the other hand, there were also many cases where the same type of question was repeated several times in a row. In the former case, it is assumed that there

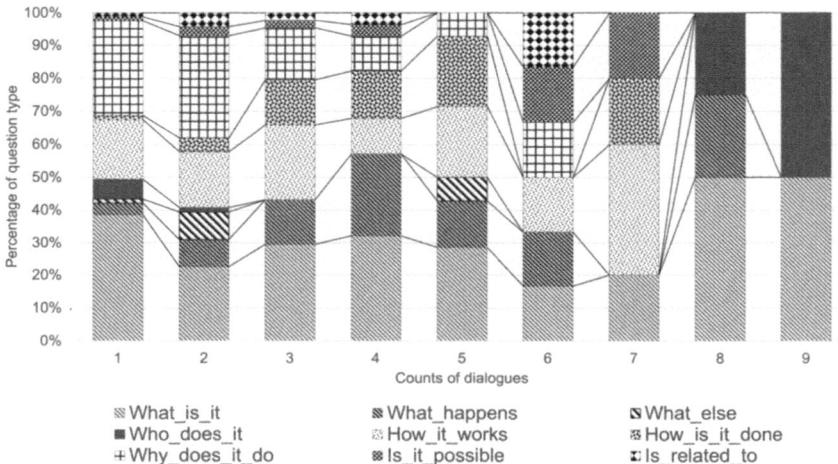

Fig. 10. Percentage of question types to counts of dialogues.

was a development of interest/attention; in the combined dialogue of How_does_it_work and Why_does_it_do, we also found a development of scientific thinking.

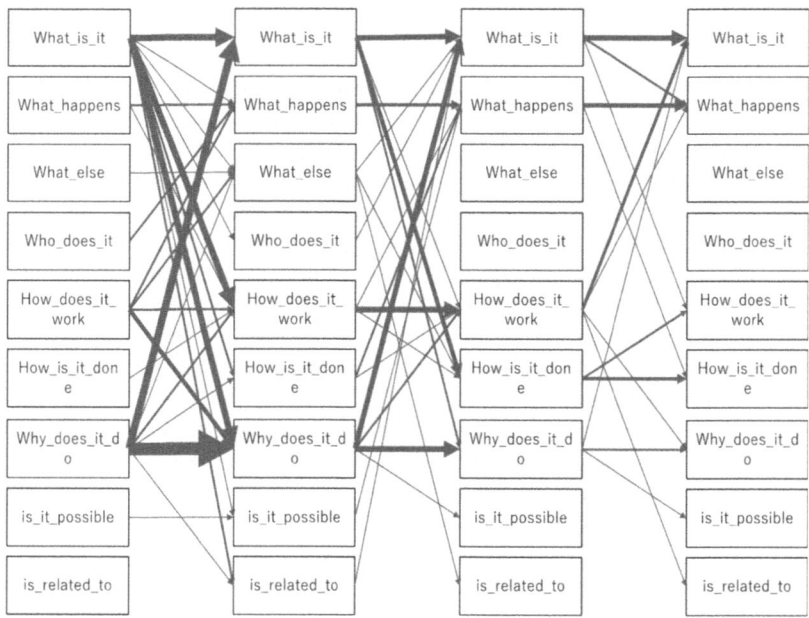

Fig. 11. Transition of question types as the dialogue progresses.

3.4 Reflection Session

After the class, the students' interaction records with ChatGPT were analyzed by ChatGPT, and the ChatGPT analysis was provided to individual students as feedback/comments. The three analyses and prompts are listed in Table 5.

The first content, "evaluation of learning attitude," is a basic reward for the student's input on a question. It is expected that by first giving praise, even if only for typing the same question as the teacher's example, students will be more open-minded and receptive to subsequent comments.

For the second content, "evaluation of interest and ideas," we asked ChatGPT to consider three perspectives inferred from the students' questions: "depth of interest," "uniqueness of ideas," and "creativity. Positive praise was given for depth of interest, and positive evaluation was given for uniqueness if the question included originality. Creativity was rated comparatively harshly. Creativity was evaluated as creative when it combined concepts and methods from different disciplines.

Finally, the third content, "Questions to Further Extend the Learning," provided students with hints to develop original ideas. This was to utilize the reasoning function of ChatGPT as a way to help students become able to ask developmental questions.

The students who received this feedback were asked to freely describe their impressions of the feedback, which were collected and categorized into seven categories as shown in Table 7. The table also shows examples of the feedback, many of which were stimulating and motivating. The number of comments for each category is shown in Fig. 12. Black bars indicate positive feedback, while white or gray bars indicate negative feedback. It was known that 88% of the responding students had a positive view of the individual feedback from the AI and a positive view of the AI's evaluation of their work.

The most prominent negative opinions were in reference to the evaluation of human nature and the comparison between humans and AI. When placing AI on par with humans in the context of education, there may be discomfort with an environment that lacks others who understand and care about students. However, students find the best of both human and AI feedback. School education may increasingly be required to live in symbiosis with AI.

Table 7. Categorized results of a free-response questionnaire for individual feedback from AI.

Opinions (excerpts)	Classifications
Many parts were written concretely and made sense to me The language was a little difficult, but I thought it was great because it gave detailed and specific thoughts and advice on the questions	Praise for memory and specificity
I thought it was interesting, with human-like, easy-to-read sentences	Evaluation of readability and interest

(*continued*)

Table 7. (*continued*)

Opinions (excerpts)	Classifications
For the first time, I was surprised that AI could give me a rating! I will do my best so that AI can give me a rating	Surprises and positive expectations for AI
I was happy to see that AI also appreciated me I was afraid that it would send them to me like a real human being It was nice that each one was carefully evaluated, but I was still more pleased with the evaluation with human feelings	Evaluation of AI and humanity
I would like to think along with AI, but when it comes to using AI, there are dangers, so I would like to use AI with care As time goes on, there are developments that I am unaware of, and in this day and age when AI such as ChatGPT can already reply so naturally, I thought it would be necessary to be careful in how I use it	Attitudes toward the use of AI
I thought it analyzed every detail of my questions and accurately captured my characteristics. I hope that AI will continue to evaluate me I hope I can consult with ChatGPT in the future about things I don't understand I think AI will play an active role in a wide range of fields	The usefulness of AI and prospects for the future
I really liked the part about questions that expand further I would like to look into questions to further expand my learning I thought it was necessary to write detailed information when asking questions I felt that the questions I asked were not original and had a strong sense of reality, so when I heard ChatGPT say, "Uniqueness is medium," I wanted to try asking more interesting questions I felt that I was analyzing things well that I was not aware of, and I felt that I would make use of this in my future studies I want to try to look at things from different perspectives because my creativity is lacking!	Willingness to improve and dig deeper into questions

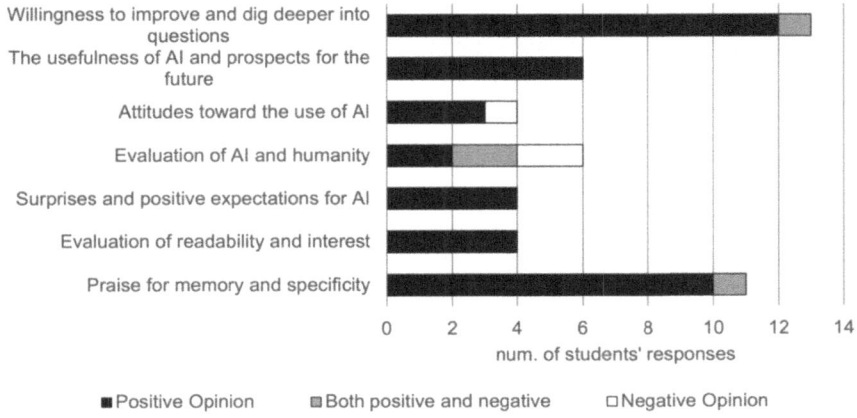

Fig. 12. Students' free descriptions of feedback from AI to students.

4 Conclusion

A trial lesson was given to middle school students to encourage them to ask their own questions through ChatGPT. The trial lesson began with a media literacy session in which students learned about the features and problems of ChatGPT. During the literacy session, students were asked what they wanted to ask the AI, and the teacher asked questions to ChatGPT in natural language. During the next class period, as an introduction to the sound unit, a hands-on session was conducted. The students asked questions to ChatGPT themselves while they were given free hands-on experience manipulating the tuning fork. Finally, we gave feedback to the students by having ChatGPT generate evaluation comments in response to the students' questions to ChatGPT during the hands-on session. Students were asked to write their thoughts on the ChatGPT comments. These took place outside of class time and were referred to as reflection sessions.

Many of the students' reflections during the literacy sessions indicated a "meta-cognition of engagement" with the AI and how they perceived themselves engaging with it. In the hands-on session, many students entered data into ChatGPT while experiencing the experience of manipulating the lab equipment themselves. Many students ended up asking a single question, similar to a web search, by submitting a single search term. However, some students repeated their questions, and a few students repeated their questions around 10 times. In the process of repeated dialogue, questions that could be linked to scientific inquiry, such as how and why physical phenomena are occurring, emerged.

The most common reason for students wanting to repeat the question multiple times during the hands-on session was that the dialogue helped them understand what they wanted to ask. In addition, sharing the student's dialogue with ChatGPT with the group and the class generated interest in the content of the dialogue. This may have had an impact on students who were not able to leave the realm of a single web search. These findings indicate that a natural language generative AI that responds to students' questions individually can be a learning partner to ignite questioning and thinking learning, provided that appropriate literacy education is provided.

A large number of students in the reflection sessions appeared to be positively receptive to the assessments from ChatGPT of their questions, while a few students expressed discomfort with the assessments from the AI. However, they also perceived the advantages of both the human and the AI. Students who can recognize the complementarity between the advantages of both may proactively explore the symbiosis between AI and humans in education.

The ChatGPT always provides certain answers to students' questions. If students are given an immediate correct answer to their questions, they may stop thinking without thinking carefully; they cannot necessarily understand everything by reading ChatGPT's answer to a single question. The development of the question by the student and the observation of the development of the GAI's answer may affect the pedagogical effectiveness of the student-GAI relationship. The ability to actively develop not only standard questions, but rather questions based on individual interests and concerns, may be a literacy in coexistence with GAI.

Acknowledgments. This work was partly funded by a Grant-in-Aid for Scientific Research (C) 19K02806 from the Ministry of Education, Culture, Sports, Science and Technology.

References

1. Lo, C.K.: What Is the Impact of ChatGPT on education? a rapid review of the literature. Educ. Sci. **13**(4), 410 (2023)
2. Javaid, M., Haleem, A., Singh, R.P., Khan, S., Khan, I.H.: Unlocking the opportunities through ChatGPT Tool towards ameliorating the education system. BenchCouncil Trans. Benchmark Stand. Eval. **3**, 100115 (2023)
3. Geerling, W., Mateer, G.D., Wooten, J., Damodaran, N.: Is ChatGPT smarter than a student in principles of economics? SSRN **2023**, 4356034 (2023)
4. Gill, S.S., et al.: Transformative effects of ChatGPT on modern education: emerging era of AI Chatbots. Internet Things Cyber-Phys. Syst. **4**, 19–23 (2024)
5. Sharma, S., Yadav, R.: Chat GPT – a technological remedy or challenge for education system. Global J. Enterprise Inform. Syst. **14**(4), 46–51 (2023)
6. Ausat, A., Massang, B., Efendi, M., Nofirman, N., Riady, Y.: Can ChatGPT replace the role of the teacher in the classroom: a fundamental analysis. J. Educ. **5**(4), 16100–16106 (2023)
7. Baidoo-Anu, D., Ansah, L.O.: Education in the era of generative Artificial Intelligence (AI): understanding the potential benefits of ChatGPT in promoting teaching and learning. J. AI **7**(1), 52–62 (2023)
8. Kasneci, E., et al.: ChatGPT for good? On opportunities and challenges of large language models for education. Learn. Individ. Differen. **103**, 102274 (2023)
9. Ministry of Education, Culture, Sports, Science and Technology (MEXT), Elementary and Secondary Education Bureau (ESB). https://www.mext.go.jp/content/20230710-mxt_shuuky o02-000030823_003.pdf. Accessed 12 Feb 2024
10. MEXT, Leading DX School. https://leadingdxschool.mext.go.jp/files/2023/08/file_ldx_230 803_01-1.pdf. Accessed 12 Feb 2024

11. Eloundou, T., Manning, S., Mishkin, P., Rock, D.: GPTs are GPTs: an early look at the labor market impact potential of large language models (2023). arXiv:2303.10130 [econ.GN]
12. Cooper, G.: Examining science education in ChatGPT: an exploratory study of generative artificial intelligence. J. Sci. Educ. Technol. **32**, 444–452 (2023)
13. Exintaris, B., Karunaratne, N., Yuriev, E.: Metacognition and critical thinking: using ChatGPT-generated responses as prompts for critique in a problem solving workshop (SMARTCHEMPer). J. Chem. Educ. **100**(8), 2972–2980 (2023)
14. Vstone Co., Ltd. https://www.vstone.co.jp/products/sota/. Accessed 12 Feb 2024

The Influencing Factors of Young Designers' Intentions to Continue Using Artificial Intelligence Generated Content Platforms

Xiangbin Peng, Junjie Li[(✉)], and Wei Li

Nanjing Forestry University, Nanjing 210037, China
lijunjie@njfu.edu.cn

Abstract. In recent years, with the rapid emergence of Artificial Intelligence Generated Content (AIGC) platforms such as ChatGPT and Midjourney, the traditional content creation process has been completely transformed. Young designers, as the group with the highest acceptance of AIGC platforms, play a pioneering role in this technological revolution. However, the factors influencing the continued usage of these platforms by young designers remain unclear, which is crucial for the commercial sustainability of AIGC platforms. To address this research gap, this study constructs the AIGC Continuous Usage Model (ACUM) based on the Expectation Confirmation Model (ECM) and the Technology Acceptance Model (TAM), analyzing the key factors influencing the continued usage of AIGC platforms by young designers. The study encompasses various subfields of design, including product design, visual design, interior design, and landscape design. We focused our research on the well-known platforms ChatGPT and Midjourney. The results indicate that perceived usefulness, satisfaction, and ease of use significantly influence the continued usage intention of AIGC platforms by users. Factors such as expected confirmation, content quality, habit, enjoyment, and system quality also indirectly affect users' intention to use these platforms. Valuable recommendations for designers include enhancing platform functionality, improving user experience and satisfaction, simplifying operation processes, ensuring content quality and system stability, and fostering user habits and enjoyment for continued usage. This study provides valuable insights for developers and young designer users of AIGC platforms, offering scientific suggestions for platform development to ensure their sustainability in the design industry.

Keywords: Satisfaction · SEM · Artificial Intelligence · Intention to use · AIGC

1 Introduction

Artificial Intelligence-Generated Content (AIGC) is emerging as a novel means of creating and consuming digital media due to its ability to automate the generation of various content types, including text, images, and videos [1–3]. This technology has the potential to significantly enhance efficiency and conserve resources by rapidly generating substantial quantities of superior content. Artificial Intelligence has profoundly influenced both research and creative methodologies within the realm of visual arts [4].

A. Coman et al. (Eds.): HCII 2024, LNCS 15375, pp. 46–67, 2025.
https://doi.org/10.1007/978-3-031-76806-4_4

In the field of image generation, Generative Adversarial Networks (GANs) have been used to produce images of remarkable photorealism. Recent research has demonstrated significant advancements in AIGC. For example, researchers have employed advanced deep learning methodologies to generate text that is both coherent and diverse in nature [5]. In 2020, OpenAI introduced the GPT-3 model, a highly versatile language model with capabilities that include machine translation, text generation, semantic analysis, and more [6].

The inaugural China AIGC Industry Summit was held in Beijing, where representatives from industry, academia, and research shared and discussed the trending topics including large-scale models, generative AI, ChatGPT, and more. The summit unveiled the first China AIGC Industry Landscape Report, which projects that the Chinese AI market will reach 17 billion RMB in 2023 and exceed 1 trillion RMB by 2030, giving rise to entirely new business models. The adoption of AIGC platforms by consumers and industries is experiencing rapid growth, representing a burgeoning industry with tremendous potential. However, in order to achieve sustainable growth and profitability, companies must address various challenges such as developing and refining business models and cultivating a strong user base.

Previous research on AIGC platforms has primarily focused on issues such as automatic artist [7, 8], genre classification [9], and style [10] through the extraction of various hand-crafted image features [4]. However, the factors that influence users' continued engagement with AIGC platforms have received comparatively less attention. This paper primarily compares the research of global scholars on users' continued engagement with AIGC platforms in order to examine the factors that influence such engagement [11–13]. The objectives of this study are twofold: Firstly, to identify the factors that influence users' continued engagement with AIGC platforms; and secondly, to determine the most suitable theoretical framework for analyzing the continuance intention of users with AIGC platforms.

In order to investigate the factors influencing the long-term use of the product by the users of the AIGC platform, two well-established models, TAM and ECM, were studied and integrated to create the research model for this study [14, 15]. The ECM has been widely utilized in studies examining users' attitudes towards Information Systems (IS) in post-adoption scenarios. It has been applied to investigate diverse contexts such as mobile data services [16], Web 2.0 usage [17], online shopping [18], e-learning [19], and electronic textbooks [20]. On the other hand, when exploring users' initial adoption of products, scholars have predominantly relied on Davis' Technology Acceptance Model (TAM). This model incorporates several theories, including immersion theory [21], social exchange theory [22], and the theory of planned behavior [23]. It introduces new theoretical variables to examine the factors influencing users' adoption and utilization of products. Building upon previous research, we have expanded the theoretical model of users' continuance intention by integrating both the ECM and TAM models. By doing so, we aim to provide a more comprehensive understanding of the factors that shape users' intentions to continue using the AIGC platform.

This research examines the continued engagement of users with AIGC platforms and identifies key factors that influence such engagement. Utilizing AIGC platforms as the subject of study and employing Structural Equation Modeling (SEM) analysis, the findings of this research can benefit both the AIGC industry and its users. On one hand, it can provide valuable insights to inform future product development and generate benefits for both AIGC and the broader industry. On the other hand, it can enhance the user experience on AIGC platforms and offer efficient design tools for art and design-related industries.

2 Theoretical Background

Prior research on AI generated art has been scant in the problem of automatic artist [7, 8], genre classification [9] and style [10] by extracting various hand-crafted image features [4].The theoretical model of the user' continuance intention is built based on the integration of [14] and TAM [26] to examine the factors influence the user's continuance intention.

2.1 ECM

Bhattacherjee first introduced ECM in 2001 based on the Expectation-Confirmation Theory (ECT) proposed by Oliver in 1980.In the field of studying users' consumer behaviour, ECT has been widely used to assess user satisfaction and consumer buying behaviour [24, 25]. However, ECT has limitations, and the model is thought to ignore potential changes in consumers after the purchase experience (Barnes 2011 p. 1).Bhattacherjee's ECM addresses this limitation by considering the impact of changes in consumer expectations on subsequent cognitive processes. This allows for a deeper understanding of how consumer satisfaction and post-purchase behaviour are influenced by pre- and post-consumption experiences.

Bhattacherjee argues that the continuity behaviour of users in information systems and the repurchase behaviour of consumers are similar. Because both behaviours follow the initial acceptance or purchase behaviour and they are both influenced by the initial experience of using the information system or product, both may lead to a change in the user's behaviour. Bhattacherjee combines the user's pre-consumption expectations, post-consumption expectations and perceived usefulness based on the TAM [26]. Bhattacherjee first proposed the ECM in 2001, which consists of four variables: conformity, perceived usefulness, satisfaction and continued intention. ECT shows that user satisfaction with the information system and perceived usefulness are related to the user's continued intention to use it. The level of user confirmation can indirectly influence users' decision to continue using through user satisfaction and perceived usefulness.

ECM is now widely used to study users' intention to use products over time. Barnes and Böhringer (2011) applied ECM to understand users' intention to continue using microblogging services and showed that users were influenced by perceived usefulness, satisfaction and habit [26]. Thong, Hong and Tam also used ECM to study users' intention to continue using e-government services [61]. Kim used ECM to predict users' intention to use mobile data services in the long term in 2010 and showed that factors such as user satisfaction and perceived usefulness had a significant impact on the intention to continue using mobile e-services [16].

2.2 Technology Acceptance Model (TAM)

TAM model is a powerful tool that has been widely used to explain the factors that influence user adoption of new devices and technologies for data communication in the field [30]. This model was suggested by Davis and has been widely used until recently [31]. The TAM model is based on the Theory of Reasoned Action (TRA) [32] and the Theory of Planned Behaviour (TPB) (Venkatesh, 2000 p. 186). These theories provide a strong theoretical foundation for ongoing research on information service use, information platform use and individual adoption behaviour. TAM was created to study the willingness of users to adopt a new information technology (IT) system [31].

External variables as antecedent variables can also have a positive impact on perceived usefulness and perceived ease of use. This, in turn, can indirectly influence a user's attitude towards the technology. Ultimately, a user's decision to use a new technology is directly determined by their behavioral intention. This intention is influenced by their attitude towards the technology, as well as by external factors. While TAM is a powerful tool for understanding why people choose to adopt or reject new technologies, it does have its limitations. For example, it cannot identify all the factors that may hinder technology acceptance. Additionally, it may not fully represent the complex relationships between different variables. Despite these limitations, TAM remains a widely used model for explaining the factors that affect the use of information systems.

In order to optimize the TAM, Davis has made several revisions to the original model. One such revision was proposed by Venkatesh and Davi (1996). In their revised version of TAM, Venkatesh and Davis argued that the attitude variable only reflects a user's emotional preferences. As a result, it does not effectively present the direct impact of perceived usefulness and perceived ease of use on users' behavioural intentions. To address this issue, Venkatesh and Davis replaced the attitude variable from TAM. They propose a revised model that focuses more directly on the relationship between perceived usefulness, perceived ease of use and users' behavioural intentions. This revised version of the TAM provides a more scientific study of how different factors influence users' decisions to adopt or reject new technologies.

TAM has been used in a wide range of studies in a number of domains. Extended TAM was used by Adi Alsyouf et al. in their study of how self-determination in health management affects users' intention to use a personal health record system [34]. Extended TAM was applied by Sri Rahayu Natasia et al. to analyse the acceptance of the NUADU platform by a group of Indonesian student users [35]. Zin et al. used the extended TAM to study the acceptance of wearable products in digital health among older adults [36].

3 Hypotheses

In order to investigate the factors that influence the willingness of users to use the AIGC platform in the long term, the researchers have constructed a comprehensive research model that integrates two renowned theories: the ECM and the TAM [31]. By merging these two models, the researchers aim to enhance their understanding of the factors that shape users' intention to continue utilizing AIGC platforms. This section presents the research variables and hypotheses, laying the foundation for further analysis and exploration.

3.1 Perceived Usefulness (PU)

Perceived usefulness refers to users' expectations and assessments of how well a product, service or system performs a specific task or meets a specific need. It reflects the extent to which users perceive the product, service or system to be useful in achieving their goals or providing the required functionality [26]. Previous research has shown a positive relationship between perceived usefulness (PU) and persistent intention in different contexts. These contexts include studies of systematic evaluation of e-texts (Stone 2013 p. 984), studies of intention to use real-time communication systems over time (Wang 2011 p. 500), studies of intention to continue using mobile service provider systems (Abbas 2015 p. 648), studies of satisfaction with use and intention to continue using online travel services [40], studies of intention to continue using e-learning systems [41], studies of intention to learn on blogs over time [42] and a study on factors influencing intention to create knowledge [43]. In the technology acceptance model, perceived usefulness refers to users' subjective perceptions of whether a particular technology or system has real benefits for their work, tasks or goals. It is the user's assessment and expectation of the usefulness of a technology and relates to the user's perceived ability of the technology or system to provide problem solving, improve efficiency, increase productivity or achieve other relevant goals [44]. Perceived usefulness not only influences users' attitudes towards use [26], but also their satisfaction and intention to continue using the information system (Barnes 2011 p. 1). Therefore, this study defines perceived usefulness as "users' perceptions of whether utilising the AIGC platform will improve their work performance". Drawing upon the preceding studies, we formulate the following hypotheses:

- **H1:** PU positively affects CI
- **H2:** PU positively affects SA

3.2 Perceived Ease of Use (PEU)

Perceived ease of use plays an important role in the study of user experience and user acceptance, and is important for evaluating and improving the design and interaction of a technology or system [26]. For the purpose of this paper, perceived ease of use refers to users' subjective evaluation of the interface design, interaction style, operational fluency and user experience during the use of the AIGC platform. It reflects whether the users' use of the AIGC platform is easy and intuitive, whether they can easily grasp and operate it, and whether it meets their needs for using the platform. By improving the perceived ease of use of the AIGC platform, user recognition and satisfaction can be enhanced, thus increasing the user engagement and sustainability of the platform. In addition, PEUs often indirectly influence users' intention to continue using information systems through PU [45], as an increase in users' perceived ease of use of an AIGC platform can positively influence users' intention to continue using the platform. In studies of online learning platforms; online travel services; and mobile service providers, PEOU was positively related to users' intention to continuously use the platform [46]. Based on the above studies, this study expects PEU to positively influence users' continued intention to use the AIGC platform and indirectly influence users' continued intention to use the AIGC platform through PU. Building on the previous research, we put forward the following hypotheses:

- **H3:** PEU positively affects CI
- **H4:** PEU positively affects PU

3.3 Confirmation (CF) and Satisfaction (SA)

According to Bhattacherjee (2001), satisfaction refers to an individual's subjective evaluation of their overall experience of using a particular product or service. Confirmation refers to the extent to which an individual's initial expectations of a product or service are affirmed or validated by their actual experience of using it. It can be concluded from previous research that the degree of expectation confirmation and perceived usefulness of users has a significant positive impact on their satisfaction with technology [47]. Barnes and Böhringer found that satisfaction influenced users' intention to use blogging services in the long term. In addition to this, the degree of confirmation of users' expectations of the service had a positive impact on the satisfaction of users' usage [48]. Kim (2010) found that satisfaction, perceived usefulness and perceived behaviour had a positive impact on the idea of using a product or service over time.Lee and Kwon (2011) found that consumers' intention to continue using online services was determined by satisfaction, perceived usefulness, familiarity and intimacy [49].Sinda Agrebi and Joël Jallais (2006) demonstrated that expectation confirmation and satisfaction have a positive impact on users' intention to continue visiting mobile websites [50]. Considering the above studies, we propose the following hypothesis:

- **H5:** CF positively affects SA
- **H6:** CF positively affects PU
- **H7:** SA positively affects CI

3.4 Quality of Content (QC)

The concept of content quality encompasses the perceived excellence, relevance, accuracy, and usefulness of the information or materials provided in a specific context [51]. In an extension of the ECM model, Gokhan and Park introduced the dimensions of information quality and system quality, finding that they positively influence confirmation. The quality of the information system plays a significant role in shaping users' perception of a website [52]. The quality of content, in particular, serves as a crucial factor in influencing users' perception of the information system's usefulness, ultimately impacting their frequency of use. System quality, as described by Chen (2010), refers to the quality of the information system's processing capabilities [53]. Additionally, Lin (2007) suggests that website quality can be assessed based on factors such as website design and interactivity [54]. Based on these arguments, we hypothesize the following:

- **H8:** QC positively affects CF
- **H9:** QC positively affects PU

3.5 Habit (HA)

Verplanken (1997) considers a habit to be an "automated pattern of behaviour displayed repeatedly by an individual in a given situation. Habits are formed through repeated behaviour and experience and are characterised by stability and permanence". Recent studies have shown that users' long-term habits of using information systems platforms in their daily lives have a significant impact on their behavioural intention to continue using the technology [55, 56]. Users' habits of using information technology products such as information technology and online learning platforms have a significant positive impact on their intention to use these products over time [48–57]. Limayem's 2008 study investigated the influence of habit on users' intention to continue using the platform by extending the research model of continuous use information systems [74]. Kang et al. used an extended ECM model to explore the relationship between how habit affects users' intention to continue using and true long-term use behaviour, and the results showed that habit has a The results showed that habit had a significant impact on users' intention to continue using the platform [58]. Based on the above research, we propose the following hypothesis:

- **H10:** HA positively affects PU

3.6 Enjoyment (EM)

According to academic definitions in the field of enjoyment psychology, enjoyment can be described as a subjective feeling that involves positive emotions, satisfaction and pleasure experienced by an individual in a given situation. The generation and experience of enjoyment is influenced by external factors such as the individual's needs, expectations, values, personality traits and environmental factors [59]. In a 2009 study by Ha and Stoel on factors influencing university students' use of e-shopping platforms, they found that users' perception of hedonic pleasure while using the platform was an important factor in determining willingness to continue using the information system [60]. Users' perceived enjoyment when using mobile morning systems has a positive impact on users' mobile commerce loyalty [61]. Hsiao and Chiou found in their study of factors influencing online game players' attitudes towards gaming that whether players can perceive enjoyment while playing online video games significantly influenced their attitudes towards online games and their willingness to play games in the long term [62]. Zhou and Lu found in their study that when users perceive enjoyment while using mobile even communication systems users' satisfaction with the platform satisfaction and the willingness to use it in the long term are significantly increased [63]. In their study of factors influencing the sustainability of Internet information systems, Thong et al. found that the factor of perceived enjoyment had a positive effect on satisfaction and intention to continue using [64]. in their study of college students' online repurchase intentions, Wen et al. found that perceived enjoyment had a significant positive effect on US college students' online repurchase persistence intentions [65] Based on these arguments, we propose the following hypothesis:

- **H11:** EM positively affects PU
- **H12:** EM positively affects PEU

3.7 System Quality (SQ)

In the field of software engineering and systems development, system quality can be defined as the attributes and characteristics that a system possesses in terms of meeting specific requirements and goals. System quality is the assessment and measurement of the overall functionality, reliability, performance, maintainability, usability and security of a system [66]. Cheng (2012) investigated the factors influencing nurses' willingness to consistently use e-learning systems and found that the system quality of online learning systems had a significant impact on the perceived ease of use of online learning platforms [67]. In a study of mobile websites, Zhou (2011) found that the system quality of mobile websites could positively influence users' perceived ease of use of the websites [68]. Based on the above arguments, we propose the following hypothesis (Fig. 1):

- **H13:** SQ positively affects PEU

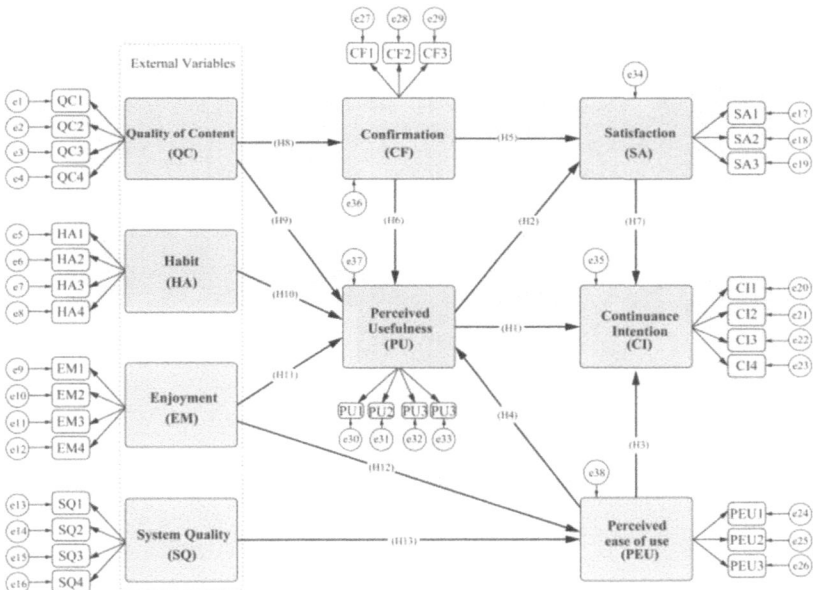

Fig. 1. The conceptual framework.

4   Research Methodology

4.1   Research Context

Midjourney and ChatGPT are the platforms currently being implemented for Artificial Intelligence Generative Content. Midjourney currently has over 16 million users. It uses artificial intelligence models to automatically generate various types of image content based on specified themes, keywords, formats, styles and other conditions, providing users with a high-quality, efficient and highly personalised content service. Midjourney has now achieved two major breakthroughs, one in understanding language and the other in creating images, and the combination of these two technologies has led to it being able to generate images at a very fast rate (Fig. 2). ChatGPT is a new artificial intelligence technology-powered AIGC platform from OpenAI. It has language understanding and text generation capabilities, in particular it generates content based on an internet corpus of real-life books, essays, conversations, etc. (Fig. 2). This enables ChatGPT to have a wide range of knowledge, as well as the ability to complete interactions and write emails, copy, essays, translations and other content based on user needs. Midjourney and ChatGPT are two of the most commonly used AIGC data platforms today.

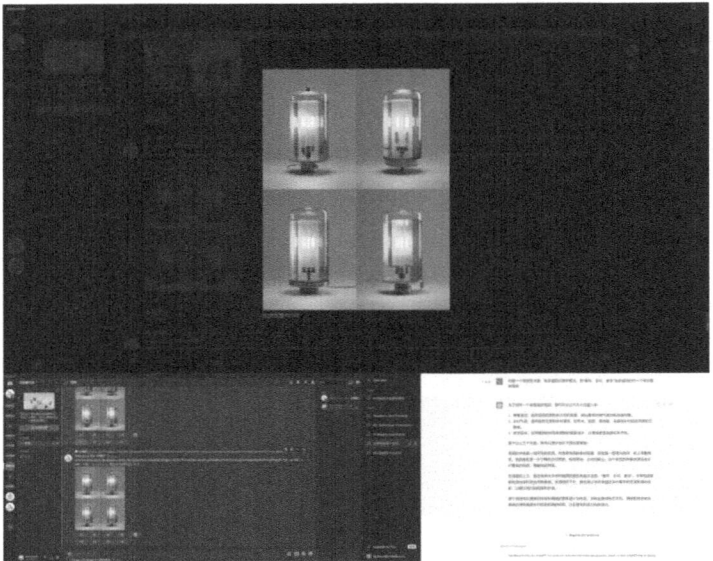

Fig. 2. Midjourney and ChatGPT.

4.2 Research Design

The questionnaires utilized in this study were carefully chosen from previous studies to ensure their applicability: perceived usefulness [26, 70, 71], perceived ease of use Davis (1989), confirmation [14, 16, 49], satisfaction [14, 58], continuance intention [14, 16], enjoyment [58, 72], habit [72, 73], quality of content [76], system quality [77, 78]. A pretest was conducted with a select group of participants to confirm the feasibility of the questionnaire. Based on the feedback received from these individuals, slight modifications were made to improve comprehension of the variable data.

The first section of the questionnaire is designed to classify respondents based on their experience with or familiarity with Midjourney and ChatGPT. This information is crucial in understanding the sample's characteristics and how they may impact the study's results. The second section gathers demographic information such as gender and living conditions, providing valuable insights into the sample's characteristics and their potential influence on the study's outcomes. The third section uses a 5-point Likert scale to measure each variable in the study through rating scale questions. Respondents indicate their level of agreement with each statement on a scale from 1 ("strongly disagree") to 5 ("strongly agree"). The specific measurement items used in this section are detailed in Table 3. Table 1 presents an overview of the demographic characteristics of the study's participants.

4.3   Sampling Strategy and Sample Collection

This study used a multi-stage approach to collect data from participants. The first stage involved conducting interviews to gather qualitative data. As the AIGC platform is an emerging content generation platform, current research suggests that the main audience served by the platform is young artistic creators, so the target audience for this study is 16–30 year olds with relevant needs. During these interviews, the researchers spoke with designers, artists, and art and design college students in Nanjing, Jiangsu Province. The main focus of the interviews was to understand the participants' current profession, their experience with Midjourneyand ChatGPT platforms, and their views on these platforms. To ensure that all participants had a basic understanding of Midjourneyand ChatGPT platforms, the researchers provided some platforms for them to experience. This allowed participants who were not familiar with Midjourneyand ChatGPT to gain a better understanding of these platforms and how they work. Through these interviews, the researchers were able to gather valuable insights into the experiences and opinions of individuals who work in creative fields and may have used Midjourney and ChatGPT platforms in their work.

Secondly, the researchers asked participants to complete a survey to gather their views on Midjourney and ChatGPT platforms. To ensure the quality and validity of the survey, the researchers conducted a pretest with 60 art and design college students. Based on the feedback from these pretest participants, the researchers made modifications and improvements to the survey. This allowed them to refine the questionnaire and improve its efficiency and quality before distributing it more widely. By taking this approach, the researchers were able to reduce the number of unqualified questionnaires and improve the practicality and scientificity of their survey. This, in turn, helped them gather more accurate and reliable data from participants.

In the third phase of the data survey for this study, we spread the data collection from schools to other parts of the community For example, in Baiqi artist studio,Nangjing Deji art gallery or other places.

In order to reduce the impact of sampling error on this experiment, the following steps are used in this paper: 1. Define the target population: clearly define the target population to be studied, i.e. the population or group to be investigated. 2. Determine the sample size: ensure the reliability of the statistical results by determining the required sample size. The size of the sample size should be determined according to the overall size, expected error and confidence level. A larger sample size can usually reduce the error.3. Random sampling: Use random sampling methods to select samples from the target population. 4. Survey implementation: Conducting a survey on a selected sample. Ensure that the questionnaire is well designed, with clear and unambiguous questions, and that the survey is conducted at the appropriate time and place. A reasonable survey process can improve the recall rate and the reliability of the data. A total of 348 questionnaires were collected for this study, excluding 36 invalid questionnaires, leaving 312 valid questionnaires, a valid rate of 89.65%.

5   Analysis and Results

5.1   Descriptive Statistics

As illustrated in Table 1, the majority of respondents (41.35%) were between the ages of 21 and 25. The gender distribution was 40.37% female and 59.63% male. In terms of education level, the largest group (39.73%) held a bachelor's degree, while those with a graduate degree made up the smallest group at 9.73%. Nearly half (47.39%) of the respondents reported using the Midjourney platform at least once a month. More than half (57.05%) of the participants had first used the Midjourney platform within the past 1–3 months, while only 11.55% had first used it within the past 9–12 months.

Table 1. Descriptive statistics of respondents' characteristics.

Demographic variable	Categories	Frequency	Percentage(%)
Age	16–20 age	97	31.09
	21–25 age	129	41.35
	26–30 age	86	27.56
Gender	Male	186	59.63
	Female	126	40.37
Educational level	Secondary school	50	16.06
	Vocational degree	107	34.28
	Bachelor degree	124	39.73
	Graduate degree	31	9.73
Usage Frequency	At least once a day	21	6.51
	At least once a week	87	27.78
	At least once a month	146	47.39
	At least once a half year	58	18.32
Platform Usage Time From the First Use	1–3 months	178	57.05
	3–6 months	52	16.66
	6–9 months	46	14.74
	9–12 months	36	11.55

5.2   The Measurement Model Assessment

This study employed SPSS 27.0 for confirmatory factor analysis and descriptive statistics, and utilized AMOS 28.0 for structural equation modeling.

This study used SPSS 27.0 for confirmatory factor analysis and descriptive statistics and AMOS 28.0 for structural equation modelling. In order to assess the fit index of the model, the CFA method proposed by Anderson and Gerbing in 1988 was used in this study [79, 80]. From Table 2, it can be observed that the model exhibited a good fit within an acceptable range. The Chi-square/df value was 1.097, falling between the suggested range of 1.0 and 3.0. The RMSEA value was 0.018, below the maximum cutoff of 0.10 [78]. The NFI $= 0.882$, IFI $= 0.988$, and CFI $= 0.988$ respectively, all surpassing the recommended threshold of 0.85 [79, 80]. Therefore, the results of this study demonstrate a favorable model fit.

Table 2. The values of fit indices.

Fit indices	Chi-square/df	RMSEA	NFI	IFI	CFI
Actual	1.097	0.018	0.882	0.988	0.988
Recommended	<3	<0.06	>0.85	>0.85	>0.85

In addition, we measured the reliability and validity of the data by combining reliability (CR) [79], Cronbach's alpha and average variance extracted (AVE). The value of Cronbach's alpha should be 0.70 or above [82]. In the data in this paper, Cronbach's alpha was between 0.794 and 0.865, so the data were satisfactory, and CR and AVE were considered acceptable if they were above 0.70 and 0.5. In our study [56], CR varied between 0.803 and 0.868 and AVE varied between 0.560 and 0.689, and these were satisfactory.

In the table presented in this study, the standardized regression coefficients represent the direct effect values between variables. These coefficients are also known as path coefficients. The table also includes information about the statistical significance of these relationships. This is indicated by the probability values (P) presented in the table. When P is less than 0.001, it is represented by "***". When P is between 0.001 and 0.01, it is represented by "**". When P is between 0.01 and 0.05, it is represented by "*". In all other cases, the P value is presented directly in the column. Using a significance level of 0.05, the researchers can determine whether there is a direct effect between two variables. If there is a significant relationship, the standardized regression coefficient indicates the strength of this effect.

The final results are shown in Table 4. The findings indicate that perceived usefulness significantly influences both behavioral intention (H1:$\beta = 0.63$) and satisfaction (H2:$\beta = 0.38$). Therefore, H1 and H2 are supported. Perceived ease of use has a significant impact on behavioral intention (H3:$\beta = 0.34$) and satisfaction (H5: $\beta = 0.24$), as well as on perceived usefulness (H6: $\beta = 0.15$), providing support for H5. Additionally, satisfaction demonstrates a positive correlation with continued intention to use (H7: $\beta = 0.42$). Content quality has a positive and statistically significant influence on confirmation (H8: $\beta = 0.25$) and perceived usefulness (H9: $\beta = 0.19$), thus validating H8 and H9. Habit directly affects perceived usefulness (H10: $\beta = 0.22$), supporting H10. Enjoyment has a positive and statistically significant impact on perceived ease of use (H12: $\beta =$

Table 3. Results of confirmatory factor analysis.

	Items and contents	Factor loading	AVE	CR	Alpha
PU	PU1: I think AIGC platforms are beneficial	0.814	0.514	0.807	0.838
	PU2: Using AIGC platforms has improved my ability in daily painting	0.744			
	PU3: Using AIGC platforms improves my efficiency in daily painting	0.709			
	PU4: Overall I find AIGC platforms to be useful for painting	0.580			
PEU	PEU1:Participating in AIGC platforms is easy	0.814	0.573	0.801	0.798
	PEU2: The tools and functions in the AIGC platforms are easy to use	0.744			
	PEU3: Learning how to use AI in the application is easy	0.709			
CF	CF1: My experience with using AIGC platforms was better than what I expected	0.762	0.649	0.847	0.846
	CF2: The service level provided by AIGC platforms was better than what I expected	0.867			
	CF3: My expectation from using AIGC platforms was satisfied as a whole	0.785			
Satisfaction	SA1: My overall experience of AIGC platforms use was very satisfying	0.712	0.576	0.803	0.794
	SA2: My overall experience of AIGC platforms use was very pleasant	0.799			
	SA3: My overall experience of AIGC platforms use was a good idea	0.764			
QC	QC1: The works created with AI are diverse in style and can meet my needs	0.794	0.577	0.845	0.845
	QC2: The works created with AI are quality and can meet my needs	0.747			
	QC3: The works created with AI are accuracy and can meet my needs	0.781			
	QC4: AIGC platforms provides required content and information	0.715			
EM	EM1: Using AIGC platforms provides me with a lot of enjoyment	0.684	0.510	0.806	0.804
	EM2: Using AIGC platforms is fun	0.741			

(*continued*)

Table 3. (*continued*)

	Items and contents	Factor loading	AVE	CR	Alpha
	EM3: Using AIGC platforms gives me pleasure	0.784			
	EM4: Using AIGC platforms makes me feel at ease	0.640			
HA	HA1: I use AIGC platforms as a matter of habit	0.709	0.546	0.828	0.827
	HA2: Using AIGC platforms has become automatic to me	0.740			
	HA3: Using AIGC platforms is natural to me	0.767			
	HA4:Using AIGC platforms has become a routine for me	0.738			
SQ	SQ1: AIGC platforms is aesthetically satisfying	0.746	0.618	0.866	0.865
	SQ2: AIGC platforms optimizes response time	0.812			
	SQ3: AIGC platforms is user friendly	0.827			
	SQ4: AIGC platforms possesses structured design	0.757			
CI	CI1: I intend to continue using AIGC platforms rather than discontinue its use	0.707	0.513	0.808	0.808
	CI2: I will keep using AIGC platforms as regularly as I do now	0.701			
	CI3: I tend to use AIGC platforms	0.710			
	CI4: I intend to increase my use of AIGC platforms in the future	0.747			

0.17), but its influence on perceived usefulness is relatively small. Furthermore, system quality is positively related to perceived ease of use (H13: $\beta = 0.26$) (Fig. 3).

Table 4. Path analysis results.

			Estimate	S.E	C.R	P	β
CI	<---	PU	0.38	0.08	5.036	***	0.63
SA	<---	PU	0.42	0.08	5.02	***	0.38
CI	<---	PEU	0.15	0.04	3.888	***	0.34
PU	<---	PEU	0.11	0.05	2.089	0.037	0.15
SA	<---	CF	0.2	0.06	3.543	***	0.24
PU	<---	CF	0.12	0.05	2.189	0.029	0.15
CI	<---	SA	0.23	0.06	4.108	***	0.42
CF	<---	QC	0.24	0.07	3.648	***	0.25
PU	<---	QC	0.14	0.05	2.726	0.006	0.19
PU	<---	HA	0.16	0.05	3.164	0.002	0.22
PU	<---	EM	0.08	0.05	1.519	0.129	0.11
PEU	<---	EM	0.18	0.07	2.438	0.015	0.17
PEU	<---	QA	0.26	0.07	3.89	***	0.26

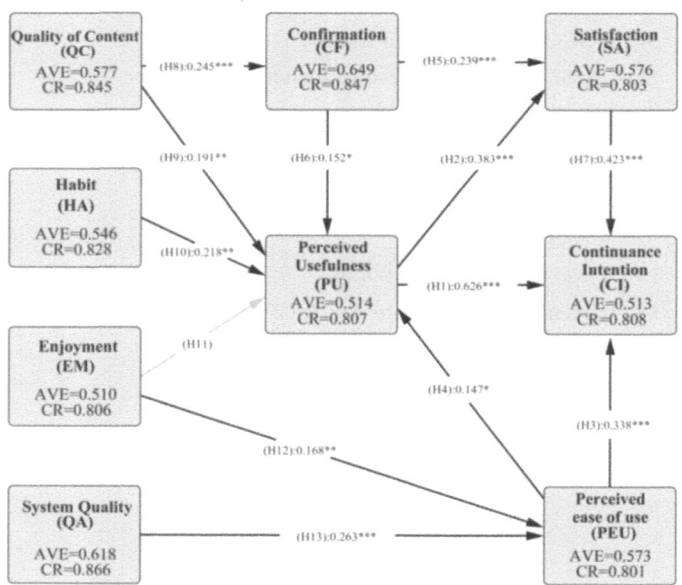

Fig. 3. Determinants of users' continuance intention of using AIGC platforms.

6 Conclusion and Suggestions

6.1 Conclusion

In the context of the explosive development of artificial intelligence, this paper constructs a new model based on TAM and ECM and adds new external variables based on the characteristics of the AIGC platform in order to provide a more specific picture of users' intention to continue using the AIGC platform. A total of 13 hypotheses were formulated and analysed in relation to the questionnaire data and SEM. The results show that all the hypotheses were successfully tested, except for H11, as shown in Table 4. The specific analysis is as follows.

In the context of the explosive development of artificial intelligence, this paper constructs a new model based on TAM and ECM, and adds new external variables based on the characteristics of the AIGC platform in order to provide a more specific description of users' intention to continue using the AIGC platform. A combination of offline interviews and questionnaires were used to collect 312 sets of valid data and the data collected were analysed using SPSS27.0 and AMOS28.0 tools. A total of 13 hypotheses were formulated for this study and the results showed that all hypotheses were successfully tested except for H11, as shown in Representation 4. The specific analysis is shown below.

As shown in Table 4, the potential factors that have a direct impact on users' intention to use the AIGC platform in the long term are perceived usefulness ($\beta = 0.626$), perceived ease of use ($\beta = 0.338$) and satisfaction ($\beta = 0.423$). Of these, perceived usefulness had the greatest impact, suggesting that the higher the perceived usefulness of the platforms users, the stronger the user's intention to use the platform in the long term. Perceived usefulness ($\beta = 0.152$) and satisfaction ($\beta = 0.239$) are directly and positively influenced by expectation confirmation, which indirectly influences users' intention to use the AIGC platform in the long term. In addition, we found that the perceived usefulness of the platform had a significant positive relationship with the satisfaction of the users ($\beta = 0.383$). Based on the above research we can find that perceived usefulness and satisfaction influence the continued intention to use the AIGC platform. In addition, the positive influence of perceived usefulness and perceived ease of use on users' intention to continue using the platform and the positive influence of perceived ease of use on perceived usefulness in the TAM model were also verified, indicating that the higher the users' perceived usefulness of using the AIGC platform, the stronger their intention to use the platform and the stronger their intention to continue using it. Perceived ease of use can also indirectly influence users' willingness to continue using the platform by positively influencing their perceived usefulness. The above estimation results suggest that the AIGC platform should focus on improving user experience during the development process, providing more content and services after users have used the platform, and improving the ease of use design in order to increase users' perceived usefulness and satisfaction with the use of the AIGC platform, thereby enhancing users' willingness to continue using it. In this study, our findings suggest that individuals' intention to continue using the AIGC platform is influenced by the other variables proposed in this study, namely enjoyment, validation, variability, content quality and habit. These potential influencing factors can indirectly affect users' intention to continue using through other variables. In addition, content quality can indirectly influence users' intention to continue using the platform by positively influencing their perceived usefulness and expectations. This suggests that the quality of content on the AIGC platform is a key factor that can influence users' intention to continue using the platform. If the platform's content is of high quality, users will have higher confirmation and perceived usefulness after using the platform. We found that habit indirectly influences users' intention to continue using the AIGC platform through perceived usefulness. Therefore, we expect that when users use the AIGC platform on a regular basis for habitual reasons, this will indirectly contribute to users' continued intention through perceived usefulness. A number of IS studies have investigated the direct or moderating effects of habit. Finally, our study found that the system quality of the AIGC platform had a direct positive effect on perceived ease of use and indirectly influenced users' continued intention.

6.2 Suggestions

Based on the above findings, this study makes the following recommendations in order to optimise user satisfaction and increase users' willingness to continue using the AIGC platform.

Technological innovation: The AIGC platform should gradually complete techno-logical innovation in order to respond to users' personalised needs, invoking the latest AI technology to complete the innovation of content processing, visual interface and evaluation feedback, improving the quality and efficiency of AI-generated content and increasing the usefulness and ease of use of the AIGC platform. The AIGC platform can also cooperate with others in the future to achieve cross-platform content creation. With the continuous improvement of the system level, the AIGC platform can provide users with better quality and more customised content and services, increasing user satisfac-tion and expectation confirmation, thus enhancing their willingness to continue using the platform.

User experience: The AIGC platform can increase users' satisfaction with the plat-form by providing better quality content, attentive services and convenient operations. The platform can also expand the channels for users, lower the threshold of use, so that more users can experience the convenient services of the AIGC platform, and encourage users to actively provide feedback and suggestions, and regularly conduct interactive exchange sessions to improve user participation and optimise user experience. Users' trust in the platform should be increased. In the future, the AIGC platform can invest more in promotion to attract the interest of more creators and increase users' satisfaction with the platform, which will in turn increase their willingness to continue using it.

Business expansion: The AIGC platform is currently a new type of module, with few links to other platforms. AIGC can open more platform ports in the future, and through multi-channel and multi-platform interventions can increase users' understanding of the platform and attract more users. At the same time, the AIGC platform can provide customised content generation services for different consumer groups (e.g. new media, design, sales, education, freelancing, etc.) and can help users optimise their creative solutions to increase their satisfaction and intention to continue using the platform. The AIGC platform should be expanded in the future to provide users with more services such as image creation, text modification, creative generation, interactive entertainment, etc. to optimise user satisfaction and continued usage of the platform.

6.3 Limitation and Recommendation for Further Studies

Firstly, the current research model does not take into account other factors that may influence users' intention to continue using the AIGC platform. The model could be extended in future studies by including more variables and examining their impact on users' intention to continue using the platform. Secondly, the model in this study only measured factors such as AIGC platform users' satisfaction with the platform and intention to continue using it at a single point in time. Changes in users' intentions towards the platform over a longer time dimension could be studied in future research, as individuals' preferences and preferences for the platform change as they gain more information and experience. Finally, as the AIGC platform is still in its emerging stage, its main audience is focused on a younger creative demographic. Therefore, the sample for this study focuses on individuals aged 16–30. As the platform develops, future studies can gradually expand the study population to improve the generalisability of the findings.

Acknowledgments. A third level heading in 9-point font size at the end of the paper is used for general acknowledgments, for example: This study was funded by X (grant number Y).

Disclosure of Interests. It is now necessary to declare any competing interests or to specifically state that the authors have no competing interests. Please place the statement with a third level heading in 9-point font size beneath the (optional) acknowledgments [1], for example: The authors have no competing interests to declare that are relevant to the content of this article. Or: Author A has received research grants from Company W. Author B has received a speaker honorarium from Company X and owns stock in Company Y. Author C is a member of committee Z.

References

1. Cao, Y., Li, S., Liu, Y., et al.: A comprehensive survey of ai-generated content (aigc): a history of generative AI from Gan to chatgpt. arXiv preprint arXiv:2303.04226 (2023)
2. Yunjiu, L., Wei, W., Zheng, Y.: Artificial intelligence-generated and human expert-designed vocabulary tests: a comparative study. SAGE Open **12**(1), 21582440221082130 (2022)
3. Poltronieri, F.A., Hänska, M.: Technical images and visual art in the era of artificial intelligence: from GOFAI to GANs. In: Proceedings of the 9th International Conference on Digital and Interactive Arts, pp. 1–8 (2019)
4. Cetinic, E., She, J.: Understanding and creating art with AI: review and outlook. ACM Trans. Multimedia Comput. Commun. Appl. **18**(2), 1–22 (2022)
5. Chen, M., Radford, A., Child, R., et al.: Generative pretraining from pixels. In: International Conference on Machine Learning, pp. 1691–1703. PMLR (2020)
6. Floridi, L., Chiriatti, M.: GPT-3: its nature, scope, limits, and consequences. Mind. Mach. **30**, 681–694 (2020)

---

[1] If EquinOCS, our proceedings submission system, is used, then the disclaimer can be provided directly in the system.

7. Cetinic, E., Grgic, S.: Automated painter recognition based on image feature extraction. In: Proceedings ELMAR-2013, pp. 19–22. IEEE (2013)
8. Keren, D.: Painter identification using local features and naive bayes. In: 2002 International Conference on Pattern Recognition, vol. 2, pp. 474–477. IEEE (2002)
9. Agarwal, S., Karnick, H., Pant, N., et al.: Genre and style-based painting classification. In: 2015 IEEE Winter Conference on Applications of Computer Vision, pp. 588–594. IEEE (2015)
10. Shamir, L., Macura, T., Orlov, N., et al.: Impressionism, expressionism, surrealism: automated recognition of painters and schools of art. ACM Trans. Appl. Percept. **7**(2), 1–17 (2010)
11. Chang, Y.P., Zhu, D.H.: The role of perceived social capital and flow experience in building users' continuance intention to social networking sites in China. Comput. Hum. Behav. **28**(3), 995–1001 (2012)
12. Deng, X., Yuan, L.: Integrating technology acceptance model with social capital theory to promote passive users' continuance intention toward virtual brand communities. IEEE Access **8**, 73061–73070 (2020)
13. Gong, X., Liu, Z., Zheng, X., et al.: Why are experienced users of WeChat likely to continue using the app?. Asia Pacific J. Market. Logist. (2018)
14. Bhattacherjee, A.: Understanding information systems continuance: an expectation-confirmation model. MIS Quar. 351–370 (2001)
15. Davis, F.D., Bagozzi, R.P., Warshaw, P.R.: User acceptance of computer technology: a comparison of two theoretical models. Manage. Sci. **35**(8), 982–1003 (1989)
16. Kim, B.: An empirical investigation of mobile data service continuance: incorporating the theory of planned behavior into the expectation–confirmation model. Expert Syst. Appl. **37**(10), 7033–7039 (2010)
17. Cheng, Y.M.: Effects of quality antecedents on e-learning acceptance. Internet Res. (2012)
18. Al-Hattami, H.M.: Determinants of intention to continue usage of online shopping under a pandemic: COVID-19. Cogent Bus. Manage. **8**(1), 1936368 (2021)
19. Prasetya, F.H., Harnadi, B., Widiantoro, A.D., et al.: Extending ECM with quality factors to investigate continuance intention to use E-learning. In: 2021 Sixth International Conference on Informatics and Computing (ICIC), pp. 1–7. IEEE (2021)
20. Gelderblom, H., Matthee, M., Hattingh, M., et al.: High school learners' continuance intention to use electronic textbooks: a usability study. Educ. Inf. Technol. **24**, 1753–1776 (2019)
21. Gao, L.: Research on the influence of interactive animation based on extended TAM model on user focus immersion in software application. Converter **2021**(7), 1109–1116 (2021)
22. Allam, H., Qusa, H., Alameer, O., et al.: Theoretical perspective of technology acceptance models: towards a unified model for social media applciations. In: 2019 Sixth HCT Information Technology Trends (ITT), pp. 154–159. IEEE (2019)
23. Nadlifatin, R., Miraja, B., Persada, S., et al.: The measurement of University students' intention to use blended learning system through technology acceptance model (TAM) and theory of planned behavior (TPB) at developed and developing regions: lessons learned from Taiwan and Indonesia. Int. J. Emerg. Technol. Learn. **15**(9), 219–230 (2020)
24. Anderson, E.W., Sullivan, M.W.: The antecedents and consequences of customer satisfaction for firms. Mark. Sci. **12**(2), 125–143 (1993)
25. Patterson, P.G., Johnson, L.W., Spreng, R.A.: Modeling the determinants of customer satisfaction for business-to-business professional services. J. Acad. Mark. Sci. **25**(1), 4–17 (1997)
26. Barnes, S.J., Böhringer, M.: Modeling user continuance behavior in microblogging services: the case of Twitter. J. Comput. Inform. Syst. **51**(4), 1–10 (2011)
27. Lee, M.C.: Explaining and predicting users' continuance intention toward elearning: an extension of the expectation–onfirmation model. Comput. Educ. **54**(2), 506–516 (2010)

28. Lee, M.C., Tsai, T.R.: What drives people to continue to play online games? An extension of technology model and theory of planned behavior. Int. J. Hum.-Comput. Interact. **26**(6), 601–620 (2010)

29. Tang, J.E., Chiang, C.: Integrating experiential value of blog use into the expectation-confirmation theory model. Soc. Behav. Pers. **38**(10), 1377–1389 (2010)

30. Taylor, P.A.T.: Understanding information technology usage: a test of competing models. Inform. Syst. Res. **6**(2), 144–176 (1995)

31. Davis, R.P., Bagozzi, P.R.W.: User acceptance of computer technology: a comparison of two theoretical models. Manage. Sci. **35**(8), 982–1003 (1989)

32. Mathieson: predicting user intentions: comparing the technology acceptance model with the theory of planned behaviour. Inform. Syst. Res. **2**(3), 173–191 (1991)

33. Venkatesh, F.D.D.: A theoretical extension of the technology acceptance model: four longitudinal field studies. Manage. Sci. **46**(2), 186–204 (2000)

34. Adi, A., et al.: The use of a Technology Acceptance Model (TAM) to predict patients' usage of a personal health record system: the role of security, privacy, and usability. Int. J. Environ. Res. Public Health **20.2**, 1347 (2023)

35. Natasia, S.R., Yuyun, T.W., Parastika, A.: Acceptance analysis of NUADU as e-learning platform using the Technology Acceptance Model (TAM) approach. Procedia Comput. Sci. **197**,512–520 (2022)

36. Zin, K.S.L.T., et al.: A study on technology acceptance of digital healthcare among older korean adults using extended tam (Extended Technology Acceptance Model). Administ. Sci. **13.2**, 42 (2023)

37. Stone, R.W., Baker-Eveleth, L.: Students' expectation, confirmation and continuance intention to useelectronic textbooks. Comput. Hum. Behav. **29**(3), 984–990 (2013)

38. Wang, W., Ngai, E.W.T., Wei, H.: Explaining instant messaging continuance intention: the role of personality. Int. J. Hum.-Comput. Interact. **28**(8), 500–510 (2011)

39. Abbas, H.A., Hamdy, H.I.: Determinants of continuance intention factor in Kuwait communication market: case study of Zain-Kuwait. Comput. Hum. Behav. **49**, 648–657 (2015)

40. Li, H., Liu, Y.: Understanding post-adoption behaviors of e-service users in the context of online travel services. Inform. Manage. **51**(8), 1043–1052 (2014)

41. Lin, W.-S., Wang, C.-H.: Antecedences to continued intentions of adopting e-learning system in blended learning instruction: a contingency framework based on models of information system success and task-technology fit. Comput. Educ. **58**(1), 88–99 (2012)

42. Tang, J.-T.E., Tang, T.-I., Chiang, C.-H.: Blog learning: effects of users' usefulness and efficiency towards continuance intention. Behav. Inform. Technol. **33**(1), 36–50 (2012)

43. Chou, S.-W., Min, H.-T., Chang, Y.-C., Lin, C.-T.: Understanding continuance intention of knowledge creation using extended expectation– confirmation theory: an empirical study of Taiwan and China online communities. Behav. Inform. Technol. **29**(6), 557–570 (2009)

44. Park, N., Rhoads, M., Hou, J., Lee, K.M.: Understanding the acceptance of teleconferencing systems among employees: an extension of the technology acceptance model. Comput. Hum. Behav. **39**, 118–127 (2014)

45. Alturki, U., Aldraiweesh, A.: Application of learning management system (LMS) during the covid-19 pandemic: a sustainable acceptance model of the expansion technology approach. Sustainability **13**(19), 10991 (2021)

46. Chiu, C.-M., Wang, E.T.G.: Understanding Web-based learning continuance intention: the role of subjective task value. Inform. Manage. **45**(3), 194–201 (2008)

47. Oliver, R.L.: A cognitive model for the antecedents and consequences of satisfaction. J. Mark. Res. **17**(4), 460–469 (1980)

48. Bhattacherjee, A., Barfar, A.: Information technology continuance research: current state and future directions. Asia Pacific J. Inform. Syst. **21**(2), 1–18 (2011)

49. Lee, Y., Kwon, O.: Intimacy, familiarity and continuance intention: an extended expectation–confirmation model in web-based services. Electron. Commer. Res. Appl. **10**(3), 342–357 (2011)
50. Agrebi, S., Jallais, J.: Explain the intention to use smartphones for mobile shopping. J. Retail. Consum. Serv. **22**, 16–23 (2015)
51. Almahamid, S., Rub, F.A.: Factors that determine continuance intention to use e-learning system: an empirical investigation. In: International Conference on Telecommunication Technology and Applications Proceedings of CSIT, vol. 5(1), pp. 242–246 (2011)
52. Alshurideh, M., Salloum, S.A., Al Kurdi, B., et al.: Understanding the quality determinants that influence the intention to use the mobile learning platforms: a practical study. Int. J. Interact. Mobile Technol. **13**(11) (2019)
53. Chen, C.W.: Impact of quality antecedents on taxpayer satisfaction with online tax-filing systems—an empirical study. Inform. Manage. **47**(5–6), 308–315 (2010)
54. Lin, H.F.: The impact of website quality dimensions on customer satisfaction in the B2C e-commerce context. Total Qual. Manag. Bus. Excell. **18**(4), 363–378 (2007)
55. Liao, C., Palviab, P., Lin, H.-N.: The roles of habit and web site quality in ecommerce. Int. J. Inf. Manage. **26**(6), 469–483 (2006)
56. Gefen, D., Straub, D.W., Boudreau, M.C.: Structural equation modeling and regression: guidelines for research practice. Commun. Assoc. Inf. Syst. **4**(7), 1–70 (2000)
57. Limayenm, M., Hirt, S.G., Cheung, C.M.K.: Habit in the context of IS continuance: theory extension and scale development (2003)
58. Kang, Y.S., Hong, S., Lee, H.: Exploring continued online service usage behavior: the roles of self-image congruity and regret. Comput. Hum. Behav. **25**(1), 111–122 (2009)
59. van der Heijden, H.: User acceptance of hedonic information systems. MIS Q. **28**(4), 695–704 (2004)
60. Ha, S., Stoel, L.: Consumer e-shopping acceptance: antecedents in a technology acceptance model. J. Bus. Res. **62**(5), 565–571 (2009)
61. Cyr, D., Head, M., Ivanov, A.: Design aesthetics leading to m-loyalty in mobile commerce. Inform. Manage. **43**(8), 950–963 (2006)
62. Hsiao, C.-C., Chiou, J.-S.: The effects of a player's network centrality on resource accessibility, game enjoyment, and continuance intention: a study on online gaming communities. Electron. Commer. Res. Appl. **11**, 75–84 (2012)
63. Zhou, T., Lu, Y.: Examining mobile instant messaging user loyalty from the perspectives of network externalities and flow experience. Comput. Hum. Behav. **27**(2), 883–889 (2011)
64. Thong, J.Y.L., Hong, S.J., Tam, K.Y.: The effects of post-adoption beliefs on the expectation–confirmation model for information technology continuance. Int. J. Hum. Comput Stud. **64**(9), 799–810 (2006)
65. Wen, C., Prybutok, V.R., Xu, C.: An integrated model for customer online repurchase intention. J. Comput. Inform. Syst. **52**(1), 14–23 (2011)
66. Gorla, N., Somers, T.M., Wong, B.: Organizational impact of system quality, information quality, and service quality. J. Strateg. Inf. Syst. **19**, 207–228 (2010)
67. Cheng, Y.M.: The effects of information systems quality on nurses' acceptance of the electronic learning system. J. Nurs. Res. **20**, 19–31 (2012)
68. Zhou, T.: Examining the critical success factors of mobile website adoption. Online Inf. Rev. **35**, 636–652 (2011)
69. Tencent. How did Midjourney succeed (2023).https://new.qq.com/rain/a/20230508A0A4 IX00. Accessed 8 May 2023
70. Kwon, O., Wen, Y.: An empirical study of the factors affecting social network service use. Comput. Hum. Behav. **26**(2), 254–263 (2010)
71. Mäntymäki, M., Salo, J.: Teenagers in social virtual worlds: Continuous use and purchasing behavior in Habbo Hotel. Comput. Hum. Behav. **27**(6), 2088–2097 (2011)

72. Lin, K.-Y., Lu, H.-P.: Why people use social networking sites: an empirical study integrating network externalities and motivation theory. Comput. Hum. Behav. **27**(3), 1152–1161 (2011)
73. Chiu, C.-M., Hsu, M.-H., Lai, H., Chang, C.-M.: Re-examining the influence of trust on online repeat purchase intention: the moderating role of habit and its antecedents. Decis. Support Syst. **53**(4), 835–845 (2012)
74. Limayem, M., Hirt, S.G.: Force of habit and information systems usage: theory and initial validation. J. Assoc. Inf. Syst. **4**(1), 3 (2003)
75. Limayem, M., Hirt, S.G., Cheung, C.M.K.: Habit in the context of IS continuance: Theory extension and scale development. In: Proceedings of the eleventh European conference on information systems (ECIS 2003). Naples, Italy, June 19–21 (2003)
76. Petter, S., DeLone, W., McLean, E.: Measuring information systems success: models, dimensions, measures, and interrelationships. Eur. J. Inf. Syst. **17**, 236–263 (2008)
77. Ho, C.L., Dzeng, R.J.: Construction safety training via e-learning: learning effectiveness and user satisfaction. Comput. Educ. **55**, 858–867 (2010)
78. Ozkan, S., Koseler, R.: Multi-dimensional students' evaluation of e-learning systems in the higher education context: an empirical investigation. Comput. Educ. **53**, 1285–1296 (2009)
79. Hair, J.F., Anderson, R.E., Tatham, R.L., Black, W.C.: Multivariate data analysis with readings, 5th edn. Macmillan, New York (1998)
80. Anderson, J.C., Gerbing, D.W.: Structural equation modeling in practice: a review and recommended two-step approach. Psychol. Bull. **103**(3), 411–423 (1988)
81. Chin, W.W., Gopal, A.: Adoption intention in GSS: Relative importance of beliefs. Data Base Adv. Inform. Syst. **26**(2–3), 42–64 (1995)
82. Nunnally, J.C., Bernstein, I.H.: Psychometric theory, 3rd edn. McGraw-Hill, New York (1994)

The Effects of Conversation Initiation Strategies in Human-Aided Service Bots: The Role of Perceived Flexibility

Xixian Peng[1,2(✉)], Mengri Yang[1,2], Lingyi Zhou[1,2], and Xinwei Wang[3]

[1] Department of Data Science and Engineering Management, School of Management, Zhejiang University, Hangzhou 310058, China
1034487553@qq.com
[2] Neuromanagement Lab, Zhejiang University, Hangzhou 310058, China
[3] Department of Information Systems and Operations Management, Business School, University of Auckland, Auckland 1142, New Zealand

Abstract. This paper delves into the realm of human-aided service bots and aims to enhance consumers' experience with online services. Through a situational experimental study, we investigate how conversation initiation (by the human agent vs. by the AI agent) affects consumers' evaluations of human-aided service bots. The results reveal a positive influence of human agent (vs. AI agent) initiation on consumers' service evaluation, which is mediated by perceived flexibility and expectation confirmation. Moreover, the study suggests a moderating role of consumers' aversion to AI. These insights contribute to a deeper understanding of designing human-aided service bots and provide valuable guidance for enhancing the overall customer experience and satisfaction, ultimately benefiting both businesses and consumers.

Keywords: Human-aided Bot · Service Agent · Conversation Initiation · Perceived Flexibility

1 Introduction

In recent years, the development of artificial intelligence (AI) technology has led to a significant transformation in various fields, one breakthrough is the emergence of intelligent customer services or AI chatbots. Market analyses indicate that the global chatbot market, which was valued at $5.7 billion in 2023, is expected to expand to $ 34.6 Billion by 2032[1]. Although chatbots are highly useful in providing quick responses and handling a large volume of user queries, there are inherent challenges in their application. For example, due to algorithmic limitations like a restricted vocabulary, inappropriate choice of words, inadequate training data, and others, chatbots might not accurately understand user queries, leading to user frustration, poor customer satisfaction, and ultimately chatbot aversion (Schuetzler et al. 2021). To avoid these issues, a recent

---

[1] Chatbot Market Report (imarcgroup.com/chatbot-market).

© The Author(s), under exclusive license to Springer Nature Switzerland AG 2025
A. Coman et al. (Eds.): HCII 2024, LNCS 15375, pp. 68–76, 2025.
https://doi.org/10.1007/978-3-031-76806-4_5

trend, especially in the e-commerce industry, is the adoption of human-aided service bots or agents to involve human agents to assist AI agents in improving the performance and acceptance of chatbot services. Human-aided agents comprise a combination of AI agents and human agents, working together as a cohesive unit through a single interface (Schuetzler et al. 2021). By leveraging this human-aided agent system, chatbots efficiently handle simple questions and requests automatically, whereas complex queries that chatbots fail to address are transferred to human agents (Rai et al. 2019).

Despite the extensive research on chatbot design, the design of human-aided service agents warrants further exploration as the combined human and AI service model introduces distinguished features that are unexplored by previous literature. One noteworthy aspect is conversation initiation, referring to whether the AI agent or the human agent starts the conversation. Numerous studies demonstrate that consumers often prefer human agents over AI agents across a variety of contexts because users perceive that robot fall short in addressing issues with flexibility and innovation, as well as lacking uniqueness and empathy (Garvey et al. 2022; Longoni et al. 2019; Yu et al. 2024). In line with this perspective, we posit that initiating interactions with human agents can significantly enhance the user's initial belief that human customer support is readily available to address AI-unresolvable issues, thereby offering an enhanced perception of flexibility. An experimental study was conducted and offered support for the positive impact of human agent (vs. AI agent) initiation on consumers' service evaluation. In addition, the results confirmed the sequential mediating role of perceived flexibility and expectation confirmation and the moderation role of consumers' aversion toward AI.

Overall, our focus on human-aided service agents and exploration of conversation initiation offers a novel perspective on chatbot design which is important but not examined in previous literature. By demonstrating shifting the conversation initiator from the human agent to the AI agent would influence consumer perceptions and evaluations, our results offer a feasible practical implication for enhancing consumers' evaluations of chatbots.

2   Theoretical Backgrounds and Hypothesis Development

2.1   Conversation Initiation in Service Context

Conversation initiation occurs when one participant takes the conversational lead. In human-human dialogue, it is common for both individuals to initiate a conversation with a ritualistic verbal exchange (Cassell et al. 2001), which contributes to the development of a closer relationship as it makes both parties responsive to each other's contributions during an interaction. Previous research on initiation in a service context has primarily focused on the differences between agents and consumers (Bergner et al. 2023; Smith et al. 1999). In the context of service failure, several researchers have suggested that organization-initiated recovery efforts enhance customers' evaluations of the service provider more than customer-initiated complaint-handling efforts (Kelley et al. 1993; Smith et al. 1999). In human-computer interaction, initiation by a brand's AI-based conversational interface induces greater perceptions of humanness and leads to more intimate consumer-brand relationships (Bergner et al. 2023). However, there is a lack of research comparing the effects of initiation by AI and human agents in human-aided bot service scenarios.

Given the established preference for humans over AI agents in varied contexts, including service provision, recovery, and decision-making (Garvey et al. 2022; Longoni et al. 2019), in our particular context, this research posits that initiating the conversation by the human agent, rather than by the AI agent, could generate more favorable perceptions among consumers, consequently elevating the service evaluation of human-aided bots. This hypothesis stems from the premise that human agents, with their capacity to offer personalized and flexible interactions (Yu et al. 2024), might counterbalance any potential skepticism towards AI, setting positive expectations for the interaction that follows. As we will delve into later, consumers' psychological perceptions can shed light on the underlying mechanisms driving this effect. Accordingly, we hypothesize:

H1: In a human-aided bot service context, conversations initiated by the human agent will lead to higher service evaluations compared to those initiated by the AI agent.

2.2 Consumers' Perceived Flexibility and Expectation Confirmation

The concept of flexibility is of great significance in discussions and deliberations within various fields. In the service literature, employee flexibility has been extensively examined as an organizational expectation, with organizations requiring employees to be flexible and proficient in multitasking activities (Jena et al. 2019). While research on the perceived flexibility of service from AI agents is limited, recent studies have indicated that human agents are generally perceived as more flexible than AI agents, particularly when consumers encounter service request rejections (Yu et al. 2024). Therefore, in the context of human-aided bot service, initiating conversations by human agents may foster a perception of enhanced adaptability and an increased capability to tailor responses to individuals' specific needs. This perception contributes to the notion that the human-aid agent service is more flexible. Thus, we hypothesize that:

H2: In a human-aided bot service context, conversations initiated by the human agent will lead to higher perceived flexibility compared to those initiated by the AI agent.

Expectation-confirmation theory is widely used in the consumer behavior literature to study consumer satisfaction, post-purchase behavior (e.g., repurchase, complaining), and service marketing (Bhattacherjee 2001). This theory posits that consumers initially develop specific expectations regarding a product or service and subsequently evaluate its performance by comparing it to their pre-existing expectations. This evaluation process determines the extent to which their initial expectations are confirmed. The variance of expectation confirmation in human-AI interaction leads to a negative impact on subsequent purchase intentions (Crolic et al. 2022).

Adapting the expectation-confirmation theory to our specific context, the improved perception of flexibility afforded by human agents helps ensure that the actual service performance more effectively meets or exceeds the initial expectations set by consumers. Consequently, this alignment between perceived service performance and initial expectations fosters a more positive service evaluation. Hence, we hypothesize that:

H3: Consumers' perceived flexibility will increase the confirmation between human-aided agents' performance and consumers' expectations.

H4: Consumers' expectation confirmation will lead to a more favorable service evaluation of human-aided agents.

2.3 Moderation Effect of Aversion Toward AI

The aversion toward AI, rooted in algorithm aversion, describes individuals' tendency to discount algorithmic decisions, engaging in this behavior either consciously or unconsciously (Mahmud et al. 2022). People tend to reject algorithms and choose human decision-makers even if algorithms outperform humans (Dietvorst et al. 2015). In contrast, algorithm appreciation acknowledges the potential of algorithms to enhance decision-making by providing data-driven insights that surpass human cognitive limitations (You et al. 2022). This perspective appreciates the consistent and on-time responses of algorithms, recognizing their capacity to supplement human labor and enhance human capabilities. Supporters of algorithm appreciation advocate for the integration of human-aided bots as a pathway to optimized outcomes and increased efficiency.

Consumers' perceived flexibility of a human-aided agent, therefore, can be contingent upon different attitudes to AI. More specifically, individuals with a high level of aversion toward AI would be more skeptical about AI-initiated service, thus perceiving the service bot as lacking flexibility. On the other hand, individuals with a low level of aversion towards AI may attribute higher flexibility to AI-initiated interactions, recognizing the potential of AI to enrich customer engagement. These divergent perceptions influence the degree of expectation confirmation and, consequently, service evaluations. Thus, we hypothesize that:

H5a: Individuals with a high level of aversion towards AI are likely to evaluate the service of human-aided bots initiated by AI agents more negatively compared to those with a low level of AI aversion.

H5b: Individuals with a high level of aversion towards AI are likely to perceive AI-initiated conversations as less flexible, which decreases the confirmation between human-aided agents' performance and consumers' expectations, ultimately leading to lower service evaluation.

The research model is depicted in Fig. 1.

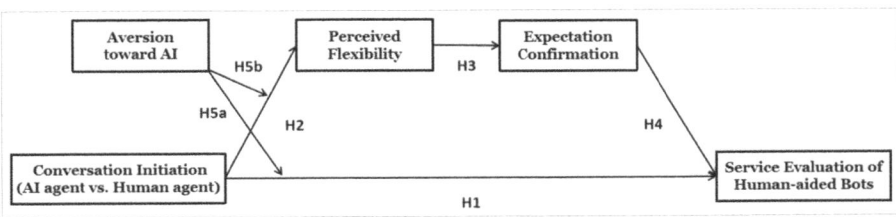

Fig. 1. Research Model

3   Empirical Overview

3.1   Participants and Procedure

239 participants (61.5% female; Mage = 31.22 years, SD = 7.27) were recruited from a crowdsourcing website named Credamo and compensated for money. One whose scores on all questions were the same was excluded from the following data analysis. We conducted a one-factor, two-level (conversation initiation: by the AI agent vs. by the human agent) between-subject study, and participants were randomly assigned to each group.

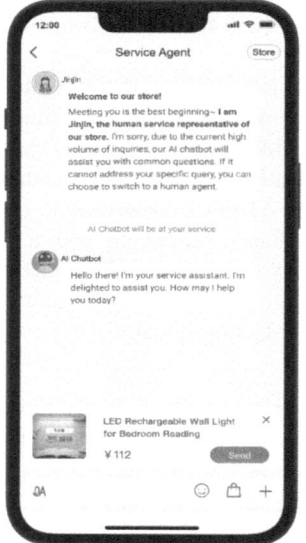 

Fig. 2. Conversation Initiation (left: human agent; right: AI agent)

We designed an online chatbot and simulated a real online service process. Participants first read a scenario in which they were asked to imagine that half a year ago they purchased a wall LED light from an online store, which was installed using double-sided adhesive tape and magnets. After using it for a while, the adhesive tape used for fixing the light naturally fell off. Participants were then instructed to contact the hybrid customer service agent of the online store to inquire about purchasing replacement adhesive tape for the wall light. The conversation proceeded in three steps. In step 1, the conversation was initiated by either a human agent or an AI agent (see Fig. 2). The agent informed the participants that the human agent was currently occupied and therefore, an AI agent would handle their inquiries. The AI agent was programmed to address common questions while giving customers the option to switch back to a human agent if needed. Moving on to Step 2, the participants sent their inquiry regarding the adhesive tape. However, due to the complexity of the question, the AI agent was unable to provide a satisfactory resolution or effectively address the issue. Finally, in Step 3, participants requested the assistance of a human agent, and promptly, a human agent intervened to provide an immediate and satisfactory resolution to the problem. (For the screenshot, see Fig. 3).

Fig. 3. Experiment Procedure (human agent-initiated)

3.2 Measurements

After the experiment, participants were asked to evaluate the service on three questions ("The service agent provides a good service," "I am satisfied with the agent's service"; "I felt uncomfortable about the service (R); *Cronbach's* $\alpha = 0.93$) (Yu et al. 2024). Participants also indicated their perceived flexibility of the agent on three questions ("The service agent has the flexibility to adapt to my request"; "The service agent has the ability to adapt to my need"; "The agent shows adequate flexibility in dealing with my problem"; *Cronbach's* $\alpha = 0.91$) (Yu et al. 2024). Expectation confirmation measurements included three items such as "my experience with using the online agent was better than what I expected" (*Cronbach's* $\alpha = 0.94$) (Bhattacherjee 2001). Finally, participants responded to background questions, like aversion toward AI ("Human should avoid social contact with AI"; "Human should not delegate important tasks to AI"; *Cronbach's* $\alpha = 0.73$).

3.3 Results

Main Effect. One-way analysis of variance (ANOVA) revealed a significant main effect of conversation initiation on service evaluation. People evaluated the service more positively if it was initiated by a human agent (Mhuman $= 5.02$, $SD = 1.47$) than by an AI agent (MAI $= 4.49$, $SD = 1.84$; F (1, 237) $= 5.96$, $p < 0.05$). Thus, H1 was supported.

Sequential Mediating Effect. A serial mediation analysis (bootstrapping samples = 5000; Process Model 6) was conducted, controlling for age, gender, and education. Results showed the sequential mediation from perceived flexibility to expectation confirmation was significant (conversation initiation → perceived flexibility → expectation confirmation → service evaluation; $b = 0.25$, $SE = 0.09$, $95\% CI = [0.08, 0.44]$; illustrated in Fig. 4). Thus, H2, H3, and H4 were all supported.

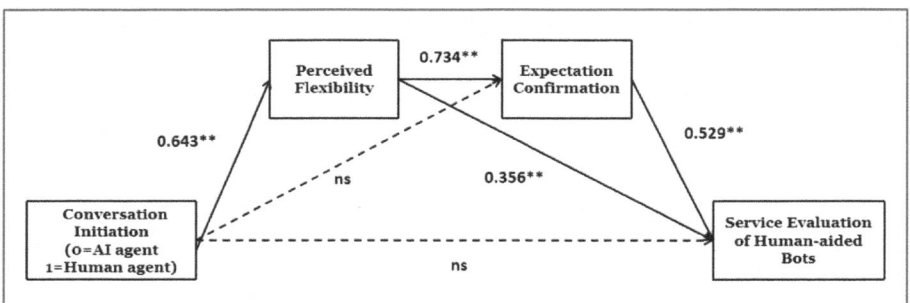

Notes: ns- not significant, * $p < 0.05$, ** $p < 0.01$

Fig. 4. The Sequential Mediating Effect

Moderating Effect. Results of a moderation analysis revealed that there was a statistically significant interaction effect between conversation initiation and consumers' aversion toward AI on service evaluation ($F (1, 232) = 4.90, p < 0.05$). As depicted in Fig. 4, individuals with a high aversion towards AI evaluated the service of a human-aided bot initiated by an AI agent more negatively, which supported H5a. Moreover, we con-ducted a moderated serial multiple mediation model of conversation initiation on service evaluation through perceived flexibility and expectation confirmation (bootstrap-ping samples = 5000; Process Model 86). The results indicated that the moderated mediation effect was significant ($Index = 0.15$, $SE = 0.07$, $95\% CI = [0.03, 0.29]$). The indirect effects as serial mediators were significant under the high aversion towards AI ($b = 0.54$, $SE = 0.15$, $95\% CI = [0.26, 0.85]$), but not significant under the low aversion towards AI ($b = 0.08$, $SE = 0.12$, $95\% CI = [-0.16, 0.32]$) Fig. 5). Thus, individuals with different levels of aversion evaluated the service initiated by an AI agent differently could be explained by the sequential mediating effect of perceived flexibility and expectation confirmation. H5b was also supported.

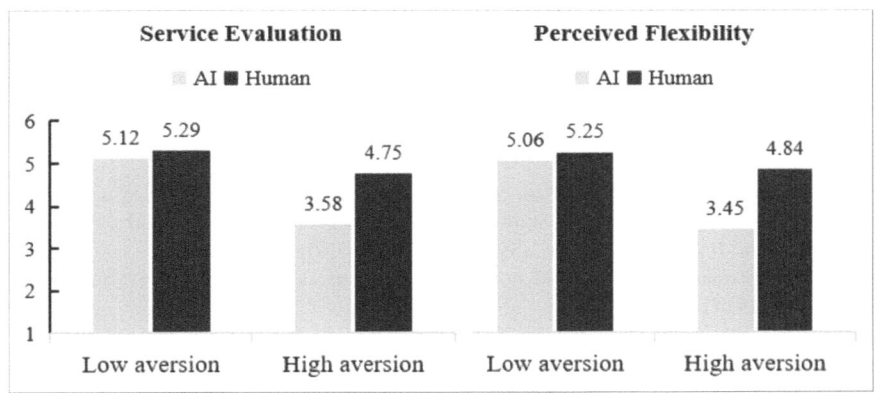

Fig. 5. The Moderation Effect

4 Conclusion

This research examines the impact of conversation initiation (by the human agent vs. by the AI agent) on service evaluation of a human-aided service bot. Results indicate that when the conversation is initiated by a human agent, consumers tend to evaluate the service more positively compared to when initiated by an AI agent. This effect is driven by consumers' perception of greater flexibility and confirmation of expectations from human-aided agents' services. Furthermore, consumers' aversion towards AI moderates these relationships. Our study sheds light on the importance of conversation initiation in the human-aided service bot field, an area that has been overlooked in previous research. The findings offer valuable insights for the e-commerce industry to improve user experience and enhance the effectiveness of chatbot services with the aid of human agents.

Acknowledgments. This work was supported by the National Natural Science Foundation of China [grant number: 72394371,72002193], the Fundamental Research Funds for the Central Universities[grant number: S20230031], and Zhejiang University – The Hong Kong Polytechnic University Joint Center.

Disclosure of Interests. The authors have no competing interests.

References

Bergner, A.S., Hildebrand, C., Häubl, G.: Machine talk: how verbal embodiment in conversational AI shapes consumer-brand relationships. J. Consum. Res. **50**(4), 742–764 (2023)

Bhattacherjee, A.: Understanding information systems continuance: an expectation-confirmation model. MIS Quart. 351–370 (2001)

Cassell, J., Bickmore, T., Campbell, L., Vilhjalmsson, H., Yan, H.: More than just a pretty face: conversational protocols and the affordances of embodiment. Knowl.-Based Syst. **14**(1–2), 55–64 (2001)

Crolic, C., Thomaz, F., Hadi, R., Stephen, A.T.: Blame the Bot: anthropomorphism and anger in customer-chatbot interactions. J. Market. (86:1), 132–148 (2022)

Dietvorst, B.J., Simmons, J.P., Massey, C.: Algorithm aversion: people erroneously avoid algorithms after seeing them err. J. Exper. Psychol. General (144:1), 114 (2015)

Garvey, A.M., Kim, T., Duhachek, A.: Bad news? send an AI. good news? send a human. J. Mark. **87**(1), 10–25 (2022)

Jena, L.K., Bhattacharyya, P., Pradhan, S.: Am I empowered through meaningful work? the moderating role of perceived flexibility in connecting meaningful work and psychological empowerment. IIMB Manage. Rev. (31:3), 298–308 (2019)

Kelley, S.W., Hoffman, K.D., Davis, M.A.: A typology of retail failures and recoveries. J. Retail. **69**(4), 429–452 (1993)

Longoni, C., Bonezzi, A., Morewedge, C.K.: Resistance to medical artificial intelligence. J. Consum. Res. **46**(4), 629–650 (2019)

Mahmud, H., Islam, A.N., Ahmed, S.I., Smolander, K.: What influences algorithmic decision-making? a systematic literature review on algorithm aversion. Technol. Forecast. Soc. Chang. **175**, 121390 (2022)

Rai, A., Constantinides, P., Sarker, S.: Next generation digital platforms: toward human-Ai hybrids. MIS Q. **43**(1), iii–ix (2019)

Schuetzler, R.M., Grimes, G.M., Giboney, J.S., Rosser, H.K.: Deciding whether and how to deploy Chatbots. MIS Q. Exec. **20**(1), 1–15 (2021)

Smith, A.K., Bolton, R.N., Wagner, J.: A model of customer satisfaction with service encounters involving failure and recovery. J. Mark. Res. **36**(3), 356–372 (1999)

You, S., Yang, C.L., Li, X.: Algorithmic versus human advice: does presenting prediction performance matter for algorithm appreciation? J. Manage. Inform. Syst. (39:2), 336–365 (2022)

Yu, S., Xiong, J., Shen, H.: The rise of Chatbots: the effect of using Chatbot agents on consumers' responses to request rejection. J. Consum. Psychol. **34**(1), 35–48 (2024)

Chatbot User Experience: Design and Evaluation

Dijana Peras[(✉)] [iD]

Faculty of Organization and Informatics, University of Zagreb, Pavlinska 2,
42000 Varaždin, Croatia
dperas@foi.unizg.hr

Abstract. The paper provides a review and systematization of the literature related to the chatbot user experience (CUX) by focusing on the chatbot's design and evaluation domain. An overview of the state of the art for each topic is provided, along with recommendations that can improve the design and evaluation of CUX. A literature review was conducted to: a) identify the methods used to design the user experience (UX) of different types of chatbots, and b) identify the methods used to evaluate the UX of different types of chatbots. The narrative approach was used to analyze the results of the selected studies. Content analysis was used to qualitatively evaluate the methods used to design and evaluate CUX. The synthesis was made to identify the key design requirements of the chatbot in terms of locus of control and duration of interaction. The paper provides: a) qualitative evaluation of the methods used to design the UX of different types of chatbots and categorization of steps of the design process in terms of chatbot functionality and purpose, b) qualitative evaluation and systematization of the methods used to evaluate the UX of different types of chatbots, and c) recommendations for the design and evaluation of chatbots concerning different types of chatbots and different categories of methods.

Keywords: Chat Agent · Chatbot · Chatterbot · Conversational Agent · Conversational Bot · Human-Chatbot Interaction · Usability · User Experience

1 Introduction

Today, chatbots are often built into applications and websites, allowing tasks to be performed via chat. They can understand users and provide them with answers similar to those provided by humans. According to Drift's report [1], the use of chatbots as a communication channel has grown by 92% since 2019. Today, chatbots usually achieve 35–40% response rates. However, 62% of customers still prefer human customer service channels over chatbots [2]. To achieve higher response rates, a better UX needs to be provided. Currently, though, little is known about the methods for designing effective human-chatbot interactions. To design a chatbot, a transition from a visual layout design and interaction mechanisms toward a conversational design is required [3]. This change in the way of interaction affects both the way of designing and evaluating CUX. Past research has covered only small fragments of the design and evaluation of CUX. Hence,

A. Coman et al. (Eds.): HCII 2024, LNCS 15375, pp. 77–93, 2025.
https://doi.org/10.1007/978-3-031-76806-4_6

the current research attempts to encompass them and provide recommendations for their use. The purpose of this paper is to provide a review of the literature related to CUX, here by focusing on two domains: design and evaluation. The goals of the paper are: a) to identify and systematize methods used to design the UX of different types of chatbots, b) to identify and systematize methods used to evaluate the UX of different types of chatbots, and c) to provide recommendations for the CUX design and evaluation concerning different types of chatbots.

The paper consists of five sections. After the introduction, an overview of the relevant background of chatbots is presented. Then the methodology is presented. The fourth section presents the results of the research. The recommendations are given in the fifth chapter, followed by the discussion made in the sixth chapter. The last chapter presents the main conclusions.

2   Background

2.1   Definition and Typology of Chatbots

A chatbot can be defined as a program that simulates and processes conversation allowing humans to interact with digital devices as if they were communicating with a person [4]. The way that chatbots are implemented varies significantly. The duration of the user's interaction with the chatbot and the locus of control for the user's engagement with the chatbot are considered to be among the most important factors that distinguish their design and affect UX [5]. According to [5], one can distinguish between chatbot-driven, user-driven, short-term relation, and long-term relation types of chatbot conversation. Chatbot-driven type offers a limited number of alternative path options, while user-driven type is designed to allow for a wider range of possible input from users and to respond more quickly to changes in that input. On the other hand, the short-term type is characterized by a user engaging with the chatbot once, without the collection of user information, while the long-term type is characterized by creating a user profile for strengthening UX across visits. This typology will serve as a basis for identifying approaches to the design and evaluation of the UX of different types of chatbots.

2.2   Chatbot User Experience

UX can be interpreted in numerous ways. According to ISO 9241-210, "It includes the users' emotions, beliefs, preferences, perceptions, comfort, behaviors and accomplishments that occur before, during, and after use" [6]. UX encompasses all aspects of the user's interaction with the company, its services, and its products [7]. Although the above definitions make it easier to understand the breadth of the UX's scope, there is still a lack of information on the dimensions that need to be considered given the context of use [8]. In addition, although there are different methods for evaluating the user interface, there is still a lack of those focusing specifically on evaluating the UX. While traditional user interfaces tend to be exposed and allow an exploration of different options and menus, a chatbot's user interface is hidden from the user [9]. The interactions cannot be fully predicted, so the evaluation of UX is harder. The current research does not provide sufficient knowledge on different methods for designing and evaluating chatbot user experience (UX), especially concerning the different types of chatbots. Steps of designing CUX can be applied by following the guidelines made by large technology companies such as Google [10], IBM [11], and Amazon [12]. The scientific literature, on the other hand, is rare.

To fill the identified research gap, this paper aims to identify and systematize various factors and dimensions of CUX and to propose guidelines for their evaluation in different contexts. The paper will address two intertwining areas - design and evaluation of UX - more broadly than what may be found within the existing body of literature on chatbots.

3   Methodology

A literature review was conducted to: a) identify the methods used to design the UX of different types of chatbots, and b) identify the methods used to evaluate the UX of different types of chatbots. Scopus, Web of Science (WoS), and ScienceDirect were chosen to collect relevant studies since they return a respectable number of papers, allow the use of the same search string, and are accessible to the author of the paper. The search string was defined based on the keywords and author's knowledge related to the research area: ('chatbot' OR 'chat agent' OR 'conversational agent' OR 'chatterbot' OR 'conversational bot') AND ('UX' OR 'usability'). The search was performed during the first quarter of 2022. For a study to be considered, it had to satisfy at least one of the following criteria: describe the method for designing CUX, or describe the method for evaluating CUX. Only papers published in English were included. Papers that did not discuss the design or evaluation of CUX, as well as papers dealing solely with technical issues related to the design of chatbots, were excluded from the research. The selection of papers was conducted in two stages: 1) the document title and abstract screening was made, which classified the papers as included or excluded, and 2) the full-text screening of the available papers was made and the data were extracted.

First, the narrative approach was used to analyze the results of the selected studies, with a description of different methodologies, processes, and methods used to develop and evaluate CUX. The next step of the research was to qualitatively evaluate the methods used to design CUX. Steps of design processes were compared and assessed to determine which seemed to represent the same category. According to the described functionality, chatbots were categorized in terms of locus of control and duration of the interaction. The initial categorization of methods, design process steps, chatbot types, and purposes was done, followed by a thorough review of the proposed categorization.

Content analysis was used to qualitatively assess the evaluation methods. The methods were first classified as traditional or newly developed/modified. Afterward, the summary was made by categorizing the method as inspection, testing, inquiry, or objective. The next step was to identify the metrics used to evaluate the UX of different types of chatbots. The typology selected to group dimensions influencing CUX was the one proposed by [13], which encompasses chatbot-related, environment-related, and user-related dimensions. As suggested by Nicolescu and Tudorache [14], chatbot-related dimensions were further divided into functional, system, and anthropomorphic dimensions, while user-related dimensions were divided into users' perceptions and attitudes during and after the interaction with a chatbot.

Finally, a set of recommendations that can improve the design and evaluation of CUX was proposed. The synthesis was made to identify the key design requirements of the chatbot in terms of locus of control and duration of interaction. Combinations of several types of questionnaires were proposed to cover the subcategories that are crucial for the specific type of chatbot.

4   Results

4.1   Paper Selection

Altogether 446 papers were obtained through the defined search string, of which 127 were duplicates. After removing the duplicates, 319 papers remained, and they were reviewed based on document title and abstract. Another 255 papers were excluded after the document title and abstract review because they did not discuss the design or evaluation of CUX. 66 papers that met the inclusion criteria were included in the next stage of the selection. The full-text screening of those papers resulted in the final set of 39 papers included in the literature review.

4.2   Qualitative Evaluation of the Selected Papers

Designing Methods. The following paragraph describes the methods used to design CUX. The results of papers that discuss the design of conversational dialogue, chatbot personality, and conversational structure will be briefly presented. As stated earlier, there is no generally accepted methodology for designing CUX. However, the papers included in the analysis followed the guidelines of the human-centered design methodology [15–18]. According to the ISO, "Human-centered design is an approach to interactive systems' development that aims to make systems usable and useful by focusing on the users, their needs and requirements, and by applying human factors/ergonomics, and usability knowledge and techniques" [6]. From a human-centered design perspective, there are many variations in how CUX can be implemented. The approach involves various steps, including understanding users' needs, analyzing users' goals, specifying requirements, prototyping, and testing. The decision on which steps to implement should consider the functionality and preferences of the users in a particular context. It is therefore crucial to specify the locus of control (chatbot-driven or user-driven type of chatbot) and the duration of the interaction (short-term or long-term type of chatbot). The steps of the methodology that were used to design the UX of different types of chatbots are presented in Table 1.

Methods for the Evaluation of CUX. Altogether, 27 papers describing the methods for evaluating CUX were identified. Traditional categorization differentiates inspection, testing, inquiry, and objective methods. A large part of the research community still relies on standard methods for evaluating CUX. However, some authors argue that using standard methods is not enough for chatbots. Therefore, new types of measuring instruments are often developed. In the subsections that follow, a qualitative analysis of the papers that used either standard or new/modified methods for the evaluation of CUX is given.

Table 1. Steps of the human-centered method used to design the UX of identified chatbot types

Steps of the design process	Chatbot type	Purpose	Ref.
1) defining the scope, 2) problem analysis, 3) content design, 4) design and implementation, 5) testing and validation, 6) prototype design	User-driven and long-term relation	Customer support	[18]
1) problem analysis, 2) personality elicitation, 3) testing and implementation, 4) prototype design	User-driven and long-term relation	Personal assistance	[17]
1) identifying needs, 2) specifying requirements, 3) chatbot learning, 4) design application, 5) design evaluation, 6) prototype design, 7) chatbot development, 8) chatbot evaluation, 9) release and use, 10) monitoring and evaluation	User-driven and long-term relation	Personal assistance	[15]
1) problem analysis, 2) design and implementation, 3) testing and validation	Chatbot-driven and long-term relation	Customer support	[16]

Standard Methods for the Evaluation of CUX. Nielsen's (1994), Norman's (2013), and Shneiderman and Plaisant's (2010) heuristics were used in [19, 20]. Additional guidelines were proposed by [19, 20]. Valério et al. [9] explored the communication strategies of chatbots by using the semiotic inspection method (SIM). Duijst [21] measured the utility, usability, and satisfaction of CUX by utilizing the Technology Acceptance Model (TAM) Questionnaire, the System Usability Scale (SUS), the Usability Metrics for UX (UMUX) Questionnaire, the PARAdigm for Dialogue Evaluation System (PARADISE), and the Questionnaire for User Interaction Satisfaction (QUIS). Also, the objective metrics (time required to complete the task, proportion of correct user redirects, proportion of calls managed by the system, call abandonment rate), and subjective metrics (SASSI questionnaire) were used to measure various aspects of UX, and the HEART framework was used to assess the quality of the UX. Different measurement instruments for evaluating chatbots (AttrakDiff, SASSI, SUISQ, MOS-X, SUS, and PARADISE) were analyzed in [8] to assess their suitability for measuring hedonistic, aesthetic, and pragmatic dimensions of the UX. Semantic ordinal scales were used to measure the usability of chatbots [22]. A combination of subjective metrics and objective metrics (bilingual evaluation understudy (BLEU)) was used to assess the usability of a chatbot [23]. A usability evaluation was performed with the SUS questionnaire, and the users' loyalty was measured with the net promoter score (NPS). Quiroz et al. [24] used SUS to measure usability, UEQ to measure pragmatic and hedonic aspects, and the Technology Trust Questionnaire to measure trust. The UEQ was also used in [25]. The perceptions of user expectations of chatbots were evaluated by collecting UX via survey and analyzing responses with a mixture of qualitative approaches [26]. In [16], objective and subjective metrics for measuring CUX were combined.

New or Modified Methods for the Evaluation of CUX. Skjuve and Brandzaeg [27] developed a new scale for measuring the social aspects of human-chatbot interaction. Rubin and Martin [28] developed a self-report Interpersonal Communication Competence Scale (ICCS) to measure 10 dimensions of competence. Several new metrics were proposed for evaluating the qualitative aspects of commercial chatbots [29]. Newly developed methods such as Godspeed, which measures human similarity, and social presence scales, which measure how (un)sociable, (in)sensitive, (im)personal, and cold/warm a particular chatbot is, were suggested in [30, 31]. Peras [32] proposed usability, performance, affect, and satisfaction metrics. Furthermore, an evaluation approach based on quantitative and qualitative metrics was proposed by [33]. An open-source questionnaire designed by Chatbottest [34] was used to evaluate a chatbot's usability. In-depth interviews on UX and motivation to use chatbots were conducted by [35]. The humanity of a chatbot and its capability to properly handle inquiries were assessed. The Self-developed Questionnaire was developed to evaluate chatbots' design, navigation, organization, and performance [36]. Chatbot Usability Questionnaire (CUQ) score for assessing the usability of chatbots was proposed in [37]. User-friendliness, information ability and equipment, language level and equipment, humanity, and business aspect were assessed by [38] to measure chatbot effectiveness. Finally, two instruments for measuring chatbot usability were developed: a diagnostic tool in the form of a checklist (BOT-Check), and a 15-item questionnaire (BOT Usability Scale, BUS-15) [39].

Several authors recognized privacy concerns as one of the factors affecting CUX. When privacy protection mechanisms fail to meet user's expectations, the perceived privacy risk increases, making it difficult to achieve user satisfaction. Privacy concerns were measured using questionnaires. The effect of privacy concerns on the user's intention to use chatbots was measured in [40, 41]. The extent to which the human-like characteristics of a chatbot influence privacy concerns was measured in [42]. Finally, Biswas [43] measured the privacy risks related to user's sentiment and location.

Summary of the Methods for the Evaluation of CUX. The descriptions of the methods used for the evaluation of CUX are listed in Table 2. Both standard methods and new/modified methods were grouped into four categories: a) inspection methods, b) testing methods, c) inquiry methods, and d) objective methods. The proposed categorization aims to help evaluators choose the right category of method for the specific context. The corresponding metrics are listed, along with their descriptions and references.

The typology selected to group the factors influencing CUX in this paper is the one proposed by Nordheim et al. [13]. The proposed typology encompasses chatbot-related, environment-related, and user-related dimensions. According to Nicolescu and Tudorache [14], the chatbot-related dimension can be further divided into functional, system, and anthropomorphic subdimensions. In contrast, the user-related dimension

Table 2. List of methods for the evaluation of CUX

Categories	Metrics	Description	Ref.
Inspection methods	Heuristics	Finding the usability problems in the design of a user interface	[19, 20]
	SIM	Assessing the ability to communicate efficiently and effectively	[9]
Testing methods	Thinking aloud	Asking the users to think aloud while executing the task	[21, 36, 37]
	Automatic recording	Screen and audio recording during the observations	[21]
	Eye-tracking analysis	Using an eye-tracking system to measure visual behavior	[33]
Inquiry methods	TAM	Measuring perceived usefulness and ease of use	[21]
	SUS	Measuring ease of use and learnability	[8, 22] -[24, 34, 36, 37]
	UMUX	Measuring effectivity, efficiency, satisfaction	[21]
	QUIS	Measuring attitude toward interface factors	[21]
	PARADISE	Measuring task success, dialogue costs, user satisfaction	[8, 21]
	SASSI	Measuring response accuracy, likeability, cognitive demand, annoyance, habitability, speed	[8, 21]
	The HEART framework	Measuring happiness, engagement, adoption, retention, task success	[21]
	AttrakDiff	Measuring hedonic and pragmatic features, attractiveness	[8]

(continued)

Table 2. (*continued*)

Categories	Metrics	Description	Ref.
	SUISQ	Measuring user goal orientation, speech features, wordiness, customer service attitude	[8]
	MOS	Evaluating the quality of artificially created speech	[8]
	MOS-X	Assessing voice characteristics	[8]
	UEQ	Measuring attractiveness, perspicuity, efficiency, dependability, stimulation, novelty	[24, 25, 36, 37]
	Self-developed Questionnaire	Assessing design, navigation, organization, performance	[36]
	Metrics	**Descriptions**	**Ref.**
	Likert scales	Measuring problem solvability, helpfulness, loyalty, satisfaction, efficiency, or overall UX	[16, 22, 26, 29, 32]
	NPS	Measuring users' loyalty	[23]
	Technology Trust Questionnaire	Measuring trust	[24]
	Contextual input	Speaking, typing, appropriateness	[26]
	Godspeed	Measuring anthropomorphism, animacy, likeability, perceived intelligence, perceived safety	[30]
	Social presence scales	Labeling the chatbot as sociable/unsociable, sensitive/insensitive, personal/impersonal	[31]

(*continued*)

Table 2. (*continued*)

Categories	Metrics	Description	Ref.
	ICC	Measuring self-disclosure, empathy, social relaxation, interaction, assertiveness, expressiveness, immediacy, supportiveness, control	[27]
	Quality of responses	The number of responses that are correct, partially correct, or not correct	[23, 29]
	Semeraro's questionnaire	Measuring impression, command, effectiveness, navigability, learnability, comprehension	[33]
	Chatbottest	Measuring answering, error management, intelligence, navigation, onboarding, personality, understanding	[34]
	CUQ	Measuring personality, onboarding, navigation, understanding, error handling, intelligence	[37]
	Interviews	Addressing experiences with the chatbot	[35]
	BOT Check	Checklist for measuring chatbot usability	[39]
	BUS-15	A 15-item questionnaire for measuring usability	[39]
	Privacy concern	Measuring privacy concern about using a chatbot	[40] - [43]
Objective methods	Efficiency	The time to complete the task	[16, 21, 22, 37]

(*continued*)

Table 2. (*continued*)

Categories	Metrics	Description	Ref.
	Effectiveness	Percentage of tasks completed, percentage of match, response type relative probability	[21, 32, 38]
	Correct transfer	The percentage of appropriately redirected users	[21]
	Containment rate	Duration of conversation	[21, 32]
	Error rate	Wrong input that passes validation, inability to enter the correct input, number of error messages	[16, 21]
	Performance	Percentage of completed tasks	[32]
	BLEU	Automatic evaluation of the quality of responses	[23]
	Conversation log analysis	Correct text output, fallback sentences, proactive sentences, percentage of positive search results	[33]
	Sentiment analysis	AWS Lex	[43]
	Location analysis	Location values dictionary	[43]

can be divided into users' perceptions and attitudes during and after interacting with a chatbot. The systematization of metrics is presented in Table 3.

Table 3. Metrics used to evaluate CUX according to the typology of chatbot factors

Dimensions	Subdimensions	Factors	Metrics
Chatbot-related	Functional	Usability	Nielsen's, Norman's, and Shneiderman's heuristics

(*continued*)

Table 3. (*continued*)

Dimensions	Subdimensions	Factors	Metrics
		Efficiency	SIM, UMUX, UEQ, Likert scale, time to complete the task
		Effectiveness	SIM, PARADISE, Semeraro
		Usefulness	TAM
		Ease of use	TAM, SUS
		Problem resolution	Likert scale, Chatbottest, CUQ
		Helpfulness	Likert scale, Semeraro et. Al
		Task success	PARADISE, HEART
		Error management	Chatbottest, CUQ
	System	Response accuracy	SASSI
		Speed	SASSI
		Speech quality	SUISQ, MOS, MOS-X
		Dependability	UEQ
		Novelty	UEQ
		Stimulation	UEQ
		Quality	BLEU
		Navigability	Semeraro, Chatbottest, CUQ
	Anthropomorphic	Attitude	QUIS
		Learnability	SUS, Semeraro et. Al
		Annoyance	SASSI
		Likeability	SASSI
		Cognitive demand	SASSI
		Habitability	SASSI
		Human similarity	Godspeed
		Social presence	Social presence scales
		Interpersonal competence	ICC related
		Impression	Semeraro

(*continued*)

Table 3. (*continued*)

Dimensions	Subdimensions	Factors	Metrics
		Comprehension	Semeraro, Chatbottest, CUQ
		Intelligence	Chatbottest, CUQ
		Personality	Chatbottest, CUQ
Chatbot-related	Anthropo-morphic	Hedonic features	AttrakDiff
		Pragmatic features	AttrakDiff
Environment-related	Privacy perceptions	Privacy	Privacy concern scale
User-related	Perceptions and attitudes during the interaction	Happiness	HEART
		Engagement	HEART
		Trust	Technology Trust Questionnaire
	Perceptions and attitudes after the interaction	Satisfaction	UMUX, PARADISE, Likert
		Adoption	HEART, Likert scale
		Overall UX	Likert scale
		Loyalty	NPS

5 Recommendations

The following section provides a set of recommendations that aim to improve the design and evaluation of CUX. First, the recommendations for the design will be given, followed by the recommendations for the evaluation of CUX.

5.1 Design of CUX

Regarding the design of CUX, the paper has identified the human-centered design approach as the most commonly used method. The methodology is flexible and provides general directions for a chatbot development process. It can help identify the reasons for reluctance to adopt a service (problem analysis), define the goals of UX, design the prototype, and examine UX in relation to the set goals and expectations of the users. The human-centered methodology can be easily applied to all types of chatbots. The following paragraphs will briefly describe the proposed design of the interaction in terms of locus of control and duration of interaction.

Chatbot-Driven Short-Term Relation Type
This type of chatbot should be designed to serve as a portal to the collection of content. It should be able to display and suggest available content to the user. Users should have the option to accept, filter, or reject content.

Chatbot-Driven Long-Term Relation Type. This type of chatbot should be designed to assist users with a certain activity. It should be able to guide the user through the activity by providing the necessary means. The sessions should be brief and frequent, initiated by different user states.

User-Driven Short-Term Relation Type of Chatbot. The design of this type of chatbot should be simple to allow users to easily enter their questions. Chatbot should be able to recognize the problem and provide appropriate solutions. Users should be able to give feedback or ask for more information after obtaining the response.

User-Driven Long-Term Relation Type of Chatbot. This type of chatbot should be designed to continuously assist users with their regular activities. It should allow a high level of personalization. The design should be simple to allow users to express their needs quickly and efficiently, through text or voice input.

5.2   Evaluation of CUX

In the following paragraphs, combinations of several types of questionnaires will be proposed to cover the subcategories that are vital for the specific type of chatbot.

Chatbot-Driven Short-Term Relation Type. Since the most important task of chatbot-driven short-term relation type of chatbot is the delivery of content, testing methods such as automatic recording and eye tracking would be beneficial to evaluate functional, system, and user-related subcategories (task success, navigability, engagement, efficiency, effectiveness, and performance). Another option is to use objective metrics, which are useful for obtaining quantitative data on the UX. Hoverer, objective metrics are not sufficient to capture the whole concept of UX. They should therefore be combined with UMUX (usability), PARADISE (effectiveness, task success, and satisfaction), and SUS (ease of use) to gain insights into the user's overall experience during the interaction.

Chatbot-Driven Long-Term Relation Type. Chatbot-driven long-term relation type is the most challenging type of chatbot, both in terms of design and evaluation of UX. The combinations of metrics suggested for evaluating the UX of user-driven long-term relation type chatbot should be utilized and expanded with SUISQ to measure politeness, friendliness, and professional attitude of a chatbot, and SASSI to measure system response accuracy, speed, likeability, and annoyance. These metrics are important since the chatbot serves as a personal guide, and therefore it should be highly functional and attractive.

User-Driven Short-Term Relation Type of Chatbot. Some basic functional, system and user-related subcategories should be measured, while anthropomorphic and privacy perceptions subcategories of chatbot-related factors are less important and can be skipped. For instance, UMUX, UEQ, and HEART can be combined to measure chatbot functional (effectivity and efficiency), system (dependability, novelty, and stimulation), and user-related (satisfaction, happiness, engagement, and adoption) dimensions. Another way of measuring the mentioned subcategories is to use the semiotic inspection method (SIM). This method is subjective by nature, so it may be best to combine it with testing methods (such as thinking aloud, automatic recording, and eye tracking) to obtain more reliable results.

User-Driven Long-Term Relation Type of Chatbot. This type should be able to memorize the user and provide personalized content. Therefore, besides functional, system, and user-related factors, anthropomorphic and environment-related dimensions should be measured. Since this type of chatbot is usually available on multiple platforms, QUIS should be used for assessing attitudes towards interface factors (visibility, terminology, system capabilities, etc.). CUQ should be used for assessing the functional, system, and anthropomorphic dimensions (personality, onboarding, navigation, understanding, responses, error handling, and intelligence) of a chatbot, while the privacy concern scale should be used for measuring environment-related dimensions (privacy perceptions of users). To measure user-related dimensions, satisfaction, adoption, and overall UX scales would be beneficial. Another option is to use the semiotic inspection method (SIM), combined with the HEART and privacy concern scale. This way, the large number of chatbot-related, environment-related, and user-related dimensions important for evaluating the UX of this specific type of chatbot would be covered.

6   Discussion

According to the results of the literature review, when it comes to the design and evaluation of CUX, no standardized design methodology or metrics exists, and no survey addresses all of the potentially important concepts of CUX. As far as the author is aware, this paper is the first to summarize the literature on how CUX has been developed and evaluated in the past. Furthermore, this paper is the first to propose guidelines for using different UX design and evaluation methods in different contexts, according to both the category of a method and the type of chatbot.

The research found that the human-centered design approach was the only method used to design CUX. The author identified which types of chatbots can benefit from human-centered design methodology, and made recommendations considering the steps of the methodology that would be desirable to adopt for different types of chatbots. The significance of the research results compared to what is already known lies in the provision of concrete design guidelines for different types of chatbots.

As for the methods for the evaluation of CUX, several authors proposed various metrics. The value of the paper lies in the systematization of the evaluation methods according to the category of method, as well as in their systematization according to the different dimensions and subdimensions of chatbot-related factors. Since there is no evaluation method covering all the factors of UX, the author proposed combinations of several types of methods to successfully evaluate the UX of different types of chatbots. The recommendations are not exhaustive, but they cover the most important factors of chatbots considering their functionality, purpose, and interaction with users. As such, they can significantly cut down the amount of time researchers and designers spend while looking for the most suitable UX design and evaluation methods.

7   Conclusion

The current paper explains the concept of CUX, describing the elements that are important for understanding it. A review of the literature revealed several different approaches to the UX, but also a variety of methods focusing on the evaluation of CUX. Papers whose authors suggested evaluating CUX using standard measurement instruments have been detected, as well as papers whose authors claimed that relying on previous ways of evaluating the UX is no longer possible and, hence, use other types of measurement instruments. The inspection, testing, inquiry, and objective methods that were primarily designed for evaluating usability problems were presented. Since they could be partially successfully applied to evaluate UX, a variety of methods for measuring the different factors of chatbots should be combined to capture the entire UX. This paper provides a valuable overview of the different factors affecting chatbot user experience that need to be considered in various contexts. The author of the paper was aware of the pros and cons of different categories of methods while writing the recommendations. However, since the detailed description of the categories of methods is out of the scope of this paper, the designers and researchers are advised to consider additional resources to verify the prerequisites for their use.

Future work should focus on identifying guidelines for using the stated evaluation methods in different contexts, here depending on available resources, since the choice of a method for evaluating CUX is often limited by factors such as time, resources, equipment, etc. Future work should also focus on providing new methods and methodologies for evaluating the aspects of UX that are more closely related to chatbots.

Acknowledgments. Dijana Peras is a PhD student at the Faculty of Organization and Informatics, University of Zagreb. The University of Zagreb contributed funds for academic mobility, which helped to cover the conference registration fee.

References

1. 2021 State of Conversational Marketing, Drift & Heinz Marketing (2020). https://www.drift.com/books-reports/conversational-marketing-trends/. Accessed 10 May 2023
2. Kergaravat, C.: Chatbot vs human: how to combine the best of both worlds. Business Insider (2024). https://www.apizee.com/chatbot-vs-human.php. Accessed 15 May 2023
3. Følstad, A., Brandtzæg, P.B.: Chatbots and the new world of HCI. interactions. Google Scholar Google Scholar Digital Library Digital Library **24**(4), 38–42 (2017)
4. What is a Chatbot | Oracle. https://www.oracle.com/chatbots/what-is-a-chatbot/. Accessed 26 Oct 2021
5. Følstad, A., Skjuve, M., Brandtzaeg, P.B.: Different chatbots for different purposes: towards a typology of chatbots to understand interaction design. Presented at the Internet Science: INSCI 2018 International Workshops, October 24–26, 2018, pp. 145–156. St. Petersburg, Russia. Revised Selected Papers 5, Springer (2019)
6. ISO 9241-210:2019 (2019). https://www.iso.org/cms/render/live/en/sites/isoorg/contents/data/standard/07/75/77520.html
7. Norman, D., Nielsen, J.: The definition of User Experience (UX). Nielsen Norman Group. https://www.nngroup.com/articles/definition-user-experience/ Accessed 20 May 2023
8. Kocabalil, A.B., Laranjo, L., Coiera, E.: Measuring user experience in conversational interfaces: a comparison of six questionnaires. Presented at the Proceedings of the 32nd International BCS Human Computer Interaction Conference, BCS Learning & Development (2018)

9. Valério, F.A., Guimarães, T.G., Prates, R.O., Candello, H.: Here's what I can do: Chatbots' strategies to convey their features to users. Presented at the Proceedings of the XVI Brazilian Symposium on Human Factors in Computing Systems, pp. 1–10 (2017)
10. Conversational Actions sunset overview. Google (2023). https://developers.google.com/ass istant/ca-sunset. Accessed 15 Jun 2023
11. Moore, R.J., An, S., Ren, G.-J.: The IBM natural conversation framework: a new paradigm for conversational UX design. Hum.-Comput. Interact. **38**(3–4), 168–193 (2023)
12. Alexa Design Guide. Amazon (2023). https://developer.amazon.com/en-US/alexa/alexa-haus Accessed 23 Jun 2023
13. Nordheim, C.B., Følstad, A., Bjørkli, C.A.: An initial model of trust in chatbots for customer service—findings from a questionnaire study. Interact. Comput. **31**(3), 317–335 (2019)
14. Nicolescu, L., Tudorache, M.T.: Human-computer interaction in customer service: the experience with AI chatbots - a systematic literature review. Electronics **11**(10), 1579 (2022)
15. Bahja, M., Hammad, R., Butt, G.: A user-centric framework for educational chatbots design and development. In: Stephanidis, C., Kurosu, M., Degen, H., Reinerman-Jones, L. (eds.) HCI International 2020 - Late Breaking Papers: Multimodality and Intelligence. HCII 2020. LNCS, vol. 12424. Springer, Cham (2020). https://doi.org/10.1007/978-3-030-60117-1_3
16. Galko, L., Porubän, J., Senko, J.: Improving the user experience of electronic university enrollment. Presented at the 2018 16th International Conference on Emerging eLearning Technologies and Applications (ICETA), pp. 179–184. IEEE (2018)
17. Ghosh, S., Pherwani, J.: Designing of a natural voice assistants for mobile through user centered design approach. Presented at the Human-Computer Interaction: Design and Evaluation: 17th International Conference, HCI International 2015, 2–7 August 2015, pp. 320–331. Los Angeles, CA, USA. Proceedings, Part I 17, Springer (2015)
18. Pricilla, C., Lestari, D.P., Dharma, D.: Designing interaction for chatbot-based conversational commerce with user-centered design. In: 2018 5th International Conference on Advanced Informatics: Concept Theory and Applications (ICAICTA), pp. 244–249. IEEE (2018)
19. Murad, C., Munteanu, C., Clark, L., Cowan, B.R.: Design guidelines for hands-free speech interaction. Presented at the Proceedings of the 20th International Conference on Human-Computer Interaction with Mobile Devices and Services Adjunct, pp. 269–276 (2018)
20. Sugisaki, K., Bleiker, A.: Usability guidelines and evaluation criteria for conversational user interfaces: a heuristic and linguistic approach. In: Proceedings of the Conference on Mensch und Computer, pp. 309–319 (2020)
21. Duijst, D.: Can we improve the user experience of chatbots with personalization. Master's thesis. University of Amsterdam (2017)
22. Bennion, M.R., Hardy, G.E., Moore, R.K., Kellett, S., Millings, A.: Usability, acceptability, and effectiveness of web-based conversational agents to facilitate problem solving in older adults: controlled study. J. Med. Internet Res. **22**(5), e16794 (2020)
23. Liu, Q., Huang, J., Wu, L., Zhu, K., Ba, S.: CBET: design and evaluation of a domain-specific chatbot for mobile learning. Univ. Access Inf. Soc. **19**(3), 655–673 (2020)
24. Quiroz, J.C., Bongolan, T., Ijaz, K.: Alexa depression and anxiety self-tests: a preliminary analysis of user experience and trust. Presented at the Adjunct Proceedings of the 2020 ACM International Joint Conference on Pervasive and Ubiquitous Computing and Proceedings of the 2020 ACM International Symposium on Wearable Computers, pp. 494–496 (2020)
25. Te Pas, M.E., Rutten, W.G., Bouwman, R.A., Buise, M.P.: User experience of a chatbot questionnaire versus a regular computer questionnaire: prospective comparative study. JMIR Med. Inform. **8**(12), e21982 (2020)
26. Zamora, J.: I'm sorry, dave, i'm afraid i can't do that: Chatbot perception and expectations. Presented at the Proceedings of the 5th International Conference on Human Agent Interaction, pp. 253–260 (2017)

27. Skjuve, M., Brandzaeg, P.B.: Measuring user experience in chatbots: an approach to interpersonal communication competence. In: Bodrunova, S., et al. (eds.) Internet Science. INSCI 2018. LNCS, vol. 11551. Springer, Cham (2019). https://doi.org/10.1007/978-3-030-17705-8_10

28. Rubin, R.B., Martin, M.M.: Development of a measure of interpersonal communication competence. Commun. Res. Rep. **11**(1), 33–44 (1994)

29. Kuligowska, K.: Commercial chatbot: performance evaluation, usability metrics and quality standards of embodied conversational agents. Professionals Center for Business Research, vol. 2 (2015)

30. Ho, C.-C., MacDorman, K.F.: Revisiting the uncanny valley theory: developing and validating an alternative to the Godspeed indices. Comput. Hum. Behav. **26**(6), 1508–1518 (2010)

31. Biocca, F., Harms, C., Burgoon, J.K.: Toward a more robust theory and measure of social presence: review and suggested criteria. Presence: Teleoperators & virtual environments, vol. 12, no. 5, pp. 456–480 (2003)

32. Peras, D.: Chatbot evaluation metrics: review paper, pp. 89–97 (2018)

33. Semeraro, G., Andersen, H.H., Andersen, V., Lops, P., Abbattista, F.: Evaluation and validation of a conversational agent embodied in a bookstore. Presented at the Universal Access Theoretical Perspectives, Practice, and Experience: 7th ERCIM International Workshop on User Interfaces for All, 24–25 October 2002, pp. 360–371. Paris, France. Revised Papers 7, Springer, 2003

34. Cameron, G., et al.: Assessing the usability of a chatbot for mental health care. In: Bodrunova, S., et al. (eds.) Internet Science. INSCI 2018. LNCS, vol 11551. Springer, Cham (2018). https://doi.org/10.1007/978-3-030-17705-8_11

35. Følstad, A., Skjuve, M.: Chatbots for customer service: user experience and motivation. In: Proceedings of the 1st International Conference on Conversational User Interfaces - CUI 2019, pp. 1–9. ACM Press, Dublin, Ireland (2019)

36. Anubharath, P., Chui, Y.P., Sng, J., Zhu, L., Tham, K., Lee, E.: Usability and user experience evaluation of Virtual Integrated Patient, pp. 18–28. ASCILITE Publications (2019)

37. Holmes, S., Moorhead, A., Bond, R., Zheng, H., Coates, V., McTear, M.: Usability testing of a healthcare chatbot: can we use conventional methods to assess conversational user interfaces?. Presented at the Proceedings of the 31st European Conference on Cognitive Ergonomics, pp. 207–214 (2019)

38. Mohelska, H., Sokolova, M.: Measuring chatbot effectiveness. In: Maci, J., Maresova, P., Firlej, K., Soukal, I. (eds.) Presented at the hradec economic days 2021, pp. 589–598 (2021). https://doi.org/10.36689/uhk/hed/2021-01-058

39. Borsci, S., et al.: The Chatbot usability scale: the design and pilot of a usability scale for interaction with AI-based conversational agents. Pers. Ubiquit. Comput. **26**(1), 95–119 (2022). https://doi.org/10.1007/s00779-021-01582-9

40. Rese, A., Ganster, L., Baier, D.: Chatbots in retailers' customer communication: how to measure their acceptance? J. Retail. Consum. Serv. **56**, 102176 (2020)

41. Cheng, Y., Jiang, H.: How do AI-driven chatbots impact user experience? Examining gratifications, perceived privacy risk, satisfaction, loyalty, and continued use. J. Broadcast. Electron. Media **64**(4), 592–614 (2020)

42. Ischen, C., Araujo, T., Voorveld, H., van Noort, G., Smit, E.: Privacy concerns in chatbot interactions. Presented at the Chatbot Research and Design: Third International Workshop, CONVERSATIONS 2019, 19–20, November 2019, pp. 34–48. Amsterdam, The Netherlands. Revised Selected Papers 3, Springer (2020)

43. Biswas, D.: Privacy preserving chatbot conversations. In: 2020 IEEE Third International Conference on Artificial Intelligence and Knowledge Engineering (AIKE), pp. 179–182. IEEE (2020)

SARD: A Human-AI Collaborative Story Generation

Ahmed Y. Radwan[1(✉)], Khaled M. Alasmari[1], Omar A. Abdulbagi[1],
and Emad A. Alghamdi[2]

[1] Department of Computer Science, ASAS AI, King Abdulaziz University,
Jeddah, Saudi Arabia
{aragabradwan,kabdualasmari,ofaridabdulbagi}@stu.kau.edu.sa
[2] Center for Research Excellence in AI and Data Science, ASAS AI,
King Abdulaziz University, Jeddah, Saudi Arabia
eaalghamdi@kau.edu.sa

Abstract. Generative artificial intelligence (GenAI) has ushered in a
new era for storytellers, providing a powerful tool to ignite creativity
and explore uncharted narrative territories. As technology continues to
advance, the synergy between human creativity and AI-generated content holds the potential to redefine the landscape of storytelling. In this
work, we propose SARD, a drag-and-drop visual interface for generating
a multi-chapter story using large language models. Our evaluation of the
usability of SARD and its creativity support shows that while node-based
visualization of the narrative may help writers build a mental model, it
exerts unnecessary mental overhead to the writer and becomes a source
of distraction as the story becomes more elaborated. We also found that
AI generates stories that are less lexically diverse, irrespective of the complexity of the story. We discovered several tendencies and restrictions in
our tool that can help drive the development of future human-AI co-
writing tools, giving useful insights for improving user experience and
the overall functioning of collaborative systems.

Keywords: Human-AI collaboration · Co-Creativity · Computational
Creativity · Large Language Models · Storytelling · Natural Language
Generation · Evaluation · Creativity

1 Introduction

Narrative expression is a fundamental element of the human experience, mani-
fested across various mediums such as written text, oral traditions, cave paint-
ings, and beyond. Generative artificial intelligence has ushered in a new era for
storytellers, providing a powerful tool to ignite creativity and explore uncharted
narrative territories [14,16]. Generative AI, a subset of artificial intelligence, has
revolutionized the way stories are crafted, providing a new avenue for creativity
and imagination. While extensive work on automated story generation has been

A. Coman et al. (Eds.): HCII 2024, LNCS 15375, pp. 94–105, 2025.
https://doi.org/10.1007/978-3-031-76806-4_7

conducted in the past 40 years [14], the rise of large language models (LLMs) is opening new frontiers for human-AI collaboration. However, integrating such capabilities with human cognitive faculties and creative processes remains challenging.

Generative AI, often associated with deep learning techniques, enables machines to produce content that mimics human-like creativity. Unlike traditional programming, which relies on explicit instructions, generative AI learns patterns and styles from vast datasets to create original and diverse content. This technology has found a unique niche in the world of storytelling, where it is employed to generate narratives, characters, and even entire stories and poems [5]. Generative AI for story creation involves training models on massive datasets comprised of diverse literary works, genres, and writing styles. These models, such as OpenAI's GPT-3 and GPT-4, learn the nuances of language, syntax, and semantics, enabling them to generate coherent and contextually relevant text. Once trained, these models can be prompted with a starting point or theme, and they autonomously produce imaginative and contextually appropriate stories.

One of the significant advantages of generative AI in story creation is its ability to break through creative barriers and expedite the writing process [16]. Exposing the model to a myriad of writing styles and genres can produce content combining elements from various sources, resulting in novel and unique narratives. This not only aids writers in overcoming creative blocks but also fosters a collaborative relationship between human creativity and machine-generated content. Generative AI should be viewed as a tool to augment human creativity rather than replace it. Writers can leverage these AI models to explore new ideas, overcome writer's block, or even collaborate with the AI in co-authoring projects. The human touch remains essential in refining and contextualizing the generated content, ensuring that it aligns with the intended emotional tone, narrative structure, and thematic elements.

2   Related Work

The use of computer programs to generate a story or parts of a story has been an interest for computer science researchers since the field's inception [14]. Initial efforts in this field utilized traditional AI algorithms, including symbolic and logical planning as well as graph traversal, to craft narratives [7,12]. These narratives often incorporated a degree of user control, allowing users to define initial goals and conditions. In recent endeavours, researchers have explored the potential of using LLMs to produce complete narratives autonomously [8], whereas others have emphasized the significance of developing AI systems that give precedence to human participation in the process of crafting stories [21].

2.1   Generative AI for Story Creation

Recent advancements in generative AI, such as GPT-4 and DALL-E2, have unlocked new possibilities for automated story generation. Numerous prototypes of AI-powered story-authoring systems have emerged. [24] developed Wordcraft, a web application for story writing with an LLM. Wordcraft consists of a traditional text editor and a set of controls that prompt an LLM to perform various writing tasks. In [22], writers interacted with AI in a "turn=taking" style to co=write short science-fiction stories. The writers discovered that the language model occasionally produces texts of subpar quality, containing words that may be challenging to comprehend. On the contrary, there are instances where it generates high-quality inspirations that propel the plot beyond what humans might anticipate. [3] explored how novelists use AI to generate stories finding that novelists find pleasure in utilizing the language model as a constraining tool to push the boundaries of their writing or as an opponent that aided them in realigning and improving their purpose. [18] investigated AI-assisted storytelling for Japanese novelists and found that while novice writers benefited from model suggestions, experts found these less useful and underwhelming.

Concerns about LLM's creativity have been raised. [19] found that LLMs aligned to human feedback, e.g., InstructGPT, generate less diverse content and increase the similarity between the writings of different writers. Addressing the lack of long-semantic coherence and relevance of outputs generated by LLMs, [23] proposed the Recursive Reprompting and Revision framework (Re3) which recursively prompt LLMs to plan, draft, rewrite, and edit. A qualitative evaluation by human evaluators found stories generated using this framework to have more coherent plots and relevance to the user install premise. [17] developed Drematron by applying language models hierarchically via prompt chaining. Drematron can help theatre and film professionals generate coherent scripts and screenplays along with titles, characters, story beats, location descriptions, and dialogues.

2.2   AI-Authoring Tools

There has been some recent work on integrating generative AI in writing assistant systems and how to best support storytellers in their writing process. These tools vary in their level of technical complexity, degrees of automation, user interactions, and level of support they provide. A common design paradigm for writing authoring tools takes the form of dialogue, where a user and the language model take turns to append content to the end of the story [3, 22, 24]. For example, [6] performed a case study on collaborative slogans and short story writing, observing that users preferred an interface design where they had a higher level of control over the interactions. Compared to the latter projects SARD provides an interactive interface, where users can control the flow of their narratives without continuous interaction with a chatbot or an excessive amount of inputs.

2.3   AI Content Quality and Novelty

Assessing the quality of content generated by AI models remains a difficult challenge, as tasks of quantifying the intricacies of narrative structure, creativity, coherence, and emotional resonance in AI-generated stories are complex. Numerous studies have approached this evaluation by assessing their generated stories with various evaluation methods. One of the most efficient methods is computer-based evaluation, where the stories generated are automatically assessed for quality, relevance, and coherence using tools and algorithms. Studies, such as [13] and [11], used pre-trained models to evaluate the fluency and diversity in AI-generated content.

After reviewing the current advancements in story generation, we observed that many existing approaches still heavily depend on human editing and interaction. In contrast, SARD minimizes the need for continuous human intervention by requiring only initial input in a straightforward manner, thus relying more on AI to drive the narrative. This makes SARD particularly user-friendly for non-writers, enabling them to create their own stories with ease and without requiring extensive expertise.

3   System Overview

SARD is a multi-chapter story generation facilitated by generative AI (see Fig. 1). It is a storyboard-based authoring tool that enables users to construct narratives through a drag-and-drop interface. SARD editor is built with ReactJS and shadcn/ui to help users to generate their own stories via a simple drag-and-drop interface. SARD is connected to generative AI models through a REST API and a WebSocket connection to the backend.

Users initiate the creation of a story by accessing the menu and selecting their preferred story genre (thrillers, science fiction, ..etc.) and structure (free, three-act story, and five-act story). Once initial story parameters are set, the users can add nodes, provided in the story elements tab, that symbolize different narrative components such as characters, actions, and relationships. These nodes can be interconnected with one another to form a complex narrative structure. Another key feature of SARD is the generation of descriptive content for characters or scenery in the story based on images provided by the user. After finishing the storyboard, the users can order events to enhance the narrative flow. The finalized user-generated storyboard is converted programmatically to prompts which are then sent to the GPT-4 model to craft a coherent and contextually rich story.

3.1 Prompt Designing

The designed several prompts for the different functionalities in SARD. Table 1 shows the prompts and their functions. We experimented with different prompts for each functionality and only included the ones that generated the best results. We designed our prompts to be as generic as possible. For example, our prompt for ensuring coherence between all chapters is:`Summarize the following chapter in a short and concise way. Make sure you include all the important events in your summary as the next chapters will depend on it: [chapter to summarize].`

We observed that this prompt helped the language model to grasp what happened in the preceding and following events. We decided to hide the prompts from the user to make them focus more on their story-writing process and less on optimizing prompts. Our decision was motivated by a previous study in which non-AI experts found it difficult to craft suitable prompts to generate intended behaviours [25].

3.2 Canvas

The canvas resembles the storyboard where story characters and different elements will be visualized as nodes. Specific nodes can be linked together through edges to form an event in the current storyboard. In addition, the optional initialization of metadata by providing character nodes with images. The simplistic interface is aimed to be user-friendly with a mini-map feature and a navigational guide to freely transport through the canvas. These functionalities streamline the user's creative workflow and provide a clear picture of how the story is developed progressively.

3.3 Setting Genre and Structure

The options tab offers two main components to writing a novel, the first one is the genre list and the second is the story structure. The genre's list provides our model to be more strict, as in the novels each genre has a way of writing and leads to a different flow of events and words. For the story structure, there are three options, free mode which lets the user have no rules in writing the story, as he may have at least one board to generate a story. There is no maximum that will make the story more creative but with the disadvantage of not following a famous structure like the others. The three-act structure consists of three main parts, an introduction, a climax, and a resolution, to represent each one in a storyboard, as it will control the flow of the story, unlike the free mode. And, for the last structure is the five-act structure, which follows *Exposition, Rising, Climax, Falling Action*, and *Resolution*. The main difference from the three-act structure it will be longer which will be more engaging in longer stories.

Table 1. The prompts used to instruct GPT-4

Functionality	Prompt
Describing a scenery	This image represents a place where events happened. Describe the place in detail. If the image has characters in it, do not describe them and ignore them. Your main focus is to describe the place and its surroundings in detail.
Describing the visual appearance of a character	Describe the character's appearance in detail for the attached image. The character name is [name] . Refrain from using pronouns, please use the character name instead. Make sure you start describing the character immediately. Do not use words like 'Certainly', or 'Okay'. If you do not receive an image, respond with nothing.
Generating a story	Write chapter [chapter number] with dialogues using the following characters' details: [characters names and details] and the relationships between them are [list of relations] . Now map it to the information you have in the following events: [list of events] , [previous chapters summary] , < [description for the place where the events happened] >. Output Length: <3000 words>. Structure of Writing: <You are writing a chapter, follow the rules to write an amazing chapter>. Take your time with the writing, perfecting this chapter.
Summarizing a chapter	Summarize the following chapter shortly and concisely. Make sure you include all the important events in your summary as the next chapters will depend on it: [chapter to summarize]

3.4   Adding Characters, Events and Actions

The story is built with three types of nodes: *character, action*, and *relationship*. The user can create one or more storyboards and drop new elements or reuse any existing story elements. The character node allows the user to add new characters as well as images to describe the character or scenes. For the action node, it offers multiple default actions to choose from, as well as a custom option that allows the user to be more specific about what he wants. Finally, the relation node is intended to bring dimension to the characters. These components are used to build the novel's events, which each include at least one character on both sides and are connected by an action node or relation. For example, the event 'Ahmad humiliated John and Ben' will be divided into four nodes combined from three characters, and a single action.

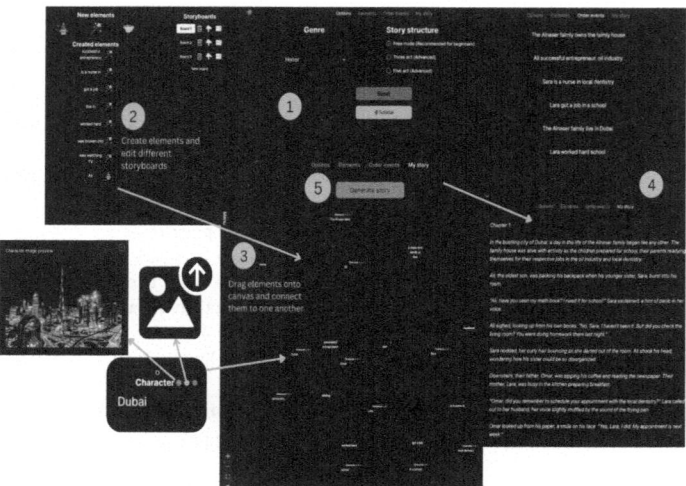

Fig. 1. SARD: Novel generation through interactive storyboard. The user starts with (1) where the user sets the story structure and genre. (2) is where the user can create and add elements, either character, action, or relationship, to their storyboard. (2) can also be used to navigate through different storyboards and set the setting with an image. When creating an element the user drags it into the canvas (3) where it is translated into a node. The user can click the green button to represent character nodes with images, and then preview them with the blue button. This node can be connected to other elements creating relationships. After the user orders events (4), they can generate their storyboards into a story (5) which is displayed in the story tab. (Color figure online)

3.5   Ordering of Events

The events sequence is of importance as it dictates the flow and coherence of the story. Based on user feedback and testing through development, we discovered that chaining events with edges can get messy and confusing very quickly. To overcome this, we added a tab for ordering events in the interface.

4   Methodology

4.1   Study 1: Evaluating the Usability and Collaborative Aspects of SARD

The primary objective of Study 1 was to assess the usability of SARD and its creativity support. To this end, the System Usability Scale (SUS) [2] and a modified version of the Mixed-Initiative Creativity Support Index (MICSI) [15] were used. The SUS scale includes 10 items (five-point Likert scale questionnaire), developed specifically to provide a reliable metric for system usability. The final score of SUS ranges from 0 to 100 and a score of 70 or above is considered to be a good indicator of system usability [1]. MICSI, an 18-item scale designed for evaluating collaborative creativity between humans and machines, encompasses five sub-scales related to Creativity Support: Enjoyment, Exploration, Expressiveness, Immersion, and Results-Worth-Effort. Each of these sub-scales involves a pair of seven-point Likert-scale questions, with the score calculated based on the mean response value for each question pair. Additionally, MICSI includes sub-scales dedicated to assessing Human-Machine Collaboration, each measured through a distinct seven-point Likert-scale question. These sub-scales address aspects like Communication, Alignment, Agency, and Partnership. A score of 5 or higher on these MICSI sub-scales indicates a positive user experience. We also allowed users to give any feedback on their use of SARD.

Participants. We recruited six university students (4 females and 2 males) to participate in the study. All the participants were graduate students in English and creative writing. The participants were aged between 22 and 25 ($M = 22.5$, $SD = 0.42$).

Task and Procedure. After obtaining participants' consent, they were given a walk-through tutorial on how to navigate the interface and use the system. Then, they were asked to generate a story of their choice using all the utilities of SARD. They were given a week to complete a story.

Results. The results of scales are presented in 2. The average score for SARD's usability was 63.75, indicating that participants had moderately positive attitudes toward the usability of SARD. This could be due to the novelty effect. Two participants indicated they initially had difficulty connecting the nodes in the canvas.

W1 *"I think how to connect the nodes was a bit challenging at first. It's hard to link nodes with each other but after some attempts, I was able to build my story "*

We also observed that some participants did not go through the tutorial we provided in the interface, and immediately started adding characters to the canvas (Fig. 2).

The scores of the MICSI sub-scales were slightly below five, as shown in 2 B, but they all expressed their satisfaction with their generated stories as they reflected in the exploratory questions as well as in their feedback in Study 2.

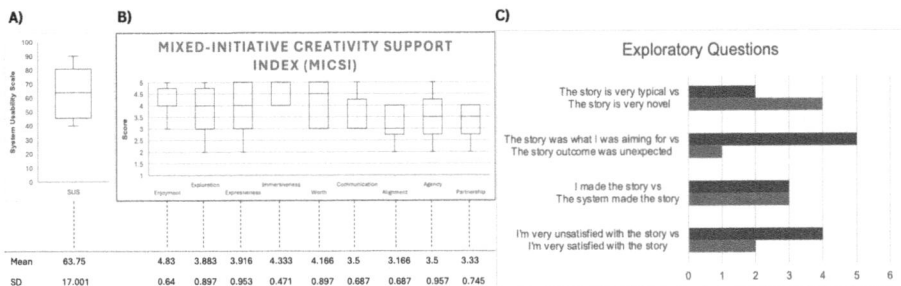

Fig. 2. Results from Study 1: (a) SUS Scores, (b) MICSI Sub-Scale Scores, (c) Exploratory Question Responses.

4.2   Study 2: Evaluating Story Quality

Understanding how writers assess systems output is crucial because it could influence their interaction and engagement with the writing assistant during the story generation process. One key characteristic of high-quality output is its textual coherence, which underlines the need for grammatically and contextually coherent output [10]. Another important facet is textual diversity which underscores the importance of offering varied system outputs to foster creativity in writing [10,20]. In Study 2, we investigated the quality and content diversity of the generated stories via quantitative and qualitative measures.

Measures. We assessed the lexical diversity of the generated stories using token-type ratios (TTR). We also conducted a semi-structured interview with the participants to solicit their opinions about the stories they generated using SARD.

4.3   Results

All participants selected a three-act story structure and developed three storyboards for each act. Our analysis of the lexical diversity of generated stories showed that the participants' stories had similar TTR ($M = 0.47$, $SD = 0.09$).

Regarding the participants' judgment of their own stories, all participants expressed their positive attitudes toward the story they generated using SARD. Specifically, they mentioned how the tool helped them to elaborate on their initial plot and extend their vocabulary.

W2 *"I like it, it creates a very advanced level of the story. It uses advanced vocabulary."*

W5 *"Honestly, I was not expecting that. I had a simple story in my mind but this tool took it to another level."*

5   Discussion

The results of our questionnaire and interviews with the participants have revealed some common patterns and themes in users' interactions with SARD, which can provide some insights for research in the realms of Natural Language Processing and Human-Computer Interaction.

5.1   Identifying Patterns in User Interactions

All writers found creating nodes to create relationships between the characters and events to help create a mental model of the story. However, a writer mentioned that she began to lose sight of her mental model of the story as she elaborated more on her story and added too many characters and events to her story canvas. While SARD summarizes and generates a plot for each chapter, it does not show it to the users. Showing a concise summary for each chapter might be helpful for users to stay oriented in their story generation process as it follows. We also observed that our participants developed their stores' characters and modified their plots repeatedly over a week. This may indicate that while our node-based system gives more flexibility and elaborateness to the story development process, it nonetheless exerts more cognitive load compared to turn-taking authoring systems.

5.2   Sense of Agency, Control, and Ownership

The user's different perceptions of AI in the co-writing process seem to impact how they interact with the tool. While some users rely heavily on AI to steer the story generation, others want more control of their story. Specifically, writers felt AI does not reflect and express what they had in their mind, despite their efforts in planning the plot of the story and how the events should flow. Some participants felt that hiding the prompts used for generating stories is limiting their ability to control their stories.

5.3   System Limitations Experienced by Participants

The participants identified some limitations in SARD. First, some participants hoped that AI could help them in brainstorming ideas and initiating some suggested plots to expiate the writing process. A participant mentioned that he used ChatGPT to brainstorm some ideas before using SARD. Second, some participants expressed disappointment or resignation when the system's output did not align with their expectations, and that adjusting nodes and reordering the event sequence did not help generate more diverse content. This echoes recent concerns on the inability of current LLMs to generate creative content on their own [4,9].

6 Conclusion and Future Work

AI-driven storytelling is an evolving landscape. In this study, we reported the findings of two studies on the usability and quality of AI-powered story generation using a custom-built interface. Our results demonstrated that the potential of human-AI co-creative systems, such as SARD, in helping novice writers generate novel stories. However, future systems need to take user's workload and their expectations of such systems into consideration. In our future work, we aim to give users more control over their story generation by allowing them to directly prompt and co-create with AI as a companion. We also aim to leverage LLMs for generating graph nodes from natural text describing story plots.

References

1. Bangor, A., Kortum, P., Miller, J.: Determining what individual SUS scores mean: adding an adjective rating scale. J. Usability Stud. **4**(3), 114–123 (2009)
2. Brooke, J.: SUS: a quick and dirty usability. Usability Eval. Ind. **189**(3), 189–194 (1996)
3. Calderwood, A., Qiu, V., Gero, K.I., Chilton, L.B.: How novelists use generative language models: an exploratory user study. In: HAI-GEN+ user2agent@ IUI (2020)
4. Chakrabarty, T., Laban, P., Agarwal, D., Muresan, S., Wu, C.S.: Art or artifice? large language models and the false promise of creativity. arXiv preprint arXiv:2309.14556 (2023)
5. Chakrabarty, T., Padmakumar, V., He, H.: Help me write a poem: instruction tuning as a vehicle for collaborative poetry writing. arXiv preprint arXiv:2210.13669 (2022)
6. Clark, E., Ross, A.S., Tan, C., Ji, Y., Smith, N.A.: Creative writing with a machine in the loop: case studies on slogans and stories. In: 23rd International Conference on Intelligent User Interfaces, pp. 329–340 (2018)
7. Dehn, N.: Story generation after tale-spin. IJCAI **81**, 16–18 (1981)
8. Fan, A., Lewis, M., Dauphin, Y.: Hierarchical neural story generation. arXiv preprint arXiv:1805.04833 (2018)
9. Franceschelli, G., Musolesi, M.: On the creativity of large language models. arXiv preprint arXiv:2304.00008 (2023)
10. Gero, K.I., Liu, V., Chilton, L.: Sparks: inspiration for science writing using language models. In: Designing Interactive Systems Conference, pp. 1002–1019 (2022)
11. Khan, A., Wang, A., Hager, S., Andrews, N.: Learning to generate text in arbitrary writing styles. arXiv preprint arXiv:2312.17242 (2023)
12. Klein, S., et al.: Automatic novel writing: a status report. University of Wisconsin-Madison Department of Computer Sciences, Tech. rep. (1973)
13. Kong, X., Huang, J., Tung, Z., Guan, J., Huang, M.: Stylized story generation with style-guided planning. arXiv preprint arXiv:2105.08625 (2021)
14. Kybartas, B., Bidarra, R.: A survey on story generation techniques for authoring computational narratives. IEEE Trans. Comput. Intell. AI in Games **9**(3), 239–253 (2016)
15. Lawton, T., Ibarrola, F.J., Ventura, D., Grace, K.: Drawing with reframer: emergence and control in co-creative AI. In: Proceedings of the 28th International Conference on Intelligent User Interfaces, pp. 264–277 (2023)

16. Lee, M., et al.: Design space for intelligent and interactive writing assistants. In: Proceedings of the ACM CHI Conference on Human Factors in Computing Systems. ACM (2024)
17. Mirowski, P., Mathewson, K.W., Pittman, J., Evans, R.: Co-writing screenplays and theatre scripts with language models: evaluation by industry professionals. In: Proceedings of the 2023 CHI Conference on Human Factors in Computing Systems, pp. 1–34 (2023)
18. Osone, H., Lu, J.L., Ochiai, Y.: BunCho: AI supported story co-creation via unsupervised multitask learning to increase writers' creativity in Japanese. In: Extended Abstracts of the 2021 CHI Conference on Human Factors in Computing Systems, pp. 1–10 (2021)
19. Padmakumar, V., He, H.: Does writing with language models reduce content diversity? ArXiv preprint arXiv:2309.05196 (2023)
20. Singh, N., Bernal, G., Savchenko, D., Glassman, E.L.: Where to hide a stolen elephant: leaps in creative writing with multimodal machine intelligence. ACM Trans. Comput.-Hum. Interact. **30**(5), 1–57 (2023)
21. Swanson, B., Mathewson, K., Pietrzak, B., Chen, S., Dinalescu, M.: Story centaur: large language model few shot learning as a creative writing tool. In: Proceedings of the 16th Conference of the European Chapter of the Association for Computational Linguistics: System Demonstrations, pp. 244–256 (2021)
22. Yang, D., Zhou, Y., Zhang, Z., Li, T.J.J., LC, R.: AI as an active writer: Interaction strategies with generated text in human-AI collaborative fiction writing. In: Joint Proceedings of the ACM IUI Workshops, vol. 10. CEUR-WS Team (2022)
23. Yang, K., Peng, N., Tian, Y., Klein, D.: Re3: generating longer stories with recursive reprompting and revision. arXiv preprint arXiv:2210.06774 (2022)
24. Yuan, A., Coenen, A., Reif, E., Ippolito, D.: Wordcraft: story writing with large language models. In: 27th International Conference on Intelligent User Interfaces, pp. 841–852 (2022)
25. Zamfirescu-Pereira, J., Wong, R.Y., Hartmann, B., Yang, Q.: Why Johnny can't prompt: how non-AI experts try (and fail) to design LLM prompts. In: Proceedings of the 2023 CHI Conference on Human Factors in Computing Systems, pp. 1–21 (2023)

Cross-Cultural Implications of Large Language Models: An Extended Comparative Analysis

Xinyang Shan[1], Yuanyuan Xu[1(✉)], Yining Wang[2], Yin-Shan Lin[3], and Yunshi Bao[4]

[1] Tongji University, Shanghai 200092, China
ecusttethys@foxmail.com
[2] Bentley University, Waltham, MA 02452, USA
[3] Northeastern University, Boston, MA 02115, USA
[4] Fairleigh Dickinson University, Teaneck, NJ 07666, USA

Abstract. This article examines the impacts of deploying large language models (LLMs) across diverse cultural contexts, emphasizing the challenges and opportunities related to their linguistic adaptability and cultural sensitivity. As globalization progresses, the necessity for LLMs to operate effectively and sensitively in multilingual and multicultural environments becomes increasingly critical. This study conducts a comprehensive multilingual analysis to explore how these models navigate linguistic nuances and cultural idiosyncrasies when generating and interpreting text. By investigating a diverse array of languages and cultural settings, the research identifies crucial challenges that current models face, such as biases and inaccuracies in languages with less digital representation. These biases not only affect the accuracy of the models but also potentially exacerbate existing social inequalities, particularly in marginalized communities. To address these challenges, this article proposes innovative strategies to enhance the cultural and linguistic effectiveness of LLMs. Firstly, it emphasizes the importance of incorporating culturally inclusive training datasets during the development phases of AI systems to ensure that the models are exposed to a diverse range of languages and cultural contexts. Secondly, it suggests integrating cultural experts into development teams to provide valuable insights into linguistic peculiarities and cultural nuances, thereby improving the models' accuracy and sensitivity. Through quantitative and qualitative methods, the study assesses the performance of LLMs across various metrics, including cultural sensitivity and user satisfaction. The quantitative analysis involves using a series of culturally specific prompts to measure the accuracy of language generation and comprehension, while the qualitative evaluation involves detailed feedback from language experts and native speakers to assess the contextual appropriateness and cultural relevance of the generated texts. The findings reveal that while LLMs perform excellently in handling resource-rich languages, there remains a significant gap in their ability to manage languages with fewer resources.

© The Author(s), under exclusive license to Springer Nature Switzerland AG 2025
A. Coman et al. (Eds.): HCII 2024, LNCS 15375, pp. 106–118, 2025.
https://doi.org/10.1007/978-3-031-76806-4_8

Keywords: Cross-Cultural Communication · Large Language Models · Multilingual Text Generation

1 Introduction

The integration of large language models (LLMs) into diverse linguistic environments presents significant opportunities and complex challenges for AI developers and users. As globalization accelerates, the need for LLMs to function effectively and sensitively in multilingual and multicultural contexts becomes increasingly critical [1]. This research delves into the impacts of deploying LLMs across different cultural settings, highlighting the challenges and possibilities associated with their linguistic adaptability and cultural sensitivity.

The significance of this work lies in its potential to enhance global communication by improving the cultural and linguistic competence of AI systems. Previous studies have shown that while LLMs, such as OpenAI's GPT series, exhibit remarkable linguistic capabilities, they often struggle with the nuances of less-represented languages, leading to biased outputs and reduced effectiveness in non-Western contexts [2–4]. Scholars' research on the Transformer architecture has laid the foundation for these models, yet there remains a critical gap in developing LLMs that are truly global in their understanding and application [5–7].

The integration of cultural sensitivity within AI systems is gaining increasing attention as these technologies reach global markets. Studies have demonstrated that AI systems trained without considering cultural diversity can perpetuate stereotypes and misunderstandings. Further research, examining user interactions with AI across different countries, has found significant variations in user satisfaction and system efficacy due to embedded cultural biases [8].

Through conducting a comprehensive multilingual analysis this article explores how LLMs manage linguistic nuances and cultural idiosyncrasies when generating and interpreting text. By investigating a diverse array of languages and cultural settings, this research identifies crucial challenges that current models face, such as biases and inaccuracies in languages with less digital representation. It also proposes innovative strategies to enhance the cultural and linguistic effectiveness of LLMs, emphasizing the importance of culturally inclusive training datasets and integrating cultural expertise into AI system development.

Through quantitative and qualitative methods, this study assesses the performance of LLMs across various metrics, including cultural sensitivity and user satisfaction. It offers insights into potential improvements that could make these models more globally adaptable and equitable. This research aims to contribute to the field by providing a pathway towards creating more culturally aware and linguistically competent AI tools, aiming for a future where technology truly understands and respects cultural diversity.

2   Literature Review

2.1   Recent Advances in Large Language Models

Recent research has significantly advanced our understanding of LLMs, particularly in their applications within multilingual environments. The Transformer architecture has laid the foundation for developing models like OpenAI's GPT-3. These models exhibit remarkable linguistic capabilities when trained on large-scale datasets predominantly in English. However, research by various scholars indicates that despite their impressive performance in language processing, these models often struggle with the nuances of less-represented languages, leading to biased outputs and reduced effectiveness in non-Western contexts [10]. This body of work highlights a critical gap in the development of LLMs that are truly global in their understanding and application.

The work by Cotterell et al. further deepens this field by exploring whether all languages are equally challenging to language-model. Their study, through an in-depth analysis of various languages, reveals unique challenges certain languages face in language modeling. By evaluating the performance of language models across different languages, this research provides valuable insights for improving the adaptability of LLMs in multilingual environments [11].

Mahowald et al. (2023) take a cognitive perspective to investigate the dissociation between language and thought in large language models. Their work demonstrates that while LLMs excel in language processing, there remains a significant gap in capturing and simulating human thought processes. This study underscores the importance of incorporating cognitive science perspectives into the development of LLMs, pointing to future research directions in this area [12].

2.2   Cultural Sensitivity in AI

As artificial intelligence technologies enter global markets, the integration of cultural sensitivity within AI systems is receiving increasing attention [13]. Research by various scholars indicates that AI systems trained without considering cultural diversity may perpetuate stereotypes and misunderstandings [14]. They advocate for a "culturally aware" training process that incorporates diverse data sources reflective of various linguistic and cultural backgrounds [15]. Similarly, other scholars have studied user interactions with AI across different countries, finding significant variations in user satisfaction and system efficacy due to the cultural biases embedded in AI models [16–18]. These studies underscore the necessity of embedding cultural understanding in AI development to prevent the reinforcement of cultural biases and ensure the equitable deployment of AI technologies globally.

The contributions of Cotterell et al. and Mahowald et al. offer important insights into the performance and improvement of LLMs in multilingual and cross-cultural contexts. Their research not only highlights the limitations of current models in handling linguistic and cultural nuances but also provides valuable directions for future improvements. By integrating these studies, this thesis aims to further advance the development of culturally sensitive and linguistically diverse AI systems, promoting effective and fair communication on a global scale [11,12].

2.3   Bias and Fairness in AI

In recent years, the issue of bias in artificial intelligence systems has received widespread attention. Particularly in large language models, biases in training data and limitations in model architecture can lead to biased outputs. This bias not only affects the accuracy of the models but also has profound negative impacts on marginalized communities. For instance, some scholars have noted that many LLMs perform poorly when handling minority languages and cultures, potentially exacerbating existing social inequalities [19,20]. Furthermore, studies have shown that biased AI systems can make unfair decisions in critical areas such as recruitment, credit evaluation, and legal judgments, further impacting the quality of life for marginalized groups [21–23].

To reduce bias in AI systems, researchers have proposed various strategies. Diversifying data sources can help train more equitable models, avoiding the influence of biased data. Some scholars suggest introducing fairness algorithms during the training process to ensure that the models treat data from different cultural and linguistic backgrounds equally [24,25]. Additionally, continuous monitoring and adjustment of models can help detect and correct bias issues promptly. Specific case studies have demonstrated that adopting these strategies can significantly improve the fairness and reliability of models, reducing negative impacts on marginalized communities [26].

2.4   Transparency and Explainability

Transparency and explainability are crucial for ensuring that AI systems are trustworthy and reliable. In LLMs, transparency can help users understand the decision-making process of the models, thereby enhancing trust. Current research aims to make LLMs more interpretable and understandable to non-experts. Some scholars have discussed the importance of increasing AI system transparency through model interpretability techniques and explainable AI (XAI) frameworks [29,30]. Scholars agree that transparent AI systems can help users identify and correct potential errors and biases, thereby improving the overall performance of the systems [31].

To enhance the transparency and explainability of AI systems, researchers have developed various methods and tools. Model interpretability techniques can reveal the decision logic within models, enabling users to better understand and trust AI systems [32]. XAI frameworks provide a systematic approach to evaluating and enhancing the interpretability of models. These tools and frameworks have been proven effective in practice, helping developers create more transparent and reliable AI systems [33].

3   Methods

The study employed a mixed-method approach, combining quantitative data anal-ysis with qualitative evaluations from language experts. Participants included a diverse group of 30 individuals, consisting of 15 males and 15 females, aged be-tween 25 and 50 years. All participants were either language professionals or na-tive speakers with advanced proficiency in their respective languages, rep-resenting English, Mandarin, Spanish, Arabic, Russian, Hindi, Bengali, Swahili, Portuguese, and Japanese. These participants were carefully selected to ensure a balanced rep-resentation of different age groups, genders, and linguistic back-grounds, which was crucial for obtaining comprehensive and unbiased feedback on the LLMs' performance. The research approach integrated both quantita-tive and qualitative methodologies to provide a comprehensive assessment of LLMs' performance across different languages and cultural contexts, allowing for a robust evaluation of the models by combining numerical data with in-depth qualitative insights.

3.1   Quantitative Analysis

The quantitative analysis involved a series of tests to measure the accuracy of language generation and comprehension by the LLMs. The performance of the models was evaluated using the following steps: Each language was tested using a set of culturally specific prompts designed to evaluate the models' linguistic accuracy and cultural relevance. These prompts were developed in consultation with linguistic experts to ensure they captured a wide range of linguistic and cultural nuances. For instance, for cultural references, the models were tasked with writing a short essay on Thanksgiving traditions in English, explaining their significance and typical activities; a short essay on Spring Festival customs in Mandarin, detailing their importance and typical activities; and a short essay on Holy Week celebrations in Spanish, discussing their significance and typical activities. The generated outputs were scored against benchmarks established by linguistic experts. These benchmarks included metrics for comprehension accu-racy and cultural sensitivity, reflecting the complexity and diversity of real-world language use. (Table 2) The performance scores were tabulated and analyzed for each language, focusing on aspects such as adaptability, handling of slang, dialect variations, contextual humor, and proverbs. The analysis also included a com-parison of the models' performance across different languages to identify any disparities or biases. To systematically evaluate the performance of the LLMs, a comprehensive scoring system was implemented, considering various aspects of linguistic and cultural competence (Table 1).

Each criterion is scored out of 10 points. The total score is the sum of all individual scores, with each criterion having a maximum score of 10 points, resulting in a total maximum score of 70 points. For each culturally specific prompt, the average score of the two prompts is calculated for each criterion. The total score is converted to a percentage, i.e., (Total Score/70) * 100.

Table 1. Evaluation Criteria and Scoring System.

Criterion	Description	Maximum Score
Comprehension Accuracy	Assesses the accuracy of the generated output's comprehension	10
Cultural Sensitivity	Evaluates the cultural relevance of the generated output	10
Adaptability	Measures the model's adaptability to different contexts	10
Slang Handling	Assesses the model's ability to handle slang	10
Dialect Variations	Evaluates the model's handling of dialectal variations	10
Contextual Humor	Measures the model's ability to understand and generate contextual humor	10
Proverbs Handling	Assesses the model's ability to handle proverbs	10
Total Score	The sum of all criteria (maximum of 70 points), converted to a percentage	70

3.2 Qualitative Analysis

The qualitative analysis provided deeper insights into the contextual appropriateness of the generated texts. Key aspects of the qualitative evaluation included:

Feedback from Native Speakers: Native speakers of each language reviewed the LLM outputs to assess the contextual appropriateness and cultural relevance of the generated texts. They provided detailed feedback on various aspects, including the use of idiomatic expressions, regional dialects, and culturally specific references.

Evaluation by Cultural Experts: Cultural experts evaluated the texts for nuances in politeness, humor, metaphorical language, and other culturally specific elements. These experts were selected based on their extensive knowledge of the cultural contexts and linguistic subtleties of the target languages.

Thematic Analysis: The feedback was thematically analyzed to identify common issues and patterns. This analysis focused on key themes such as politeness levels, humor, and metaphorical language usage, which varied significantly across cultures. Thematic analysis also helped in understanding the broader cultural implications of the models' outputs.

Iterative Refinement: The qualitative insights were used in an iterative process to refine the models. This involved adjusting the training data and model parameters to better handle the identified issues. The refined models were then re-evaluated using the same qualitative criteria to ensure improvements in cultural sensitivity and contextual appropriateness.

The insights gained from the qualitative analysis were crucial in understanding the practical limitations of current LLM training datasets and identifying areas for improvement. This comprehensive evaluation methodology ensured that the study not only assessed the current performance of LLMs but also provided actionable recommendations for enhancing their cultural and linguistic capabilities.

3.3 Detailed Process Description

Participants were recruited through professional networks and linguistic organizations to ensure high proficiency and expertise. A demographic survey was conducted to ensure diversity in age, gender, and linguistic background. Linguistic experts from each language group collaborated to create culturally specific prompts, which included a mix of formal and informal scenarios, idiomatic expressions, and culturally significant references. The LLMs were tasked with generating responses to the prompts in each language, and the generated responses were collected and anonymized for unbiased evaluation.

For the quantitative analysis, linguistic experts evaluated the responses based on predefined benchmarks. Metrics included accuracy, fluency, cultural relevance, and sensitivity. Scores were recorded and statistically analyzed to compare performance across languages. In the qualitative analysis, native speakers and cultural experts reviewed the responses in detail. Feedback sessions were conducted where reviewers discussed the appropriateness and accuracy of the LLMs' outputs, and common themes and issues were identified through thematic analysis.

Based on the qualitative feedback, the training data and model parameters were adjusted. The models were retrained and tested again using the same set of prompts and evaluation criteria. This cycle was repeated until noticeable improvements were observed in the models' performance. The refined models underwent a final round of both quantitative and qualitative evaluations, and the results were compared to the initial performance to assess the effectiveness of the refinements. This detailed process ensured a thorough and balanced evaluation of LLMs, highlighting their strengths and areas for improvement in handling cross-cultural and multilingual tasks.

4 Results

The results of this study highlighted a pronounced disparity in performance across different languages, revealing significant insights into the capabilities and limitations of large language models (LLMs) in handling linguistic and cultural diversity.

4.1 Quantitative Results

The quantitative analysis showed varying degrees of success in the models' ability to comprehend and generate text across different languages. The performance metrics indicated that LLMs excel in languages with extensive digital re-sources but struggle with those having less representation. Specifically, the com-prehension accuracy and cultural sensitivity scores varied widely, as summarized in Table 2

Table 2. Performance Analysis of Large Language Models Across Different Cultural Contexts.

Language	User Feedback Themes	Total Score (as %)
English	Highly adaptable, minor nuances missed	95.4%
Mandarin	Strong in formal contexts, struggles with slang	90.4%
Spanish	Good performance, occasional formal/informal mix-ups	88.7%
Arabic	Difficulties with dialect variations	80.4%
Russian	Effective for standard use, less so for regional idioms	84%
Hindi	Struggles with contextual humor and proverbs	78.4%
Bengali	Limited data affects performance	72%
Swahili	Very basic comprehension, needs significant improvement	68.3%
Portuguese	Generally effective, some issues with European vs. Brazilian variations	85.6%
Japanese	Performs well with standard language, less so with politeness levels	87.6%

These results illustrate that LLMs are generally more accurate and culturally sensitive in languages like English and Mandarin, which have abundant digital resources. In contrast, languages such as Bengali and Swahili, which have less digital representation, showed significant gaps in performance. This discrepancy underscores the need for more robust and culturally diverse training datasets to enhance the models' effectiveness across all languages.

4.2   Qualitative Results

The qualitative analysis provided deeper insights into the contextual appropriateness of the generated texts. Feedback from native speakers and cultural experts highlighted several key themes.

Politeness and Formality: The models generally performed well in understanding and generating polite and formal language in English, Mandarin, and Japanese. However, they struggled with informal speech and slang, particularly in languages like Hindi and Swahili.

Humor and Metaphors: Cultural nuances in humor and metaphorical language posed significant challenges for the models. For instance, English and

Spanish texts often lacked the subtlety needed to convey humor accurately, while Arabic and Russian outputs showed difficulties with metaphorical expressions.

Dialectal Variations: The models were less effective in handling regional dialects and idiomatic expressions. This issue was particularly evident in Arabic, where dialectal differences significantly impacted the accuracy and cultural relevance of the generated texts. The qualitative feedback emphasized the practical limitations of current LLMs training datasets, which often lack the cultural depth needed to handle nuanced language use across different contexts. Native speakers and cultural experts consistently pointed out areas where the models' outputs failed to capture the subtleties of their languages, leading to potential misunderstandings or culturally insensitive responses.

5   Discussion

The findings of this study reveal critical insights into the functionality of large language models (LLMs) across various linguistic and cultural landscapes, underscoring significant implications for the future of AI development. This section explores these implications, particularly emphasizing the importance of embedding cultural diversity within the AI training processes. Incorporating cultural experts into AI development teams could greatly enhance the cultural competence of these models, ensuring that they are more attuned to the subtle nuances of different cultures and languages.

The potential benefits of such integration are manifold. Firstly, cultural experts can provide invaluable insights into linguistic idiosyncrasies and cultural nuances that are often overlooked by technologists. This can lead to more accurate and sensitive AI outputs, reducing the risk of cultural misinterpretations and biases that can alienate users or lead to miscommunications. Furthermore, strategies such as the creation of diverse focus groups to continuously test and provide feedback on AI systems can mitigate existing biases and prevent new ones from forming.

The pronounced disparity in performance between languages with extensive online resources and those with less digital presence underscores the critical need for more inclusive training datasets. The study's findings highlight several important implications for the development of LLMs. First, increasing the diversity of training data to include more languages and dialects is essential for improving the models' global adaptability, helping to mitigate biases and enhance the models' ability to generate culturally sensitive outputs. Second, integrating cultural experts into the AI development process can provide valuable insights into linguistic idiosyncrasies and cultural nuances that are often overlooked, leading to more accurate and sensitive AI outputs and reducing the risk of cultural misinterpretations and biases. Finally, establishing diverse focus groups to continuously test and provide feedback on AI systems can help identify and address existing biases, ensuring that the models remain responsive to the evolving needs of global users.

Comparing our findings with similar studies, such as those by Cotterell et al. and Mahowald et al., it becomes evident that while some advancements have been made in improving LLMs' performance across various languages, there remains a significant gap in achieving true cultural sensitivity [11,12]. For instance, Cotterell et al. demonstrated that language models perform worse on languages with complex inflectional morphology, suggesting that these models are not yet fully capable of handling linguistic diversity. Similarly, Mahowald et al. emphasized the distinction between formal linguistic competence and functional linguistic competence, indicating that while LLMs excel at formal linguistic tasks, they often struggle with functional tasks that require deeper understanding and contextual awareness. Our study corroborates these findings and further emphasizes the necessity of proactive measures to address these issues.

The importance of transparency and explainability in AI systems has been highlighted. As discussed by various researchers, transparent AI systems enable users to understand and trust the decision-making processes of LLMs, thereby reducing the likelihood of misinterpretations and fostering greater acceptance of AI technologies [34]. Our findings support this notion, suggesting that enhanced transparency and continuous feedback mechanisms are vital for developing culturally competent AI systems.

Our study not only confirms the existing challenges in the field but also provides a comprehensive framework for addressing them. By focusing on cultural diversity, transparency, and continuous feedback, we can develop LLMs that are more equitable, reliable, and globally adaptable. Compared to the in-depth analyses by other researchers, our study provides a broader perspective on the integration of cultural competence in AI, aiming to create technology that truly understands and respects cultural diversity.

6   Conclusion

This study highlights the potential of large language models to enhance global communication, contingent upon significant advancements in cultural and linguistic inclusivity. The findings reveal a pronounced disparity in performance between languages with extensive online resources and those with less digital presence, underscoring the critical need for more robust and culturally diverse training datasets. To address these challenges, the study advocates for a strategic framework focused on creating more culturally competent AI systems.

Integrating cultural expertise in the AI development process is essential. Cultural experts can provide invaluable insights into linguistic idiosyncrasies and cultural nuances that are often overlooked by technologists, leading to more accurate and sensitive AI outputs. This integration helps reduce the risk of cultural misinterpretations and biases that can alienate users or lead to miscommunications. Additionally, establishing diverse focus groups to continuously test and provide feedback on AI systems can help identify and address existing biases, ensuring that the models remain responsive to the evolving needs of global users.

By expanding training datasets to encompass a wider range of languages and cultural contexts, AI developers can enhance the global adaptability of their technologies. Such improvements are crucial for building trust and facilitating the ethical deployment of AI across varied cultural landscapes. This study contributes to the field by providing a pathway toward creating more culturally aware and linguistically competent AI tools, aiming for a future where technology truly understands and respects cultural diversity.

In reflecting on the comprehensive and insightful work done by Cotterell et al. (2020) and Mahowald et al. (2024), we acknowledge the depth and rigor of their analyses, which provide a strong foundation upon which our research builds. Their meticulous examination of linguistic complexities and the cognitive aspects of LLM performance set a high standard, inspiring our efforts to further explore and address the cultural dimensions of AI systems.

References

1. Liu, C. C., Koto, F., Baldwin, T., et al.: Are multilingual LLMs culturally-diverse reasoners? An investigation into multicultural proverbs and sayings. arXiv preprint arXiv:2309.08591 (2023)
2. Beguš, G., Dąbkowski, M., Rhodes, R.: Large linguistic models: analyzing theoretical linguistic abilities of LLMs. arXiv preprint arXiv:2305.00948 (2023)
3. Muñoz-Ortiz, A., Gómez-Rodríguez, C., Vilares, D.: Contrasting linguistic patterns in human and LLM-generated text. arXiv preprint arXiv:2308.09067 (2023)
4. Lin, Y. T., Chen, Y. N.: Taiwan LLM: bridging the linguistic divide with a culturally aligned language model. arXiv preprint arXiv:2311.17487 (2023)
5. Yamazaki, K., Vo, K., Truong, Q. S., et al.: VLTinT: visual-linguistic transformer-in-transformer for coherent video paragraph captioning. In: Proceedings of the AAAI Conference on Artificial Intelligence, vol. 37(3), pp. 3081–3090 (2023)
6. Deng, J., Yang, Z., Chen, T., et al.: TransVG: end-to-end visual grounding with transformers. In: Proceedings of the IEEE/CVF International Conference on Computer Vision, pp. 1769–1779 (2021)
7. Lan, G., Liu, X. Y., Zhang, Y., et al.: Communication-efficient federated learning for resource-constrained edge devices. IEEE Trans. Mach. Learn. Commun. Netw. (2023)
8. Challen, R., Denny, J., Pitt, M., et al.: Artificial intelligence, bias and clinical safety. BMJ Qual. Saf. **28**(3), 231–237 (2019)
9. Stanley, B.: The reshaping of Christian tradition: western denominational identity in a non-western context. Stud. Church Hist. **32**, 399–426 (1996)
10. İlhan, B., Gürses, B. O., Güneri, P.: Addressing inequalities in science: the role of language learning models in bridging the gap. Int. Dental J. (2024)
11. Cotterell, R., Mielke, S. J., Eisner, J., Roark, B.: Are all languages equally hard to language-model?. ArXiv preprint arXiv:1806.03743 (2018)
12. Mahowald, K., Ivanova, A.A., Blank, I.A., et al.: Dissociating language and thought in large language models: a cognitive perspective. arXiv preprint arXiv:2301.06627 (2023)
13. Mengesha, Z., Heldreth, C., Lahav, M., et al.: I don't think these devices are very culturally sensitive - Impact of automated speech recognition errors on African Americans. Front. Artif. Intell. **4**, 725911 (2021)
14. McIntosh, T. R., Liu, T., Susnjak, T., et al.: A culturally sensitive test to evaluate nuanced GPT hallucination. IEEE Trans. Artif. Intell. (2023)

15. Haim, G., Gal, Y., Gelfand, M., et al.: A cultural sensitive agent for human-computer negotiation. In: Proceedings of the 11th International Conference on Autonomous Agents and Multiagent Systems, vol. 1, pp. 451–458 (2012)

16. Parra, C.M., Gupta, M., Dennehy, D.: Likelihood of questioning AI-based recommendations due to perceived racial/gender bias. IEEE Trans. Technol. Soc. **3**(1), 41–45 (2021)

17. Schwartz, R., Schwartz, R., Vassilev, A., et al.: Towards a standard for identifying and managing bias in artificial intelligence. US Department of Commerce, National Institute of Standards and Technology (2022)

18. Kulesz, O.: Culture, platforms and machines: the impact of artificial intelligence on the diversity of cultural expressions. In: Intergovernmental Committee for the Protection and Promotion of the Diversity of Cultural Expressions, vol. 12 (2018)

19. Nguyen, X. P., Aljunied, S. M., Joty, S., et al.: Democratizing LLMs for low-resource languages by leveraging their English dominant abilities with linguistically-diverse prompts. arXiv preprint arXiv:2306.11372 (2023)

20. Tian, G., Xu, Y.: A study on the typeface design method of Han characters imitated Tangut. Adv. Educ. Hum. Soc. Sci. Res. **1**(2), 270–270 (2022)

21. Ntoutsi, E., Fafalios, P., Gadiraju, U., et al.: Bias in data-driven artificial intelligence systems-an introductory survey. Wiley Interdisc. Rev. Data Min. Knowl. Disc. **10**(3), e1356 (2020)

22. Langer, M., König, C.J., Back, C., et al.: Trust in artificial intelligence: comparing trust processes between human and automated trustees in light of unfair bias. J. Bus. Psychol. **38**(3), 493–508 (2023)

23. Hagendorff, T., Bossert, L.N., Tse, Y.F., et al.: Speciesist bias in AI: how AI applications perpetuate discrimination and unfair outcomes against animals. AI Ethics **3**(3), 717–734 (2023)

24. Roselli, D., Matthews, J., Talagala, N.: Managing bias in AI. In: Companion Proceedings of the 2019 World Wide Web Conference, pp. 539–544 (2019)

25. Nazer, L.H., Zatarah, R., Waldrip, S., et al.: Bias in artificial intelligence algorithms and recommendations for mitigation. PLOS Digit. Health **2**(6), e0000278 (2023)

26. Ehsan, U., Liao, Q.V., Muller, M., et al.: Expanding Explainability: Towards Social Transparency in AI Systems. Springer, Cham (2021)

27. Larsson, S., Heintz, F.: Transparency in artificial intelligence. Internet Policy Rev. **9**(2) (2020)

28. Das, A., Rad, P.: Opportunities and challenges in explainable artificial intelligence (XAI): a survey. arXiv preprint arXiv:2006.11371 (2020)

29. Arrieta, A.B., Díaz-Rodríguez, N., Del Ser, J., et al.: Explainable Artificial Intelligence (XAI): concepts, taxonomies, opportunities and challenges toward responsible AI. Inf. Fus. **58**, 82–115 (2020)

30. Adadi, A., Berrada, M.: Peeking inside the black-box: a survey on explainable artificial intelligence (XAI). IEEE Access **6**, 52138–52160 (2018)

31. Holzinger, A., Saranti, A., Molnar, C., Biecek, P., Samek, W.: Explainable AI methods - a brief overview. In: Holzinger, A., Goebel, R., Fong, R., Moon, T., Müller, K.-R., Samek, W. (eds.) xxAI - Beyond Explainable AI: International Workshop, Held in Conjunction with ICML 2020, July 18, 2020, Vienna, Austria, Revised and Extended Papers, pp. 13–38. Springer International Publishing, Cham (2022). https://doi.org/10.1007/978-3-031-04083-2_2

32. Hanif, A., Zhang, X., Wood, S.: A survey on explainable artificial intelligence techniques and challenges. In: 2021 IEEE 25th International Enterprise Distributed Object Computing Workshop (EDOCW), pp. 81–89. IEEE (2021)

33. Ali, S., Abuhmed, T., El-Sappagh, S., et al.: Explainable Artificial Intelligence (XAI): what we know and what is left to attain Trustworthy Artificial Intelligence. Inf. Fus. **99**, 101805 (2023)
34. Chamola, V., Hassija, V., Sulthana, A.R., et al.: A review of trustworthy and explainable artificial intelligence (XAI). IEEE (2023)

Research on the Influence of the Artificial Intelligence Chatbots' Service Quality on the Consumers' Purchase Intention

Zhuoqi Teng(✉) [ID], Aocheng Wu [ID], and Zhaoran Song [ID]

College of Business Administration, Henan Finance University, Zhengzhou, China
tengzhuoqi@hafu.edu.cn

Abstract. With the swift advancement of artificial intelligence (AI) technology and the escalating prevalence of online transactions, AI chatbots have become ubiquitous in e-commerce and various other sectors. In numerous e-commerce contexts, the widespread deployment of AI chatbots can result in substantial cost and time savings. Serving as a vital conduit between consumers and businesses, the implementation of AI chatbots significantly influences consumers' purchasing decisions and compliant behaviors, contingent upon the quality of service provided. Hence, it is critical to investigate the relationship between AI chatbots and consumers' propensity for service engagement and compliant behavior. This research establishes a theoretical framework wherein the information quality and interaction quality of AI chatbots are positioned as independent variables, with customer compliance and consumer purchase intentions as dependent factors. A survey was meticulously crafted for empirical investigation. Post-analysis, the ensuing conclusions were deduced: the quality of information positively affects perceived trust; the quality of interaction exerts a substantial positive effect on perceived usefulness and trust; perceived usefulness significantly enhances user compliance, yet its influence on purchase intent remains insignificant; trust positively influences both user compliance and purchase intent. Based on these findings, this study endeavors to proffer strategic recommendations and guidelines for the optimal utilization of chatbots within e-commerce platforms.

Keywords: AI chatbot service quality · perceived usefulness · user compliance · purchase intention · structural equation modeling

1 Introduction

AI stands as a pivotal technology reshaping the future, profoundly influencing economic development, societal advancement, and the very fabric of human existence [1]. Over time, AI has been pervasively integrated to bolster decision-making and elevate problem-solving efficacy across diverse sectors, including healthcare [2], education, public services, industry, media, and commerce [3]. The advent of real-time customer interactions via chat interfaces has surged in popularity as a paradigm for delivering immediate customer support within e-commerce spheres. With online transactions growing exponentially, AI's deployment in e-commerce chat services, particularly AI chatbots, has become widespread. As an inevitable trend of our times, AI chatbots empower businesses to enhance customer experiences and meet their expectations through real-time interactions in the digital marketplace. These chatbots have pioneered conversational commerce and introduced innovative methods for businesses to engage with the global community, primarily through customer communication [4]. Studies project that chatbots could trim global business costs by an estimated $1.3 trillion by accelerating response times, enabling agents to focus on other tasks, and handling up to 30% of customer service queries. Amidst an annual tally of 2.65 trillion customer service requests, chatbots are capable of addressing 80% of routine issues [5]. As a primary vehicle for enhancing communication efficiency between consumers and businesses, AI chatbots play an indispensable role in e-commerce shopping. The majority of consumers seek more detailed product or service information, which AI chatbots readily provide, thereby serving a practical function in conserving consumers' time by obviating the need to sift through extensive descriptions. Moreover, interacting with chatbots can mitigate purchase risks, dispel uncertainties, and foster trust, thus fulfilling an emotional role.

In conclusion, the key to swaying consumer purchase intentions lies in crafting AI chatbots that align with consumer desires. This investigation delves into how AI chatbots foster consumer perceptions of utility and trust, thereby increasing the likelihood of consumers heeding chatbot recommendations and fostering the intent to purchase. Through dissecting the attributes of AI chatbots' service quality, this research devises a theoretical model wherein the information and interaction quality of AI chatbots serve as independent variables, perceived usefulness and trust as intermediary factors, and user compliance and purchase intention as outcome measures. Upon rigorous analysis and validation of this model, the study endeavors to provide e-commerce businesses with insights into how the characteristics of AI chatbots impact consumer purchasing decisions. The goal is to aid businesses in tailoring or enhancing this technology based on the findings, integrating it into e-commerce services to propel the growth of e-commerce ventures.

2 Theoretical Background and Hypotheses Development

2.1 User Compliance and Purchase Intention

"Compliance" refers to "responding to specific types of communication (requests) in particular default ways [6]." Research into compliance is centered on diverse methods aimed at fostering adherence to regulations. Among the most studied and employed techniques for compliance is the 'foot-in-the-door' (FITD) approach. This strategy exploits individuals' intrinsic motivation for consistency [6]. The tactic involves initially posing a minor request to the intended individual, which almost invariably elicits an affirmative response. Once compliance has been achieved, the initial solicitor or an associated party presents a larger, typically connected, request [6].This scenario also applies to interactions with AI dialogue systems, whereby when users initially agree to and fulfill a smaller request posed by the dialogue system, they are more likely to comply with subsequent service feedback requests [7]. User compliance in this study refers to the specific type of response users make when faced with requests presented by merchants, that is, whether users handle requests and prompt responses in the manner expected by the merchant.

Purchase intention is the likelihood of consumers in an e-commerce environment to consume a product or service, representing the subjective approval of consumers towards the product or service and serving as a crucial measurement indicator prompting purchase behavior. Consumers' purchase intention on e-commerce platforms is closely related to their communication with customer service [8]. With the widespread introduction of AI chatbot customer service, based on the distinction between machines and humans, what impact does this have on purchase intention, and which factors play a dominant, mediating role? This constitutes the main objective of this study.

2.2 Perceived Usefulness

Perceived usefulness, a critical factor among the multitude of variables that can sway information technology (IT) adoption, significantly impacts whether people embrace or spurn IT. The perceived usefulness that consumers experience in their interactions with AI chatbots reflects the effortlessness and efficacy with which the human-machine interface fulfills designated objectives effectively, efficiently, and satisfactorily [9]. Chatbots perceived to be more useful are likely to furnish consumers with an enhanced experience. If consumers deem the service rendered by the chatbot as useful, they are inclined to recognize the chatbot's performance and may well yield to the chatbot's requests. Consequently, this study posits the ensuing hypothesis:

H1a: Perceived usefulness positively influences user compliance.

In the realm of e-commerce, chatbots assume a pivotal role in delivering standardized services by engaging in direct conversations or messaging with consumers [10]. Such personalized service experiences can lead consumers to perceive the information and services provided by the chatbot as valuable. It is this perceived usefulness that can pique consumers' interest in the products offered, as scholarly research suggests that the correlation between perceived usefulness and purchase intent originates from the context of technology acceptance [11]. Yet, this relationship may equally hold sway within the purchasing context, given humanity's inherent proclivity for seeking rewards or benefits remains unaltered [12]. A wealth of studies has demonstrated that perceived usefulness significantly and positively influences the intention to purchase [13, 14]. In light of these findings, this study posits the following hypothesis:

H1b: Perceived usefulness positively influences consumer purchase intention.

2.3 Trust

Trust is defined as "the willingness of a party to be vulnerable to the actions of another party, based on the expectation that the other will perform a particular action important to the trustor, irrespective of the ability to monitor or control that other party" (Mayer & Davis, 1995). This definition highlights that trust embodies a subjective belief one party holds about another throughout their interaction [15]. It is the cornerstone for establishing and sustaining relationships, acting as a foundational element for collaborative behaviors within interpersonal connections [16]. AI-driven chatbots, serving as social entities (roles) that mimic human-like attitudes or emotions, can proficiently nurture and uphold such trust-based linkages. These bots are equipped to dispense expert assistance and services, communicate authentic and reliable information, thus forming a critical link in fostering buyer-vendor ties. Chatbots' inherent traits lead consumers to view them as dependable, which in turn increases their likelihood to be enticed by online sellers and continue making purchases, an effect mirrored in heightened purchase intentions [17]. Indeed, robust trust relationships within e-commerce settings have been empirically shown to positively influence purchase intent [18]. Consequently, this research puts forth the subsequent hypothesis:

H2a: Trust positively influences consumer purchase intention.

The trust that consumers place in chatbots can significantly impact their trust in the provider whom the chatbot represents [19]. This trust may lead consumers to fulfill the requests made by the chatbot in the manner intended by the merchant—that is, consumers are more likely to adhere to the seller's preferences. Furthermore, studies have shown that trust in chatbots positively influences consumers' intentions to reuse them [19]. As consumers repeatedly utilize chatbots, not only do they obtain information, but chatbots may also present them with minor requests. This can increase the likelihood of consumers making repeated, small commitments, eventually leading to agreement on a more substantial focal request. This phenomenon aligns with research on the 'foot-in-the-door' compliance technique, which suggests that smaller requests are more effective in persuading individuals to concur with the requester's viewpoint (Burger 1999), culminating in heightened compliance from consumers. Thus, this research puts forth the ensuing hypothesis:

H2b: Trust positively influences user compliance.

2.4 Service Quality of AI Chatbots

AI chatbot services represent not only a novel entrant into the realm of service providers but also herald a groundbreaking approach to service delivery. AI chatbots, while anthropomorphic in design, possess distinct strengths and limitations when benchmarked against their human counterparts. For instance, they excel in computational prowess and learning aptitude, yet fall short in the realms of empathy and emotional attunement. Despite certain shortcomings—such as an inability to engage in profound emotional exchanges with customers—AI chatbots are ill-equipped to tackle complex issues that still necessitate human customer service intervention. In the consumer journey, AI chatbots often stand as the initial point of contact within an organization, serving as the first "representative" encountered. Many consumers are compelled to engage with these bots prior to making a purchase decision. It is only upon encountering challenges beyond the bots' resolving capabilities that consumers redirect their inquiry towards human representatives. Consequently, the standard of service rendered by AI chatbots is pivotal in shaping customer satisfaction and loyalty toward the organization. This research endeavor aims to dissect the correlation between the service quality of AI chatbots and the ensuing trust and perceived utility, examining this relationship through the prism of two key components: information quality and interaction quality.

Information Quality. Information quality, as one of the characteristics of AI chatbots, pertains to the specialization of chatbots in exhibiting agent expertise and delivering credible information [20]. Consumers anticipate that chatbots will attentively hear out their issues, diagnose problems accurately, and furnish them with the necessary information [10]. In subsequent research, it has been identified that to foster positive perceptions of chatbots and enhance the communication experience, the interaction with chatbots must be fluid, precise, and thorough [10]. If the information conveyed is both dependable and displays a high level of professionalism, consumers are likely to respond favorably to the evaluation of chatbots [10]. This favorable response may stem from consumers' perception of chatbots as effective due to the receipt of high-quality information. Hence, this study posits the following hypothesis:

H3a: The quality of information provided by AI chatbots positively influences perceived usefulness.

Consumers also place their trust in chatbots due to their professional knowledge and integrity. Beyond merely answering immediate queries, when chatbots comprehend the context during a conversation, consumers are likely to perceive them as engaging personally [21], thus viewing chatbots as entities that resemble human-like interactions. Additionally, honesty, meticulous phrasing, and an aversion to deception are characteristics associated with being trustworthy [22]. Furthermore, information that comes across as dependable, unbiased, and equitable is deemed trustworthy. Consequently, this study proposes the following hypothesis:

H3b: The quality of information provided by AI chatbots positively influences trust.

Interaction Quality. Interaction within the service process encompasses not only the interpersonal communication between consumers and service personnel but also a variety of forms of interaction, including those among consumers, systems, and devices [23]. When customers engage in efficient interaction and receive prompt feedback from the chatbot, the interaction is deemed effective [24]. This implies that AI chatbots are adept at delivering precise information and steering consumers towards their consumption objectives. Effective interaction enhances consumers' receptiveness to the information dispensed by the chatbot and encourages them to provide feedback. Leveraging this interaction, chatbots can offer augmented information and more in-depth guidance. In such interactive dialogues, chatbots can efficiently achieve set goals and furnish consumers with heightened satisfaction. Through these dialogues, consumers progressively acknowledge the value of the information or services proffered by chatbots, viewing their interactions as beneficial. Hence, this study posits the following hypothesis:

H4a: The interaction quality between AI chatbots and consumers positively influences perceived usefulness.

Additionally, some scholars have posited that humanoid agents, or AI chatbots, can endow participants with an augmented sense of interaction with others [25]. In the context of a chat environment, elevated levels of information interactivity fortify the sense of presence [26]. The more intense the sense of presence experienced by consumers during their interaction with chatbots, the greater the emotional closeness or social connection they perceive. This amplified sense of connectedness can consequently result in favorable assessments of the agent and bolster consumers' trust in chatbots [27]. Thus, this study advances the following hypothesis:

H4b: The interaction quality between AI chatbots and consumers positively influences trust.

3   Research Methodology

The scales utilized in this study were developed based on the theoretical constructs identified in the literature review provided above. Specifically, the two items pertaining to information quality were principally adapted from the scales formulated by Wang & Strong [28] and YiMing Zheng [29]. The two items addressing interaction quality were primarily derived from the scales established by Parasuraman et al. [30]. The three items associated with perceived usefulness were chiefly adapted from scales created by Rose et al. [31]. The two items concerning trust were mainly drawn from the scales developed by Gefen et al. [32]. The four items related to user compliance were primarily based on scales devised by Yi & Gong [33]. Lastly, the three items linked to purchase intention are predominantly sourced from scales crafted by Bock [34]. In aggregate, the instrument comprises 16 items in total.

The survey questionnaire in this study was primarily disseminated online. To address the potential issue of inadequate cognitive understanding of the questionnaire design during distribution, respondents were provided with a concise outline highlighting key considerations within the questionnaire. They were instructed to meticulously read through explanations of relevant concepts and view explanatory videos to validate their genuine responses. As a gesture of gratitude, small gifts were offered as incentives. Upon completion, the questionnaires were promptly collected. In the end, throughout the approximately two-week period of distributing and gathering the questionnaires, a total of 472 responses were amassed. Out of these, 14 invalid questionnaires were discarded due to a lack of e-commerce experience, culminating in 458 valid questionnaires, which represents an efficacy rate of 97.03%. Furthermore, the validity of the developed scales was assessed using principal component analysis via SPSS 22.0, while Amos 24.0 was employed to verify our measures and structural model.

4   Empirical Results

4.1 Demographics of Samples

Among the 458 samples collected in this questionnaire, 40.6% of the respondents are males while 59.4% are females. In terms of age distribution, 288 respondents are mainly young people between the ages of 18 and 25, accounting for 62.9% of the total sample, which indicates that most of the respondents in this questionnaire are young people, and this group is also the main group involved in online shopping. The education level of the respondents was mainly undergraduate, accounting for 75.5%; The monthly income of the survey respondents is mainly less than 3,000-yuan, accounting for more than half, about 55.7%. Detailed data are shown in Table 1 below.

Table 1. Demographic Analysis Results

Variable	Answer	Frequency	Percentage (%)
Gender	Male	186	40.6
	Female	272	59.4
Age(years)	21–30	360	80.8
	31–40	45	9.8
	Over 40	43	9.4
Educational background	High school and below	34	7.4
	College	408	88.8
	College above	17	3.7
Household incomes	Below 3000RMB	255	55.7
	3000–5000RMB	82	17.9
	5000–8000RMB	91	19.9
	Above 8000RMB	14	6.6

4.2 Reliability and Validity

In order to verify the reliability and validity of the measures used in this study, we calculated Cronbach's α and conducted a principal component analysis. The results are shown in Table 2.

Table 2. Measurement of constructs

Variable	Item	Component						Cronbach's α
		1	2	3	4	5	6	
User Compliance	UC2	0.685	0.77	0.250	0.217	0.284	0.168	0.879
	UC1	0.641	0.328	0.217	0.206	0.042	0.355	
	UC4	0.590	0.234	0.219	0.184	0.480	0.217	
	UC3	0.580	0.361	0.323	0.110	0.313	0.248	
Purchase Intention	PI3	0.321	0.732	0.267	0.228	0.219	0.149	0.869
	PI2	0.217	0.681	0.218	0.191	0.333	0.327	
	PI1	0.442	0.644	0.247	0.222	0.153	0.126	
Perceived Usefulness	PU2	0.315	0.151	0.765	0.273	0.102	0.213	0.776
	PU1	0.118	0.309	0.653	0.193	0.355	0.232	
	PU3	0.332	0.333	0.618	0.082	0.254	0.255	

(*continued*)

Table 2. (*continued*)

Variable	Item	Component						Cronbach's α
		1	2	3	4	5	6	
Information Quality	IFQ2	0.223	0.080	0.190	0.809	0.278	0.145	0.795
	IFQ1	0.136	0.323	0.166	0.804	0.111	0.197	
Trust	T2	0.203	0.283	0.220	0.272	0.737	0.212	0.831
	T1	0.404	0.238	0.346	0.274	0.557	0.082	
Interaction Quality	ITQ2	0.130	0.221	0.292	0.145	0.252	0.777	0.735
	ITQ1	0.411	0.146	0.170	0.243	0.063	0.708	
Total Eigenvalues		9.291	0.901	0.749	0.653	0.536	0.493	
Variance Explained Cumulative		16.218	14.566	13.641	12.012	11.276	11176	
Variance Explained		16.218	30.784	44.426	56.438	67.714	78891	

Lastly, the discriminant validity of the measurement model was examined. In this case, discriminant validity does exist when the results calculated by (ø ± 2 x standard error) formula exclude value of 1 with 95% of confidence interval. Table 3 suggests that value of 1 is outside the interval between Lower value and Upper value, which proved the discriminant validity.

Table 3. Discriminant Validity Test Results

	Estimate	SE	Lower	Upper
Information Quality<->Interaction Quality	0.701	0.041	0.619	0.783
Information Quality<->Perceived Usefulness	0.703	0.036	0.631	0.775
Information Quality<->Trust	0.789	0.036	0.717	0.861
Information Quality<->User Compliance	0.708	0.035	0.638	0.778
Information Quality<->Purchase Intention	0.722	0.033	0.656	0.788
Interaction Quality<->Perceived Usefulness	0.86	0.03	0.8	0.92
Interaction Quality<->Trust	0.768	0.039	0.69	0.846
Interaction Quality<->User Compliance	0.863	0.028	0.807	0.919
Interaction Quality<->Purchase Intention	0.797	0.034	0.729	0.865
Perceived Usefulness<->Trust	0.907	0.024	0.859	0.955
Perceived Usefulness<->User Compliance	0.902	0.019	0.864	0.94
Perceived Usefulness<->User Compliance	0.873	0.022	0.829	0.917

(*continued*)

Table 3. (*continued*)

	Estimate	SE	Lower	Upper
Trust<->User Compliance	0.915	0.021	0.873	0.957
Trust<->Purchase Intention	0.884	0.024	0.836	0.932
User Compliance<->Purchase Intention	0.921	0.016	0.889	0.953

4.3 Testing Measurement Model

We test our measurement model under AMOS 21.0 program by performing confirmation factor analysis. Results indicated that the model fits this study well (GFI = .959, CFI = .986, TLI = .981, IFI = .986, NFI = .968, RMSEA = .042) with all C.R. above 1.96.

4.4 Testing Hypotheses

Tested by structural equation model analysis of AMOS21.0 program, the hypotheses revealed good fits with the results of $\chi2 = 210.413$ (DF = 95 P = .000), GFI = .944, CFI = .976, TLI = .970, IFI = .977, NFI = .958, RMSEA = .052. In detail, the analysis results showed all of the hypotheses accepted except the H3a and H1b (Table 4).

Table 4. Hypotheses Testing Result Summary

Hypothesis Path	Estimate	S.E	C.R	P-value	Results
H1a: PU→UC	0. 317	0. 121	2.630	0.009	Accepted
H1b: PU→PI	0. 234	0. 137	1.702	0.089	Rejected
H2a: T→PI	0. 702	0.128	5.505	***	Accepted
H2b: T→UC	0. 627	0. 112	5.582	***	Accepted
H3a: IFQ→PU	-0.091	0.057	−1.006	0.314	Rejected
H3b: IFQ→T	0. 161	0. 082	1.971	0.049	Accepted
H4a: ITQ→PU	1.031	0.113	9.105	***	Accepted
H4b: ITQ→T	0. 885	0. 098	9.012	***	Accepted

5 Conclusions and Implications

This study explores how AI chatbots influence consumers' purchase intention by examining the effects of AI chatbots' service quality on perceived usefulness and trust, which in turn impact consumers' purchase intention and user compliance. The main research conclusions are as follows:

The quality of information provided by AI chatbots does not significantly affect perceived usefulness. This may be because the current application of AI technology in e-commerce platform chatbots is not mature enough, so chatbots cannot provide consumers with accurate and valuable information. The information provided by AI chatbots does not make consumers perceive it as useful, and most people even believe that AI chatbots provide a lot of useless information. This information does not help consumers to accurately understand the information of products or services when shopping on e-commerce platforms. Most people believe that the quality of information provided by AI chatbots does not significantly affect perceived usefulness.

Other hypotheses are significant, indicating that the information quality in the characteristics of AI chatbots has a positive impact on customer-perceived trust, and interaction quality has a positive impact on perceived usefulness and trust, thereby affecting user compliance and purchase intention.

According to the theoretical hypothesis model of AI chatbots' service quality constructed in this study for consumers' purchase intention, it can be seen that AI chatbots' service quality affects perceived usefulness and trust, thereby affecting consumers' purchase intention. Therefore, the application of well-designed chatbots can effectively stimulate consumers' purchase intention.

AI chatbots should be able to more effectively predict customer needs and purchasing behavior, and provide personalized recommendations. It uses AI to analyze collected user data, considering customer information, preferences, historical purchasing behavior, third-party data, and contextual information to provide customers with high-quality information. This enhances consumers' perceived usefulness and trust, thereby increasing their purchase intention.

In addition to displaying content to consumers, AI chatbots can also interact better with consumers. Ineffective interactions may raise questions from consumers interested in the product about their upcoming purchase plans. Therefore, e-commerce companies should upgrade the interaction between chatbots and consumers. During the communication process with consumers, chatbots need to be proactive rather than passive, not only providing information about products but also actively inquiring about consumer needs. Additionally, chatbots should not ignore consumer requests. It is also necessary to encourage customers to follow some calls to action, which can help maintain a close relationship between customers and businesses.

References

1. Schuetzler, R.M., Giboney, J.S., Grimes, G.M., Nunamaker, J.F.: The influence of conversational agent embodiment and conversational relevance on socially desirable responding. Decis. Support Syst. **114**, 94–102 (2018)
2. Valtolina, S., Barricelli, B.R., Di Gaetano, S.: Communicability of traditional interfaces VS chatbots in healthcare and smart home domains. Behav. Inform. Technol. **39**, 108–132 (2020)
3. Hellwig, J., Huggett, S., Siebert, M., Jayabalasingham, B.: Artificial intelligence: how knowledge is created, transferred, and used (2019). https://doi.org/10.17632/7ydfs62gd6.2
4. Top 7 Benefits of Chatbots for Your Business. Digital Doughtnut https://www.digitaldough nut.com/articles/2017/october/top-7-benefits-of-chatbots-for-your-business
5. Techlabs, M.: Can Chatbots Help Reduce Customer Service Costs by 30%? Medium (2018). https://chatbotsmagazine.com/how-with-the-help-of-chatbots-customer-ser vice-costs-could-be-reduced-up-to-30-b9266a369945

6. Cialdini, R.B., Goldstein, N.J.: Social influence: compliance and conformity. Annu. Rev. Psychol. **55**, 591–621 (2004)
7. Schneider, D., Klumpe, J., Adam, M., Benlian, A.: Nudging users into digital service solutions. Electron Mark. **30**, 863–881 (2020)
8. Li, L., Yuan, L., Tian, J.: Influence of online E-commerce interaction on consumer satisfaction based on big data algorithm. Heliyon **9**, e18322 (2023)
9. Petre, M., Minocha, S., Roberts, D.: Usability beyond the website: an empirically-grounded e-commerce evaluation instrument for the total customer experience. Behav. Inform. Technol. **25**, 189–203 (2006)
10. Chung, M., Ko, E., Joung, H., Kim, S.J.: Chatbot e-service and customer satisfaction regarding luxury brands. J. Bus. Res. **117**, 587–595 (2020)
11. Davis, F.D., Bagozzi, R.P., Warshaw, P.R.: User acceptance of computer technology: a comparison of two theoretical models. Manage. Sci. **35**, 982–1003 (1989)
12. Bhattacherjee, A.: Understanding information systems continuance: an expectation-confirmation model. MIS Q. **25**, 351–370 (2001)
13. Moslehpour, M., Pham, V.K., Wong, W.-K., Bilgiçli, İ: E-Purchase intention of taiwanese consumers: sustainable mediation of perceived usefulness and perceived ease of use. Sustainability **10**, 234 (2018)
14. Osburg, V.-S., Yoganathan, V., Brueckner, S., Toporowski, W.: How detailed product information strengthens eco-friendly consumption. Manag. Decis. **58**, 1084–1099 (2019)
15. Pennington, R., Wilcox, H.D., Grover, V.: The role of system trust in business-to-consumer transactions. J. Manag. Inf. Syst. **20**, 197–226 (2003)
16. Li, D., Browne, G.J., Wetherbe, J.C.: Why do internet users stick with a specific web site? a relationship perspective. Int. J. Electron. Commer. **10**, 105–141 (2006)
17. Farivar, S., Turel, O., Yuan, Y.: A trust-risk perspective on social commerce use: an examination of the biasing role of habit. Internet Res. **27**, 586–607 (2017)
18. Gibreel, O., AlOtaibi, D.A., Altmann, J.: Social commerce development in emerging markets. Electron. Commer. Res. Appl. **27**, 152–162 (2018)
19. Benbasat, I., Wang, W.: Trust in and adoption of online recommendation agents. J. Assoc. Inform. Syst. **6** (2005)
20. Huang, A.H., Chen, K., Yen, D.C., Tran, T.P.: A study of factors that contribute to online review helpfulness. Comput. Hum. Behav. **48**, 17–27 (2015)
21. Roy, S.K., Shekhar, V., Lassar, W.M., Chen, T.: Customer engagement behaviors: the role of service convenience, fairness and quality. J. Retail. Consum. Serv. **44**, 293–304 (2018)
22. Hilligoss, B., Rieh, S.Y.: Developing a unifying framework of credibility assessment: construct, heuristics, and interaction in context. Inf. Process. Manage. **44**, 1467–1484 (2008)
23. Svensson, G.: The interactive interface of service quality: a conceptual framework. Eur. Bus. Rev. **18**, 243–257 (2006)
24. Wang, X., Lin, X., Spencer, M.K.: Exploring the effects of extrinsic motivation on consumer behaviors in social commerce: revealing consumers' perceptions of social commerce benefits. Int. J. Inf. Manage. **45**, 163–175 (2019)
25. Kim, Y., Sundar, S.S.: Anthropomorphism of computers: is it mindful or mindless? Comput. Hum. Behav. **28**, 241–250 (2012)
26. Sundar, S.S., Go, E., Kim, H.-S., Zhang, B.: Communicating art, virtually! psychological effects of technological affordances in a virtual museum. Int. J. Hum.-Comput. Interact. **31**, 385–401 (2015)
27. Go, E., Sundar, S.S.: Humanizing chatbots: the effects of visual, identity and conversational cues on humanness perceptions. Comput. Hum. Behav. **97**, 304–316 (2019)
28. Wang, R.Y., Strong, D.M.: Beyond accuracy: what data quality means to data consumers. J. Manag. Inf. Syst. **12**, 5–33 (1996)

29. Zheng, Y., Zhao, K., Stylianou, A.: The impacts of information quality and system quality on users' continuance intention in information-exchange virtual communities: an empirical investigation. Decis. Support Syst. **56**, 513–524 (2013)
30. Parasuraman, A., Zeithaml, V.A., Berry, L.L.: A conceptual model of service quality and its implications for future research. J. Mark. **49**, 41–50 (1985)
31. Rose, S., Clark, M., Samouel, P., Hair, N.: Online customer experience in e-retailing: an empirical model of antecedents and outcomes. J. Retail. **88**, 308–322 (2012)
32. Gefen, D., Karahanna, E., Straub, D.W.: Trust and TAM in online shopping: an integrated model. MIS Quart. 51–90 (2003)
33. Yi, Y., Gong, T.: Customer value co-creation behavior: scale development and validation. J. Bus. Res. **66**, 1279–1284 (2013)
34. Bock, G.-W., Lee, J., Kuan, H.-H., Kim, J.-H.: The progression of online trust in the multi-channel retailer context and the role of product uncertainty. Decis. Support Syst. **53**, 97–107 (2012)

Designing XAI Chatbots to Enhance Learner Self-efficacy in Education

Valerie Vera[1], Jonathan Fu[2(✉)], and Matthew J. Irvin[1]

[1] University of South Carolina, Columbia, SC 29208, USA
lookingv@email.sc.edu, irvinmj@mailbox.sc.edu
[2] Chapin High School, Chapin, SC 29036, USA
jonathanztfu@gmail.com

Abstract. Self-efficacy is crucial for self-regulated learning (SRL), helping learners overcome obstacles and achieve educational goals. This study introduces ALLURE, a multimodal AI platform with an XAI-driven chatbot for teaching Rubik's Cube solving to enhance self-efficacy. We analyzed interactions of college students using interviews, think-aloud protocols, and observational notes. Preliminary findings show that while XAI-driven chatbots can boost self-efficacy, their effectiveness varies. These results highlight the need for educational chatbots to cater to diverse learning needs. The study provides insights into developing XAI-driven chatbots with transparent, personalized interactions to support self-efficacy and competence in educational settings.

Keywords: Explainable AI · Chatbot · Self-efficacy · HCI · Self-regulated Learning

1 Introduction

AI-driven chatbots have become valuable tools in education, facilitating self-regulated learning (SRL) skills and self-efficacy [1, 2]. Self-efficacy, the belief in one's capacity to achieve specific goals, significantly impacts learner motivation and approach [3, 4]. It is highly indicative of learners' self-regulatory skills, enabling persistent application in the face of difficulties [5]. While previous studies have explored chatbots' effects on SRL [6–8], further research is needed to understand their impact on online learners' self-efficacy, considering learner characteristics, prior knowledge, and interaction patterns [9–11]. As XAI chatbots evolve, transparency becomes crucial [12]. Explainable AI (XAI) can decode the "black box" of AI, potentially enhancing self-efficacy. Despite the promising role of XAI in education, research on its integration with educational chatbots is still in its early stages, necessitating further exploration of how XAI technologies can improve learning outcomes.

This study empirically examines the impact of an XAI-driven chatbot on learners' self-efficacy for SRL using ALLURE, an AI-driven platform for teaching Rubik's Cube solving. It addresses gaps in understanding how educational chatbots can be designed to enhance self-efficacy [13] and how variations in learner interactions, represented through

A. Coman et al. (Eds.): HCII 2024, LNCS 15375, pp. 131–137, 2025.
https://doi.org/10.1007/978-3-031-76806-4_10

personas, affect self-efficacy [11]. The study aims to apply XAI chatbot technology to examine its effect on perceived self-efficacy in SRL. The overarching research question to guide this work is:

RQ: How can we design an XAI-driven chatbot in an online multimodal learning platform to enhance learners' self-efficacy for SRL?

2   Related Work

SRL is a cyclical process where learners plan, organize, self-monitor, and self-evaluate towards achieving their goals [14–16]. Many learners lack optimal SRL skills, but enhancing self-efficacy can improve these skills [17]. Given the importance of self-efficacy in SRL, we developed an XAI-driven chatbot for an online multimodal learning platform to support self-efficacy and foster effective SRL strategies.

Educational chatbots can enhance accessibility [18], foster problem-solving [19], and increase learning efficiency [1]. While the current chatbot research has focused on reasoning, knowledge retention, and engagement [1], the impact on self-efficacy is less explored [4, 13, 20]. Behavioral aspects like interaction and transparency also need more attention [21]. XAI addresses AI's "black box" issue with transparency [22], enhancing usability and trustworthiness, thereby supporting self-efficacy [23, 24]. This study examines how XAI-driven chatbots impact self-efficacy through user interactions illustrated by various personas. We use ALLURE platform with an embodied XAI chatbot Rubik's Cube solving, to explore this relationship. The Rubik's Cube, requiring complex problem-solving, serves as an ideal case to study self-efficacy's influence on learning approaches and coping behaviors.

3   Methods

3.1   ALLURE Platform

ALLURE (Fig. 1) uses visual and natural language interfaces to guide users in solving the white cross of the Rubik's Cube, employing a scaffolding design to decode AI's "black box." The AI agent initially learns the white cross using DeepCubeA [26] and provides visual cues, while the chatbot, Ally, offers natural language explanations and step-by-step visualizations to enhance learners' self-efficacy [27]. The platform includes a tutorial and nine AI solution scenarios with XAI visualizations. Ally, the interactive chatbot, can communicate with users through breaking down complex solutions into manageable steps using text and 3D visuals, interacts with learners via the RASA framework [28], and converts complex algorithmic explanations from first-order logic into natural language. Learners communicate with Ally to express subgoals, manipulate a virtual cube, and propose algorithmic solutions, which the Inductive Logic Programming system translates into logic programs and then back into natural language for verification.

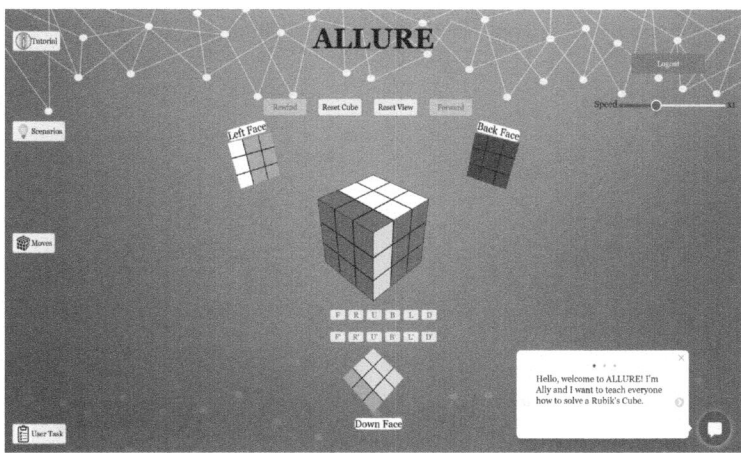

Fig. 1. ALLURE Platform.

3.2 Study Participants

We recruited 70 university participants in the United States using convenience sampling through flyers and emails. In a pre-survey, most participants were aged 18 to 20, identified as Caucasian or Asian, and female.

3.3 Procedure and Data Analysis

We designed ALLURE with an embodied chatbot, randomly assigning 70 participants to our user experiment. Participants completed a pre-survey covering demographics, Rubik's Cube knowledge, learning abilities, and self-efficacy, using items adapted from validated scales [29]. Among them, 38 participants completed their tasks (Table 1). The pre-survey included six Mental Rotations Test questions [30] to assess spatial skills. Participants then engaged in 45–95 min of usability testing, interacting with ALLURE to solve the white cross while verbalizing their thought processes [30]. After usability testing, participants underwent a semi-structured interview on user satisfaction and completed a post-survey measuring platform satisfaction, self-efficacy [29], chatbot usability [31], trustworthiness, and spatial reasoning skills [30].

We transcribed users' think-aloud and interview recordings, and then coded them in NVivo 14 using an emic/etic approach [32]. Data analysis yielded three high-level categories: perceived self-efficacy, persona, and SRL, with 33 corresponding codes. Each participant was assigned one of seven personas based on the most salient code. Descriptive statistics and logistic regression analysis showed that the chatbot, STEM background, and self-reported skill levels did not significantly affect task completion, but gender did, with males more likely to complete the task. Additionally, the study participants rated the chatbot's trustworthiness moderately positive on a 5-point Likert scale (Table 2).

Table 1. User Task Completion

ALLURE	# of Participants Who Completed the User Task	Mean	Std. Deviation
With Chatbot (n = 70)	38	0.543	0.502

Table 2. Perceptions of Chatbot Trustworthiness

Mean	Median	Std. Deviation	Min	Max
3.152	3.00	1.26	1.00	5.00

4 Preliminary Findings

In our preliminary qualitative thematic analysis, we identified seven distinctive user personas (Table 3) among which the theme was most prevalent, and also provided chatbot design implications respectively.

Table 3. Identified Personas

Persona	Definition	# of Participants	Chatbot Design Implications
Adherent	User who carefully reads the instructions and does not veer from the platform's directions	13	• Provide personable encouragement
Critical Thinker	User who compares their experience with the physical Rubik's Cube and tries to apply their experiences to the virtual Rubik's Cube	23	• Integrate responsive learning paths
Explorer	User who explores all functionalities of the platform, such as out of curiosity	21	• Provide hints when users are "stuck," rather than full solutions
Goal-Oriented	User who narrows in on a task and is determined to complete it as efficiently as possible	17	• Integrate responsive learning paths

(continued)

Table 3. (*continued*)

Persona	Definition	# of Participants	Chatbot Design Implications
Independent	User who wants to learn on their own and does not want to ask for help	10	• Integrate responsive learning paths
Kinesthetic	User who uses their hands to imagine a physical interaction with a Rubik's Cube	14	• Provide personable encouragement
Self-Critical	User who expresses self-criticism or self-consciousness over their performance on the platform	26	• Interject with hints or additional guidance through dynamic feedback

5 Discussions

This research highlights the need for designing XAI UIs that translate AI outputs to support learners' self-efficacy for SRL through chatbot design. Our preliminary findings address gaps in how chatbots impact self-efficacy based on learner characteristics and emphasize the importance of adaptive, personalized feedback to cater to diverse learning needs. Effective chatbots act as motivational scaffolds, providing timely and tailored cues that align with learners' perceived performance. However, feedback misalignment can negatively affect learners, especially those with low self-efficacy. The study underscores the necessity for chatbots to offer adaptive feedback informed by ongoing assessments of learner progress and emotions. Although XAI technologies hold promise for enhancing feedback personalization, further development is needed to maximize their benefits in educational contexts.

Acknowledgments. The authors would like to thank all the study participants for their participation and support. This project was partially funded by the University of South Carolina's Institute of Rural Education and Development (PI: Dr. Matthew J. Irin) and College of Computing and Engineering.

Disclosure of Interests. The Authors have no competing interests to declare that are relevant to the content of this article.

References

1. Deng, X., Yu, Z.: A meta-analysis and systematic review of the effect of chatbot technology use in sustainable education. Sustainability **15**, 4 (2023)
2. Okonkwo, C.W., Ade-Ibijola, A.: Chatbots applications in education: a systematic review. Comput. Educ. Artific. Intell. **2** (2021)

3. Chang, D.H., Lin, M.P.-C., Hajian, S., Wang, Q.Q.: Educational design principles of using AI Chatbot that supports self-regulated learning in education: goal setting, feedback, and personalization. Sustainability **15**, 17, 12921–12921 (2023)
4. Lee, Y.-F., Hwang, G.-J., Chen, P.-Y.: Impacts of an AI-based chabot on college students' after-class review, academic performance, self-efficacy, learning attitude, and motivation. Educ. Technol. Res. Develop. **70**, 5, 1843–1865 (2022)
5. Bandura, A.: Human agency in social cognitive theory. Am. Psychol. **44**, 1175–1184 (1989)
6. Caprara, G.V., et al.: Longitudinal analysis of the role of perceived self-efficacy for self-regulated learning in academic continuance and achievement. J. Educ. Psychol. **100**(3), 525–534 (2008)
7. Bernacki, M.L., Nokes-Malach, T.J., Aleven, V.: Examining self-efficacy during learning: variability and relations to behavior, performance, and learning. Metacogn. Learn. **10**(1), 99–117 (2014)
8. Yildiz Durak, H.: Conversational agent-based guidance: examining the effect of chatbot usage frequency and satisfaction on visual design self-efficacy, engagement, satisfaction, and learner autonomy. Educ. Inf. Technol. **28**(1), 471–488 (2022)
9. Lajoie, S.P., Poitras, E.G., Doleck, T., Huang, L.: Time in various phases of self-regulation and problem-solving performance in an Intelligent Tutoring System. Educ. Inf. Technol. **28**(5), 5605–5620 (2022)
10. Song, D., Kim, D.: Effects of self-regulation scaffolding on online participation and learning outcomes. J. Res. Technol. Educ. **53**(3), 249–263 (2020)
11. Labadze, L., Grigolia, M., Machaidze, L.: Role of AI chatbots in education: systematic literature review. Int. J. Educ. Technol. High. Educ. **20**, 1 (2023)
12. Weitz, K.: Towards human-centered AI: psychological concepts as foundation for empirical XAI research. IT – Inform. Technol. **64**, 1–2, 71–75 (2022)
13. Chang, C.Y., Hwang, G.J., Gau, M.L.: Promoting students' learning achievement and self-efficacy: a mobile chatbot approach for nursing training. British J. Educ. Technol. **53**, 1, 171–188 (2022)
14. Winne, P.H.: A cognitive and metacognitive analysis of self-regulated learning. Routledge, City (2011)
15. Zimmerman, B.J.: Self-regulated learning and academic achievement: an overview. Educ. Psychol. **25**, 1, 3–17 (1990)
16. Zimmerman, B.J.: Attaining self-regulation: a social cognitive perspective. Academic Press, City (2000)
17. Zimmerman, B.J.: Models of self-regulated learning and academic achievement. Springer, City (1989)
18. Wollny, S., Schneider, J., Di Mitri, D., Weidlich, J., Rittberger, M., Drachsler, H.: Are we there yet? - a systematic literature review on chatbots in education. Front Artif. Intell. **4**, 654924 (2021)
19. Benvenuti, M., et al.: Artificial intelligence and human behavioral development: a perspective on new skills and competences acquisition for the educational context. Comput. Hum. Behav. **148** (2023)
20. Essel, H.B., Vlachopoulos, D., Tachie-Menson, A., Johnson, E. E., Baah, P.K.: The impact of a virtual teaching assistant (chatbot) on students' learning in Ghanaian higher education. Int. J. Educ. Technol. High. Educ. **19**, 1, 57–57 (2022)
21. Hasan, M.R., Chowdhury, N.I., Rahman, M.H., Syed, M.A.B., Ryu, J.: Analysis of the user perception of chatbots in education using a partial least squares structural equation modeling approach, vol. 1 (2023)
22. Farrow, R.: The possibilities and limits of XAI in education: a socio-technical perspective. Learn. Media Technol. **48**(2), 266–279 (2023)

23. Khurana, A., Alamzadeh, P., Chilana, P.K.: ChatrEx: designing explainable chatbot interfaces for enhancing usefulness, transparency, and trust. IEEE Computer Society, City (2021)
24. Weitz, K., Schlagowski, R., André, E.: Demystifying artificial intelligence for end-users: findings from a participatory machine learning show. Springer International Publishing, City, Cham (2021)
25. Pruitt, J., Grudin, J.: Personas. ACM, City (2003)
26. Agostinelli, F., McAleer, S., Shmakov, A., Baldi, P.: Solving the Rubik's cube with deep reinforcement learning and search. Nature Mach. Intell. **1**(8), 356–363 (2019)
27. Kim, N.J., Belland, B.R., Walker, A.E.: Effectiveness of computer-based scaffolding in the context of problem-based learning for stem education: bayesian meta-analysis. Educ. Psychol. Rev. **30**, 2, 397–429 (2018)
28. Bocklisch, T., Faulkner, J., Pawlowski, N., Nichol, A.: Rasa: open source language understanding and dialogue management (2017)
29. Betz, N., Hackett, G.: Mathematics Self-Efficacy Scale (MSES). City (1993)
30. Vandenberg, S.G., Kuse, A.R.: Mental rotations, a group test of three-dimensional spatial visualization. Percept. Mot. Skills **47**(2), 599–604 (1978)
31. Borsci, S., et al.: The chatbot usability scale: the design and pilot of a usability scale for interaction with AI-based conversational agents. Person. Ubiquitous Comput. **26**, 1, 95–119 (2022)

Improving Knowledge Asymmetry in Group Discussions with Smart Assistants

Hongfei Wu[1]([✉]), Chiju Chao[1], Zhijie Yi[2], and Zhiyong Fu[1]

[1] Department of Information Design, Tsinghua University, Beijing 100084, China
wuhongfeiiiii@gmail.com, zjr21@mails.tsinghua.edu.cn,
fuzhiyong@tsinghua.edu.cn
[2] Beijing Normal University, Beijing 100875, China
yzj@mail.bnu.edu.cn

Abstract. This study aimed to explore the role of smart assistants in alleviating knowledge asymmetry in interdisciplinary group discussions. Due to diverse disciplinary backgrounds and foundational knowledge differences, group members struggle to engage effectively in group discussions. To address this issue, we introduced a smart assistant named CaseAssistant, designed to provide relevant information for discussions, thereby promoting cognitive consensus among participants. Through qualitative research, including user interviews, semi-structured group discussions, and observer feedback, we deeply analyzed the impact of CaseAssistant on enhancing discussion efficiency, reducing participant workload, and expanding the depth and breadth of discussions. The findings indicate that the introduction of smart assistants can lower the workload of group members, promotes cognitive consensus, and effectively improves the quality and efficiency of group discussions.

Keywords: Smart Assistant · Group Discussions · Knowledge Asymmetry · Wizard of Oz

1 Introduction

Group discussion is characterized by the collaborative engagement of multiple individuals in exploring, examining, and investigating specific problems, topics, or issues, with the ultimate objective of problem-solving or consensus-building. Numerous studies have substantiated that this goal-oriented mode of communication facilitates collective cognition, idea exchange, and the generation of positive outcomes, ultimately enhancing participant satisfaction [10, 22]. Furthermore, it has been demonstrated that group discussion contributes to attaining consensus, thereby rendering group decision-making more systematic and rational.

College students are required to participate in exchanges and discussions among different majors. However, due to a lack of exposure to foundational courses in other disciplines, college students must spend extra effort understanding the opinions or professional terms expressed by their peers from different disciplinary backgrounds when participating in group discussions. This situation is called "knowledge asymmetry."

A. Coman et al. (Eds.): HCII 2024, LNCS 15375, pp. 138–150, 2025.
https://doi.org/10.1007/978-3-031-76806-4_11

In the context of China's active promotion of interdisciplinary construction, this phenomenon of "knowledge asymmetry" is increasingly prevalent and urgently needs to be addressed. As Max Kemman [13] pointed out, Knowledge asymmetry especially poses risks in collaborative settings where the distance between forms of expertise is considerable, with little overlap of conceptual or methodological understanding. It affects not just the research outcomes but also the development of mutual trust. The knowledge asymmetry can be unfriendly for members who lack relevant knowledge, ultimately leading them into the "spiral of silence" [18]. Specifically, when confronted with a problem, members with insufficient knowledge may observe that no other members are posing questions, causing them to be concerned that their uncertainties may slow down the pace of discussion or even be criticized. Consequently, they may remain silent, ultimately becoming "non-contributors." This situation widens the contribution gap among members, affecting the quality and innovation of group discussions.

We're attempting to deploy a smart assistant to improve knowledge asymmetry in group discussions. Through a series of user studies, we've designed unique behavioral patterns for the assistant that will help it better engage in group discussions and improve knowledge asymmetry.

2   Research Question

This study aims to explore the potential and effects of using smart assistants in reducing knowledge asymmetry during group discussions. Specifically, we focus on how to design a smart assistant named CaseAssistant, which can provide timely and relevant information to participants in interdisciplinary exchanges, thereby promoting cognitive consensus and discussion efficiency. Additionally, this research assesses the specific impacts of CaseAssistant on the group discussion process and outcomes, including participants' cognitive load and the depth and breadth of discussions.

3   Related Work

Our research is focused on using smart assistants to improve knowledge asymmetry in group discussions and is related to the following three topics.

3.1   Conversation-Oriented Smart Assistant

Conversation-oriented smart assistants interact with users through text or voice, answering their questions. They perform natural language processing and respond with natural language [1, 6, 23, 28]. For example, ChatGPT, developed by OpenAI [6], can accurately handle complex natural language dialogues and customer experience interview chatbots [23]. Moreover, mobile communication platforms like LINE, WeChat, Slack, and Telegram have integrated various chatbot-supporting technologies.

3.2 Smart Assistant in Group Discussion

Users can often find conversation-oriented smart assistants or chatbots in online group chats. Their functions are diverse, such as GremoBot [20], which guides group discussions away from negative vocabulary and can perform emotion regulation. Another example is GROUPFEEDBOT [14], which helps with time management, encourages lurkers to participate and summarizes opinions. These studies focus on conversation-oriented smart assistants participating in group chats on online social platforms.

We have referenced these studies in our work, which aims to design a smart assistant that can provide appropriate discussion information to group members based on rules and support group discussions.

4   User Study

Our study was conducted in three stages. In the first stage, we conducted a user study among teachers and students on campus regarding the characteristics of smart assistants in group discussions. Based on the results, we formulated the response strategies of the smart assistant. In the second stage, we deployed an online whiteboard tool and arranged for participants to engage in validation. Participants were asked to complete semi-structured group discussions. In the third stage, we invited observers with different disciplinary backgrounds to describe user behavior. Finally, we qualitatively analyzed the results using workload comparisons, morpheme analysis, and theme analysis.

4.1   User Needs

We conducted user research to investigate the characteristics of smart assistants in group discussions. Through advertisements on WeChat Moments, we recruited six teachers and graduate students from our university who were asked to participate in a 30-min semi-structured interview. The recruitment criteria were (a) having experience using six or more smart assistant products and (b) having participated in at least four interdisciplinary discussions with 3 to 6 participants within the past month. Based on user research, we have organized the main issues and needs.

Interdisciplinary students from varied backgrounds face difficulties understanding each other and achieving consensus. Participants believe that smart assistants should help group members access information from various perspectives related to the discussion topic to facilitate as much consensus as possible among group members.

Discussions can easily deviate from their intended direction and fail to progress. Discussion smart assistants should assist group members in managing their time and attention, preventing them from spending too much time on limited issues, which could lead to a loss of focus.

Additionally, participants also expressed a desire for smart assistants to have task execution capabilities, such as searching for relevant information and documenting the discussion process. However, these functions have already been well implemented in previous research and development [12, 14, 25], so this paper will not discuss them further.

4.2   CaseAssistant

Based on the previous study, we proposed CaseAssistant. We designed two response strategies for CaseAssistant centered around providing information.

Promote Cognitive Consensus. CaseAssistant matches information with high similarity to the descriptions of group members in the corpus based on the content and keywords of the group members' discussions. This information includes news, policies, and cases. This strategy aims to improve knowledge asymmetry and promote cognitive consensus among group members.

Discussion Framework Support. CaseAssistant matches appropriate discussion frameworks based on the discussion topic. At the same time, CaseAssistant proactively provides participants with information from different perspectives according to the framework. this strategy aims to prevent group members from becoming overly engaged in limited discussions (Fig. 1).

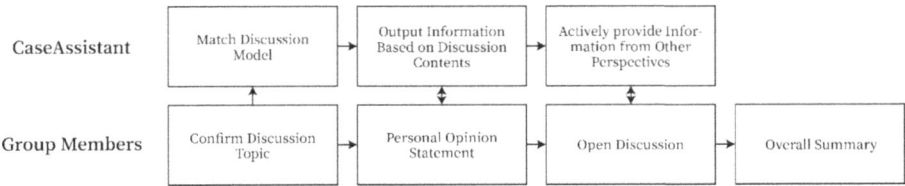

Fig. 1. The discussion flow of group members in the qualitative study and the information exchange method between CaseAssistant and group members.

5   Methodology

This section will present the details and methodology of the study.

5.1   Study Design

We carried out a qualitative study involving four groups. The participants ($N = 16$) were evenly distributed among the four groups, with each group comprising four individuals. They were instructed to engage in two semi-structured group discussions using the Future Triangle [8] model, each lasting approximately one hour. The second discussion was facilitated with the aid of CaseAssistant.

5.2   Procedure

Before the qualitative study, participants were briefly introduced to the experiment and informed that CaseAssistant would provide them with information based on specified rules. Only the second task would incorporate CaseAssistant's assistance in the discussion. Participants were instructed to complete the NASA-TLX after each of the two tasks. At the end of the qualitative study, participants were required to partake in a semi-structured focus group interview [16], lasting approximately 10 min, to document their experience with CaseAssistant's involvement in the discussion. Later, observers from design, psychology, and computer science documented the participants' usage behavior.

5.3 Participants

We recruited 24 participants and observers (17 female) with different disciplinary backgrounds through a WeChat public account questionnaire registration channel. They originated from various disciplines and were not acquainted with each other. A human moderator was also designated during the experiment to introduce the topic and manage the process.

5.4 Wizard of Oz

To evaluate the potential of the smart assistant, CaseAssistant, in mitigating knowledge asymmetry in group discussions, we employed the "Wizard of Oz" method for simulation. This approach allowed the researchers to mimic the responses of the smart assistant without the need to develop a fully functional system, thus enabling rapid iteration and testing of different design concepts. Through this method, we explored the potential utility of CaseAssistant in natural group discussion settings and gathered preliminary data on its impact on discussion efficiency and cognitive consensus. This provided valuable insights for further system development and optimization.

5.5 Task

We established two semi-structured group discussion tasks: designing a future food product and conceptualizing a future vehicle. Each group was required to engage in discussions based on the assigned task themes. In the end, participants were asked to summarize their proposed products in writing, ensuring they conformed to the task themes. We selected topics reflecting objectives commonly found in real-life situations, as they necessitate collaborative efforts from participants with varying backgrounds and prevent instances where individuals are unable to contribute due to a lack of understanding of the objectives.

5.6 Tools

This qualitative study used the Future Triangle, BroadMix, and a corpus to support group discussion.

Future Triangle. The Future Triangle is a simple and intuitive method for visualizing future scenarios, proposed by Inayatullah (2002, 2008) [8]. It consists of three dimensions: future pull, present push, and past gravity. Participants are required to discuss topics based on these dimensions, and it is commonly used in brainstorming sessions to explore consensual futures. In this experiment, the future triangle was utilized to depict the outcomes of participants' discussions.

BroadMix. BroadMix is a cloud-based real-time collaboration tool. It supports multi-device connectivity and provides a drawing board that enables multiple users to draw, write, and add labels simultaneously. The entire experiment was conducted synchronously on BroadMix [5]. At the beginning of the experiment, participants were instructed to familiarize themselves with the tool and use it to complete a self-introduction task.

Corpus. We prepared an extensive collection of materials highly relevant to the discussion themes, including future design cases, news reports, and related keyword definitions. Before the qualitative study, we conducted a small-scale pilot test using the prepared content. Based on the pilot test results, we further enriched and adjusted the materials in the corpus to better align with the themes and directions of the current discussion.

5.7 Analysis Methods

We collected data from the qualitative study. The data included the content of the discussions, speakers, and speaking time. First, we employed the NASA-Task Load Index (NASA-TLX) to comparatively assess the workload of participants while completing the two discussion tasks. NASA-TLX is a multidimensional rating scale designed to obtain workload estimates immediately during or after one or multiple operators perform a task [11]. We collected the NASA-TLX for each task at the end of both tasks. Second, we utilized Python to tokenize the discussion content, removing meaningless words and compared the number of words used by group members during the two discussions. By comparing the word count of group members in the two tasks, we inferred the quality of the thematic discussions. Third, we invited observers to participate in semi-structured focus group interviews, during which they were asked to describe the users' behavior (characterize user's usage behavior) observed throughout the experiment. Two researchers then employed thematic analysis to summarize the observers' descriptions of user behavior into participant suggestions and observer insights.

6 Results

Our research findings are presented through three aspects: workload comparison, morpheme analysis, and participant interviews. We assessed the impact of CaseAssistant on discussion facilitation across two tasks. Simultaneously, thematic coding was applied to participants' behaviors, experiences, and observers' descriptions, integrating these into distinct themes. These themes highlight the advantages and disadvantages of using CaseAssistant in group discussions, alongside suggestions from participants and insights from observers.

6.1 Workload Comparison

The results indicate that utilizing CaseAssistant in discussions led to a lower overall workload for participants compared to direct discussions, with an average workload reduction of about 11%. This suggests that CaseAssistant effectively reduces group members' workload and enhances discussion efficiency (Table 1).

Table 1. This table shows the workload comparison results before and after the qualitative study.

Sample Number	Group A		Sample Number	Group B		Sample Number	Group C		Sample Number	Group D	
	Task 1	Task 2		Task 1	Task 2		Task 1	Task 2		Task 1	Task 2
a1	46	42	b1	46	39	c1	56	51	d1	33	26
a2	52	33	b2	48	32	c2	48	47	d2	39	44
a3	64	62	b3	38	42	c3	57	56	d3	39	37
a4	60	43	b4	39	37	c4	35	32	d4	18	12
Average	55.5	45		42.75	37.5		49	46.5		32.25	29.75

6.2 Morpheme Analysis

Comparison revealed that the number of words in the second task was more than that in the first task, with an average increase of about 4.38. This implies that the participation of CaseAssistant can help group members discuss concepts related to the topic more thoroughly and effectively, promoting the expansion of the depth and breadth of group discussions (Fig. 2).

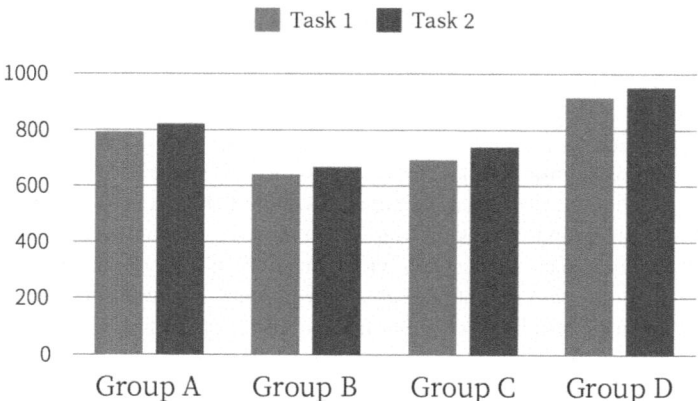

Fig. 2. Comparison of the number of words used by group members in the two group experiments. The growth rates of words used before and after groups A, B, C, and D are 3.5%, 4.3%, 6%, and 3.7%.

6.3 Participant Interviews

Participants' behaviors, experiences, and observers' descriptions were recorded. Subsequently, two researchers employed thematic analysis [4] to categorize these open-ended responses into distinct themes. These themes highlighted both the advantages and disadvantages of using CaseAssistant in group discussions, in addition to providing participant suggestions and observer insights. We coded a total of 96 units, forming three themes.

Theme 1: Advantages. This theme includes 39 units, forming three sub-themes.

T1.1: Helping Participants Otain and Supplement Effective Information, Promoting Cognitive Consensus (20 units). CaseAssistant creates a favorable environment for group discussions by promoting cognitive consensus among group members. One participant described their feelings about CaseAssistant: "While discussing with everyone, I searched for a lot of things privately. CaseAssistant played the role of a'search engine,' helping me complete the search for materials, which was very helpful to me." Another participant said, "It can tell me some issues to tackle." Another participant mentioned, "There were some topics I didn't dare to talk about until CaseAssistant brought them up."

T1.2: Shifting Perspectives, Breaking Silence, and Promoting Communication (7 units). When the group discussion fell silent, CaseAssistant's information played a good role in enabling members to restart discussions based on that information. In the second group experiment, a participant stated, "when we were discussing'sky travel,' CaseAssistant provided us with the idea of'underground travel,' giving me some new ideas." researchers believe, "this can help group members break out of their current thinking bottlenecks."

T1.3: Focusing on Design Ideas, Helping Members Reach Consensus (12 units). Without CaseAssistant's participation, participants need to process and discuss more information, especially irrelevant information, which increases their workload and makes it difficult to grasp valuable topics. An observer said, "CaseAssistant's information helps group members confirm the value of discussion topics and advance the product innovation process." Another said, "it helps discussants understand the development level of technology and enhances their confidence in the possibility of their designs."

Theme 2: Disadvantages. This theme includes 18 units, forming three sub-themes.

T2.1: Weakening individual statements of group members (6 units). CaseAssistant provides a lot of information, making it more prominent in discussions and weakening other group members' statements. One participant said, "Sometimes the information provided by CaseAssistant can limit some ideas." Researchers believe, "Although CaseAssistant has a role in focusing on design ideas, it can also easily become an'opinion leader,' affecting human creativity."

T2.2: Interrupting Open Discussions or Personal Statements of Participants (5 units). Using voice output in the smart assistant for group discussions seems to be unpopular. one participant Said, "I had to listen to CaseAssistant's 1-2-min speech patiently, and then I needed to try hard to recall the previous discussion ideas." Another participant thought, "CaseAssistant's interruptions are slightly abrupt, affecting subsequent user communication."

T2.3: The Intentions and Rules of the Smart Assistant are Opaque, making it Difficult to Understand (7 units). Although CaseAssistant's information provision is effective for most participants, an observer described another feeling participants had when facing the information provided by CaseAssistant: "Participants do not understand CaseAssistant's rules and try to guess the intention behind the provided information." One observer also said, "CaseAssistant's behavior logic is incomprehensible. for example, what information it can provide, whether the information is insufficient, and why it suddenly provides information…" Another observer suggested, "CaseAssistant should provide motivation when giving out information to help participants understand the purpose of interrupting the discussion." These results reflect people's distrust of smart assistants, possibly stemming from complex or opaque rule design, causing participants to doubt the accuracy or relevance of the results.

Theme 3: Participant Suggestions and Observer Observations. The theme of participant suggestions and observer observations includes 13 units, forming three sub-themes.

T3.1: Less Interruption and Adding a question-asking Feature (8 units). Through focus groups, we learned about the disturbances experienced by participants. participants suggested, "CaseAssistant could be in the form of a pop-up robot, which would be more noticeable to me and not interrupt me." Researchers believe, "popup robots are more flexible and easier to interact with, and users don't have to listen to the long speeches of smart assistants, especially when the content is not accurately matched."

T3.2: Anthropomorphic Features (2 units). We found that group members had expectations for CaseAssistant's anthropo-morphism, and designers could consider incorporating personality factors in the design process of smart assistants to enhance user experience. A researcher said, "CaseAssistant's statements have sparked several discussions among group members about its 'values.'"

T3.3: capturing Keywords like "Wake up" and Providing Corresponding Help (3 units). Many participants had prior experience with "wake-up" operations and hoped that smart assistants could respond to explicit confusion, making the discussion process smoother. One participant said, "Maybe we can add the capture of keywords like'I don't know,' and in such cases, provide some proactive help."

7 Discussion

7.1 Design Principles

Based on the experimental results and participant feedback of CaseAssistant, we propose the following design suggestions to enhance the effectiveness and practicality of smart assistants in group discussions:

Respond to Users Timely. Smart assistants participating in group discussions should avoid over-answering questions or frequently interrupting conversations to prevent negative effects such as user communication interference, privacy invasion, or dependency. ensure timely responses when users actively ask questions. Smart assistants need to judge when to participate in discussions and when to remain silent in different contexts.

Establish User Trust in Smart Assistants. Transparency of rules and intentions is crucial for building trust. If the rules of the smart assistant are opaque, its effectiveness will be significantly reduced, and users will have to expend extra effort guessing why the smart assistant made certain puzzling actions or responses. Transparent rules and intentions can accelerate the trust-building process.

Emphasize Tool Attributes. Users are accustomed to receiving information in text form and have a low acceptance of voice output. They prefer to see such smart assistants as a tool rather than a "person". Although anthropomorphic features of the assistant are mentioned in the participant suggestions section, such features should be built on top of its tool attributes.

7.2   How Should Smart Assistants Engage in Group Discussions?

Based on the findings from various experiments and thorough investigations, two researchers have detailed the key aspects of how smart assistants can be effectively integrated into group discussions. These aspects outline a structured approach for smart assistants to enhance the group discussion process, ensuring that their participation is both effective and constructive.

Independent Thinking Phase. At the outset of the discussion, group members should independently ponder the topic, forming their insights and ideas. During this process, smart assistants ought to refrain from interfering with the members' process of independent thought.

Information Acquisition Phase. Group members will access a variety of informational resources provided by smart assistants, such as news, research reports, and case studies, to aid in their understanding of the discussion topic. Smart assistants can employ natural language processing technology to answer questions or provide further explanations and clarifications of the information.

Free Discussion Phase. Leveraging the information available and that provided by the smart assistant, group members engage in open discussions. Smart assistants can record the content of the discussions, manage discussion time, and encourage fewer vocal members to participate, ensuring an equitable discussion environment.

Decision Support Phase. In the face of differing opinions and discussion deadlocks, smart assistants can offer decision support, suggest solutions based on the information provided by the group, and help members ascertain the value of the discussion topic.

Summary Phase. After the discussion, group members summarize the content, sharing their conclusions and recommendations. Smart assistants can augment this summary with additional content based on the discussion overview, ensuring the comprehensiveness and depth of the discussion outcomes.

7.3   Considering Using AIGC in Group Discussions

Compared to users independently filtering through massive amounts of information, AIGC can autonomously recommend the most appropriate content to users, helping them save time. These applications can obtain the information users need by asking questions. However, we found that the quality of answers from AIGC largely depends on the clarity of user questions. If users want high-quality, accurate answers, they must precisely define their questions. According to Naomi Miyake, Donald A. Norman [17], and others, the prerequisite for asking questions is having a certain level of knowledge.

Therefore, when some students face "knowledge asymmetry," it may not be a wise choice to employ LLM (Large Language Model) without thoughtful modifications.

In addition, since they cannot access real literature data, AIGC sometimes generates fictional information [9], such as fictional literature references, news, or cases, making it difficult for users to judge the accuracy of the information provided by AIGC. To understand the feasibility of AIGC participating in group discussions, we asked ChatGPT questions using the text records from the qualitative study. We restated the two rules defined for CaseAssistant to ChatGPT and asked it to provide us with feedback based on the rules. The version of ChatGPT used was the ChatGPT Mar 14 Version. We compared the feedback from ChatGPT with the feedback from CaseAssistant (Fig. 3).

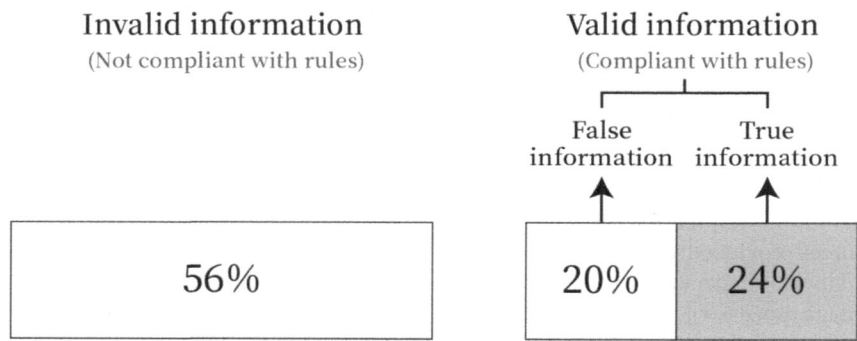

Fig. 3. Results of the information type output from asking ChatGPT questions using text records.

In the feedback from the qualitative study, the probability of ChatGPT providing information that matched CaseAssistant was 44 percent. This included some false information, with a probability of outputting false information at 20%. The probability of outputting other answers was 56%, with most of these answer types being summaries or suggestions. Only 24% of the information was both in compliance with the rules and true.

Although AIGC shows considerable comprehension and creativity and performs well in multi-turn, multi-intent conversations, the results indicate that to apply AIGC as a smart assistant in specific scenarios, such as group discussions, it still needs to be adjusted and optimized for the context.

In Future work, we aim to deploy LLM in group discussions, adhering to the strategies and conclusions derived from this paper. We intend to further investigate the potential of LLM in participating in group discussions.

8 Contribution

Previous research on the application of smart assistant in group discussions has primarily focused on encouraging participation from less active members [14] and avoiding negative vocabulary [20]. However, there has been limited exploration into addressing knowledge asymmetry within these discussions. This gap becomes increasingly significant with the global push towards interdisciplinary collaboration, where knowledge asymmetry in group discussions is becoming more pronounced. Addressing this challenge, our study introduces CaseAssistant, a smart assistant designed to improve knowledge asymmetry by aiding group members in retrieving relevant information and examples. This not only reduces the workload of participants but also enhances discussion efficiency and promotes cognitive consensus among group members. Our research specifically targets the issue of knowledge asymmetry in group discussions and enriches the design strategies for smart assistants participating in such settings. Through a series of experiments and interviews, we have contributed to the understanding of how smart assistants can be effectively integrated into group discussions to facilitate better communication, idea exchange, and consensus-building among participants with diverse knowledge backgrounds. Our work provided valuable insights for the future development of smart assistants participating in group discussions.

9 Conclusion

This study explored the possibility of using smart assistants to improve knowledge asymmetry in group discussions. We designed a Wizard of Oz approach to simulate a smart assistant called CaseAssistant, which can provide suitable information and cases based on the discussion content of group members, reducing their workload and promoting cognitive consensus.

References

1. AbuShawar, B., Atwell, E.: ALICE chatbot: Trials and outputs. Computación y Sistemas **19**(4), 625–632 (2015)
2. Aharon, D.: Introducing cloud text-to-speech powered by deepmind WaveNet technology, 09 April 2023. https://cloud.google.com/blog/products/ai-machine-learning/introducing-cloud-text-to-speech-powered-by-deepmind-wavenet-technology
3. Backlog. [n.d.]. Project management software for virtual teams: backlog, 09 April 2023. https://nulab.com/backlog/
4. Braun, V., Clarke, V.: Using thematic analysis in psychology. Qual. Res. Psychol. **3**(2), 77–101 (2006)
5. BroadMix. [n.d.]. Online whiteboard tool oardmix, 09 April 2023. https://boardmix.cn/
6. ChatGPT. [n.d.]. Introducing ChatGPT, 09 April 2023. https://openai.com/blog/chatgpt
7. Fast, E., Chen, B., Mendelsohn, J., Bassen, J., Bernstein, M.S.: IRIS: a conversational agent for complex tasks. In: Proceedings of the 2018 CHI Conference on Human Factors in Computing Systems, pp. 1–12 (2018)
8. Fergnani, A.: Futures Triangle 2.0: Integrating the Futures Triangle with Scenario Planning. Foresight (2020)

9. Haman, M., Školník, M.: Using ChatGPT to conduct a literature review. Account. Res., 1–3 (2023)
10. Hamann, K., Pollock, P.H., Wilson, B.M.: Assessing student perceptions of the benefits of discussions in small-group, large-class, and online learning contexts. Coll. Teach. **60**(2), 65–75 (2012)
11. Hart, S.G.: NASA-task load index (NASA-TLX); 20 years later. In: Proceedings of the Human Factors and Ergonomics Society Annual Meeting, vol. 50, pp. 904–908. Sage publications, Los Angeles (2006)
12. iFLYTEK. [n.d.]. Make notes easier, 09 April 2023. https://iflynote.com/home
13. Kemman, M.: Knowledge asymmetry in interdisciplinary collaborations and how to reduce it, 09 April 2023. https://i2insights.org/2019/02/26/knowledge-asymmetry/
14. Kim, S., Eun, J., Oh, C., Suh, B., Lee, J.: Bot in the bunch: facilitating group chat discussion by improving efficiency and participation with a chatbot. In: Proceedings of the 2020 CHI Conference on Human Factors in Computing Systems, pp. 1–13 (2020)
15. Medhi Thies, I., Menon, N., Magapu, S., Subramony, M., O'Neill, J.: How do you want your chatbot? an exploratory Wizard-of-Oz study with young, urban Indians. In: Bernhaupt, R., Dalvi, G., Joshi, A., K. Balkrishan, D., O'Neill, J., Winckler, M. (eds.) Human-Computer Interaction - INTERACT 2017. INTERACT 2017. Lecture Notes in Computer Science(), vol. 10513. Springer, Cham (2017). https://doi.org/10.1007/978-3-319-67744-6_28
16. Mishra, L.: Focus group discussion in qualitative research. TechnoLearn Int. J. Educ. Technol. **6**(1), 1–5 (2016)
17. Miyake, N., Norman, D.A.: To ask a question, one must know enough to know what is not known. J. Verbal Learn. Verbal Behav. **18**(3), 357–364 (1979)
18. Noelle-Neumann, E.: The spiral of silence a theory of public opinion. J. Commun. **24**(2), 43–51 (1974)
19. Palmeiro, A.R., van der Kint, S., Vissers, L., Farah, H., de Winter, J.C.F., Hagenzieker, M.: Interaction between pedestrians and automated vehicles: a Wizard of Oz experiment. Transport. Res. F: Traffic Psychol. Behav. **58**(2018), 1005–1020 (2018)
20. Peng, Z., Kim, T., Ma, X.: GremoBot: exploring emotion regulation in group chat. In: Conference Companion Publication of the 2019 on Computer Supported Cooperative Work and Social Computing, pp. 335–340 (2019)
21. Petousi, D., Katifori, V., Roussou, M., Ioannidis, Y.: The dialogue facilitator bot: reflections on design and evaluation. In: 2022 International Conference on Interactive Media, Smart Systems and Emerging Technologies (IMET), pp. 1–8. IEEE (2022)
22. Pollock, P.H., Hamann, K., Wilson, B.M.: Learning through discussions: comparing the benefits of small-group and large-class settings. J. Polit. Sci. Educ. **7**(1), 48–64 (2011)
23. Sidaoui, K., Jaakkola, M., Burton, J.: AI feel you: customer experience assessment via chatbot interviews. J. Serv. Manag. **31**(4), 745–766 (2020)
24. Sutoyo, R., Chowanda, A., Kurniati, A., Wongso, R.: Designing an emotionally realistic chatbot framework to enhance its believability with AIML and information states. Proc. Comput. Sci. **157**(2019), 621–628 (2019)
25. Tencent. [n.d.]. Tencent Meeting,09 April 2023. https://meeting.tencent.com/
26. Toxtli, C., Monroy-Hernández, A., Cranshaw, J.: Understanding chatbot-mediated task management. In: Proceedings of the 2018 CHI Conference on Human Factors in Computing Systems, pp. 1–6 (2018)
27. Xiao, Z., Zhou, M.X., Chen, W., Yang, H., Chi, C.: If I hear you correctly, building and evaluating interview chatbots with active listening skills. In: Proceedings of the 2020 CHI Conference on Human Factors in Computing Systems, pp. 1–14. Manuscript submitted to ACM, p. 12 (2020)
28. Zhou, L., Gao, J., Li, D., Shum, H.-Y.: The design and implementation of xiaoice, an empathetic social chatbot. Comput. Linguis. **46**(1), 53–93 (2020)

Interacting in Social Media

In the Wake of the Woke: Reinvigorating Brand Conversation at the Crossroads of Policy and Politics M&M's Superbowl 2023 Campaign

Karine Berthelot-Guiet[✉]

CELSA, Sorbonne University, Paris, France
karine.berthelot-guiet@sorbonne-universite.fr

Abstract. This paper proposes exploring the contemporary transformations of so-called "conversational" forms of brand communication on social media in the theoretical framework and methodological approaches presented above. After almost 20 years of brand presence on social media promoting conversation between brands and consumers, this type of communication, like all forms of advertising, must have reached a stage of maturity and diminished capacity for differentiation. To analyze this phenomenon, we chose to focus on the communications proposals of M&M's brand, which, in early 2023, created a communications "event" on its social media with strong social and political commentary.

We will then try to understand how the claim to a social and political voice can be part of the tactics of reinvigorating Brand Conversation by playing on the life of the city (policy) as much as on political opinions and victimizations (politics) currently alive in the USA. We will examine the possible strategic aims of this hyperadvertising and its legitimacy to intervene in the public arena by making social judgments and political statements.

Keywords: Advertising · Conversation · Digital Literacy

1 Introduction

1.1 The Framework of the French Communication Sciences

This paper is part of a French approach to communication sciences, which emphasizes the analysis of communication processes and their changes over time to consider metamorphoses rather than revolutions. In France, whether the terms "information" and "communication" are used separately or together, whether the communication is interpersonal or collective, mediatized or not, political, cultural, corporate, etc., information and communication sciences cover a wide field, ranging from documentation to commercial communication.

As one of the founders of the "Sciences de l'Information et de la Communication" points out: "Communication is a process of change, a process of transformation." It is "a science that defines itself only partly by its object, but more by what it seeks to explain in the objects it studies, by the explanatory models it proposes, one could say its paradigms" [1]. Whatever the objects and methodologies, all involve elaborating a communication question, which generally requires an approach that interweaves numerous concepts from the humanities and social sciences in the classical sense. The identity of this discipline in the French scientific landscape is to propose an approach that is resolutely interdisciplinary and fully communication.

However, in this discipline, not all objects and concepts are equal as in others. Recognition is uneven. In France, consumerism, advertising, branding, and brand discourse are among the most persistently unpopular topics. Research in these fields has not yet been encouraged. As a result, academic careers in the human sciences are equally complex. In France, consumerism and advertising are still too often the subject of an academic wasteland. In 2024, theoretical reflection on these topics needs to be revised. Even today, it is not easy to work on advertising within the framework of the humanities, social sciences, and communication, as it remains an object of research deemed lacking theorization, dedicated to applied research, or even to producing case studies in the service of business and capitalism. We are among the few researchers who believe it is necessary to conceptualize, describe, and analyze the social discourses of the media and commerce and the social and cultural circulations that shape their presence in the media and the public sphere. We consider media, commercial, advertising, and brand discourses social and cultural discourses. We analyze these market mediation processes by giving equal importance to communication processes, communication products (advertisements, brand films, museums, websites, social media, etc.), and what professionals (advertisers, communication, and media specialists) write or say publicly about them.

1.2 A Sociosemiotic Method

We regularly apply a socio-semiotic approach focusing on the negotiation of meaning in the interpretation process, continuous semiosis, and creative appropriation. Over the past thirty years, we have developed an assertive theoretical approach to commercial mediation in our laboratory. Together with other colleagues, we have led the eponymous line of research that links these issues to semiotics, sociology, economics, anthropology, and political analysis.

Contemporary approaches in French information and communication sciences, which deserve to be better known outside the French-speaking world, form the basis of the analysis we intend to develop here. More precisely, we will mobilize researchers in French communication studies interested in conceptualizing, describing, or analyzing social, media, and commercial discourses. They aim to understand how these discursive elements, broadly defined as speech, images, and all media products, circulate between different social and media spaces, constructing their media and public presence. In this respect, media, commercial, advertising, and brand discourses are social discourses that carry out market mediation processes.

This specific point of view is neither psychological, sociological, or semiotic. French information and communication sciences allow us to develop intermediate positions based on earlier analyses, such as the problematization developed by Barthes and Baudrillard of consumption as a social and symbolic system, essentially a system of signification linked to a sociological system of distinction, albeit determined by economic aspects [2–5]. Our methodology addresses signs and meanings related to consumption objects and discourses in their specific sociological, economic, cultural, and communication contexts.

This paper draws on long-term research that gives equal importance to the communication process, the products of communication (advertisements, branded films, museums, websites, social media, etc.), and what professionals say. This implies working on openly commented uses to reach practices and thus find a way toward users' uses, representations, and creative appropriations. This is different from reception studies, as they have been developed in media studies and are limited to media uses, even if some of the receivers' perspectives are considered to choose a socio-semiotic approach that deals with the negotiation of meaning in the process of interpretation, with the infinite semiosis in progress, and with creative appropriation, or "poaching," as De Certeau describes it [6].

1.3 Socio-semio-Communication Analysis

This method takes what people think, say, and do - including advertising and marketing professionals. This point of view implies a "creative methodology" in research. We need to find the right methods to challenge the theory each time. Using existing methods is generally the rule, but certain subjects and research objects require specific methods resulting from in-depth theoretical analysis. Choosing the best set and architecture of qualitative methods, not based on statistics or being unable to give quantitative results, is a major challenge to question a research topic theoretically appropriately.

In this respect, micro-scale approaches are our choice, particularly and paradoxically, to achieve macro-analysis. Numerous highly detailed analyses of small elements ultimately lead to processing a large corpus of small things and enable valuable and unexpected results that we would have obtained through something other than direct macro-analysis. Our theoretical position on methodology is that of a social-semio-communication approach. In 1996, Semprini [7] adopted a sociosemiotic perspective to analyze general and advertising communication as a social discourse to identify the meaning "articulated" by social discourses and to understand how these discourses interact.

The ambition of sociosemiotics is to analyze the meaning within the socio-cultural space that produces and circulates it. Like other communication manifestations, advertising offers more general discursive forms. Semprini, for example, points out that Benetton advertisements (in the era of the "provocative" campaigns) more broadly invite us to question the legitimacy of an enunciation that oscillates between economic and political discourse. From this perspective, the sociosemiotic approach includes the study of formal mechanisms for the circulation of social discourses and the systems of actors that each discourse sets up. Semprini insists on studying the possible worlds generated by the relationship between textual, discursive, and socio-cultural spaces. Meaning is the dynamic result of interweaving textual, discursive, and socio-cultural spaces.

This paper proposes exploring the contemporary transformations of so-called "conversational" forms of brand communication on social media in the theoretical framework and methodological approaches presented above. After almost 20 years of brand presence on social media promoting conversations between brands and consumers, this type of communication, like all forms of advertising, must have reached a stage of maturity and diminished capacity for differentiation.

Indeed, the primary role of advertising, in which we include the brand conversation, is to ensure the brand's communication existence, according to the principle of the "advertising cry." To exist and make the brand and its discourse exist, advertising must first exist as a message. Many of its transformations over time have been generated by this necessity: support changes, formats, the search for appropriate technical innovations, and tactical or strategic choices. It is always a question of ensuring the possibility of a discourse of existence—all the more reason as consumers become increasingly advertising literate, offline and online. We will see how advertising professionals have been trying to make online discourse difficult to spot, contour, and criticize. In this respect, old advertising forms, abandoned for the ethical problems they posed, such as "réclame" and advertising hype, have been joined by contemporary forms, such as dark patterns, to sneak in or force their way in. The erosion of differentiation, and therefore the ability to have value as an "advertising cry," also affects brand conversation on social media. Conversations are being transformed for greater visibility. To analyze this phenomenon, we chose to focus on the communications proposals of M&M's brand, which, in early 2023, created a communications "event" on its social media with strong social and political commentary.

We will then try to understand how the claim to a social and political voice can be part of the tactics of reinvigorating Brand Conversation by playing on the life of the city (policy) as much as on political opinions and victimizations (politics) currently at work in the USA. We will examine the possible strategic aims of this hyperadvertising. We can remember the ten years of advertising communications (the 1990s) by the Benetton clothing brand. These campaigns were one after the other, bathed in controversy and controversy generated by the fact that a clothing brand believes it is legitimate to intervene in the public arena by making social judgments and political statements.

2 Advertising Establishing a Brand's Existence: From a Cry to a Conversation

Since its earliest days, advertising has faced a major and virtually unique communication problem. To be a message in the full sense of the term and fulfill its ultimate mission of convincing receivers to buy a product or service or support a cause, it must first capture the attention of people not looking for it. We are faced with an extreme case here: advertising is a type of communication that's extremely expensive to produce and put into circulation, even though almost nobody wants to receive it, let alone expects to.

Much of the history of advertising and the evolution of its content, media, and formats can be reread in this light. The incessant evolutions and transformations, the strong propensity to adopt new technologies almost as soon as they appear, and the multiplication of professional discourses that emphasize the obligation of contemporaneity imposed on advertising are just a few snippets of an overall system that seeks to create large or small communication events to enable advertising to fulfill its primary role as a discourse of brand existence.

2.1 The Advertising Cry: A Necessity

Since advertising began in Europe, promotional communication has developed according to two logics that are sometimes difficult to reconcile:

- the first is a tension between publicizing and announcing things so everyone knows about them and publicizing things so people buy them;
- the second is a hesitation between the desire to exert influence through messages that are as hidden as possible and the need to ensure that they are received, which sometimes requires a certain degree of outrageousness.

This latter necessity often becomes primary for advertising messages as the various media and supports develop and become successively saturated, whether really or supposedly. To sell, advertising must first exist in the stream of promotional messages; the semiotic equivalence of a cry can materialize this. In our earlier work, we proposed to call this discursive logic "advertising cry." [8].

The "cry" is designed to attract attention. Historically, it was one of the first modes of advertising expression that found an incarnation in the now-forgotten figures of the town crier, newspaper crier, and fairground crier. From the Middle Ages to the mid-20th century, the town crier was responsible for making certain official announcements heard around the town, informing people of newspaper headlines so that they could buy them, and providing information on merchandise. Today, despite the media transformations, advertising remains, first and foremost, a message that needs to be heard, and messages act like a cry to arrest the customer in the hope that he or she will become a receiver of the message. Before rhetorical, commercial, or aesthetic effectiveness, the main challenge is to exist, and the saturation of media spaces increases the risk of an ad failing to reach its intended audience.

From the adoption of lithography, first in black and white, then in increasingly exuberant colors, to the promotional speeches of influencers, contemporary versions of the woman and the sandwich man already present in Benjamin [9]. Efforts were initially focused on giving the advertising message a high profile capable of catching people's attention and, eventually, leading them to give interpretation a few seconds. Thus, until the 1960s, advertising agencies tended to focus on the poster's gigantic size, recognizable graphism, and logotype, often accompanied by a brand character. The proliferation of advertising poster printing in the USA led to the development of a specific typography, almost dedicated to, and therefore recognizable and attributable to, commerce and its advertising. Floch [10] points out that the typeface used is Egyptian, typical of the early days of commercial communication in the USA. Indeed, commercial posters and signs from the turn of the nineteenth and twentieth centuries essentially used this typography.

Over time, each new technical and media possibility was almost immediately spotted if it had the advertising potential to ensure the message's visibility. At the same time, formats sought to polarize these new possibilities to make the most of them. Cinema, for example, moved swiftly from the in-theater poster on the curtain to the beginnings of the film, which had a great deal of advertising potential. Similarly, radio-enabled advertisements in France are sung ritornellos that can still be heard humming around villages. The arrival of television advertising, albeit late in France's case, put the advertising film on a similar scale to radio, tightening up the filmed message, emphasizing the slogan and song, and hammering out repetition.

Over the years, advertisers have regularly, both through an appetite for technical novelties and an ability to detect the assets they represent, one after the other, nurtured, preserved, and often revived the advertising cry. At the same time, they have evolved over the decades in line with the changes they wanted to bring to their profession and the social judgment that goes with it. Whether they are graduates of prestigious universities and even doctors, as has been the case in the USA since the beginning of the 20th century, or trained on the job and then in schools run by professionals before finding a place in universities and business schools, as is the case in France, advertising professionals have to deal with the bad opinion that the least correct of their practices can arouse over time: misleading, charlatanic advertising, "réclame" designed, in France, to deceive readers by playing on the trust they have in the discourse of journalists from the press titles to which they subscribe. This context was conducive to the rise of a general suspicion of advertising. It undermined its ability to serve sales and made it difficult for the advertising cry to function properly.

2.2   The Advertising Cry: The Brand as Specific Mediation

Brand discourses, specifically advertising discourses, are largely built around the need to establish the brand's existence. At the same time, advertising discourse is highly determined by its production's internal and external conditions. From the nineteenth century onwards, advertising is one of the two market mediations specifically used to serve the brand. Producers of goods and merchandise invented brands to bypass the mediation of retailers and merchants; it soon became clear that brands could not find their place and function without being carried by a medium - the package - and brought to the public's attention by advertising. From then on, advertising played a complex role in communicating the brand's existence.

To be effective, advertising must guarantee that the brand is easily recognizable both in-store and on social media. This is why advertising messages are discourses of legitimization and declaration of existence for the brand. They can only fulfill this role if they exist as messages. Advertising is rarely a discourse that people seek out or devote attention to. The advertising message must integrate a major imperative from its conception: it must exist as a message and, therefore, begin by attracting the attention of a person who will become the receiver. Many professional advertising techniques are dedicated to this task and attempt to attract attention in the short, medium, and sometimes long term. Advertising serves two purposes: to deliver a message and to bring recognition, notoriety, and legitimacy to the brand. We propose to explore this as an "advertising cry."

When brands were created as a form of commercial mediation, they became part of a long-standing system in which retailers, shopkeepers, etc., cohabited. Producers and manufacturers started brands, packaging, and advertising in hopes of controlling and imposing them on sellers to gain easier access to buyers. This process affects the market system, as signs gradually represent products. Trademarks create trust in a sign that guarantees the quality of the product it represents. The focus shifts to brand and communication.

From the perspective of information and communication sciences, a brand is the union of processes and mediations. "Both communicating and communicated" could be rephrased as "both the ones communicating and the ones being comm. It is at once an economic, semiotic, social, and cultural artifact linked to multiple mediations:

- historically, the brand is a market mediation,
- It is a form of social mediation that contributes to differentiation as well as communication and publicity,
- it is a symbolic mediation that substitutes sign value for use value,
- It is a form of cultural mediation that helps us understand the everyday environment and connect it to a system of values in an anthropological sense.

The brand acts as a mediator of communication, setting the tone for the exchanges associated and interactions as the central point for all advertising messages, which align to convey the brand's superior qualities. The brand encapsulates excellence in a single goal, often mass motions, aiming to facilitate commercial exchanges. In *Le système des objets*, Baudrillard [3] asserts that the entire advertising system is an immense metaphor for the brand. Advertising is the discourse of the brand, and language becomes an "object of consumption, a fetish." In advertising discourse, consumerism industrializes both language and material production. Baudrillard's work explores and affirms the role and type of mediation the brand assumes in the advertising system. This system aims to produce connivance by summoning a work of meaning that functions through signifying impressionism. The latter refers to a significant system that condenses the meaning of various objects, giving them their unique identity. Finally, the brand serves a dual function of signaling the product and symbolically affixing a warning flag. It also condenses multiple emotional connotations to sell the product. Baudrillard calls the brand a "supersign".

The advertising message brings together a range of elements, products, and discourses, with the brand being both the starting and ending point, all in constant circulation. It is essential to consider internal and external constraints when defining advertising discourse, as they significantly impact its form. All the more so since advertising must provide worldly knowledge about the product(s) whose brand is the market mediator: it must ensure "stability of content and create a contextualization that favors the selection of the right referent by nourishing the media of knowledge shared by the interlocutors." Advertising thus acts as a vast defining contextualization, Associating the brand with a universe; all the elements of the advertising message contribute to connotatively defining the brand.

Advertising discourse is under pressure due to constraints. It must balance brand enhancement and semiotic condensation to produce effective messages. Advertising creates language that is both highly suggestive and obviously commercial. Indeed, advertising messages naturalize their commercial nature through the mythical mediation of the brand. It activates potential meanings and neutralizes present ones in a Barthesian sense, functioning as a myth. The brand has a powerful symbolic operativity and displays the plasticity of the myth's conceptualization; It does not hide anything but distorts and masks its commodity nature through the naturalization of commodity ideology, much like a myth. Therefore, brands are communication matrices that transform any element conceived in their terms into a system of signs impregnated with commodity ideology, enabling consumption and/or symbolic appropriation. The commercial discourse places the ideology of consumption at the center of the brand's mythology.

The presence of a brand in a discourse engages the latter in advertising. Where there is a brand, there is theoretical advertising since the mere presence of the brand in a discourse engages the latter in a mercantile semiotic predilection. "We use the term advertising to refer to all forms of branded communication." In other words, the definition of advertising discourse is brand = advertising. When a brand initiates a conversation, it becomes part of the advertising realm. Brand speeches are essentially a means for showcasing and promoting brands. They play a crucial role in establishing the identity and status of a brand and serve as a reference point for customers. Advertising acts as a mediator in this process, reinforcing the message of the brand's existence through a discourse of meta-mediation.

3   The Advertising Cry: Tactics and Strategies for Brand Existence

Ensuring that an advertising message is noticed has been a requirement for centuries. One of the earliest methods for advertising was through the town crier. The town crier was stationed at crossroads and in squares, and their responsibility was to attract the attention of passers-by using a bell or drum to gather them and form an audience. An advertising message needs an audience to be noticed, whether it is through sight, sound, or text. Some advertising messages are designed to act as a warning to stop consumers in their tracks. Professionals in the field of advertising implement two types of action to achieve their goals. These actions are two complementary aspects of what is known as the advertising cry. The first type is tactical and short-term, and it involves using advertising techniques to attract immediate attention. The second type is strategic, focusing on achieving long-term or mid-term goals.

3.1   The Advertising Cry: Tactics

Here, the term "advertising cry" refers to the short-term tactics used to ensure the existence of a product. "The technique is designed to capture attention and generate interest." While long-term strategies can establish a more durable presence, advertising always assumes the role of an "existence teller." Regardless of how complex contemporary advertising and consumption trends have become, all brand discourses must effectively communicate and guarantee their existence. As consumption is a part of our daily lives, advertising has also undergone significant transformations. It has developed both tactical and strategic solutions to remain relevant, particularly since the rise of brands as key players in the consumption industry. A comprehensive redefinition can be evaluated by considering the broader perspective that time and the researcher's expertise permit. In general, there are two strategies to reconsider the issue of advertising discourse: either to dissociate from it and find new forms of communication or to intensify it by emphasizing certain features. These communication proposals evolve around the issue of brand existence. They suggest that advertising discourse, disseminated through several media channels like press, billboards, television, radio, cinema, and the Internet, is not enough to guarantee a brand's communication existence strategy by itself.

From a tactical perspective, many commercial messages we receive today still rely on an alert that seeks to establish contact with potential receivers. Such messages' form and/or content often resemble a cry for attention. One example is the teasing technique employed in advertising, where the message is delivered in two or more stages. In the first stage, the message is designed to be intriguing and not signed by the brand. The aim is to pique the audience's curiosity and encourage them to seek out the second message, which is delivered later and reveals the brand. In such cases, curiosity is the driving force behind the message.

Ads that provoke visual and/or intellectual cries are tactical cries. Discreet methods are also used for emotional appeal. Our prior research in French press ads found attention-grabbing linguistic tools. Over time, advertising has adopted various tactical methods to sustain its attractiveness in rapidly changing contexts. However, it has also sought more strategic solutions to fulfill this purpose. To achieve this goal, contemporary forms of brand communication play around with the advertising form. Some advertising speeches use tactics like creating an alarm to grab attention, teasing techniques, provoking emotions, using foreign languages, linguistic errors, and hyperneological terms to grab the audience's attention. This helps in establishing and maintaining contact with the audience. Some companies, such as Benetton, have used provocative ads to attract attention.

3.2 Advertising, Unadvertising, and Hyperadvertising

Continuous transformation drives the evolution of advertising as a field, with new techniques, technologies, supports, and media constantly being identified to renew discourse and increase visibility while remaining contemporary. However, this extraordinary ability to identify and adapt is not always enough to maintain the "advertising cry" function in a multi-factorial, evolving context. Brand managers in companies and agencies face a complex economic and social context affecting the brand. Today's media often reflect a common sentiment that is distrustful and resistant towards advertising. People tend to evaluate brands based on their actions and the behavior of the companies that own them. It has become normal and socially acceptable to express one's disapproval of advertising openly. Maintaining the value of advertising cry over the long term is a significant challenge in this context. Moreover, in societies and environments where advertising is omnipresent, it punctuates or accompanies daily life. Advertising professionals believe that traditional forms of advertising are no longer effective due to the rise of anti-advertising sentiment and the saturation of traditional advertising spaces. However, the advertising industry relies on agencies to find new sources of growth to sustain their business. In professional practices, two types of strategy [11] have emerged amidst this context:

– the first, uncovered and worked on by Marti, consists of minimizing advertising forms by erasing them as far as possible: this is unadvertising,
– the second approach focuses on maximizing advertising aspects. This can be achieved through quantitative work that involves creating new media or transforming existing ones into media, as described by Marti. Alternatively, qualitative work can be

undertaken, which involves transforming advertising through strong aestheticization and hypertrophied semiotization. This approach is known as hyperadvertising (Berthelot-Guiet.)

The names "unadvertising" and "hyperadvertising" are cross-disciplinary research results. They are used to give a name and logic to various professional productions that are often produced on an ad hoc basis. From a professional point of view, these terms are more like product placement, brand content, sponsoring, programming, conversational marketing, and so on.

Unadvertising aims to minimize traditional forms of advertising through communication strategies.

- Entering pre-existing media forms (product placement in television, cinema, games, or television programming). This also includes sponsoring television programs.
- Imitating either existing media productions (consumer magazines, branded web series or games) or cultural productions or devices such as branded short movies ("Prada presents A Therapy," directed by Roman Polanski, starring Ben Kingsley and Helen Bonham Carter), branded cookbooks such (Philadelphia, Oreos), or branded exhibitions and museums.
- Adopting forms of communication that are supposed to redistribute communication roles, as is the case with YouTube channels and so-called social media or media.

Hyperadvertising works on the hypertrophy of advertising aspects. The aim is not to hide the nature of the message but, on the contrary, to maximize the advertising presence. When this work is quantitative, it is generally a search for the continuous creation of media to transform everyday elements into ephemeral or perennial advertising media. When the work is qualitative, it increases the semiotic density of the message through creative and/or sophisticated aesthetic work. New advertising formats, such as long TV ads requiring exceptional film work or high-quality magazine ads on glossy paper, are being explored.

3.3 Brands and Digital Social Media: The Source of the Ideal of Conversation

Conversational marketing has its roots in the world of professional marketing and advertising. It originated from "The Clue Train Manifesto," written by American consultants in 1999, explicitly referred to as the source of the conversational marketing myth. It argues that e-commerce is essentially a conversation between people. This perspective is based on an idealized vision of commercial conversation from the pre-industrial era when the traditional marketplace was always the hub of commercial communication, facilitating various exchanges, negotiations, and person-to-person information.

The pre-capitalist conversation is described as genuine and direct and disappeared during the industrial era until the advent and the rise of the Internet, which enables content production and exchange via interposed applications. From this point onwards, the authors make several semantic and presuppositional shifts: the pre-industrial conversation between customer and salesperson around the product(s) or even the sale becomes a conversation between individual buyers or consumers about products and consumption. This web conversation inherits the attributes of its great ancestor and is irenic and idealized. Moreover, this conversation is constructed as opposed to influential communication, i.e., advertising and "public relations," renamed "bonimenteurs."

The conversation built up in the Cluetrain Manifesto is a vox populi, an ideal exchange that's supposed to be genuine and truthful. Personal feedback is especially valorized, especially for brands and their communication issues. At the time, brands, or rather their managers, were to consider the birth of online conversation and learn to participate and even lead it. Emphasis is being placed on the highly perceptible artificiality of brand communications, described as the "current homogenized 'voice' of business." The way is paved for consulting agencies to help brands "enter the conversation" by explaining "how to talk," particularly by identifying those among their employees who have this ability.

Since this text was first published, marketing conversation has mostly stayed the same regarding its definition and contours; it remains a hybrid production, largely consensual, both innate (for consumers) and to be learned (for brands). It is based on a vision of horizontal communication, seeking to erase hierarchical positions and relationships of power or influence. In this way, it is opposed to the top-down verticality of advertising linked to the dominant hierarchical position of brands. Since 2018, the "conversation" between brand and consumer takes place, for the most part, via social media and media, and has evolved between several modalities: the soliloquy when the brand is not followed, the dissensus for brands often challenged in a new form of long-term crisis communication, the pure commercial argument for brands that engage in hard selling between couponing and putting the consumer to work through numerous mini-surveys, the conversation in a few ultimately exceptional cases and the brand's discourse of existence or advertising. These hyper-advertising forms ensure a strong, repetitive presence for the brand reduced to its main totems, namely the name and logotype. The discussion of the brand conversation shows that professionals are trying to draw a line, or even an opposition, between "good" communication, which is transparent and non-manipulative, akin to information, and "bad" communication, which is opaque, manipulative, and advertising.

4 Brand Conversation: How to Stop the Erosion of Differentiation

4.1 Conversation, Digital Literacy, Changes in the Online Brand Landscape: The Risk of Indifferentiation

The strong development of the omnipresence of brands in social media creates a form of differentiation between brands, as it does every time a new form of media or a new medium appears that usually works for several years. When it fades, it is difficult to guarantee the functioning of a discourse of existence, and brands sometimes choose to return to old formats, however disparaged they may have been. We propose to explore contemporary transformations of so-called 'conversational' brand forms within the theoretical framework and methodological approaches presented above. After almost 20 years of brand presence on social media and the promotion of the notion of conversation between brands and consumers, this form of communication, like all forms of advertising, must have reached a stage of maturity and diminished capacity for differentiation. Consumers are developing advertising literacy skills for offline advertising and digital avatars. Professionals have tried to thwart the ability of participants to recognize and criticize advertising. In this respect, old forms, abandoned because of ethical problems, such as "réclame" and hype, come back and meet contemporary forms, such as dark patterns, to sneak in or force their way in. The erosion of differentiation, and therefore the ability to have value as an "advertising rallying cry," also affects brand conversations on social media. Conversations are being transformed for greater visibility.

To analyze this phenomenon, we chose to focus on the communication proposals of the M&M's brand, owned by the Mars Group, which created a communication "event" on its social media between 21 January and 13 February 2023, the day of the Super Bowl final, with a strong social and political commentary. The Super Bowl is a major advertising moment in the USA. The candy brand M&Ms has been mentioned for a long time as one of the most important brands that take part in this "advertising show" every year [12, 13]. "[14]. From M&M's USA Facebook page, we have compiled a corpus of posts and comments. We have analyzed this Facebook account repeatedly since 2017, and it provides some points of comparison. Since the brand's Facebook France account did not address the issue of accusations of wokism against two of the brand's mascots (Green and Purple), we collected a corpus via the Europresse database of the national and regional French press by entering the keyword.

M&M's changed the shoes of its female "spokescandy" named "Green" and added "Purple" to the group in 2022. To the general indifference, apart from the repeated remarks or attacks of Carlson Tucker, the star host of the Fox News channel, a Trumpist who specializes in exploiting the anger of his viewers, he considered the two characters "woke."

On 5 January 2023, after a classic New Year's greeting, M&M's posted the following message: "I thought they would at least last for Women's History Month. The new campaign is ridiculous and offensive", "Glad to see more companies recognizing all the traditionally excluded and marginalized people and groups in our society. #leadership".

– a response to the brand's request to nominate a person: "XX is doing AMAZING WORK!!! She has done an amazing job changing her life and so many lives around her, and I cannot praise her enough or tell you how proud I am of her!!!! She deserves everything".

On 21 January, encouraging people to order for Valentine's Day, a post returns to the classic area of commerce.

The controversy began on 22 January, the day of the Lunar New Year, which M&M's celebrates on Facebook with a short cartoon featuring Green and Purple with the following message: "Let's bring good luck and good vibes into this #LunarNewYear! #ForAll-Funkind". This post polarised followers into three groups: cons, pros, and meta-analysis. Comments on the shoes soon got out of hand. A multi-polemic debate ensued between those who wanted the traditional costume back and those who argued that the outfit was inappropriate for a woman.

Politically charged exchanges between conservatives and progressives abound, with the brand's characters seen as the promotion of inappropriate representations. Right-wing and left-wing extremism were both denounced. Some comments emphasized that a brand, or even the manufacturer of the sweets, had no right to intervene in this area, and others immediately suggested a tactical communication calculation on the part of the brand.

The "controversy" escalated when the brand announced the withdrawal of the little characters in several posts, allegedly under pressure from conservative discourses accusing them of "wokism." Maya Rudolph then replaced them. She is a former Saturday Night Live guest and an outspoken Democrat. The brand unveiled her as its new face and announced plans to launch shell-shaped sweets. Some of its followers, however, continued to take the situation seriously: "Who in their right mind thought it was a good idea to replace fictional characters with a real person because of politically charged artificial controversies? Don't they know how much hate and negative attention she's going to get now? By trying to appease everyone, they've made both sides hate this girl, lol." most comments emphasized the advertising nature of the maneuver, especially with the date of the Super Bowl final so close: "This is a marketing campaign before her Super Bowl ad. People really need to chill out. My goodness, all this fuss over chocolate. It's just sweets, people. Get over it." Criticism of the brand for exploiting a political controversy is strong: "Not real! Now we're politicising sweets. I've never thought of the M&M spokes as anything other than cute characters associated with a popular and successful brand. I have never once thought about their 'sexuality' or 'inclusivity.' They are iconic characters for the M&M brand... Period... Nothing more, nothing less. Getting rid of them is a disgrace, and allowing your company to be influenced by a "news reporter" (and I use the term loosely) is nothing short of pathetic."

The brand stepped up to the plate and ended the hoax without acknowledging it at any point on 13 February 2023, the day of the Super Bowl final. The brand's Facebook USA account changed its profile picture to show the seven mascots with their new, redesigned attributes, including the white "green" sneakers, which again sparked many comments. On the same day, the end of the so-called mascot exclusion during the Super Bowl was announced with an image of the same mascots, with the caption, "They're back for good."

During the same period, no single post related to the issue on M&M's France Facebook account existed. However, the French national and regional press reported and broadcast the alleged adventures of the brand's international mascots. Between 21 January and 13 February, 33 press articles mention the brand, 32 of which refer to either the disappearance/reappearance of the brand's mascots, the "mystery" or the marketing coup and 22 of which address the issue of the controversy surrounding the mascots, presented as an accusation of being "woke," "too woke," "suffering the pain of the American right" because of "their ecological policies."

Before the 13 February denouement, the issue was generally taken very seriously. Brand managers' statements were cited as sources to be taken at face value, as this excerpt from the Huffington Post website of 21 January 2023 shows: "Even the shoes on candy can cause polarization. Referring to these changes, M&M's said on a message on Monday that it had not expected them to disrupt the internet. However, we now understand," the confectioner added, "that even the shoes on candy can be polarizing and that was the last thing we wanted as our goal is to bring people together. As a result, the company has announced that it has decided to take the characters off the air indefinitely. In the new advertising campaigns, comedian and humorist Maya Rudolph will replace the animated creatures." A second article, published on 13 February, announced the return of the mascots but maintained a serious tone, recalling the controversial choices made by the brand and the criticism from the American right.

In the national press, on January 26, 2023, Le Monde ran the headline "Les bonbons M&M's, ligne de front dérisoire dans la guerre culturelle aux Etats-Unis" ("M&M's candies, a derisory frontline in the cultural war in the United States").Le Point magazine returned to the issue 4 times during the period.

The French press, which took things very seriously and treated M&M's campaign accordingly, did not admit to having been duped and went out of its way to treat the issue seriously, recognizing the "cleverly orchestrated coup by M&M's" (advertising by implication) (Le Point 13/02), acknowledging a marketing mastery while maintaining a serious treatment, returning to the societal and political issues surrounding wokism in the USA: "Mars has clearly won this round of the cultural war, which is not the case in the USA." The French papers then point out that Mars is not the only company involved in this way in American or international domestic politics (Coca-Cola).

5   Conclusion: Advertising Literacy and Brand Conversation

This M&M's controversy is interesting, not only because it reveals an aspect of American political life in the classic sense of the term but also because M&M's is a brand that has been confronted with advertising digital literacy for a long time and knows how to deal with it.

5.1   M&M's and Advertising Digital Literacy: A Long Relationship

A semio-communicational analysis of M&M's Facebook accounts between 2015 and 2019 has enabled us to show that their participants and subscribers were, for many of them, fully aware of the advertising character of the posted messages and that communication professionals were in charge of participating, on behalf of the brand, in these exchanges and produce them (Berthelot-Guiet, 2015; Berthelot-Guiet, 2019). The brand is omnipresent, and its discursive content is very closely linked to its advertising discourse in traditional media. The messages posted online are, in fact, variations on their advertising show, and those who react or comment on them express their appreciation of the "show" in writing, often with simple interjections, the written expression of the joy of the show and laughter, and emojis representing applause and laughter. The M&M's Facebook pages were ultimately a hyper-advertising production in which the brand was omnipresent, with discursive content strongly linked to their advertising discourse. The advertising spectacle is so obvious that participants refer to the "authors" of these messages as marketing and advertising professionals: "Simultaneous faint, candle falls to the floor…. The absolute best M&M commercial ever!!!!!!" "every time it's a hit… You, advertisers, are crazy." The hyperadvertising nature of these brand communications attracts participants willing to voluntarily receive, several times a week, advertising content from brands they have chosen. We cannot know whether they are all consumers and/or buyers of these brands, but they are certainly voluntary consumers of their advertising discourse and signs.

An evaluation by the same audience of the advertising quality of the messages produced accompanies this consumption of brand signs. Commentators can make aesthetic, narrative, or even strategic judgments about what they consider good advertising for the brand. The advertising spectacle goes hand in hand with developing an amateur critique of advertising productions that bears witness to an advertising culture. These kinds of remarks do not go unheeded, as the M&M's brand chose to highlight during the final of the 2022 Super Bowl. The brand produced its usual annual advertising film and a film featuring film critics singing the praises of an unseen film until one of them points out that it is just an advert and is put in his place by the others. The play on the confusion between short films and commercials, available on the mmschocolate Facebook page and YouTube channel, is well done.

When participants write to the "authors" of these messages and not to the brand, they refer to them by their profession (advertisers), fully recognizing the advertising nature of these communications. Literacy in action shows that participants can appreciate a brand and its advertising enough to choose to register on a social media site and receive their chosen advertising content several times a week. An evaluation by the same audience of the advertising quality of the messages produced often accompanies this consumption of brand signs. This demonstrates a capacity for aesthetic, narrative, and even strategic judgment regarding what can be considered good advertising for a specific brand (Berthelot-Guiet, 2020). The advertising show is thus accompanied by an amateur critique rooted in an advertising culture. Audiences interact with brands on social media in an informed and consensual way. This literacy is double-edged, however, as the general public has quickly realized that the presence of brands on social media makes it easy to express criticism or complaints about them to a wide audience. This is why, for some brands, social media has become the site of a new type of "permanent" crisis communication.

5.2   Advertising Show, Social and Political Conversation

Over the year, M&M's dropped most of its advertising shows and deployed a completely different form of content, close to that of many other brands. The brand's posts mainly presented the different flavors and pastry recipes incorporating the candies, asking participants about their preferences and even getting them to vote. The conversation had thus become a classic promotional pitch. In this context, the non-explicit choice to return to showmanship by staging a brand amid live crisis communication is noteworthy.

However, the choices made by the brand's communications department are far from trivial: the discourse is situated in a classic register of tactical existence discourse, provocation, and commentary on the polemics underway in American society around the "woke" question. The brand initially indicated that it was giving in to conservative polarization. The brand then went beyond the social issue to the political level, in the dual sense of political politics and city life management. The hoax makes a mockery of the anti-woke rhetoric and the pressure that a section of the American political class exerts on star brands in such cases.

The revelation of the hoax during the Superbowl final and the triumphant return of the mascots make a mockery of the issues that run through society. This raises the question of a brand's legitimacy to intervene in politics and policy. Where Benetton had largely failed and abandoned its increasingly socially and politically engaged ads, M&M's usual light-hearted, humorous show tone allows it to hold a discourse that would be difficult for any other brand to bear.

When, in the 1990s, Benetton sought to shock in order to awaken social and political awareness but failed to win the assent of receivers, other brands, more discreetly, began to advertise with "the means of expression of the political sphere" and taking over the source of political debate and "this shift from the commercial to the political is in itself an important indicator of changing attitudes." [15].

What is more, the strong regeneration of the brand's speeches and follower participation on social media showed, from the very first days, the extent to which a large proportion of participants were not fooled, calling the brand's choices a joke or a hoax in the run-up to the Superbowl, and demonstrating a high level of digital advertising literacy. The type of discursive relationships established by the brand over many years makes it possible, despite the evolution towards a more promotional form, for communications teams to produce this complex advertising form and, above all, to make it acceptable because it is subject to comment and the exercise of literacy. These few days in the life of M&M's mascots on social media show that brands claim legitimacy to intervene in the societal and political field and that their claim is understood and discussed by their followers, who demonstrate a strong advertising literacy.

This shows a considerable deployment of digital advertising literacy around M&M's. Where followers used to show signs of appreciation for an advertising show (2015–2020), we now find a much broader judgment on the legitimacy of speaking out in the societal and political field and the value given to a brand's discourse in this area. Participants quickly remind others that they are talking about sweets, cartoons, etc. and that they need to keep their wits about them. It is all part of the show, but to be taken precisely as such, with hindsight. Perhaps this answers Jeanneret's questions more positively than we could have predicted: Better still, are we letting advertisers "play" on the founding values of the Republic and democracy [...]? Can advertising dispense us from analyzing the political situation, satiating us with clichés and fantasies when we urgently need to act, to invent new practices, new forms of democracy? Can advertising dispense us from analyzing the political situation? [16].

In conclusion, an analysis of the presence of certain brands on digital social media shows that brands strongly activate both types of power of representation in these systems. Through publicity, they achieve a form of ubiquity and omnipresence in everyday life. This power of presence is crucial and gives them access to the second stage of power of representation, according to Marin: "power of the institution, authorization, and legitimization as the result of the reflexive operation of the device on itself."

Conversation, aka advertising, is, therefore, a logic of power.

References

1. Meyriat, J.: Dimensions sociales du document, Sciences de la société, 68 (2006)
2. Barthes, R.: Mythologies. The Noonday Press, New York (1991)
3. Baudrillard, J.: The System of Objects. Verso, London (1996)
4. Berthelot-Guiet, K.: Paroles de Pub. La Vie Triviale de la Publicité, Le Havre, Éditions Non Standard (2013)

5. Fuat-Firat, A., Dholakia, N.: Consuming People, From Political Economy to Theaters of Consumption. Routledge, London (1998)
6. de Certeau, M.: The Practice of Everyday Life. University of California Press, Berkeley (1984)
7. Semprini, A.: Analyser la communication. L'Harmattant, Paris (1996)
8. Berthelot-Guiet, K.: The digital "Advertising Call": an archeology of advertising literacy. In: Meiselwitz, G. (eds.) Social Computing and Social Media. Participation, User Experience, Consumer Experience, and Applications of Social Computing. HCII 2020. Lecture Notes in Computer Science(), vol. 12195. Springer, Cham (2020). https://doi.org/10.1007/978-3-030-49576-3_21
9. Benjamin, W.: The Arcade Project. Belknap Press (1982)
10. Floch, J.M.: La voie des logos. Le face-à-face des logos IBM et Apple. Identités visuelles, Paris, PUF, pp. 43–78 (1995)
11. Patrin-Leclère, V., Marti de Montety, C., Berthelot-Guiet, K.: La fin de la publicité. Tours et contours de la dépublicitarisation, Le Bord de l'eau, Paris (2014)
12. Hartmann, W., Klapper.: Super Bowl Ads. Market. Sci. 37(1), 78–96 (2017)
13. McAllister, M.: Super Bowl advertising as a commercial celebration. Commun. Rev. 3(4), 403–428 (1999)
14. O'Barr, W.: Super bowl commercials: America's annual festival of advertising A1. Adv. Soc. Rev. 13(1) (2012)
15. Souchier, E.: La publicité comme détournement du politique. Commun. Lang. 93, 36 (1992)
16. Jeanneret, Y.: Manipuler les idées et les désirs, Publicité et politique, Le monde diplomatique, p. 28, Décembre 1994

Emoji Retrieval from Gibberish or Garbled Social Media Text: A Novel Methodology and a Case Study

Shuqi Cui, Nirmalya Thakur[✉], and Audrey Poon

Department of Computer Science, Emory University, Atlanta, GA 30322, USA
{nicole.cui,audrey.poon}@emory.edu, nirmalyathakur@ieee.org

Abstract. Emojis, considered an integral aspect of social media conversations, are widely used on almost all social media platforms. However, social media data may be noisy and may also include gibberish or garbled text which is difficult to detect and work with. Most naïve data preprocessing approaches recommend removing such gibberish or garbled text from social media posts before performing any form of data analysis or before passing such data to any machine learning model. However, it is important to note that such gibberish or garbled text may have been an emoji(s) in the original social media post(s) and failure to retrieve the actual emoji(s) may result in the loss or lack of contextual meaning of the analyzed social media data. The work presented in this paper aims to address this challenge by proposing a three-step reverse engineering-based novel methodology for retrieving emojis from garbled or gibberish text in social media posts. The development of this methodology also helped to unravel the reasons that could lead to the generation of gibberish or garbled text related to data mining of social media posts. To evaluate the effectiveness of the proposed methodology, the model was applied to a dataset of 509,248 Tweets about the Mpox outbreak, that has been used in about 30 prior works in this field, none of which were able to retrieve the emojis in the original Tweets from the gibberish text present in this dataset. Using our methodology, we were able to retrieve a total of 157,748 emojis present in 76,914 Tweets in this dataset by processing the gibberish or garbled text. The effectiveness of this methodology has been discussed in the paper through the presentation of multiple metrics related to text readability and text coherence which include the Flesch Reading Ease, Flesch Kincaid Grade Score, Coleman Liau index, Automated Readability Index, Dale Chall Readability Score, Text Standard, and Reading Time for the Tweets before and after the application of the methodology to the Tweets. The results showed that the application of this methodology to the Tweets improved the readability and coherence scores. Finally, as a case study, the frequency of emoji usage in these Tweets about the Mpox outbreak was analyzed and the results are presented.

Keywords: Emoji · Social Media · Big Data · Data Analysis · Natural Language Processing

1   Introduction

The emergence of social media platforms coupled with their ubiquitousness and inter-connectedness has resulted in a tremendous increase in the amount of time individuals have been spending on social media in the last decade and a half [1]. On average, a person spends 143 min per day on social media [2] and owns 8.4 social media accounts [3]. On a global scale, about 5 billion people use social media platforms [4]. This extensive adoption of social media results in the generation of tremendous amounts of Big Data. Mining and analysis of this Big Data has attracted the attention of researchers from different disciplines for various use cases such as understanding, interpreting, anticipating, and predicting the patterns of social media discourse, sentiment analysis, subjectivity analysis, opinion mining, topic modeling, misinformation detection, and toxicity analysis, just to name a few [5–8]. Emojis, considered an integral aspect of social media conversations, are widely used on almost all social media platforms [9]. For example, on Facebook Messenger more than 900 million emojis are sent every day, half of all the comments on Instagram include an emoji, and one in five Tweets includes an emoji [10, 11]. However, social media data is noisy [12] and prior works in this field have also stated that the issues with social media data include gibberish or garbled text [13, 14] which is difficult to detect [15]. In this context, we define "gibberish" or "garbled" text as text that contains characters outside the character set of all human-readable languages and such characters cannot be comprehended by humans. Table 1 represents a few Tweets that contain garbled or gibberish text for further clarification of the definition.

Table 1. Examples of Tweets that contain gibberish or garbled text

Tweet #1: Actually the K is silent. It is pronounced MONEYPOX ðŸ□µðŸ™ŠðŸ™^ðŸ'°ðŸ'°ðŸ'°ðŸ'°ðŸ'°ðŸ'°ðŸ'°ðŸ'°ðŸ'µðŸ''ðŸ'°ðŸ''ðŸ'µð Ÿ'µðŸ''ðŸ'¶ðŸ'¶ðŸ'°ðŸ''ðŸ'µðŸ''ðŸ''ðŸ''ðŸ''ðŸ'µðŸ'°ðŸ'°ðŸ'°ðŸ'°ðŸ'°ð Ÿ'°ðŸ'°ðŸ'°ðŸ'°ðŸ'°ðŸ'°ðŸ'µðŸ'µðŸ'µðŸ'µðŸ'µðŸ'°ðŸ'°ðŸ'µðŸ'µðŸ'°
Tweet #2: @MaureenStroud @MatthewNewell67 @nuhope2022 @handmadekathy @JimeeLiberty @volpiranyas @pawley_robert @PremChamp1 @PLHartungRN @FvckYourFear @Cdoglover1 @BlueBear0386 @doom37455413 @provaxtexan @The_Aussie_Luke @GhostDancer2022 @TsuDhoNimh @ogilville1 @AngryFleas @BadC19TestTakes @LizNYC13 @mcfunny @Chelle389 @SkepticalMutant @swedishchf @KStateTurk @itisjustmebabe @YellowstoneRan1 @Nockit1 @andylumm @KathyGa28615606 @richykirsh @theanswer50 @HighJanky @GeoffSchuler @NoMisinfoToday @ConsequentialBr @JonDaley7 @TonyBaduy @noonienoodie @doritmi @sammy44231 @zeetubes @JonathanHannah @Monstercoyliar @tomsirolimus @SallyJiggles @AndrewLazarus4 @butterednoodIe It seems that every few weeks they have something new and ridiculous. The whole monkey pox thing that someone tried to pin on the vaccines was just..ðŸ˜³ðŸ™„ðŸ¤¡ðŸ˜µâ€□ðŸ'«ðŸ˜µâ€□ðŸ'«ðŸ˜µâ€□ðŸ'«ðŸ˜µâ€□ðŸ'«ðŸ˜µâ€□ðŸ'«

(continued)

Table 1. (*continued*)

Tweet #3: Now they got something called monkeypox that's out ðŸ¤¦ðŸ¾â€â™€ï¸ðŸ¤¦ðŸ¾â€â™€ï¸ðŸ¤¦ðŸ¾â€â™€ï¸ðŸ¤¦ðŸ¾â€â™€ï¸ðŸ¤¦ðŸ¾â€â™€ï¸ðŸ¤¦ðŸ¾â€â™€ï¸
Tweet #4: Monkey pox whispers in work. Anyone fooled by this fear a second time ðŸ¤¦â€â™€ï¸ðŸ¤¦â€â™€ï¸ðŸ¤¦â€â™€ï¸ðŸ¤¦â€â™€ï¸ðŸ¤¦â€â™€ï¸ðŸ¤¦â€â™€ï¸ðŸ¤¦â€â™€ï¸
Tweet #5: @GBNEWS Of course he would ðŸ™„is his relevance waning like the fear of the rona has cue monkey poxðŸ¤ðŸ¤ðŸ¤ðŸ¤ðŸ¤ðŸ¤ðŸ¤ðŸ¤ðŸ¤ðŸ¤ðŸ¤®ðŸ®ðŸ®ðŸ®ðŸ®ðŸ®ðŸ®ðŸ®ðŸ®ðŸ®ðŸ’ŠðŸ’ŠðŸ’ŠðŸ’ŠðŸ’ŠðŸ’ŠðŸ’ŠðŸ’ŠðŸ’ŠðŸ’ŠðŸ’Š

In the last few years, there have been multiple works related to the detection or prediction of emojis in social media texts (reviewed in Sect. 2). The ongoing and past Mpox outbreaks in different parts of the world [16–19] and conversations about the same on social media platforms have also been investigated in multiple research projects in this field (reviewed in Sect. 2). However, the methodologies proposed in prior works in this field for the prediction or detection of emojis are not highly accurate as none of those algorithms identify the root cause that led to the generation of a gibberish character(s) instead of an emoji in the mined version of a social media post. Furthermore, none of the prior works related to the analysis of social media posts about the ongoing and past Mpox outbreaks have focused on the retrieval of emojis from gibberish or garbled text. Addressing this research challenge serves as the main motivation for this work. The rest of this paper is organized as follows. In Sect. 2, a review of recent works in this field is presented. Section 3 discusses the methodology which is followed by the results in Sect. 4. Section 4 is followed by the conclusion section which concludes the paper and summarizes the scope of future work in this field.

2   Literature Review

The work of Chouhan et al. [20] showed that data gathered from live-streaming platforms frequently involves emojis, emotes, and emoticons, and understanding the usage of the same is vital in comprehending the discussions on live-streaming platforms. Kumar et al. [21] utilized machine learning and deep learning algorithms to predict emojis in text-based data where the emojis were not mined correctly or were missing. Nusrat et al. [22] used Bert to predict the most appropriate emoji for a given text. Their model achieved an overall accuracy of 75% and was more accurate as compared to other emoji prediction models at that time. The work of Kone et al. [23] concluded that emojis are a "visual language" that enables users to communicate their feelings. Ranjan et al. [24] studied the relationship between English words and emojis to predict the latter. They trained their model using concepts of Multinomial Naive Bayes and LSTMs to predict emojis in Tweets. Stoikos et al. [25] utilized a BERTmoticon model to predict missing emojis in social media texts. They applied the model to Tweets about COVID-19. The findings of their work showed that since WHO's declaration of COVID-19 as a global pandemic, there has been a spike in the usage of emojis on social media platforms, specifically emojis that are associated with feelings of sadness. Inan et al. [26] used concepts of classification from machine learning to predict emojis in Tweets. They tested their model on a dataset of Tweets and their approach achieved a 0.901 F1 score. Kumar et al. [27] proposed an on-device pipeline to insert emojis in appropriate locations in texts based on concepts of semantic analysis. Barbieri et al. [28] developed a methodology that used concepts of word embedding in vectorial space to predict emojis in social media texts. A similar approach was used by Gupta et al. [29]. However, the work of Gupta et al. [29] also incorporated the time and location information associated with social media texts to improve the accuracy of emoji predictions. Their methodology achieved an overall accuracy of 73.32%. Shobana et al. [30] developed a deep neural network for predicting emojis in texts where the underlying emojis were missing or not mined correctly. Their methodology used concepts of text semantic analysis and achieved an overall accuracy of 86%. Barbieri et al. [31] studied the semantics behind emojis and developed a model for the prediction of emojis in tweets. Zhao et al. [32] developed a dataset of Emoji-embedded Tweets and post-response pairs to study their learning method for persona-aware emoji-embedded dialogue.

Sv et al. [33] studied public attitudes towards the Mpox outbreak. They performed sentiment analysis on 556,403 English Tweets about the Mpox outbreak, published between June 1, 2022, and June 25, 2022. The findings showed that the percentage of neutral, positive, and negative tweets was 41.6%, 28.82%, and 23.01%, respectively. A similar study of sentiment analysis of Tweets about the Mpox outbreak was performed by Ng et al. [34]. They used 352,182 tweets published between May 6, 2022, and July 23, 2022. Cooper et al. [35] analyzed Tweets about Mpox published between May 1, 2022, and July 23, 2022. The findings of their work showed that 48,330 tweets were written by LGBTQ + individuals or advocates and the most common sentiment present in these Tweets was fear or sadness. Iparraguirre-Villanueva et al. [36] developed a sentiment analysis model using CNN and LSTM to perform sentiment analysis of Tweets about Mpox. Their model achieved an overall accuracy of 83%. D'souza et al. [37] studied 70,832 Tweets published between May 01, 2022, and September 07, 2022, that contained the terms #monkeypox, #MPVS, #stigma, or #LGBTQ +. The results of their study showed that the LGBTQ + community faced hate on Twitter as a result of stigma, misinformation, and misinterpretation related to the Mpox outbreak. Zuhanda et al. [38] analyzed a dataset of 5000 Tweets about Mpox published on August 5, 2022. The findings showed that fear was the most prevalent emotion expressed in the Tweets. Knudsen et al. [39] studied Tweets about Mpox published between May 18, 2022, and September 19, 2022. The findings of their work showed that 82% of the Tweets expressed incorrect information about Mpox. Bengesi et al. [40] studied Tweets about Mpox for sentiment analysis. They proposed a methodology that used TextBlob annotation, Lemmatization, Vectorization, and a Support Vector Machine for performing sentiment analysis. Their approach achieved an overall accuracy of 93.48%. Farahat et al. [41] performed sentiment analysis of 8532 Tweets about Mpox published between May 22, 2022, and August 5, 2022. The findings of their work showed that the percentage of neutral, positive, and negative tweets was 48%, 37%, and 15%, respectively.

In summary, even though multiple research works have been conducted in this field thus far, two major research gaps still remain:

- Emojis may be represented as garbled or gibberish text during the data mining process of posts (for example: Tweets) from social media platforms. The process of predicting emojis to replace gibberish text has achieved considerable attention from the scientific community in the last few years. However, the developed algorithms are not highly accurate as they don't investigate or identify the root cause that led to the generation of a gibberish character(s) instead of an emoji(s) in the mined version of a social media post. So, the predicted emoji(s) by the existing algorithms may not always be correct. As emojis are a crucial aspect of communication on social media platforms, incorrect emojis may completely change the meaning of a sentence. For example, if we consider these two statements – "Did your friend really die? 😂" and "Did your friend really die? 😭". The first sentence contains the "face with tears of joy" emoji. It is an emoji that represents crying with laughter facial expression. The second statement contains the "loudly crying face" emoji. This emoji depicts a face with an open mouth and streams of heavy tears flowing from closed eyes. In this context, between the two emojis, the "loudly crying face" emoji would be appropriate. However, if an algorithm (incorrectly) predicts the "face with tears of joy" emoji at the end of this sentence, it would be inappropriate for the given context.
- Sentiment analysis of Tweets continues to attract the attention of researchers from different disciplines. Considering emojis is crucial for performing sentiment analysis [42–47]. Most naïve data preprocessing approaches recommend removing gibberish or garbled texts from social media posts (for example: Tweets) before performing any form of data analysis or before passing such data to any machine learning model [48, 49]. While it is true that the gibberish or garbled text would have a negative effect on the data analysis task or on the training of any machine learning algorithm (not just for sentiment analysis), it is important to note that the gibberish text or garbled text contains meaning (for instance, it may represent one or more emojis) which would get lost if such data was directly deleted. Prior works in this field, for example [50], have followed such naïve data preprocessing approaches i.e. ignoring the garbled or gibberish text in social media content prior to data analysis and machine learning-based model development.

Addressing these gaps with an aim to contribute to the advancement of research in this field, serves as the main motivation for this research work. A detailed discussion of the methodology is presented in Sect. 3.

3 Methodology

This section presents the methodology that was developed to address the research challenge of retrieving emojis from gibberish or garbled text by proposing a three-step reverse engineering-based novel methodology. The first step of this approach uses concepts of Natural Language Processing and Information Retrieval to detect garbled or gibberish text in social media posts. The second step uses concepts of Reverse Engineering, Data Analysis, and Information Processing to infer the underlying cause for the generation of the garbled or gibberish text in a social media post. The final step reverse engineers the process to restore the emojis as were present in the original post on a social media platform. A detailed discussion of the working of this methodology is presented later in this section. The flowchart shown in Fig. 1 presents an overview of this methodology as well as an overview of the research work and the case study that was performed.

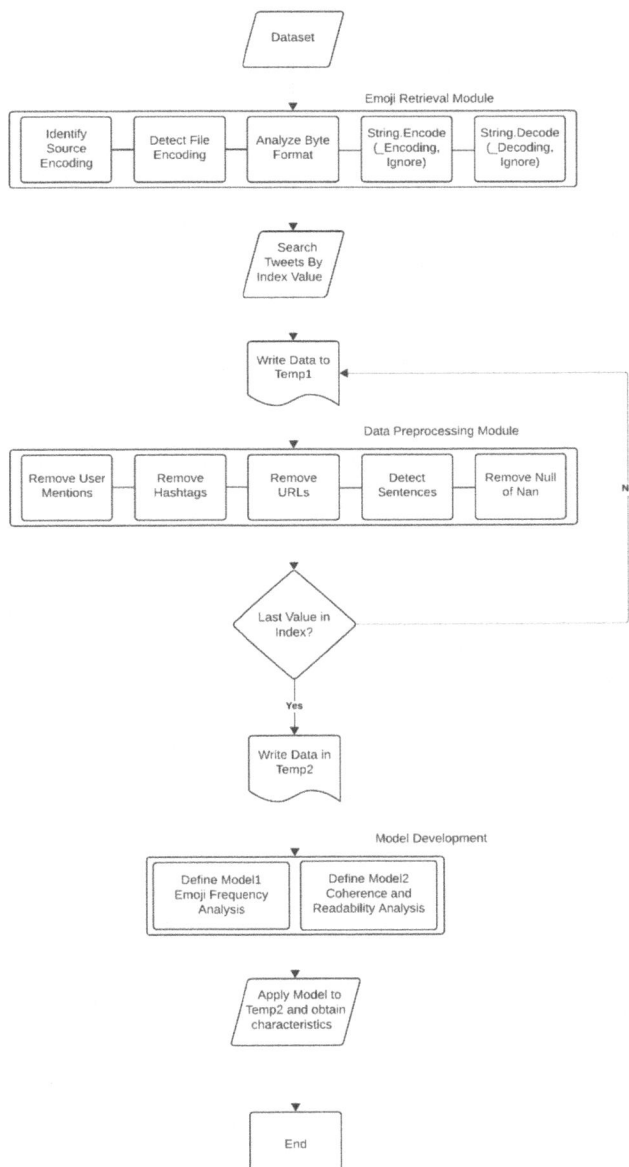

Fig. 1. A flowchart that represents an overview of the methodology and the specifics of the case study that was performed.

The development of this methodology also helped to unravel the reasons that could lead to the generation of gibberish or garbled text related to data mining of social media text. The work showed that gibberish or garbled text may be generated by computer programs or algorithms during the data mining process from a social media platform due to one or more of the following scenarios:

- Text from social media platforms is decoded in a format different from the source text during the data mining process.
- Mismatch of default encoding across applications or platforms or programs during the data analysis process, or machine learning algorithm development process where social media data was used.
- The application of incorrect encoding for storage or retrieval of data files containing social media data.

To evaluate the effectiveness of the proposed reverse engineering-based methodology for retrieving emojis from garbled or gibberish text, we wrote a Python program to implement and apply the same to a dataset of 509,248 Tweets about the Mpox outbreak published on Twitter between May 21, 2022, to November 11, 2022 [51]. This dataset was specifically selected for the evaluation of this methodology for multiple reasons. First, several Tweets in this dataset contain gibberish or garbled text. Second, even though this dataset has been used in about 30 prior works involving data analysis of Tweets related to the Mpox outbreak, for example [52–55], none of those works focused on retrieving emojis from the gibberish or garbled text which is present in several Tweets in this dataset. Third, different parts of the world are currently experiencing an outbreak of Mpox including the United States where the number of cases in 2024 is nearly double as compared to the number of cases of Mpox in the United States around the same time last year [56, 57].

As shown in Fig. 1, the Emoji Retrieval Module contains multiple functions that are associated with specific tasks. These tasks include identifying source encoding, detecting file encoding, analyzing byte format, performing string encoding, and performing string decoding. In this context, the source encoding refers to the encoding used in the character set (for example: English) used to publish content on a social media platform (for example: Twitter) that belongs to the list of encoding patterns accepted by that platform. Here, "file encoding" refers to the type of encoding in the output file(s) by a data mining program, algorithm, or software to retrieve that content from that social media platform. Upon identification of any garbled or gibberish text, the second step of our methodology uses a brute force approach to identify the exact cause of the garbled or gibberish text and the exact encoding patterns that represent the values of "source encoding" and "file encoding". More specifically, in this step, the algorithm iterates through a list of all encoding patterns in Python 3.12 to identify the value of the "file encoding". Table 2 shows these codecs by name and the languages for which the encoding is likely used [58]. For the development of this approach, the encodings supported by Python 3.12 were used for two reasons. First, Python 3.12 was the most recent version of Python at the time of development of this methodology. Second, the list of encodings supported by Python 3.12 is more than the list of encodings supported by old versions of Python [59–63]. Upon identification of the "file encoding", our algorithm uses a reverse engineering-based methodology to identify the source encoding. More specifically, it processes emojis using every encoding-to-encoding conversion using the value of the "file encoding" to determine the value of the "source encoding". Thereafter, using the values of the "source encoding" and "file encoding" it reverse engineers the process to retrieve the gibberish or garbled text to its original form that represented one or more emojis. The remainder of Fig. 1 shows the steps that we performed for the case study on this dataset to evaluate the effectiveness of our methodology. The results that highlight the effectiveness of this methodology are presented in Sect. 4.

Table 2. Encodings supported by Python 3.12

Codec	Languages
ascii	English
big5	Traditional Chinese
big5hkscs	Traditional Chinese
cp037	English
cp273	German
cp424	Hebrew
cp437	English
cp500	Western Europe
cp720	Arabic
cp737	Greek
cp775	Baltic languages
cp850	Western Europe
cp852	Central and Eastern Europe
cp855	Bulgarian, Byelorussian, Macedonian, Russian, Serbian
cp856	Hebrew
cp857	Turkish
cp858	Western Europe
cp860	Portuguese
cp861	Icelandic
cp862	Hebrew
cp863	Canadian
cp864	Arabic
cp865	Danish, Norwegian
cp866	Russian
cp869	Greek
cp874	Thai

(continued)

Table 2. (*continued*)

Codec	Languages
cp875	Greek
cp932	Japanese
cp949	Korean
cp950	Traditional Chinese
cp1006	Urdu
cp1026	Turkish
cp1125	Ukrainian
cp1140	Western Europe
cp1250	Central and Eastern Europe
cp1251	Bulgarian, Byelorussian, Macedonian, Russian, Serbian
cp1252	Western Europe
cp1253	Greek
cp1254	Turkish
cp1255	Hebrew
cp1256	Arabic
cp1257	Baltic languages
cp1258	Vietnamese
euc_jp	Japanese
euc_jis_2004	Japanese
euc_jisx0213	Japanese
euc_kr	Korean
gb2312	Simplified Chinese
gbk	Unified Chinese
gb18030	Unified Chinese
hz	Simplified Chinese
iso2022_jp	Japanese
iso2022_jp_1	Japanese
iso2022_jp_2	Japanese, Korean, Simplified Chinese, Western Europe, Greek
iso2022_jp_2004	Japanese
iso2022_jp_3	Japanese
iso2022_jp_ext	Japanese
iso2022_kr	Korean
latin_1	Western Europe

(*continued*)

Table 2. (*continued*)

Codec	Languages
iso8859_2	Central and Eastern Europe
iso8859_3	Esperanto, Maltese
iso8859_4	Baltic languages
iso8859_5	Bulgarian, Byelorussian, Macedonian, Russian, Serbian
iso8859_6	Arabic
iso8859_7	Greek
iso8859_8	Hebrew
iso8859_9	Turkish
iso8859_10	Nordic languages
iso8859_11	Thai languages
iso8859_13	Baltic languages
iso8859_14	Celtic languages
iso8859_15	Western Europe
iso8859_16	South-Eastern Europe
johab	Korean
koi8_r	Russian
koi8_t	Tajik
koi8_u	Ukrainian
kz1048	Kazakh
mac_cyrillic	Bulgarian, Byelorussian, Macedonian, Russian, Serbian
mac_greek	Greek
mac_iceland	Icelandic
mac_latin2	Central and Eastern Europe
mac_roman	Western Europe
mac_turkish	Turkish
ptcp154	Kazakh
shift_jis	Japanese
shift_jis_2004	Japanese
shift_jisx0213	Japanese
utf_32	all languages
utf_32_be	all languages
utf_32_le	all languages
utf_16	all languages

(*continued*)

Table 2. (*continued*)

Codec	Languages
utf_16_be	all languages
utf_16_le	all languages
utf_7	all languages
utf_8	all languages
utf_8_sig	all languages

4   Results and Discussions

This section presents the results of this research work. To show the effectiveness of the proposed three-step reverse engineering-based novel methodology for retrieving emojis from garbled or gibberish text in social media posts, we have presented Table 3. In Table 3, we revisit Table 1 and show the processing of those Tweets using our methodology that results in the retrieval of all the emojis (from the gibberish or garbled text) as were present in these original Tweets on Twitter.

In a similar way, using this methodology we were able to retrieve all the emojis from the garbled or gibberish text in this dataset. There were a total of 76914 Tweets containing garbled or gibberish text and upon passing the same through our methodology we were able to retrieve the actual emojis that were used in these Tweets. A total of 157748 emojis were retrieved during this process. We evaluated the effectiveness of the application of this methodology to this dataset using multiple metrics related to text readability and text coherence which include the Flesch Reading Ease, Flesch Kincaid Grade Score, Coleman Liau index, Automated Readability Index, Dale Chall Readability Score, Text Standard, and Reading Time for the Tweets before and after the application of the methodology. Twitter allows a user to publish a Tweet containing up to 280 characters and users may or may not use all the characters. In fact, studies have shown that depending on the subject matter users on Twitter may post short or long Tweets [64, 65]. Therefore, it is crucial to investigate the performance of our methodology on Tweets of different lengths (in terms of the number of characters). So, we grouped the Tweets in this dataset into four groups as outlined below:

- Group 1 = length of Tweets less than or equal to 70 characters
- Group 2 = length of Tweets greater than or equal to 71 characters but less than 141 characters
- Group 3 = length of Tweets greater than or equal to 141 characters but less than 211 characters
- Group 4 = length of Tweets greater than 211 characters

Figure 2 shows the evaluation of these metrics for all these groups before applying our methodology and Fig. 3 shows the evaluation of these metrics for all these groups after applying our methodology.

Table 3. Results of applying our methodology to the Tweets from Table 1

Tweet #1 from Table 1 (before applying our methodology): Actually the K is silent. It is pronounced MONEYPOX

ðŸ□µðŸ™ŠðŸ™ˆðŸ’ºðŸ’ºðŸ’ºðŸ’ºðŸ’ºðŸ’ºðŸ’ºðŸ’ºðŸ’µðŸ’ðŸ’ºðŸ’ðŸ’µðŸ'µðŸ'ðŸ'¶ðŸ'¶ðŸ'ºðŸ'·ðŸ'µðŸ'ðŸ'ðŸ'ðŸ'ðŸ'µðŸ'ºðŸ'ºðŸ'ºðŸ'ºðŸ'ºðŸ'ºðŸ'ºðŸ'ºðŸ'ºðŸ'ºðŸ'µðŸ'µðŸ'µðŸ'µðŸ'µðŸ'ºðŸ'ºðŸ'µðŸ'µðŸ'ºðŸ'º

Tweet #1, from Table 1, after processing the same using our methodology:
Actually the K is silent It is pronounced MONEYPOX

Tweet #2 from Table 1 (before applying our methodology): @MaureenStroud @MatthewNewell67 @nuhope2022 @handmadekathy @JimeeLiberty @volpiranyas @pawley_robert @PremChamp1 @PLHartungRN @FvckYourFear @Cdoglover1 @BlueBear0386 @doom37455413 @provaxtexan @The_Aussie_Luke @GhostDancer2022 @TsuDhoNimh @ogilville1 @AngryFleas @BadC19TestTakes @LizNYC13 @mcfunny @Chelle389 @SkepticalMutant @swedishchf @KStateTurk @itisjustmebabe @YellowstoneRan1 @Nockit1 @andylumm @KathyGa28615606 @richykirsh @theanswer50 @HighJanky @GeoffSchuler @NoMisinfoToday @ConsequentialBr @JonDaley7 @TonyBaduy @noonienoodie @doritmi @sammy44231 @zeetubes @JonathanHannah @Monstercoyliar @tomsirolimus @SallyJiggles @AndrewLazarus4 @butterednoodIe It seems that every few weeks they have something new and ridiculous. The whole monkey pox thing that someone tried to pin on the vaccines was just..ðŸ˜³ðŸ™„„ðŸ¤¡ðŸ˜µâ€□ðŸ'«ðŸ˜µâ€□ðŸ'«ðŸ˜µâ€□ðŸ'«ðŸ˜µâ€□ðŸ'«ðŸ˜µâ€□ðŸ'«

Tweet #2, from Table 1, after processing the same using our methodology:
@MaureenStroud @MatthewNewell67 @nuhope2022 @handmadekathy @JimeeLiberty @volpiranyas @pawley_robert @PremChamp1 @PLHartungRN @FvckYourFear @Cdoglover1 @BlueBear0386 @doom37455413 @provaxtexan @The_Aussie_Luke @GhostDancer2022 @TsuDhoNimh @ogilville1 @AngryFleas @BadC19TestTakes @LizNYC13 @mcfunny @Chelle389 @SkepticalMutant @swedishchf @KStateTurk @itisjustmebabe @YellowstoneRan1 @Nockit1 @andylumm @KathyGa28615606 @richykirsh @theanswer50 @HighJanky @GeoffSchuler @NoMisinfoToday @ConsequentialBr @JonDaley7 @TonyBaduy @noonienoodie @doritmi @sammy44231 @zeetubes @JonathanHannah @Monstercoyliar @tomsirolimus @SallyJiggles @AndrewLazarus4 @butterednoodIe It seems that every few weeks they have something new and ridiculous. The whole monkey pox thing that someone tried to pin on the vaccines was just

---

Tweet #3 from Table 1 (before applying our methodology): Now they got something called monkeypox that's out
ðŸ¤¦ðŸ□¾â€□â™€Ì□ðŸ¤¦ðŸ□¾â€□â™€Ì□ðŸ¤¦ðŸ□¾â€□â™€Ì□ðŸ¤¦ðŸ□¾â€□â™€Ì□ðŸ¤¦ðŸ□¾â€□â™€Ì□ðŸ¤¦ðŸ□¾â€□â™€Ì□

Tweet #3, from Table 1, after processing the same using our methodology:
Now they got something called monkeypox thats out

(*continued*)

Table 3. (*continued*)

Tweet #4 from Table 1 (before applying our methodology): Monkey pox whispers in work. Anyone fooled by this fear a second time ðŸ¤¦â€â™€ï,ðŸ¤¦â€â™€ï,ðŸ¤¦â€â™€ï,ðŸ¤¦â€â™€ï,ðŸ¤¦â€â™€ï,ðŸ¤â€â™€ï,ðŸ¤¦â€â™€ï,ðŸ¤¦â€â™€ï,□
Tweet #4, from Table 1, after processing the same using our methodology: Monkey pox whispers in work Anyone fooled by this fear a second time 🤦‍♀🤦‍♀🤦‍♀🤦‍♀🤦‍♀🤦‍♀🤦‍♀🤦‍♀
Tweet #5 from Table 1 (before applying our methodology): @GBNEWS Of course he would ðŸ™,,is his relevance waning like the fear of the rona has cue monkey poxðŸ'¤ðŸ'¤ðŸ'¤ðŸ'¤ðŸ'¤ðŸ'¤ðŸ'¤ðŸ'¤ðŸ'¤ðŸ¤®ðŸ¤®ðŸ¤®ðŸ¤®ðŸ¤®ðŸ¤®ðŸ¤®ðŸ¤®ðŸ¤®ðŸ¤®ðŸ'‰ðŸ'‰ðŸ'‰ðŸ'‰ðŸ'‰ðŸ'‰ðŸ'‰ðŸ'‰ðŸ'‰ðŸ'‰ðŸ'‰ðŸ'‰
Tweet #5, from Table 1, after processing the same using our methodology: GBNEWS Of course he would 🙈 is his relevance waning like the fear of the rona has cue monkey pox 🧼🧼🧼🧼🧼🧼🧼🧼🧼🧼🧼🧼🤮🤮🤮🤮🤮🤮🤮🤮🤮🤮✏✏✏✏✏✏✏✏✏✏✏

These Tweets are presented here in "as is" form after obtaining the same from the Tweet IDs of the used dataset and after processing the same using the proposed methodology. These Tweets do not represent or reflect the views, opinions, beliefs, or political stances of the authors of this paper.

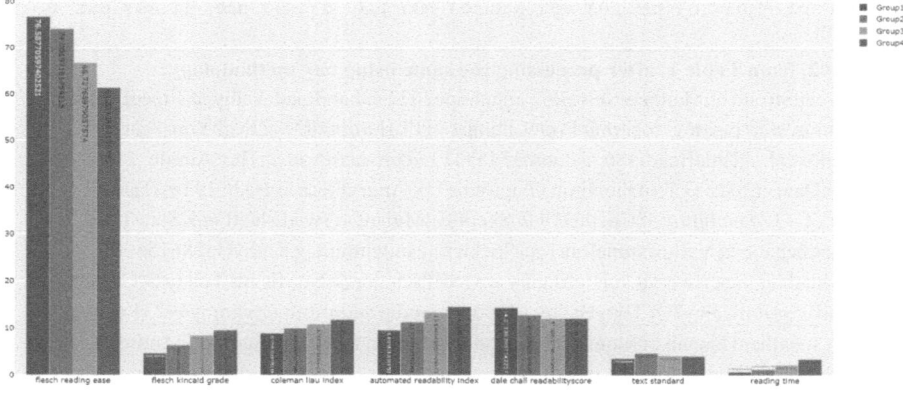

Fig. 2. Evaluation of different metrics before applying our methodology

The improvement of most of these metrics upon the application of our methodology indicates the effectiveness of the same related to text readability and coherence. For instance, for Group 1, the average Automated Readability Index improved from 9.41 to 6.15. The average Automated Readability Index is a number that approximates the grade level needed to comprehend a given text. In other words, for this metric, a lower score indicates better readability. Similarly, for Group 1, the average Dale Chall Readability Score changed from 14.21 to 10.59. The reading time for Group 1, Group 2, Group 3,

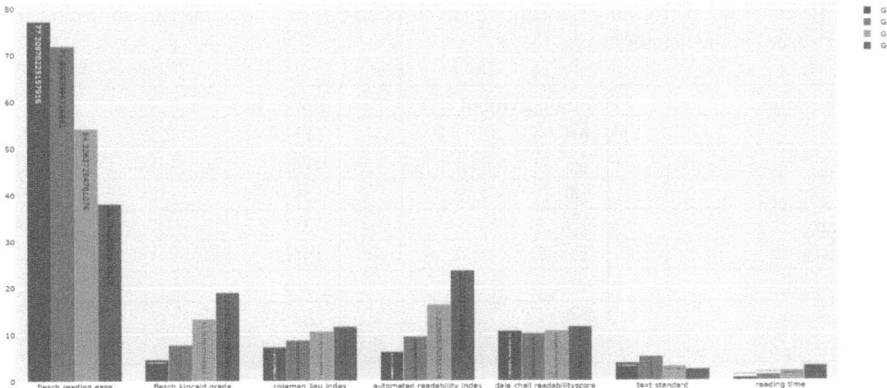

Fig. 3. Evaluation of different metrics after applying our methodology

and Group 4 before applying our methodology was 0.66, 1.24, 2.12, 3.38. After applying our methodology, the reading time for all these groups improved to 0.58, 1.19, 2.07, and 3.13, respectively.

To further support the scientific contributions of this work, we performed a frequency analysis of all the emojis present in this dataset as none of the prior works that used this dataset were able to retrieve any emoji(s) from the gibberish or garbled text present in the Tweets. The results of the same (top 40 emojis are shown for the paucity of space) are presented in Table 4.

The work presented in this paper has a couple of limitations. First, the second step of our methodology uses a brute force approach to identify the exact cause of the garbled or gibberish text and the exact encoding patterns that represent the values of "source encoding" and "file encoding". So, from the time complexity standpoint, there is scope for improvement in this regard which was not addressed in this paper. Second, the list of encodings supported by Python 3.12 was used for the development of this methodology as the encodings supported by Python 3.12 are more than old versions of Python. Python 3.12 was the most recent version of Python at the time of development of this methodology. However, future versions of Python may support a higher number of encodings. As any new encoding patterns that future versions of Python may support were not stated on python.org [66] at the time of development of this methodology, this probable limitation could not be addressed at this point.

Table 4. Results from performing frequency analysis of emojis (top 40 emojis are shown for the paucity of space) in the dataset

Emoji Name	Emoji Symbol	Frequency
joy	😂	11328
sob	😭	9120
rofl	🤣	6795
thinking	🤔	4217
facepalm	🤦	3038
male_sign	♂	2761
roll_eyes	🙄	2685
female_sign	♀	2680
weary	😩	2335
shrug	🤷	2240
woozy_face	🥴	2033
see_no_evil	🙈	1723
flushed	😳	1685
clown_face	🤡	1520
nauseated_face	🤢	1394
skull	💀	1388
speak_no_evil	🙊	1375
vomiting_face	🤮	1292
eyes	👀	1252
syringe	💉	1212
mask	😷	1079
unamused	😒	1053
point_down	👇	990
rotating_light	🚨	956
hear_no_evil	🙉	955
grimacing	😬	933
satisfied	😆	929
sweat_smile	😅	923
dizzy_face	😵	816
dizzy	💫	776
wink	😉	755
100	💯	753
upside_down_face	🙃	738
melting_face	🫠	708
microbe	🦠	692
tired_face	😫	627
raised_eyebrow	🤨	583
scream	😱	577
smiling_face_with_tear	🥲	572
zany_face	🤪	556

5   Conclusion

Emojis, an essential component of social media posts, are extensively used on almost all social media platforms. However, social media data is prone to noise, and prior works in this area have also acknowledged the presence of gibberish text in social media posts, that is difficult to identify and work with. In the recent past, multiple studies have focused on identifying and predicting the presence of emojis in social media posts containing gibberish text. However, those algorithms are not highly accurate as those algorithms do not investigate or identify the root cause for the generation of gibberish text in the mined version of the social media posts. Therefore, the emojis generated by these algorithms may not consistently align with the intended meaning of an analyzed social media post(s). Furthermore, emojis play a vital role in the development of various Natural Language Processing algorithms. Conventional data preprocessing approaches often advise the deletion of such gibberish or garbled text from social media posts, such as Tweets, prior to performing any data analysis or providing such posts as input to a machine learning model. In this context, it is crucial to note that such gibberish or garbled text may contain meaningful information, such as emojis, which would be lost if simply deleted.

The work presented in this paper aims to address this challenge by proposing a three-step reverse engineering-based novel methodology for retrieving emojis from garbled or gibberish text in social media posts. The development of this methodology also helped to unravel the reasons that could lead to the generation of gibberish or garbled text related to data mining of social media text. To evaluate the effectiveness of the proposed methodology, it was applied to a dataset of 509,248 Tweets about the Mpox outbreak which has been used in several prior works related to sentiment analysis and other analyses of Tweets about Mpox. However, none of those works retrieved the emojis from the garbled or gibberish text in this dataset. Upon applying our methodology to this dataset, we were able to successfully retrieve all the emojis from the garbled or gibberish text in this dataset. There were a total of 76914 Tweets containing garbled or gibberish text and upon passing the same through our methodology we were able to retrieve the actual emojis that were used in these Tweets. A total of 157748 emojis were retrieved during this process. The effectiveness of the application of this methodology to this dataset has been discussed in the paper through the presentation of multiple metrics related to text readability and text coherence which include the Flesch Reading Ease, Flesch Kincaid Grade Score, Coleman Liau index, Automated Readability Index, Dale Chall Readability Score, Text Standard, and Reading Time for the Tweets before and after the application of the methodology. The results showed that the application of this methodology to the Tweets improved the readability and coherence scores.

As per the best knowledge of the authors, no similar work has been performed in this field thus far. Future work would involve improving the time complexity and integrating the methodology as a Python package that can be imported into Python programs for emoji retrieval from gibberish or garbled texts in social media posts.

Disclosure of Interests. The authors have no competing interests to declare that are relevant to the content of this article.

References

1. Aichner, T., Grünfelder, M., Maurer, O., Jegeni, D.: Twenty-five years of social media: a review of social media applications and definitions from 1994 to 2019. Cyberpsychol. Behav. Soc. Netw. **24**, 215–222 (2021). https://doi.org/10.1089/cyber.2020.0134
2. Global daily social media usage 2024. https://www.statista.com/statistics/433871/daily-social-media-usage-worldwide/. Accessed 30 Mar 2024
3. Belle Wong, J.D.: Top social media statistics and trends of 2024. https://www.forbes.com/advisor/business/social-media-statistics/. Accessed 30 Mar 2024
4. Number of worldwide social network users 2027. https://www.statista.com/statistics/278414/number-of-worldwide-social-network-users/. Accessed 30 Mar 2024
5. Rodríguez-Ibánez, M., Casánez-Ventura, A., Castejón-Mateos, F., Cuenca-Jiménez, P.-M.: A review on sentiment analysis from social media platforms. Expert Syst. Appl. **223**, 119862 (2023). https://doi.org/10.1016/j.eswa.2023.119862
6. Dhiman, D.B.: Ethical issues and challenges in social media: A current scenario. SSRN Electron. J. (2023). https://doi.org/10.2139/ssrn.4406610
7. Thakur, N., Han, C.: An exploratory study of tweets about the SARS-CoV-2 Omicron variant: insights from sentiment analysis, language interpretation, source tracking, type classification, and embedded URL detection. COVID. **2**, 1026–1049 (2022). https://doi.org/10.3390/covid2080076
8. Thakur, N.: A large-scale dataset of Twitter chatter about online learning during the current COVID-19 Omicron wave. Data (Basel) **7**, 109 (2022). https://doi.org/10.3390/data7080109
9. Ge, J., Gretzel, U.: Emoji rhetoric: a social media influencer perspective. J. Mark. Manag. **34**, 1272–1295 (2018). https://doi.org/10.1080/0267257x.2018.1483960
10. World Emoji Day statistics —. https://worldemojiday.com/statistics. Accessed 30 Mar 2024
11. Smileys, People: Emoji statistics. https://emojipedia.org/stats. Accessed 30 Mar 2024
12. Tang, J., Chang, Y., Liu, H.: Mining social media with social theories: a survey. https://www.cse.msu.edu/~tangjili/publication/Tang-Chang-Liu.pdf. Accessed 30 Mar 2024
13. Agarwal, N., Yiliyasi, Y.: Information quality challenges in social media. In: MIT International Conference on Information Quality (2010)
14. Social Data Mining for Crime Intelligence: Contributions to Social Data Quality Assessment and Prediction Methods. https://bradscholars.brad.ac.uk/handle/10454/16066. Accessed 30 Mar 2024
15. Date, D.#: P., Sg-, P.L.C., Reply-to:, S.-22, Jabot, C.: Correct UTF-8 handling during phase 1 of translation. https://www.open-std.org/jtc1/sc22/wg21/docs/papers/2021/p2295r0.pdf. Accessed 03 May 2024
16. Mohapatra, R.K., et al.: Transmission dynamics, complications and mitigation strategies of the current mpox outbreak: a comprehensive review with bibliometric study. Rev. Med. Virol. **34** (2024). https://doi.org/10.1002/rmv.2541
17. Cuetos-Suárez, D., Gan, R.K., Cuetos-Suárez, D., Arcos González, P., Castro-Delgado, R.: A review of mpox outbreak and public health response in Spain. Risk Manag. Healthc. Policy. **17**, 297–310 (2024). https://doi.org/10.2147/rmhp.s440035
18. Masirika, L.M., et al.: Ongoing mpox outbreak in Kamituga, South Kivu province, associated with monkeypox virus of a novel Clade I sub-lineage, Democratic Republic of the Congo, 2024. Euro Surveill. 29 (2024). https://doi.org/10.2807/1560-7917.es.2024.29.11.2400106
19. Multi-country outbreak of mpox, External situation report#33, 31 May 2024. https://www.who.int/publications/m/item/multi-country-outbreak-of-mpox--external-situation-report-33--31-may-2024. Accessed 07 Jun 2024

20. Chouhan, A., Nanda, D., Jain, J., Pattni, K., Kurup, L.: Emotion prediction of comments in Twitch.Tv livestream environment. In: Fong, S., Dey, N., Joshi, A. (eds.) ICT Analysis and Applications. Lecture Notes in Networks and Systems, vol. 517. Springer, Singapore (2023). https://doi.org/10.1007/978-981-19-5224-1_40

21. https://ijadst.com/ajradmin/certificates/138/IJADST_20210438.pdf. Accessed 04 May 2024

22. https://www.researchgate.net/profile/Muhammad-Nusrat-2/publication/373649914_Emoji_Prediction_in_Tweets_using_BERT/links/64f5ea6348c07f3da3d86513/Emoji-Prediction-in-Tweets-using-BERT.pdf. Accessed 04 May 2024

23. Kone, V.S., Anagal, A.M., Anegundi, S., Jadekar, P., Patil, P.: Emoji prediction using bi-directional LSTM. ITM Web Conf. **53**, 02004 (2023). https://doi.org/10.1051/itmconf/20235302004

24. Ranjan, R., Yadav, P.: Emoji prediction using LSTM and Naive Bayes. In: TENCON 2021 - 2021 IEEE Region 10 Conference (TENCON). IEEE (2021)

25. Stoikos, S., Izbicki, M.: Multilingual emoticon prediction of tweets about COVID-19. In: Nissim, M., Patti, V., Plank, B., Durmus, E. (eds.) Proceedings of the Third Workshop on Computational Modeling of People's Opinions, Personality, and Emotion's in Social Media, pp. 109–118. Association for Computational Linguistics, Barcelona, Spain (Online) (2020)

26. Inan, E.: An active learning based emoji prediction method in Turkish. Int. J. Intell. Syst. Appl. Eng. **8**, 1–5 (2020). https://doi.org/10.18201/ijisae.2020158882

27. Kumar, S., Harichandana, B.S.S., Arora, H.: VoiceMoji: a novel on-device pipeline for seamless emoji insertion in dictation. In: 2021 IEEE 18th India Council International Conference (INDICON). IEEE (2021)

28. Barbieri, F., Ronzano, F., Saggion, H.: What does this emoji mean? a vector space skip-gram model for twitter emojis (2016)

29. Gupta, A., et al.: Context-aware emoji prediction using deep learning. In: Dev, A., Agrawal, S.S., Sharma, A. (eds.) Artificial Intelligence and Speech Technology. AIST 2021. Communications in Computer and Information Science, vol. 1546. Springer, Cham (2022). https://doi.org/10.1007/978-3-030-95711-7_22

30. Shobana, J., Amudha, S., Kumar, S.: Emoji anticipation and prediction using deep neural network model. In: 2022 International Conference on Power, Energy, Control and Transmission Systems (ICPECTS). IEEE (2022)

31. Barbieri, F., Ballesteros, M., Saggion, H.: Are emojis predictable? In: Proceedings of the 15th Conference of the European Chapter of the Association for Computational Linguistics, vol. 2, Short Papers. Association for Computational Linguistics, Stroudsburg, PA, USA (2017)

32. Zhao, S., et al.: PEDM: A multi-task learning model for persona-aware Emoji-embedded dialogue generation. ACM Trans. Multimed. Comput. Commun. Appl. **19**, 1–21 (2023). https://doi.org/10.1145/3571819

33. Sv, P., Ittamalla, R.: What concerns the general public the most about monkeypox virus? – a text analytics study based on Natural Language Processing (NLP). Travel Med. Infect. Dis. **49**, 102404 (2022). https://doi.org/10.1016/j.tmaid.2022.102404

34. Ng, Q.X., Yau, C.E., Lim, Y.L., Wong, L.K.T., Liew, T.M.: Public sentiment on the global outbreak of monkeypox: an unsupervised machine learning analysis of 352,182 twitter posts. Publ. Health **213**, 1–4 (2022). https://doi.org/10.1016/j.puhe.2022.09.008

35. Cooper, L.N., et al.: Analyzing an emerging pandemic on Twitter: Monkeypox. Open Forum Infect. Dis. **10** (2023). https://doi.org/10.1093/ofid/ofad142

36. Iparraguirre-Villanueva, O., et al.: The public health contribution of sentiment analysis of Monkeypox tweets to detect polarities using the CNN-LSTM model. Vaccines (Basel) **11**, 312 (2023). https://doi.org/10.3390/vaccines11020312

37. Dsouza, V.S., et al.: A sentiment and content analysis of tweets on monkeypox stigma among the LGBTQ+ community: a cue to risk communication plan. Dialogues Health. **2**, 100095 (2023). https://doi.org/10.1016/j.dialog.2022.100095

38. Zuhanda, M.K., Syofra, A.H.S., Mathelinea, D., Gio, P.U., Anisa, Y.A., Novita, N.: Analysis of twitter user sentiment on the monkeypox virus issue using the NRC lexicon. Mantik **6**, 3854–3860 (2023). https://doi.org/10.35335/mantik.v6i4.3502

39. Knudsen, B., Høeg, T.B., Prasad, V.: Analysis of tweets discussing the risk of Mpox among children and young people in school (May–October 2022): a retrospective observational study. BMJ Paediatr. Open. **8**, e002236 (2024). https://doi.org/10.1136/bmjpo-2023-002236

40. Bengesi, S., Oladunni, T., Olusegun, R., Audu, H.: A machine learning-sentiment analysis on Monkeypox outbreak: an extensive dataset to show the polarity of public opinion from twitter tweets. IEEE Access. **11**, 11811–11826 (2023). https://doi.org/10.1109/access.2023.3242290

41. Farahat, R.A., Yassin, M.A., Al-Tawfiq, J.A., Bejan, C.A., Abdelazeem, B.: Public perspectives of monkeypox in Twitter: A social media analysis using machine learning. New Microbes New Infect. **49–50**, 101053 (2022). https://doi.org/10.1016/j.nmni.2022.101053

42. Chen, Y., Yuan, J., You, Q., Luo, J.: Twitter sentiment analysis via bi-sense emoji embedding and attention-based LSTM. In: Proceedings of the 26th ACM International Conference on Multimedia. ACM, New York (2018)

43. Lou, Y., Zhang, Y., Li, F., Qian, T., Ji, D.: Emoji-based sentiment analysis using attention networks. ACM Trans. Asian Low-resour. Lang. Inf. Process. **19**, 1–13 (2020). https://doi.org/10.1145/3389035

44. Thakur, N., Patel, K.A., Poon, A., Shah, R., Azizi, N., Han, C.: A comprehensive analysis and investigation of the public discourse on twitter about exoskeletons from 2017 to 2023. Future Int. **15**, 346 (2023). https://doi.org/10.3390/fi15100346

45. Liu, C., et al.: Improving sentiment analysis accuracy with emoji embedding. J. Safety Sci. Resil. **2**, 246–252 (2021). https://doi.org/10.1016/j.jnlssr.2021.10.003

46. Grover, V.: Exploiting emojis in sentiment analysis: a survey. J. Inst. Eng. (India): Series B **103**(1), 259–272 (2021). https://doi.org/10.1007/s40031-021-00620-7

47. Thakur, N., Cui, S., Khanna, K., Knieling, V., Duggal, Y.N., Shao, M.: Investigation of the gender-specific discourse about online learning during COVID-19 on Twitter using sentiment analysis, subjectivity analysis, and toxicity analysis. Computers. **12**, 221 (2023). https://doi.org/10.3390/computers12110221

48. Calisir, E., Brambilla, M.: The problem of data cleaning for knowledge extraction from social media. In: Pautasso, C., Sánchez-Figueroa, F., Systä, K., Murillo Rodríguez, J. (eds.) Current Trends in Web Engineering. ICWE 2018. Lecture Notes in Computer Science(), vol. 11153. Springer, Cham (2018). https://doi.org/10.1007/978-3-030-03056-8_10

49. Batrinca, B., Treleaven, P.C.: Social media analytics: a survey of techniques, tools and platforms. AI Soc. **30**, 89–116 (2015). https://doi.org/10.1007/s00146-014-0549-4

50. http://www.jacet-hokkaido.org/JACET_RBET_pdf/2019/Sato_2019.pdf. Accessed 04 May 2024

51. Thakur, N.: MonkeyPox2022Tweets: A large-scale Twitter dataset on the 2022 Monkeypox outbreak, findings from analysis of Tweets, and open research questions. Infect. Dis. Rep. **14**, 855–883 (2022). https://doi.org/10.3390/idr14060087

52. Malaeb, D., et al.: Knowledge, attitude and conspiracy beliefs of healthcare workers in Lebanon towards Monkeypox. Trop. Med. Infect. Dis. **8**, 81 (2023). https://doi.org/10.3390/tropicalmed8020081

53. Mohbey, K.K., Meena, G., Kumar, S., Lokesh, K.: A CNN-LSTM-based hybrid deep learning approach for sentiment analysis on Monkeypox tweets. New Gener. Comput. **42**, 89–107 (2024). https://doi.org/10.1007/s00354-023-00227-0

54. Subramani, N., Veerappampalayam Easwaramoorthy, S., Mohan, P., Subramanian, M., Sambath, V.: A gradient boosted decision tree-based influencer prediction in social network analysis. Big Data Cogn. Comput. **7**, 6 (2023). https://doi.org/10.3390/bdcc7010006

55. Hassani, H., Komendantova, N., Rovenskaya, E., Yeganegi, M.R.: Social intelligence mining: unlocking insights from X. Mach. Learn. Knowl. Extr. **5**, 1921–1936 (2023). https://doi.org/10.3390/make5040093

56. https://www.who.int/westernpacific/emergencies/mpox-outbreak. Accessed 04 May 2024

57. https://wonder.cdc.gov/nndss/static/2024/11/2024-11-table968.html. Accessed 04 May 2024

58. Encodings supported by Python 3.12. https://docs.python.org/3.12/library/codecs.html. Accessed 07 Jun 2024

59. Encodings supported by Python 2.5. https://docs.python.org/2.5/lib/standard-encodings.html. Accessed 07 Jun 2024

60. Encodings supported by Python 2.6, https://docs.python.org/2.6/library/codecs.html. Accessed 07 Jun 2024

61. Encodings supported by Python 2.7. https://docs.python.org/2.7/library/codecs.html. Accessed 07 Jun 2024

62. Encodings supported by Python 3.0. https://docs.python.org/3.0/library/codecs.html. Accessed 07 Jun 2024

63. Encodings supported by Python 3.1. https://docs.python.org/3.1/library/codecs.html. Accessed 07 Jun 2024

64. Java, A., Song, X., Finin, T., Tseng, B.: Why we Twitter: understanding microblogging usage and communities. In: Proceedings of the 9th WebKDD and 1st SNA-KDD 2007 Workshop on Web Mining and Social Network Analysis. ACM, New York (2007)

65. Jansen, B.J., Zhang, M., Sobel, K., Chowdury, A.: Twitter power: tweets as electronic word of mouth. J. Am. Soc. Inf. Sci. Technol. **60**, 2169–2188 (2009). https://doi.org/10.1002/asi.21149

66. Python. https://www.python.org/. Accessed 07 Jun 2024

SerendipitySeeker: A Novel SNS Viewer Designed to Broaden Perspectives by Encountering Diverse Information

Tomonari Kamba[✉] [iD]

Information Networking for Innovation and Design, Toyo University, 1-7-11 Akabanedai, Kita-ku, Tokyo 115-8650, Japan
kamba@iniad.org

Abstract. The "follow" and "friend" mechanisms on social networking sites, combined with their widespread adoption, have led to the emergence of filter bubbles. Within these bubbles, individuals predominantly encounter opinions that reflect their own, thereby creating echo-chambers. In these chambers, ideas can become radicalized within isolated clusters, leading to societal divisions and potential confrontations. This study introduces SerendipitySeeker, a social networking service (SNS) viewer developed to address these issues. Some recommendation systems have attempted to include content outside typical user preferences to promote unexpected discoveries and mitigate personalization risks. However, according to the self-determination theory, individuals are more inclined to act based on intrinsic motivations than external directives. Considering this, we created interactive maps to position SNS messages on multiple axes, such as positive/negative and subjective/objective, using a language-model API. These maps are seamlessly integrated into an SNS viewer to broaden users' informational horizons. Preliminary testing of SerendipitySeeker with 12 participants demonstrated its potential effectiveness. Users actively engaged with the map, shifting their content consumption from a linear pattern to a more comprehensive exploration.

Keywords: Serendipity · SNS · Filter bubble

1 Introduction

Generally, social networking services (SNSs) have a "friend" or "follow" system, where users follow the posts of other users who make posts, they are interested in. Consequently, the articles they see daily tend to be only those posted by users with interests and views similar to their own, a phenomenon known as filter bubbles [1]. This approach can result in virtual clusters of users sharing similar views and interests on various topics, and the views within these clusters can sometimes become radicalized. This phenomenon is called an echo chamber [2]. Because it is generally easy to reshare other users' posts on SNSs, users may spread extreme information without thorough consideration. The distortion and radicalization of human cognition through SNSs can deepen division and conflict in the world, leading not only to argumentative disputes, but also to global instability and wars.

A. Coman et al. (Eds.): HCII 2024, LNCS 15375, pp. 190–200, 2025.
https://doi.org/10.1007/978-3-031-76806-4_15

This problem is closely related to personalization, recommendations, and targeting technologies. These technologies are extremely effective from a business perspective and are often used to increase the effectiveness of advertisements and consumer purchases. Even if they do not lead to direct product purchases, they are used to display information of interest to users on websites to increase dwell time. This is also applied to SNS, where posts that the platform estimates "will be of interest to users" are displayed preferentially as "recommendations," even to users who do not follow them [3]. These technologies are effective for efficiently delivering information of interest to users; however, in the long term, they may cause users' interests to become narrower, deeper, and more acute, or may reduce their exposure to a wider range of information.

These issues have previously been identified, with warnings about their social implications. Moreover, a range of theoretical and technical solutions have been proposed to tackle these problems. One of the most important is the promotion of serendipitous and fortunate opportunities to encounter information. This study is based on the same awareness of the issues, but instead of giving users serendipity from the outside, our system, SerendipitySeeker, aims to make users aware that information has various perspectives and to increase their internal motivation for information exploration.

2 Related Research

2.1 Personalization, Recommendation, and Targeting

Some personalization is user-driven, in which the user sets the site to his/her preferred color or sets the weather forecast for his/her area of residence to be constantly displayed; however, here, we discuss automatic personalization. Techniques in which a system learns the interests of users based on their browsing behavior and prioritizes the display of articles that are likely to be of interest to them have been used since the very early days of the Web [4] and remain an important issue today [5, 6]. The same technique is now applied to advertisements and is called "targeting" from the perspective of the ad provider.

Recommendation is a similar term that is often used, particularly in online shopping. Content-based filtering, which is based on direct relationships between products, as well as social filtering, recommends products based on similarities in purchasing behavior among people. It was proposed in the very early days of the Web [7] and continues to improve in various ways.

2.2 Serendipity

These mechanisms have considerable business value in that they are currently being applied to all aspects of the web, and it might be possible to state that this synergy with social networking has affected the current filter bubble and echo chamber problems.

One way to mitigate this issue is to promote serendipitousness. Mechanisms that provide information that not only directly interests or responds to the user, but also leads to unexpected discoveries or new interests are being considered. For example, Jasim et al. studied a method for recommending not only information of interest to the user, but also randomly scattered information or information that deviates from the user's interests [8]. Kotkov et al. summarized the types of serendipity and their use in recommendation systems and presented a proposed measurement method for online news [9]. Smets et al. showed that both the recommendation algorithm and the user interface are important for promoting serendipity [10]. Björneborn indexes how much serendipity is gained by users in physical libraries [11]. There are also systems that measure opportunities for serendipity in digital spaces with reference to this index [12–15]. Grace et al. showed the complexity of recommending recipes for personal cooking, comparing "what the user will like" to "what the user will be surprised at" [16].

2.3 Human Motivation

Let us now change our perspective and consider human motivation for information exploration. Deci and Ryan's self-determination theory is a detailed theory that humans are more likely to act when they are intrinsically motivated than when they are extrinsically motivated [17, 18]. A simplified example illustrates this: an idea conceived independently is more likely to inspire action than an idea suggested by others. Considering this classification, "recommendation" and the user interface style itself are "external motivations" to the user. If this is the case, to encourage serendipity, we must first increase human motivation to search for information.

3 Proposed System

To encourage serendipity, it is important not only to mix information from new perspectives on specific information sites but also to increase the internal motivation of many people to be exposed to information from more diverse perspectives. This study proposed SerendipitySeeker, an SNS viewer with an interactive positioning map.

The system constantly displays an interactive positioning map of posts or posters next to a list of post timelines or search results. This allows SNS users to always be aware that there are different viewpoints and claims from the posts they are viewing, and in some cases, that the posts they are reading are extreme. Moreover, by using our system, users can quickly access information from different positions on a map. Below is an overview and initial evaluation of SerendipitySeeker for X (Twitter) posts. There are two views, one that looks at the timeline of the posts and the other that looks at the search results, each of which is shown below.

3.1 Timeline View

Figure 1 illustrates this timeline. The posts are displayed on the left side of the screen on the timeline and a position map of the posters is displayed on the right side. A circle on the positioning map corresponds to a single poster, and the radius of the circle reflects the number of followers (in Fig. 1, all the posters shown are celebrities with more than one million followers; therefore, the circles appear to be of almost the same size). Positioning on the map is based on the automatic classification of the poster's last 10 posts using linguistic analysis Application Programming Interfaces (APIs) such as ChatGPT on the

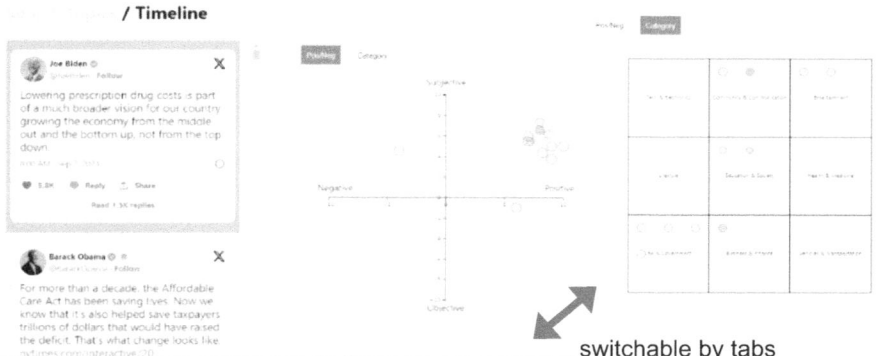

Fig. 1. Timeline View

Web. The circle corresponding to the poster, highlighted with a bright yellow frame on the left timeline, is also highlighted in yellow on the map. The maps can be categorized into (a) positive/negative, and (b) content types.

- (a) Positive-negative: On the x-axis, the poster's posts are more positive further to the right and more negative further to the left; the higher the y-axis, the more subjective, and the lower the y-axis, the more objective the post.
- (b) Content categories: Classified into the following nine categories: Tech and Electronics, Community and Communication, Entertainment, Lifestyle, Education Society, Health and Medicine, Law and Government, Business and Finance, and Vehicles and Transportation.

When a user scrolls down and up the list on the left side of the map to switch between focused posts, the yellow highlighted circle on the map also changes. Conversely, when a user clicks on a poster on the map, the left-side list scrolls down or up to the most recent post of the poster, and the post is focused upon.

3.2   Search View

Figure 2 shows a screen of the keyword searches for the posts. The left side of the screen displays the searched posts in a list format (in order of latest arrival), and the right side is a map showing the positioning of each post in terms of "positive/negative" and "subjective/objective". Unlike in the timeline view, a single circle displayed on the map corresponds to a single post, not a poster. The size of the circle reflects the number of "likes" for that post.

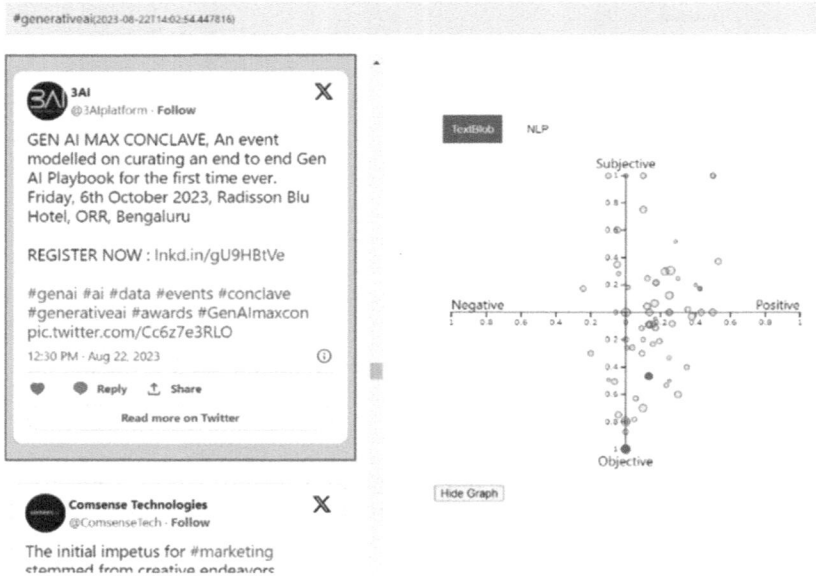

Fig. 2. Search View

3.3 System Architecture

Figure 3 shows the system architecture of the SerendipitySeeker. The proposed system comprises two components.

- API Server (FAST API Server): This component retrieves, parses, and delivers posts to the User Interface (UI) server.
- UI Server (React Server): Accessible via a browser that provides the user interface.

The API server retrieves the posts to be displayed in both the timeline and search views and stores the results of sentiment analysis and the content category classification of individual posts in a database. The implementation uses Python and the FastAPI framework. In the database of the timeline view, the sentiment analysis of each poster is performed by combining 10 latest posts of a given poster into a single post, and then sending it to the ChatGPT API as "quantify these posts on two axes, positive/negative and subjective/objective, in order to map them." The Google NLP API [19] is used for content category classification. It classifies content into 28 categories, and each category is mapped onto one of the nine categories on the content category map using a mapping list. To reduce the number of categories in the mapping from 28 to 9, all the categories were given to ChatGPT, and a dialogue was conducted with the following content: "Please determine the categories and display positions so that these can be displayed on the screen in the nine categories that are easy for humans to understand." As for the positive and negative analysis for the search results, TexBlob API [20] is used owing to its response speed. Each post is analyzed independently and its context is not considered.

The UI server is implemented using the React framework. It retrieves data from the API server, provides a timeline, and the search results. Users freely switch between these views. The current screen configuration is intended for a large screen such as a PC.

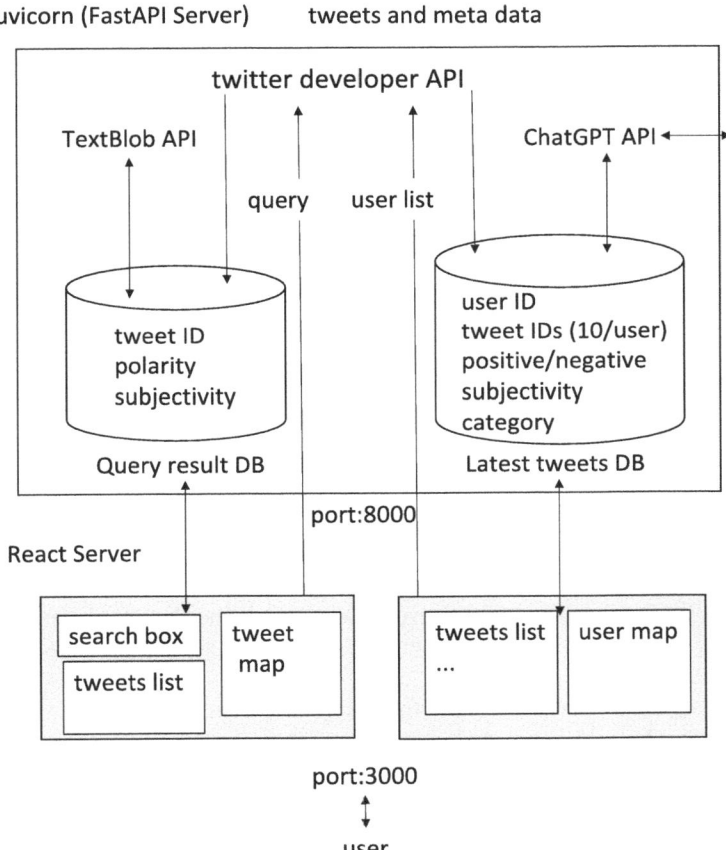

Fig. 3. System Architecture

4   User Interface Evaluation

To confirm the fundamental effectiveness of SerendipitySeeker, we evaluated whether users voluntarily and actively used the interactive positioning map.

4.1 Experiment Setup

The experiment involved 12 participants, who were undergraduate or graduate students aged between 20 and 25 years, who were recruited from the author's informatics department. An honorarium of approximately $10 was offered for participation in the experiment. The posts and search keywords were a mixture of Japanese and English. The native language of the subjects was Japanese, however, they had basic English proficiency and sufficient browsing experience of X. All experiments were conducted on the same PC, the browser, and browser size. User operations were recorded with the consent of the participants.

The evaluation experiment required approximately 30 min per person. Seven of the 12 participants used the SerendipitySeeker. For the other five users, all maps were hidden in both the timeline and search views, displaying only a list of posts. When the map was hidden, the right column of the map was left blank and no other changes were made. The subjects were given a one-minute explanation of how to use the system. The following instructions were provided to the participants:

1. View posts freely in the timeline view (10 min).
2. View posts freely in the search view (10 min).
3. Fill out the questionnaire

The settings for use were as follows:

(1) In the timeline view, the user does not log into X, and the system displayed the most recent 10 posts by each of the 20 celebrities prepared in advance. In total, 200 posts were viewed.
(2) The search view displayed search results for ten predefined keywords, such as "global warming" and "Generative AI. " There were 25 results, and 250 submissions for each keyword.
(3) The questionnaire consisted of the following three items, all of which were rated on a 5-point scale from 1 (not at all appropriate) to 5 (very appropriate).

- Q1: Appropriate placement of the posters in the positive/negative map of the timeline view
- Q2: Appropriate poster placement in the category map in the timeline view
- Q3: Appropriate placement of posts in the positioning map of the search results.

4.2 Results

User Behavior on the Timeline View. In the timeline view, the average number of user operations on the positive-negative map was 11.4 (standard deviation 6.8) per person during the 10-min period, and the average number of operations on the categorical map was 7.1 (standard deviation 10.7). When both were added, the total number of operations on the map in 10 min averaged 18.6 (standard deviation 15.5), indicating active map use.

The number of map operations significantly varied from user to user. Some users frequently browsed the map while selecting posters, whereas others did not operate the map much while scrolling through the list of posts. However, according to the post-experiment questionnaire, even users who rarely clicked on the map looked it frequently while scrolling through the list of posts to determine the positions of the posters they were looking at.

User Behavior on the Search View

The history of user operations in the search results view, counted every minute, is shown in Fig. 4. In (a), the number of clicks on the search keyword list is always higher when there is no map display (orange line) than when there is a positioning map display (blue line). Instead, as shown in (b), the user constantly clicked on the map when it is present. This indicates that when viewing the search results, users did not view the posts in order, but mainly viewed the posts by selecting them on the positive-negative map. The total number of operations on the map over a 10-min period averaged 21.7 (standard deviation 12.8). Figure 4(c) reveals a decline in article views by users without map use after 7 min owing to rapid content browsing. In contrast, steady engagement was observed with map use, indicating longer and more deliberate exploration.

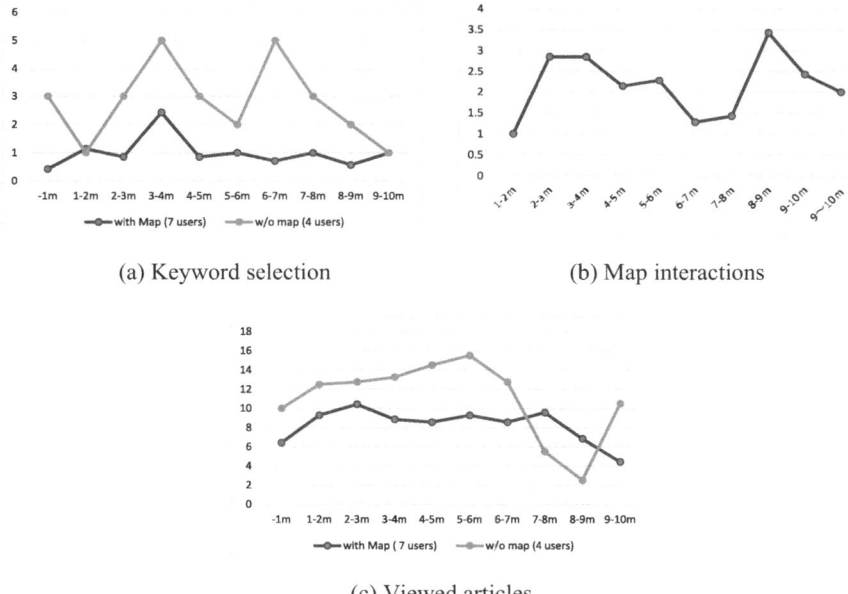

(a) Keyword selection   (b) Map interactions

(c) Viewed articles

Fig. 4. Average Trends in User Behaviors per Minute during the Experiment (N = 12)

Questionnaire Result. Responses were obtained from six of the seven participants for whom the map was displayed (the highest score was 5).

- Q1 (Appropriate placement on the poster positive-negative map of the timeline view): 4 for all
- Q2 (Appropriate placement on the poster category map in the timeline view): mean 3.5 (standard deviation 1.0))

- Q3 (Appropriate placement on the positioning map in the search view): mean 3.7 (standard deviation 0.59)

For the positive-negative map, the timeline is considered more accurate than the search view because the last 10 posts are analyzed linguistically when determining the placement of each poster in the timeline view, whereas only one post is analyzed in the search results view. One possible reason for the low evaluation of the category map in Q2 is that the posters selected for this experiment were celebrities with numerous followers. For instance, if a user known for academic or sports prominence is categorized under "entertainment" based on their last ten posts, this classification might seem dubious to users familiar with their usual content.

5   Discussions

5.1   Validity of Map Display

Although the interactive positioning map will be useful for users to know the positioning of a post or poster and to be aware that there are multiple viewpoints and opinions for any kind of issue, we must note that some technical and linguistic analysis limitations always exist for the map. For example, in positioning the posters, only 10 recent posts were analyzed for each poster. In positioning the search results, each post was analyzed without considering its context. Although these points will improve gradually, there may be limitations in increasing the accuracy of linguistic analysis because SNSs are not places where all people write comments with sufficient consideration. For instance, in a sentiment analysis conducted on Twitter, there is a report indicating the significant challenges in enhancing classification accuracy [21].

5.2   Screen Design

Left and Right Alignments of the Submission List with Map. The list of posts is displayed on the left, and an interactive map is displayed on the right. The reason for this was to emphasize that the position of the post list did not change during the evaluation experiment regardless of whether the map was displayed on the same browser. However, in general, users tend to look at the left side of the screen first and then at the right side. Therefore, if the map is displayed on the left side of the screen instead of on the right side, users may have more opportunities to easily look at the map, and interaction with the map may increase.

Ratio of the Widths of the Post List and Map. Both the list and map each occupies 50% of the browser size on the current system. If we want to widen the map, the post list would narrow, and vice versa. Of course, it is desirable that users can change the width of the post list and map, but the default display ratio would be important. This is not only a design issue, but also a question of how to strike a balance between people seeing individual opinions and being aware of their positionings.

Color Scheme for Focused and Unfocused Users and Posts. In the current implementation, the color is bright yellow when the focus is on the post and light blue when it is not. When interacting with the map, users quickly notice the change in the circle color when selecting a new one. However, when navigating a list of posts, they may not realize the corresponding changes in the highlighted items on the map. How user operation will change owing to the color difference is a subject for future studies.

6 Conclusion

To increase serendipity, it is necessary to increase the users' internal motivation to search for information. We implemented SerendipitySeeker, which displays an interactive positioning map using a list of posts. User evaluations showed that users actively operated the map, confirming its effectiveness. Further studies and experiments are required to determine whether this encourages users to explore diverse opinions more actively. SNSs serve as portals for browsing various types of information and as a platform that influences the views of many people. By transforming SNS into spaces where users are constantly reminded of the diverse viewpoints in the world, we can alleviate filter bubbles and echo chambers, potentially reducing conflicts among people.

Acknowledgments. This study was supported by JSPS KAKENHI Grant Number JP23K11205.

References

1. Pariser, E.: The Filter Bubble: What the Internet is Hiding from You. Penguin, UK (2011)
2. Diaz Ruiz, C., Nilsson, T.: Disinformation and echo chambers: how disinformation circulates on social media through identity-driven controversies. J. Public Policy Mark. **42**(1), 18–35 (2023)
3. Narayanan, A.: Understanding Social Media Recommendation Algorithms, 23-01 Knight First Amendment Institute (2023)
4. Kamba, T., Bharat, K., Albers, M.C.: The Krakatoa chronicle – an interactive, personalized, newspaper on the web. In: Proceedings of the Forth International Conference on World Wide Web, pp.159–170 (1995)
5. Thurman, N.: Personalization of news. In: Vos, T.P., Hanusch, F., Dimitrakopoulou, D., Geertsema-Sligh, M., Sehl, A. (eds.) The International Encyclopedia of Journalism Studies. Wiley-Blackwell, Massachusetts (2018)
6. Bozdag, E.: Bias in algorithmic filtering and personalization. Ethics Inf. Technol. **15**, 209–227 (2013)
7. Shardanand, U., Maes, P.: Social information filtering: algorithms for automating "Word of Mouth". In: CHI 1995 Proceedings, pp. 210–217 (1995)
8. Jasim, M., Collins, C., Sarvghad, A., Mahyar, N.: Supporting serendipitous discovery and balanced analysis of online product reviews with interaction-driven metrics and bias-mitigating suggestions. In: CHI 2022 Proceedings, Article No. 9, April 2022
9. Kotkov, D., Medlar, A., Glowacka, D.: Rethinking serendipity in recommender systems. In: CHIIR 2023, March 19023, 2023, Austin, Tx, USA (2023)

10. Smets, A., Michiels, L., Bogers, T., Björneborn, L.: Serendipity in recommender systems beyond the algorithm: a feature repository and experimental design. CEUR Workshop Proc. **3222**, 46–66 (2022)

11. Björneborn, L.: Serendipity dimensions and users' information behavior in the physical library interface. Inform. Res. **13**(1), Paper 370 (2008)

12. McCay-Peet, L., Toms, E.: Measuring the dimensions of serendipity in digital environments. Inform. Res. **16**(3), Paper 483 (2011)

13. Thudt, A., Hinrichs, U., Carpendale, S.: The bohemian bookshelf: supporting serendipitous book discoveries through information visualization. In: CHI 2012 Proceedings, pp. 1461–1470 (2012)

14. Palmonari, M., Uboldi, G., Cremaschi, M., Ciminieri, D., Bianchi, F.: DaCENA: serendipitous news reading with data contexts. In: Gandon, F., Guéret, C., Villata, S., Breslin, J., Faron-Zucker, C., Zimmermann, A. (eds.) The Semantic Web: ESWC 2015 Satellite Events. ESWC 2015. Lecture Notes in Computer Science(), vol. 9341. Springer, Cham (2015). https://doi.org/10.1007/978-3-319-25639-9_26

15. Beale, R.: Supporting serendipity: using ambient intelligence to augment user exploration for data mining and web browsing. Int. J. Hum. Comput. Stud. **65**(5), 421–433 (2007)

16. Grace, K., Finch, E., Gulbransen-Diaz, N., Henderson, H.: Q-Chef: the impact of surprise-eliciting systems on food-related decision-making. In: CHI 2022 Proceedings, Article No. 11, pp. 1–14, April 2022

17. Deci, E.L., Ryan, R.M.: Intrinsic Motivation and Self-Determination in Human Behavior. Springer, New York (1985)

18. Ryan, R.M., Deci, El.L.: Self-Determination Theory: Basic Psychological Needs in Motivation, Development, and Wellness. Guilford Publishing, New York (2017)

19. Google Cloud Natural Language API. https://cloud.google.com/natural-language/docs/basics. Accessed 27 April 2024

20. TextBlob sentiment analysis. https://textblob.readthedocs.io/en/dev/advanced_usage.html. Accessed 27 April 2024

21. Zimbra, D., Abbasi, A., Zeng, D., Chen, H.: The state-of-the-art in Twitter sentiment analysis: a review and benchmark evaluation. ACM Trans. Manage. Inform. Syst. **9**(2), 1–29 (2018). Article no. 5

Gaming Privacy Concerns in an Online Social Networking Environment from a User Perspective

Stacy Nicholson[✉] and Robert J. Hammell II

Towson University, 8000 York Road, Towson, MD 21252, USA
{snicholson,rhammell}@towson.edu

Abstract. Gaming is one of the most popular and profitable forms of entertainment and leisurely activity amongst individuals of all ages. However, behind the scenes of online gaming, there is a massive amount of data collection and processing that may pose risks to the privacy of millions of players. This study explores players privacy concerns associated with Instant Games on Facebook, and gameplay behavior that can impact their privacy in a social networking environment. It discusses privacy concerns affecting players from a user perspective, players gaming actions towards privacy and investigates their protective behavior on social networking sites. A survey and game app testing were conducted to collect and analyze pertinent data. The findings showed that 77% of participants were concerned with the amount of personal information being shared with the Instant Games apps. In addition, the participants top concerns were tracking and third-party application access to user information. The findings shed light on the fact that games played on social networking platforms such as Facebook can impact the user's privacy and raise serious concerns. It also highlights the mismatch between user-stated privacy concerns and actual gameplay behavior (the "privacy paradox"). This research contributes to the ongoing conversation about data privacy and privacy concerns. Learning about user privacy concerns with games is crucial to safeguard personal information, maintain a safe gaming environment, and shape the future of the gaming industry in a way that respects and protects user privacy.

Keywords: Privacy Concerns · Players · Gaming · Facebook · Social Games · Protective Behaviors · Instant Games

1 Introduction

Privacy concerns on social networking sites have been a popular topic of discussion in recent years, and the issue is only becoming more significant. Social networks allow users to engage with a variety of online content to entertain themselves, share information, buy products, and interact with friends, family, and their peers. In addition, they allow users to partake in contents, products, and services offered by third-party companies. For instance, free-to-play social casual games such as Basketball FRVR, 8 Ball Pool, and Words with Friends are examples of third-party game products available online on

A. Coman et al. (Eds.): HCII 2024, LNCS 15375, pp. 201–219, 2025.
https://doi.org/10.1007/978-3-031-76806-4_16

Facebook [1]. Facebook hosts these social casual games referred to as Instant Games (IG) as an entertainment source for its users and allows third-party game companies to access users' data, gain a wider audience, gain revenue, and build traction to their games [2]. While IG provides entertainment for users, they have the potential to pose privacy and security threats and violations to the users [3–7].

Gaming data is a valuable asset that contains significant amounts of high value player's information such as personal information, behavioral traits, playstyle, social network connections (friends, family, and peers), gaming activity, financial data, and game preferences to a name a few [5, 7]. This information about players can be used to track, profile users, recognize their playstyle, target ads, and spark various cyber-criminal activities towards the players and the gaming company.

According to Statista, Facebook is the world's most used online social networking platform [8, 9]. Further, there are over 1000 free third-party IG available on the Facebook platform [1]. Thus, user privacy on Facebook is of particular interest. Data breaches or excessive harvesting of players gaming data can lead to the users' privacy and security being compromised. An example is the Cambridge Analytica data breach, where a third-party personality quiz app violated 87 million Facebook users' privacy by taking personal data without the users' consent [10] [11]. In another incident, more than 530 million Facebook users had their information (including names, birth dates, and phone numbers) posted to a hacker website [12]. There has been a lack of research on IG third-party applications on Facebook. Little to no work has been found in the literature relating specifically to IG data sharing with respect to security exposure, privacy concerns, gaming behavior towards privacy, and privacy control options.

This study explores users' privacy concerns associated with Instant Games on Facebook, and gameplay behavior that can impact their privacy in a social networking environment. The focus is on identifying and understanding users' privacy concerns surrounding casual Instant Games on Facebook from a user perspective, players actions towards privacy, and their protective behavior employed on social networking sites (SNS). The results show that players are not just fearful about how Facebook shares their personal information with IG app companies, but also have concerns related to the use and abuse of their personal information. The following research questions (RQ) were investigated that directly relate to the subject matter being discussed.

- RQ#1-What are the privacy concerns related to IG on Facebook?
- RQ#2-What are the players gameplay actions towards privacy?

The remainder of this paper is organized as follows: A review of pertinent literature to help understand the issues and research is presented next. Section 3 explains the methodology used to conduct the research. Then the essential analysis results are presented and discussed in Sect. 4. Section 5, discussion, conclusions, and future study directions are offered. Finally, Sect. 6 contains information on the study limitations and ethical considerations.

2 Literature Review

This section provides relevant information on several concepts that will provide helpful insight and perspective into the research conducted in this paper.

2.1   Online Games

Online gaming has seen a significant increase over the past few years, drawing the young and the old to invest their time in playing games online. Online Games (OG) are types of games that can be played online via social networks such as Facebook. IG are types of OG that have become very popular on Facebook, thereby raising interest in areas that need to be examined, such as data privacy and security. One continuous growing concern is users' unknowingly giving out sensitive information to individuals not affiliated with Facebook, which has the potential to cause the users privacy and security to be violated [7]. With regards to IG further study is needed to examine other concerns more directly related to IG online game play due to the diverse nature of the Facebook platform.

2.2   Overview of Privacy Issue with Facebook

Privacy has become a common social problem instead of a social public good [13]. Facebook has faced several privacy concerns since the company's revenue model involves the oversharing of information about its users. There is a need for users to be more conscious of how third parties are taking advantage of personal data through third party applications which are hard to control. A study conducted by [14], found that users' intention to use Facebook privacy settings will be influenced by many factors such as subjective norms where the user is influenced by their peers to determine their privacy setting level. In addition, the user's information security awareness will play a role in safeguarding their personal data from third parties that access user data provided through Facebook Application Programming Interface (API) and Terms of Service (TOS). Facebook APIs allow developers to tap into the social network and add Facebook functionality to their applications which grants them access to user's information on Facebook [15].

2.3   Personal Information and Gaming Risk

Gaming companies collect all kinds of personal information associated with players. When it comes on to online gaming the types of data collected includes name, location, age, IP addresses, profiles information when linked with social networking sites, credit card information for in-game purchases, game activity and so on [5, 7, 16]. According to [16] a larger privacy concern arises when the user's game profile data on one platform is linked with other personal information from their social networking account, thus, making user profiling easier and less complex to perform. Furthermore, users may not be aware that their social networking profile and personal information are being shared with these gaming companies when they play games on a social networking site such as Facebook [17]. The lack of knowledge and awareness about the types and amount of their personal data being shared with and collected by these game companies may result in users not adjusting their privacy settings to reduce the amount of information that is shared.

Other privacy risk factors affecting players is the theft of their login credentials, in-game currency and malware conducted by hackers [18, 19]. Users that have social media accounts and credit card information linked to these game apps run the risk of having their privacy and data being compromised. The users and their social network connections are both at risk when it comes to the collection of their personal information. Online gamers are faced with various security threats such as malware, phishing, ransomware, and identify theft [3–5, 19, 20]. For instance, players can be scammed into divulging financial records, identifying data or account information to cybercriminals [5, 21, 22].

2.4 Privacy Awareness Impact and Concerns

Privacy awareness influences individuals' behavior, particularly those who use social network services, and influences their decisions regarding the disclosure of personal information. By promoting privacy awareness, individuals and organizations can protect themselves against privacy breaches and identity theft [23]. Authors in [24] note that privacy awareness showed negative impact on self-disclosure and privacy concerns. That is, users' privacy worries will increase as their privacy knowledge increases and the users' desire to self-disclose will decrease. This argument is also supported by research relating to privacy concerns [25]. Furthermore, [26] indicated that privacy awareness and gender play a significant role in explaining the users concerns for information privacy. This in turn can render insight into the user's privacy-protective behaviors.

Privacy concerns can be impacted by both positive and negative privacy awareness, in that, positive privacy awareness can play a key role in mitigating privacy concerns. It can act as a shield against privacy breaches and identity theft, especially in the digital age where personal information is frequently collected and shared [17, 23, 27]. It can further lead to informed decisions about personal information disclosure and cultivate trust between companies and customers [27]. Conversely, negative privacy awareness might worsen privacy problems. When people are unaware of who is collecting their personal information, how it is collected, or how it will be used, users may not think about privacy concerns [17, 28]. This lack of awareness might result in unfavorable feelings, causing users to shun dangers associated with information sharing. Furthermore, those who are unaware of the value of privacy may unintentionally divulge sensitive information, resulting in catastrophic consequences such as identity theft [17, 29–31]. Thus, both positive and negative privacy awareness are important factors in generating privacy concerns.

2.5 Privacy Paradox vs. Privacy Trade off

The term "privacy paradox" suggests that while users are concerned about their privacy, their behavior is different from their concerns [32–35]. That is, users tend to continue to use services and disclose personal data even though they are concerned about privacy. Prior study also mentioned the complexity of the "privacy paradox" suggesting further research is needed to unlock this phenomenon [34]. This paradox can be attributed to a number of factors such as: 1) users' awareness of their right to privacy, and 2) users may not consider their personal data as a risk factor [34, 36, 37]. On the other hand, "privacy trade-off" looks at assessing the benefits gained from sharing information against the privacy risks or perceived value [38].

3 Methodology

3.1 Research Design

An empirical approach was used in this study to comprehend and analyze relevant data related to the research questions posed in this study. The first aim was to understand the user's gaming privacy concerns directly related to Instant Games (social casual games on Facebook). The second objective was to investigate the players' gameplay actions towards privacy and its impact on the users. The study was carried out using an online survey and IG gaming experiment for the collection of pertinent data. The approach taken in this study was influence by past research [7, 17] investigating Instant Games on Facebook. The participants did not need to have any prior experience playing IG on Facebook since, all participants had to play an Instant Game before completing the survey.

3.2 Participants

Participants were recruited from the Computer and Information Sciences Department at Towson University through large group emails. Participants ranged in age from 18 to 35, with the majority falling in the 18–22 age group. The sample consisted of 75% male and 25% female participants after data cleaning. A total of 62 participants took part in the study. These College students in the Computer Science and Information technology area were chosen as the target population as they align with the age group that mostly plays games online [39] and to assess the role higher education plays in users privacy concerns and actions towards protecting their privacy. Participants were required to be familiar with social media and be 18 or older. Participants who completed the study did not receive any monetary compensation.

3.3 Survey Instrument and Procedure

A web-based survey was developed and distributed using Qualtrics survey software. Participants were given a link to complete the online questionnaire right after playing the game. The survey was designed to collect data related to users' gaming privacy concerns, gaming actions towards privacy, and protective behaviors in a social network (such as Facebook). The questionnaire included demographic questions (age, gender, education level, etc.), privacy concerns, IG gameplay, etc.– see Appendix.

Privacy Concerns. Privacy concern here examines the players concerns as it relates to playing IG on Facebook and Sharing Personally Identifiable Information (PII) (name, photo, location, etc.) and other personal data with third-party social casual gaming apps. It also looked at associated concerns while playing a game on Facebook.

Gaming Actions Towards Privacy. Explores the users' actions taken before playing an IG app as it relates to assisting in the protection of their privacy and data. It also helped to investigate player protective behavior towards privacy.

3.4   Gameplay Procedure and Instruments

A gaming experiment was conducted to generate game experience for all participants on Facebook and for the collection of relevant gaming data. A mobile emulator device was used to conduct the game experiments with, along with the IG apps on Facebook. This approach was adopted from a prior study [7, 17] that used the same method to generate real-time gaming experience for the participants.

Game App Selection. The game apps selected were classified as popular games played on the Facebook Instant Games platform. Two game apps were chosen: "Solitaire Farm: Harvest Seasons" by SoftGames Mobile Entertainment Services, and "Basketball FRVR" – offered by FRVR. Apart from been classified as popular games on Facebook, both free-to-play (F2P) games were easy to play. The IG games, as noted in a prior study [7] had homogeneous features regarding the users' data being requested and the permission/privacy setting; that is, each game chosen has the same default data requirement statement. For instance, the default data requirements message for Basketball FRVR was:

"Basketball FRVR will receive your name, profile picture, preferred language, and friends list. On Facebook, your friends, and fellow players can see your gaming activity".

3.5   Pilot Testing

Several instances of pilot testing of the questionnaires were done by the researcher, and by a small test group of students in the Computer and Information Sciences Department. From the pilot study and gameplay activity evaluations, final modifications were made to the questionnaires before the main study was conducted.

3.6   Data Analysis

The evaluation phase involved the use of the SPSS statistical program and NVivo software to clean, validate and analyze the data collected from the surveys. The survey included multiple response questions where participants could select more than one answer. They could select from zero to all the options; participants were instructed to select all the options that applied to them. Questions that included an open-ended response section were categorized into themes using thematic coding analysis. Closed ended questions with multiple select options were represented in the findings as percentage of cases.

4   Results

The findings will first introduce the demographics of the respondents in general. Then pertinent findings regarding the reach questions are presented. This section highlights players concerns, determinants associated with gaming privacy concerns, gaming action and players protective behaviors as it relates to casual Instant Games gameplay. Afterwards, a discussion on the findings and its impacts are discussed.

4.1 Demographic Characteristics of Participants

The total number of participants accepted out of 62 participants that met the requirements and after cleaning the data was N = 53. Demographic characteristics that were gathered included: gender, age group, education level, and computer skill level.

- Most participants were in the 18 to 22 age group (81%); 17% were aged 23–26 and 2% were aged 30–35.
- 40 (75%) of the respondents were male and 13 (25%) were female.
- Most of the participants were Juniors (24 = 45%); 12 (23%) were sophomores and 17 (32%) were seniors. No freshmen participated in the study
- 26 (50%) of the participants rated themselves as having moderate computer skills, while 22 (42%) said they were at the advanced level. 1 (2%) rated themselves as a beginner while 3 (6%) felt they were experts.
- In terms of social media outlet use, most of the participants had used one or more social media sites, but only 35 (66%) of the participants used Facebook.

4.2 Privacy Concerns

This section presents findings related to Research Question 1 (RQ#1): What are the privacy concerns related to IG on Facebook? The participants were provided with 12 options in the order given in Table 1 and could select all options that they think applied, as well as volunteering other options not included in the list.

The findings indicated that the highest privacy concerns conveyed were tracking (option 10) and access to user personal information given to the game apps (option 2), with each concern being selected by 34 participants (64.2%), as shown in Table 1. The next highest was abuse of user's profile information (option 1), and data sharing (option 7), with each indicated by 30 participants (56.6%). One participant expressed the following "Selling of personal information for financial benefit" as another reason for their concern as a volunteered option.

Overall, when it came to the participants rating of their privacy concerns directed at IG on Facebook, the concern level is HIGH with 73% of participants expressing this sentiment. 6% rated their concern level as LOW, with 21% selecting NEUTRAL.

IG Data Sharing Privacy Concerns. On Facebook, the user's personal identifiable data, device details, and other personal information can be shared with these third-party IG apps, which has the potential to compromise the user's personal data and privacy. To expand on the players' privacy concerns this section examines the cross-data sharing aspect of gameplay in a social networking environment by evaluating the frequency of participants' concerns with regards to data sharing.

The participants were asked whether they thought their gaming data had been shared with other entities apart from Facebook. The findings showed that 81% of participants (43/53) were aware of this, while 15% of participants (8/53) expressed that they were not sure; only 4% said their data were not shared.

The number of participants concerned with the amount of personal information being shared with the IG apps was high. Among the participants, 77% said they were concerned with this sharing, while 23% said they were not.

Table 1. Participant's privacy concerns with Instant Games

#	Items	Frequency	Percent
1	Abuse of user's profile information	30	56.6%
2	Access to user personal information given to third-party applications	34	64.2%
3	Leakage of user personal identifiable information and other personal data	29	54.7%
4	Identity theft	20	37.7%
5	Accessibility (limiting what get access and shared)	21	39.6%
6	Information misuse	28	52.8%
7	Data sharing	30	56.6%
8	Cyberstalking	16	30.2%
9	Phishing Scams	20	37.7%
10	Tracking	34	64.2%
11	Friends and Family can see my gaming activity	18	34.0%
12	Amount of personal information collected	23	43.4%
13	Others, please specify	1	1.9%

In terms of their acceptance of the types of personal data being shared by Facebook with the IG apps (these included: the user's name, profile picture, friends list, etc.), only 5 (9.4%) indicated it was acceptable to share; 23 (43.4%) respondents stated that it was somewhat acceptable, 17 (32.1%) were neutral, and 8 (15.1%) found it unacceptable.

Overall, 34 (64%) of participants expressed that they were highly concerned to concerned about the way in which Facebook shared their data with the IG app (see

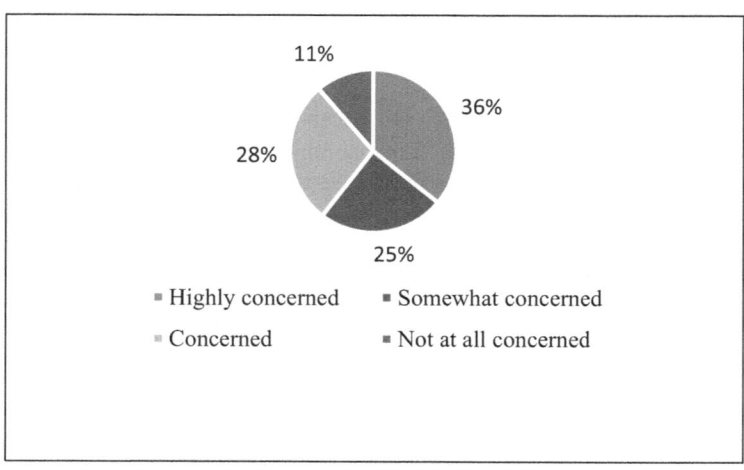

Fig. 1. User's level of concerns with how Facebook shares their data with IG.

Fig. 1). 25% were still somewhat concerned, while only 11% were not at all concerned. This indicates that Facebook data sharing practices are still a concern for its users, even if they find some aspects acceptable.

4.3 Privacy Control Options

This section explores how players feel about the adequacy of the privacy settings that are available to protect their data and privacy. The effect of privacy control has the potential to influence privacy concerns which in turn can affect gaming privacy concerns.

When asked how satisfied they were with the privacy settings provided by Facebook to protect their privacy, 27 (51%) users expressed that they were not sufficient. Less than 50% of participants indicated that to some extent they found the settings enough to protect their privacy on Facebook. The approximately 50/50 split was interesting, given the privacy concerns that were indicated previously.

Of the 53 respondents, a whopping 70% indicated that the privacy settings on Facebook were very helpful or helpful or somewhat helpful to limit or deny what gets shared, accessed, and collected by the game app. 28% said the settings were not helpful; 2% said that they did not know, see Fig. 2.

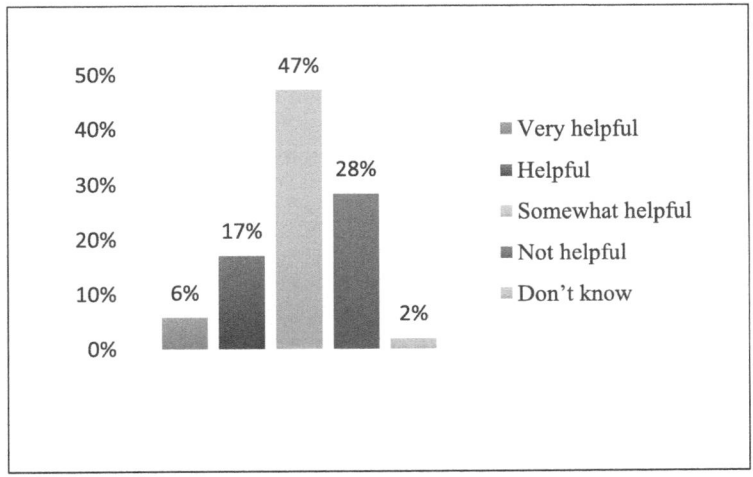

Fig. 2. User perception on how helpful the privacy settings on Facebook are to limit data access and collection by IG apps.

4.4 Data Collection Concerns

Data collection is another factor that can contribute to players privacy concerns-specifically how they feel about the amount and types of information being collected by game apps. When the participants were asked about how they perceived the IG data collection practices based on the default data requirement statement given, 43% (23 participants) found it acceptable, while 25% found it unacceptable (13 participants). Furthermore, 32% (17 participants) indicated that to some extent they found it acceptable. To further expands on this their reasons behind their 'not or somewhat acceptable' responses, which were indicated by 30 participants, an open-ended question was used.

Five main themes were generated from the respondent's responses to the follow up open-opened question; these were (1) tracking, (2) personal information, (3) game activity disclosure, (4) friends list, and (5) ads targeting, see Fig. 3. The results showed that the main reason for their data collection concerns was the collection of personal information, as indicated by 46.6% of respondents. This implies that the current data collection practice may adversely affect users and their connections on Facebook. Secondly, when it came to the instant games accessing their friends list, 21.2% of respondents indicated an issue with their friends and family members contact information being given out and made known automatically by default to the games. Participants expressed this in their responses such as:

P58 - "I have a concern with, allowing others to see my friends list."

P11- "I don't think that they need my friends and family's info and my location to play this game."

P55- "I don't think a small game needs your photo, personal info, and a list of your friends to make your experience better."

The third theme area of concern was the game activity disclosure. Concerns with the disclosure of their game activity to people in their friend's network and outside players was indicated by 16.8% of respondents. The respondents expressed that they wanted to keep their game activity private from others as noted in some of their responses.

P25- "I do not want the games that I play to be shared with my friends."

P42- "I may not want all of my activity public on Facebook."

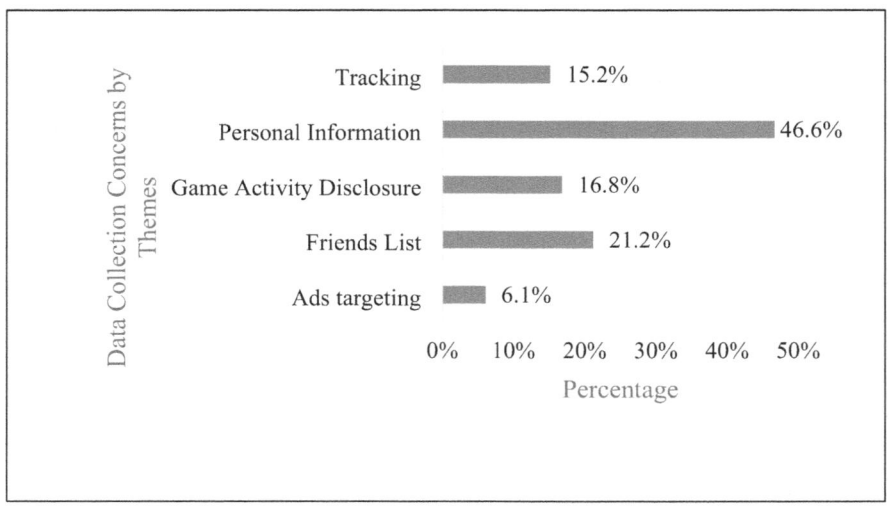

Fig. 3. Data collection concerns by themes.

The last two themes that emerged were location tracking and Ads targeting, which were noted in the respondents' responses as their concerns regarding data collection.

When asked about how invasive they found the IG app's data collection to be, 19 out of 53 participants (36%) expressed that the collection practice was invasive to very invasive. 20 (37.7%) participants found it somewhat invasive, 13 (24.5%) were neutral, and only 1 person (1.9%) indicated there was no issue with the data collection requirements see in Fig. 4. This shows that nearly three-quarters of the participants (73.7%) leaned towards feeling that the app's data collection process was invasive to some degree.

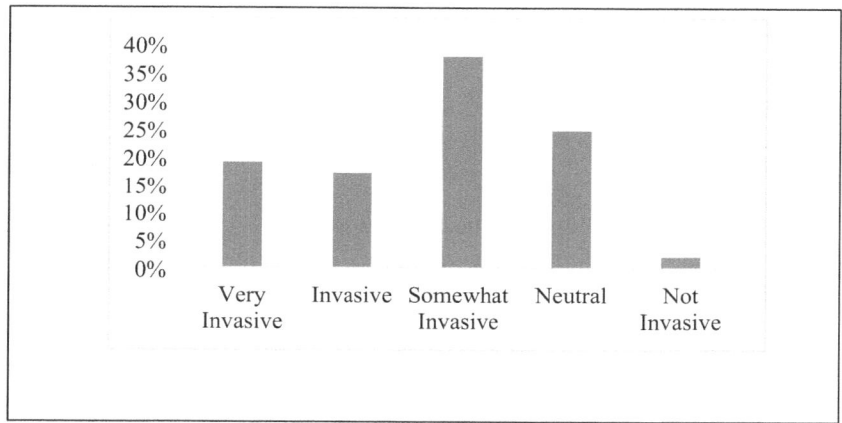

Fig. 4. Users' perspective on how invasive they find the IG app data request.

4.5   Gameplay Action Towards Privacy

This section analyzes the players action towards protecting their privacy when playing an IG on Facebook. Thus, it presents key information to answer research question 2 (RQ#2): What are the players gameplay actions towards privacy?

A list of 6 multiple choice options were presented in random order, with the "other" option given for respondents to provide further feedback, see Table 2. The participants could select all options that relate to them. The results are represented as 'percent of cases', which means that values in this category account for a certain percentage of all cases (i.e. the number of respondents). Percent of cases total will be more than a 100%, but the individual proportions can be understood as the predominance of that option in the survey sample.

The findings showed that the vast majority of respondents chose to click play (94.3% or 50/53) to start the game rather than reviewing or editing any privacy settings (see Table 2). Less than half of the respondents 17% (9/53) chose to review the types of personally identifiable information (PII) and other personal data they were consenting to give access to. By not reviewing the app permissions to see what is being accessed and collected by the game apps, the users may inadvertently put their privacy and social

Table 2. Player's gameplay privacy action towards IG on Facebook.

Privacy actions	n	% of respondents
Read privacy policy	7	13.2%
Review permissions	9	17.0%
Click Play	50	94.3%
Change who can see your game app activities	5	9.4%
Edit the game app permissions	4	7.5%
Other (game ranking)	1	1.9%

activities at risk of being exploited or misused. This gives raise to another issue of informed consent when users are blindly opting to agree to something just to enjoy the benefits of online gameplay and socialization without fully understanding the possible risks. In the findings this is seen further when only 8% of respondents indicated that they edited the game app permission before clicking play. Furthermore, a very small percentage (24.5%, 13/53) of respondents opted to do some other privacy related actions before clicking play such as reading the privacy policy (13.2% of participants).

5   Discussion and Conclusion

The goal of the study was to understand and analyze the extent to which casual social games can impact the user's privacy by exploring Instant Games (IG) on Facebook. The study explored users' privacy concerns, and gameplay behavior that can impact their privacy in a social networking environment. Two research questions were investigated to obtain direct responses from players regarding their Instant Game gameplay experience.

5.1   RQ#1 - What Are the Privacy Concerns Related to IG on Facebook?

Instant Games played on Facebook had a high concern level (73% of participants) when it came to data privacy concerns. The top four privacy concerns were (1) tracking, (2) access to user personal information given to the game apps, (3) abuse of user's profile information and (4) data sharing. The number one concern was tracking, which may affect where users decide to play games or how they connect to these gaming platforms. For instance, privacy conscious users for instance may opt to use protective measures that include the use of a Virtual Private Network (VPN) to prevent being tracked online.

When it comes onto the respondent's data sharing concerns, the findings indicates that Facebook data sharing practices are still a concern for its users, even if they find some aspects acceptable. The results show that when it comes to personal information being shared with IG third party apps, 77% of participants expressed concerns. Their concerns stem from the potential of having their data being exposed to the wrong entities, the purpose of the data sharing, and the use of their data. This concern may contribute to some players' unwillingness to disclose personal information about themselves when gaming or continue to play games on Facebook. Additionally, privacy conscious players may more likely increase their use of privacy protective measures as echoed in associated prior studies regarding online privacy [40].

The result showed that 81% of participants were aware that when they play an IG their gaming data is shared with entities other than Facebook. Although players were aware of the data sharing, only 9.4% found Facebook data sharing practice acceptable, while 8 (15.1%) found it unacceptable. However, most of the respondents (43%) said that to some degree they found it acceptable. This shows that if users accept Facebook data sharing practices with social games such as IG, they may be more inclined to play these social games on Facebook. And they may be more open to having their personal information and gaming activities shared with these third-party game apps as well.

The type and quantity of personal information collected by games apps can contribute to the users' privacy concerns. The results indicate that user perception varies significantly when it comes to IG data collection: 43% of participants found it acceptable, while 25% found it unacceptable. Between these two data points sits 32% of participants indicating that to some extent they found it acceptable. Furthermore, the finding also indicates five main themes behind players concerns towards data collection being done by the IG apps that include: personal information (47%), friends list (21%), game activity disclosure (17%), tracking (14%) and Ads targeting (6%). Personal information data collection was the top concern among the players. These findings suggest that the user perceptions of data collection can influence their gaming privacy concerns.

The results also indicated that 36% of participants expressed that the collection practice for IG apps was invasive to very invasive. This shows that if the users find the IG apps data collection practice invasive, they may or may not decide to continue to play these games on Facebook. Additionally, they may not trust the IG app to have their best interest when it comes to their privacy and even safety.

Another factor to consider with regards to privacy concerns is privacy controls. The level of privacy control that players have over their personal information can influence their privacy concerns. That is, if players do not find the privacy controls sufficient to protect their data or feel like they have enough control over their data this can become a growing privacy concern. The findings indicate that slightly over 50% of participants did not find the privacy settings provided by Facebook adequate to protect their privacy. This can result in the players losing trust in the Facebook gaming platform. Furthermore, players may decide to no longer play games on that platform, especially among individuals that have a high regard for data privacy.

In an associated prior study [41], the authors suggest that users' perceptions of Personal Information Control (PIC) have a significant impact on their information sharing behaviors. The study indicates that higher PIC on SNS represents more control for the users, while lower PIC reduces control. Privacy controls are meant to lessen privacy concerns; however, if users feel that they lack adequate control over their data or lose trust in the entities collecting their data this can impact their privacy concerns.

5.2 RQ#2 - What Are the Players Gameplay Actions Towards Privacy?

The players gaming actions towards privacy as it relates to research question #2 indicates that a privacy paradox exists as majority of the participants chose to "click play" to start the game even though they had high privacy concerns. Furthermore, the players gameplay actions towards privacy indicates that most players may "not to occasionally not" protect their privacy while playing games online which can impact them in a negative manner. From a negative standpoint the results indicated that 94.3% of respondents choose to "click play" first, without taking any other actions to help enhance their privacy or to limit the game app from accessing certain personal information about them such as their name, profile photo, friends list, etc. this can put the users and their associated friend contacts in a vulnerable position, especially in the event of a data breach or other cybercriminal activity.

The results also indicated that despite the concerns about privacy, the majority of the users fail to adjust their behavior to protect their data and privacy before gameplay. This reveals that there is a mismatch between participants stated privacy concerns and their actual gameplay behavior which implies a privacy paradox; this corresponds with other prior studies [34, 42]. From the authors perspective another viewpoint on this is that this failure to adjust their behavior to protect their data could also stem from user not being aware that their personal data can become at risk and their privacy potentially violated. Furthermore, their gameplay action may be one of a privacy versus benefit trade-off, in that socialization and entertainment overshadow the perceived privacy risks and privacy concerns. This is a matter that needs to be considered since the user does not have full control over their data and how it gets shared with third-party game apps or services associated with Facebook.

The players protective behavior towards protecting their data and privacy is surprisingly very low, as the findings show less than 20% of the players decided to review the privacy policy, which can help them to some extent to know what types of data the game collects and how it will be used. Furthermore, less than 20% reviewed and edited the permissions to help control to some degree who can access and see their information. The finding shows that to some extent players are taking steps towards protecting their privacy and data while gaming. These gameplay actions towards privacy include reviewing and editing the game permissions beforehand, adjusting the privacy settings on Facebook and reading the privacy policy. However, this is not done enough, hence the need for game developers, and the gaming platform itself, to help increase privacy-protecting behaviors by increasing privacy-preserving features and functionality. The results further showed that higher education can influence users' privacy concerns to some extent, but it does not necessarily impact their actions towards protecting their privacy when gaming.

The contributions in this paper are a key step towards understanding players privacy concerns and gaming behavior relating to IG on Facebook. The information compiled in this paper can serve as a basis for Facebook and game developers to understand users' privacy concerns, aid with privacy impact assessments and further research into the impact of gaming via a social networking site.

6 Study Limitations and Ethical Considerations

The study has some limitations, the first of which is the sample size. The sample was not a full representation of the targeted student population since no freshman took part in the study. The findings from the sample may not be generalizable. Expanding the research to include non-technical participants and a wider public demographic would add more to the research work. However, the findings still yield strong significant results that contributes to the body of knowledge. This study complied with ethical guidelines for research involving human subjects. An Institutional Review Board (IRB) approval was obtained before starting the study. Each participant had to sign a consent form before taking part in the study.

Appendix- Survey Measures

The survey questions and possible responses are shown below. Note that the questionnaire was presented in a much more user-friendly manner; it is condensed here for space considerations.

Demographic Information.

1. Age Range: 18–22; 23–26; 27–30; 30–35; 36–40; 40–45; 45–50; 51+
2. Gender: How do you identify?
   Male/ non-binary (neither male nor female) / Female
3. Education level:
   Freshman / Sophomore / Junior / Senior / Graduate student
4. How would you rate your computer skills level?
   Beginner / Moderate / Advance / Expert level

Social Media Activities

5. Have you used any of the following social media outlets?
   Facebook / Twitter / Snapchat / Instagram / None

Facebook Instant Games

6. Before playing the Instant Game which of the following is something that you do? (Select all that apply)
   Read privacy policy / Review permissions / Click Play / Change who can see your game app activities / Edit the game app permissions / Others, please specify _____

7. How concerned are you about how Facebook shares your data with the Instant Game app?
   Highly concerned / Somewhat concerned / Low concerned / Not at all concerned.
8. Please rate your level of acceptability with the types of data being shared by Facebook with the Instant Game app.
   Acceptable / Somewhat acceptable / Neutral/ Unacceptable
9. Before playing an Instant Game, the following "data required" statement showing information that will be collected by the game, is shown in sample screenshot #1 below: Do you find the data being collected by the game app acceptable?

Basketball FRVR will receive your name, profile picture, preferred language and friends list. On Facebook, your friends and fellow players can see your gaming activity. ☑ Edit This

Yes /Somewhat /No

10. If your answer is no or somewhat to the question before (prior) please state your reasons.
11. On a scale of 1–10, please rate your privacy concern with the Instant Game you just played (1–4 = Low concern, Neutral = 5–6 and 7–10 = High concern)
12. What are your privacy concerns regarding the Instant Game that you just played on Facebook? (Select all that apply)

    Abuse of user profile information / Access to user personal information given to Third-party application / Leakage of user personal identifiable information and other personal information / Identity theft / Accessibility (limiting what get access and shared) / Information misuse / Data sharing / Cyberstalking / Phishing Scams / Tracking / Friends and Family can see my gaming activity / Others, please specify.
13. Are you concerned with the amount of personal information being shared with the Instant Game app?

    Yes /No
14. Please rate how invasive you find the Instant Game app data collection requirements?

    Very Invasive / Invasive / Somewhat Invasive / Neutral / Not Invasive
15. Apart from Facebook do you think your Gaming data has been shared with others?

    Yes /No / Not sure
16. Did you find the current privacy setting provided by Facebook to its users adequate (enough) to protect its user privacy?

    Yes / Somewhat / No
17. Please rate how helpful the current privacy settings on Facebook are to limit or deny what gets shared, accessed, and collected by the game app.

    Very helpful / Helpful/ Somewhat helpful/Not helpful /Don't know.

References

1. Facebook: Instant Games [Internet] (2020). Accessed 2020 Oct 14. https://www.facebook.com/games/instantgames
2. TechCrunch: Facebook opens Instant Games to all developers [Internet] (2018). Accessed 2022 Apr 24. https://techcrunch.com/2018/03/15/facebook-opens-instant-games-to-all-developers/
3. Kröger, J.L., Raschke, P., Campbell, J.P., Ullrich, S.: Surveilling the gamers: privacy impacts of the video game industry. SSRN Elec. J. 1–23 (2021). Accessed 13 Feb 2023. https://www.ssrn.com/abstract=3881279
4. Micro, T.: Data Privacy and Online Gaming: Why Gamers Make for Ideal Targets - Security News [Internet] (2015). Accessed 1 May 2023. https://www.trendmicro.com/vinfo/us/security/news/online-privacy/data-privacy-and-online-gaming-why-gamers-make-for-ideal-targets
5. Polygon: The dangers of in-game data collection [Internet] (2019). Accessed 15 Apr 2022. https://www.polygon.com/features/2019/5/9/18522937/video-game-privacy-player-data-collection
6. Lab, K.: Online Gaming Scams during Pandemic. How to Stay Safe [Internet] (2023). Accessed 2 May 2023. https://www.kaspersky.com/resource-center/threats/coronavirus-gaming-scams

7. Nicholson, S., Chakraborty, J., Ali-Gombe, A., II Hammell, R.J.: Data sharing and exposure: findings from descriptive and network analysis of instant games on Facebook. Inform. Syst. Comput. Acad. Profession. (2021). Accessed 13 Jan 2022. https://iscap.us/proceedings/con isar/2021/pdf/5613.pdf

8. Statista Research Department: Most popular social networks worldwide as of July 2021, ranked by number of active users [Internet] Statista, pp. 2–3 (2021). https://www.statista. com/statistics/272014/global-social-networks-ranked-by-number-of-users/

9. Statista: Facebook MAU worldwide 2023 [Internet] (2024). Accessed 21 May 2024. https:// www.statista.com/statistics/264810/number-of-monthly-active-facebook-users-worldwide/

10. Isaak, J., Hanna, M.J.: User data privacy: Facebook, Cambridge analytica, and privacy protection. Computer (Long Beach Calif) **51**, 56–59 (2018)

11. BBC News: Meta settles Cambridge Analytica scandal case for $725m - [Internet]. Accessed 20 Apr 2023. https://www.bbc.com/news/technology-64075067

12. CNET.: Facebook says data from 530M users was obtained by scraping, not hack - [Internet (2021). Accessed 19 Feb 2024. https://www.cnet.com/news/privacy/facebook-says-data-leak-is-from-old-vulnerability-that-no-longer-exists/

13. Fairfield, J., Engel, C.: Privacy as a public good. In: Miller, R.A., (ed.) Duke Law J. pp. 95–128 (2015). https://www.cambridge.org/core/product/identifier/9781316658888%23CT-bp-4/type/book_part

14. Read, K., van der Schyff, K.: Modelling the intended use of Facebook privacy settings. SA J. Inform. Manag. **22** (2020). http://www.sajim.co.za/index.php/SAJIM/article/view/1238

15. Facebook.: Instant Games SDK [Internet] (2021). Accessed 4 Mar 2021. https://developers. facebook.com/docs/games/instant-games/sdk/fbinstant6.3

16. Office of the Privacy Commissioner of Canada.: Gaming and personal information: playing with privacy - Office of the Privacy Commissioner of Canada [Internet] (2019). Accessed 2 May 2023. https://www.priv.gc.ca/en/privacy-topics/technology/mobile-and-digital-devices/ digital-devices/gd_gc_201905#h1

17. Nicholson, S., Hammell II, R.J., Chakraborty, J., Ali-gombe, A.: User awareness and privacy regarding instant games on Facebook. In: HCI International Conference 2022 (2022). Accessed 13 Mar 2023. https://doi.org/10.1007/978-3-031-22131-6_46

18. Security Magazine: The pressures the online gaming community faces when it comes to cybersecurity |28 Oct 2020| [Internet]. Security Magazine 2020. Accessed 2 May 2023. https://www.securitymagazine.com/articles/93764-the-pressures-the-online-gam ing-community-faces-when-it-comes-to-cybersecurity

19. TechRadar Pro: Thousands of online gaming accounts hit in major cyberattack | TechRadar [Internet] (2021). Accessed 2 May 2023. https://www.techradar.com/news/thousands-of-onl ine-gaming-accounts-hit-in-major-cyberattack

20. Zhao, C.: Cyber security issues in online games. In: AIP Conference Proceedings, American Institute of Physics Inc. (2018)

21. kaspersky: Online Gaming Risks & Game Security [Internet]. Accessed 26 Mar 2024. https:// www.kaspersky.com/resource-center/threats/top-10-online-gaming-risks#:~:text=Dangers% 20of%20online%20gaming%201%20Malware%20and%20viruses,scripting%20...%208% 20DDoS%20attacks%20...%20More%20items

22. Newsweek: Millions of EA Origin Gamer Accounts Put at Risk of Being Taken Over by Hackers Due to Bugs: Cyber Experts [Internet] (2019). Accessed 2 May 2023. https://www.newsweek.com/electronic-arts-ea-origin-account-takeover-hacking-cybercrime-check-point-cyberint-1445976

23. Privacytemplate: What is Privacy Awareness: Understanding the Importance of Protecting Personal Information - privacytemplate.com [Internet] (2023). Accessed 17 Apr 2024. https:// privacytemplate.com/what-is-privacy-awareness/

24. Zlatolas, L.N., Welzer, T., Heričko, M., Hölbl, M.: Privacy antecedents for SNS self-disclosure: the case of Facebook. Comput. Hum. Behav. **45**, 158–167 (2015)

25. Budak, J., Rajh, E., Recher, V., Škare, V., Škrinjarić, B., Žokalj, M., et al.: The Extended Model of Online Privacy Concern [Internet] (2018). http://www.eizg.hr

26. Benamati, J.H., Ozdemir, Z.D., Smith, H.J.: An empirical test of an Antecedents – Privacy Concerns – Outcomes model, vol. 43, pp. 583–600 (2016). https://doi.org/10.1177/016555 1516653590. Accessed 6 May 2023

27. Paspatis, I., Tsohou, A., Kokolakis, S.: How is privacy behavior formulated? a review of current research and synthesis of information privacy behavioral factors. multimodal technologies and interaction 2023, vol. 7, p. 76 (2023). Accessed 17 Apr 2024. https://www.mdpi.com/2414-4088/7/8/76/htm

28. Hsu, C.L., Liao, Y.C., Lee, C.W., Chan, L.K.: Privacy Concerns and Information Sharing: The Perspective of the U-Shaped Curve. Front Psychol. **13**, 771278 (2022). Accessed 17 Apr 2024. www.frontiersin.org

29. Zhang. S., Chi-Wai Kwok, R., Benjamin Lowry, P., Liu, Z., Paul Benjamin Lowry, P.: Does more accessibility lead to more disclosure? exploring the influence of information accessibility on self-disclosure in online social networks (2014)

30. Pew Research Center.: Views of data privacy risks, personal data and digital privacy laws in America [Internet] (2023). Accessed 17 Apr 2024. https://www.pewresearch.org/internet/2023/10/18/views-of-data-privacy-risks-personal-data-and-digital-privacy-laws/

31. Firewall Times: Facebook Data Breaches: Full Timeline Through 2023 [Internet] (2023). Accessed 12 Apr 2024. https://firewalltimes.com/facebook-data-breach-timeline/#:~:text=Facebook%20Data%20Breaches%3A%20Full%20Timeline%20Through%202023% 201,Users%20Found%20on%20Exposed%20Server%20...%20More%20items

32. Barth, S., de Jong, M.D.T.: The privacy paradox – Investigating discrepancies between expressed privacy concerns and actual online behavior – a systematic literature review. Telemat. Inform. **34**, 1038–1058 (2017). https://linkinghub.elsevier.com/retrieve/pii/S07365 85317302022

33. Barnes, S.B.: A privacy paradox: social networking in the United States. First Monday. **11**, 5 (2006)

34. Kokolakis, S.: Privacy attitudes and privacy behaviour: a review of current research on the privacy paradox phenomenon. Comput. Secur. 122–134. Elsevier Ltd. (2017)

35. Gerber, N., Gerber, P., Volkamer, M.: Explaining the privacy paradox: a systematic review of literature investigating privacy attitude and behavior. Comput. Secur. **77**, 226–261 (2018)

36. Gerber, N., Gerber, P., Volkamer, M.: Explaining the privacy paradox: a systematic review of literature investigating privacy attitude and behavior. Comput. Secur. **77**, 226–261 (2018). https://linkinghub.elsevier.com/retrieve/pii/S0167404818303031

37. Bongiovanni, I., Renaud, K., Aleisa, N.: The privacy paradox: we claim we care about our data, so why don't our actions match? [Internet] (2020). Accessed 20 Mar 2024. https://theconversation.com/the-privacy-paradox-we-claim-we-care-about-our-data-so-why-dont-our-actions-match-143354

38. Pew Research Center.: Americans' opinions on privacy and information sharing [Internet]. Accessed 20 Apr 2023. https://www.pewresearch.org/internet/2016/01/14/privacy-and-information-sharing/

39. Statista: U.S. video gamers age 2022 [Internet] (2022). Accessed 7 Apr 2023. https://www.statista.com/statistics/189582/age-of-us-video-game-players/

40. Baruh, L., Secinti, E., Cemalcilar, Z.: Online privacy concerns and privacy management: a meta-analytical review. J. Commun. **67**, 26–53 (2017)

41. Mutambik, I., Almuqrin, A., Liu, Y., Alhossayin, M., Qintash, F.H.: Gender differentials on information sharing and privacy concerns on social networking sites: perspectives from users. J. Glob. Inf. Manag. **29**, 236–255 (2021)
42. Taddicken, M.: The 'Privacy Paradox' in the social web: the impact of privacy concerns, individual characteristics, and the perceived social relevance on different forms of self-disclosure. J. Comput.-Media. Commun. **19**, 248–273 (2014). Accessed 11 May 2023. https://academic.oup.com/jcmc/article/19/2/248/4067550

A Labeled Dataset for Sentiment Analysis of Videos on YouTube, TikTok, and Other Sources About the 2024 Outbreak of Measles

Nirmalya Thakur[1]([✉]), Vanessa Su[2], Mingchen Shao[1], Kesha A. Patel[2], Hongseok Jeong[1], Victoria Knieling[3], and Andrew Bian[4]

[1] Department of Computer Science, Emory University, Atlanta, GA 30322, USA
nirmalyathakur@ieee.org, {katie.shao,peter.jeong}@emory.edu
[2] Department of Mathematics, Emory University, Atlanta, GA 30322, USA
{vanessa.su,kesha.patel}@emory.edu
[3] Program in Linguistics, Emory University, Atlanta, GA 30322, USA
victoria.knieling@emory.edu
[4] Goizueta Business School, Emory University, Atlanta, GA 30322, USA
andrew.bian@emory.edu

Abstract. Since the beginning of 2024, several countries have been experiencing an outbreak of measles. In the modern-day Internet of Everything lifestyle, social media platforms such as YouTube and TikTok have gained widespread popularity on a global scale due to their ability to facilitate the easy creation and dissemination of videos. During virus outbreaks of the recent past, videos on social media platforms played a crucial role in keeping the global population informed and updated regarding various aspects of the outbreaks. As a result in the last few years, researchers from different disciplines have focused on the development of datasets of videos published on YouTube, TikTok, and similar websites. No prior work in this field has focused on the development of a dataset of videos about the ongoing outbreak of measles, published on social media platforms. The work of this paper aims to address this research gap and presents a dataset that contains the data of 4011 videos about the ongoing outbreak of measles published on 264 websites on the internet between January 1, 2024, and May 31, 2024, available at https://dx.doi.org/10.21227/40s8-xf63. These websites primarily include YouTube and TikTok, which account for 48.6% and 15.2% of the videos, respectively. The remainder of the websites include Instagram and Facebook as well as the websites of various global and local news organizations. For each of these videos, the URL of the video, title of the post, description of the post, and the date of publication of the video are presented as separate attributes in the dataset. After developing this dataset, sentiment analysis (using VADER), subjectivity analysis (using TextBlob), and fine-grain sentiment analysis (using DistilRoBERTa-base) of the video titles and video descriptions were performed. This included classifying each video title and video description into (i) one of the sentiment classes i.e. positive, negative, or neutral, (ii) one of the subjectivity classes i.e. highly opinionated, neutral opinionated, or least opinionated, and (iii) one of the fine-grain sentiment classes i.e. fear, surprise, joy, sadness, anger, disgust, or neutral. These results are presented as separate attributes in the dataset for the training and

A. Coman et al. (Eds.): HCII 2024, LNCS 15375, pp. 220–239, 2025.
https://doi.org/10.1007/978-3-031-76806-4_17

testing of machine learning algorithms for performing sentiment analysis or subjectivity analysis in this field as well as for other applications. Finally, this paper also presents a list of open research questions that may be investigated using this dataset.

Keywords: Measles · Big Data · Dataset · Sentiment Analysis · Subjectivity Analysis · Data Analysis · Natural Language Processing · Data Science

1   Introduction

Measles is a highly transmissible viral illness caused by a single-stranded and enveloped RNA virus [1]. Despite the availability of an effective measles vaccine for more than 40 years, annually there are approximately 20 million cases of measles on a global scale and measles continues to be among the leading causes of death in young children [2, 3]. The risk of measles has been significantly increased by the COVID-19 pandemic [4, 5]. Furthermore, due to the impact of COVID-19 on the healthcare sector, from 2020 to 2022, more than 61 million doses of measles vaccines were missed or deferred on a global scale [6]. As a result, since the beginning of 2024, multiple countries have been experiencing outbreaks of measles. The countries include – Kazakhstan (21,740 cases), Azerbaijan (13,720 cases), Yemen (13,676 cases), India (13,220 cases), Iraq (11,595 cases), Ethiopia (9,042 cases), Kyrgyzstan (7,601 cases), Russian Federation (7,594 cases), Pakistan (5,812 cases), and Indonesia (5,648 cases). To add to this, the number of cases of measles in the United States since the beginning of 2024 has already exceeded the number of cases of measles recorded in the United States in 2023 [6].

Among the various types of web services and applications, online videos are currently "dominating the internet" [7]. On average, an individual watches 17 hours of videos on the internet per week [8] as online videos serve as a rich and seamless resource of information related to various topics including recent issues, global challenges, pandemics, virus outbreaks, emerging technologies, and trending matters [9]. In the last few years, social media platforms such as YouTube and TikTok have become popular amongst all groups as such platforms provide a seamless way for users to create and disseminate information in the form of videos [10, 11]. On a global scale, YouTube is the second most frequented website on the internet after google.com. It is accessible in 100 nations and 80 languages, with users collectively streaming approximately 5 billion videos daily [12, 13]. In terms of worldwide traffic on YouTube, the United States takes the lead with 11.67 billion, followed by South Korea (8.25 billion), India (4.2 billion), Brazil (3.59 billion), Germany (3.49 billion), and other countries [14]. In addition to this, more than 122 million individuals engage with YouTube daily, constituting roughly a quarter of global internet activity [15]. On a global scale, TikTok ranks 5th in the list of most popular social media platforms [16]. At present the number of active users on TikTok is 1.7 billion and this number is projected to increase to 2.25 billion by 2027 [17]. In 2024, TikTok has been the 3rd most downloaded mobile application on a global scale [18], and on average, each user spends 58 minutes and 24 seconds on TikTok on a daily basis [19]. In terms of the worldwide traffic on TikTok, the United States takes the lead with 148 million, which is followed by Indonesia (126.8 million), Brazil (98.6 million),

Mexico (74.2 million), Vietnam (67.7 million), Russia (58.6 million), Pakistan (54.4 million), Philippines (49.1 million), Thailand (44.4 million), Turkey (37.7 million), and other countries [20].

During virus outbreaks of the recent past, social media platforms such as YouTube and TikTok served as crucial sources for the global population to stay informed and updated related to those virus outbreaks [21, 22]. Video datasets serve as valuable data resources for the investigation of diverse research questions related to creating, viewing, reacting, and disseminating video-based content on the internet. As a result in the last few years, researchers from different disciplines have focused on the development of datasets of videos published on YouTube, TikTok, and similar websites. The ongoing outbreak of measles which has been declared a public health emergency [23], epidemic [24], and a national incident [25] in different parts of the world has resulted in a concern about public health on a global scale. So, in the last few months, researchers from different disciplines have investigated the same as well as studied prior outbreaks of measles for insight related to the current outbreak. However, no prior work in this field has focused on the development of a dataset of videos about the ongoing outbreak of measles published on YouTube, TikTok, and other websites on the internet. To add to this, there are other research gaps that still exist in this field (discussed in Sect. 2). Addressing these gaps with an aim to contribute to the advancement of research in this field serves as the main motivation for this work. The rest of this paper is structured as follows. Section 2 presents a review of recent works in this field and discusses the research gaps that exist. Section 3 discusses the methodology that was followed for the development of this dataset. The results are presented in Sect. 4 which also includes a list of open research questions that may be investigated using this dataset. The conclusion is presented in Sect. 5 where the scientific contributions of this work are summarized and the scope for future work in this field is outlined.

2 Literature Review

Real et al. [26] developed a dataset that contains the URLs of YouTube videos for object detection. This dataset contains about 380,000 videos and the duration of each of these videos is approximately 19 seconds. Loh et al. [27] developed a dataset of YouTube videos for modeling internet traffic and streaming analysis. The dataset comprises 80 network scenarios, encompassing 171 distinct bandwidth settings. These settings were tested in a total of 5,181 tests with limited bandwidth, 1,939 runs with emulated 3G/4G traces, and 4,022 runs with pre-defined bandwidth variations. The work of Xu et al. [28] involved the development of a YouTube dataset for sequence-to-sequence video object segmentation. The dataset contains 3252 video clips and 78 types of common objects and human activities. Similar video datasets for object segmentation were developed by Li et al. [29], Jain et al. [30], Ochs et al. [31], Perazzi et al. [32], and Pont-Tuset et al. [33]. The number of videos these datasets contain is 14, 96, 59, 50, and 90, respectively. Lall et al. [34] collected watch history data of 243 YouTube users over a period of 1.5 years and developed a dataset. Their dataset contains a total of 1.8 million YouTube videos. Le et al. [35] developed a dataset of YouTube videos that contains 23,738 videos in four categories: comedy, travel and events, education, science and technology. Their dataset contains YouTube videos published over 12 years from 72 channels.

Qian et al. [36] developed a dataset of 283,582 TikTok videos for human activity recognition. The videos from this dataset represent 386 different hashtags related to human behavior. The work of Ng et al. [37] involved preparing a dataset of about 7000 videos from TikTok. The authors specifically focused on collecting videos where TikTok users demonstrated their participation or completion of trending challenges on TikTok. Basch et al. [38] collected 100 videos from TikTok containing #climatechange. 73 videos from this collection focused on at least one aspect of climate change. Fiallos et al. [39] developed a dataset of 1495 TikTok videos to understand the categories of knowledge and learning opportunities from TikTok. The dataset contains videos with different hashtags out of which #learnontiktok represents the primary hashtag for knowledge and learning opportunities. Shutsko et al. [40] developed a dataset of 1000 TikTok videos to analyze the trends of popularity of different subject matters on TikTok. The work of Abdaljaleel et al. [41] involved the assessment of information about the measles vaccine on social media platforms including YouTube and TikTok. The analysis of videos from these platforms showed that a majority of the videos (61.8%) were created by lay individuals and not medical professionals, healthcare providers, or journalists. Hussain et al. [42] performed an analysis of YouTube videos regarding measles. The findings showed that about 32% opposed vaccination against measles. Yiannakoulias et al. [43] analyzed content about measles vaccines as disseminated in YouTube videos. The findings from their analysis of 134 YouTube videos showed that 48.51% of the videos were in favor of getting vaccinated for measles, 19.40% of the videos were against getting vaccinated for measles, and 32.09% of the videos didn't communicate an opinion for or against getting vaccinated for measles.

To summarize, even though multiple works exist related to the development of datasets of YouTube videos, datasets of TikTok videos, and investigation of prior outbreaks of measles, there are multiple research gaps that exist in these areas of research. These research gaps are outlined as follows:

- No prior work in this field has focused on the development of a dataset of videos about the ongoing outbreak of measles published on YouTube, TikTok, and other websites on the internet.
- None of the video datasets in this field have attributes that assign an overall sentiment of positive, negative, or neutral to the video descriptions or video titles. To add to this, none of these datasets have attributes that assign a label such as anger, disgust, fear, joy, neutral, sadness, or surprise, to the video descriptions or video titles after performing fine-grain sentiment analysis.
- No prior work related to the development of a dataset of videos has attributes that categorize the video descriptions or video titles into one of the subjectivity classes - highly opinionated, neutral opinionated, and least opinionated, based on the degree of opinion expressed in each video.
- No prior work has presented the results of performing overall sentiment analysis, fine-grain sentiment analysis, or subjectivity analysis of videos related to the ongoing outbreak of measles from YouTube, TikTok, and other websites on the internet.
- None of these works that focused on the development of video datasets present datasets that contain the data of videos from YouTube, TikTok, Instagram, and

Facebook as well as some of the popular news organizations such as cbsnews.com, nbcnews.com, msn.com, dailytelegraph.com.au, apnews.com, cnn.com.

The work presented in this paper aims to address these research gaps. The step-by-step methodology that was followed for the completion of this research work is discussed in Sect. 3.

3 Methodology

Figure 1 presents an overview of the methodology that was followed in this research work that resulted in the development of this dataset that contains the data of 4011 videos about the ongoing outbreak of measles published on 264 websites on the internet between January 1, 2024, and May 31, 2024, available at https://dx.doi.org/10.21227/40s8-xf63. These websites primarily include YouTube and TikTok, which account for 48.6% and 15.2% of the videos, respectively. The remainder of the websites includes Instagram and Facebook, as well as the websites of various global and local news organizations such as cbsnews.com, nbcnews.com, msn.com, dailytelegraph.com.au, apnews.com, cnn.com, etc.

For collecting data from YouTube, the YouTube API was used [44]. For the rest of the websites, the data was collected manually by the co-authors of this paper by using a keyword search on Google followed by visiting each of these websites. The keywords that were used for collecting the data included "measles" and "MMR vaccine". More specifically, if the title or description of a video contained either of these keywords that video was included in the development of the first version of the dataset. During the data collection process for the development of the first version of the dataset, for each video about measles, the URL of the video, the title of the post, the description of the post, and the date of publication of the video were collected. For websites such as tiktok.com, instagram.com, and a few news sources, as a separate video title and video description are not published, the value of the video title was used as the value of the video description. As this research work specifically focuses on the 2024 outbreak of measles, the time range for data collection was set as January 1, 2024, and May 31, 2024 (the most recent date at the time of submission of the camera-ready version of this paper to HCII 2024) and the data of videos published before January 1, 2024, were removed from the dataset. Thereafter, data preprocessing of the video titles and video descriptions was performed by writing a program in Python 3.11.5 installed on a computer with a Microsoft Windows 10 Pro operating system. The data preprocessing included (a) removal of characters that were not alphabets, (b) removal of URLs, (c) removal of hashtags, (d) removal of user mentions, (e) detection of English words using tokenization, (f) stemming, (g) removal of stop words, and (h) removal of numbers.

Finally, edge cases were also removed from the dataset by manual review of the video titles and video descriptions. This manual review was performed by the co-authors of this paper. In this context, we define edge cases as video titles or video descriptions that met our search criteria but were not related to the ongoing outbreak of measles (for example [45]). Thereafter, the preprocessed versions of the video titles and video descriptions were analyzed using VADER for Sentiment Analysis [46], TextBlob for Subjectivity Analysis [47], and DistilRoBERTa-base for fine-grain sentiment analysis [48].

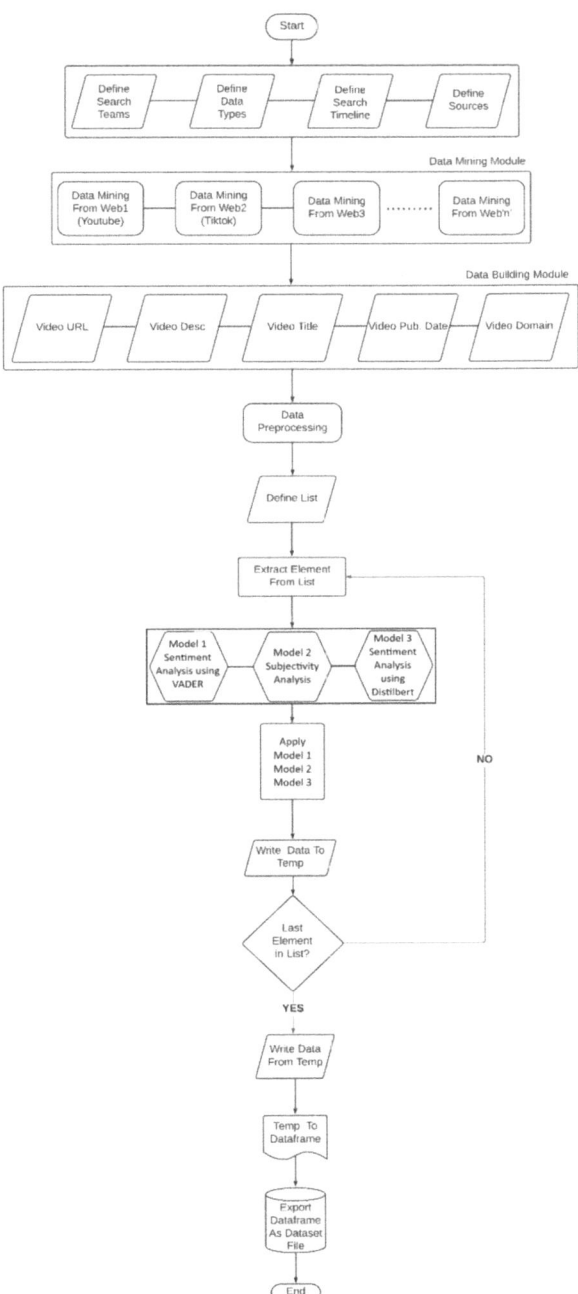

Fig. 1. A flowchart that represents an overview of the methodology that was followed for the development of this dataset.

VADER (Valence Aware Dictionary and sEntiment Reasoner) is a lexicon and rule-based sentiment analysis tool that is specifically attuned to sentiments expressed in social media [46]. VADER can analyze a given text and categorize it as either positive, negative, or neutral. In addition, it can identify the compound sentiment score and the magnitude of sentiment represented in a given text, ranging from 0 to + 4 for positive sentiment and 0 to –4 for negative sentiment. There are multiple factors as a result of which VADER was used for sentiment analysis in this work even though several other approaches for sentiment analysis exist. First, studies have shown that VADER demonstrates outstanding efficiency with respect to both precision and efficacy [49–51]. Second, VADER effectively addresses the limitations faced by several other sentiment analysis approaches [52–55]. Finally, VADER has attracted the attention of researchers from different disciplines for solving research problems that focused on performing sentiment analysis of conversations on the internet related to recent virus outbreaks [56–60]. TextBlob is a lexicon-based analyzer that uses a set of predefined rules to perform sentiment analysis and subjectivity analysis. The sentiment score lies between − 1 to 1, where − 1 identifies the most negative words such as 'disgusting', 'awful', and 'pathetic', and 1 identifies the most positive words like 'excellent', and 'best'. The subjectivity score lies between 0 and 1. It represents the degree of personal opinion, if a sentence has high subjectivity i.e., close to 1, it means that the text contains more personal opinion than factual information. For fine-grain sentiment analysis, the specific model that was used was DistilRoBERTa-base [48]. This model can analyze a text and categorize it into one of the fine-grain sentiment classes - anger, disgust, fear, joy, neutral, sadness, or surprise. This model is a fine-tuned checkpoint of DistilRoBERTa-base and has been used in multiple prior works in this field that involved performing fine-grain sentiment analysis [61–63]. The results of applying VADER to the descriptions and titles of these videos were compiled and added as two new attributes – "VADER_Description" and "VADER_Title" to the dataset. These two attributes present the classification of video descriptions and video titles as positive, negative, or neutral using VADER. The results of subjectivity analysis were also compiled and added as two new attributes - "Subjectivity_Description" and "Subjectivity_Title", where the video descriptions and video titles are classified as Highly Opinionated, Neutral Opinionated, or Least Opinionated. These subjectivity or opinion classes based on the output from TextBlob were defined based on multiple prior works in this field where TextBlob was used for performing subjectivity analysis (for example: [64, 65]).

Finally, the results of applying DistilRoBERTa-base to the descriptions and titles of these videos to perform fine-grain sentiment analysis were also compiled and added as two different attributes – "FineGrainSentiment_Description" and "FineGrainSentiment_Title", where the video descriptions and video titles are classified as anger, disgust, fear, joy, neutral, sadness, or surprise. These results are discussed in detail in Sect. 4, which also presents the results of data analysis and a list of open research questions that may be investigated using this dataset.

4   Results and Discussions

This section presents the results of this research work. The dataset that was developed is available at https://dx.doi.org/10.21227/40s8-xf63. This dataset is compliant with the FAIR (Findability, Accessibility, Interoperability, and Reusability) principles for scientific data management [66]. The dataset is findable, as it has a unique and permanent DOI, which has been assigned by IEEE Dataport. The dataset can be accessed online by any individual on the internet by directly visiting the DOI of the dataset. It is interoperable due to the use of a .csv file that can be downloaded, read, and analyzed across different operating systems and applications. The dataset is reusable as the video-related information, such as the URLs of the videos, titles of the posts, descriptions of the posts, the dates of publication of the videos, overall sentiment classes, fine-grain sentiment classes, and subjectivity classes from the dataset file can be used for free for the development of any types of programs or algorithms any number of times without any requirement to purchase any subscription or credits per use.

The results of the data analysis are shown in Figs. 2, 3, 4, 5, 6 and 7. The results of sentiment analysis using VADER in Figs. 2 and 3 show that for the video titles, 62.78% were neutral, 20.04% were positive, and 17.18% were negative and for the video descriptions 40.46% were neutral, 39.42% were positive, and 20.12% were negative. The results of subjectivity analysis using TextBlob from Figs. 4 and 5 show that for the video titles, the distribution of the classes highly opinionated, neutral opinionated, and least opinionated were 5.93%, 17.85%, and 76.22%, respectively, and for the video descriptions, the distribution of these opinion classes was 10.07%, 27.25%, and 62.68%, respectively. The results of sentiment analysis using DistilRoBERTa-base showed that for the video descriptions, the distribution of fine-grain sentiment classes of fear, surprise, joy, sadness, anger, disgust, and neutral was 26.18%, 2.17%, 3.44%, 8.63%, 2.34%, 0.42%, and 56.82%, respectively and for the video titles the distribution of these fine-grain sentiment classes was 18.37%, 2.22%, 1.20%, 6.31%, 2.12%, 0.82%, and 68.96%, respectively. In this context, the authors would like to clarify that the sentiment class, subjectivity class, and fine grain sentiment class assigned to each video title and video description in this dataset, are presented in *as-is* form after obtaining the same from the outputs of VADER, TextBlob, and DistilRoBERTa-base, respectively. These outputs as well as the video data present in this dataset do not represent or reflect the views, opinions, beliefs, or political stances of the authors of this paper.

YouTube and TikTok, being among the top five globally popular social media platforms are popular for video-based content creation and dissemination on a wide range of topics. Prior works have shown that the nature and intensity of sentiments on YouTube and TikTok vary from topic to topic [67–71]. For instance, the work of Shevtsov et al. [72] showed that in the context of the 2020 presidential elections in the United States, the sentiment towards the presidential candidates was predominantly negative. In [73], the authors concluded that in terms of conspiracy theories related to COVID-19 on YouTube, the distribution of sentiment was 46.9% positive, 31.0% neutral, and 22.1% negative. In [74], the authors showed that the sentiment towards vaccinations on YouTube was primarily negative (52%) in 2017. However, this changed to primarily positive (54%) in 2018.

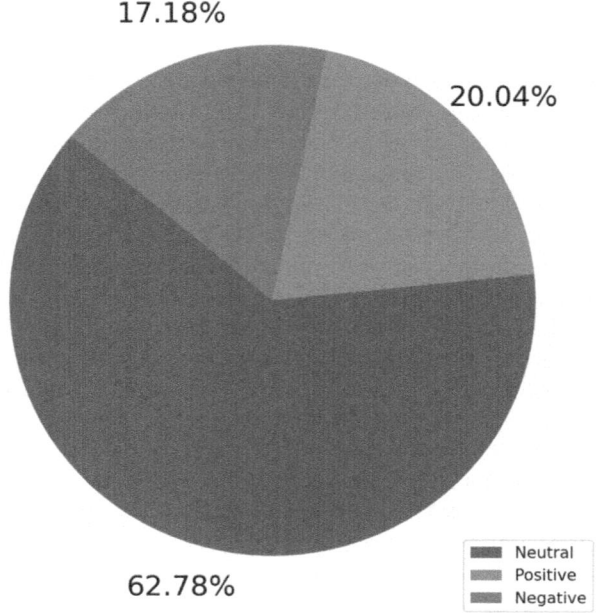

Fig. 2. Results of Sentiment Analysis of the Video Titles using VADER

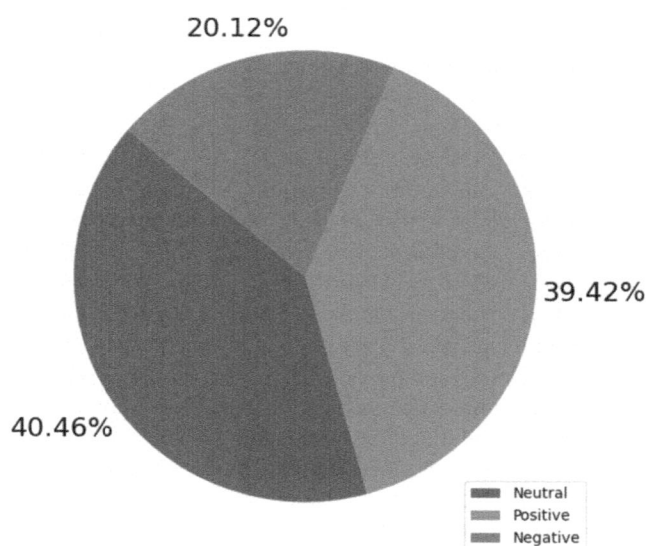

Fig. 3. Results of Sentiment Analysis of the Video Descriptions using VADER

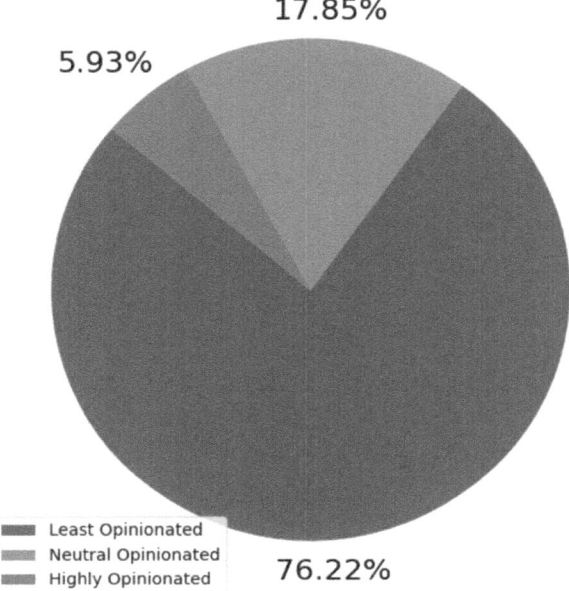

Fig. 4. Results of Subjectivity Analysis of the Video Titles using TextBlob

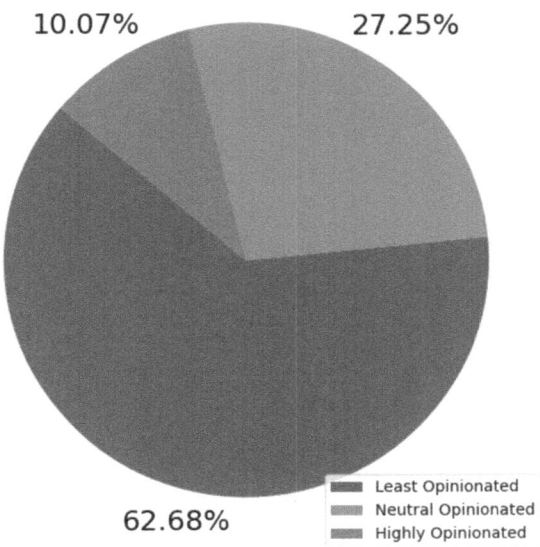

Fig. 5. Results of Subjectivity Analysis of the Video Descriptions using TextBlob

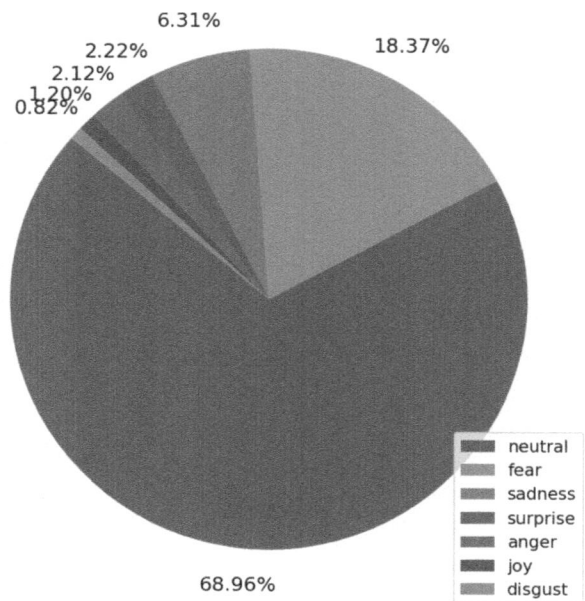

Fig. 6. Results of Fine-Grain Sentiment Analysis of the Video Titles using DistilRoBERTa-base

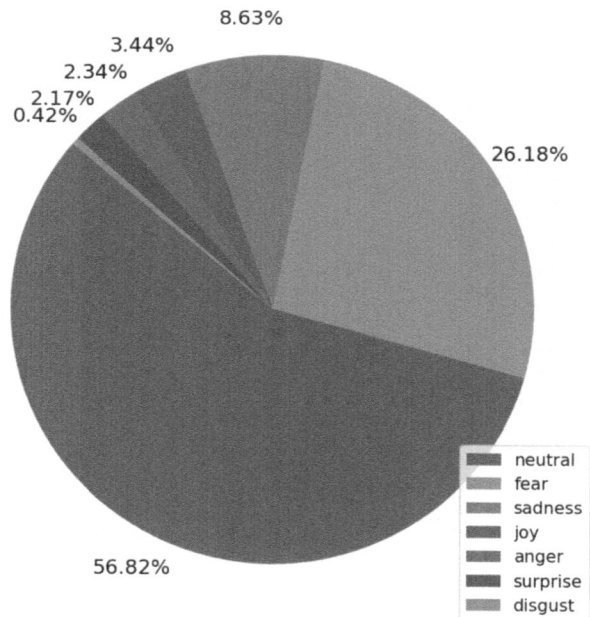

Fig. 7. Results of Fine-Grain Sentiment of the Video Descriptions using DistilRoBERTa-base

The work of Rachmawati et al. [75] showed that TikTok videos containing #samasam-abelajar were primarily neutral (57.06%). In this paper, the findings of sentiment analysis show that the percentage of videos with neutral sentiment is higher than the percentage of videos with other sentiments. There may be multiple reasons that support this finding. First, the videos of this dataset have been published on YouTube, TikTok, Instagram, Facebook, and other websites such as cbsnews.com, nbcnews.com, msn.com, dailytele-graph.com.au, apnews.com, cnn.com, etc. since the beginning of this year. Many of these websites are news channels that are likely to present the facts as compared to presenting their opinions (positive or negative) related to the ongoing measles outbreak. For a video that presents only factual information, the assigned label from sentiment analysis using VADER and DistilRoBERTa-base would be neutral. Second, the ongoing outbreak of measles, similar to the virus outbreaks of the recent past, isn't a topic for which the global population is expected to have negative opinions (unlike the 2020 Presential Elections in the United States as per the findings of Shevtsov et al. [72]). As a result, the majority of the videos in this dataset are not associated with a negative sentiment.

A list of open research questions is presented next, which may be investigated using this dataset:

- Performing topic modeling of the video descriptions to identify the themes or focus areas related to the creation and dissemination of videos about the ongoing outbreak of measles.
- Performing aspect-based sentiment analysis of these videos to investigate the specific topics or focus areas regarding the ongoing measles outbreak associated with positive or negative sentiments or one of the fine-grain sentiment classes of fear, surprise, joy, sadness, anger, or disgust.
- Performing a case study of different supervised learning models in machine learning to determine the optimal model for identification of the overall sentiment, the fine-grain sentiment, or the subjectivity expressed in these videos.
- Detecting sarcasm expressed in video descriptions or video titles to identify the trends of sarcasm (using the dates of publications of the videos that are present in the dataset) about the ongoing outbreak of measles on social media platforms such as YouTube, TikTok, Instagram, and Facebook and analyzing any similarities or differences in those trends.
- Investigation of any correlations between the length of video titles (or descriptions) and the overall sentiment, fine-grain sentiment, or subjectivity in the videos.
- Analyzing the usage of hashtags in video descriptions related to the ongoing outbreak of measles on YouTube and TikTok to identify the popular hashtags associated with positive, negative, and neutral videos.
- Detecting distinct users (from the video URLs that are present in the dataset) who published these videos on TikTok and YouTube. Thereafter, identifying the types of users (for example, medical professionals, healthcare organizations, etc.) who posted the majority of positive, negative, and neutral videos.
- Performing Content Value Analysis and analysis of the credibility of information in these videos to rank the video sources from highest credibility to lowest credibility regarding information about the ongoing measles outbreak on social media platforms such as YouTube, TikTok, Instagram, and Facebook.

- Develop a binary classifier to categorize the video sources as a news source or not a news source. Thereafter, identifying the role of news sources in the dissemination of information about the ongoing outbreak of measles.
- Detecting misinformation expressed by the different video sources to analyze the degree of misinformation dissemination per video source related to the ongoing outbreak of measles.
- Detecting fake news regarding measles expressed by the different video sources to analyze the degree of misinformation dissemination per video source.
- Identification of conspiracy theories expressed in videos about the ongoing measles outbreak to infer which platform(s) has been playing a greater role in the creation and dissemination of conspiracy theories.
- Detecting satire related to measles expressed in video descriptions and the trends of the satire on social media platforms such as YouTube, TikTok, Instagram, and Facebook on a weekly or biweekly basis (using the date of publication of these videos which is present in the dataset).
- Identification of hate speech or abusive language in videos about the ongoing outbreak of measles published on social media platforms such as YouTube, TikTok, Instagram, and Facebook to determine the trends of the same.
- Detection, identification, and ranking of trending topics for video publication on the internet related to the ongoing outbreak of measles.
- Detection of communities on social media platforms such as YouTube, TikTok, Instagram, and Facebook that support or do not support each other regarding the ongoing outbreak of measles based on the analysis of reaction videos and related characteristics.

This dataset and the open research questions presented in this paper are expected to advance research and development in this field. Furthermore, the findings of this paper are also expected to contribute to the development of video recommendations related to the ongoing outbreak of measles. The methodology used by modern-day video recommendation systems is either collaborative filtering or content-based filtering [76]. Collaborative filtering algorithms evaluate components of user behavior related to watching videos such as ratings, likes, dislikes, watch time, favorites, etc. to create a profile of each user as per their interests. Then, the algorithm pairs the user with other users with similar behavior. Thereafter, it analyzes similar behaviors to develop video recommendations for similar users [77]. However, collaborative filtering-based video recommendations have a "cold start" problem as many users on the internet do not like, dislike, or rate videos. Such systems also require a considerable amount of data for the identification of similar users [78, 79]. Therefore, content-based filtering approaches for video recommendations have been gaining popularity in the recent past [80]. Content-based filtering approaches take into account multiple characteristics of videos for recommending videos to users. The concept of content-based video recommendations is used by multiple video streaming platforms [80]. As this paper presents the findings of sentiment analysis, fine-grain sentiment analysis, and subjectivity analysis and the assignment of sentiment, fine-grain sentiment, and subjectivity classes to each video in this dataset, this work is also expected to contribute towards the development of content-based video recommendation systems related to the ongoing measles outbreak.

The work presented in this paper has a few limitations. First, VADER and DistilRoBERTa-base were used for performing sentiment analysis and fine-grain sentiment analysis. To add to this, TextBlob was used for performing subjectivity analysis. These three algorithms use unsupervised learning and have been widely used for sentiment analysis, fine-grain sentiment analysis, and subjectivity analysis in several prior works in this field [81–86]. However, none of these algorithms are 100% accurate. Second, other than YouTube, the video data (i.e. the URL of the video, title of the post, description of the post, and the date of publication of the video) from sources such as TikTok, Instagram, Facebook, and websites of global and local news channels, presented in this dataset was collected by the co-authors of this paper by manually visiting different websites (discussed in Sect. 3). As stated in prior works where manual labeling was used [87, 88], manual labeling may be associated with minor human errors. Third, even though it is not stated in the description of the DistilRoBERTa-base model [48], we observed that this model is able to process up to 512 characters for performing fine-grain sentiment analysis. To address this limitation of the model, for video descriptions and video titles that exceeded its processing limit, we passed the first 512 characters to the model. Finally, the findings of sentiment analysis, fine-grain sentiment analysis, and subjectivity analysis as presented in this paper are based on the videos that are available in this dataset. The ongoing outbreak of measles continues to affect multiple geographic regions of the world. As a result, multiple videos related to this outbreak are getting published on the internet every day. Therefore, if sentiment analysis, fine-grain sentiment analysis, and subjectivity analysis of videos about the ongoing outbreak of measles are performed at any time in the near future, depending on the global reaction, views, opinions, and responses towards the outbreak at that time, the results may vary as compared to the results presented in this paper.

5   Conclusion

Measles is a highly contagious viral illness produced by a single-stranded RNA virus and prior works in this field have shown a substantial rise in the susceptibility to measles as a direct consequence of the COVID-19 pandemic. Since the beginning of 2024, several countries have been experiencing an outbreak of measles. Online videos are currently exerting a dominant influence on the internet. Social media platforms such as YouTube and TikTok have gained widespread popularity across many demographics on a global scale due to their ability to facilitate the easy creation and sharing of videos. During virus outbreaks of the recent past, social media platforms such as YouTube and TikTok played a vital role in keeping the worldwide public informed and up to date on the outbreaks. Video datasets serve as valuable data resources for the investigation of diverse research questions related to the creation and dissemination of video-based content on the Internet. As a result in the last few years, researchers from different disciplines have focused on the development of datasets of videos published on YouTube, TikTok, and similar websites. However, no prior work in this field has focused on the development of a dataset of videos about the ongoing outbreak of measles published on YouTube, TikTok, and other websites on the internet. To add to this, there are other research gaps that still exist in this field. The work of this paper aims to address these research gaps and presents a dataset that contains the data of 4011 videos about the ongoing outbreak of measles uploaded on 264 websites on the internet between January 1, 2024, and May 31, 2024, available at https://dx.doi.org/10.21227/40s8-xf63. These websites primarily include YouTube and TikTok, which account for 48.6% and 15.2% of the videos, respectively. The remainder of the websites include Instagram and Facebook as well as the websites of multiple global and local news organizations such as cbsnews.com, nbcnews.com, msn.com, dailytelegraph.com.au, apnews.com, cnn.com, etc. For each of these videos, the URL of the video, title of the post, description of the post, and the date of publication of the video are presented as separate attributes in the dataset. The work of this paper also included performing sentiment analysis (using VADER), subjectivity analysis (using TextBlob), and fine-grain sentiment analysis (using DistilRoBERTa-base) of the video titles and video descriptions. These results are presented as separate attributes in the dataset. The dataset complies with the FAIR principles of scientific data management. The paper also presents a list of open research questions that may be investigated using this dataset. As per the best knowledge of the authors, no similar work has been done in this field thus far. Future work in this area would include extending the dataset as well as investigating the presented research questions and research directions.

Disclosure of Interests. The authors have no competing interests to declare that are relevant to the content of this article.

References

1. Bester, J.C.: Measles and measles vaccination: a review. JAMA Pediatr. **170**, 1209 (2016). https://doi.org/10.1001/jamapediatrics.2016.1787
2. Measles — United States, January 4–April 2 (2015). https://www.cdc.gov/mmwr/preview/mmwrhtml/mm6414a1.htm. Accessed 29 Mar 2024
3. Gastañaduy, P.A., Goodson, J.L., Panagiotakopoulos, L., Rota, P.A., Orenstein, W.A., Patel, M.: Measles in the 21st century: progress toward achieving and sustaining elimination. J. Infect. Dis. **224**, S420–S428 (2021). https://doi.org/10.1093/infdis/jiaa793
4. Durrheim, D.N., Andrus, J.K., Tabassum, S., Bashour, H., Githanga, D., Pfaff, G.: A dangerous measles future looms beyond the COVID-19 pandemic. Nat. Med. **27**, 360–361 (2021). https://doi.org/10.1038/s41591-021-01237-5
5. Soodejani, M.T., Basti, M., Tabatabaei, S.M., Rajabkhah, K.: Measles, mumps, and rubella (MMR) vaccine and COVID-19: a systematic review. Int. J. Mol. Epidemiol. Gen. **12**, 35 (2021)
6. CDCGlobal: Global measles outbreaks. https://www.cdc.gov/globalhealth/measles/data/global-measles-outbreaks.html. Accessed 29 Mar 2024
7. Ouyang, S., Li, C., Li, X.: A peek into the future: Predicting the popularity of online videos. IEEE Access. **4**, 3026–3033 (2016). https://doi.org/10.1109/access.2016.2580911
8. Weekly time spent with online video worldwide 2018–2023. https://www.statista.com/statistics/611707/online-video-time-spent/. Accessed 29 Mar 2024
9. Rosenthal, S.: Media literacy, scientific literacy, and science videos on the Internet. Front. Commun. **5** (2020). https://doi.org/10.3389/fcomm.2020.581585
10. Elgedawy, R., et al.: Security advice for parents and children about content filtering and circumvention as found on YouTube and TikTok (2024). http://arxiv.org/abs/2402.03255

11. Cuesta-Valiño, P., Gutiérrez-Rodríguez, P., Durán-Álamo, P.: Why do people return to video platforms? millennials and centennials on TikTok. Media Commun. **10**, 198–207 (2022). https://doi.org/10.17645/mac.v10i1.4737

12. Mohsin, M.: 10 YouTube statistics that you need to know in 2023. https://www.oberlo.com/blog/youtube-statistics. Accessed 01 May 2024

13. Top websites in the World - March 2024 most visited & popular rankings. https://www.semrush.com/website/top/. Accessed 01 May 2024

14. Blogger, G.M.I.: Youtube statistics 2024 (demographics, users by country & more). https://www.globalmediainsight.com/blog/youtube-users-statistics/. Accessed 01 May 2024

15. YouTube app user engagement in selected markets 2023. https://www.statista.com/statistics/1287283/time-spent-youtube-app-selected-countries/. Accessed 01 May 2024

16. Biggest social media platforms 2024. https://www.statista.com/statistics/272014/global-social-networks-ranked-by-number-of-users/. Accessed 01 May 2024

17. TikTok users worldwide 2027. https://www.statista.com/forecasts/1142687/tiktok-users-worldwide. Accessed 01 May 2024

18. Most downloaded apps worldwide 2024. https://www.statista.com/statistics/1448008/top-downloaded-mobile-apps-worldwide/. Accessed 01 May 2024

19. Duarte, F.: Average time spent on TikTok statistics (2024). https://explodingtopics.com/blog/time-spent-on-tiktok. Accessed 01 May 2024

20. Lin, Y.: TikTok users by country. https://www.oberlo.com/statistics/tiktok-users-by-country. Accessed 01 May 2024

21. de Guzman, A.B., Mesana, J.C.B., Manuel, M.E., Arcega, K.C.A., Yumang, R.L.T., Miranda, K.N.V.: Examining intergenerational family members' creative activities during COVID-19 lockdown via manifest content analysis of YouTube and TikTok videos. Educ. Gerontol. **48**, 458–471 (2022). https://doi.org/10.1080/03601277.2022.2046372

22. Comeau, N., Abdelnour, A., Ashack, K.: Assessing public interest in Mpox via Google trends, YouTube, and TikTok. JMIR Dermatol. **6**, e48827 (2023). https://doi.org/10.2196/48827

23. https://abcnews.go.com/Health/measles-outbreak-american-samoa-declared-public-health-emergency/story?id=98826831. Accessed 01 May 2024

24. Romania declares measles epidemic as infant dies in hospital. https://www.vaccinestoday.eu/stories/romania-declares-measles-epidemic-as-infant-dies-in-hospital/. Accessed 01 May 2024

25. Prater, E.: Measles cases are mounting in the US as the UK declares a 'national incident' over the disease. What parents need to know to keep their kids safe. https://fortune.com/well/2024/01/27/measles-cases-rise-us-uk-world-symptoms-vaccine-hesitancy-covid-pandemic/. Accessed 01 May 2024

26. Real, E., Shlens, J., Mazzocchi, S., Pan, X., Vanhoucke, V.: YouTube-BoundingBoxes: a large high-precision human-annotated data set for object detection in video. In: 2017 IEEE Conference on Computer Vision and Pattern Recognition (CVPR). IEEE (2017)

27. Loh, F., Wamser, F., Poignée, F., Geißler, S., Hoßfeld, T.: YouTube dataset on mobile streaming for Internet traffic modeling and streaming analysis. Sci. Data. **9**, 1–12 (2022). https://doi.org/10.1038/s41597-022-01418-y

28. Xu, N., et al.: YouTube-VOS: sequence-to-sequence video object segmentation. In: Ferrari, V., Hebert, M., Sminchisescu, C., Weiss, Y. (eds.) Computer Vision – ECCV 2018. ECCV 2018. Lecture Notes in Computer Science(), vol. 11209. Springer, Cham (2018). https://doi.org/10.1007/978-3-030-01228-1_36

29. Li, F., Kim, T., Humayun, A., Tsai, D., Rehg, J.M.: Video segmentation by tracking many figure-ground segments. In: 2013 IEEE International Conference on Computer Vision. IEEE (2013)

30. Jain, S.D., Grauman, K.: Supervoxel-consistent foreground propagation in video. In: Fleet, D., Pajdla, T., Schiele, B., Tuytelaars, T. (eds.) Computer Vision – ECCV 2014. ECCV 2014. Lecture Notes in Computer Science, vol. 8692. Springer, Cham (2014). https://doi.org/10.1007/978-3-319-10593-2_43

31. Ochs, P., Malik, J., Brox, T.: Segmentation of moving objects by long-term video analysis. IEEE Trans. Pattern Anal. Mach. Intell. **36**, 1187–1200 (2014). https://doi.org/10.1109/tpami.2013.242

32. Perazzi, F., Pont-Tuset, J., McWilliams, B., Van Gool, L., Gross, M., Sorkine-Hornung, A.: A benchmark dataset and evaluation methodology for video object segmentation. In: 2016 IEEE Conference on Computer Vision and Pattern Recognition (CVPR). IEEE (2016)

33. Pont-Tuset, J., Perazzi, F., Caelles, S., Arbeláez, P., Sorkine-Hornung, A., Van Gool, L.: The 2017 DAVIS Challenge on Video Object Segmentation (2017). http://arxiv.org/abs/1704.00675

34. Lall, S., Agarwal, M., Sivakumar, R.: A YouTube dataset with user-level usage data: baseline characteristics and key insights. In: ICC 2020 - 2020 IEEE International Conference on Communications (ICC). IEEE (2020)

35. Le, T., Nguyen-Thi, M.-V., Le, H., Vo, Q.-T., Le, T., Nguyen, H.T.: EnTube: A Dataset for YouTube Video Engagement Analytics (2022). https://doi.org/10.21203/rs.3.rs-2085784/v1

36. Qian, Y., Sun, Y.: Tik Tok Actions: A Tik Tok-Derived Video Dataset for Human Action Recognition. http://arxiv.org/abs/2402.08875. Accessed 01 May 2024

37. Ng, L.H.X., Tan, J.Y.H., Tan, D.J.H., Lee, R.K.-W.: Will you dance to the challenge?: predicting user participation of TikTok challenges. In: Proceedings of the 2021 IEEE/ACM International Conference on Advances in Social Networks Analysis and Mining. ACM, New York (2021)

38. Basch, C.H., Yalamanchili, B., Fera, J.: #climate change on TikTok: a content analysis of videos. J. Commun. Health **47**, 163–167 (2022). https://doi.org/10.1007/s10900-021-01031-x

39. Fiallos, A., Fiallos, C., Figueroa, S.: Tiktok and education: Discovering knowledge through learning videos. In: 2021 Eighth International Conference on eDemocracy and eGovernment (ICEDEG), pp. 172–176. IEEE, Los Alamitos (2021)

40. Shutsko, A.: User-generated short video content in social media: a case study of TikTok. In: Meiselwitz, G. (eds.) Social Computing and Social Media. Participation, User Experience, Consumer Experience, and Applications of Social Computing. HCII 2020. Lecture Notes in Computer Science(), vol. 12195. Springer, Cham (2020). https://doi.org/10.1007/978-3-030-49576-3_8

41. Abdaljaleel, M., Barakat, M., Mahafzah, A., Hallit, R.R.: TikTok content on measles-rubella vaccine in Jordan: a cross-sectional study highlighting the spread of vaccine misinformation. JMIR Preprints (2023)

42. Hussain, A., Ali, S., Ahmed, M., Hussain, S.: The anti-vaccination movement: a regression in modern medicine. Cureus (2018). https://doi.org/10.7759/cureus.2919

43. Yiannakoulias, N., Slavik, C.E., Chase, M.: Expressions of pro - and anti-vaccine sentiment on YouTube. Vaccine **37**, 2057–2064 (2019). https://doi.org/10.1016/j.vaccine.2019.03.001

44. YouTube data API. https://developers.google.com/youtube/v3. Accessed 07 Jun 2024

45. getcartermusic: No baby at all by THE MEASLES [music video]. https://www.youtube.com/watch?v=fr1H5j56kv4. Accessed 07 Jun 2024

46. Hutto, C., Gilbert, E.: VADER: a parsimonious rule-based model for sentiment analysis of social media text. In: Proceedings of the International AAAI Conference on Web and Social Media, vol. 8, pp. 216–225 (2014). https://doi.org/10.1609/icwsm.v8i1.14550

47. TextBlob: Simplified Text Processing — TextBlob 0.18.0.post0 documentation. https://textblob.readthedocs.io/. Accessed 01 May 2024

48. J-hartmann/emotion-english-distilroberta-base · hugging face. https://huggingface.co/j-hartmann/emotion-english-distilroberta-base. Accessed 01 May 2024

49. Liu, B.: Sentiment Analysis: Mining Opinions, Sentiments, and Emotions. Cambridge University Press, Cambridge (2020)
50. Vyas, V., Uma, V.: Approaches to sentiment analysis on product reviews. In: Advances in Business Information Systems and Analytics, pp. 15–30. IGI Global, Hershey (2019)
51. Ribeiro, F.N., Araújo, M., Gonçalves, P., André Gonçalves, M., Benevenuto, F.: SentiBench - a benchmark comparison of state-of-the-practice sentiment analysis methods. EPJ Data Sci. 5 (2016). https://doi.org/10.1140/epjds/s13688-016-0085-1
52. Islam, M.R., Zibran, M.F.: A comparison of dictionary building methods for sentiment analysis in software engineering text. In: 2017 ACM/IEEE International Symposium on Empirical Software Engineering and Measurement (ESEM), pp. 478–479. IEEE (2017)
53. Nguyen, H., Veluchamy, A., Diop, M., Iqbal, R.: Comparative study of sentiment analysis with product reviews using machine learning and lexicon-based approaches. SMU Data Sci. Rev. 1, 7 (2018)
54. Saha, S., Showrov, M.I.H., Rahman, M.M., Majumder, M.Z.H.: VADER vs. BERT: a comparative performance analysis for sentiment on coronavirus outbreak. In: Satu, M.S., Moni, M.A., Kaiser, M.S., Arefin, M.S. (eds.) Machine Intelligence and Emerging Technologies. MIET 2022. Lecture Notes of the Institute for Computer Sciences, Social Informatics and Telecommunications Engineering, vol. 490. Springer, Cham (2023). https://doi.org/10.1007/978-3-031-34619-4_30
55. Borrelli, F.M., Challiol, C.: Comparing and evaluating tools for sentiment analysis. In: XI Jornadas de Cloud Computing, Big Data and Emerging Topics (La Plata, 27 al 29 de junio de 2023) (2023)
56. Thakur, N., Han, C.: An exploratory study of tweets about the SARS-CoV-2 Omicron variant: insights from sentiment analysis, language interpretation, source tracking, type classification, and embedded URL detection. COVID 2, 1026–1049 (2022). https://doi.org/10.3390/covid2080076
57. Thakur, N.: Sentiment analysis and text analysis of the public discourse on Twitter about COVID-19 and MPox. Big Data Cogn. Comput. 7, 116 (2023). https://doi.org/10.3390/bdcc7020116
58. Anoop, V.S., Sreelakshmi, S.: Public discourse and sentiment during Mpox outbreak: an analysis using natural language processing. Publ. Health 218, 114–120 (2023). https://doi.org/10.1016/j.puhe.2023.02.018
59. Bengesi, S., Oladunni, T., Olusegun, R., Audu. H.: A machine learning-sentiment analysis on Monkeypox outbreak: an extensive dataset to show the polarity of public opinion from Twitter tweets. IEEE Access. 11, 11811–11826 (2023). https://doi.org/10.1109/access.2023.3242290
60. Thakur, N.: MonkeyPox2022Tweets: a large-scale Twitter dataset on the 2022 Monkeypox outbreak, findings from analysis of Tweets, and open research questions. Infect. Dis. Rep. 14, 855–883 (2022). https://doi.org/10.3390/idr14060087
61. Butt, S., Sharma, S., Sharma, R., Sidorov, G., Gelbukh, A.: What goes on inside rumour and non-rumour tweets and their reactions: a psycholinguistic analyses. Comput. Human Behav. 135, 107345 (2022). https://doi.org/10.1016/j.chb.2022.107345
62. Kuang, Z., Zong, S., Zhang, J., Chen, J., Liu, H.: Music-to-text synaesthesia: generating descriptive text from music recordings (2022). http://arxiv.org/abs/2210.00434
63. Rozado, D., Hughes, R., Halberstadt, J.: Longitudinal analysis of sentiment and emotion in news media headlines using automated labelling with transformer language models. PLoS ONE 17, e0276367 (2022). https://doi.org/10.1371/journal.pone.0276367
64. Melton, C.A., Olusanya, O.A., Ammar, N., Shaban-Nejad, A.: Public sentiment analysis and topic modeling regarding COVID-19 vaccines on the Reddit social media platform: a call to action for strengthening vaccine confidence. J. Infect. Public Health 14, 1505–1512 (2021). https://doi.org/10.1016/j.jiph.2021.08.010

65. Melton, C.A.: Mining public opinion on COVID-19 vaccines using unstructured social media data (2022)
66. Wilkinson, M.D., et al.: The FAIR guiding principles for scientific data management and stewardship. Sci. Data. **3**, 1–9 (2016). https://doi.org/10.1038/sdata.2016.18
67. Kaushik, L., Sangwan, A., Hansen, J.H.L.: Automatic sentiment extraction from YouTube videos. In: 2013 IEEE Workshop on Automatic Speech Recognition and Understanding. IEEE (2013)
68. Oksanen, A., et al.: Pro-anorexia and anti-pro-anorexia videos on YouTube: sentiment analysis of user responses. J. Med. Internet Res. **17**, e256 (2015). https://doi.org/10.2196/jmir.5007
69. Isnan, M., Elwirehardja, G.N., Pardamean, B.: Sentiment analysis for TikTok review using VADER sentiment and SVM model. Proc. Comput. Sci. **227**, 168–175 (2023). https://doi.org/10.1016/j.procs.2023.10.514
70. Southwick, L., Guntuku, S.C., Klinger, E.V., Seltzer, E., McCalpin, H.J., Mer-chant, R.M.: Characterizing COVID-19 content posted to TikTok: public sentiment and response during the first phase of the COVID-19 pandemic. J. Adolesc. Health. **69**, 234–241 (2021). https://doi.org/10.1016/j.jadohealth.2021.05.010
71. Heyder, C., Hillebrandt, I.: Short vertical videos going viral on TikTok: an empirical study and sentiment analysis. In: Redler, J., Schmidt, H.J., Baumgarth, C. (eds.) Forum Markenforschung 2021. Springer Gabler, Wiesbaden (2023). https://doi.org/10.1007/978-3-658-39568-1_7
72. Shevtsov, A., Oikonomidou, M., Antonakaki, D.: Analysis of Twitter and YouTube during USelections 2020. http://arxiv.org/abs/2010.08183. https://doi.org/10.1145/nnnnnnn.nnnnnnn
73. Thakur, N., Cui, S., Knieling, V., Khanna, K., Shao, M.: Investigation of the misinformation about COVID-19 on YouTube using topic modeling, sentiment analysis, and language analysis. Computation (Basel) **12**, 28 (2024). https://doi.org/10.3390/computation12020028
74. Porreca, A., Scozzari, F., Di Nicola, M.: Using text mining and sentiment analysis to analyse YouTube Italian videos concerning vaccination. BMC Publ. Health. **20** (2020). https://doi.org/10.1186/s12889-020-8342-4
75. Rachmawati, F., Wibowo, A.A., Arianto, I.D.: Sentiment analysis #samasamabelajar public relations campaign based on big data on Tik-Tok. In: Proceeding of the International Conference on Economics and Business, vol. 1, pp. 377–388
76. Da'u, A., Salim, N.: Recommendation system based on deep learning methods: a systematic review and new directions. Artif. Intell. Rev. **53**, 2709–2748 (2020). https://doi.org/10.1007/s10462-019-09744-1
77. Herlocker, J.L., Konstan, J.A., Riedl, J.: Explaining collaborative filtering recommendations. In: Proceedings of the 2000 ACM Conference on Computer-Supported Cooperative Work. ACM, New York (2000)
78. Schein, A.I., Popescul, A., Ungar, L.H., Pennock, D.M.: Methods and metrics for cold-start recommendations. In: Proceedings of the 25th Annual International ACM SIGIR Conference on Research and Development in Information Retrieval. ACM, New York (2002)
79. Ma, H., Zhou, T.C., Lyu, M.R., King, I.: Improving recommender systems by incorporating social contextual information. ACM Trans. Inf. Syst. **29**, 1–23 (2011). https://doi.org/10.1145/1961209.1961212
80. Li, Y., Wang, H., Liu, H., Chen, B.: A study on content-based video recommendation. In: 2017 IEEE International Conference on Image Processing (ICIP). IEEE (2017)
81. Nanli, Z., Ping, Z., Weiguo, L., Meng, C.: Sentiment analysis: a literature review. In: 2012 International Symposium on Management of Technology (ISMOT). IEEE (2012)
82. Medhat, W., Hassan, A., Korashy, H.: Sentiment analysis algorithms and applications: a survey. Ain Shams Eng. J. **5**, 1093–1113 (2014). https://doi.org/10.1016/j.asej.2014.04.011

83. Wankhade, M., Rao, A.C.S., Kulkarni, C.: A survey on sentiment analysis methods, applications, and challenges. Artif. Intell. Rev. **55**, 5731–5780 (2022)
84. Birjali, M., Kasri, M., Beni-Hssane, A.: A comprehensive survey on sentiment analysis: approaches, challenges, and trends. Knowl. Based Syst. **226**, 107134 (2021). https://doi.org/10.1016/j.knosys.2021.107134
85. Singh, N.K., Tomar, D.S., Sangaiah, A.K.: Sentiment analysis: a review and comparative analysis over social media. J. Ambient. Intell. Humaniz. Comput. **11**, 97–117 (2020). https://doi.org/10.1007/s12652-018-0862-8
86. Hussein, D.M.E.-D.M.: A survey on sentiment analysis challenges. J. King Saud Univ. - Eng. Sci. **30**, 330–338 (2018). https://doi.org/10.1016/j.jksues.2016.04.002
87. Zhang, L., Tong, Y., Ji, Q.: Active image labeling and its application to facial action labeling. In: Forsyth, D., Torr, P., Zisserman, A. (eds.) Computer Vision – ECCV 2008. ECCV 2008. Lecture Notes in Computer Science, vol. 5303. Springer, Heidelberg (2008). https://doi.org/10.1007/978-3-540-88688-4_52
88. Woods, D.D.: Behind Human Error. Ashgate Publishing, London (2010)

Evaluating Real-Time Emotional Responses Using Bullet Screen Sentiment Analysis: Evidence from Electrodermal Activity

Zhao Xu[1], Qingchuan Li[1(✉)], and Yao Song[2,3]

[1] School of Humanities and Social Sciences, Harbin Institute of Technology, Shenzhen, China
liqingchuan@hit.edu.cn
[2] College of Literature and Journalism, Sichuan University, Chengdu, China
yao.song@scu.edu.cn
[3] Digital Convergence Laboratory of Chinese Cultural Inheritance and Global Communication, Sichuan University, Chengdu, China

Abstract. Bullet screens are attracting increasing attention as a way to express emotions and interact on short video platforms. Prior studies have used natural language processing (NLP) to analyze bullet screen sentiment in order to evaluate public opinion trends regarding a specific topic, movie, or product. However, few studies have investigated the effectiveness of using bullet screen sentiment analysis to predict real-time emotional responses. Thus, this study examined whether and to what extent bullet screen sentiment analysis can be used to evaluate and predict real-time emotional responses to videos by employing physiological electrodermal activity (EDA) measurements. A behavioral experiment was conducted in which eight college students wore a set of wireless galvanic skin sensors while watching three music videos (MVs) in random or-der. The participants' EDA data, including skin conductance responses and peak amplitudes, were then analyzed. Meanwhile, the sentiments expressed in the bullet screen comments on the three MVs were analyzed using three dictionary-based sentiment analysis algorithms: SnowNLP, BosonNLP, and Hel-loNLP. The bullet screen sentiment analysis and physiological measurement results were then compared using descriptive and correlation analyses. The bullet screen sentiment parameters were found to significantly correlate with the EDA measurements. This study confirms the effectiveness of using bullet screen sentiment analysis to predict participants' real-time emotional responses, providing a convenient and flexible way for enterprises and governments to detect public opinion trends and take action accordingly.

Keywords: Sentiment Analysis · Bullet Screen · Emotional Response · EDA

1 Introduction

Social media have become important platforms for people to communicate, obtain information, and share ideas in their daily lives [1]. On such platforms, people can express their opinions and emotions in multiple convenient ways, such as by posting comments, blogs, images, and videos. Recently, due to the prevalence of 5G networks and smartphones, the mobile application market has witnessed exponential growth in short video platforms such as TikTok, Kwai, and Bilibili [2]. According to China Internet Network Information Center data [3], the number of users watching videos (including short videos) online had reached 1044 million by June 2023, comprising 96.8% of all Chinese Internet users.

Against this backdrop, bullet screen, a new technology for commenting on videos, have emerged, enabling users to express their emotions and thoughts and respond to other users' comments in a more engaging and enjoyable way than traditional social medias. Bullet screens present users' comments dynamically from right to left on a video screen, with each comment appearing synchronously with a video's timeline. By superposing videos and comments in the same screen area, bullet screens enable viewers to read and share opinions in real time while watching videos online [4]. Thus, bullet screens blur the boundaries between content and comments, creating an interactive and immersive viewing experience. They allow users not only to communicate with others watching the same video at the same time but also to see the feelings and thoughts expressed by previous viewers [4]. Overall, bullet screens can help viewers express the most authentic opinions, further influencing others' judgments and experiences [5]. Moreover, they can reflect public opinion trends and emotional responses to specific topics of social interest, movies, brands, or products. For example, they can be used as a means of reviewing movies in real time. Sun et al. [6] used the number of comments on bullet screens to assist in locating a movie's highlights. By comparing the bullet screen results with the subjective reviews of 22 movie critics, they confirmed the effectiveness of using bullet screens for movie reviews [6]. Furthermore, bullet screen sentiment analysis based on natural language processing (NLP) has been widely used to detect and classify users' opinions [7]. Zhu developed a filtering method for video bullet screens based on a semantic analysis framework [8] that can help users select the bullet screen content that they want to view. Yang et al. developed a system to use bullet screen content for video retrieval in order to provide a user-friendly search mechanism [9].

Since bullet screens convey viewers' emotional responses, they can be used by enterprises and governments to understand public opinion trends and take action accordingly [10]. For example, by obtaining and analyzing customer feedback on bullet screens, enterprises can quickly adjust their operation strategies. However, because bullet screen comments vary in length and contain ambiguous emotional expressions, it is quite challenging to use NLP for bullet screen semantic analysis [11]. Furthermore, there is a lack of studies on the effectiveness of using bullet screen sentiment analysis to predict viewers' real-time emotional responses. To fill these research gaps, this study employed physiological electrodermal activity (EDA) signal measurements to identify participants' real-time emotional responses. By comparing the results of physiological measurements and sentiment analysis, this study aimed to explore the effectiveness of bullet screen sentiment analysis in predicting emotional responses and monitoring public opinion.

2 Literature Review

2.1 Bullet Screen Sentiment Analysis

According to the strength of interactivity, bullet screens can be categorized into three types: subtitle, bullet screen video, and live site [9]. When using subtitles, viewers can see comments but cannot respond to them. In the video type, users can access both previous and current messages and express their own thoughts. In the live site type, real-time communications are displayed, while previous interactions are not accessible. As opinion monitoring requires obtaining as much user feed-back as possible, the video type has been the most widely studied. According to Yan et al. [12], this type of bullet screen can provide benefits to both platforms and their users. With regard to users, it can satisfy their needs for leisure and socialization and has become highly popular in China, South Korea, and Japan [13]. For platforms, it can provide a new virtual ecosystem due to its high interactivity, thus increasing user stickiness [14]. However, most research has focused on how to design the form, content, and functionality of bullet screens to create a better user experience, whereas few studies have used NLP to analyze bullet screen comments [11]. Given that understanding users' emotional responses through bullet screen comments is an effective way of monitoring public opinion, there is a need to examine how to analyze such responses.

Sentiment analysis is a branch of affective computing, which aims to evaluate people's emotional states using text analysis approaches [5]. Sentiment analysis, one of the most important text mining technologies, has been widely used in review analysis [15] and multimedia content aggregation [16]. This type of analysis usually includes text extraction, text preprocessing, sentiment information extraction, and sentiment polarity judgment [17], aiming to classify sentiments as positive, negative, or neutral [7]. The main types of sentiment analysis are dictionary-based and machine learning–based [14]. The former determines the sentiment of a text based on existing dictionaries and analysis rules, while the latter determines sentiment categories based on deep neural networks and manually annotated corpora [7]. Because users tend to use colloquial and varied expressions on bullet screens, it is difficult to conduct comprehensive manual annotation using machine learning methods. Thus, dictionary-based methods were deemed more appropriate for this study. To minimize the possible limitations of using a single semantic resource, multiple dictionary sources were employed.

2.2 Physiological Measurements for Emotional Responses

Although sentiment analysis can detect people's negative or positive judgments on a specific topic, video, or product, its effectiveness in predicting real-time emotional responses needs to be further evaluated. Behavioral measurements have been extensively used for emotion detection and recognition based, for instance, on facial expressions, gestures, postures, and body movements [18]. However, behavioral measurements may not be very accurate in detecting emotional responses because people can deliberately manipulate or control their behaviors to conceal their true feelings [18]. For this reason, physiological measurements are emerging as a more valid way of detecting emotional responses in real time. Physiological functions such as skin electrical activity and respiratory activity are extremely sensitive to emotional changes [19]. Thus, by analyzing physiological signals using electrocardiography (ECG), electrodermal activity (EDA) measurements, skin temperature (SKT) measurements, and photoplethysmography (PPG), Jang et al. successfully classified three kinds of emotional responses, including boredom, pain, and surprise, induced by various sounds, achieving a prediction accuracy of 84.7% [20].

EDA is one of the most promising ways of measuring emotional responses, such as stress, tension, and excitement, in the field of psychology [20]. Generally, EDA is measured as reflected by changes of the skin's ability to conduct electricity, which is referred to as the skin conductance change (SCC). More specifically, the general level of SCC is known as the skin conductance level (SCL), which is measured through changes over a relatively long period. Transient or sudden SCC, on the other hand, is known as the skin conductance response (SCR), which is measured through changes over a shorter period and tends to correlate with the appearance of experimental stimuli. Since this study focused on emotional responses to various videos over a short period, SCR metrics were used as the main physiological data. Specifically, amplitude (AMP) is one of the main parameters of the level of SCR and reflects the strength of a response to a change in potential. Thus, the AMP calculated for a period after the appearance of an experimental stimulus can represent the intensity of the emotional response induced by this stimulus.

In summary, this study aimed to assess the effectiveness of bullet screen sentiment analysis in predicting emotional responses to videos by measuring students' EDA signals, including SCR and AMP. To this end, several NLP techniques were employed to analyze the sentiments expressed in bullet screen comments on three popular music videos (MVs). Meanwhile, the students' real-time emotional responses to MV were then detected based on the EDA signals. By examining the relationship between the sentiment analysis results and the physiological measurements, we aim to answer the following research question: whether and to what extent can bullet screen sentiment analysis predict real-time emotional responses to videos?

3   Methodology

3.1   Participants

Fifteen college student participants were recruited through offline and online advertisements and leaflets. The participants were required to be older than 18 years and not to have watched the MVs used in the experiment over the previous three months. After removing invalid data, the experimental data of eight participants were used in the analysis. The participants were informed of the potential benefits and risks of participating and of their right to withdraw at any time with no consequences and provided informed consent. After completing the experiment, each participant received a reward of RMB 20.

3.2   Experimental Setup and Tasks

The experiment was conducted in a secluded and quiet laboratory under strictly controlled conditions. Illuminance was maintained at 440 lx, and humidity was maintained at 50%–60%. The participants were asked to randomly watch three MVs on a 27-in. Dell P2719H monitor with a resolution of 1920 × 1080 px, wearing wired semi-in-ear earphones. To collect EDA data, wireless galvanic skin sensors (ErgoLab), including a smart wearable ear clip sensor and a smart wearable finger sensor, were placed on each participant's ears and fingers. Specifically, the smart wearable ear clip was connected to a sensor that placed on the participants' back to capture EDA data (Fig. 1). A laptop computer was used to collect the data.

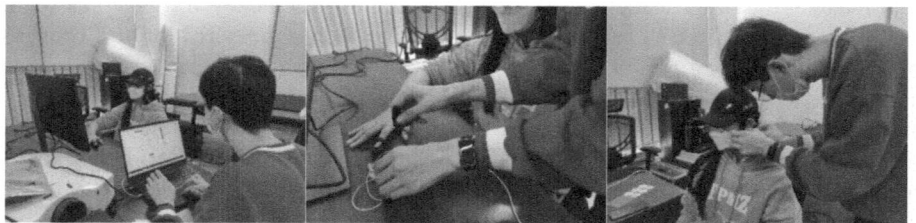

Fig. 1. The experiment setup.

Three MV clips were used in the experiment: "See You Again" [21] from the movie *Fast & Furious 7* (MV1), "Let It Go" [22] from the animated movie *Frozen* (MV2), and "Sugar" [23], a song by the pop band Maroon 5 (MV3). For the sake of consistency, all three MVs were downloaded from Bilibili, one of the most popular online video websites with active bullet screen features, in October 2023. MV1 lasted 3 min and 48 s, MV2 lasted 3 min and 38 s, and MV3 lasted 5 min and 1 s. Screenshots of the MVs are shown in Fig. 2.

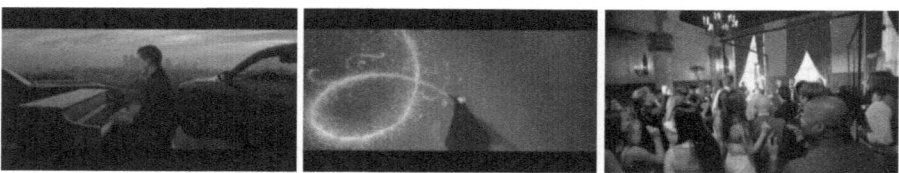

Fig. 2. Examples of MV screenshots used in the experiment.

3.3 Experimental Procedure

The participants were asked to sign informed consent forms that included matters of experiment confidentiality, data collection, and the right to withdraw at any time for any reason. Then, with an experimenter's help, the wireless galvanic skin sensors were placed on the participants' fingers and ears (connected with the sensors placed on the backs). The participants were free to adjust their chairs and earphones at will. To ensure reliable emotional response measurements, the participants were instructed to be as relaxed and engaged as possible and to quit the experiment if they felt discomfort at any time.

Before the experiment, a pilot test was performed to ensure that the sensors collected data properly. The MV volume was maintained at 24%–26%. After watching each MV, the participants were asked to take a break for 15 s with their eyes closed to minimize emotional response overlaps between the three MVs and reduce possible fatigue. The duration of the experiment for each participant was approximately 20 min.

3.4 Data Analysis

Bullet Screen Sentiment Analysis. Emotional changes are mostly caused by the intensity fluctuations in an MV's plot and music. For example, people tend to have more intense emotional responses during climaxes and less intense responses during other, less exciting parts. Therefore, before the sentiment analysis, three music experts were asked to help divide each MV into sections based on the compositional structure of popular songs. The basic structure consisted of eight segments: intro, verse, prechorus, chorus, interlude, bridge, solo, and outro. However, it should be noted that not all MVs included all segments. The segmentation of each MV is shown in Table 1. The subsequent sentiment analyses were based on the music structure of each MV.

Bullet screen comments on the three MVs were crawled from Bilibili [9, 14], and their sentiments were analyzed using the third-party Python libraries Requests and bs4. A total of 1200 bullet screen comments were obtained for each MV. Three dictionary-based sentiment analysis algorithms were used to identify the sentiment in each comment: SnowNLP, BosonNLP, and HelloNLP. SnowNLP is an NLP class library for Python. Based on its trained dictionary algorithm, it assigns each sentiment a score ranging from 0 to 1, with lower scores indicating more negative emotional responses and higher scores indicating more positive emotional responses. BosonNLP [24] uses a sentiment dictionary based on various data sources, such as microblogging, news, and forums. Negative sentiment scores indicate negative emotional responses, while positive scores indicate positive responses. Larger values indicate stronger emotional responses. HelloNLP [25] is a Chinese semantic-processing algorithm that calculates and returns the positive and negative sentiment values (both greater than zero) of a text separately and uses the larger of the two to indicate a positive or negative sentiment. To harmonize the format of the HelloNLP scores with those of the other two algorithms, the positive sentiment value was subtracted from the negative sentiment value as the final sentiment score of HelloNLP in this study.

Because the number of bullet screen comments during different segments of an MV can reflect viewers' levels of activities, the sum of comments (Num-Sum) during each MV segment was used as a sentiment parameter. The sentiment score of all bullet screen comments during each segment was used as another parameter. Using the three dictionary-based sentiment analysis algorithms, three sentiment score parameters were obtained: Snow-Sum, Boson-Sum, and Hello-Sum.

EDA Data Analysis. EDA data were collected from the finger and back, through the smart wearable finger sensor and smart wearable ear clip sensor respectively. The data with more pronounced waveforms were selected for the analysis. The sampling frequency of all EDA sensors was 64 Hz. All data were subjected to noise reduction by Gaussian filtering with a window size of 5. Since this study focused on emotional

Table 1. Segmentation of each MV used in the experiment.

MV	Sequence	Time Range (s)	Segment
MV1	1	0–10	Intro
	2	10–39	Chorus 1
	3	39–74	Solo 1
	4	74–101	Chorus 2
	5	101–117	Interlude
	6	117–149	Solo 2
	7	149–173	Pre-chorus
	8	173–197	Chorus 3
	9	197–228	Outro
MV2	1	0–15	Intro
	2	15–43	Verse 1
	3	43–60	Pre-chorus
	4	60–88	Chorus 1
	5	88–120	Bridge
	6	120–147	Chorus 2
	7	147–183	Verse 2
	8	183–211	Chorus 3
	9	211–218	Outro
MV3	1	0–42	Intro
	2	42–58	Verse 1
	3	58–74	Pre-chorus 1
	4	74–106	Chorus 1
	5	106–122	Verse 2
	6	122–138	Pre-chorus 2
	7	138–171	Chorus 2
	8	171–194	Bridge
	9	194–258	Chorus 3
	10	258–301	Outro

responses within a short period, the SCR data were extracted for further analysis according to a moderately sensitive peak recognition criterion, with parameters including a maximum climb time of 4 s, a maximum half-life of 4 s, and a minimum amplitude of 0.03 micro-Siemens (μS). The activation responses to stimuli (MV segments, e.g., intro, and outro) in the SCR data were set to 1–4 s, and the continuity SCR parameter and the AMP parameter in response to the stimuli were analyzed accordingly. The continuity

SCR parameter was the level of skin surface conductivity sampled in micro-Siemens at 0.25 s intervals, which reflected the overall change in emotional arousal across MV segments. The AMP parameter was the magnitude of the skin conductivity response elicited by different MV segments, which was discretely distributed in micro-Siemens within MV segments.

Previous studies have generally performed summing and averaging calculations for EDA parameters to represent emotional arousal levels and stimulus response intensity [18]. Accordingly, this study used the overall and average SCR and AMP values in the analysis, termed SCR-Sum, SCR-Mean, AMP-Sum, and AMP-Mean.

After obtaining the sentiment analysis results and physiological EDA data, the parameters were normalized because each was expressed in a different unit and had a different value range. A descriptive analysis of the sentiment analysis results and EDA data was then performed for each MV segment. Subsequently, a correlation analysis of the sentiment analysis results and EDA data was performed.

4 Results

4.1 Demographic Information

After removing the invalid samples, the data of five male and three female participants were used in the analyses. The participants had an average age of 22 (SD = 2.2) years (range: 18–24 years). Two participants were undergraduate students, and six were graduate students.

4.2 Descriptive Analysis for Sentiment Scores and EDA Data

The EDA data reflecting the participants' emotional responses to the three MVs (SCR-Sum, SCR-Mean, AMP-Sum, and AMP-Mean) and the sentiment analysis results (Num-Sum, Snow-Sum, Boson-Sum, and Hello-Sum) are presented in Fig. 3. Due to wide variations in their distribution, the EDA parameters of SCR-Mean and AMP-Mean for MV2 and MV3 were excluded from the visualization. The EDA and sentiment data for the outro segment of MV1 were also excluded be-cause this segment was too short for reliable AMP data to be captured from most participants.

The descriptive analysis results indicated that the participants' emotional responses measured based on EDA data exhibited a trend similar to that revealed by the bullet screen sentiment analysis results. This similarity was also reflected in the changes in each parameter during the MV segments. For example, in MV1 (Fig. 3-a), several EDA and sentiment parameters showed the same increasing and decreasing trends from solo 1 to interlude and from solo 2 to outro. Likewise, during most of MV2 (Fig. 3-b), all EDA and sentiment parameters exhibited similar increasing and decreasing trends, with five (AMP-Sum, SCR-Sum, Num-Sum, Snow-Sum, and Hello-Sum) showing the lowest values during the pre-chorus segment. In MV3 (Fig. 3-c), the increases and decreases in EDA and sentiment values were also similar, with all six parameters exhibiting the lowest values during verse 2. These findings suggest that the bullet screen sentiment analysis results generally correlated with the emotional responses determined through the EDA measurements.

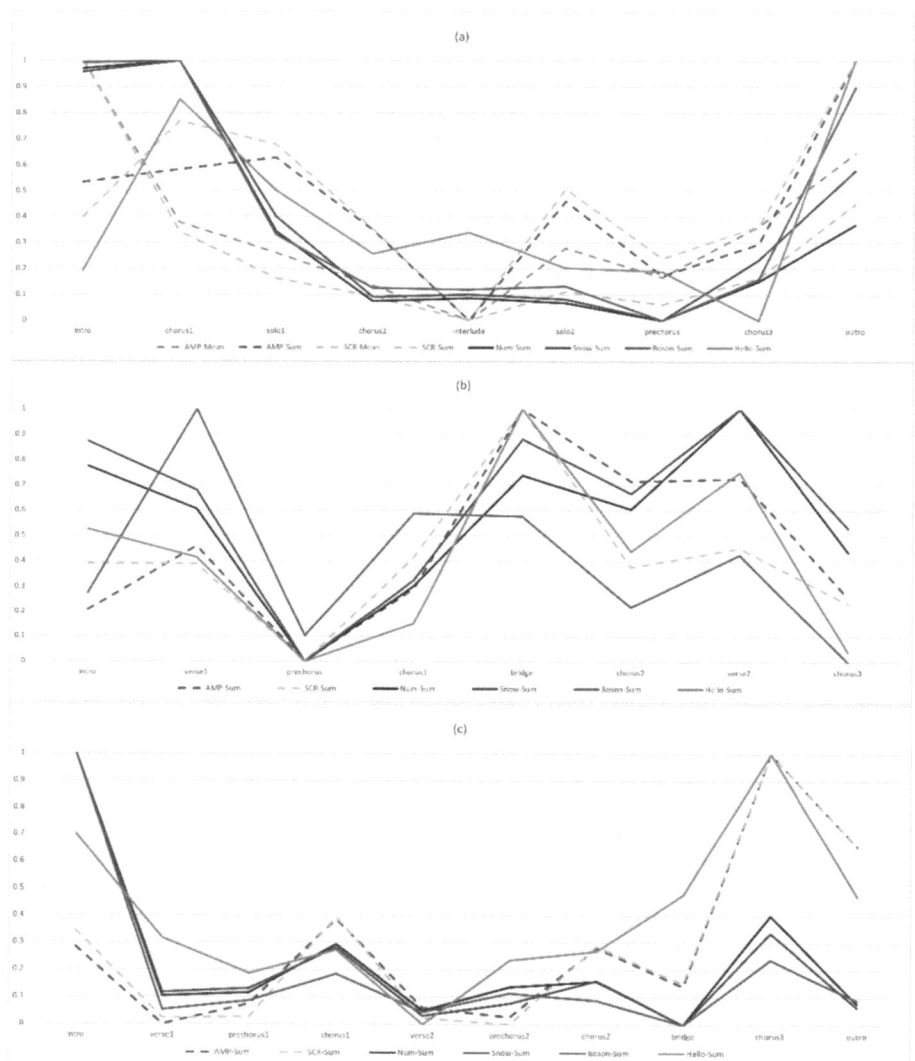

Fig. 3. Visualization of the descriptive data for the EDA (dashed lines) and sentiment (solid lines) parameters: (a) MV1; (b) MV2; (c) MV3.

4.3 Correlation Analysis for Sentiment and EDA Data

The Shapiro–Wilk (S–W) test was used to check data normality. Because the data were not normally distributed in the case of MV1 and MV3, Spearman correlation analysis was performed to assess the relationships between the EDA and sentiment parameters for these MVs. For MV2, Pearson correlation analysis was used, as the data showed a normal distribution.

The correlation results for MV1 are shown in Table 2. Significant positive correlations were observed between AMP-Sum and Snow-Sum ($p < 0.05$), AMP-Sum and Boson-Sum ($p < 0.01$), AMP-Sum and Num-Sum ($p < 0.05$), SCR-Sum and Boson-Sum ($p < 0.01$), AMP-Mean and Snow-Sum ($p < 0.05$), AMP-Mean and Boson-Sum ($p < 0.01$), AMP-Mean and Num-Sum ($p < 0.05$), SCR-Mean and Snow-Sum ($p < 0.01$), SCR-Mean and Boson-Sum ($p < 0.01$), and SCR-Mean and Num-Sum ($p < 0.01$). Thus, the BosonNLP and SnowNLP sentiment scores showed the most significant correlations with the emotional responses determined through the EDA measurements, followed by the number of bullet screen comments and the HelloNLP sentiment analysis results.

Table 2. Spearman correlations (r) between EDA and sentiment parameters for MV1.

EDA Parameters		Sentiment Parameters			
		Snow-Sum	Boson-Sum	Hello-Sum	Num-Sum
	AMP-Sum	0.667*	0.800**	0.650	0.667*
	SCR-Sum	0.650	0.817**	0.617	0.650
	AMP-Mean	0.717*	0.850**	0.100	0.717*
	SCR-Mean	0.817**	0.917**	0.200	0.817**

Note: * $p < 0.05$; ** $p < 0.01$

Table 3 presents the correlation analysis results for MV2. Significant and positive relationships were observed between AMP-Sum and Snow-Sum ($p < 0.05$), AMP-Sum and Hello-Sum ($p < 0.01$), and SCR-Sum and Hello-Sum ($p < 0.01$). The HelloNLP sentiment analysis results showed the most significant correlations with the emotional responses determined through the EDA measurements, followed by the Snow-Sum sentiment scores. However, no statistically significant correlations were found between the number of bullet screen comments and the EDA data.

Table 3. Pearson correlations (r) between EDA and sentiment parameters for MV2.

EDA Parameters		Sentiment Parameters			
		Snow-Sum	Boson-Sum	Hello-Sum	Num-Sum
	AMP-Sum	0.708*	0.367	0.856**	0.690
	SCR-Sum	0.667	0.467	0.864**	0.606

Note: * $p < 0.05$; ** $p < 0.01$

Table 4 shows the correlation results for MV3. Significant positive correlations were found between AMP-Sum and Hello-Sum ($p < 0.01$) and between SCR-Sum and Hello-Sum ($p < 0.01$). The HelloNLP sentiment analysis results exhibited the only significant correlations with the EDA data, indicating that this algorithm was more effective than the other two in predicting the participants' emotional responses. However, no statistically significant correlations were revealed between EDA data and the sentiment results based on other NLP approaches.

Table 4. Spearman correlations (r) between EDA and sentiment parameters for MV3.

EDA Parameters		Sentiment Parameters			
		Snow-Sum	Boson-Sum	Hello-Sum	Num-Sum
	AMP-Sum	0.225	0.161	0.770**	0.455
	SCR-Sum	0.286	0.222	0.805**	0.430

Note: * p < 0.05; ** p < 0.01

5 Discussion

The purpose of this study was to investigate whether bullet screen comments can reflect students' emotional responses to MVs and to explore the feasibility of public opinion monitoring through bullet screen sentiment analysis based on NLP methods. Using three dictionary-based sentiment analysis algorithms, various sentiment parameters were obtained. Moreover, to accurately capture emotional responses, galvanic skin sensors were used to collect EDA data from the participants while they watched three MVs in a behavioral experiment. Thus, the participants' emotional responses were analyzed based on their skin conductance responses and changes. Descriptive and correlation analyses of the EDA data and sentiment results were then performed, which indicated significant correlations between bullet screen comment sentiments and emotional responses measured through the EDA parameters.

A visualization of the descriptive analysis showed that the participants exhibited relatively high emotional sensitivity to the MV contents. These results are consistent with prior research indicating that videos offer a more engaging and interactive user experience than traditional social media platforms [2]. Specifically, both the bullet screen sentiments and the EDA data changed significantly with the different segments of the MVs used in the experiment. For example, the participants' emotional responses were more enthusiastic in the first third of MV1 ("See You Again"), then dropped to a lower level, and rose again at the end. In MV 2 ("Let It Go"), the participants reacted more intensely to the overture, the bridge, and the two main choruses. In MV3 ("Sugar"), they reacted more intensely to the three choruses after overture. Overall, the observed high emotional sensitivity to MVs confirmed the great potential of exploring students' viewpoints and emotions by obtaining real-time user data, such as comments and opinions [6, 26].

The descriptive analysis also showed that the bullet screen sentiment parameters (Num-Sum, Snow-Sum, Boson-Sum, and Hello-Sum) and the EDA parameters (SCR-Sum, SCR-Mean, AMP-Sum, and AMP-Mean) exhibited a certain degree of similarity, indicating consistency between bullet screen sentiments and the participants' real emotional responses. The correlation analysis further confirmed the effectiveness of using bullet screen sentiment analysis to predict emotional responses. Accordingly, the research question was addressed. These findings suggest that enterprises and governments can use bullet screen sentiment analysis to understand public opinion trends [10].

The results also showed that sentiment analysis using the dictionary-based sentiment analysis algorithms outperformed the number of bullet screen comments in predicting the participants' emotional responses. However, the three NLP algorithms had varying predictive power with different MVs. For example, the HelloNLP-based analysis outperformed the analyses based on the other two algorithms in MV2 and MV3 but failed to accurately predict the participants' emotional responses to MV1. Moreover, the analysis using BosonNLP had better performance in predicting the participants' emotional responses to MV1 than to MV2 and MV3. The reason for this is that, for different MV styles and contents, students may vary contents and styles when posting bullet screen comments, making NLP-based bullet screen comments analysis challenging [11]. Therefore, we recommend that researchers and partitioners employ several NLP algorithms simultaneously to accurately detect emotional responses to videos when conducting bullet screen sentiment analysis.

6 Conclusion

With the development of Internet features such as live streaming and short video platforms, bullet screens have attracted increasing attention. By measuring real-time emotional responses using EDA data, this study confirmed the effectiveness of using bullet screen sentiment analysis based on NLP approaches to predict emotional responses to videos. Thus, bullet screen sentiment analysis provides a convenient and flexible means by which enterprises and governments can monitor public opinion trends. However, more in-depth research is needed. All experimental materials used in this study were MVs, which tend to trigger positive emotional responses. Therefore, it is necessary to study the effectiveness of using bullet screen sentiment analysis to evaluate viewers' emotional responses to different kinds of videos and with various cultural backgrounds. Moreover, future research should compare more types of NLP algorithms to improve the prediction accuracy of bullet screen sentiment analysis.

Acknowledgments. This study was funded by the National Natural Science Foundation of China [grant number 62207008] and General Program of Stable Support Plan for Universities in Shenzhen [grant number GXWD20231129154726002].

Disclosure of Interests. The authors have no competing interests to declare that are relevant to the content of this article.

References

1. Kaplan, A.M., Haenlein, M.: Users of the world, unite! the challenges and opportunities of social media. Bus. Horiz. **53**(1), 59–68 (2010). https://doi.org/10.1016/j.bushor.2009.09.003
2. Lin, B., Chen, Y., Zhang, L.: Research on the factors influencing the repurchase intention on short video platforms: a case of China. Plos One **17**(3) (2022). https://doi.org/10.1371/journal.pone.0265090
3. China Internet Network Information Center (CNNIC). The 52nd Statistical Report on China's Internet Development (2023). https://www.cnnic.com.cn/IDR/ReportDownloads/202311/P020231121355042476714.pdf
4. Djamasbi, S., Hall-Phillips, A., Liu, Z., Li, W., Bian, J.: Social viewing, bullet screen, and user experience: a first look. In: 2016 49th Hawaii International Conference on System Sciences (HICSS), pp. 648–657. IEEE (2016)
5. Yadollahi, A., Shahraki, A.G., Zaiane, O.R.: Current state of text sentiment analysis from opinion to emotion mining. ACM Comput. Surv. **50**(2), 1–33 (2018). https://doi.org/10.1145/3057270
6. Sun, S., Wang, F., He, L.: Movie summarization using bullet screen comments. Multimedia Tools Appl. **77**, 9093–9110 (2018)
7. Saberi, B., Saad, S.: Sentiment analysis or opinion mining: a review. Int. J. Adv. Sci. Eng. Inf. Technol. **7**(5), 1660–1666 (2017)
8. Zhu, B.: Video bullet screen filtering method and device. LCN201510628104.1 (2015)
9. Yang, X., Binglu, W., Junjie, H., Shuwen, L.: Natural language processing in "Bullet Screen" application. In: 2017 International Conference on Service Systems and Service Management, pp. 1–6. IEEE (2017)
10. Gupta, A., Tyagi, M., Sharma, D.: Use of social media marketing in healthcare. J. Health Manag. **15**(2), 293–302 (2013). https://doi.org/10.1177/0972063413489058
11. Fersini, E.: Sentiment analysis in social networks: a machine learning perspective. In: Sentiment Analysis in Social Networks, pp. 91–111. Elsevier (2017). https://doi.org/10.1016/B978-0-12-804412-4.00006-1
12. Yan, J., Pan, Y., Yun, T.: Analysis of Chinese video website barrage language based on the influence of the ACGN culture. Int. J. Internet Broadcasting Commun. **13**(2), 195–207 (2021)
13. Yu, S., Zhu, H., Jiang, S., Zhang, Y., Xing, C., Chen, H.: Emoticon analysis for Chinese social media and e-commerce: the AZEmo system. ACM Trans. Manag. Inf. Syst. **9**(4), 1–22 (2018). https://doi.org/10.1145/3309707
14. Hsieh, Y.H., Zeng, X.P.: Sentiment analysis: An ERNIE-BiLSTM approach to bullet screen comments. Sensors **22**(14), 5223 (2022)
15. Haddi, E., Liu, X., Shi, Y.: The role of text pre-processing in sentiment analysis. Procedia Comput. Sci. **17**, 26–32 (2013). https://doi.org/10.1016/j.procs.2013.05.005
16. Tan, S., Ngo, C.-W., Tan, H.-K., Pang, L.: Cross media hyperlinking for search topic browsing. In: Proceedings of the 19th ACM International Conference on Multimedia, 243–252 (2011). https://doi.org/10.1145/2072298.2072331
17. Matsumoto, S., Takamura, H., Okumura, M.: Sentiment classification using word subsequences and dependency sub-trees. In: Ho, T.B., Cheung, D., Liu, H. (eds.) Advances in Knowledge Discovery and Data Mining. PAKDD 2005. Lecture Notes in Computer Science, vol. 3518. Springer, Berlin, Heidelberg(2005). https://doi.org/10.1007/11430919_37
18. Rahman, J.S., Hossain, M.Z., Gedeon, T.: Measuring observers' EDA responses to emotional videos. In: Proceedings of the 31st Australian Conference on Human-Computer-Interaction, pp. 457–461 (2019)
19. Kim, J., André, E.: Emotion recognition based on physiological changes in music listening. IEEE Trans. Pattern Anal. Mach. Intell. **30**(12), 2067–2083 (2008)

20. Jang, E.H., Park, B.J., Park, M.S., Kim, S.H., Sohn, J.H.: Analysis of physiological signals for recognition of boredom, pain, and surprise emotions. J. Physiol. Anthropol. **34**(1), 1–12 (2015)
21. Music Private Collection. Charlie Puth's "See You Again" explodes with fire! Cherish the people around you! Bilibili (23 October 2021). https://www.bilibili.com/list/watchlater?bvid= BV1qU4y1F73A&oid=676186170
22. Music for Classmates Jun. HDR Frozen theme song "Let It Go" by Idina Menzel 2160P! My phone is a little bit stuck! Bilibili (20 February 2022). https://www.bilibili.com/list/watchl ater?bvid=BV1RR4y1L76K&oid=339176835
23. G_callen. [4K] Maroon 5 – Sugar. Bilibili (23 March 2021). https://www.bilibili.com/list/wat chlater?bvid=BV1gh411D753&oid=204834300
24. Petrichoryi. Sentiment analysis of text based on sentiment dictionary. CSND (30 April 2020). https://blog.csdn.net/Petrichoryi/article/details/105861462
25. Chen, M.: Hellonlp/Sentiment-Analysis. Github (2023). https://github.com/hellonlp/sentim ent-analysis/tree/master/sentiment_analysis_dict/dict
26. Liu, L., Suh, A., Wagner, C.: Watching online videos interactively: the impact of media capabilities in Chinese Danmaku video sites. Chin. J. Commun. **9**(3), 283–303 (2016)

Can Identity Information Really Promote Social Support in Internet Communities?

Yuqiao Yan and Jia Dai[✉]

Tsinghua University, Tsinghua, China
jiadai@tsinghua.edu.cn

Abstract. The present study aims to explore the relationship between information disclosure and social support among depressed patients on social media, and further investigate the impacts of communication index, negative emotion index, and the proportion of first-person singular pronouns on social support. Through linear regression analysis of 1040 Weibo data, the study finds that the overall model is significant and can explain about 15% of the variation in social support. Personal information disclosure and communication index are positively correlated with social support, while negative emotion index is negatively correlated with social support. Although the proportion of first-person singular pronouns is negatively correlated with social support, its impact is relatively small. These results suggest that on social media, depressed patients can obtain more social support through moderate disclosure of personal information and effective communication, while the expression of negative emotions may reduce social support. The study also finds that there may be complex interactions among variables that jointly affect the acquisition of social support. These findings provide valuable references and suggestions for the use of social media by depressed patients, emphasizing the importance of focusing on information disclosure, communication styles, and emotional expression when seeking social support. Meanwhile, the research results also imply that encouraging moderate information disclosure and effective communication may help improve the level of social support for depressed patients, provided that patient privacy and safety are protected. In addition, future research can further optimize the measurement methods of relevant indicators and deeply explore the interaction mechanisms among variables, in order to provide more precise and effective guidance for social media intervention among depressed patients.

Keywords: Depression · social media · Information Disclosure · Social Support

1 Introduction

In recent years, depression has become a highly notable medical and social issue. Topics related to depression awareness, prevention system construction, stigma, and discrimination towards patients with depression have increasingly garnered public attention.

A study on the relationship between text features and response effects of Weibo's su-per topic "patients with depression" based on cue filtered out theory.

Individuals with depression often bear not only the burden of the illness but also face verbal discrimination and social exclusion, leaving them in a more challenging and isolated state. With the rise of social media, online communities such as post bars, WeChat groups, and microblogging hashtags have become spaces for some depression patients to exchange medical information, seek emotional comfort, and resist the stigmatization of the illness.

Realistically, statistics related to depression reveal its profound impact on Chinese society. The "Study on the Burden of Mental Disorders and Health Service Utilization in China" (abbreviated as the Chinese Mental Health Survey, CMHS), organized by Professor Huang Yueqin from Peking University Sixth Hospital, is a research project supported by the National Health Commission and the Ministry of Science and Technology. It was jointly completed by 44 institutions nationwide over three years (2013–2015) and represents the first national epidemiological survey of mental disorders among adults in China. The research findings were published online in "Lancet Psychiatry" on February 18, 2019, and September 21, 2021. The study indicates that the lifetime prevalence rate of depression in China is 6.9%, and the 12-month prevalence rate is 3.6%. Based on these estimations, there are over 95 million people with depression in China, surpassing cancer as the second leading cause of disease burden after cardiovascular and cerebrovascular diseases. Additionally, the distribution of depressive disorders in China is characterized by a higher prevalence among women compared to men, unemployed individuals compared to those employed, and individuals who are separated, widowed, or divorced compared to those who are married or cohabiting. Most individuals with depressive disorders experience social dysfunction, and the utilization of health services for depressive disorders is low, with inadequate treatment rates. Therefore, there is a need for the government to develop plans to increase the availability, accessibility, and acceptability of health resources to improve the utilization of health services for individuals with depressive disorders.

When exploring social support and interaction among individuals with depression, this study focuses on "microblogging hashtags." Firstly, depression-related hashtags on Sina Weibo have become virtual spiritual spaces for many depression-related audiences to seek warmth due to their instant publishing, diverse interactivity, and flexible anonymity that combines both acquaintance and stranger social networking. These hashtags have a significant user base and a certain degree of social representativeness. Secondly, social connection data (likes, replies, retweets, friend relationships) in Sina Weibo hashtags are easy to observe and obtain, facilitating the control of quantitative research variables and ensuring high reliability. Thirdly, this study introduces the perspectives of social capital and weak tie theory and cue-filtered theory. Posts in Sina Weibo hashtags feature diverse textual content. Due to Weibo's broadcasting media characteristics targeting non-specific audiences, posters have significant freedom in disclosing their personal social identity information. The textual data exhibits clear hierarchical layers, aligning with the quantitative analysis requirements of the study.

In further exploring Sina Weibo hashtags, this study selects the hashtag "Depression Patients" as the research object. As one of the top three hashtags related to depression themes on Sina Weibo (with 764,000 posts for "Depression," 24,000 for "Depression

Hashtag," and 13,000 for "Depression Patients"), it has significant influence and a concentrated participant base (mostly confirmed patients). Additionally, its textual content filters out information weakly related to social interactions among depression patients (such as fan support for idol singers' depression-related songs). Thus, it becomes the focal observation object for this study.

2 Literature Review

Cue-filtered theory is rooted in social information processing theory derived from interpersonal communication. It explains that the lack of nonverbal cues in computer-mediated online relationships can impair the establishment of interpersonal relationships within online groups. The theory proposed by Culnan and Markus (1987) suggests that the absence of identity cues in online environments, such as real-world identity, gender, physical appearance, and social class, can diminish the quality of interpersonal interactions. In hyperrealistic online spaces, individuals' ability to judge others in interactive situations declines, and uncertainty increases, leading to a range of deviant behaviors in virtual spaces, such as poor information quality, deception, and abuse. Participants engage in more self-enhancing behaviors and emotional expressions, reducing public self-awareness.

In the 2002 publication "The Handbook of Interpersonal Communication," scholars Walther and Parks divided cue-filtered theory into three parts: Cues Filtered Out, Cues to Choose by, and Cues Filtered In. The first part, Cues Filtered Out, suggests that certain types of information may be communicated more effectively in one medium than another. The second part, Cues to Choose by, emphasizes that the ability of a medium to objectively convey the quantity and content of information affects users' choices of medium, communication processes, and audience effects, as highlighted by Media Richness theory. The third part, Cues Filtered In, rejects the aforementioned viewpoint and argues that nonverbal cues do not restrict the exchange of personalized viewpoints between communicators. Instead, it assumes that communicators in cyberspace, like in other environments, are motivated to act, reducing uncertainty in interpersonal communication and developing affinity.

In the realm of online interactions, a prominent characteristic of Cue Filtered Theory is the lack of sincerity and authenticity. Within the context of online support groups, researchers have discovered that a higher number of identity cues tend to enhance users' attention, leading to a more self-centered response to help-seeking posts and fostering more positive perceptions towards others (Li & Li 2015; Guegan et al. 2017). The revelation of one's genuine social identity is found to promote discussions and participation within online communities, subsequently augmenting group identification and creative expressions (Guegan et al. 2017). Tanis and Postmes (2005; 2007) examined how the amount of identity cues affects interactive outcomes in computer-mediated networks, finding that while more identity cues positively influence interpersonal relationship perceptions, they simultaneously reduce the sense of unity and entitativity.

Social Support Theory, originally emerging from sociology, has been applied to describe social relationships pertaining to physical health since the 1970s. In this study, social support refers to specific, supportive, or aid-oriented behaviors exhibited by others, constituting extrinsic social activities for the supported individual (Gu Donghui 2002). Social support is conceptualized as the interdependent relationship between individuals or between an individual and a group. This reliance can enhance resilience against short-term challenges, stress, and social deprivation (Vinokur et al. 1987). Research by Lawndale and Haven (1968) found that elderly individuals engaging with close acquaintances can effectively reduce depressive symptoms, while Locke (1989) posited that social support aids in protecting self-concept, thereby mitigating psychological stress reactions. In China, Xiao Shuiyuan et al. (1987) was among the first to explore the relationship between social support and physical and mental health, utilizing medical record matching methods to study the impacts of social psychological factors like stress and social support on peptic ulcer. Cohen and Wills (1985) categorized social support into four types based on the distinctive nature of the resources provided: emotional, informational, social companionship, and instrumental support.

In the context of depression, patients often exhibit a pronounced sense of stigma in their daily social interactions, tending to avoid or withdraw from discussions about their illness, which can exacerbate anxiety symptoms (Cui Xiangjun 2012). When confronted with illness-related details mentioned by others, patients may become more sensitive, tense, and uneasy, leading to increased aggression or a further reduction in social expectations (Cui Xiangjun et al. 2012). Zhang Junli's (2011) research indicates that depressive self-stigma tends to rise with age among depressed individuals, correlating negatively with self-efficacy and positively with social avoidance. Huang Guanlan et al. (2021) observed that depressed patients use more first-person singular pronouns and negative emotion words in their language, reflecting social isolation and reduced sensitivity to others' positive expressions.

In light of these findings, the present study aims to investigate whether the disclosure of personal identity information in help-seeking posts within the "Depression Patients Super Topic" is associated with the social support received. Specifically, the research hypothesizes that a higher level of personal information disclosure will correlate positively with social support (Hypothesis 1). Additionally, it explores whether narrative style and dissemination indices are related to the social support received (Hypothesis 2).

The study seeks to address a gap in the literature by examining the applicability of Cue Filtered Theory and Social Support Theory within the unique context of online depression communities. By understanding the factors that influence social support in these settings, we can better design interventions and platforms that effectively support individuals with depression.

2.1 Hypotheses

1. Hypothesis 1: In the context of microblogging hashtags dedicated to depression sufferers, there is a positive correlation between the "Exposure of identity clues" described by the subjects in their original posts and the "Social Support" they receive. (Independent variable: Personal Information Disclosure; Dependent variable: Social Support)
2. Hypothesis 2: Under the hashtags related to depression sufferers, the Social Support received by the subjects is correlated with variables such as Communication Index, Negative Emotion Index, and Proportion of First-Person Singular usage.

3. Hypothesis 3: The Social Support received by the subjects is more influenced by the variables mentioned in Hypothesis 2, suggesting that the independent variable in Hypothesis 1 is not the sole factor affecting Social Support.

2.2 Research Methodology

This study employs a four-step approach comprising data mining, expert scoring, machine learning, and regression analysis to rigorously investigate the hypotheses.

Dependent variable: social support			
	Agent	Categorization	Details
Content	Supporters: "4 types of social support"	Emotional support*	empathy/ sympathy
			encouragement/ resassurance
			care/ physical affection
			universality/ interrelationship
		Informational support	provide advice, referrals or knowledge (Bambina, 2007)
		Instrumental support	offering help or assistance in a tangible way, providing money and services
	Help-seeker	The coding method is the same as that in the above table. Three types of support are required	
*	Yoo, W et al., (2014) Giving and Receiving Emotional Support Online: Communication Competence as a Moderator of Psychosocial Benefits for Women with Breast Cancer. Comput Human Behav. 2014 Jan; 30: 13–22.		
Independent variable: Self Disclosure			
	Coding type	Categorization	Details
Self-disclosure : reveal private information about themselves in Weibo	Anonymous (Scott, 2004)	visusal anonymity	Scott, C. R. (2004). Benefits and drawbacks of anonymous online communication: Legal challenges and communicative recommendations. In S. Drucker (Ed.), Free speech yearbook (Vol. 41, pp. 127–141). Washington, DC: National Communication Association.
		discursive anonymity	
	Social context cues (Kiesler, Siegel, & McGuire, 1984; Sproull & Kiesler, 1986).	demographic data	How Social Context Cues in Online Support-Seeking Influence Self-Disclosure in Support Provision. DOI: 10.1080/01463373.2015.1078389 link:https://escholarship.org/content/qt4 jj2k41s/qt4jj2k41s.pdf?t=o2ppz4
		personal characteristics	
	Social presence (Bente, Ruggenberg, Kramer, & Eschenburg, 2008; Chuah et al., 2013; Reeves & Nass,1996). (Tanis & Postmes, 2007; Zheng, Veinott, Bos, Olson, & Olson, 2002).	None-verbal cues, use of emoticons, avatars	
		Basic user information: user picture, user name and ID, automatic reply after paying attention to the original user - sense of interaction	

Data Mining and Initial Scale Design: The study mines help-seeking information, replies, and "@" mentions from hashtags dedicated to depression sufferers on microblogging platforms. Random samples of textual information and comments are extracted from original posts. The initial scales for clue filtering and online social support are developed based on existing literature, as illustrated in the accompanying diagram.

Expert Scoring and Text Processing: This study analyzes microblog posts, comment data, and the number of likes/retweets/comments from 200 bloggers in the "Depression" section of a popular microblogging platform. Text processing is performed using Support Vector Machines (SVM) for machine learning. Twenty experts with PhDs in psychology are invited to score the text features, identity clue exposure, and social support in the comment section, resulting in a text type-social support score table.

Data Mining and Processing: Utilizing data mining techniques, posts, dissemination patterns, and comment data from approximately 1000 bloggers in the "Depression" section are collected. Based on the previously developed scoring table, corresponding scores for identity clue exposure and social support are calculated. Additionally, the Qingbo public opinion analysis system is used to calculate scores for other variables mentioned in Hypothesis 2: Communication Index, Negative Emotion Index, and Proportion of First-Person Singular usage in the original posts.

Machine Learning and Regression Analysis: Two regression methods, Random Forest and Decision Tree, are employed to train the dataset. Predictive analysis of independent and dependent variables is conducted against actual results to determine the optimal regression model. This model is then used for regression analysis to draw conclusions.

2.3 Data Results and Analysis

Through a rigorous data screening and comparison process, this study ultimately gathered and analyzed 1,040 original microblog posts from the Depression-related hashtags on Sina Weibo. These data were sourced from the original content posted under hashtags related to depression by individuals affected by the condition. After preprocessing and coding, relevant metrics for both independent and dependent variables were extracted. The independent variables comprised personal information disclosure, communication index, negative emotion index, and the proportion of first-person singular pronouns, while the dependent variable was social support.

2.4 Descriptive Statistics

The dataset encompassed 1,040 samples, with each sample corresponding to five variables. All variables were quantitative in nature, meaning they could be measured and represented numerically. Prior to conducting further analysis, a basic statistical description of the dataset was undertaken to gain an overview of the data's general characteristics.

The overall sample characteristics are as follows:

Variable name	sample size	Max	min	mean	Standard deviation	median	variance	kurtosis	skewness	CV
Exposure of identity clues	1040	8.906	3.438	6.295	1.317	6.188	1.735	−0.822	0.288	0.209
Negative Emotion Index	1040	4.8	1.6	3.385	0.738	3.4	0.545	−0.976	−0.003	0.218
Comuuication idenx	1040	5	1	3.206	1.035	3	1.071	−1.041	−0.063	0.323
Proportion of first person singular pronouns	1040	5	2	3.458	0.738	3.583	0.544	−0.717	−0.462	0.213

2.5 Exposure of Identity Clues

The maximum value of this variable is 8.906, and the minimum value is 3.438, indicating a wide range of variation. The mean value is 6.295, and the median is 6.188, suggesting a relatively symmetric data distribution. The standard deviation is 1.317, and the variance is 1.735, indicating some degree of dispersion in the data. The coefficient of variation is 0.209, implying relatively low data volatility. However, the Shapiro-Wilk (S-W) normality test results reveal that the data do not follow a normal distribution (P = 0.000***), which should be carefully considered during subsequent inferential statistical analyses.

2.6 Communication Index

The maximum value of the Communication Index is 5, and the minimum value is 1, with a mean of 3.206. The median is 3, which is close to the mean, indicating a relatively uniform data distribution. The standard deviation is 1.035, and the variance is 1.071, showing some dispersion. The coefficient of variation is 0.323, which is relatively high, suggesting stronger data volatility. Similarly, the S-W normality test indicates that the data do not follow a normal distribution (P = 0.000***).

2.7 Negative Emotion Index

The maximum value of the Negative Emotion Index is 4.8, and the minimum value is 1.6, with a mean of 3.385. The median is 3.4, which is very close to the mean, indicating a relatively symmetric data distribution. The standard deviation is 0.738, and the variance is 0.545, showing a relatively low degree of dispersion. The coefficient of variation is 0.218, implying lower data volatility. Nonetheless, the S-W normality test still indicates that the data do not follow a normal distribution (P = 0.000***).

2.8 Proportion of First-Person Singular Pronouns

The maximum value for the proportion of first-person singular pronouns is 5, and the minimum value is 2, with a mean of 3.458. The median is 3.583, slightly higher than the mean, suggesting a possible slight right skew in the data distribution. The standard deviation is 0.738, and the variance is 0.544, indicating some dispersion. The coefficient of variation is 0.213, which is relatively low. However, the S-W normality test results reveal that the data do not follow a normal distribution (P = 0.000***).

2.9 Social Support

The maximum value for social support is 9.2, and the minimum value is 2.4, with a mean of 6.623. The median is 6.8, slightly higher than the mean, indicating a possible slight left skew in the data distribution. The standard deviation is 1.357, and the variance is 1.843, showing some degree of dispersion. The coefficient of variation is 0.205, which is relatively low. As with the previous variables, the S-W normality test indicates that the data do not follow a normal distribution (P = 0.000***).

The data for all variables do not follow a normal distribution, which necessitates careful consideration when selecting appropriate non-parametric test methods for subsequent inferential statistical analyses. The means and medians of the variables are relatively close, indicating relatively symmetric data distributions; however, the standard deviations and variances of some variables are higher, showing some dispersion. The coefficients of variation suggest varying levels of volatility among the variables, with the Communication Index exhibiting the highest volatility and the Negative Emotion Index the lowest.

2.10 Support Vector Regression (SVR) Analysis

This step employs Support Vector Regression (SVR) for regression analysis, aiming to explore the relationship between social media behavior and social support among individuals with depression. During the data preprocessing stage, the raw data were cleaned, encoded, and standardized to ensure data quality and consistency. Subsequently, the processed data were divided into training and testing sets for model training and evaluation.

The SVR model parameters used in this study are as follows: the penalty coefficient is 1, the kernel function is linear, the kernel coefficient is scale, the kernel constant is 0, the highest degree of the kernel function is 3, the error convergence condition is 0.001, and the maximum number of iterations is 1000. The model training time is 0.035 s, the data splitting ratio is 0.7, and no data shuffling or cross-validation was performed.

	MSE	RMSE	MAE	MAPE	R2
learn	1.589	1.26	0.979	15.039	0.143
test	1.676	1.295	0.993	15.168	0.075

The evaluation results of the model indicate that the Mean Squared Error (MSE) for the training set is 1.589, the Root Mean Squared Error (RMSE) is 1.26, the Mean Absolute Error (MAE) is 0.979, the Mean Absolute Percentage Error (MAPE) is 15.039%, and the Coefficient of Determination (R2) is 0.143. For the test set, the MSE is 1.676, the RMSE is 1.295, the MAE is 0.993, the MAPE is 15.168%, and the R2 is 0.075. It can be observed that the model exhibits similar performance on both the training set and the test set, but the overall prediction effectiveness is mediocre, with relatively low R2 values.

Prediction Results and Analysis:

MSE	1.614838692528339
RMSE	1.2707630355531825
MAE	0.9829034461924887
R2	0.12284980864175976
MAPE	15.077472341450438

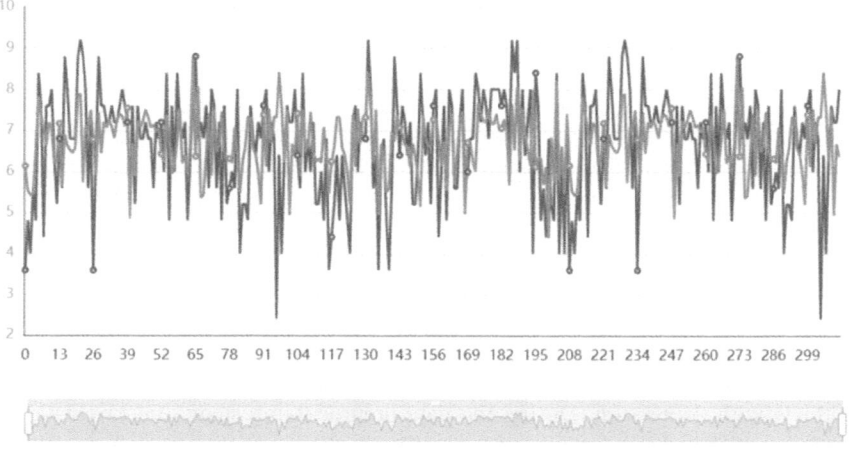

Based on the comparison between the model's predicted results and the actual outcomes, we observed that the predicted results had an MSE of 1.6148, an RMSE of 1.2708, an MAE of 0.9829, an R2 of 0.1228, and a MAPE of 15.0775%.

These metrics suggest that the model's predictive performance is not satisfactory, particularly due to the low R2 value, indicating a poor fit of the model to the data. While the model's predictions are close to the actual values in some cases, there are significant deviations in others. This could be attributed to the model's inability to adequately capture nonlinear relationships in the data or the influence of other unknown factors.

2.11 Decision Tree Regression

Given the unsatisfactory performance of the Support Vector Regression (SVR) model, we constructed a Decision Tree Regression model based on the data characteristics. We then trained and evaluated this model. During the data preprocessing stage, we cleaned, encoded, and standardized the raw data to ensure its quality and consistency. Subsequently, we divided the processed data into training and test sets for model training and evaluation.

The parameters of the regression model are as follows: the criterion for splitting nodes is 'friedman_mse', the strategy for selecting the best split is 'best', the maximum proportion of features considered for splitting is 'None', the minimum number of samples required to split an internal node is 2, the minimum number of samples required to be at a leaf node is 1, the minimum weight required to be at a leaf node is 0, the maximum depth of the tree is 10, the maximum number of leaf nodes is 50, and the threshold for impurity in splitting nodes is 0. The model training took 0.018 s, with a data split ratio of 0.7, and no shuffling or cross-validation was performed. Based on the training results, the structure of the decision tree is shown in the figure.

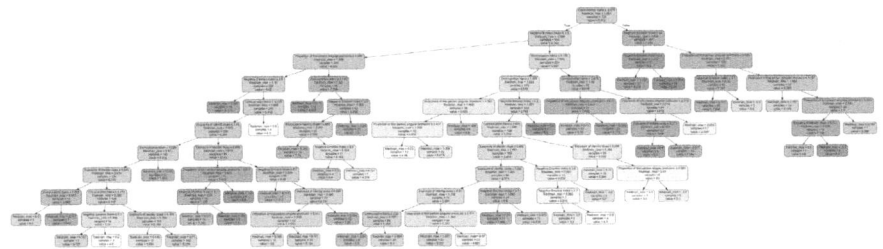

The model evaluation results indicate that for the training set, the Mean Squared Error (MSE) is 0.464, the Root Mean Squared Error (RMSE) is 0.681, the Mean Absolute Error (MAE) is 0.484, the Mean Absolute Percentage Error (MAPE) is 7.784%, and the Coefficient of Determination (R^2) is 0.75. For the test set, the MSE is 0.496, the RMSE is 0.704, the MAE is 0.49, the MAPE is 7.826%, and the R^2 is 0.726. It can be observed that the model exhibits similar performance on both the training set and the test set, with good overall prediction effectiveness indicated by the relatively high R^2 values.

	MSE	RMSE	MAE	MAPE	R2
learn	0.464	0.681	0.484	7.784	0.75
test	0.496	0.704	0.49	7.826	0.726

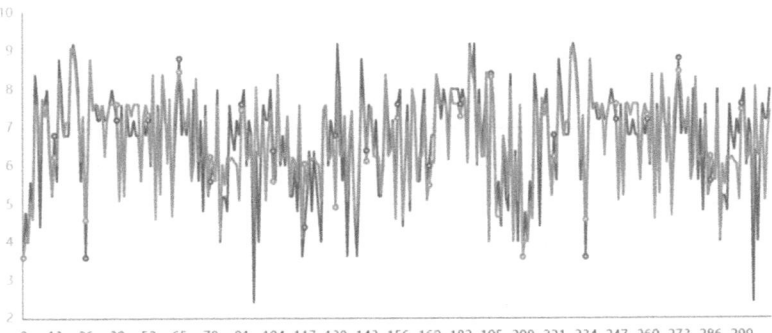

Based on the comparison between the model's predicted results and the actual outcomes, we observed that the Mean Squared Error (MSE) of the predictions is 0.4736, the Root Mean Squared Error (RMSE) is 0.6882, the Mean Absolute Error (MAE) is 0.4856, the Coefficient of Determination (R2) is 0.7427, and the Mean Absolute Percentage Error (MAPE) is 7.7967%. These metrics suggest a satisfactory predictive performance of the model, particularly due to the high R2 value, indicating a good fit of the model to the data.

2.12 Linear Regression Analysis

Using linear regression analysis, we explored the relationship between personal information disclosure (Exposure of identity clues) and social support (Social Support) within the context of depression-related hashtags. Furthermore, we examined the correlations between social support and several other variables, including the communication index (Communication Index), negative emotion index (Negative Emotion Index), and the proportion of first-person singular pronouns (Proportion of first-person singular pronouns).

Linear regression analysis results n = 1040									
	Non standardized coefficient		Standardization coefficient	t	P	VIF	R2	Adjust R 2	F
	B	Standard error	Beta						
constant	6.479	0.467	–	13.864	0.000***	–	0.154	0.151	F = 47.022 P = 0.000***
Exposure of identity clues	0.113	0.031	0.11	3.651	0.000***	1.112			
Negative Emotion Index	–0.452	0.069	–0.246	–6.52	0.000***	1.74			
Comuuication idenx	0.449	0.04	0.342	11.22	0.000***	1.136			
Proportion of first person singular pronouns	–0.138	0.069	–0.075	–1.992	0.047**	1.741			
dependent variable:Social Support									

Note: * * *, * *, * * represent significance levels of 1%, 5%, and 10%, respectively

2.13 Overall Model Evaluation

Based on the regression analysis, the model has an R2 value of 0.154 and an adjusted R2 of 0.151, indicating that it can explain approximately 15.1% of the variation in the dependent variable, social support. The F-value of 47.022, significant at the 1% level, suggests that the model is statistically significant overall. Despite the limited explanatory power, these results hold some valuable insights in the context of social media research.

Impact of Variables on Social Support

1. Personal Information Disclosure: The unstandardized coefficient is 0.113, with a standardized coefficient of 0.11 and a t-value of 3.651, significant at the 1% level. This indicates a positive association between personal information disclosure and social support, suggesting that greater disclosure leads to more social support. This finding supports Hypothesis 1, highlighting that disclosing more personal information in depression-related hashtags can foster trust and empathy, ultimately increasing social support. However, it's essential to strike a balance in disclosing personal information to avoid privacy breaches and safety concerns.

2. Negative Emotion Index: The unstandardized coefficient is –0.452, with a standardized coefficient of –0.246 and a t-value of –6.52, significant at the 1% level. This negative correlation suggests that higher expressions of negative emotions are associated with lower social support. This aligns with our expectations and previous research, indicating that negative emotional expressions can evoke discomfort and avoidance behaviors, leading to reduced social support. Therefore, it's advisable for individuals with depression to maintain a positive and optimistic attitude on social media while expressing emotions.

3. Communication Index: The unstandardized coefficient is 0.449, with a standardized coefficient of 0.342 and a t-value of 11.22, significant at the 1% level. This positive correlation suggests that effective communication is associated with higher social support. This finding aligns with our expectations and common sense, indicating that clear and effective communication can enhance information transmission, trust, and empathy, leading to increased social support. Depression patients can improve communication effectiveness by using clear and concise language on social media while actively engaging in interactions and discussions.

4. Proportion of First-Person Singular Pronouns: The unstandardized coefficient is –0.138, with a standardized coefficient of –0.075 and a t-value of –1.992, significant at the 5% level. This negative association suggests that a higher proportion of first-person singular pronouns is related to lower social support, albeit with a relatively small effect size. This might indicate that excessive self-focus or isolation reflected in pronoun usage could reduce social support. However, interpretation should be cautious, considering that pronoun usage might also be influenced by individual expression habits and contexts. Future research could employ more nuanced metrics and methodologies to further explore this relationship.

2.14 Interactions and Impact Among Variables

Beyond examining the individual impacts of these variables on social support, it's essential to consider their interactions and combined effects. For instance, personal information disclosure and communication index might interactively influence social support acquisition. Disclosing more personal information while adopting effective communication strategies could further enhance social support. Conversely, inappropriate communication might hinder the benefits of information disclosure.

Similarly, there might be a relationship between the negative emotion index and the proportion of first-person singular pronouns. Excessive use of first-person singular pronouns might reflect self-focus or isolation, which could exacerbate negative emotion expression and perception, thereby negatively impacting social support. Therefore, it's crucial to consider these interactive effects when interpreting regression results.

2.15   Hypothesis Validation

The regression analysis results allow us to validate and discuss the proposed hypotheses. Hypothesis 1 is supported, indicating a positive association between personal information disclosure and social support. However, the extent of disclosure should be balanced to prevent privacy breaches. Hypothesis 2 is partially supported, with communication index positively related to social support and negative emotion index negatively related. The proportion of first-person singular pronouns has a significant but minor impact, warranting cautious interpretation. Hypothesis 3 is somewhat supported, with the communication index exerting the strongest influence on social support, followed by the negative emotion index and then personal information disclosure. This suggests that while personal information disclosure is beneficial, effective communication and emotional expression might be more critical in seeking social support.

2.16   Summary and Discussion

This study delves into the relationship between information disclosure and social support among depression patients on social media, further examining the impacts of communication index, negative emotion index, and the proportion of first-person singular pronouns on social support. The findings provide a new perspective on depression patients' social media usage and offer valuable insights for more effective social support provision. While the model's explanatory power is limited, with R2 and adjusted R2 indicating approximately 15% variance explained in social support, the results hold academic and practical significance in the complex social media research landscape. They suggest that additional unconsidered factors might significantly influence social support. The significant positive correlation between personal information disclosure and social support underscores the importance of balanced disclosure in fostering empathy and trust on social media platforms, emphasizing the need for privacy and safety considerations. The negative association between negative emotion index and social support highlights the beneficial role of maintaining a positive attitude in attracting social support. The positive correlation between communication index and social support underscores the critical role of effective communication in social support acquisition. Finally, the study acknowledges the complex interactions among these variables and their potential combined effects on social support, calling for a more comprehensive and nuanced approach in future research.

References

Culnan, M.J., Markus, M.L.: Information technologies. In: Jablin, F.M., Putnam, L.L., Roberts, K.H., Porter, L.W. (eds.) Handbook of Organizational Communication: An Interdisciplinary Perspective. Sage Publications, Inc., pp. 420–443 (1987)

Walther, J.B., Parks, M.R.: Cues filtered out, cues filtered in: computer mediated communication and relationships. In: Miller, G.R. (ed.) The Handbook of Interpersonal Communication. Sage Publications, pp. 529–563 (2002)

Guegan, J., Segonds, F., Barre, J., Maranzana, N., Mantelet, F., Buisine, S.: Social identity cues to improve creativity and identification in face-to-face and virtual groups. Comput. Hum. Behav. **77**, 140–147 (2017). https://doi.org/10.1016/j.chb.2017.08.043

Tanis, M., Postmes, T.: Two faces of anonymity: paradoxical effects of cues to identity in CMC. Comput. Hum. Behav. **23**, 955–970 (2007). https://doi.org/10.1016/j.chb.2005.08.004

Vinokur, A., Schul, Y., Caplan, R.D.: Determinants of perceived social support: Interpersonal transactions, personal outlook, and transient affective states. J. Pers. Soc. Psychol. **53**(6), 1137–1145 (1987). https://doi.org/10.1037/0022-3514.53.6.1137

Simmons, A.J.: Locke's state of nature. Polit. Theory **17**(3), 449–470 (1989). https://doi.org/10.1177/0090591789017003005

Cohen, S., Wills, T.A.: Stress, social support, and the buffering hypothesis. Psychol. Bull. **98**(2), 310–357 (1985). https://doi.org/10.1037/0033-2909.98.2.310

Gui, Y., Gu, D.H., Zhu, G.H.: The impact of social networks on job search: an empirical study of laid-off workers in Shanghai. In: World Economic Forum (ed.) (volume/issue not provided), pp. 45–51. (Note: Volume/issue and page numbers might need verification.) (2002)

Xiao, S.Y., Yang, D.S.: The influence of social support on physical and mental health. In: Chinese Mental Health Journal (ed.) (volume/issue not provided), pp. 184–187 (1987). (Note: Volume/issue and page numbers might need verification.)

Cui, X.J., et al.: A correlational study on stigma and coping styles in patients with depression. Chin. J. Health Psychol. **20**(06), 814–815 (2012)

Zhang, J.L.: The relationship between depression self-stigma, self-efficacy, and social avoidance. Dissertation, Henan University (2011)

Huang, G.L., Zhou, X.L.: Language use patterns of patients with depression. Progress Psychol. Sci. **29**(05), 838–848 (2021)

Ma, X., Yu, H.: The current situation and adjustment strategy of depression communication in social media. Youth Journalist **12**, 39–40 (2019)

Ji, J.L., Xu, M.Q.: A study on comorbid anxiety disorders in depression and schizophrenia. J. Clin. Psychiatry **01**, 9–11 (2004)

Fintech, Consumer Behavior and the Business Environment

Consumer Behavior in Electronic Word of Mouth: A Bibliometric Approach

Jorge Cruz-Cárdenas[1,2](✉) ⓘ, Parvaneh Saeidi[1,2] ⓘ, Ekaterina Zabelina[3] ⓘ,
Olga Deyneka[4] ⓘ, Carlos Ramos-Galarza[5] ⓘ, and Andrés Palacio-Fierro[6] ⓘ

[1] Facultad de Administración y Negocios, Universidad Indoamérica, Quito, Ecuador
{jorgecruz,parvanehsaeidi}@uti.edu.ec
[2] Research Center in Business, Society and Technology, ESTec, Universidad Indoamérica,
Quito, Ecuador
[3] Department of Psychology, Chelyabinsk State University, Chelyabinsk, Russia
katya_k@mail.ru
[4] Department of Political Psychology, St. Petersburg State University, St. Petersburg, Russia
osdeyneka@yandex.ru
[5] Facultad de Psicología, Pontificia Universidad Católica del Ecuador, Quito, Ecuador
ca-ramos@puce.edu.ec
[6] Universidad Internacional del Ecuador (UIDE), Quito, Ecuador
anpalaciofi@uide.edu.ec

Abstract. Electronic word of mouth (eWOM) is a consumer behavior that involves the dissemination of communications about brands, products, and companies with clear positive or negative valence. eWOM is attracting great attention from academics and practitioners, which is reflected in the growing number of publications on the subject. Thus, the present study aims to contribute to the organization and description of this knowledge through the use of bibliometric techniques. This study analyzes a documentary corpus of 2,331 eWOM documents existing in the Scopus database. The descriptive analysis of this body of documents confirms a rapid growth in the pace of publication. The data further highlight eWOM as a multidisciplinary academic field with a center of gravity in business, management, and accounting. However, the analysis shows a great predominance of institutions and researchers from developed and emerging countries. The analysis of the co-occurrence of terms leads to the identification of three thematic clusters: (1) search and use of eWOM by the consumer, (2) the consumer's experience and satisfaction in the consumption of services, and (3) the consumer behavior in the generation of eWOM. The analysis of the overlay visualization of terms allows us to verify an evolution in research interest from the orientation to lay the theoretical foundations of eWOM to the current interest in delving into search behavior and the use of eWOM in decision making. Finally, the present study formulates the theoretical and practical implications of these findings.

Keywords: consumer behavior · electronic word of mouth · eWOM

A. Coman et al. (Eds.): HCII 2024, LNCS 15375, pp. 271–281, 2025.
https://doi.org/10.1007/978-3-031-76806-4_20

1 Introduction

In general, word of mouth (WOM) is a type of informal communication that some consumers direct to others, and its whose content refers to goods, services, brands, or companies [1]. The usefulness of the information transmitted by WOM to consumers lies in the reduction of cognitive effort, risk, and uncertainty both before and after the purchase [2–4]. Therefore, WOM has a significant impact on consumers' purchasing decisions [5, 6].

With the rapid advancement of technologies and the spread of social networks and other digital spaces, the largest amount of WOM has moved to the digital world, a consumer behavior now called electronic word of mouth (eWOM). Thus, eWOM is a type of communication behavior that involves human–computer interaction [7]. The content of the communication is information about brands, products, or companies with a clear positive or negative valence, and the spread of the information is very fast, as it is distributed in the digital space [8]. Among these digital spaces of propagation are social networks (e.g., Facebook, Instagram, and TikTok), blogs, forums, question-and-answer sites, and e-commerce places. The impact that eWOM has on society is twofold. At the micro or individual level, eWOM influences consumer decision making [9–12]. At an aggregate level, eWOM can mark the destiny of brands and organizations and can also be the basis for the dissemination of more responsible consumer behaviors, that is, United Nations' Sustainable Development Goal 12 [13].

Academic and scientific production regarding eWOM has experienced rapid growth in recent years [14]. In scenarios of rapid knowledge growth, efforts aimed at organizing and structuring said knowledge become necessary [15]. This is precisely the objective of the present study, which uses a methodological approach based on bibliometric techniques. Previous studies have also sought to organize and systematize the existing body of knowledge on eWOM. To do this, scholars have used approaches such as meta-analyses [e.g., 9, 11], systematic literature reviews [e.g., 1, 7], and bibliometric approaches [e.g., 14]. However, two distinctive characteristics of the present study are its updated dataset and its greater coverage of documents. Formally, the general objective of this study is to establish through bibliometric techniques the characteristics and structure of the existing body of knowledge on eWOM.

This article is organized into various sections. Beyond this introduction to the study and its general objective, Section objective, "Methods," details the techniques and decisions adopted in obtaining a dataset of documents published on eWOM, which totaled 2,331. In Sect. 3, "Analysis of the corpus of documents," we performed various analyses using two bibliometric techniques—productivity and science mapping [14, 17]—to assess and structure the documentary body on eWOM. Section 4, "Discussion, conclusions, and recommendations," concludes the paper by summarizing the most important findings and presenting recommendations for future research and professional practice.

2 Methods

The present study was divided into three stages that Donthu et al. [14] recommended for bibliometric studies: (1) formulating the research objectives, (2) designing the study methodology, and (3) obtaining the research outcomes. Stage 1, that is, the formulation of objectives, was addressed in the "Introduction" section. Stage 2 is addressed here in the Methods section. Stage 3 will be addressed in Sects. 3 and 4. The study followed the guidelines contained in the Preferred Reporting Items for Systematic reviews and Meta-Analyses (PRISMA) statement [18]. The general objective guiding the study was to establish the characteristics and structure of the existing body of knowledge on eWOM.

To deploy the search strategy, several decisions were adopted. First, the Scopus database was chosen considering three crucial characteristics: its quality criteria for content inclusion, its accessibility, and its broad coverage [19]. A second decision was related to the search string to be used. For this, an exploratory study was carried out in the Scopus database. As a starting point, it was decided that two types of content should be present simultaneously: (1) the type of discipline or approach, with "consumer" being the starting term and (2) the behavior to be studied, being "electronic word of mouth." For each of these terms, frequent alternative terms were searched in the Scopus database. Once these alternative terms were analyzed, the search string was defined as follows: ("consumer" OR "customer") AND ("electronic word-of-mouth" OR "electronic word of mouth" OR "electronic word of mouths" OR "ewom" OR "e-wom").

The search for relevant documents was performed on March 5, 2024. The search was carried out on titles, abstracts, and keywords. The first search result returned 2,452 documents. Two types of delimitations were imposed on the document group. A first delimitation was to select only articles, conference papers, books, and book chapters, that is, documents that have gone through an editorial review process. A second delimitation concerned language. Thus, only documents published in English were selected, which allowed for science mapping bibliometric analyses. No temporal delimitation was imposed. The application of the delimitations finally reduced the initial group to 2,331 documents. We then obtained the set of relevant documents and applied two groups of analyses: performance analysis of science actors and science mapping [20]. These analyses are described in the following section.

3 Analysis of the Corpus of Documents

A first group of analyses was aimed at establishing the performance of the main actors in science, such as institutions, countries, and journals. To this end, the study began by establishing trends in the volume of annual publications of documents in the area under analysis. The results obtained and presented in Fig. 1 underscore a trend of rapid growth that is consistent with previous studies [14]. However, although in general terms, this growth pattern exists in the volume of publications on consumer behavior in eWOM, two phases were visually identified. A first phase was located between 2006 and 2013. In this first phase, only modest growth in publication volume was observed. A second phase was identified from 2014 to the present. This second phase was characterized by accelerated growth (steeper curve) in the volume of publications in this area of studies on human–computer interaction.

Regarding the disciplines that contribute the most to studies on consumer behavior and eWOM, Table 1 presents the panorama found.

As shown in Table 1, business and management, computer science, and social sciences were the areas that contributed the most to eWOM studies, a panorama that has

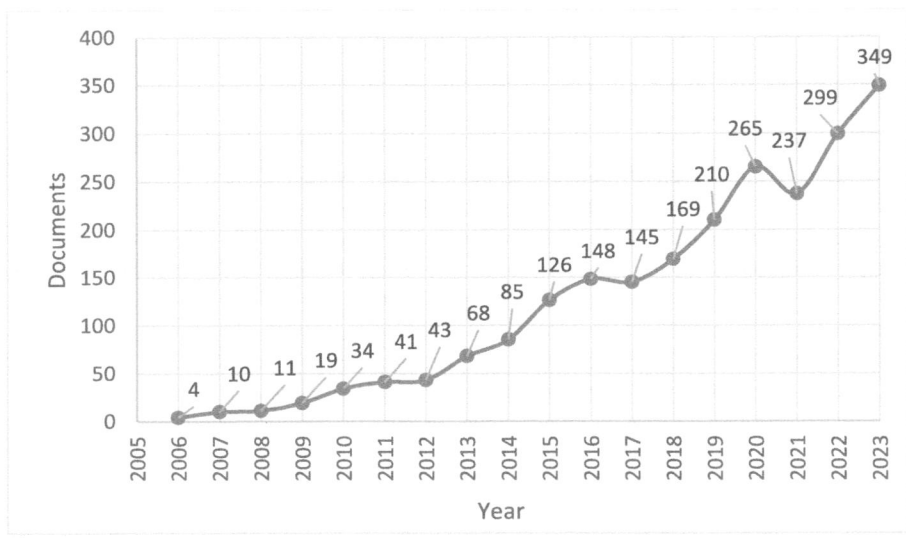

Fig. 1. Historical evolution of the volume of published documents (source: Scopus)

Table 1. Areas of knowledge contributing to eWOM

Subject area	Documents	%
Business, management, and accounting	1470	63.1%
Computer science	791	33.9%
Social sciences	528	22.7%
Economics, econometrics, and finance	363	15.6%
Decision sciences	223	9.6%
Engineering	222	9.5%
Psychology	156	6.7%
Arts and humanities	108	4.6%

been observed in other areas of study of human–computer interaction [21]. However, the greater contribution of some areas over others was also salient. Clearly, eWOM emerged as a multidisciplinary field of study whose center of gravity in business, management, and accounting (63.1% of the documents were linked to this area). Additionally, it should be noted that in Table 1, the percentages add up to more than 100%, given that the Scopus database can assign multiple disciplinary areas to the same document.

Another important aspect in the study of performance in the area of eWOM is determining the main document publication formats. Table 2 presents this information, showing that the dominant form of publication was article (75.6% of the documents). Conference papers followed at a good distance (16%). These results may be due to the area of knowledge that contributes the most—business, management, and accounting—where the frequent form of publication is articles.

Table 2. Types of documents in eWOM publication

University/Institution	Documents	%
Article	1762	75.6%
Conference paper	373	16.0%
Book chapter	190	8.1%
Book	6	0.3%
TOTAL	2331	100%

Another aspect addressed in the bibliometric analysis of performance was the main publication sources. Table 3 presents the most relevant sources, using the publication of 30 or more documents as a cut-off point. As shown in the table, three publication sources stand out from the others: "Developments in Marketing Science Proceedings of the Academy of Marketing Science," "Journal of Business Research," and "Sustainability." The first two sources of publication are a proceeding and a journal focused on the area of business administration. The third publication source is a multidisciplinary journal. Other sources presented in Table 3 are journals focused on the topic of services and technologies. This interest in eWOM from journals specializing in the subject of services could be attributed to consumers' intensive use of eWOM in the world of services, given the difficulty of pre-purchase evaluation, typical of intangibles [22].

Table 3. Main publication sources

Source title	Documents
Developments in Marketing Science, Proceedings of the Academy of Marketing Science	71
Journal of Business Research	60
Sustainability Switzerland	50
International Journal of Hospitality Management	35
International Journal of Contemporary Hospitality Management	34
Journal of Retailing and Consumer Services	34
Internet Research	33
Computers in Human Behavior	32

A final bibliometric approach to the performance in the thematic field of eWOM evaluated the countries as research actors. Table 4 presents this information. It is necessary to clarify that considering that a single document can have several authors, the same document can be simultaneously linked to several countries. As Table 4 shows, the United States leads eWOM research, with 20.1% of the documents signed by one or more authors assigned to institutions or universities in the United States. The rest of the list is a combination of both developed and emerging countries.

Table 4. Top countries in eWOM research

University/Institution	Documents	%
United States	468	20,1%
China	270	11,6%
India	226	9,7%
United Kingdom	208	8,9%
Taiwan	153	6,6%
South Korea	145	6,2%
Spain	139	6,0%
Indonesia	135	5,8%
Malaysia	122	5,2%

A second group of analysis was aimed at mapping science in the area of eWOM. Among the various possible tools, co-occurrence networks of terms and the overlay visualization of terms were chosen [23, 24]. For the application of these two types of tools, the contents of the titles and abstracts of the 2,331 documents were chosen and the Vosviewer software version 1.6.20 was used [24]. Initially, 31,240 unique words and terms were identified. A minimum frequency of occurrence of 30 was imposed as a restriction on this group of words [21]. Additionally, terms that did not contribute to the analysis were removed [21]. Thus, terms linked to the type of documents and their component parts were removed (e.g., "abstract," "paper," and "practical implication") and terms linked to the methodology of the study (e.g., "quantitative approach," "questionnaire," and "structural equation modeling"). The application of these two delimitations led to the final selection of 260 words and terms for the analyses.

As indicated, the first tool used for science mapping was the co-occurrence network of terms. This analysis seeks to establish thematic clusters based on the content of the selected documents [23, 24]. These clusters are a good approximation of the areas or lines of research on the topic of interest [15]. Figure 2 shows the results obtained.

Figure 2 shows the three thematic clusters. Each cluster is represented with a different color; additionally, the terms or words are represented as nodes, where the size of the node is proportional to the frequency with which the term appears in the body of documents [24]. The clusters obtained are described below.

Cluster 1 (red color, 118 items) had "intention" and "purchase intention" as its main nodes. Other notable nodes were "engagement," "social network," "credibility," "online shopping," and "outcome." Thus, this cluster was associated with the behavior of searching for and using eWOM in purchase decision making. Cluster 2 (green, 109

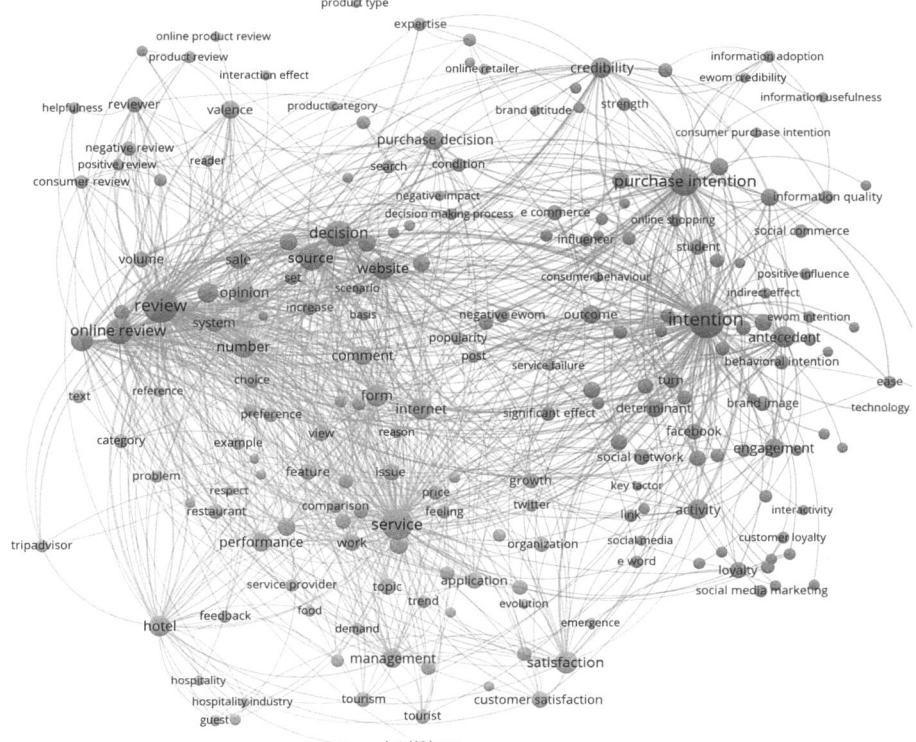

Fig. 2. Co-occurrence network of terms

terms) presented the word "service" as its main node. Other notable nodes were "satisfaction," "performance," "hotel," "comment," "management," and "opinion." Therefore, this cluster was associated with the consumer experience of service consumption and satisfaction (i.e., the onset of eWOM). Cluster 3 (blue color, 33 items) had the word "decision" as its main node. Other important nodes were "review," "online review," "valence," "negative review," "positive review," and "website." This cluster was therefore associated with the behavior of generating eWOM.

A second tool that was used for science mapping was the overlay visualization of terms. Figure 3 presents the results obtained.

The interpretation of graphical results from the overlay visualization of terms is also based on colors and nodes. However, unlike the analysis of the co-occurrence network of terms, in the overlay visualization of terms, the colors represent the popularity of a term in the timeline. Thus, the terms represented in purple and green nodes are those that were most frequently used years ago, while the terms whose nodes are represented in yellow are currently popular terms [24]. This graphic representation is a good approximation of the evolution of research interest over time [21, 24].

As shown in Fig. 3, there has been a historical evolution in the interest and emphasis of research on eWOM. Years ago, interest was concentrated in terms such as "source,"

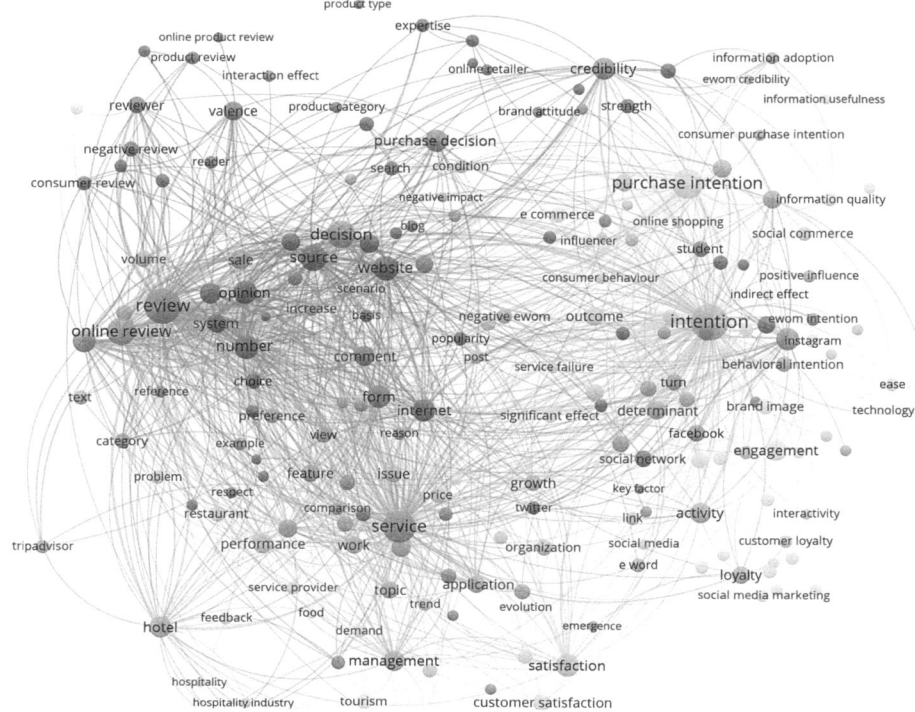

Fig. 3. Overlay visualization of terms

"website," "internet," "product category," "valence," "reviewer," "consumer review," and "negative review." Thus, initially, the interest focused on laying the foundations of the general theory of eWOM and general consumer behavior in this practice. Figure 3 further shows the current popular terms (yellow color) as "purchase intention," "e-commerce," "engagement," "customer satisfaction," "information quality," and "online shopping." Thus, the current emphasis of the research on eWOM was on consumer behavior in the search for and use of eWOM in decision making.

4   Discussion, Conclusions, and Recommendations

Consumer behavior in eWOM is a rapidly growing academic and scientific area. This trend observed by previous studies [e.g., 14] was confirmed by the present study, which also found that after a stage of modest growth, in 2014, the stage of accelerated growth began. This growth trend not only justifies the present study but also allows us to recommend the eWOM area as an attractive area for future studies.

The present study found a multidisciplinary character in eWOM studies. This characteristic has been observed in other studies on human–computer interaction [e.g., 21]. This finding makes sense because knowledge from a range of disciplines is needed to grasp the complexity of the interaction of people and technology. Obviously, depending on the specific topic of the study, the center of gravity (discipline with the most contribution) will change. In this case, we found that eWOM has a center of gravity in business, management, and accounting. For this reason, the recommendation is to form multidisciplinary teams to capture the complexity of behaviors, such as eWOM and others linked to human–computer interaction.

Performance measures by country in eWOM research show a predominance of developed and emerging countries and very little presence of developing countries. The present study therefore joins the call by previous studies on human–computer interaction, which have noted this aspect and proposed more research in other settings, such as developing countries [21]. Such future study efforts on human–computer interaction in developing countries may have a single-country focus or be based on comparative studies. More studies in developing countries will allow testing existing knowledge and its generalization possibilities [25] or generating completely new knowledge.

Previous studies, such as Donthu et al. [14], found a fragmented and dispersed panorama of thematic clusters on consumer behavior in eWOM, identifying a total of 11. The present study updated this finding by analyzing a greater number of documents and finding a more concentrated panorama. Thus, three thematic clusters were identified: (1) the search for and use of eWOM by the consumer in decision making, (2) the experience and satisfaction of the consumer in the consumption of services, and (3) consumer behavior in the generation of eWOM. Clusters 1 and 3 are directly associated with the use and issuance of eWOM, two types of actions that were also noted by King et al. [7]. Cluster 2 refers more to the service experience, which is plausible, considering that services, being intangible, are more difficult to evaluate before purchasing than goods [22]; therefore, eWOM can have a central value in providing information. Thus, this finding of the present study of three thematic clusters in eWOM research allows future studies to better position their research efforts.

Another interesting finding of the present study was observed in the analysis of the overlay visualization of terms. Here, an evolution in research interest emerges from the efforts to lay general theoretical foundations on eWOM behavior to today's interest in consumer behavior in the search for and use of eWOM in decision making. This finding is also presents a useful future research direction in eWOM.

Regarding recommendations for professional practice, organizations should implement integrated eWOM management. Thus, organizations must understand that eWOM is a behavior that fuels consumer decision making, particularly in situations of risk and difficult evaluation [2, 4]. Subsequently, consumers receiving eWOM will become senders of their experiences, thereby further developing the eWOM process. Finally, nonprofit organizations should consider the potential of eWOM to modulate responsible consumption behaviors.

References

1. Westbrook, R.A.: Product/consumption-based affective responses and postpurchase processes. J. Mark. Res. **24**(3), 258–270 (1987)
2. Eliashberg, J., Jonker, J.J., Sawhney, M.S., Wierenga, B.: MOVIEMOD: an implementable decision-support system for prerelease market evaluation of motion pictures. Mark. Sci. **19**(3), 226–243 (2000)
3. Dowling, G.R., Staelin, R.: A model of perceived risk and intended risk-handling activity. J. Consum. Res. **21**(1), 119–134 (1994)
4. Widayati, C.C., Ali, H., Permana, D., Nugroho, A.: The role of destination image on visiting decisions through word of mouth in urban tourism in Yogyakarta. Int. J. Innov. Creat. Change. **12**(3), 177–196 (2020)
5. East, R., Romaniuk, J., Chawdhary, R., Uncles, M.: The impact of word of mouth on intention to purchase currently used and other brands. Int. J. Mark. Res. **59**(3), 321–334 (2017)
6. Iyer, R., Griffin, M.: Modeling word-of-mouth usage: a replication. J. Bus. Res. **126**, 512–523 (2020)
7. King, R.A., Racherla, P., Bush, V.D.: What we know and don't know about online word-of-mouth: a review and synthesis of the literature. J. Interact. Mark. **28**(3), 167–183 (2014)
8. Hennig-Thurau, T., Gwinner, K.P., Walsh, G., Gremler, D.D.: Electronic word-of-mouth via consumer-opinion platforms: What motivates consumers to articulate themselves on the Internet? J. Interact. Mark. **18**(1), 38–52 (2004)
9. Babić, A., Sotgiu, F., de Valck, K., Bijmolt, T.H.A.: The effect of electronic word of mouth on sales: a meta-analytic review of platform, product, and metric factors. J. Mark. Res. **53**(3), 297–318 (2016)
10. Erkan, I., Evans, C.: The influence of eWOM in social media on consumers' purchase intentions: an extended approach to information adoption. Comput. Hum. Behav. **61**, 47–55 (2016).
11. Ismagilova, E., Slade, E.L., Rana, N.P., Dwivedi, Y.K.: The effect of electronic word of mouth communications on intention to buy: a meta-analysis. Inf. Syst. Front. **22**, 1203–1226 (2020)
12. Shankar, A., Jebarajakirthy, C., Ashaduzzaman, M.: How do electronic word of mouth practices contribute to mobile banking adoption? J. Retail. Consum. Serv. **52**, 101920 (2020)
13. United Nations: Sustainable Development (2015). https://sdgs.un.org/goals
14. Donthu, N., Kumar, S., Mukherjee, D., Pandey, N., Lim, W.M.: How to conduct a biblio metric analysis: an overview and guidelines. J. Bus. Res. **133**, 285–296 (2021)
15. Cruz-Cárdenas, J., Zabelina, E., Guadalupe-Lanas, J., Palacio-Fierro, A., Ramos-Galarza, C.: Covid-19, consumer behavior, technology, and society: a literature review and bibliometric analysis. Technol. Forecast. Soc. Change. **173**, 121179 (2021)
16. Cheung, C.M.K., Thadani, D.R.: The impact of electronic word-of-mouth communication: a literature analysis and integrative model. Decis. Support. Syst. **54**(1), 461–470 (2012)
17. Noyons, E.C.M., Moed, H.F., Van Raan, A.F.J.: Integrating research performance analysis and science mapping. Scientometrics **46**, 591–604 (1999)
18. Page, M.J., McKenzie, J.E., Bossuyt, P.M., Boutron, I., Hoffmann, T.C., Mulrow, C.D., et al.: The PRISMA 2020 statement: an updated guideline for reporting systematic reviews. BMJ **372**, n71 (2021)
19. Pranckuté, R.: Web of Science (WoS) and Scopus: the titans of bibliographic information in today's academic world. Publications **9**(1), 12 (2021)
20. Guleria, D., Kaur, G.: Bibliometric analysis of ecopreneurship using VOSviewer and RStudio bibliometrix, 1989–2019. Libr. Hi. Tech. **39**(4), 1001–1024 (2021)

21. Cruz-Cárdenas, J., Zabelina, E., Deyneka, O., Palacio-Fierro, A., Guadalupe-Lanas, J., Ramos-Galarza, C.: Smartphones and higher education: mapping the field. In: Salvendy, G., Wei, J. (eds.) Design, Operation and Evaluation of Mobile Communications. HCII 2023. Lecture Notes in Computer Science, vol. 14052. Springer, Cham (2023). https://doi.org/10.1007/978-3-031-35921-7_17

22. Litvin, S.W., Goldsmith, R.E., Pan, B.: Electronic word-of-mouth in hospitality and tourism management. Tour. Manag. **29**(3), 458–468 (2008)

23. Van Eck, N.J., Waltman, L.: Software survey: VOSviewer, a computer program for bibliometric mapping. Scientometrics **84**(2), 523–538 (2010)

24. Van Eck, N.J., Waltman, L.: Manual for Vosviewer version 1.6.20 (2023). https://www.vosviewer.com/documentation/Manual_VOSviewer_1.6.15.pdf

25. Cruz-Cárdenas, J., Zabelina, E., Deyneka, O., Guadalupe-Lanas, J., Velín-Fárez, M.: Role of demographic factors, attitudes toward technology, and cultural values in the prediction of technology-based consumer behaviors: a study in developing and emerging countries. Technol. Forecast. Soc. Change. **149**, 119768 (2019)

A Hybrid Multi-criteria Decision-Making Model for Supplier Selection Based on Secure International Commerce: A Case Study of the Lithography Industry

Genett Isabel Jiménez-Delgado[1](✉) [ID], Hugo Hernandez-Palma[2] [ID],
Dionicio Neira-Rodado[3] [ID], Bellanith Lucena-León Castro[4,5],
Anderson Nieto-Granados[6], Dairo Novoa[7], Felipe Acosta-Ortega[8],
Osman Redondo-Bilbao[9] [ID], and Jairo Martinez-Ventura[10]

[1] Department of Industrial Engineering, Institución Universitaria de Barranquilla IUB,
Barranquilla, Colombia
gjimenez@unibarranquilla.edu.co
[2] Faculty of Engineering, Industrial Engineering Program, Corporación Universitaria
Iberoamericana IBERO, Bogotá, Colombia
hugo.hernandez@ibero.edu.co
[3] Department of Productivity and Innovation, Universidad de La Costa CUC,
Barranquilla, Colombia
dneira1@cuc.edu.co
[4] International Business Program, Corporación Universitaria Americana,
Barranquilla, Colombia
bellanithlucena@americana.edu.co,
bleonca36518@universidadean.edu.co
[5] Doctorate of Project Management. Universidad EAN, Bogotá, Colombia
[6] Faculty of Engineering, Corporación Universitaria Iberoamericana IBERO, Bogotá, Colombia
anderson.nieto@ibero.edu.co
[7] Management of Tourism Enterprises Program, Universidad del Atlántico,
Barranquilla, Colombia
daironovoa@mail.uniatlantico.edu.co
[8] Faculty of Economic, Accounting and Administrative Sciences, Business Administration
Program, Fundación Universitaria de Popayan, Popayan, Colombia
felipe.acosta@docente.fup.edu.co
[9] Accounting Program, Corporación Politécnico Costa Atlántica, Barranquilla, Colombia
[10] Faculty of Economic Sciences, Corporación Universitaria Latinoamericana CUL,
Barranquilla, Colombia
academico@ul.edu.co

Abstract. The lithography industry has experienced significant changes and significant growth in the market in recent years, driven by technological advances and specific demands from various sectors, as well as the increase in international trade and the search for new clients in the face of unstable local markets. After the Covid-19 pandemic. In international trade, supplier selection is critical to guarantee quality, availability, efficiency, and security in commercial operations, specifically in the lithography industry, where sensitive materials and products are handled. Therefore, developing models for choosing safe suppliers is essential to entering and remaining in markets as competitive as international ones. This paper proposes a novel hybrid approach that integrates F-AHP, DEMATEL, and TOPSIS techniques for selecting suppliers that facilitate compliance with standards for Secure International Commerce in the lithography industry supply chain. To this end, the methodological approach consisted first of applying the fuzzy analytical hierarchy process (F-AHP) to determine the weights of the criteria and sub-criteria under conditions of uncertainty. Next, the Decision-Making Evaluation and Testing Laboratory (DEMATEL) was used to establish the main influencers in selecting suppliers for safe trade. Finally, the Technique for Order of Preference by Similarity to Ideal Solution (TOPSIS) was implemented to identify weaknesses that affect secure trade in the supply chain. The proposed approach was validated with a case study in the lithography industry. The main findings reveal that "Quality", "Economy", and "Management certifications" are essential factor, and the most influential criteria are "Management certifications" and "Quality".

Keywords: Multi-Criteria Decision-making · Fuzzy AHP · DEMATEL · TOPSIS · Supplier Selection · Secure International Commerce · Customer Satisfaction · Lithography industry

1 Introduction

The lithography industry plays a crucial role globally, providing primary technology for producing printed materials. This industry is essential for creating books, magazines, brochures, packaging, and other graphic products, allowing the mass reproduction of high-quality images and texts to disseminate information and visual communication. Additionally, it provides employment opportunities in graphic design, printing, and production of related equipment. As reported by Mordor Intelligence [1], the EUV lithography market size is estimated at $10.34 billion in 2024 and is expected to reach $17.81 billion in 2029, growing at an annual compound of 11.5% during the period 2024–2029. On the other hand, the lithographic industry has revealed increasing confidence in almost all markets worldwide after the restrictions generated by the COVID-19 pandemic despite the current economic uncertainties [2]. The growth prospects for the sector are promising, given the rise of Internet of Things (IoT) and artificial intelligence (AI) technologies that have increased demand for photolithography, as well as the production of smaller, more powerful, and more efficient semiconductor devices. Efficient technologies for IoT and AI drive the need for advanced lithography [1].

However, the lithography industry faces challenges requiring attention and innovative solutions. One of the main challenges is the constant evolution of printing technology, which requires the acquisition and updating of specialized equipment, supplies, and software and the training of workers. Another challenge is optimizing production and administrative processes to achieve greater efficiency and reduce delivery times. Likewise, using sustainable and environmentally friendly printing techniques is an increasingly relevant technological challenge for the lithographic industry. Likewise, future projections in the demand of the lithographic industry require companies to search for new markets, especially at an international level, for which they must continually improve their processes and guarantee an efficient and secure supply chain. A typical key factor that causes the challenges raised above is the selection of suppliers. Adequate selection and management of suppliers benefit companies in their overall performance [3].

Regarding the selection and evaluation of suppliers, different authors [4–7] have determined that this is a multifactorial or multicriteria decision-making problem, given that quantitative and qualitative criteria are involved in quality, costs, innovation, and sustainability, among others. Others are considered by the purchasing departments in the selection and evaluation of suppliers. Due to the above, the supplier selection and evaluation process has challenges to resolve. The first challenge is incorporating multiple criteria appropriate to the context and particularities of the purchasing process [8]. The second challenge is the empirical nature of the selection and evolution processes, whether due to a lack of knowledge in the use of robust quantitative techniques, the absence of the implementation of management systems, not involving the interested arts in the selection processes, and the lack of training of the personnel who make the decisions in the selection and evaluation of suppliers [9] and the third challenge lies in the objectivity in the judgments on the part of the decision-makers when selecting or evaluating the suppliers, either due to bias or ambiguity in the evaluation process [10]. These challenges pose the development and application of objective, robust, and reliable methodologies and techniques that ensure not only an effective process in terms of the objective of having high-quality suppliers but also an efficient one by optimizing process resources (time, materials, etc.) and effective with an impact on the continuous improvement of both suppliers and the processes and products offered.

As mentioned by Karbassi, Fernandes, Hanne, Abdi, F, and Homayoun [10], multi-criteria decision analysis (MCDA) is an area of study of increasing development and application, which involves a set of methodologies and techniques to reduce uncertainty and risk in the identification and weighting of criteria used in the selection of suppliers as well as in their objective and appropriate classification. The application of MCDM models for supplier selection has incorporated technical, economic, social, and environmental criteria [11–13], and its use has extended to the food industry [7], Oil and Gas [14], and construction [15].], health [16], among others. The main MCDM techniques applied include AHP, ANP, DEMATEL, TOPSIS, and ELECTRE, as well as their diffuse, intuitionistic, and neutrosophic variants. Despite the extensive development of techniques for multi-criteria decision-making, in the context of the lithographic industry, their application is still limited, especially considering supplier selection criteria that minimize problems in the supply chain. Supply and promote the prevention of anti-money laundering and counterterrorism financing risk (AML/CFT) to access international markets.

This paper proposes a novel hybrid supplier selection approach to facilitate secure trade in the lithography industry. Multicriteria methodologies have demonstrated their ability to support companies' decision-making processes, reconciling subjectivity, inconsistencies, and uncertainty [17–19]. From the managerial implications, the results obtained can support companies to establish robust processes and good practices in the selection of safe suppliers, as well as to implement strategies that allow them to face the technological, commercial, and environmental challenges that raise safe trade by increasing the quality, efficiency and safety of suppliers.

The rest of the paper is structured as follows. Section 2 presents the literature review of MCDM in supplier selection. Section 3 defines the methodology design. Section 4 shows the results and discussion of the methodological approach applied in a real lithography company. Finally, conclusions and further research opportunities are exposed in Sect. 5.

2 Literature Review

Multi-criteria models for evaluating important aspects that lead to correct decision-making are of great relevance in any company in the productive sector. Product quality and customer satisfaction are vital in the current competitive business landscape. This is particularly relevant in the lithography industry, which operates in the dynamic printing, paper bag manufacturing, and high-security product supply sectors. The following state of the art explores the various cases and exposes the critical concepts for contextualizing the study carried out in this project.

It begins with the analysis of supply and supply chains. Within supply chain management, as mentioned [3], a necessary process is the supply of raw materials and inputs, which is required to carry out any company's missional and operational process. As seen today, as mentioned by [20, 21], the supply chain has become an aspect that contributes to productivity and competitiveness in different mining industries, such as copper, gold, coal, and nickel, among others.

On the other hand, it is necessary to consider a theoretical approach to logistics and purchasing processes to determine their impact on the organization's value chain, which can raise awareness of the importance of the processes in companies. Purchasing is a fundamental part of customer satisfaction, as mentioned by [22]. As explained by [23], efficient procurement management can generate savings, guarantee the quality of products and services, and maintain solid relationships with suppliers.

A study, like the one being developed, in which a multicriteria model is used for supplier selection in an automotive company, was carried out by [24], highlighting the relevance of this process. In the study by [25], the evaluation of suppliers is underlined as a determining factor of competitive business management. On the other hand, [26] addresses the selection of suppliers in the construction industry from a sustainability perspective, particularly in emerging economies. [27] detail the strategies necessary for selecting and evaluating whether a supplier is suitable, considering that suppliers are essential when discussing competitiveness and quality. [28] their study explains that they were forced to apply a research instrument with 11 criteria for selecting suppliers to the 186 clients and 75 suppliers registered in the National Chamber of Aquaculture of Ecuador to improve the quality system of the shrimp relating to its price and other criteria that were evaluated to the supplier where they must comply with the standards and regulations established by international organizations.

In the Colombian context, large companies have a lot of potential to carry out similar studies [29] based on the literature, there can be thousands of analyses to determine the criteria and standards necessary for the optimal development of supplier evaluation. For his part, [30] comments that risk is a fundamental factor in knowing how far we are willing to go to determine which criteria are more important than others. Each organization draws its differentiated factor when selecting a supplier, where we decide which is the best alternative; this is developed through a multicriteria methodology, where aspects that become decisive and that can change the direction of the selection are considered. Likewise, [31] states that suppliers' selection, evaluation, and classification are fundamental stages when creating and establishing a supply chain, so it is efficient and effective. As mentioned by [32], evaluating and selecting a supplier is a critical and complex decision due to several imprecise and subjective criteria.

It is worth highlighting that the multicriteria model, in conjunction with other methodologies such as fuzzy TOPSIS AHP, is highly applicable to any company in the productive sector that requires optimizing its processes, and to do so requires the selection, choice, and evaluation of elements, suppliers., etc., that allow them to increase their operational results [33] presents an innovative and effective supplier performance evaluation model based on the Hesitant Fuzzy TOPSIS method. The study was applied in an automotive company with eight suppliers and ten criteria, comparing it with similar previous models [34] mentions that decision-makers often face complicated decision problems with intangible and conflicting criteria. Numerous multicriteria decision-making (MCDM) methods have been proposed to handle measuring the priorities of contradictory tangible and intangible criteria and, in turn, use them to choose the best alternative for a decision. According to [35] and [36], the evaluation of suppliers is carried out to support decision-making in an agile and reliable manner, which requires the identification of critical variables and parameters that intervene in the process; said guide is established within the qualitative, quantitative analysis. [37] uses a fuzzy TOPSIS approach to evaluate teleworkers' technical conditions during a pandemic [38] uses fuzzy AHP method for assessing occupational health and safety conditions in land cargo transportation [39] explain a combined AHP-TOPSIS approach for evaluating the innovation and integration of management systems in the logistic sector.

Finally, the role of the lithographic industry is highlighted, which is highly demanded by other companies since they oversee the creation of their corporate and advertising image with high-quality and innovative ideas, considering that advertising plays a vital role. Therefore, attracting customers can boost recognition at a commercial level. For this reason, applying multicriteria models, as stated by [40] and [41] is an approach used to make complex decisions in situations where multiple criteria or factors that may impact decision-making must be considered. Instead of relying on a single criterion, several relevant criteria are considered to evaluate and compare different options.

3   Methodology

The methodology consists of a hybrid multi-criteria decision-making (MCDM) approach to select suppliers that facilitate secure international trade in the lithography industry, which, in addition to selecting suppliers, allows identifying significant weaknesses that affect their performance as secure suppliers and improve their performance through specific intervention plans that guide suppliers towards good practices in the prevention of anti-money laundering and counterterrorism financing risk (AML/CFT) to access international markets. The proposed approach combines the F-AHP, DEMATEL, and TOPSIS techniques under a 5-phase scheme (Fig. 1).

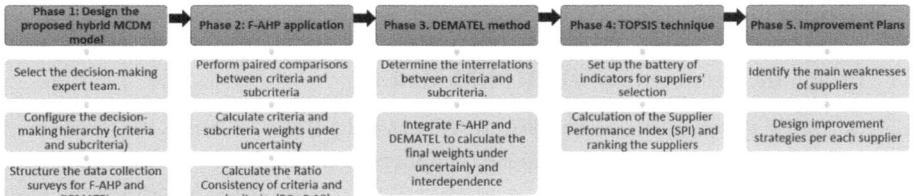

Fig. 1. The proposed hybrid MCDM framework for supplier selection of lithography industry

Phase 1. *Design the proposed hybrid MCDM model*: IIn this first phase, the team of decision-making experts was selected, considering their experience in purchasing and supply chain management and the lithography industry. The team of experts validated the criteria and sub-criteria to be considered in selecting suppliers based on secure international trade using the F-AHP and DEMATEL techniques. Then, the decision-making hierarchy was configured with the evaluation criteria and sub-criteria through the literature review and the experts' opinions. Next, the data collection instruments were structured for the application of the F-AHP and DEMATEL methods.

Phase 2. *F-AHP application*: In this stage, the F-AHP method was used to calculate the relative weights of the criteria and sub-criteria, considering the uncertainty in the expert team's paired comparisons, which are represented as triangular numbers [42–44]. As the main result of F-AHP, the most important criteria, and subcriteria were determined, which will be the basis for improvements in the supplier selection process that promote safe international trade.

Phase 3. *DEMATEL method*: In this phase, the DEMATEL method determines the relevant interdependencies between criteria and sub-criteria [45]. DEMATEL allows the identification of influence criteria (dispatchers) and effect criteria (receivers) [46]. In addition, this method evaluates the strength of the interrelationships to design improvement strategies sustained over time [47]. Then, the results of FAHP and DEMATEL [4, 47] are integrated to obtain the weights of the criteria and sub-criteria, considering uncertainty and interdependencies.

Phase 4. *TOPSIS technique*: In this phase, TOPSIS is applied to calculate the Supplier Performance Index (SPI) [48], considering a set of indicators that represent the different criteria of the evaluation model. Then, the suppliers were classified based on the SPI from highest to lowest to identify the suppliers with the best and lowest performance, which will require specific improvement plans.

Phase 5. *Improvement Plans*: In this late stage, based on the Supplier Performance Index (SPI) and the ranking of the lithographic suppliers, the GAPS [49] and critical sub-criteria that affect the performance of the evaluated suppliers were identified to respond to the requirements and good practices in secure international commerce. Finally, intervention plans were defined to improve suppliers' performance and facilitate the prevention of AML/CFT risks to access international markets.

4 Results

4.1 Design the Proposed Hybrid MCDM Model

As a result of the first phase, the F-AHP/DEMATEL/ TOPSIS multi-criteria hybrid decision model was designed to evaluate suppliers that support companies in secure international trade. First, I select the team of experts who participated in the identification and validation of the criteria and sub-criteria, as well as their importance and influence for the proposed model. The expert profiles are as follows:

- Three managers with more than 5 years in the lithography industry (Head of Production Department, Head of Supplies Department, Head of Quality Management).
- Two consultants (professional in industrial engineering with a master's degree in Logistics, professional in industrial engineering with a master's degree in administrative engineering) both with 10 years of experience as a consultant in Supply Chain Management, Standards ISO 9001, ISO 14001, and BASC in manufacturing companies.
- Two academicians (professionals in industrial engineering with a master's degree in industrial engineering) with more than 10 years of experience in application of MCDM methods, supply chain management and Integrated Management Systems in companies of manufacturing and services.

Subsequently, a hybrid MCDM model was designed composed of 6 criteria and 18 sub-criteria, were chosen based on the pertinent scientific literature, the international management standards (ISO 9001, ISO 14001, BASC), and the expert's opinion (See Fig. 2). A description of each criterion can be found in Table 1.

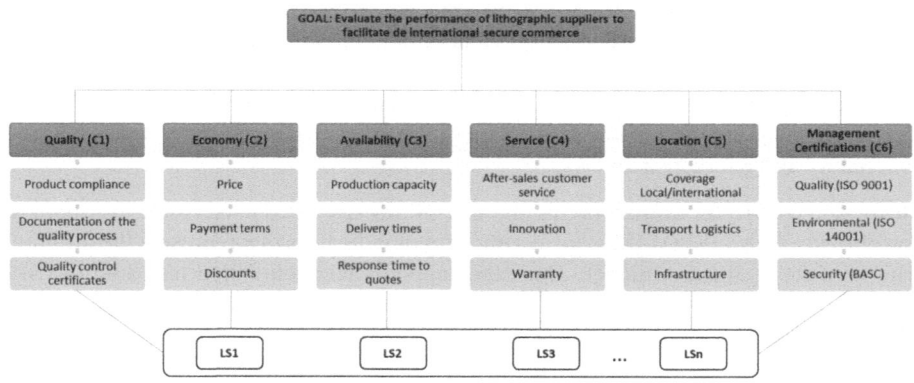

Fig. 2. MCDM model to evaluate the performance of lithographic suppliers.

Then, the surveys were designed to collect the experts' judgments regarding importance (F-AHP) and influence (DEMATEL) through paired comparisons between criteria and sub-criteria. Figure 3 shows an example of the F-AHP and DEMATEL surveys.

Table 1. Description of criteria

Criterion	Subcriteria	Criterion description
Quality (C1)	Product compliance (SC1) Documentation of the quality process (SC2) Quality control certificates (SC3)	This criterion evaluates the conformity to the product, according to quality. Quality represents a determining factor for competitiveness and organizational survival, which is why the management of organizations manages and implements procedures to offer it [50]
Economy (C2)	Price (SC4) Payment terms(SC5) Discounts (SC6)	This factor examines the economic advantages of suppliers in the product purchasing process. The economic criteria directly impact profitability, competitiveness, cost savings, and the selection and negotiation process with suppliers [51]
Availability (C3)	Production capacity (SC7) Delivery times (SC8) Response time to quotes (SC9)	This criterion analyzes the supplier's availability in terms of its production capacity, delivery times, and timeliness in responding to quotes. Lack of availability can negatively affect supply chain management and company performance [52]
Service (C4)	After-sales customer service (SC10) Innovation (SC11) Warranty (SC12)	This dimension considers the supplier's ability to offer a high level of service, including aspects such as warranties, innovation, and post-sales customer service. Service quality is considered an alternative for companies to obtain a competitive and sustainable advantage in a globalized economic environment [53]

(*continued*)

Table 1. (*continued*)

Criterion	Subcriteria	Criterion description
Location (C5)	Coverage Local/international (S13) Transport logistics (SC14) Infrastructure (SC15)	This aspect evaluates the supplier's reach in terms of distance, logistical transportation, and infrastructure. Location can also affect the availability and cost of products and services [54]
Management certifications (C6)	Quality (ISO 9001) (SC16) Environmental (ISO 14001) (SC17) Security BASC (SC18)	This domain verifies the implementation of management standards evidenced in certifications such as ISO 9001, ISO 14001, and BASC. Supplier certification is a path toward improving the supply chain management of the organization that contracts its services [55]

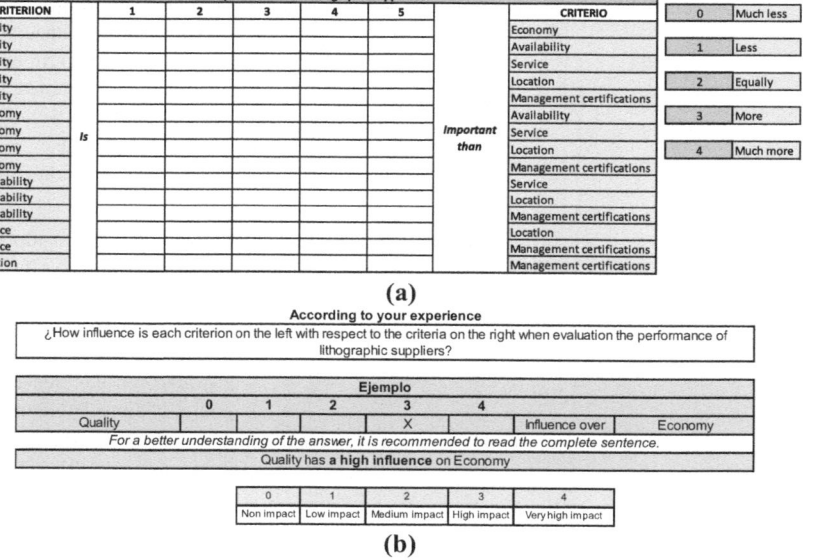

Fig. 3. Data collection tools for a) F-AHP and b) DEMATEL evaluation.

4.2 F-AHP Application

After collecting the paired comparisons by the team of experts, the results of the second phase are presented, with the importance of the criteria and subcriteria obtained from the F-AHP method. According to Table 2 and Fig. 4a, "Economy" (GW = 21.6%) and "Quality" (GW = 21.3%) are the most important criteria when evaluating suppliers that facilitate secure trade in the lithographic industry. No less important are the requirements "Availability" (GW = 18.8%), Management certifications (GW = 13.5%), "Customer Service" (GW = 12.7%), and "Location" (GW = 12.1%). The above shows that, in addition to price and quality, other relevant factors determine the selection of suppliers

Table 2. Global and local weights of criteria and subcriteria by using F-AHP technique*

Criterion / Subcriterion	GW	LW	CR
QUALITY (C1)	**0.213**		**0.013**
Product compliance (SC1)	0.07	0.33	
Documentation of the quality process (SC2)	0.10	0.45	
Quality control certificates (SC3)	0.05	0.22	
ECONOMY (C2)	**0.216**		**0.016**
Price (SC4)	0.12	0.55	
Payment terms(SC5)	0.04	0.20	
Discounts (SC6)	0.05	0.25	
AVAILABILITY (C3)	**0.188**		**0.018**
Production capacity (SC7)	0.07	0.38	
Delivery times (SC8)	0.09	0.47	
Response time to quotes (SC9)	0.03	0.15	
SERVICE (C4)	**0.127**		**0.003**
After-sales customer service (SC10)	0.04	0.30	
Innovation (SC11)	0.04	0.34	
Warranty (SC12)	0.05	0.36	
LOCATION (C5)	**0.121**		**0.026**
Coverage Local/international (S13)	0.02	0.14	
Transport logistics (SC14)	0.07	0.58	
Infrastructure (SC15)	0.03	0.27	
MANAGEMENT CERTIFICATION (C6)	**0.135**		**0.003**
Quality (ISO 9001) (SC16)	0.05	0.36	
Environmental (ISO 14001) (SC17)	0.04	0.28	
Security BASC (SC18)	0.05	0.36	

* CR for Criteria = 0.03

that facilitate the adoption of good practices for safe international trade, including mul-tifactor intervention plans for developing suppliers as allies—Strategic in the search for new markets.

On the other hand, as seen in Fig. 4b, the top five of the most relevant sub-criteria were identified. In this sense, "Price" (GW = 11.91%), "Documentation of the quality process" (GW = 9.55%), "Delivery times" (GW = 8.89%), "Transport logistics" (GW = 7.09%), and "Production capacity" (GW = 7.08%), demonstrating that the selection of a safe supplier depends on a variety of factors ranging from economic profile, level of quality, availability and location, which guarantee a chain of supply with quality standards, flexibility, opportunity in balance with the costs of companies in the lithography sector.

Finally, consistency ratios were calculated to evaluate the reliability of the experts' judgments (see Table 2). In this regard, all CR values are less than 0.1, which demon-strates consistency in the paired comparisons made by the experts. The above is due to the design of the data collection instrument, with a short and easy-to-apply evaluation scale and a training process, which reduces inconsistencies and encourages the participation of experts in the validation process of the criteria and sub-criteria in the decision-making process.

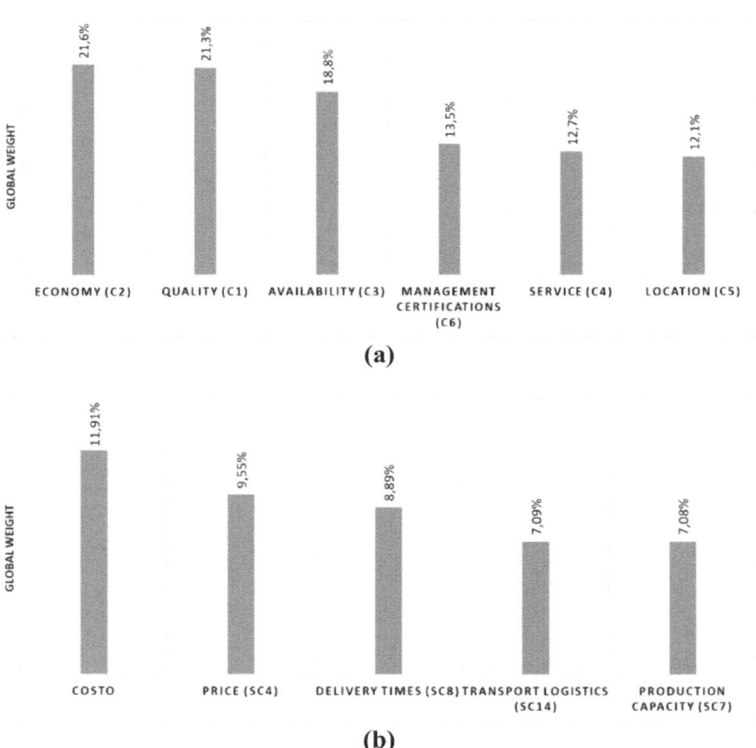

Fig. 4. Ranking for a) criteria and b) subcriteria F-AHP.

4.3   DEMATEL Method and Integration of F-AHP/DEMATEL Methods

In this phase, the DEMATEL method was applied to determine the interrelationships between the criteria and sub-criteria and identify the sending and receiving factors (see Table 3) by calculating the value of prominence (D + R) and relationship (D-R). The results obtained show that "Management Certifications" (C6), "Quality" (C1), and "Location" (C5) are the influencing criteria, which is why they are essential elements in the development of intervention plans for performance improvement for suppliers and, in general, of the supply chain process towards compliance with standards in safe international trade. Furthermore, "Economy" (C2) has the highest D + R value (6.76), which reveals that this criterion has a greater degree of relationship with the other criteria (Quality, Availability, Service), which is why it is an element that is affected by the other supplier evaluation criteria. Regarding the subcriteria, the main Dispatchers were "Documentation of the quality process" (SC2), "Quality control certificates" (SC3), "Payment terms" (SC5), "Discounts" (SC6), "Production capacity" (SC7), "Response time to quotes" (SC9), "Innovation" (SC11), "Coverage Local/international" (S13), and "Quality (ISO 9001)" (SC16).

On the other hand, the interdependencies between the criteria and sub-criteria were represented using an impact map, as shown in Figs. 5a-5b. The green arrows show unidirectional interdependencies, while the orange arrows show bidirectional interrelationships. As an example, in Fig. 5a, it is observed that "Management Certifications" (C6) undoubtedly influence most of the criteria (Quality, Economy, Quality, Availability, and Service), as does the "Quality" Criterion. Exerts a significant influence on the "Economy," "Availability," and "Service" criteria. In addition, bidirectional relationships were detected between "Quality" - "Management Certifications." These findings show the need to improve quality standards at the level of products, services, and processes, as well as the adoption and certification of international standards such as ISO 9001, ISO 14001, and BASC to improve the performance of suppliers with an impact on the chain—supply of the lithographic industry. Implementing various management systems allows companies to obtain benefits such as increased income, reduced costs, optimal management of resources, and improved customer and stakeholder satisfaction [56, 57]. Likewise, in Fig. 5b, it is evident that "Quality control certificates" (SC3) exert a significant influence on the sub-criteria "Product compliance" (SC1) and "Documentation of the Quality process" (SC2). In this sense, it is recommended that support strategies be implemented for suppliers to certify their processes based on quality, environment, and safe trade standards. Meaningful bidirectional relationships are also evident between the criteria "Quality" – "Economy", "Quality – "Availability", and "Availability" – "Economy", which reveals the influence of these criteria on the selection of suppliers.

Finally, the weights resulting from F-AHP and the normalized matrix of the evaluations of the DEMATEL experts are integrated to obtain the global and local weights of the criteria and sub-criteria under conditions of uncertainty and considering the influence of the factors and subfactors in the decision-making process. Table 4 shows the final global and local weights. The results show that the criteria "Quality" (GW = 19.6%), "Economy" (GW = 19.2%) and "Management certifications" (GW = 18.9%) are the

Table 3. Dispatchers and receivers for criteria and subcriteria

	D + R	D - R	DISPATCHER	RECEIVER
C1	6.43	0.26	X	
SC1	12.46	−1.39		X
SC2	12.35	0.32	X	
SC3	12.75	1.07	X	
C2	6.76	−0.53		X
SC4	5.79	−0.91		X
SC5	5.14	0.67	X	
SC6	5.19	0.24	X	
C3	5.79	−0.20		X
SC7	6.09	0.36	X	
SC8	6.31	−0.98		X
SC9	5.35	0.62	X	
C4	4.68	−0.72		X
SC10	5.89	−0.55		X
SC11	5.15	1.27	X	
SC12	6.37	−0.72		X
C5	4.66	0.16	X	
SC13	12.73	0.51	X	
SC14	12.53	−0.23		X
SC15	9.39	−0.27		X
C6	5.39	1.03	X	
SC16	6.47	0.26	X	
SC17	2.94	−0.18		X
SC18	5.76	−0.09		X

most important in the selection of suppliers that facilitate the adoption of good practices and allow safe international trade, so the strategies to be implemented to improve supplier performance must consider these criteria.

4.4 TOPSIS Technique

In this last stage, the TOPSIS technique was used to classify the suppliers of a lithographic company, considering the performance criteria for safe international trade in 5 suppliers of lithography inks to classify the suppliers according to the level of performance and identify opportunities for improvement for each company or the supplier selection process. To this end, a set of selection indicators was designed, considering

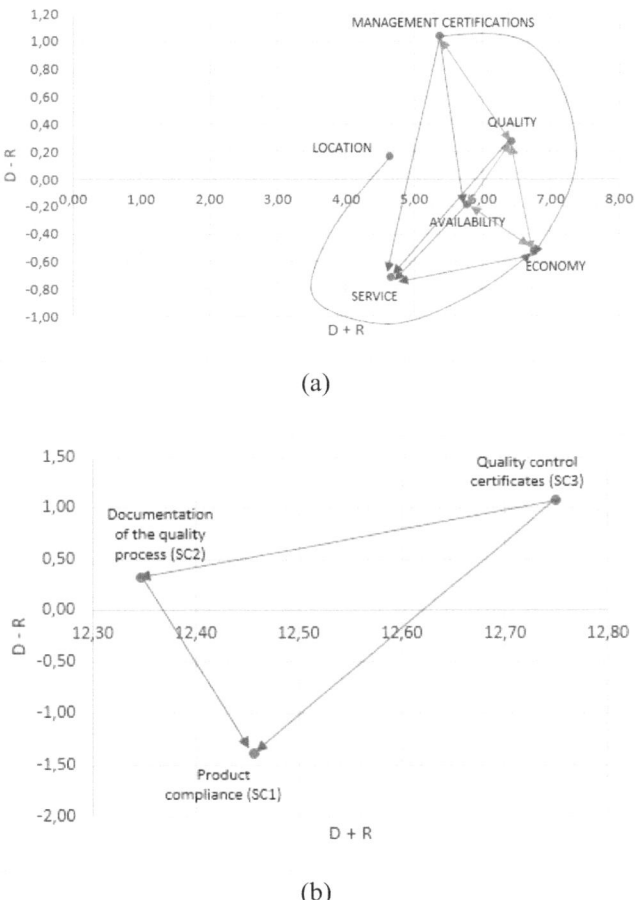

(a)

(b)

Fig. 5. Impact digraph maps for a) criteria and b) Quality subcriteria.

the subcriteria of the proposed evaluation model. Subsequently, the formulation of the TOPSIS technique [58] was applied, with which the TOPSIS decision matrix, the normalized matrix R, the weighted and normalized decision matrix, and the values of the separations of the ideal positive solution (PIS) were obtained. And negative ideal (NIS) and finally the calculation of the Closeness Coefficient, which for this study was called the Supplier Performance Index (SPI). Using this indicator, the company established the classification of its suppliers taking into account the following scale (Low performance – Rejected suppliers: 0% < SPI ≤ 48% || Medium performance – Approved suppliers with monitoring: 49% < SPI ≤ 74% || High performance – Approved suppliers: 75% < SPI ≤ 100%).

Table 5 shows the initial matrix with the values of the selection indicators for each evaluated supplier and decision subcriterion. Figure 6 shows the ranking of suppliers according to the Supplier Performance Index (SPI). According to the results obtained,

Table 4. F-AHP -DEMATEL Local and global weights of criteria and subcriteria

Criterion/Subcriterion	GW	LW
QUALITY (C1)	**0.196**	
Product compliance (SC1)	0.297	0.058
Documentation of the quality process (SC2)	0.271	0.053
Quality control certificates (SC3)	0.432	0.085
ECONOMY (C2)	**0.192**	
Price (SC4)	0.238	0.046
Payment terms(SC5)	0.407	0.078
Discounts (SC6)	0.356	0.068
AVAILABILITY (C3)	**0.164**	
Production capacity (SC7)	0.344	0.056
Delivery times (SC8)	0.276	0.045
Response time to quotes (SC9)	0.381	0.062
SERVICE (C4)	**0.119**	
After-sales customer service (SC10)	0.330	0.039
Innovation (SC11)	0.306	0.036
Warranty (SC12)	0.364	0.043
LOCATION (C5)	**0.140**	
Coverage Local/international (S13)	0.547	0.077
Transport logistics (SC14)	0.227	0.032
Infrastructure (SC15)	0.227	0.032
MANAGEMENT CERTIFICATION (C6)	**0.189**	
Quality (ISO 9001) (SC16)	0.570	0.108
Environmental (ISO 14001) (SC17)	0.136	0.026
Security BASC (SC18)	0.294	0.056

the supplier with the worst performance is LS1 (SPI = 35%), which shows that this supplier is unsuitable for the company and requires immediate interventions to improve its processes to continue as a supplier to the company. Company. On the other hand, it is observed that suppliers LS2 and LS3 (SPI = 68% and SPI = 66%) are the best performers considering the proposed evaluation criteria. However, these suppliers, like LS4 and LS5, were classified as approved suppliers with monitoring, so they require action plans to improve their performance and be ranked as high-performing suppliers.

The proposed methodology also enabled the identification of the critical factors that affect compliance as safe suppliers and the establishment of improvement plans for suppliers and the company's supplier management process. Table 6 shows the critical factors for each supplier.

Table 5. TOPSIS decision matrix D for evaluate the performance of lithographic suppliers

	LS1	LS2	LS3	LS4	LS5	PIS (A +)	NIS (A-)	W
SC1	2	3	3	2	2	**3**	**1**	0.058
SC2	2	2	2	2	2	**2**	**1**	0.053
SC3	1	2	2	2	1	**2**	**1**	0.085
SC4	1	1	2	2	1	**2**	**1**	0.046
SC5	2	2	2	2	2	**2**	**1**	0.078
SC6	1	2	2	1	1	**2**	**1**	0.068
SC7	1	2	2	2	1	**2**	**1**	0.056
SC8	2	2	3	3	2	**3**	**1**	0.045
SC9	1	2	1	1	2	**2**	**1**	0.062
SC10	1	2	2	1	2	**2**	**1**	0.039
SC11	1	2	2	1	1	**2**	**1**	0.036
SC12	1	2	2	1	2	**2**	**1**	0.043
SC13	2	2	2	2	2	**2**	**1**	0.077
SC14	3	2	3	3	2	**3**	**1**	0.032
SC15	2	2	2	2	2	**2**	**1**	0.032
SC16	1	2	2	2	2	**2**	**1**	0.108
SC17	1	2	1	1	1	**2**	**1**	0.026
SC18	1	1	1	1	1	**2**	**1**	0.056

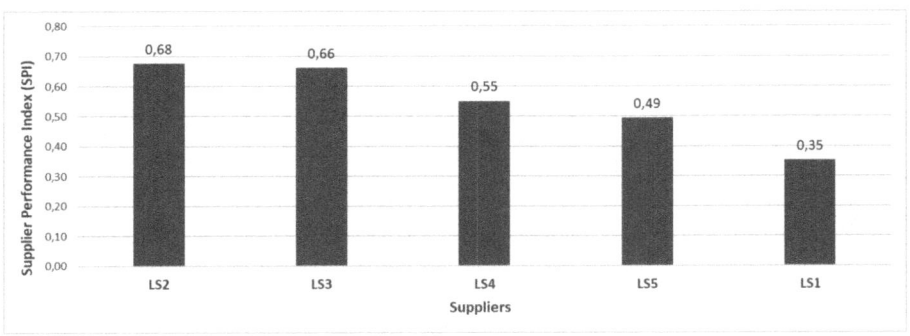

Fig. 6. Ranking of lithographic suppliers

4.5 Improvement Plans

In this last phase, different strategies were designed to improve the performance of suppliers in the lithography industry [59]. In this sense, the proposed strategies focused on subcriteria with values that were furthest from ideal performance. Firstly, it was

Table 6. Critical Factor for Suppliers via TOPSIS method

Supplier	Criteria	Critical subcriteria
LS2	Economy (C2) Availability (C3) Location (C5) Management certifications (C6)	• Price (SC4) • Delivery times (SC8) • Transport logistics (SC14) • Security BASC (SC18)
LS3	Availability (C3) Management certifications (C6)	• Response time to quotes (SC9) • Environmental (ISO 14001) (SC17) • Security BASC (SC18)
LS4	Quality (C1) Economy (C2) Availability (C3) Service (C4) Management certifications (C6)	• Product compliance (SC1) • Discounts (SC6) • Response time to quotes (SC9) • After-sales customer service (SC10) • Innovation (SC11) • Warranty (SC12) • Environmental (ISO 14001) (SC17) • Security BASC (SC18)
LS5	Quality (C1) Economy (C2) Availability (C3) Service (C4) Location (C5) Management certifications (C6)	• Product compliance (SC1) • Quality control certificates (SC3) • Price (SC4) • Discounts (SC6) • Production capacity (SC7) • Delivery times (SC8) • Innovation (SC11) • Transport logistics (SC14) • Environmental (ISO 14001) (SC17) • Security BASC (SC18)
LS1	Quality (C1) Economy (C2) Availability (C3) Service (C4) Management certifications (C6)	• Product compliance (SC1) • Quality control certificates (SC3) • Price (SC4) • Discounts (SC6) • Production capacity (SC7) • Delivery times (SC8) • Response time to quotes (SC9) • After-sales customer service (SC10) • Innovation (SC11) • Warranty (SC12) • Quality (ISO 9001) (SC16) • Environmental (ISO 14001) (SC17) • Security BASC (SC18)

identified in all suppliers that do not have quality certifications, especially ISO 14001 environmental management and BASC secure trade, which affects product quality, cost optimization, availability and customer service.. This finding agrees with different studies [60, 61], which stated that companies must implement management systems based on processes that allow them to meet their corporate objectives and work hand in hand with different interest groups by implementing good quality practices. Safe environment and trade. In this sense, the following strategies are recommended:

- Establish clear procedures with the quality, environment, and international secure commerce criteria suppliers must meet to be selected.
- Alliances with suppliers to formulate company certification projects before public and private entities.
- Training suppliers on good practices in quality management, environment, and safe trade.

Another deficiency evidenced by TOPSIS in LS1, LS2, LS4, and LS5 is the high costs of inputs for the industry, especially paper, cardboard, and inks, by more than 100%, due to the effects generated by the COVID-19 pandemic., the increase in the international exchange rate, and the lack of cost systems that affect the ability of companies to compete, allowing them to optimize costs, offer discounts, and increase the profitability of companies [62]. As proposed strategies to address these deficiencies, the following are suggested:

- Implement production cost systems.
- Commercial agreements with clients, with discounts according to the supplier's financial conditions.
- Develop continuous improvement projects (LSS, DES, among others).

Deficiencies in availability are evident in LS1, LS2, LS3, and LS5, with lower compliance in the quantities of products requested, high delivery times, and response to quotes. Due to the growing demand for lithography supplies [63], suppliers must improve their processes to respond in terms of capacity and timeliness to the needs of their clients. In this sense, the following initiatives are proposed:

- Implement projects to improve production processes and sales channels using Lean and Six Sigma tools.
- Expand the database of national and international suppliers to improve the capacity and response time of the supply chain.
- Developing combined supply chains through collaborating with suppliers to develop forecasting models, capacity planning and management, and service level agreements.

Finally, another weakness identified is the failure to introduce new technologies or innovative approaches in its products, services, or processes (LS1, LS5, and LS4), which affects its ability to compete in a market whose trend is oriented towards technological advances., the development of new products and eco-friendly products. To overcome these deficiencies, the following alternatives are proposed:

- Alliances with universities, research, and technological development centers to strengthen R&D capabilities.
- Adoption of industry 4.0/5.0 technologies for process improvement (artificial Intelligence, IoT, RFID, Blockchain, among others).
- Alliances between industry and suppliers to develop innovative products that generate joint beneficial income.

The above shows that the proposed model can support the supplier selection process robustly and practically and continuously improve supplier performance in the short and long term.

5   Conclusions and Future Work

The supply chains of the lithography industry present constant challenges due to the increase in demand for lithography products, customer needs for quality products, shorter response times and customer service, and the optimization of operational costs to face variations in input prices. In addition, the concerns of different stakeholders related to the safety of products sent for international trade, the use of inputs and development of eco-friendly products, and technological advances. When the supply chain cannot respond effectively and efficiently to multiple demands, negative consequences are generated that affect both the organization and customers, such as decreased sales, lost opportunities for new local and international customers, a decrease in customer satisfaction, the increase in production and operational costs, as well as loss of reputation and corporate value. In this sense, it is important to structure this process from one of its essential aspects, the selection of suppliers with a multifactorial perspective, considering different factors that drive the adoption of good practices for safe commerce to improve the supply chain response. Despite various initiatives detected in the literature and at a practical level to improve the supply chain and the supplier selection process, the level of development is limited in the lithographic industry. On the other hand, robust approaches are required to improve decision-making in uncertain environments and consider economic factors, quality, availability, service, Location, and management certifications that support safe commerce and efficient and effective responses to scenarios of complexity.

This study proposes a hybrid approach for managing secure suppliers in the lithographic industry by integrating the F-AHP, DEMATEL, and TOPSIS methods. The proposed approach was validated through a real case in a lithographic company for selecting input suppliers with the participation of four ink-supplying companies. Among the highlighted results, F-AHP identified that the most relevant factors in the selection and management of suppliers for secure commerce are "Economy" (GW = 21.6%), "Quality" (GW = 21.3%), and "Availability" (GW = 18.8%). DEMATEL evidenced that "Management Certifications" (D-R = 1.03), "Quality" (D-R = 0.26), and "Location" (D-R = 0.16) are the most influential criteria in the selection and development of improvement plans in supplier management for secure international trade. Likewise, "Economy" was identified with the highest D + R value (6.76), denoting the high relationship between the quality, availability, and service criteria, which impact the economic factor. On the other hand, the integration of F-AHP − DEMATEL revealed the final global weights, considering uncertainty and interdependence. The results showed that "Quality" (GW = 19.6"), "Economy" (GW = 19.2"), and "Management certifications" (GW = 18.9") are the most weighted criteria for the evaluation model. TOPSIS identified that LS2 and LS3 (SPI = 68% and SPI = 66%) are the suppliers with the best performance for secure international trade. Finally, improvement strategies were established for both the managers of the supplier companies and the lithographic company to improve safe trade practices and resolve weaknesses in the certification of management standards, product conformity, cost optimization, and security practices. R&D, response, and delivery times. On the other hand, collaborative networks, alliances, and investments in infrastructure and technology are essential for improving the supply chain response in the lithographic industry. The study's limitations are 1) the number of suppliers evaluated in the project is limited, although sufficient to support the robustness and practical applicability of the proposed approach; 2) The approach does not consider variations in model indicators and interval data according to expert panel validation.

The research's practical implications and contribution to this study involve identifying critical factors when selecting safe suppliers for international commerce. In addition, a holistic approach to selecting suppliers was proposed, which is helpful for managers, professionals, and researchers involved with logistics and the supply chain based on a real case study. In future work, the proposed model is proposed to be strengthened through hybrid fuzzy and intuitionistic approaches and compared with other traditional MCDM methods. Furthermore, it will investigate the importance and interdependence between the criteria and sub-criteria in the worldwide lithographic industry. Future research may incorporate supply chain risk analysis to respond to critical events and Authorized Economic Operator (AEO) standards.

References

1. Mordor Intelligence, Análisis de participación y tamaño del mercado de litografía ultravioleta extrema tendencias y pronósticos de crecimiento 2024–2029 (2024). https://www.mordorint elligence.com/es/industry-reports/extreme-ultraviolet-lithography-market. Accessed 23 Mar 2024
2. Drupa, The 9th Global Trends Report (2024). https://www.drupa.com/en/Media_News/News/Global_Trends_Reports/Global_Trends_Overview#gtr. Accessed 23 Mar 2024
3. Ocampo-Murillo, H., Quintero-Garzon, M.: Selección de proveedores de insumos críticos en términos de sostenibilidad, a través de la metodología multicriterio, en una empresa del sector azucarero. Entramado **16**(2) (2020). https://doi.org/10.18041/1900-3803/entramado.2.6436
4. Ortiz-Barrios, M., Kucukaltan, B., Carvajal-Tinoco, D., Neira-Rodado, D., Jiménez, G.: Strategic hybrid approach for selecting suppliers of high-density polyethylene. J. Multi-criteria Decis. Analy. (2017). https://doi.org/10.1002/mcda.1617
5. Ho, W., Xiaowei, X., Dey, P.K.: Multi-criteria decision-making approaches for supplier evaluation and selection: a literature review. Eur. J. Oper. Res. **202**(1), 16–24 (2010)
6. Yildizbasi, A., Arioz, Y.: Green supplier selection in new era for sustainability: a novel method for integrating big data analytics and a hybrid fuzzy multi-criteria decision making. Soft. Comput. **26**, 253–270 (2022)
7. Ortiz-Barrios, M., Miranda-De la Hoz, C., López-Meza, P., Petrillo, A., Felice, F.: A case of food supply chain management with AHP, DEMATEL, and TOPSIS. J. Multi-Criteria Decis. Analy. (2019). https://doi.org/10.1002/mcda.1693
8. Yazdani, M., Chatterjee, P., Kazimieras-Zavadskas, E., Hashemkhani-Zolfani, S.: Integrated QFD-MCDM framework for green supplier selection. J. Cleaner Product. **142**(4), 3728–3740 (2017). https://doi.org/10.1016/j.jclepro.2016.10.095
9. Karbassi-Yazdi, A., Fernandes-Wanke, P., Hanne, T., Abdi, F., Homayoun-Sarfaraz, A.: Supplier selection in the oil & gas industry: a comprehensive approach for multi-criteria decision analysis. Socio-Econ. Planning Sci. **79** (2022). https://doi.org/10.1016/j.seps.2021.101142
10. Ortiz-Barrios, M., Cabarcas-Reyes, J., Ishizaka, A., et al.: A hybrid fuzzy multi-criteria decision making model for selecting a sustainable supplier of forklift filters: a case study from the mining industry. Ann. Oper. Res. **307**, 443–481 (2021). https://doi.org/10.1007/s10479-020-03737-y

11. Awasthi, A., Govindan, K., Gold, S.: Multi-tier sustainable global supplier selection using a fuzzy AHP-VIKOR based approach. Int. J. Prod. Econ. **195**, 106–117 (2018). https://doi.org/10.1016/j.ijpe.2017.10.013
12. Chong, W., Barnes, D.: An integrated model for green partner selection and supply chain construction,. J. Cleaner Product. **112**(3), 2114–2132 (2016). https://doi.org/10.1016/j.jclepro.2015.02.023
13. Büyüközkan, G., Güleryüz, S., Karpak, B.: A new combined IF-DEMATEL and IF-ANP approach for CRM partner evaluation. Int. J. Prod. Econ. **191**, 194–206 (2017). https://doi.org/10.1016/j.ijpe.2017.05.012
14. Wang, C.-N., Tsai, H.-T., Ho, T.-P., Nguyen, V.-T., Huang, Y.-F.: Multi-Criteria decision making (MCDM) model for supplier evaluation and selection for oil production projects in Vietnam. Processes **8**(2), 134 (2020). https://doi.org/10.3390/pr8020134
15. Cengiz, A.E., et al.: A multi-criteria decision model for construction material supplier selection. Procedia Eng. **196**, 294–301 (2017)
16. Barrios, M.A.O., De Felice, F., Negrete, K.P., Romero, B.A., Arenas, A.Y., Petrillo, A.: An AHP-Topsis integrated model for selecting the most appropriate tomography equipment. Int. J. Inf. Technol. Decis. Mak. **15**, 861–885 (2016). https://doi.org/10.1142/S021962201640006X
17. Lu, H., et al.: A rough multi-criteria decision-making approach for sustainable supplier selection under vague environment. Sustainability **10**(8), 2622 (2018)
18. Alkahtani, M., et al.: Comparison and evaluation of multi-criteria supplier selection approaches: a case study. Adv. Mech. Eng. **11**(2), 1687814018822926 (2019)
19. Jayant, P., Gupta, S.K., Khan, G.M.: TOPSIS-AHP based approach for selection of reverse logistics service provider: a case study of mobile phone industry. Procedia Eng. **97**, 2147–2215 (2014). https://doi.org/10.1016/j.proeng.2014.12.458
20. Gahona-Flores, O.F., Juárez-Rubio, F.: Metodologías para seleccionar proveedores en la cadena de suministro de la minería del cobre en Chile. Información tecnológica **33**(3), 107–116 (2022). https://doi.org/10.4067/s0718-07642022000300107
21. Collier, D.A., Evans, J.R.: Administración de operaciones (2019)
22. Acero, L.C.P.: Administración de la producción, Ecoe Edici (2019)
23. Arenal Laza, C.: Gestión de compras en el pequeño comercio, 1st ed. Logroño (2022)
24. Manello, A., Calabrese, G.: The influence of reputation on supplier selection: an empirical study of the European automotive industry. J. Purch. Supply Manag. **25**(1), 69–77 (2019). https://doi.org/10.1016/j.pursup.2018.03.001
25. Ortiz Torres, M., Marquez Sanchez, F., Oramas Santos, O., Marrero Ancizar, Y.: Methodology for the evaluation of suppliers. case study: specialized company importer, exporter and distributor for science and technology. Rev. Espacios **39**(27), 24 (2018)
26. Niaz Tushar, Z., Mainul Bari, A.B.M., Ahmad Khan, M.: Circular supplier selection in the construction industry: a sustainability perspective for the emerging economies. Sustain. Manufact. Serv. Econ. **1** (2022). https://doi.org/10.1016/j.smse.2022.100005
27. Espejel-García, A., Ramírez-García A.G., León-Balderrama, J.I., Barrera-Rodríguez, A.I.: Estrategia de desarrollo de proveedores de una empacadora de aguacate (Persea americana Mill) cultivar Hass en Michoacán, México. Estudios Sociales **32**(59) (2022). https://doi.org/10.2307/40184061
28. Pacheco Molina, A.M., Pupo Francisco, J.M., Parra Ochoa, E.B.: Criterios para la selección de proveedores en el sector camaronero ecuatoriano. Rev. Espacios **40**(14), 7 (2019)
29. Cano, J.A., Ayala, C.J.: Oportunidades de investigación a partir del análisis de revisiones de literatura de selección de proveedores. In: Proceedings of the 33rd International Business Information Management Association Conference, IBIMA 2019: Education Excellence and Innovation Management through Vision, pp. 7018–7027 (2019)

30. Parra, C., Osorio, J., Escandón, J.: Multi-Criteria methodology for the selection of suppliers under risk considerations. Scientia et Technica Año XXIV **24**(02), 07, (2019). https://revistas. utp.edu.co/index.php/revistaciencia/article/view/19681
31. Restrepo, R., Villegas, J.G.: Supplier evaluation and classification in a Colombian motor-cycle assembly company using data envelopment analysis. Acad. Rev. Latinoamericana de Administración **32**(2), 159–180 (2019). https://doi.org/10.1108/ARLA-04-2017-0107
32. Granillo-Macías, R., González-Hernández, I.J.: Selection and evaluation of third party logis-tics in the supply chain: a systematic review. Cuadernos de Gestion **21**(2), 7–18 (2021). https://doi.org/10.5295/cdg.191141rg
33. Junior, F.R.L., Hsiao, M.: A hesitant fuzzy TOPSIS model to supplier performance evaluation. DYNA (Colombia) **88**(216), 126–135 (2021). https://doi.org/10.15446/dyna.v88n216.88320
34. Thomas, L.S., Daji, E.: Criteria for evaluating multi-criteria decision-making methods. EconsPapers **14**(3), 1250 (2015)
35. Ramírez Cano, Y., Graciano, S.: Ochoa, Guia para la selección y evaluación de proveedores en una empresa del sector retail ubicada en Medellin, Universidad de Antioquia Facultad de Ingeniería, Departamento de ingeniería industrial, Universidad De Antioquia (2021)
36. Peña Florez, L.A., Rodríguez-Rojas, Y.L.: Evaluation and selection of providers proce-dure based on the hierarchical analysis process and a mixed integer/linear programming. Procedimiento de Evaluación y Selección de Proveedores Basado on Lineal Entera Mixta **23**, 230–251 (2018). https://revistas.udistrital.edu.co/index.php/reving/article/view/13316/14221
37. Stephanidis, C., et al. (eds.): HCII 2021. LNCS, vol. 13097. Springer, Cham (2021). https://doi.org/10.1007/978-3-030-90966-6
38. Jimenez-Delgado, G., Balmaceda-Castro, N., Hernández-Palma, H., de la Hoz-Franco, E., García-Guiliany, J., Martinez-Ventura, J.: An integrated approach of multiple correspondences analysis (MCA) and fuzzy AHP method for occupational health and safety performance evaluation in the land cargo transportation. In: Duffy, V. (eds.) Digital Human Modeling and Applications in Health, Safety, Ergonomics and Risk Management. Human Body and Motion. HCII 2019. Lecture Notes in Computer Science(), vol. 11581, pp. 433–457. Springer, Cham. (2019). https://doi.org/10.1007/978-3-030-22216-1_32/COVER
39. Jiménez-Delgado, G., Santos, G., Félix, M.J., Teixeira, P., Sá, J.C.: A Combined AHP-TOPSIS approach for evaluating the process of innovation and integration of management systems in the logistic sector. In: Stephanidis, C., et al. HCI International 2020 – Late Breaking Papers: Interaction, Knowledge and Social Media. HCII 2020. Lecture Notes in Computer Science(), vol. 12427, pp. 535–559. Springer, Cham. (2020). https://doi.org/10.1007/978-3-030-60152-2_40
40. Martinez Martinez, M.M., Rozo Rodriguez, Y.: Estructura y elementos de control interno para micro y pequeñas empresas litográficas de Caucasia, Universidad de Antioquia (2021)
41. Zavadskas, E.K., Turskis, Z., Kildiene, S.: State of art surveys of over-views on MCDM/MADM methods. Technol. Econ. Dev. Econ. **20**(1), 165–179 (2014). https://doi.org/10.3846/20294913.2014.892037
42. Ayhan, M.B.: A fuzzy AHP approach for supplier selection problem: A case study in a gear motor company (2013). arXiv preprint arXiv:1311.2886
43. Kilincci, O., Onal, S.A.: Fuzzy AHP approach for supplier selection in a washing machine company. Expert Syst. Appl. **38**(8), 9656–9664 (2011)
44. Ortíz-Barrios, M., Neira-Rodado, D., Jiménez-Delgado, G., Hernández-Palma, H.: Using FAHP-VIKOR for operation selection in the flexible job-shop scheduling problem: a case study in textile industry. In: Tan, Y., Shi, Y., Tang, Q. (eds.) Advances in Swarm Intelligence. ICSI 2018. Lecture Notes in Computer Science(), vol. 10942. Springer, Cham (2018). https://doi.org/10.1007/978-3-319-93818-9_18

45. Jimenez-Delgado, G., et al.: Improving the performance in occupational health and safety management in the electric sector: an integrated methodology using fuzzy multicriteria approach. In: Duffy, V.G., (ed.) HCII 2020. LNCS, vol. 12199, pp. 130–158. Springer, Cham (2020). https://doi.org/10.1007/978-3-030-49907-5_10
46. Su, C.M., Horng, D.J., Tseng, M.L., Chiu, A.S., Wu, K.J., Chen, H.P.: Improving sustainable supply chain management using a novel hierarchical grey-DEMATEL approach. J. Cleaner Prod. **134**, 469–481 (2016)
47. Wei, P.L., Huang, J.H., Tzeng, G.H., Wu, S.I.: Causal modeling of web-advertising effects by improving SEM based on DEMATEL technique. Int. J. Inf. Technol. Decis. Making **9**(05), 799–829 (2010)
48. Shanian, A., Savadogo, O.: TOPSIS multiple-criteria decision support analysis for material selection of metallic bipolar plates for polymer electrolyte fuel cell. J. Power Sour. **159**(2), 1095–1104 (2006)
49. Jimenez-Delgado, G., Alcazar-Franco, D., García-Tamayo, D., Oliveros-Eusse, P., Gomez-Diaz, M.: Evaluating the performance in the environmental management and reverse logistics in companies of plastic sector: an integration of Fuzzy AHP, DEMATEL and TOPSIS methods. In: Stephanidis, C., et al., HCI International 2021 - Late Breaking Papers: HCI Applications in Health, Transport, and Industry. HCII 2021. Lecture Notes in Computer Science(), vol. 13097. Springer, Cham (2021). https://doi.org/10.1007/978-3-030-90966-6_36
50. Jimenez, G.: Procedimientos para el mejoramiento de la calidad y la implantación de la Norma ISO 9001 aplicado al proceso de Asesoramiento **22** (2016)
51. Verdecho, M.-J., Alarcón-Valero, F., Pérez-Perales, D., Alfaro-Saiz, J.-J., Rodríguez-Rodríguez, R.: A methodology to select suppliers to increase sustainability within supply chains. CEJOR **29**(4), 1231–1251 (2020). https://doi.org/10.1007/s10100-019-00668-3
52. Ramirez Cano, Y.V., Graciano Ochoa, S.: Guía para la Selección y Evaluación de Proveedores en una Empresa del Sector Retail, Repositorio Institucional Universidad de Antioquia **1**, 31 (2021)
53. Silva Treviño, J.G., Macías Hernández, B.A., Tello Leal, E., Delgado Rivas, J.G.: La relación entre la calidad en el servicio, satisfacción del cliente y lealtad del cliente: un estudio de caso de una empresa comercial en México, Scielo **15**, 50–56 (2021)
54. Yazdani, M., Pamucar, D., Chatterjee, P., Torkayesh, A.E.: A multitier sustainable food supplier selection model under uncertainty. Oper. Manag. Res. **15**(1–2), 116–145 (2022). https://doi.org/10.1007/s12063-021-00186-z
55. Jimenez, G., Novoa, L., Ramos, L., Martinez, J., Alvarino, C.: Diagnosis of initial conditions for the implementation of the integrated management system in the companies of the land cargo transportation in the City of Barranquilla (Colombia). In: Stephanidis, C., (eds.) HCI International 2018 – Posters' Extended Abstracts. HCI 2018. Communications in Computer and Information Science, vol. 852. Springer, Cham (2018). https://doi.org/10.1007/978-3-319-92285-0_39
56. Trierweiller, A., Bornia, A., Gisi, M., Spenassato, D., Severo-Peixe, B., Rotta, M.: An exploratory survey on the topic integrated management systems. Braz. J. Oper. Prod. Manage. **13**(2), 184–193 (2016)
57. Nunhes, T., Ferreira, L.C., Oliveira, O.J.: Evolution of integrated management systems research on the journal of cleaner production: identification of contributions and gaps in the literature. J. Clean. Prod. **139**(15), 1234–1244 (2016)
58. Ortíz-Barrios, M., Petrillo, A., De Felice, F., Jaramillo-Rueda, N., Jiménez-Delgado, G., Borrero-López, L.: A Dispatching-fuzzy AHP-TOPSIS model for scheduling flexible job-shop systems in industry 4.0 context. Appl. Sci. **11**, 5107 (2021). https://doi.org/10.3390/app11115107

59. Gutierrez, A., Kothari, A., Mazuera, C., Schoenherr, T.: Un nuevo nivel de colaboración con proveedores (2020). https://www.mckinsey.com/capabilities/operations/our-insights/taking-supplier-collaboration-to-the-next-level/es-CL. Accessed 23 Mar 2024
60. Jimenez, G., Zapata, E.: Metodología integrada para el control estratégico y la mejora continua, basada en el Balanced Scorecard y el Sistema de Gestión de Calidad: aplicación en una organización de servicios en Colombia. In: 51a Asamblea Anual del Consejo Latinoamericano de Escuelas de Administración CLADEA 2016, pp. 1–20, Medellin, Colombia (2016)
61. Uribe, K., Guerrero, A.: Diseño de estrategias de producción más limpia para el proceso de litografía en la imprenta de comando ejército. Universidad Libre Seccional Bogotá (2017). https://repository.unilibre.edu.co/bitstream/handle/10901/11260/Entrega%20OK%20DISE%C3%91O%20DE%20ESTRATEGIAS%20DE%20PRODUCCION%20%281%29.pdf?sequence=1&isAllowed=y. Accessed 23 Mar 2024
62. Ordoñez, S., Wbaldo, E.: Propuesta de un sistema de costos para la empresa tipografía y litografía arte clásico SAS de la ciudad de Cali. Universidad Antonio Nariño (2022). https://repositorio.uan.edu.co/server/api/core/bitstreams/8bd755ef-3d13-43d6-b4a1-87e8024dee06/content. Accessed 23 Mar 2024
63. Business Research. Tamaño del mercado de tintas de litografía, participación, crecimiento y análisis de la industria por tipo (a base de agua, a base de solventes, otros), por aplicación (impresión comercial, embalaje, publicación, otros) e información regional y pronóstico para 2031 (2024). https://www.businessresearchinsights.com/es/market-reports/lithography-inks-market-111640. Accessed 24 Mar 2024

Fast Food Affinity Among the Tertiary Students of Bangladesh: A Case Study

Tasnim Tabassum Lamya[1](✉) [iD] and Mohammad Shidujaman[2](✉) [iD]

[1] Department of Disaster Management and Resilience, Bangladesh University of Professionals (BUP), Dhaka 1216, Bangladesh
tasnimlamya217@gmail.com

[2] Department of Computer Science and Engineering, School of Engineering, Technology and Science, Independent University, Bangladesh (IUB), Dhaka 1229, Bangladesh
shidujaman@iub.edu.bd

Abstract. People's preference for fast food is growing due to its ease and accessibility. The threat exists over the health effects of fast food, especially among young people and adolescents. This paper aims to explore the reasons that are causing fast-food affinity to rise among university-level students - taking the case of Bangladesh University of Professionals. This mixed methods research was conducted using a case study methodology. Quantitative and qualitative data were collected from the interested participants of BUP using a questionnaire survey and in-depth interviews. A total of 47 participants participated in the questionnaire survey and 09 in the in-depth interviews. The findings of this research demonstrate how social influence and everyday routine can influence university students to make their own food choices. Results showed all the participants consume fast food at least once a week. This study also showed a positive correlation between the duration of stay at the campus, food price and fast-food intake among the participants.

Keywords: University students · fast food · consumption factors · affinity · health impacts

1 Introduction

People's affinity for fast food is increasing because of its convenience and availability. Fast food—a self-explanatory name, refers to the food items that can be processed and served with minimum preparation and effort [22] to the consumers as dine-in or takeaway [33]. Some of the commonly known and most available fast-food items are but are not limited to, snacks (e.g., burgers, pizza, fries, nachos, sandwiches, shingara, buns and bread), and hot beverages (e.g., tea, coffee, cola). These easy grab-n-eat foods, prepared from pre-packed or pre-processed, items have gained popularity over home-cooked food because of 1) no dine-in requirement, 2) quick service 3) easy accessibility and availability [11, 21], 4) time or structural constraints for home cooking, 5) reasonable pricing and good taste [36], and effective marketing [18].

Despite its popularity, fast-food items are of concern for its health impacts, particularly among young adults and adolescents [28]. University students admire international food chain brands [30], such as McDolad's [17] regardless of their geographic location, even though they might not be available in most developing countries [37]. On average 97.4% of university students consume fast-food regularly [23]. Several works of literature [4, 5, 13, 41] demonstrated a positive correlation between increased fast-food intake and obesity, or health issues, such as type II diabetes or high blood sugar and cholesterol, particularly among young adults. This is because most fast-food items contain less nutritional value than home-cooked food, and high carbohydrates, cholesterol, sugar or salt may cause substantial health hazards [33]. For instance, artificially sweetened drinks, such as juice or cola that contain high concentrations of sugar might provide instant energy but cannot satisfy a young adult's bodily requirement or craving for solid food [20], thereby, encouraging repetitive or more consumption of other unhealthy food choices available around them. Fast food, thus, not only causes future threats to health but hurts consumers' economy [22].

Additionally, long-term consumption of unhealthy fast foods [31] may cause digestive, immune, inflammatory, cardiovascular, obesity, and other health problems [35]. Not all fast food, however, is unhealthy. Some menu items may have a lower concentration of these elements than others, and some fast-food restaurants may offer healthier selections [8]. Students who are in threat of such risk, are the future of the nation [28].

The intake of takeout and fast food is growing in popularity among young adults in the emerging nation of Bangladesh [3, 23, 31, 37]. Obesity in younger generations is caused by fast food consumption [18]. 98.5% of total Bangladeshi university students show an affinity for fast food and more than 20% of them consume fast food daily [3]. In this paper, I have examined the factor that works behind to create affinity among people [30]. The outcomes of this study will help to understand the influencing factor of rising fast-food affinity and contribute to further research finding its solution.

The broader objective of this research is to understand why the fast-food affinity growing among the tertiary level students of Bangladesh – taking Bangladesh University of Professionals (BUP) as a case. I explore this broad research question by addressing the following sub-research questions:

1. What is the consumption pattern?
2. What factors influence the fast-food intake?

In answering the first question, I explored the type and frequency of fast-food intakes through a questionnaire survey. The second question was explored using qualitative data collected through in-depth one-to-one interviews. Altogether the findings of this study help understand the reasons for growing fast-food affinity among the tertiary level students of Bangladesh.

It is necessary to find the type of fast-food items consumed by tertiary students, along with the intake frequency to understand food habit patterns [3]. Understanding the factors influencing their fast-food affinity may help in taking measures to terminate or lessen unhealthy food habits among the young adults of the country. Thus, this study contributes to minimizing the potential health risks associated with poor eating habits by revealing the patterns, frequency and causes of affinity for unhealthy fast-food items among tertiary-level students.

2 Literature Review

2.1 History of Fast Food

With time, food intake has been evolving all around the world. Since humanity started living in towns and cities, commercial street foods have been eaten almost all around the world [33]. Any historical article reveals instances of street-sold, ready-to-eat food from the last two millennia [33]. In the Middle Ages, marketplaces of towns in North America, the Middle East and South Asia were marked for selling items such as fried meat kibbe, sausages, olives, nuts, and several additional snacks [33]. Famous traveller Marco Polo from the 13th century has mentioned barbequed meats, deep-fried delicacies, and roast lamb as the market selling foods of Chinese. In his period, he claimed that Asia's street-selling food variety is more enriched compared to his birthplace Italy [33]. Fast food is nevertheless connected with the American way of life, but it also originated in the United States, according to the [22]. In the last 60 years, there have been significant modifications in eating habits. Before the economic expansion of the 1950s in the United States, for instance, the house was the principal location for food production and consumption [36]. In ancient Greece and Rome, inns and taverns often supplied meals to those away from home for a cause [22]. This pattern persisted for a considerable period [22]. Although taverns and coffee houses were popular gathering places in the 17th century, the concept of dining out for entertainment did not become widespread in Western civilization until the late 18th century [22]. Eventually, the fast-food industry developed.

2.2 Classification of Fast-Food

The author argued that since the creation, fast meals have been intended to be consumed on the run, although they often do not need conventional utensils and are eaten with the hands [22]. Common fast-food menu options include fish and chips, sandwiches, hamburgers, fried chicken, French fries, pizza, and ice cream [9]. Some fast-food restaurants provide salad bars, healthy grains, buns, grilled chicken, and lean meats to cater to more nutrition-conscious clients [11]. Moreover, a handful of fast-food establishments publish a nutritional breakdown of their menu items. Fast-food items can be categorized as such; all menu items having a dough crust and toppings that are classified as pizza, including basic salad veggies as well as those with meat or pasta, burger food that is in the form of burger with a bread bun including vegetable or chicken or beef excluding breakfast burgers, chicken food items such fried chicken, nuggets etc. omitting chicken burger, sides includes fries, chips, wedges etc., fluid-based beverages, such as milkshakes, fruit smoothies, carbonated soft drinks, tea, coffee, and hot chocolate, sandwiches filled with pieces of bread and wraps excluding breakfast menu items and burgers, breakfast morning menu items only served as breakfast including rotis muffins cupcakes, rice items including biriyani, fried rice, khichuri, tahari etc. [38]. Nonetheless, the consumption of fast food is increasing all around the world eventually [1].

2.3 Changes in Consumption Pattern

Fast food was thought to be the food of the only developed country initially [6]. Eventually, affinity towards this kind of mouth-watering food has spread all around the world, significantly among the young generation [6]. In India annually, the fast-food sector is growing at a 40% rate [16]. McDonald's was the first restaurant chain to use an assembly line approach [22]. Some consider White Castle the first chain restaurant [22]. In the era of globalization, the international chain has spread its impact all around the world. Globalization refers to the process through which businesses and other organizations gain worldwide sway or begin functioning globally (Merriam-Webster, n.d.). In our country, McDonald's has no branches. However, people, especially private university students, admire them so much that they already miss having it without even experiencing it once [37]. Many items of fast food are born abroad and came here eventually [1]. Here it may change by getting a hint of Bengali masala to get accustomed to our taste buds [12]. However, the main structure of the typical fast-food items has remained the same coming in here, for instance- pizza from Italy [3]. Various factors have impacts on choosing such items to be consumed.

In a comparative study between international and Chinese students in China, authors have found poor dietary practices among their university students [28]. International students tend to have more affected hood habits due to migration [35]. As they live away from home, they intake a smaller number of vegetables, perhaps because of the slower and more difficult process to have them. Another cause of such affinity towards fast food might be the family culture [42]. Some students carry the food habit, that is practised in their family despite being home away [36]. If there is already a practice of having fast-food items in the family, it can increase among tertiary-level students. Some students eat fast food due to peer influence. The author has claimed that students consume more fast food when they are with friends, especially friends who are more likely to eat such foods [36]. They often build up or change their eating preference under the influence of trends, friend networks, etc. Ongoing this manner, they develop some influences, often undesirable diets, for instance, fizzy drinks and other fast-food items [6]. Among them, fast-food and carbonated beverage consumption was high [35]. Fast-food culture is rising among the new generation [16, 42]. Comparative, elder people are more likely to choose healthy food than them in comparison [16, 35].

Advances in study life at the tertiary level, the accessibility of fast food, and the speed of movement all contributed to an increase in the consumption of fast food. Food prices influence food selections. Native culture tends to influence food intake decisions [10]. Those who grew up eating junk food or convenience foods recall loving and consuming fast food as adults [16]. Brought up has an impact on choosing and diverting food habits. Another study on college students in South Asia found that South Asia college students are practising unhealthy dietary increasingly [27]. These students influence other students while growing up and attending university [27]. Financial flexibility to skip meals and hectic schedules motivate the intake of fast food [29]. Individuals with lower socio-economic status are more prone to eating fast food. Others contend there is a benefit of physical closeness to fast-food establishments and intake of fast food [22, 36]. The students seemed to be more involved with the developing culture of having such food. They remain outside the home most of the time [29]. Amid this situation, it may seem the easiest option to choose from, in a university student's perception [9]. They might think of this as a blessing that saves time and money [43]. However, it can be a curse wrapped up in a temporary blessing attire [16]. The health impacts gradually become significant.

2.4 Health Impacts

Health is wealth- the proverb is for all, but it is more important for university students. Health nourishment at such an age is critical [15]. Their poor health habit development and health consequences can impact them individually, the nation's development and their families today or tomorrow adversely [16]. Regular fast-food intake is related to lousy health consequences, including being overweight or obese, according to research [36]. Nowadays, health risks regarding diabetes, cardiovascular diseases, and cancers have increased at an alarming rate. According to the World Health Organization, lifestyle and dietary factors are the reasons for 80% of such chronic diseases [25]. More obesity and overweight are seen among university students [37]. Research on American students gives an overview that, 75% of pupils of 20 to 27 years old are overweight or obese [6]. Even most of them find it hard to shed extra body fat [6]. It shows that fast-food consumption is proportional to fat-associated dietary habits [12]. It often causes by-products like food intolerance and fatigue due to various health conditions [15, 41]. Fast food consumption can immediately cause numbness, tightness and a burning sensation in boys [15]. Another study references in this regard that, food-related tweets can reveal a lot about overweight, diabetes rate, political views, and home topographical location and other information [6]. Fast food, an industrial-formed product, offers low vitamins, minerals, fibre and amino acids but high calories [14, 15]. Often such food items contain harmful colours. On the other hand, having up properly balanced and nutritional diet can pave the way to overcome health sufferings and reduce health risk. Again, knowledge of proper nutrition is significant for maintaining a healthy diet. Understanding a community's attitude, and belief regarding nutritional food is important to improve their health. Contrarily, inappropriate knowledge and belief can lead to more health destruction [35].

Fast food consumption is highly dense in calories, thus increasing health risk, and weight gain. If institutional nutritional education is given to them, it might reduce junk food consumption [27]. It can grow affinity towards addiction among the students. As a result, the generation can grow unhealthy and less productive [35]. So, we can see that this affinity works as a Domino effect to create other problems. A domino effect or chain reaction is the cumulative impact generated when a single incident sets off a series of similar occurrences [19]. To solve these issues, it is needed to establish a proper guideline for the consumers by evaluating real factors considering our culture in terms of Bangladesh.

3 Research Methodology

The philosophical orientation of researchers is the foundation for research work. Thereby, research methodology begins with the theoretical orientation of the researcher, i.e., the set of beliefs that guides the research, determines the purpose of the study takes a particular knowledge stance. The guiding principle for this research was the subjectivist view, meaning it sought to believe what we observed during this research [7]. Since this study was conducted taking BUP as the case to generate detailed evidence within a limited period and resources, the methodology for this research was the case study. Although some researchers may argue that a case study is not a methodology but a method because of the focus on a single case, other scholars [39] justified it as a methodology for its ability to guide researchers in generating a sufficient level of understanding by providing a rationale for the research designed [40]. When the research subject is broad, a single case can help generate more accurate results for the selected phenomenon by producing an opportunity for familiarity and better attachment with the research subject and environment [26].

Data is collected from all 22 departments of the BUP (Bangladesh University of Professionals [2]. I purposively selected students studying 2 years and above level considering the aim of this research. I thereafter set an open invitation through social media platforms (WhatsApp groups, and Facebook groups like Conjugated BUPians) by posting the survey questionnaire. Data was collected from the students who participated willingly. Thus, participants were selected for this study through convenience sampling [32]. A total of 47 students of BUP took part in this survey. Thus, the participants selected for this study regardless of their gender, race or religion. The survey data collected through this convenience sampling helped me to answer the sub-research questions one and two. After the first phase of the survey, I collected data using qualitative in-depth interviews among the survey participants. At the end of my survey questionnaire, I send an open invitation to express interest for an in-depth discussion. I received 10 expressions of interest, among which I interviewed six. The in-depth interviews were conducted using a specific theme. The interviews were recorded using an Android phone following the ethical guidelines of BUP. This university campus is situated in Mirpur DOHS. It is administrated by Bangladesh Army in a restricted area, due to safety concerns. The conversation was left under the lead of the participant unless the researcher had any specific query. On average each interview's duration was about 30 to 40 min. The rest participants were not available during the data collection period.

Although it may appear that the number of participants for this research was low, it can be assured that this smaller number did not affect the data quality and quality of research needed for this thesis. The convenience sampling [32] used in this study allowed the participation of individuals to fall into the arena of targeted research and needed experiences, thereby, helping produce data and analysis that was required to establish the level of understanding required for this study.

This study was conducted using a mixed-methods research approach. The quantitative data were analysed using Microsoft Excel was used to generate statistical analysis. The qualitative data were analysed using thematic coding, and identified according to the specific objectives set for this thesis.

4   Result and Discussion

4.1   Perception of Fast Food

Under this segment results will be showing about respondents' thoughts on when they hear the term 'fast food' and if the nutritional information influences their food habits or not. The respondents were asked what is the first thing that comes to their mind when they hear the term 'fast food'. The question was open-ended, and the feedback showed varied results. But most people said 'pizza', 'burger', 'pasta'. The word burger, pizza, chicken fries, pasta, French fries and sandwich was mentioned 17, 9, 5, 4, 1 and 1 times, respectively.

Apart from mentioning the items some people made interesting statements. Three of the respondents mentioned 'delicious', one referred to fast food as a 'quick way to mitigate hunger', one said 'pricy' and another one said 'costly'. One respondent answered, 'Fast food is pricy and unhealthy', one said- 'Maybe it's different from other food and also tasty', and another student said, 'Fast food is a massive business. There is a whole wealth of fast-food restaurants each of them specializing in a variation of food-burgers, chicken, pizza etc.', another statement was just 'weight gain'. One mention about fast-food restaurants- Chillox, Khana's, BFC etc. One said, 'I don't prefer fast food'.

The respondents were asked if nutritional information of the food, influences their food intake or not. They showed average concern about the fact as most (33%) of them, said sometimes it has effects on their choice, most of the time not. (Fig. 1).

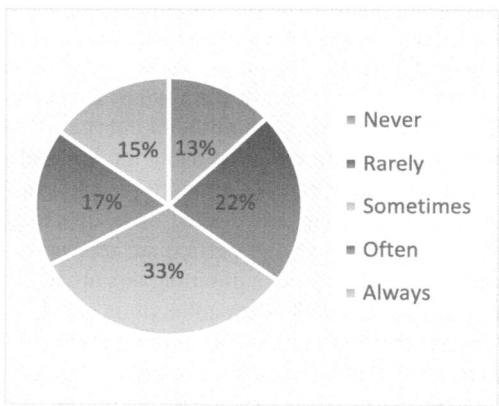

Fig. 1. Response about how frequently the nutritional information influences food choice

4.2 Impact on Food Habit Due to Lifestyle

They were asked if they lived with their family or resided in any hostel or mess. Most (60%) of them live with their families and 40% said they reside in a hostel or mess. The respondents were asked if they do any work like a part-time job or tuition to earn in addition to their studies. Most (63%) of the respondents were found to engage in different types of part-time jobs. Under this segment results will be showing about respondents' staying period at the university campus on average, food source/s of food they use during this time, response about carrying home-cooked food and its efficiency, response about the consumption of food items bought from campus food sources, response about their preference and causes of eating out, and eating in the campus, response about the preferred items they eat out and frequency of eating out, ordering online for food weekly. Lastly, the segment would show results about their consumption of instantly and easily prepared food like noodles, canned food, and frozen food, at home.

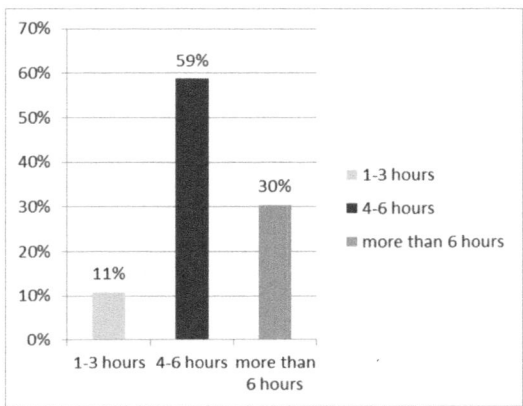

Fig. 2. Response about their staying period on a university campus

The results show that most (59%) respondents spend 4–6 h daily on the university campus which is a quite good amount of time to get hungry. (Fig. 2).

When the respondents were asked if they carry food from home or not- most (70%) seemed not to take the hassle of carrying home-cooked food. But among those (28%) who manage to carry home-cooked food, 43% of them said that the home-cooked food that they carry would serve them for the whole day need, 21% said carried food does not serve them for the whole day when they remain in the campus, 36% said maybe or maybe not. Finally, among these people who said their carried home-cooked food is not enough to serve for the day long, again were asked if they buy additional food to meet their hunger and energy purpose. 100% of them said they would buy food from nearby sources in response.

Respondents have mentioned the food sources nearby they use to get food while being on campus. Those are given below in Table 1.

Again, despite carrying home-cooked food 37% of the people said they preferred to eat outside food 42% said they would stick to home-cooked food. Then 37% of people were asked why they prefer outside food over homely, cooked food the answer was an open-ended question. There were various statements such as 'As we must stay in BUP for a long hour, after eating heavy meals that I usually bring from home I feel hungry at the end of the day. Hence, I eat snacks and tea/coffee from here, 'Because bringing food from home is a bit of a struggle. Just buying something from outside is more convenient.' 'By the time I go home, it becomes evening. So, I get hungry and must purchase one item to eat.', 'Depends on my mood', 'I cannot cook properly', 'Less hassles', 'Tastes better'.

The respondent students mentioned, alone or/and with other items.

Table 1. Food sources on the campus and their popularity among the students

Source	Several respondents use this option
BUP Vista	40 people
FBS cafeteria	40 people
3rd place	40 people
MIST canteen	16 people
Staff canteen	2 people
AD canteen	7 people
Restaurants from Mirpur 12	2 people
Roadside cart	05 people

Tea coffee 36 times, shingara 25 times, wedges 24 times, samucha 19 times, khichuri 19 times, daal-vaat 15 times, beverage drink 16 times, fried rice 14 times, vegetable, and roti 11 times, burger 10 times, patis 10 times, sandwiches 6 times, chicken rolls 5 times, hot dogs 5 times, biriyani 4 times, pizza 3 times.

The respondent students mentioned, alone or/and with other items.

- All menu items having a dough crust and toppings that are classified as pizza- 22 response
- Including basic salad veggies as well as those with meat or pasta-12 times
- Burger food that is in the form of a burger with a bread bun including vegetable chicken or beef excluding breakfast burgers – 12 times
- Chicken foods such as fried chicken, nuggets etc. omitting chicken burgers– 23 times
- Sides include fries, chips, wedges etc.- 24 times
- Fluid-based beverages, such as milkshakes, fruit smoothies, carbonated soft drinks, tea, coffee, and hot chocolate - 27 times
- Sandwiches filled with breads and wraps excluding breakfast menu items and burgers- 10 times
- Breakfast morning menu items only served as breakfast including rotis muffins cupcakes- 7 times
- Rice items including biriyani, fried rice, khichuri, tahari etc.- 25 times

The respondents were asked how much they like to eat out, and they responded on a scale between 1 to 5 depending on likelihood, where 5 refers to maximum affinity. Respectively among the students 11% rated eating out to like least as 1, 26% rated eating out to like as 2, 35% rated eating out to like as 3, 20% rated eating out to like as 4 and 9% rated eating out liking the most as 5.

Again, among the 47 respondents 17 people said weekly one or two times they might go out or take away orders for fast-food items, 12 people said it's five to six times a week, 3 people said it's more than seven times a week and rest 15 said they go for such food items for monthly one word two times. Again, when it was specifically asked, if they ordered takeaway or not, 35% said yes, 41% said no and the rest 24% answered maybe. Afterwards, for the 35% of students who say that they order online takeaway,

I investigated the frequency. 73% and 27% of them respectively said weekly 1–2 times and 3–4 times.

In response to the question, 'Do you consume food at home that can be prepared instantly (like noodles, canned food, frozen food, and food that is easily made in the microwave)?' 78% of the respondents said yes, 7% no and rest 15% answered maybe.

4.3   Food Availability and Quality

The responses about the most convenient food source in BUP, and responses on rating campus canteen's foods from different perspectives, between 1 to 5 depending on like-lihood, 5 counts for the best. And, it will display the results of responses about their purchase ability influence, staying duration influence on food choice. BUP canteen was reported as the most (76%) convenient food source among them. (Fig. 3). When they were asked for the reasons for the BUP canteen being convenient, 25%, 50%, 15%, and 10% considered time, distance, quality, and price, respectively.

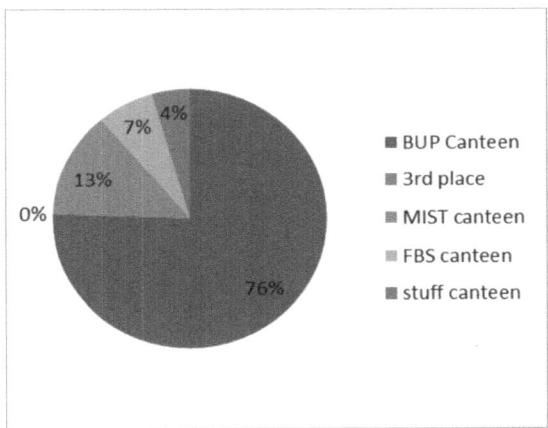

Fig. 3. Response about convenient food sources in BUP

Then they were asked if there were more options available here and if they prefer food available here, 63% said yes, and 15% said no (Fig. 4).

The respondents were asked rate the canteen's food's quality, food's pricing justifi-cation, food's taste, food availability, food hygiene, food service, food ambiance, food convenience on a scale between 1 to 5, where 5 refers to best and 1 to worst. The results are given below in graph: (Fig. 5, 6).

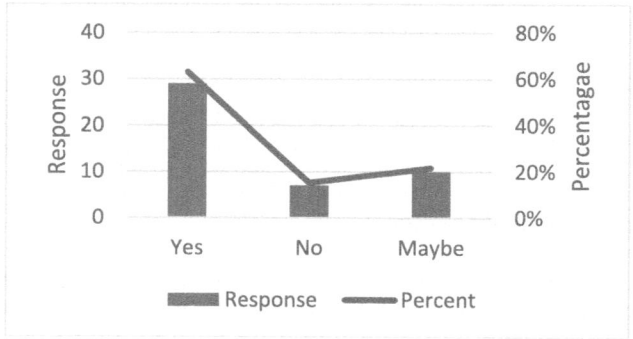

Fig. 4. Response on food availability impacting the choice

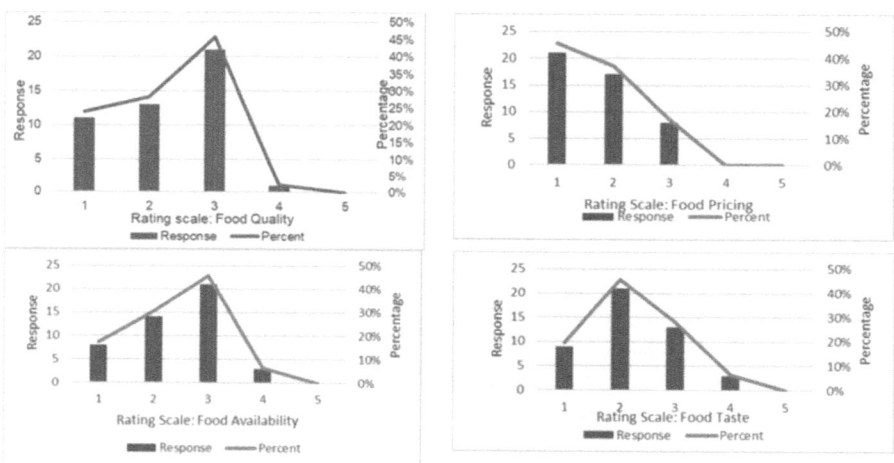

Fig. 5. Rating campus canteen's food's quality, pricing, availability and taste (between 1 to 5 depending on likelihood, 5 counts for best)

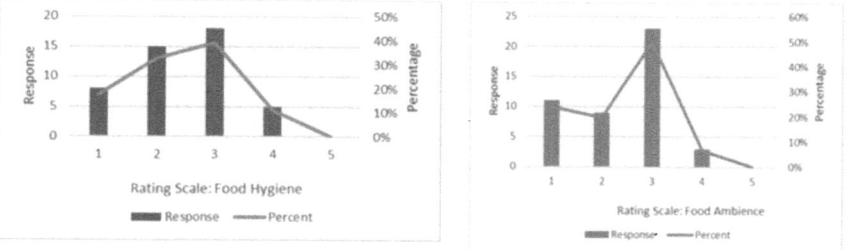

Fig. 6. Rating campus canteen's food's hygiene and ambience (between 1 to 5 depending on likelihood, 5 counts for best)

4.4   Fast-Food Intake Frequency

Respondents show the results of responses about the number of taken meals per day, responses on fast food becoming a basic need, and responses on fast food becoming a main meal option.

Most (23 of 47) of the respondents have said they have 3–4 times meals per day, and some (13) of the respondents said it's 1–2 times (Fig. 7). When they were asked if fast food has become a basic need for them or not, a significant number of people (22%) answered in the affirmative. In response, a significant number (15%) of them said they take fast food as a meal, but most (43%) of them said they intake fast food for both-meal and snack purposes.

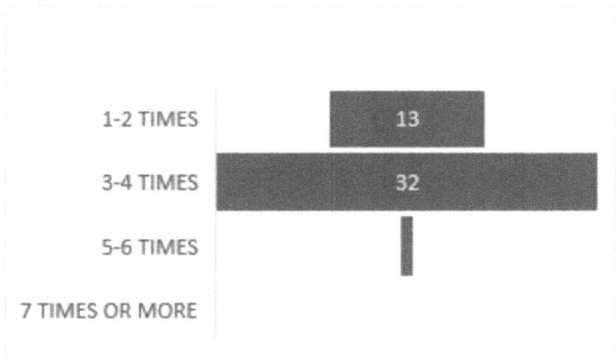

Fig. 7. Response on the number of taken meals per day by the respondents

In response to how often they consume fast-food on a weekly basis, most (44%) of them said 1 to 2 times (Fig. 8 left). When they were asked if fast-food has become a basic need for them or not, a significant number of people (22%) answered in affirmative (Fig. 8 right).

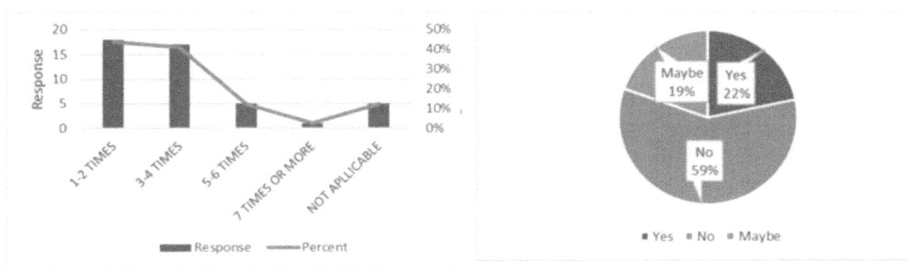

Fig. 8. Response on fast food consumption frequency weekly (left) and response on fast-food becoming a basic need (right)

4.5 Influencing Factors

When the respondents were asked about the causes of why people consume fast food, they stated various reasons. Among them 33 people said it's because fast has is very tasty, 22 people said fast-food restaurants are the only place for entertainment or hangout, five of the people said to avoid unhygienic hostel food, 17 of them said to eat with family or friends they consume fast-food, 19 of them said fast-food offers various item of menu that attracts to consume fast-food more. 13 of the people said to follow the ongoing fast-food consuming trend they feel like eating more such items, 11 of them said it's cost-efficient, 17 of them said due to limited time, 14 of them stated media influence as the cause, 14 of them said promotional influence as the reason, 27 of them said fast-food offers quick service that's why they feel affinity to consume fast-food more (Fig. 9 left). The respondents were asked if moving out of the family influenced their eating habits, and most (39%) answered in the affirmative (Fig. 9 right). Again, they were asked if social media has any influence on their purchasing of food. The results show that most of them (46%) think social media has a great impact in such regard.

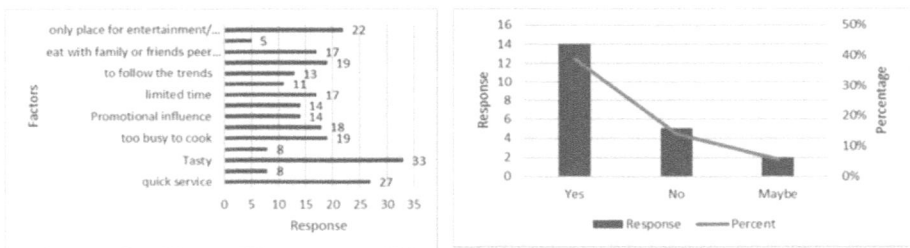

Fig. 9. Response on factor that influence fast-food intake (left) and response on the change of eating habit for moving out of the family (right)

4.6 Results Showing the Factors Influencing the Fast-Food Intake from In-Depth Interviews

Time. The study has found that students tend to eat from the BUP cafeteria, especially the fast-food items as it will save time. The students follow a hectic class schedule for a day. Talking to them, I have come to know that most of the time between two back-to-back classes, they get only a 15-min break time. Again, the academic building is 14 stories, with a very limited lift facility. Whereas food sources all are on the ground floor. It is quite tough for them to get down, eat and get back to class within the break time. Nujhat, a respondent from masters said, 'Oh I have fast foods more while being at BUP such as - sandwiches while standing for the elevator.' So, their class routine, along with the availability of a lift facility influences them to go for fast-food options more. The students who have class on the higher floor need to manage extra time to take the stairs or elevator. Again, the short time influences them to take fast food on the go. As a consequence, they go for singara, samucha, fries, and burger options more than the rice items like vaat-daal, tehari, and khichuri, which would require them to sit and eat.

Long Distance From Residence and Transportation. I have found out that, the distant places' students get transportation facility mostly for once, at around 6 am to 8 am, to reach the varsity. And again, once or twice to get back in the late afternoon. So, most of them need to stay for longer periods on the campus. If they carry food from home, in most cases, the food cannot be served for a day-long time. In addition, they need to eat snack items from BUP canteens. And the rest of the students cannot even bring home-cooked food. As their bags are already really heavy, and/or due to schedule they do not get enough time to prepare food and have to start the day very early in the morning. One of the respondents said, 'Though the quantity of oil in these foods is a lot still we buy these food as it is not possible to bring homemade food. As the distance between my home and university is quite long, I am not able to bring food from home.' So, they need to compromise with their schedule, lessening the sleep time to get home-cooked food.

Hostel/ Mess Life. The respondents who reside in a hostel or mess, tend to grow more affinity towards fast food. Most of them have complained that the hostel food is tasteless, so they are pushed to eat outside food. And again, outside foods offer lucrative fast-food items. With time they develop a habit of eating such types of food items. Fatiha said, 'Mostly I have rice items other than fast food, twice or thrice a week, despite having the option. It's more like a habit now.' Students have reported that the situation has pushed them to develop a habit of eating fast food over time.

Friends and Family, Social Media, Promotion. Both being on the campus or outside of the campus, people are influenced by their surrounding people (friends, family). Here Mahedul said: 'Whenever I'm with my friends I insist them to eat wedges'. Again, if eating out is a practice in the family, respondents who belong to such a family are more likely to choose fast-food items over traditional food. Again, in the modern era, everyone has access to Facebook and other social media. It is noticed that young people are more likely to eat fast-food items with friends and family and post them on social media. When the post reaches others, others feel like doing the same. It is an invisible but strong influence that they feel from their friends and family. Fast-food restaurant promotion works as the same as it reaches the audience.

Price. The students remarkably rated the BUP can food sources with poor marking. They said the BUP canteen's food is always spicy and oily. Apart from that, they find it cost-beneficial to choose shingara type fast-food over rice items like vaat-daal. Rafi said, 'If I eat 2 shingaras it with cost 16 taka but fulfill the hunger, on the other hand, a plate of vaat-daal-curry would cost me more than 40 takas.' So, pricing and quantity are found to influence the choice of food. The campus canteen is referred to as a beneficiary project, less considerate towards the students.

Shortage of Resources and Dissatisfaction with the Campus Canteen. Limited food sources are offered near the campus. As the campus is situated in a restricted area, online food delivery sources are not easy to get. So, whenever they get time, they go to Mirpur 12, Alubdi area to grab more variety of food. One of the respondents said, 'I would like to mention, that whenever we get much time in between the classes we prefer to go outside BUP - i.e.: Mirpur, Shagufta, Obokash etc. Because there we get so many variations of food whereas, in BUP, we get only the same foods always.' But the fact is mostly eating at the campus canteen has built up their fast-food eating tendency. Again, the Mirpur 12 area mostly offers fast-food items, but with better taste and pricing. One said, 'Oh think the quality of BUP's food is not good at all. They are oily and overpriced.' But again, they cannot but eat the food of BUP canteen fast-food.

4.7 Discussion

Types and Patterns of Fast-Food Intake. Fast-food items like burgers, pizza pasta, fries, wedges, etc. are globally known and famous among students [4, 29]. From my study, I have found out that students at Bangladesh University of Professionals prefer fast-food items over traditional rice items. They often go for hassle-free and less time-consuming food items on the go, such as sandwiches, fries, shingara, samucha, and wedges, So, here similarity is found with the other studies. Most of the participants of my study population remain at the campus for 4–6 h. Home-cooked food hardly can be served for such a long period. This period of stay makes them bound to eat fast food at least 1–2 times per day. Here they do not get enough options to value the nutrition information that much. The more the students remain on the campus the more they are prone to fast-food intake [23]. A study in India also shows students are more likely to consume fast food the longer they are on campus [16].

According to the participants of the study, as the campus is situated in a restricted area there are limited options of food sources to offer them. However, the BUP canteen is the most convenient option as a food source among them. However, it is not satisfactory to them due to being business oriented, rather than student-friendly. Most of the students said this canteen's food options are overpriced, spicy and oily. However, they cannot but eat from the canteen. Hence, they are building up a habit of eating fast food. Outside of BUP, the students are more likely to eat fast food once or twice every week on average.

Major Influencing Factors

- **Price:** Price influences the choice. Most of the respondents were from families with annual income is up to 2 lacs. Authors have claimed that income can be an influencing factor in the intake of more fast food [18]. Also, from the result I have seen that students have a limited amount of money to spend on food purposes. For that, they often, settle their hunger by eating low-price fast-food items like shingara, burgur etc. rather than having a full meal. On the contrary, if the students make income, they go out to eat often with friends. The lifestyle family brought up and, the friends surrounding also influenced their food intake.
- **Surrounding and brought up:** I have found, that students who reside with family tend to have better food habits than those who are residing in a hostel or mess. Studies indicate that friends and family have a great influence on any person to build up food habits [16]. In my study, students claim that hostel food tastes worse than BUP food, so they go for fast-food options more. Again, much availability and social influence, promotion all along create such surroundings to push them towards fast food. Research finds that fast-food companies have flourished more with the help of social media [38]

- **Routine:** Their hectic routine leaves them with no choice but to eat fast. It is known that fast food is famous for providing ease by taking on the go [29]. It remains the quick solution to their busy schedule.

5   Conclusion

The students do not get enough facilities to prioritize healthy food over fast food. The purpose of the study was to find out the root causes of why fast-food affinity is increasing among tertiary-level students. I ran a case study-based research to reach the goal and, the outcome indicates unhealthy type and frequency of fast-food consumption along with the influencing factors such as price, hectic routine, surroundings and social impact. Now ways to control the influencing factors are needed to develop to save university-going students. Otherwise, the affinity will grow more with time and befall upon the mass health destruction. Also, we know of the fact that this level of students is an asset for the country's development. Fast food can impact the whole nation. So, it is important to figure out why students are growing fast-food affinity among themselves to lead towards the solution. The urge is significant to solve the problem for the betterment of all.

References

1. Arslan, N., Aslan Ceylan, J., Hatipoğlu, A.: The relationship of fast-food consumption with sociodemographic factors, body mass index and dietary habits among university students. Nutrition Food Sci. **53**(1), 112–123 (2023)
2. Bangladesh University of Professionals (BUP). (n.d.). https://bup.edu.bd/settings/about-show. Accessed 25 Nov 2022
3. Bipasha, M.S., Goon, S.: Fast food preferences and food habits among students of private universities in Bangladesh. South East Asia J. Public Health **3**(1), 61–64 (2013)
4. Braithwaite, I., Stewart, A.W., Hancox, R.J., Beasley, R., Murphy, R., Mitchell, E.A.: Fast-food consumption and body mass index in children and adolescents: an international cross-sectional study. BMJ Open **4**(12), e005813 (2014). https://doi.org/10.1136/bmjopen-2014-005813
5. Brindal, E., Mohr, P., Wilson, C., Wittert, G.: Obesity and the effects of choice at a fast-food restaurant. Obes. Res. Clin. Pract. **2**(2), 71–142 (2008). https://doi.org/10.1016/j.orcp.2008.03.004
6. Chowdhury, M.R., Subho, M.D.R.H., Rahman, M.M., Islam, S., Chaki, D.: Impact of fast-food consumption on health: a study on university students of Bangladesh. In: 2018 21st International Conference of Computer and Information Technology (ICCIT), 1–6 (2018)
7. Crotty, M.J.: The foundations of social research: Meaning and perspective in the research process. The Foundations of Social Research, 1–256 (1998)
8. Fast food effects: Short-term, long-term, physical, mental, and more. (n.d.). https://www.medicalnewstoday.com/articles/324847#summary. Accessed 5 Dec 2022
9. Fleischhacker, S.E., Evenson, K.R., Rodriguez, D.A., Ammerman, A.S.: A systematic review of fast-food access studies. Obes. Rev. **12**(5), e460–e471 (2011)
10. García Bulle Bueno, B., et al.: Effect of mobile food environments on fast food visits. Nat. Commun. **15**(1), 2291 (2024)
11. Gerend, M.A.: Does calorie information promote lower-calorie fast food choices among college students? J. Adolesc. Health. **44**(1), 84–86 (2009)

12. Goon, S., Bipasha, M.S., Islam, M.S.: Fast food consumption and obesity risk among university students of Bangladesh. Eur. J. Prev. Med. **2**(6), 99–104 (2014)
13. Jaworowska, A., Blackham, T., Davies, I.G., Stevenson, L.: Nutritional challenges and health implications of takeaway and fast food. Nutr. Rev. **71**(5), 310–318 (2013). https://doi.org/10.1111/nure.12031
14. Khan, A.: Role of student and progress of country. https://www.nation.com.pk/25-Jun-2016/role-of-student-and-progress-of-country
15. Khatatbeh, M., Momani, W., Altaani, Z., Al Saad, R., Al Bourah, A.R.: Fast food consumption, liver functions, and change in body weight among university students: a cross-sectional study. Int. J. Prev. Med. **12** (2021)
16. Khongrangjem, T., et al.: A study to assess the knowledge and practice of fast-food consumption among Pre-University students in Udupi Taluk, Karnataka. Clin. Epidemiol. Glob. Health **6**(4), 172–175 (2018)
17. Kumar, H., Palaha, R., Kaur, A.: Study of consumption, behavior and awareness of fast food among university hostlers. Asian J. Clin. Nutr. **5**(1), 1 (2013)
18. Mazariegos, S., Chacón, V., Cole, A., Barnoya, J.: Nutritional quality and marketing strategies of fast-food children's combo meals in Guatemala. BMC Obesity **3**(1), 52 (2016). https://doi.org/10.1186/s40608-016-0136-y
19. Merriam-Webster. (n.d.). Dictionary by Merriam-Webster: America's most-trusted online dictionary. https://www.merriam-webster.com/. Accessed 5 (2022)
20. Meruelo, A.D., et al.: How do anger and impulsivity impact fast-food consumption in transitional age youth? AJPM Focus **3**(3), 100208 (2024)
21. Needham, C., Orellana, L., Allender, S., Sacks, G., Blake, M.R., Strugnell, C.: Food retail environments in greater Melbourne 2008–2016: longitudinal analysis of intra-city variation in density and healthiness of food outlets. Int. J. Environ. Res. Public Health, **17**(4) (2020). https://doi.org/10.3390/ijerph17041321
22. Ngozika, E.B., Ifeanyi, O.E.: A review on fast foods and family lifestyle. Int. J. Curr. Res. Biol. Med. **3**(4), 26–30 (2018)
23. Onurluba\cs, E., Yilmaz, N.: Fast food consumption habits of university students. J. Food Agric. Environ. 12–14 (2013)
24. Organization, W.H., others.: A guide to healthy food markets (2006)
25. Perlstein, R., McCoombe, S., Shaw, C., Nowson, C.: Medical students' perceptions regarding the importance of nutritional knowledge and their confidence in providing competent nutrition practice. Public Health **140**, 27–34 (2016)
26. Perry, C.: Processes of a case study methodology for postgraduate research in marketing. Eur. J. Mark. **32**(9/10), 785–802 (1998)
27. Saha, S., Al Mamun, M.A., Kabir, M.R.: Factors affecting fast food consumption among college students in South Asia: a systematic review. J. Am. Nutr. Assoc. **41**(6), 626–636 (2022)
28. Sajjad, M., Bhatti, A., Hill, B., Al-Omari, B.: Using the theory of planned behavior to predict factors influencing fast-food consumption among college students. BMC Public Health **23**(1), 987 (2023)
29. SharhidaZawani, S., et al.: Trends of fast-food consumption among public university students. Turk. J. Comput. Math. Educ. (TURCOMAT) **12**(3), 1618–1624 (2021)
30. Shetu, S.N.: Application of Theory of Planned Behavior (TPB) on fast-food consumption preferences among generation Z in Dhaka City, Bangladesh: an empirical study. J. Foodserv. Bus. Res. **27**(3), 320–355 (2024)
31. Stender, S., Dyerberg, J., Astrup, A.: Fast food: unfriendly and unhealthy. Int. J. Obesity (2005), **31**(6), 887–890 (2007). https://doi.org/10.1038/sj.ijo.0803616

32. Tafaghodtari, M.: Qualitative inquiry: new alternatives for the applied linguist-Patricia A. Duff, Case study research in applied linguistics. New York: Lawrence Erlbaum, 2008. Pp. ix+ 233. ISBN 978–08058–2359–2 (paperback). -Zoltán Dörnyei, Research methods in applied linguistics. Oxford: Oxford University Press, 2007. p. 336. ISBN 978–019–442258–1 (paperback). -Joseph Maxwell, Qualitative research design: An interactive approach. London: Sage, 2005. Pp. xiv+ 175. ISBN 0–7619–2608–9 (paperback).-Keith Richards, Qualitative inquiry in TESOL. New York: Palgrave Macmillan, 2003. Pp. xxv+ 323. ISBN 1–4039–0135–4 (paperback). Language Teaching, **42**(2), 272–282 (2009)
33. Tillotson, J.E.: Fast food-through the ages part 1. Nutr. Today **43**(2), 70–74 (2008)
34. Turnitin - Class Portfolio. (n.d.).https://www.turnitin.com/s_class_portfolio.asp?r=91.583 5747124316&svr=55&lang=en_us&aid=45069&cid=36676098. Accessed 8 Dec 2022
35. ul Haq, I., et al.: A comparative study of nutritional status, knowledge attitude and practices (KAP) and dietary intake between international and Chinese students in Nanjing, China. Int. J. Environ. Res. Public Health, **15**(9) (2018). https://doi.org/10.3390/ijerph15091910
36. Woodhall-Melnik, J., Matheson, F.I.: More than convenience: the role of habitus in understanding the food choices of fast-food workers. Work Employ Soc. **31**(5), 800–815 (2017)
37. Zaman, S., Selim, N., Joarder, T.: McDonaldization without a McDonald's: globalization and food culture as social determinants of health in urban Bangladesh. Food, Cult. Soc. **16**(4), 551–568.z (2013)
38. Ziauddeen, N., Fitt, E., Edney, L., Dunford, E., Neal, B., Jebb, S.: Variability in the reported energy, total fat and saturated fat content in fast food products across ten countries. Public Health Nutr. **1**, 1–8 (2015). https://doi.org/10.1017/S1368980015000336
39. Creswell, J.W.: Controversies in mixed methods research. Sage Handb. Qual. Res. **4**(1), 269–284 (2011)
40. Moon, K., Brewer, T.D., Januchowski-Hartley, S.R., Adams, V.M., Blackman, D.A.: A guideline to improve qualitative social science publishing in ecology and conservation journals. Ecol. Soc. **21**(3) (2016)
41. Firoz, M., Islam, M.M., Shidujaman, M., Islam, A., Habib, M.T.: University student's mental stress detection using machine learning. In: Seventh International Conference on Mechatronics and Intelligent Robotics (ICMIR 2023), vol. 12779, pp. 757–767. SPIE (2023)
42. Wang, J., Weng, Y., Shidujaman, M., Ahmed, S.U.: A multilevel perspective for social innovation: three exemplary case studies in collaborative communities toward sustainability. In: Kurosu, M., Hashizume, A. (eds.) Human-Computer Interaction. HCII 2023. Lecture Notes in Computer Science, vol. 14014, pp. 366–391. Springer, Cham (2023). https://doi.org/10. 1007/978-3-031-35572-1_25
43. Sultana, A., Hasan, M., Shidujaman, M., Premachandra, C.: Sentiment analysis with deep learning methods for performance assessment and comparison. In: 2024 International Conference on Image Processing and Robotics (ICIPRoB), pp. 1–6. IEEE (2024).

Innovation in Neuromarketing for the Implementation of Consumer Purchase Decisions

Diva Liceth Mendoza Ocasal[1,2] , Aida Luz Vargas Lugo[1,2] ,
Alba Marina Rueda Olivella[1,2] , Alexandra Camila Vásquez Sarmiento[1,2(✉)] ,
and Pabla Peralta Miranda[1,2]

[1] Universidad de la Costa, Barranquilla, Colombia
{dmendoza32,arueda7,avargas40,avasquez19}@cuc.edu.co,
Pperaltamir@umiminuto.edu.co
[2] Uniminuto, Barranquilla, Colombia

Abstract. This research analyzed the influence of innovation in marketing through the tools derived from the studies of cognitive neuroscience and its relationship with marketing; these two areas have generated a new trend called neuromarketing, which is a new way of applying knowledge about the functioning of the brain and its effect on purchasing decisions; this type of study allows organizations to learn new innovative strategies on how to attract customers and influence the purchasing decisions of consumers, neuroscientific studies applied to marketing use technological tools to identify tastes or preferences when making purchases. In this article, an analysis was conducted on the relationship between the brain's sensory responses to marketing stimuli and the purchase decision. A sample of 123 university students was taken for the study; the metrics were performed in three phases: In the first phase, images of distinguished brand graphics were used; in the second phase, pictures of the brands with all the elements that compose it were presented, and in the third phase, a video was shown of a commercial with A.I. about a recognized brand. The scientific method is quantitative, experimental level, and cross-sectional in scope. The evaluation was carried out through a Likert-type survey to measure the consumers' purchase decision-making. For the analysis, advanced statistical techniques of SSPS were used; the conclusion of the study allowed us to know the relationship between brain stimuli generated by marketing and consumer purchase decisions; the results show a greater inclination towards stimuli with movement used with A.I.; these provide information that could help in the development of business strategies, this research can also be used by the scientific community, to continue developing similar studies to understand what mechanisms are most effective in influencing consumer purchasing decisions and ultimately increase their success in the market.

Keywords: neuromarketing · neurosciences · innovation · consumer · purchasing decisions

A. Coman et al. (Eds.): HCII 2024, LNCS 15375, pp. 324–332, 2025.
https://doi.org/10.1007/978-3-031-76806-4_23

1 Introduction

In the field of neuromarketing, innovation has become a critical factor in understanding and leveraging consumer decision-making; according to Damásio's theory of emotions, emotions, when intense enough, provoke a physical reaction that includes decision-making and can be measured, recording the brain's responses to certain stimuli. As we move into the digital age, traditional marketing strategies are no longer sufficient to capture the attention and persuade consumers. Therefore, the need arises to explore new ways to influence decision-making using neuroscience-based techniques. However, there are still challenges and unanswered questions in this field, posing a problem requiring further research and the development of innovative solutions [1, 2].

In this research, we focus on learning how neuromarketing can leverage cutting-edge technology to improve the understanding of consumer decision-making and develop innovative marketing strategies [2].

The objective of this research is to analyze the relationship between cognitive neuroscience and marketing through the application of technological tools in an innovative way to understand the most relevant marketing factors in consumers when deciding to make a purchase. In recent years, neuromarketing has leveraged neuroscience studies using cutting-edge technology, such as functional magnetic resonance imaging and eye tracking, to understand consumer decision-making better and develop more innovative marketing strategies. (2) [3] In addition, the neuromarketing field has been able to use the latest research in cognitive neuroscience to develop more innovative marketing strategies.

Understanding consumer decision-making is critical to the success of any marketing strategy. In today's era, where technology is advancing by leaps and bounds, neuromarketing has emerged as an innovative discipline that uses advanced techniques to analyze and understand the brain processes that influence purchasing decisions. Damasio's theory of emotions states that emotion comes first, and only if it is sufficiently intense does the consumer become aware of that feeling. The somatic marker hypothesis holds that decisions are made in different situations, in favorable or unfavorable conditions. Therefore, the body first perceives emotions because they provoke a physical reaction to environmental stimuli. These stimuli can be smells, colors, and textures of objects and images that influence the consumer's perception, and this perception influences the result [4].

In neuromarketing, emotions are examined by measuring and recording the brain's reactions to a given stimulus presented to consumers. However, despite recent advances in this area, there still needs to be a gap in how to take full advantage of cutting-edge technology to improve understanding of consumer decision-making and develop more effective and innovative marketing strategies. Therefore, it is crucial to conduct research that addresses this issue and explores the possibilities of using cutting-edge neuromarketing technology to improve the understanding and prediction of consumer decisions. (3) [5, 6].

Neuromarketing or consumer neuroscience uses tools such as EEG to detect brain waves and analyze the effects of advertising on the brain through exposure to commercial stimuli, neurofeedback, and eye tracking to explore neurophysiological or biological aspects applied to marketing, conducting research on consumer preferences, improving predictability of behavior and segmenting customers, adding value to market research; These neuroscience tools make it possible to measure the cognitive, emotional and behavioral responses of customers. This can help researchers better understand customers' genuine reactions to marketing campaigns and the stimuli generated by them [5, 7, 6].

Another tool that is very useful for the study of neuromarketing is eye tracking, a technique that consists of the use of electronic devices, such as eye detection sensors, which allow observing in real time where the consumer looks; it will enable knowing what focuses on and which areas are activated with greater intensity in his brain. These data are detected by infrared lights that provide the most significant information on preferences and stimuli. [8].

1.1 Neuromarketing for Consumer Decision Making

[9] According to the trends generated by Industry 4.0, there is a relationship between brand image and consumers' self-image; the brand has to reflect the image they have of themselves, and through the brand, they express their cognitions and emotions derived from the perception they have of themselves. A precondition for brand loyalty is created if the brand image matches the consumer's image. Consumers often buy brands they believe will bring them closer to an ideal personal and social image. However, self-image is based on an imaginary idea that the consumer experiences on an emotional level, hence the importance of understanding emotions in consumers to design business strategies that come close to customers' expectations and desires. The model of an idealized self-image implies that the consumer will choose a brand that corresponds to his self-perception; therefore, decision-making has a subjective component that is highly permeated by paradigms, cultural, phylogenetic, and imagery based on beliefs, emotions, and consumer status. From a neuroscience perspective, the brain interprets the perception of the environment through the stimuli generated by marketing-derived brands, processing the information that influences the purchase decision [9, 10].

1.2 The Purchase Decision and Brand Advertising

There is innovation in advertising within the strategies of companies to promote their brands. The trend of digital technologies in the last decade has accelerated with the use of A.I., interconnected electronic devices, big data, and machine learning models, among others. The use of technologies impacts social networks, and the fame of influencers is used to promote the products of brands; celebrities become characters that influence through promoting a positive body image; in this way, celebrities relate their brand with corporate brands, that is some of the strategies, influencers use social networks to promote successful and healthy lifestyles, this helps them to build trust with their audience while improving the image of the brand. Companies use technologies to design marketing strategies and thus gain access to a wider audience. [2, 8, 10].

1.3 Technological Innovation

Innovation is essential in marketing, and artificial intelligence can be used in several ways. One of them is machine learning, which can be used to predict customer behavior and future consumer preferences. It can also be used to evaluate the effectiveness of marketing campaigns in product design [11, 12].

Another innovation recently used in neuromarketing is virtual reality; this technology allows users to interact between the digital and the physical; the experiences lived are reflected in the brain as if they were real, so this type of technology helps in understanding consumer behavior [13].

In this research, we intend to know how innovation in neuromarketing influences the realization of consumer purchasing decisions. To answer this question, we use a methodology that we describe below:

1.4 Methodology

Measurement and Theoretical Model. One of the objectives was to measure the perception of consumers when choosing to buy or feel the impulse by only observing the graphic that identifies the brand in the recognition of the brand itself and its elements and its reaction to advertising with artificial brand intelligence for the purchase decision-making process (Table 1).

Table 1. Thus, the theoretical model evaluated is shown in Fig. 1:

Source: Own elaboration.

2 Theoretical Model

The measurement was carried out using a direct collection instrument on young university students between the ages of 17 and over 25 years old. Taking as reference the independent variable "Brand consumers" before the cognitive, emotional, and sensorial stimuli regenerated by brand advertising, the sample was 123 students. The instrument was applied in three phases:

In the first phase, the sample observed only graphics of recognized brands, and subsequently, the reactions of brand recognition and feelings that awakened and inspired the purchase decision-making were validated.

In the second phase, the sample observed the complete images of recognized brands, including all their components, such as graphics, names, logos, colors, and slogans. The reactions of what attracted the most attention in the image and brand recognition were validated for the purchase decision-making process.

In the third phase, the sample observed an advertising video of a recognized brand with the application of artificial intelligence; subsequently, the reactions of stimuli in front of the advertising and impulse for the purchase decision and relevance of the use of artificial intelligence to awaken the desire to buy were validated.

2.1 Models' Statistics

The analysis of the binary logistic regression is presented, where it is expected to demonstrate the influence of advertising and technological progress in the purchase decision of consumers, which is the reaction to the stimuli applied in the observation of successful brand graphics: observation of complete images of successful brands and finally the observation of advertising commercials with artificial intelligence.

The independent variable is "Brand consumers," and the independent variables are the cognitive, emotional, and sensory stimuli regenerated by brand advertising.

From the formulation:

$$log(1 - pp) = \beta0 + \beta1x1 + \beta2x2 + \beta nxn$$

log(1-pp) of the logarithm of odds (the odds ratio) of the purchase decision being made as a function of the independent variables β = stimuli towards the need to buy, preferences and of brands and emotion for acquiring a purchase.

It is reformulated in the three phases as the independent variables.

The occurrence probability of success in the purchase decision will be tested against the different stimuli where, in each phase, they increase for exponential validation according to the age ranges of the sample.

3   Results

A binary logistic regression analysis was performed using SPSS software, which demonstrated the influence of advertising and technological progress on consumers' purchasing decisions. In this research, in the first phase, it was observed that the purchase intentionality after watching only graphics of recognized brands. In the second phase, complete images of successful brands were presented, making evident the purchase preferences of consumers; finally, an analysis of advertising commercials with artificial intelligence was made, where a greater interest in the cognitive, emotional, and sensory stimuli generated in the video was noted, which impacted on a greater interest in purchase in consumers.

3.1 Results of Binary Logistic Regression Model

The objective of the binary logistic regression analysis for our study was to determine which independent variables (or combinations of them) significantly impact the probability that a customer will make a purchase.

3.2 Purchase Decision Probabilities

In the first phase, the analysis focused on observing the reaction of potential consumers to the observation of the images of the graphics of the recognized brands. In this sense, the coding parameters that determined the probability of purchase decisions in consumers were observed.

Coding of categorical variables

		Fre-quency	Parameter coding		
			(1)	(2)	(3)
Ages	Under 17 years of age	2	1,000	,000	,000
	Between 17 and 21 years old	44	,000	1,000	,000
	Between 22 and 25 years old	58	,000	,000	1,000
	Over 25 years old	19	,000	,000	,000

Own source.

Variables in the equation

		B	Standard error	Forest	Gl	Say.	Exp(B)	95% C.I. for EXP(B)	
								Lower	Upper
Step 1a	Ages	,370	,256	2,083	1	,149	1,448	,876	2,392
	Constant	-,840	,727	1,334	1	,248	,432		

a. Variables specified in step 1: Ages.

Own Source. According to the results of the binary logistic model, the dependent variable (the need to buy) increases by 2,392 times in the face of the cognitive effects and stimuli of the brand graphics shared by the organizations, ensuring brand recognition as the number of buyers or consumers of products and services increases.

In the second phase of observation of recognized brands: In the second phase of observation of images of Recognized Brands: Post-observation coding parameters of images of Recognized Brands are observed; stimulus reaction in the recognition of preferred brands as an option to purchase.

Variables in the equation

		B	Standard error	Forest	Gl	Say.	Exp(B)	95% C.I. to EXP(B) Lower	Upper
Step 1a	Ages	-,221	,282	,611	1	,434	,802	,461	1,395
	Constant	1,619	,821	3,889	1	,049	5,049		

a.   Variables specified in step 1: Ages.

Own Source. Given the observation of images of recognized brands, the results of the binary logistic model show that the variable in recognition of the brand that drives young people to make purchase decisions is expected to increase 1,395 times as the number of buyers or consumers of products increases.

It is analyzed in that although it is true that the impact in the observation of the brand graph presents a greater probability in the influence for making purchase decisions, it is also observed an expected likelihood of success in the brand recognition of young people as this population of consumption and use of products grows.

In the third phase of observation of the video of a recognized brand commercial with the use of Artificial Intelligence:

Variables in the equation

		B	Standard error	Forest	Gl	Say.	Exp(B)	95% C.I. to EXP(B) Lower	Upper
Step 1a	Ages	,404	,258	2,446	1	,118	1,498	,903	2,486
	Constant	-,867	,731	1,407	1	,236	,420		

a.   Variables specified in step 1: Ages.

Source: Own Elaboration. After observing the video of the well-known brand commercial using artificial intelligence, the results of the binary logistic model in which it is expected that the variable in arousing emotions towards the decision to purchase the product increases 2,486 times as the number of buyers or consumers of products increases.

It is proven that the trend of buying behavior in young people considerably influences the stimuli that reach the brain and send messages of attitudes, feelings, and emotions for the purchase decision; it is proven that the information of advertising messages with the use of artificial intelligence will allow to emit emotions and desires of purchase in consumers, leading them to the identification and recognition of the brand.

4   Conclusions

Finally, innovation in neuromarketing is given through the use of technologies in combination with more excellent knowledge of how the brain works, the reactions that consumers have to the stimuli generated by the marketing of brands, and their effect on profitability.

The results of the three phases in which this study was carried out allow us to deduce that the use of advertising with the application of artificial intelligence generates a more significant effect through sensory stimuli that would enable selling experiences rather than products in themselves, where the main actors are the consumers, highlighting in the results that the new generations have a high tendency in the use of technologies, in different scenarios. Technological innovation in advertising messages motivates consumers more than buying products and services, awakening the desire to generate experiences in their use or consumption.

This type of research allows us to focus marketing towards the sensory experience through technology.

References

1. Damasio, A.R., Everitt, B.J., Bishop, D.: The Somatic Marker Hypothesis and the Possible Functions of the Prefrontal Cortex [and Discussion] (1996). http://www.jstor.org/stable/3069187
2. Jukic, D.: Beyond brand image: a neuromarketing perspective. Commun. Today **14**(1), 22–38 (2023). https://doi.org/10.34135
3. Gill, R., Singh, J.: A study of neuromarketing techniques for proposing a cost-effective information-driven decision-making framework. In: Materials Today: Proceedings, Elsevier Ltd, pp. 2969–2981 (2020). https://doi.org/10.1016/j.matpr.2020.08.730
4. Bechara, A., Damasio, A.R.: The somatic marker hypothesis: a neural theory of economic decision. Games Econ. Behav. **52**(2), 336–372 (2005). https://doi.org/10.1016/j.geb.2004.06.010
5. Dias, A.M.: From 'Neurosciences Applied to Marketing' to 'Integrative Neuromarketing (2012). http://www.cienciasecognicao.org
6. Oikonomou, V.P., Georgiadis, K., Kalaganis, F., Nikolopoulos, S., Kompatsiaris, I.: A sparse representation classification scheme for the recognition of affective and cognitive brain processes in neuromarketing. Sensors **23**(5) (2023). https://doi.org/10.3390/s23052480
7. Khushaba, R.N., Wise, C., Kodagoda, S., Louviere, J., Kahn, B.E., Townsend, C.: Consumer neuroscience: assessing the brain response to marketing stimuli using electroencephalogram (EEG) and eye tracking. Expert Syst. Appl. **40**(9), 3803–3812 (2013). https://doi.org/10.1016/j.eswa.2012.12.095
8. Mikalef, P., Sharma, K., Chatterjee, S., Chaudhuri, R., Parida, V., Gupta, S.: All eyes on me: Predicting consumer intentions on social commerce platforms using eye-tracking data and ensemble learning. Decis. Support Syst. 114039 (2023). https://doi.org/10.1016/j.dss.2023.114039
9. da Rocha, A.B., de Oliveira, K.B., Espuny, M., da Motta Reis, J.S., Oliveira, O.J.: Business transformation through sustainability based on industry 4.0. Helion E10015 (2022). https://doi.org/10.1016/j.heliyon.2022.e10015
10. Cerna, K.S.J., Guerra, M.D.P.M., Ortiz, C.P.C.: Relationship between neuromarketing and brand positioning of a company in the retail sectorǀrelación entre el neuromarketing: y el posicionamiento de marca de una empresa del sector retail. Univ. Soc. **14**(1), 554–563 (2022)

11. Mashrur, F.R., et al.: An intelligent neuromarketing system for predicting consumers' future choice from electroencephalography signals. Physiol. Behav. **253** (2022). https://doi.org/10.1016/j.physbeh.2022.113847

12. Alcañiz, M., Bigné, E., Guixeres, J.: Virtual reality in marketing: a framework, review, and research agenda. Front. Psychol. **10**, 20 Frontiers Media S.A. (2019). https://doi.org/10.3389/2019.01530

13. Hilken, T., Chylinski, M., de Ruyter, K., Heller, J., Keeling, D.I.: Exploring the frontiers in reality-enhanced service communication: from augmented and virtual reality to neuro-enhanced reality. J. Serv. Manag. **33**(4–5), 657–674 (2022). https://doi.org/10.1108/JOSM-11-2021-0439

14. Peyravi, B., Nekrošienė, J., Lobanova, L.: Revolutionised technologies for marketing: theoretical review with a focus on artificial intelligence. Bus. Theory Pract. **21**(2), 827–834 (2020). https://doi.org/10.3846/btp.2020.12313

A Systematic Literature Review of User Interface Personalization: Findings from Automated Teller Machines (ATM) and Related Domains

Luis Moquillaza(✉) ⓘ and Freddy Paz ⓘ

Pontificia Universidad Católica del Perú, Lima 32, San Miguel, Perú
luisf.moquillaza@pucp.edu.pe, fpaz@pucp.pe

Abstract. In the rapidly evolving landscape of technology consumption, users increasingly seek personalized experiences that extend beyond mere functional fulfillment. Personalization, which tailors user interfaces to individual preferences, has proven to enhance user satisfaction and engagement. Despite its advantages, the widespread integration of personalization remains limited across various frequently used product and service domains. Automated Teller Machines (ATMs), serving as a pivotal channel for numerous banking transactions, are favored by consumers for their convenience. However, the prevalent use of ATMs is often accompanied by a suboptimal user experience, primarily due to a neglect of user attitudes, perceptions, and knowledge in their design. In this sense, this study conducts a systematic literature review to identify personalization actions, challenges in implementation, and methodologies in the ATM domain and related areas to understand how they positively impact the user experience. For this, the protocol proposed by Kitchenham was followed. The findings underscore the importance of integrating user interface personalization seamlessly into the system to enhance user satisfaction and reduce average usage time. Moreover, the research highlights the challenges of incorporating personalization during development, emphasizing the need for careful selection of information sources and addressing concerns related to data privacy. The paper concludes by offering valuable insights into the state of personalization in the ATM domain, providing a foundation for future research to enhance user experiences in this critical domain.

Keywords: User Interface · Personalization · Systematic literature review · Automated teller machine · Human-computer interaction

1 Introduction

In recent years, consumers of technology products and services have developed an expectation for a personalized experience on user interfaces that goes beyond just meeting their functional needs [1]. Personalization enhances the user experience by considering the user's requirements and preferences. Research studies, such as the one conducted by Epsilon, reveal a positive impact on user perception following the implementation of personalization: 80% of users are more likely to make purchases from organizations that offer personalized experiences [2]. Despite the advantages it offers to organizations and the positive impact on user experience, personalization has not been widely implemented across various product and service domains that are frequently used.

ATMs are the most commonly used channel by bank customers for conducting their transactions. This preference arises from their ability to ease the burden on branches and provide customers with convenient transaction options [3]. However, despite their widespread usage, ATMs often deliver a subpar user experience due to a lack of consideration for user attitudes, perceptions, and knowledge [4]. In addition, according to Aguirre, there is a lack of clear guidance on the design of user interfaces in ATMs, resulting in a failure to consider the needs of the end-users interacting with them [5].

In this paper, a systematic literature review has been carried out in which personalization actions, application challenges and personalization methodologies have been identified in order to know the state of personalization in the ATM domain and related areas and to understand how it positively impacts the user experience. This research could prove valuable for design specialists and professionals, offering guidance on the selection of methods and the implementation of redesign proposals to improve the usability of graphical interfaces of ATMs. In addition, it could serve as a basis for developing customization proposals in this area, allowing interfaces to be adapted to the specific needs of users.

The structure of the paper is as follows: Sect. 2 shows the most relevant concepts and their use in this research. Section 3 details the planning and execution of the systematic literature review, while Sect. 4 shares the results obtained. Finally, Sect. 5 presents the conclusions and future work of the research.

2   Theoretical Background

This section presents the most relevant concepts present in this research. Since the purpose of the study is to discuss the state of the art on ATM graphical interface customization processes reported in the literature, concepts related to this topic of interest have been defined that have allowed the development of this research. The understanding and contextualization of these concepts is fundamental for the exhaustive analysis and subsequent discussion of the findings obtained in the framework of this research.

2.1   ATM

The ATM is an electronic banking service point that allows customers to perform simple transactions (as if it were a bank teller) without the presence of an employee [6]. Despite the growth and preference for digital accounts, ATMs are still necessary as they are the most used source to get cash, a capability that digital alternatives do not provide [7].

According to one of the main banking institutions in Peru (BCP), an increase in the transactions made in the coming years is expected, which are currently 13.7 million per month of which 78% correspond to cash withdrawals. Therefore, to meet the demand, an increase of 7% in the number of ATMs is expected by the end of 2022 [8].

2.2 User Interface

The user interface refers to the components of an interactive system that provide information and control to the user so that the user can complete specific tasks in the system [9]. For example, an ATM interface displays elements that represent the banking operations that can be performed by the user. The user can interact by activating one of them and the interface communicates by changing the status and displaying a response.

2.3 Personalization

Personalization is defined in the context of software applications as the ability to personalize communication with the client based on knowledge of their preferences and behavior during the interaction [10]. This includes adapting the content of the user interface shown to him according to the context and his needs [11].

For example, a user who has visual difficulty interacting with web pages always activates Zoom when reading. Personalization of the user interface would occur if, by taking information about the user's preferences on the size of the typography of the web pages he visits, the size of these pages is increased by default without the user having to do it on his own.

3   Planning and Executing a Systematic Literature Review

This section describes the search process that has been employed to obtain relevant studies on personalization in the ATM and its associated domains. The literature review aimed to identify case studies, challenges, difficulties, methodologies and tools related to personalization in the ATM and related domains. For this systematic literature review, the protocol proposed by B. Kitchenham [12] was used.

3.1 Objectives of the Systematic Literature Review

The objectives of the systematic literature review were:

- Understand user interface personalization actions and how they enhance the user experience in the ATM and related domains.
- Identify and analyze the challenges and difficulties encountered when applying user interface personalization in the ATM and related domains.
- Collect the methodologies and tools that are employed, within the area of data analysis, for user interface personalization in the ATM and related domains.

3.2 Research Questions

To achieve the objectives of the review, the following research questions were formulated:

- Through what actions does the personalization of the user interface contribute to improving satisfaction in the ATM domain or related domains?
- What are the challenges in performing user interface personalization in the ATM or related domains, and how have they been addressed?

- What user information is considered to carry out personalization based on their inter-action and what are the methodologies or techniques employed in the ATM or related domains?

In order to guide the search for studies based on the concepts described in the posed review questions, PICOC criteria were employed [13]. The PICOC criteria are as follows: (1) Population, in which the evidence is collected, (2) Intervention, refers to the aspects to be examined within the population and the methodology used to conduct the research, (3) Comparison, involves making comparisons between interventions, (4) Outcomes, pertaining to what is anticipated to be derived from the systematic review, and (5) Context, which refers to the setting or circumstances in which the identified case studies were conducted. This pertains to the specific scenarios or conditions under which the case studies took place.

Table 1 presents the PICOC criteria that have been defined for the concepts present in the review questions posed. In this research, the comparison criterion was not considered because the objective of this review is not to compare personalization applications but to obtain information about them.

Table 1. Definition of concepts using PICOC criteria

Criterion	Description
Population	Software products (ATM or related)
Intervention	Personalization
Outcomes	Challenges, tools, techniques, case studies
Context	User experience

3.3 Search Strategy

Following the Kitchenham protocol used for this review, key concepts were defined based on the PICOC criteria shown in Table 1. Synonyms of these concepts were also defined. Table 2 shows the key concepts that were used to establish search strings, this process is detailed in Sect. 3.5.

Table 2. Key concepts base on PICOC criteria

Keyword	Synonyms	PICOC criteria
Software	module	Population
ATM	automated teller machine, cash machine, automated banking machine	Population

(continued)

Table 2. (*continued*)

Keyword	Synonyms	PICOC criteria
personalization	personalized UX, personalized experience, hyper – personalization, personalisation	Intervention
challenge	barrier, bump, impediment, obstacle	Outcomes
technique	data analytics, data mining, approach, method, procedure, study case	Outcomes
user experience	user interface, UX, HCI	Context

3.4 Search Engines

For the review, we have taken into account search engines that have relevance both in the area of Computer Science and Software Engineering. The search engines selected for this review are shown below:

- Scopus (http://www.scopus.com)
- IEEE Digital Library (http://ieeexplore.ieee.org)
- Web of Science (https://www.webofscience.com)

3.5 Search Strings

Following the search strategy of the systematic review, search strings containing the terms defined in Table 2 were defined. On the one hand, those belonging to the same criterion were grouped and their synonyms were related using the OR operator. As a result, the following chains were formed:

```
C1: ("software" OR "module" OR "atm" OR "automated teller
machine" OR "cash machine" OR "automated banking ma-
chine")
C2: ("personalization" OR "hyper-personalization" OR
"personalisation" OR "personalized UX" OR "personalized
experience" OR "personalized content" OR "adaptive de-
sign")
C3: ("challenge*" OR "barrier*" OR "bump*" OR "impedi-
ment*" OR "obstacle*" OR "study case*" OR "technique*" OR
"data analytics" OR "data mining" OR "approach" OR
"method*" OR "procedure*" OR "framework*")
C4: ("user experience" OR "user interface" OR "user pref-
erence*" OR "human-computer interaction" OR "UX" OR "UI"
OR "user-centered design")
```

Subsequently, the different criteria were related using the AND operator. In this way, the string (C1 AND C2 AND C3 AND C4) was formed. Additionally, this string was adapted according to the syntax used by the selected search engines as seen in Table 3.

Table 3. Search strings

Search Engines	Resulting Search Engine
Scopus	TITLE-ABS-KEY(("software" OR "module" OR "atm" OR "automated teller machine" OR "cash machine" OR "automated banking machine") AND ("personalization" OR "hyper-personalization" OR "personalisation" OR "personalized UX" OR "personalized experience" or "personalized content" OR "adaptive design") AND ("challenge*" OR "barrier*" OR "bump*" OR "impediment*" OR "obstacle*" OR "study case*" OR "technique*" OR " data analytics" OR " data mining" OR "approach" OR "method*" OR "procedure*" OR "framework*") AND ("user experience" OR "user interface" OR "user preference*" OR "human-computer interaction" OR "UX" OR "UI" OR "user-centered design"))
IEEE Digital Library	("All Metadata": "software" OR "All Metadata": "module" OR "All Metadata": "atm" OR "All Metadata": "automated teller machine" OR "All Metadata": "cash machine" OR "All Metadata": "automated banking machine") AND ("All Metadata": "personalization" OR "All Metadata": "hyper-personalization" OR "All Metadata": "personalisation" OR "All Metadata": "personalized UX" OR "All Metadata":"personalized experience" OR "All Metadata": "personalized content" OR "All Metadata": "adaptive design") AND ("All Metadata": "challenge" OR "All Metadata": "barrier" OR "All Metadata": "bump" OR "All Metadata": "impediment" OR "All Metadata": "obstacle" OR "All Metadata": "study case" OR "All Metadata": "technique" OR "All Metadata": "data analytics" OR "All Metadata": "data mining" OR "All Metadata": "approach" OR "All Metadata": "method" OR "All Metadata": "procedure" OR "All Metadata": "framework") AND ("All Metadata": "user experience" OR "All Metadata": "user interface" OR "All Metadata": "user preference" OR "All Metadata": "human-computer interaction" OR "All Metadata": "UX" OR "All Metadata": "UI" OR "All Metadata": "user-centered design")
Web of Science	TS = ((software OR module OR atm OR automated teller machine OR cash machine OR automated banking machine) AND (personalization OR hyper-personalization OR personalisation OR personalized UX OR personalized experience or personalized content OR adaptive design) AND (challenge* OR barrier* OR bump* OR impediment* OR obstacle* OR study case* OR technique* OR data analytics OR data mining OR approach OR method* OR procedure* OR framework*) AND (user experience OR user interface OR user preference* OR human-computer interaction OR UX OR UI OR user-centered design))

3.6 Inclusion and Exclusion Criteria

In order to select scientific articles, inclusion criteria have been established to identify those relevant articles that allow us to obtain information to answer the review questions. The inclusion criteria defined are the following:

- **CI1:** The paper defines the concept of personalization within the area of Computer Engineering or related.
- **CI2:** The paper presents a software solution that personalizes user interaction in the ATM or related domain.
- **CI3:** The paper provides information about the challenges, difficulties or problems that prevent the implementation of a personalized user experience in the ATM or related domain.
- **CI4:** The paper details methodologies or protocols employed to personalize user interaction such as data analytics and related approaches.
- **CI5:** The paper describes a case study in which a personalization was applied to an IT solution in order to improve the user experience.

In order to discard articles that are not relevant to answer the review questions, exclusion criteria were established. Criterion CE1 is defined for articles that are not related to personalization in the area of Computer Science. Similarly, criterion CE2 rules out studies that do not provide information on personalization methodologies or tools. Criterion CE3 is established to discard articles that deal with the concept of customization instead of personalization, which is a different approach even though it is part of the HCI field. Finally, criterion CE4 was applied to exclude studies that did not use English or Spanish as their language. The exclusion criteria are presented below:

- **CE1:** The article does not relate to the concept of personalization in the area of Computer Engineering or related fields.
- **CE2**: The article does not contain relevant information on personalization methodologies.
- **CE3:** The article presents a case study in which customization is applied instead of personalization.
- **CE4:** The article is written in a language other than English or Spanish.

3.7 Documents Found

The search was conducted in March 2023. The search strings defined above were used in the corresponding search engines and a total of 839 results were obtained. Table 4 shows a breakdown of the articles obtained. After applying the defined inclusion and exclusion criteria, a total of 23 selected articles were obtained. Table 5 shows the list of these articles.

Table 4. Search results by search engines

Search Engines	Results	Duplicates	Relevant
Scopus	324	0	12
IEEE Digital Library	62	7	8
Web of Science	453	54	3
Total	**839**	**61**	**23**

Table 5. Selected papers

Paper	Title
L1 [14]	Towards Better Service Personalization: Reinforcement Learning with Guarantee of User Preference
L2 [15]	Personalized Long- and Short-term Preference Learning for Next POI Recommendation
L3 [16]	Dynamic User Interface Personalization Based on Deep Reinforcement Learning
L4 [16]	Personalization of User Interaction with Corporate Information Providing System Based on Analysis of User Preferences
L5 [17]	A Novel Data Mining Testbed for User Centred Modelling and Personalisation of Digital Library Services
L6 [18]	Traveler information in ITS: A Model-Driven Engineering approach to its personalization
L7 [19]	Exploiting Reinforcement Learning to Profile Users and Personalize Web Pages
L8 [20]	A Dynamical Extension Framework Supporting for Personalized Information Portal
L9 [21]	Model-Based Personalization within an Adaptable Human-Machine Interface Environment that is Capable of Learning from User Interactions
L10 [22]	XCS for Personalizing Desktop Interfaces
L11 [23]	Multimodality and Personalisation. En Enabling Technologies for Mobile Services: The MobiLife Book
L12 [24]	A Framework for Personalized Service Website based on TAM
L13 [25]	Describing Interfaces in the Framework of Adaptive Interface Ecosystems
L14 [26]	Automated personalization of input methods and processes
L15 [27]	Evaluating Multiple User Interactions for Ranking Personalization Using Ensemble Methods
L16 [28]	Deep Sequential Recommendation for Personalized Adaptive User Interfaces
L17 [29]	Analyzing Interaction for Automated Adaptation – First Steps in the IAAA Project
L18 [30]	User interface adaptation based on user feedback and machine learning
L19 [31]	A model driven architecture approach for user interface generation focused on content personalization
L20 [32]	Automatic construction of personalized customer interfaces
L21 [33]	Adaptive user interfaces and universal usability through plasticity of user interface design
L22 [34]	Engineering Adaptive Model-Driven User Interfaces
L23 [35]	Design and evaluation of an adaptive icon toolbar. User Modeling and User-Adapted Interaction

4 Results of the Systematic Review

4.1 Response to Question P1

To answer the first review question posed (Through what actions does the personalization of the user interface contribute to improving satisfaction in the ATM domain or related domains?) a total of 8 studies were identified. These identified a total of 4 personalization actions, which are presented in Table 6. No studies were found within the scope of ATM to answer this question.

Table 6. Personalization actions reported in the studies

Personalization Actions	Papers	Number of papers
Adaptation of the user interface according to preferences	L6, L9, L11, L12	4
Restriction of information to that which is of interest to the user	L5, L8	2
Suggestions based on user preferences	L10, L12	2
Adaptation of the interface font size	L7	1

The first personalization action relates to adapting the user interface based on user preferences. The logic behind adapting the user interface is related to making the interaction with the application as natural as possible [23] so that the goal is to dynamically generate interfaces that consider the user's preference [21, 24]. Also, it is possible to change the interface in order to change the sequence of interaction in the processes by hiding or showing options according to the needs [18]. The improvements that have been identified in the review are related to the perceived usefulness of the application, the usefulness of the content displayed, the versatility to take into account changes in preferences, and the reduction in usage time [18, 21, 23, 24].

The second personalization action relates to the restriction of information to that which is of interest to the user. In systems whose domain is closely linked to the state, legislation usually does not allow storing enough information to generate complex models of user needs [17]. This is why the improvement proposed for this context is related to user categorization and information segmentation [17]. Likewise, the information displayed can be improved by taking into account the role of the user and the information consulted [20]. The literature review shows us that defining a personalized path according to the user category helps to improve access to relevant information [17, 20].

The third personalization action relates to suggestions based on user preferences. Within the domain of desktop and web applications, user information is usually obtained implicitly in order to perform personalization, using the number of clicks, time of use, etc. [22, 24]. However, information can also be obtained through the use of feedback windows [24] and suggestions [22]. Initially, notification windows are shown in a general way in order to create a model of their preferences that will later give their outputs in these same [22, 24]. In this way, the review allows us to identify that personalized notifications will allow anticipating the user's actions, which improves their level of satisfaction and average usage time [22, 24].

Finally, the fourth personalization action relates to adapting the font size of the interface. The current approach in the web domain focuses on adapting the entire user interface, however, there is another approach in which specific elements that the user considers relevant are taken into account [19]. The lack of personalization in the formatting of fonts in the interface (font size, font phase, etc.) generates a barrier to use. The review shows that after taking into account the user's activity when choosing their settings in the interface, a model can be created that adapts the default fonts according to the needs, which helps to improve usability and user experience [19].

4.2 Response to Question P2

To answer the second review question (What are the challenges in performing user interface personalization in the ATM or related domains, and how have they been addressed?) a total of 10 studies were identified, which are presented below in Table 7. From these, 6 challenges were identified that should be taken into account when developing a user interface personalization in order to improve the user experience, as well as some measures that can mitigate the effects of these challenges. No studies were found within the scope of ATM to answer this question (Table 7).

Table 7. Challenges in performing personalization reported in the studies

Challenges to consider in personalization	Papers	Number of papers
Interface without support for personalization	L14, L21, L22	3
Data selection	L2, L12, L21	3
User learning speed of the personalized interface	L21, L23	2
Marked user preferences	L1, L3	2
Complexity of the tasks to be personalized	L22, L23	2
User privacy	L4, L20	2

The first challenge in implementing personalization is related to the interfaces which do not support personalization. During the software design period personalization is usually not taken into consideration as part of the design of user interfaces [26, 34]. This is partly because only scenarios that can be anticipated and which interfaces would be affected by personalization are considered [26, 34]. Likewise, the lack of a consensus on the methodology of adaptive (personalized) user interfaces generates that some approaches are used that do not allow to implement it correctly [33]. Faced with this challenge, the literature review suggests a refactoring of the interfaces of the system to be personalized, for which the relevant elements are identified, the interface is grouped into sections and the presentation of the interface is optimized. All this without affecting the functionalities provided by the system [33, 34].

The second challenge in carrying out personalization is related to the selection of information. Personalization depends to a large extent on the ability to select the appropriate user information from what we have available, which in some cases could be scarce [15, 24]. This information is what will allow the modeling of the user's needs to evolve, so limiting the space for modeling is going to influence the degree of final personalization delivered [24, 33]. The literature review shows us that one solution to deal with information selection is to employ a machine learning based methodology. This would employ only the interaction of the user with the system learning patterns, preferences and would be able to elaborate changes in the interface [15].

The third challenge in carrying out personalization is related to the speed at which the user learns about the personalized interface. Personalization of the user interface implies a change at the visual level that can have negative effects [35]. Constant changes in the interface can confuse and hinder the user's ability to learn to use the system and memorize the flows [33, 35]. The literature review proposes as a solution to section the user interface into groups, so that a fixed structure is maintained, applying personalization on these sections separately [35].

The fourth challenge to carry out personalization is related to the user's preference settings. During personalization, the user may have preferences that he/she considers to be overriding. The modeling time and information required means that sometimes short-term preferences are taken into account and long-term (overriding) preferences are ignored [14]. Likewise, when adding rules in order to take into account specific preferences identified in the user, it could be the case that a previous preference no longer complies with these new rules and is discarded [14, 16]. The literature review proposes as a solution a component that measures the user's satisfaction with the current preferences (through feedback at the end of the interaction) and can perceive if by taking into account the new preferences a primordial one that significantly affects the user's experience was discarded in order not to omit it [14].

The fifth challenge to carry out personalization is related to the complexity of the tasks to be personalized. The personalization capabilities applied in the system are influenced by the complexity of the task to be performed by the user [34]. More complex tasks can benefit from personalization, while for simple ones it could be counterproductive [34, 35]. The literature review shows that it is necessary to correctly identify which elements to personalize in order not to hinder the tasks according to the system where it is being applied [34, 35].

Finally, the sixth challenge to carry out personalization is related to user privacy. The information used to identify the needs to be covered must be aligned with the protection of user privacy established by the organization or legislation [16]. The concern on the part of the user about how such information is obtained should be clarified [32]. The literature review shows that contextual information from the user's interaction with the system can be used instead of information that could be sensitive [16, 32].

4.3 Response to Question P3

To answer the third review question (What user information is considered to carry out personalization based on their interaction and what are the methodologies or techniques employed in the ATM or related domains?), a total of 20 studies were identified. From

these, 5 sources of information were identified that are used as part of the user interface personalization process and it is crucial to choose the methodology that suits the
availability of these. No studies were found within the scope of ATM that answer this
question.

Table 8. Sources of information for implementing personalization reported in the studies

Sources of information used in personalization	Papers	Number of papers
Interaction with interface elements	L5, L6, L8, L13, L14, L19, L20, L22	8
Feedback on implemented actions	L4, L7, L12, L15, L18	5
Flow chosen to perform a task	L1, L14, L16	3
Historical user information	L2, L7, L15	3
Contextual user information	L10, L17	2

The first source of information used to carry out personalization is the interaction
with the interface elements. The information generated by the user's interaction with the
system is very useful to implement personalization. The choice of the elements that make
up the interface allows identifying user preferences and categorizing them according to
these through profiles [17]. Some methodologies even define attributes to these elements
so that, taking into account the relevance given to them by the user, they are adapted
in the interface. To achieve these, a weight is assigned to the user's preference on the
element and an algorithm is in charge of finding the optimal distribution [18, 25, 26,
31, 32]. Likewise, information about the choice of interface elements allows us another
approach focused on segmenting the content in which the user might be most interested
[20]. Additionally, approaches whose goal is focused on reducing interface usage time
employ interaction information to define a minimum set of actions to complete a task.
With this set they minimize the interface to what is necessary for the specific user [34].

The second source of information used to carry out personalization is the feedback
on the implemented actions. The feedback windows with which the user interacts are
another source of information to be taken into account. Based on the user's responses,
personalization actions are suggested that could fit the user's profile [16, 24]. Likewise, through the reward/punishment method, it is possible to evaluate whether the
personalization has been to the user's liking or whether it requires adjustments [19, 30].
Additionally, a set of actions for which the user has a higher perception of usefulness
can be generated and compared with profiles similar to theirs in order to personalize
with actions with which they are also likely to share a preference [27].

The third source of information used to perform personalization is the flows chosen
to perform a task. This information is useful to define a set of actions that the user
performs when interacting with the system, which allows optimizing the experience

[14]. Likewise, methods employing machine learning are able to identify user patterns throughout the interaction flow in order to design an optimal flow [26, 28].

The fourth source of information used to carry out personalization is the user's historical information. Historical user information is very useful in order to take into account the preferences that characterize the user and perceive their change in the short and long term, are employed by methods to generate an action that is attached to this trend [15, 19]. Likewise, other methods employ it to perform a ranking of the user's most recurrent elements and actions in order to assign a priority to them when adapting the user interface and to make some more accessible than others [27].

Finally, the fifth source of information used to carry out the personalization is related to the user's contextual information. There are methods that use the sensors of the end devices used by the user to obtain contextual information to create a model of the user [22]. Likewise, one can take the approach of performing testing scenarios with groups of users in order to obtain feedback and confirmation on the personalization performed on the interfaces [29].

5 Conclusions and Future Work

After carrying out a systematic review of the literature, it was found that there are no articles that directly address personalization in the ATM domain. Even so, relevant conclusions have been obtained regarding customization in user interfaces and its implementation.

First of all, when it comes to personalization implementation it has been concluded that user interface personalization should be integrated in such a way that it feels natural as part of the system itself. Actions should be aligned to meet the preferences of the specific user, so sometimes the user is categorized according to their preferences in order to provide relevant content. As a result, it is intended that the user perceives a positive feeling about the content and the usefulness of the suggestions and adapted elements. It is also intended to increase the level of satisfaction and reduce the average time of use by anticipating the user's actions.

Secondly, regarding the challenges to be managed in the implementation of personalization it has been identified that the degree of personalization of user interfaces is usually not taken into account during development. This is due to the impossibility of predicting specific scenarios according to the user. In the same line, it is necessary to know how to adequately choose the sources of information that will be used to perform the customization, since sometimes this information is scarce or not accessible due to data privacy, which is a recurrent concern of users. Likewise, it is necessary to take into account that constant changes to the interface may generate difficulties in learning to use the system. As a solution, the literature suggests a refactoring of the interface by selecting relevant elements that are grouped into sections that are later optimized independently. In addition, due to the time and information needed for modeling, short-term preferences may sometimes be prioritized over long-term ones, leading to the neglect of overriding preferences. Proposed in the literature review is a solution involving a component that evaluates user satisfaction with current preferences, gauged through feedback provided at the interaction's conclusion.

Thirdly, regarding the sources of information used for personalization one source of information used to carry out personalization is the interaction with the interface elements. This information allows identifying user preferences and categorizing them according to these through profiles. Other source of information is the feedback on the implemented actions. The feedback windows through which the user interacts provide valuable information for personalization. Actions are suggested based on user responses, and their satisfaction is evaluated through reward/punishment methods. Furthermore, actions perceived as more useful by the user can be generated and compared with similar profiles to personalize preferences effectively. In addition, historical user information is useful in order to take into account the preferences that characterize the user and perceive their change trough time.

Finally, as future work in the ATM domain, it is suggested to address the lack of personalization options based on the conclusions obtained from this systematic review as a starting point. This improvement implies the integration of personalization in a way that is natural for the user, taking into account his preferences. The use of information sources that take advantage of the data generated through interaction with the user is recommended. In addition, it is important to note that information from transaction records could be used in ATMs to obtain useful data, as long as the user's privacy is respected. Likewise, it is essential to consider changes to the interface without compromising the speed of user learning. For this, using segmentation on the user screen is an appropriate option.

Acknowledgments. This study is highly supported by the Section of Informatics Engineering of the Pontifical Catholic University of Peru (PUCP) - Peru, and the "HCI, Design, User Experience, Accessibility & Innovation Technologies" Research Group (HCI-DUXAIT). HCI-DUXAIT is a research group of PUCP.

References

1. Mehul, R.: Everything You Need to Know About the Personalization in UX Design. Medium (2021). https://medium.muz.li/everything-you-need-to-know-about-the-personalization-in-ux-design-72497c0f61f
2. Epsilon Marketing. The power of me: The impact of personalization on marketing performance (2018). https://www.slideshare.net/EpsilonMktg/the-power-of-me-the-impact-of-personalization-on-marketing-performance/1
3. Curran, K., King, D.: Investigating the human computer interaction problems with automated teller machine navigation menus. Interact. Technol. Smart Educ. 5(1), 59–79 (2008). https://doi.org/10.1108/17415650810871583
4. Valenzuela, R., Moquillaza, A., Paz, F.: Usability in automated teller machines interfaces: a systematic literature review. In: Soares, M.M., Rosenzweig, E., Marcus, A., (eds.), Design, User Experience, and Usability: UX Research, Design, and Assessment, pp. 275–294. Springer International Publishing (2022). https://doi.org/10.1007/978-3-031-05897-4_20
5. Aguirre, J., Benazar, S., Moquillaza, A.: Applying a UCD framework for ATM interfaces on the design of QR withdrawal: a case study. In: Marcus, A., Rosenzweig, E., (eds.), Design, User Experience, and Usability. Case Studies in Public and Personal Interactive Systems, pp. 3–19. Springer International Publishing (2020). https://doi.org/10.1007/978-3-030-49757-6_1

6. Weng, Y., Xia, S., Liang, S., Soares, M.: Usability Testing of Bank of China Automatic Teller Machine, pp. 189–199 (2020). https://doi.org/10.1007/978-3-030-49757-6_13
7. Hellmann, R.: In a mobile banking era, the ATM is more important than ever|ATM Marketplace (2018). https://www.atmmarketplace.com/blogs/in-a-mobile-banking-era-the-atm-is-more-important-than-ever/. Accessed 22 April 2023
8. Vasquez, L.: BCP: Transacciones por cajeros automáticos crecerán en los próximos años. La Cámara (2022). https://lacamara.pe/bcp-transacciones-por-cajeros-automaticos-creceran-en-los-proximos-anos/
9. International Organization for Standardization: Ergonomics of human-system interaction — Part 210: Human-centred design for interactive systems (ISO Standard No. 9241–210:2019), (2019). https://www.iso.org/standard/77520.html
10. Dyche, J.: Model Driven Architecture (2002). Addison-Wesley Educational Publishers, USA (2002)
11. Browne, D., Totterdell, P., Norman, M.: Adaptive User Interfaces. Academic Press, Computer and People Series, USA (1990)
12. Kitchenham, B., Charters, S.: Guidelines for performing Systematic Literature Reviews in Software Engineering (Issue EBSE 2007–001) (2007)
13. Petticrew, M., Roberts, H.: Systematic Reviews in the Social Sciences: A Practical Guide. In Systematic Reviews in the Social Sciences: A Practical Guide. Blackwell Publishing (2006). https://doi.org/10.1002/9780470754887
14. Mao, Z., Li, J., Tei, K.: Towards better service personalization: reinforcement learning with guarantee of user preference. In: 2022 IEEE 20th Jubilee International Symposium on Intelligent Systems and Informatics (SISY), 000391–000396 (2022). https://doi.org/10.1109/SISY56759.2022.10036280
15. Wu, Y., Li, K., Zhao, G., Qian, X.: Personalized long- and short-term preference learning for next POI recommendation. IEEE Trans. Knowl. Data Eng. **34**(4), 1944–1957 (2022). https://doi.org/10.1109/TKDE.2020.3002531
16. Silva, K.G.G.H., Abeyasekare, W.A.P.S., Dasanayake, D.M.H.E., Nandisena, T.B., Kasthurirathna, D., Kugathasan, A.: Dynamic user interface personalization based on deep reinforcement learning. In: 2021 3rd International Conference on Advancements in Computing (ICAC), 25–30 (2021). https://doi.org/10.1109/ICAC54203.2021.9671076
17. Almaghrabi, M.A., Chetty, G.: A novel data mining testbed for user centred modelling and personalisation of digital library services. In: 2017 IEEE 13th International Conference on e-Science (e-Science), pp. 434–435 (2017). https://doi.org/10.1109/eScience.2017.58
18. Brossard, A., Kolski, C., Abed, M., Uster, G.: Traveler information in ITS: a model-driven engineering approach to its personalization. In: 2014 International Conference on Advanced Logistics and Transport (ICALT), pp. 91-96 (2014). https://doi.org/10.1109/ICAdLT.2014.6864092
19. Ferretti, S., Mirri, S., Prandi, C., Salomoni, P.: Exploiting reinforcement learning to profile users and personalize web pages. In: 2014 IEEE 38th International Computer Software and Applications Conference Workshops, pp. 252–257 (2014). https://doi.org/10.1109/COMPSACW.2014.45
20. Chen, N., Zhang, L., Luo, D.: A dynamical extension framework supporting for personalized information portal. In: 2010 International Conference on E-Business and E-Government, pp. 439–442 (2010). https://doi.org/10.1109/ICEE.2010.119
21. Garzon, S.R., Cebulla, M.: Model-based personalization within an adaptable human-machine interface environment that is capable of learning from user interactions. In: 2010 Third International Conference on Advances in Computer-Human Interactions, pp. 191-198 (2010). https://doi.org/10.1109/ACHI.2010.12
22. Shankar, A., Louis, S.J.: XCS for personalizing desktop interfaces. IEEE Trans. Evol. Comput. **14**(4), 547–560 (2010). https://doi.org/10.1109/TEVC.2009.2021466

23. Klemettinen, M.: Multimodality and personalisation. In: Enabling Technologies for Mobile Services: The MobiLife Book, pp. 153–184. Wiley (2007). https://doi.org/10.1002/978047 0517895.ch5

24. Pei, Z., Zhenxiang, Z.: A framework for personalized service website based on TAM. In: 2006 International Conference on Service Systems and Service Management, vol. 2, pp. 1598–1603 (2006). https://doi.org/10.1109/ICSSSM.2006.320784

25. Sánchez, A.J., Hernández, E., de la Prieta, F., Corchado, J.M., Rodríguez, S.: Describing interfaces in the framework of adaptive interface ecosystems. In: Moura Oliveira, P., Novais, P., Reis, L.P., (Eds.), Progress in Artificial Intelligence, pp. 38–49. Springer International Publishing (2019). https://doi.org/10.1007/978-3-030-30244-3_4

26. Augstein, M., Neumayr, T.: 3 Automated personalization of input methods and processes, 67–102. De Gruyter Oldenbourg (2019). https://doi.org/10.1515/9783110552485-003

27. Durão, F., Cabral, B., Manzato, M., Fortes, A.: Evaluating Multiple User Interactions for Ranking Personalization Using Ensemble Methods, p. 721 (2018). https://doi.org/10.18293/ SEKE2018-112

28. Soh, H., Sanner, S., White, M., Jamieson, G.: Deep sequential recommendation for personalized adaptive user interfaces. In: Proceedings of the 22nd International Conference on Intelligent User Interfaces, pp. 589–593 (2017). https://doi.org/10.1145/3025171.3025207

29. Neumayr, T., Kern, D., Augstein, M., Kurschl, W., Altmann, J.: Analyzing interaction for automated adaptation – first steps in the IAAA project. Int. J. Electr. Telecommun. 61 (2015). https://doi.org/10.1515/eletel-2015-0020

30. Mezhoudi, N.: User interface adaptation based on user feedback and machine learning. In: Proceedings of the Companion Publication of the 2013 International Conference on Intelligent User Interfaces Companion, pp. 25–28 (2013). https://doi.org/10.1145/2451176.2451184

31. Bacha, F., Oliveira, K., Abed, M.: A model driven architecture approach for user interface generation focused on content personalization. In: 2011 Fifth International Conference on Research Challenges in Information Science, pp. 1–6 (2011). https://doi.org/10.1109/rcis. 2011.6006839

32. Price, B., Greiner, R., Häubl, G., Flatt, A.: Automatic construction of personalized customer interfaces. In: Proceedings of the 11th International Conference on Intelligent User Interfaces, pp. 250–257 (2006). https://doi.org/10.1145/1111449.1111501

33. Miraz, M.H., Ali, M., Excell, P.S.: Adaptive user interfaces and universal usability through plasticity of user interface design. Comput. Sci. Rev. 40, 100363 (2021). https://doi.org/10. 1016/j.cosrev.2021.100363

34. Akiki, P.A., Bandara, A.K., Yu, Y.: Engineering adaptive model-driven user interfaces. IEEE Trans. Software Eng. 42(12), 1118–1147 (2016). https://doi.org/10.1109/TSE.2016.2553035

35. Debevc, M., Meyer, B., Donlagic, D., Svecko, R.: Design and evaluation of an adaptive icon toolbar. User Model. User-Adap. Inter. 6(1), 1–21 (1996). https://doi.org/10.1007/BF0012 6652

Video Banking Adoption and Challenges
A Focus on the Austrian Market

Martin Stabauer[(✉)] and Bernd Zeller

Johannes Kepler University, Linz, Austria
`martin.stabauer@jku.at`

Abstract. This study addresses the underexplored area of video banking in the Austrian market, aiming to understand its current status, potential, and challenges. By developing a theoretical model based on UTAUT 2 and TAM 3, we conducted a quantitative survey with 1,119 participants. The findings reveal that video banking adoption in Austria is low, with only 7% having used the service, despite 40% indicating a potential willingness to use it if actively offered by their banks. Satisfaction among current users is high at around 80%, suggesting positive experiences for those who engage with the service. Concerns about data protection or technology play only a minor role, these disadvantages mentioned in the literature thus seem to be less pronounced than others. The frequently cited trust in well-known Austrian banks appears to mitigate many of these concerns. The explanation for the low usage seems to lie much more in the lack of active promotion than in the lack of acceptance. Two-thirds of respondents were unsure if their bank offered video banking services, even though such services were widely available among the institutions examined. Also, age does not have the moderating effect as it does in other studies. Our research contributes to the existing literature by highlighting the unique characteristics of the Austrian banking sector and providing empirical data on customer attitudes towards video banking.

Keywords: Accessibility and Assistive Technologies · Digital Transformation · Video Banking · Fintech

1 Introduction

Video banking is a technological innovation that allows customers to conduct banking transactions and consultations through video conferencing platforms. It has emerged as a significant advancement in the financial services sector and is provided to their customers by many banking institutions. It allows for extending banking services to remote areas and meet shifting consumer preferences, especially in the context of the COVID-19 pandemic. In the literature, the terms "video consultation" and "video banking" are frequently employed interchangeably, referring to essentially the same concept. This concept, in its broadest interpretation, entails facilitating communication between customers and advisors over the internet through established technologies, rather than representing a novel approach.

Empirical studies on consumer adoption are scarce, but generally show a positive trajectory in the acceptance of video banking, driven by convenience, and the personalization of services. Some indicate that customers appreciate the ability to conduct complex banking transactions or seek advice without visiting a branch, particularly for demographics with constrained mobility or those residing in underserved regions. However, acceptance varies considerably in many studies, with younger, tech-savvy populations exhibiting higher levels of adoption, while older generations show hesitance, often citing concerns over security and privacy.

The acceptance and expansion of video banking are not without challenges. Regulatory compliance, particularly in the realms of data protection and privacy, presents a significant hurdle. Financial institutions must navigate a complex web of regional and global regulations, such as the General Data Protection Regulation (GDPR) in Europe, ensuring that video banking services comply with stringent standards for customer data protection and transaction security.

Regarding payment and banking, German-speaking countries and specifically Austria show some specific characteristics. The Austrian banking landscape is very much characterized by a small-scale structure, a high density of bank branches and a very high density of ATMs. With 125 inhabitants per bank employee, Austria ranks fourth in the EU [10]. In earlier studies, the number of free-to-use ATMs was one of the three most important criteria for private customers when choosing a bank. The branch structure, on the other hand, was perceived less important and is also unprofitable as cross-subsidization of other business sectors is required to maintain branch density.

To date, the aforementioned specifics of the Austrian market remain unexplored within existing literature, necessitating a focused investigation. This study aims to address this research gap by examining the current status, potentials, and challenges of video banking with a focus on the Austrian banking market. To achieve this, a theoretical acceptance model is developed and tested using a quantitative survey (N = 1,119), answering the research question:

RQ: What is the current status of video banking in the Austrian banking market and what are its potentials and challenges?

2   Related Work

The needs of bank customers are subject to ongoing changes, presenting banking institutions with entirely new challenges. In the past, bank branches were always seen by customers as a symbol of accessibility and proximity [18]. However, nowadays, banking transactions are being routinely conducted online [6]. Many activities that were previously handled manually by branch staff have now been digitized and detached from their former physical location. Other studies confirm this trend, indicating that both customer foot traffic and the use of in-person services at branches are decreasing [14]. As a result, branch opening hours are being reduced, negatively impacting accessibility and, consequently, customer satisfaction [8].

Another significant factor is the changing competition from direct banks and various FinTech companies. These institutions offer Austrian bank customers significantly cheaper, sometimes even free, products due to their much lower costs resulting from minimal advisory services and hardly any physical branches. Often, these are niche offerings ("unbundling of a bank") that focus on specific areas such as payment transactions, credit brokerage, or securities trading [11]. Additionally, 45% of Austrian bank customers would be willing to open an account with globally established tech companies if attractive financial products were offered [13]. However, in terms of data protection, domestic banks are trusted the most, while tech companies rank much lower [2]. This fact may be the most important asset of the established banking sector.

The changing needs of employees must also be considered. As in many other industries, specialists are in short supply in the banking sector. In addition to salary, requirements for flexibility and work-life balance are essential criteria for attracting highly qualified employees [9]. The traditional culture of physical presence in banks can be alleviated by allowing online consultation appointments from home offices, which can meet these needs.

Potential advantages in the literature can be summarized as follows:

- Cost reductions for banks due to lower rent and ancillary expenses
- Reduced personnel requirements for banks
- Increased efficiency for banks
- Positive impact on product sales
- Customer retention even when customers relocate
- Nationwide accessibility for banks and customers
- Time savings for customers due to the absence of travel and waiting times
- Cost savings for customers
- Consultation appointments possible outside of regular bank hours
- Better compatibility with professional and family commitments
- Location-independent consultations
- Flexible working hours and the possibility of working from home for advisors

However, potential disadvantages can be found as well:

- Spatial distance
- Lack of personal contact
- High cognitive demands
- Data protection concerns
- Higher security requirements for banks and customers
- Fatigue from intensive use of video telephony
- Increased complexity due to media disruptions
- Technical barriers among different demographic groups
- Communication difficulties
- Increased competitive pressure for banks
- Evening working hours for employees

Table 1 provides a synopsis of findings from prior investigations, predominantly centered on analyzing the German, Swiss, and US markets. The values in the "Usage" column represent the percentage of the sample in each study that has already used video banking, ranging from 5% to 11% depending on the study design and timing. The "Satisfaction" column shows the percentage of respondents who were satisfied with their previous video banking experiences, generally around 80%. The "Potential" column indicates the proportion identified by the respective study authors as potential future users, typically about 40%. All these values are also reflected in our study, as detailed in Sect. 4.

Table 1. Overview of previous studies

Usage	Satisfaction	Potential	Reference
7%	80%	-	[1]
11%	-	-	[3]
-	-	40%	[4]
10%	-	-	[5]
-	-	29%	[7]
5%	77%	39%	[12]
-	85%	42%	[17]

3   Methodology

3.1   Theoretical Model

Methodologically, we adopt a framework based on factors delineated in the Unified Theory of Acceptance and Use of Technology 2 (UTAUT 2) by Venkatesh et al. [16], as this model has been conceptualized with a special focus on consumers. We make use of wide parts of the questionnaire developed in this paper to inquire about Austrian consumers' perceptions and preferences. *Price Value* was removed from the original UTAUT 2 model, due to the fact that video banking is offered by all observed banks without costs for consumers. *Use Behavior* as one of the original dependent variables was omitted as well. The actual usage is too limited to obtain valid data and test the construct. Our model solely aims to investigate the impacts of individual constructs on the intention to use. This aligns with the findings of the literature review, which indicated that the group of individuals who would use video consultations is a more valid measure than the small group that has already used them due to the lack of active offerings.

To better suit our special scenario of inquiry, we expanded upon our model with two additional factors drawn from the Technology Acceptance Model 3 (TAM 3) proposed by Venkatesh & Bala [15]. The first one is *Relevance* in the light of earlier research mentioning low demand for or even rejection of video banking, although we see that between 30 and 40% of consumers would utilize video banking if offered actively. The second one is *Computer Anxiety*, also mainly due to the aforementioned potential rejection of video banking by customers which could be driven by technical issues or concerns. This, combined with multiple studies mentioning the fear of personal and financial information falling into wrong hands, also leads to the hypothesis of *Security Concerns* having an influence on *Behavioral Intention*. Yang et al. [19] also show an influence of perceived risks on consumer acceptance in the context of mobile banking.

Moreover, we introduce two potential moderating variables: *Underage Children in the Household*, and *Standard Weekly Working Hours*, both hypothesized to exert significant influence due to the fact that new working environments (e.g., working from home or from abroad) and the demand for an optimized work-life balance play an increasing roll in consumer demands.

All these variables and their connections need to be tested and therefore lead to 48 hypotheses in total, which can be summarized as follows, whereby *IV* and *MV* should be replaced with all the independent variables and moderating variables in Fig. 1:

H$_{1x}$: There is a significant effect of *IV* on *Behavioral Intention*.

H$_{2x}$: There is a significant moderating effect of *MV* on the relationship between *IV* and *Behavioral Intention*.

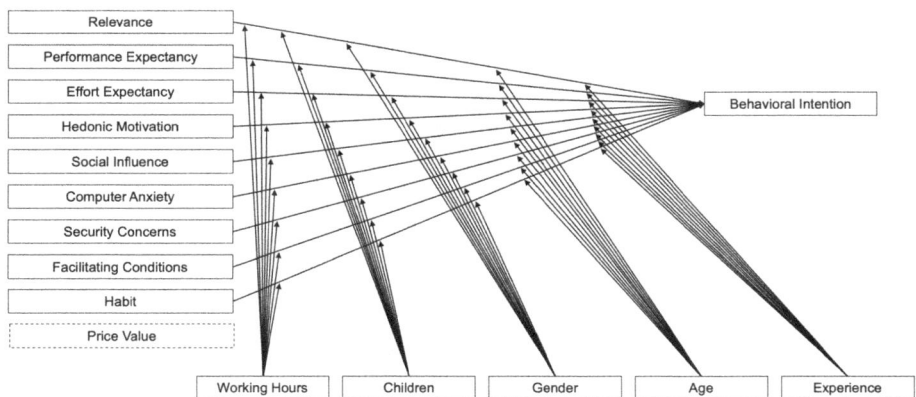

Fig. 1. Hypothesized Acceptance Model

3.2   Online Questionnaire

The proposed model underwent empirical validation through an online survey involving consumer clients of Austrian banking institutions. The questionnaire comprised questions based on the respective batteries of questions from UTAUT

2 and TAM 3, slightly adapted to fit the topic of video banking. The construct of *Security Concerns* was represented by questions from Yang et al. [19], while *Underage Children in the Household* was measured using a simple Yes/No question and *Standard Weekly Working Hours* was divided into 6 steps.

The questionnaire was active from March to April 2023 and sent out to over 14,000 consumer clients of Austrian banking institutions. The final sample after correction covered 1,119 participants, out of which were 49.2% female and 50.8% male. 30.4% had underage children in the household. The age groups were rather evenly distributed, Fig. 2 shows the numbers.

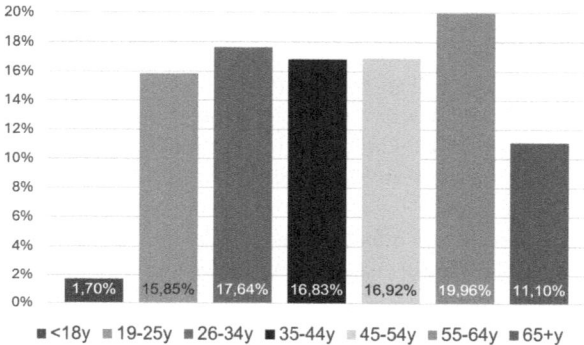

Fig. 2. Age Groups

Figure 3 shows the distribution of standard weekly working hours among the participants. The respective question asked comprised both hours of professional work and studies.

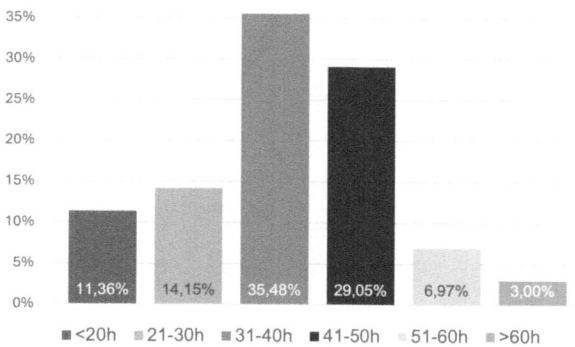

Fig. 3. Standard Weekly Working Hours

Four questions in the survey were aimed at the participants' previous experiences with video banking. However, there were only 22 participants with such experiences, which does not allow for statistical analyses. This is the reason, why the independent variable *Habit* and the dependent variable *Use Behavior* had to be removed from the model.

4 Results

Approximately 35% of participants possessed a rudimentary understanding of video banking, yet merely 7% had utilized the service to date. Some of the main reasons why video consultations have not been used so far include "no need" (57%), "prefer in-person consultations only" (33%), and "no active offer from my bank" (32%). If their own bank only offered video calls, this would completely or partially decrease the bank's value for 61% of respondents. On the other hand, offering video banking as an additional service would hardly increase the value of their bank (M = 3.02, SD = 1.45).

Remarkably, 65% of respondents were uncertain whether their banking institution provided video banking, despite the widespread availability of such services among the institutions under scrutiny. Moreover, 40% expressed an interest in utilizing video banking in the future, contingent upon its availability or better timing. Additionally, 85% had used video telephony for other use cases before, these include 81% private calls, 66% business calls, and 33% for educational purposes. The statement "Video calls or video conferences have become a habit for me" is somewhat or completely agreed with by 45% of respondents, while only 34% disagree.

38% of participants indicated a willingness to engage in pure video consultation services if banking fees were reduced by half, underscoring the significance of cost considerations in consumer decision-making, a finding consistent with previous research. On the other hand, 36% would prefer to pay the full fees to have both personal and online consultation.

We also investigated which channels consumers prefer for consultations in various use cases. These use cases included opening a checking account, applying for a credit card, obtaining insurance, making an investment, securing financing, or acquiring a consumer loan. The channels examined comprised in-person consultation, telephone consultation, email, video banking, live chat, and online via a website or app. The results were generally consistent, with in-person consultation ranking first across all use cases. The highest preferences, exceeding 50%, were observed for financing and investments, while the lowest (26%) was for applying for a credit card. In the latter case, online channels (website and email at 18% each) and telephone (17%) followed, with video banking receiving its comparatively lowest rating of 14%. In most other use cases, telephone, live chat, and email were the least preferred channels. Video consultation was most favored for obtaining insurance (19%) and for consultations regarding investments (18%) and financing (17%), primarily at the expense of the online channel, which had the lowest scores in these contexts (7%, 9%, and 4%, respectively).

To summarize, our main findings indicate a coefficient of determination (R^2) of 0.579, which demonstrates a statistically significant relationship, as evidenced by an F-statistic of $F(8, 498) = 86.362$, $p < .001$. This means, that the model as described, demonstrates high quality and explained variance.

Among some of the examined determinants, namely *Relevance, Performance Expectancy, Hedonic Motivation*, and *Social Influence*, notable correlations were observed. Unlike prior investigations, *Effort Expectancy*, and *Computer Anxiety* did not exhibit significant associations in our analysis, prompting their exclusion from the model. The same applies to the moderator variable *Age*, for which - somewhat surprisingly - no significant influence on any of the independent variables could be demonstrated. The variable *Habit* could not be included in the final acceptance model due to the small number of people who already had prior experience with online banking; and the variable *Price Value* was already previously omitted because the banking institutions offer their online banking services free of charge to consumers.

Table 2 shows relevant statistical values regarding the identified independent variables in the model, i.e., Cronbachs Alpha (α), mean value (M), standard deviation (SD), correlation coefficient (R), unstandardized regression coefficient (B) and significance level (Sig.). This indicates that the intention to use video consultations would increase by a factor of 0.3 if the perceived relevance could be increased by a factor of 1. From this, strategic insights can be derived regarding specific areas where management should focus to enhance the intention to use video consultations.

Table 2. Independent Variables in the Model

Construct	α	M	SD	R	B	Sig.
Relevance	.83	2.97	1.23	.65	.30	<.001
Performance Expectancy	.87	2.97	0.89	.62	.25	.001
Effort Expectancy	.91	3.40	1.03	.38	−.00	.988
Hedonic Motivation	.96	2.59	1.28	.68	.28	<.001
Social Influence	.93	2.05	1.22	.51	.18	<.001
Computer Anxiety	.88	2.06	1.12	−.27	−.07	.199
Security Concerns	.76	3.04	1.14	−.35	−.15	<.001
Facilitating Conditions	.64	3.58	1.22	.28	.09	.030

We tested the influences of all 5 moderating variables on each of the 8 independent variables. 9 of these 40 potential hypotheses could be confirmed, an overview is shown in Table 3, which includes relevant statistical values, i.e., the coefficient of determination (R^2), the change of this statistic caused by the moderator (ΔR^2), the probability of error (p-Value) and the F-statistic F(HC3). The moderation effects are found to have a modest impact. Notably, experience as a moderator of effort expectancy, which influences usage intention, stands out with a 2.25% increase in explained variance.

Table 3. Significant Moderating Variables in the Model

Moderator	Variable	R^2	ΔR^2	p-Value	F(HC3)
Working Hours	Performance Exp.	.3836	.0076	.0417	4.1603
Working Hours	Computer Anxiety	.0874	.0114	.0020	9.6068
Children	Performance Exp.	.3923	.0049	.0188	5.5374
Children	Effort Expectancy	.1683	.0043	.0221	5.2560
Gender	Relevance	.4591	.0024	.0338	4.5159
Gender	Security Concerns	.1215	.0037	.0499	3.8539
Experience	Performance Exp.	.1844	.0225	.0001	15.9659
Experience	Social Influence	.3014	.0064	.0185	5.5740
Experience	Facilitating Cond.	.1194	.0135	.0060	7.5779

Figure 4 summarizes the aforementioned relations. Dashed boxes and lines show variables with low significance or moderating effects on variables with low significance. The omitted constructs *Habit*, *Price Value*, and *Use Behavior* are left out of consideration in this representation.

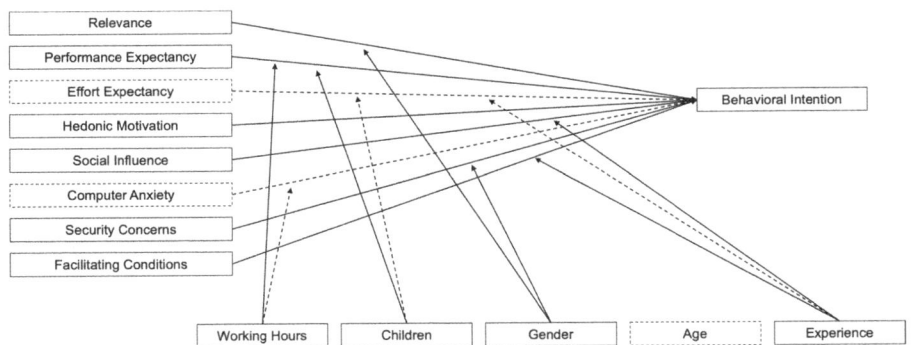

Fig. 4. Final Acceptance Model

5 Conclusion

Although video conferences are generally very widespread and established, video consultations in banks have so far been used very little. This is shown by the survey in this study and the existing literature. The reasons for this are diverse. One group sees no need for video consultations or prefers to be advised in person at the bank branch. On the other hand, there is a group of around 40% who would use video consultations, but many of them have not been actively offered this option so far. Concerns about data protection or technology play only a minor role, these disadvantages mentioned in the literature thus seem to be less pronounced than others. The frequently cited trust in well-known Austrian banks appears to mitigate many of these concerns. The explanation for the low usage seems to lie much more in the lack of active promotion than in the lack of acceptance.

The Austrian banking sector is characterized by a highly fragmented structure, a dense network of bank branches, and an extensive distribution of ATMs. While the latter is costly, it has a direct impact on customer satisfaction. According to the literature, the number of free ATMs available is one of the three most crucial criteria for customers when choosing a bank. Conversely, the branch network holds less significance and is financially unsustainable, necessitating cross-subsidization from other business areas to maintain branch density. It is particularly noteworthy that 8 out of the 10 largest banks in Austria offer video consultations, yet this service remains underutilized. Expert interviews with executives and department heads of major Austrian banks reveal that regional banks especially prefer to maintain their competitive advantage through in-person consultations at local branches. Video consultations are perceived negatively, as they standardize advisory services, potentially undermining the unique selling propositions of these banks.

This issue is complex and ambivalent. On one hand, the benefits of video consultations include retaining customer loyalty during relocations and accessing an unrestricted customer base, which also exposes banks to competitors beyond their traditional geographic boundaries. Thus, resisting the adoption of video consultations is viable only until established banks begin to intensively promote these services, thereby intensifying competition. Given the significant potential of video consultations, an avoidance strategy appears questionable. A hybrid model with a streamlined branch network could be an effective solution, integrating both traditional and digital channels to maximize benefits.

To summarize, our findings show that the acceptance of video banking is a multifaceted phenomenon influenced by technological, societal, and regulatory factors. Its evolution from a niche service to a mainstream banking channel underscores the dynamic interplay between innovation and consumer behavior. Financial institutions would be well-advised to intensify their promotion of video banking services, increase their visibility, and to refine their video banking offerings. Ongoing research, and adaption to emerging trends and challenges will be crucial for maximizing its potential benefits and mitigating associated risks. Future studies should further explore the long-term impacts of video banking on the financial landscape, particularly in relation to digital inclusivity, security, and the changing nature of customer-bank relationships.

References

1. Berg, A.: Digital Finance - wie die Digitalisierung die Finanzbranche verändert (2021). https://www.bitkom.org/sites/default/files/2019-05/bitkom-prasentation_digital_finance_21_05_2019_final.pdf
2. EY: Digitalisierungsstudie 2018 Österreich (2019). https://assets.ey.com/content/dam/ey-sites/ey-com/de_at/news/2019/03/ey-studie-versicherungen-in-oesterreich-2019.pdf
3. FMVÖ: Wert der Veränderung (2021). https://www.xn--fmv-una.at/wp-content/uploads/2021/FMVStudieWertderVernderungApril2021_1058_DE.pdf
4. Gruber, J.L., Bouché, G.: Umdenken im Vertrieb – Die Digitalisierung des Privatkundengeschäftes. In: Seidel, M. (ed.) Banking & Innovation 2017. F, pp. 31–48. Springer, Wiesbaden (2017). https://doi.org/10.1007/978-3-658-15785-2_3
5. Hafner, N.: #getintouch - Customer Touchpoints im Banking. Technical report, Hochschule Luzern Wirtschaft Institut für Finanzdienstleistungen, Zug (2020)
6. Kleine, J., Jolmes, M.: Smart Channel Banking. Zeitschrift für das gesamte Kreditwesen, pp. 32–37, March 2019
7. Müller, M.: Video Banking in the context of multichannel banking: customer perception analysis of the video banking offer on the example of the Mainzer Volksbank, Ph.D. thesis, University of Applied Sciences Worms, Worms (2016)
8. Oberle, S., Hein, H., Lahmann, M.: Bankberatung der Zukunft: Die Chancen der Digitalisierung im Retail Banking nutzen (2016). https://www.soprasteria.de/docs/librariesprovider2/sopra-steria-de/publikationen/studien/bankberatung-der-zukunft-2016-austria.pdf
9. Richardson, N., Antonello, M.: People at work 2022: a global workforce view (2022). https://www.adpri.org/wp-content/uploads/2022/04/PaW_Global_2022_GLB_US-310322_MA.pdf
10. Saravia, F.: Banking in Europe: EBF facts and figures 2021 (2022). https://www.ebf.eu/wp-content/uploads/2022/01/FINAL-Banking-in-Europe-EBF-Facts-and-Figures-2021.-11-January-2022.pdf
11. Smolinski, R., Bodek, M.C.: Start-up Garage als kollaborative Innovationsschmiede. In: Schallmo, D.R.A., Rusnjak, A., Anzengruber, J., Werani, T., Lang, K. (eds.) Digitale Transformation von Geschäftsmodellen. SBMI, pp. 531–555. Springer, Wiesbaden (2021). https://doi.org/10.1007/978-3-658-31980-9_22
12. Sonnenberg, A.K.: Deutsche sind Schlusslicht bei der Nutzung von Video-Bank-Beratungen, aber Potenzial vorhanden (2021). https://yougov.de/economy/articles/36542-deutsche-sind-schlusslicht-bei-der-nutzung-von-vid?redirect_from=/news/2021/06/22/deutsche-sind-schlusslicht-bei-der-nutzung-von-vid/
13. Sopra Steria: Banking experience report 2022 (2022). https://www.soprasteria.com/industries/financial-services/dbx-report-transform-your-bank-in-2023/dbx-report-2022
14. Terliesner, S.: In eine neue Arbeitswelt aufbrechen. Bankmagazin **70**(2–3), 12–17 (2021). https://doi.org/10.1007/s35127-021-0676-4
15. Venkatesh, V., Bala, H.: Technology acceptance model 3 and a research agenda on interventions. Decis. Sci. **39**(2), 273–315 (2008). https://doi.org/10.1111/j.1540-5915.2008.00192.x
16. Venkatesh, V., Thong, J.Y., Xu, X.: Consumer acceptance and use of information technology: extending the unified theory of acceptance and use of technology. MIS Q. **36**(1), 157–178 (2012). https://doi.org/10.2307/41410412

17. Vidyo: Video banking report 2018 - how to capture and create value from video banking (2018). https://info.vidyo.com/rs/syntellect/images/Vidyo-2018-Video-Banking-Survey-PDFVersion.pdf
18. Wannhoff, J.: Digitalisierung und Fintechs – das traditionelle Bankgeschäft im Wandel. In: Neue Erlösquellen oder Konsolidierung? – Geschäftsmodelle der Banken und Sparkassen auf dem Prüfstand, pp. 31–47. Springer, Wiesbaden (2018). https://doi.org/10.1007/978-3-658-18994-5_2
19. Yang, Y., Liu, Y., Li, H., Yu, B.: Understanding perceived risks in mobile payment acceptance. Ind. Manage. Data Syst. **115**(2), 253–269 (2015). https://doi.org/10.1108/IMDS-08-2014-0243

Financial Literacy Through Design Lens: A Scoping Review

Omar Valdiviezo[✉] [iD]

CIAUD, Research Centre for Architecture, Urbanism and Design,
Lisbon School of Architecture, Universidade de Lisboa, Lisbon, Portugal
omar.valdiviezo@gmail.com
https://ciaud.fa.ulisboa.pt/

Abstract. Financial literacy is a topic being researched from different perspectives, foci, and lenses, with theoretical to practical aims, with different instructional media supports, either printed or technological. However, given the key role of design in crafting literacy efforts, it has not been extensively researched from the design field and its sub-disciplines namely interaction design, experience design, information design, communication design, graphic design, or co-design, among others. Design facilitates an adequate articulation of a message for its audience, thus it is fundamental to analyse it from this perspective as a novel way to address financial literacy interventions, the development and deployment of its resources at different scales, either for individuals, communities, organisations or even, the government. Through a scoping literature review, this article presents a summary of the most relevant literature in financial literacy and design, analysed using design lens namely as design and its sub-disciplines playing a central role in the research process and/or its outcomes. Tentatively, I outline gaps and future research between financial literacy and design. Recently, technology advancements are being utilised to create tools that help all kinds of users, from children to retirees, to overcome financial illiteracy and achieve sustainable financial well-being.

Keywords: Financial literacy · Design lens · Scoping review · Financial education · Sustainable Development Goals · Financial education for Quality Education

1 Introduction

Over the last several years, the topic of financial literacy (FL) has gained interest and relevance for governments, institutions, organisations and individuals alike [19,24,58]. Since 2008, the research output has increased significantly, which may be explained as a result of the global financial crisis that took place in that year and the relevance of the topic for that crisis [2,28,43]. Recently, the COVID-19 pandemic, its health and work related effects as well as the prior effects of the 2008 worldwide recession, the subprime housing crisis, its grounds

A. Coman et al. (Eds.): HCII 2024, LNCS 15375, pp. 361–380, 2025.
https://doi.org/10.1007/978-3-031-76806-4_26

and impacts in almost every sector of society pointed out the importance of FL before, during, and after an economic crisis [39,44,72]. Furthermore, in some regions of the world, current wars are impacting unevenly as some countries rely on the production outputs of the countries involved in the military conflicts or have set sanctions that affect the flow of products or services disrupting their current and future availability by generating scarcity, increasing prices and unforeseen risks [9,89].

The Organisation for Economic Co-operation and Development (OECD) together with the European Union (EU) define FL as the "*combination of financial awareness, knowledge, skills, attitudes, and behaviours necessary to make sound financial decisions and ultimately achieve individual financial well-being*" [75]. Governments and institutions alike in countries either from the Global South or North follow this definition [65,67]. FL seeks to equip individuals with knowledge about money and its management that potentially foster awareness of the impact of money-related decisions and behaviours [78].

Currently, there are research works which argue the impact of FL nationwide or governmental strategies [24,56], others focus on determining which are the most relevant concepts to learn, understand, and master [94], or how to measure FL on adults or individuals [7,75] but there is a shortage of studies that focus on how to involve design into literacy interventions.

In this preliminary work, I aimed to present a scoping review [5] of FL interventions, actual designs, proofs of concept, prototypes, or works in progress reported as research contributions that employed design. I was guided by the following research questions (RQ):

- *RQ1: Which design lenses are employed in the design or implementation of FL interventions?*
- *RQ2: What are the FL dimensions -knowledge, behaviours, and/or attitudes- addressed in FL interventions?*

To this end, I expect to advance the body of knowledge by identifying published research works about FL and analysing them under the design lens umbrella.

The remainder of the paper is organised as follows: First, I present related work on scoping reviews, systematic literature reviews or bibliometric analysis in FL, as well as how FL and design are framed for this study. Then, I expound on the methodological steps followed in this scoping review. Next, I summarised key findings from FL as well as from design lens perspectives, and finally, I describe my conclusions, limitations, and recommendations for future research.

2   Background and Related Work

During the last decade, a few scoping, systematic literature reviews, or bibliometric analyses in FL and/or financial education (FE) have been published to examine different aspects, factors, foci, or research trends [2,10,19,28,29,43,50, 57,71,84,90,100]. FL is coupled with many other research fields, areas and topics such as: Economics, Finance, Business and Management, Psychology, Education and Educational Research, Mathematics, Gender, Medicine for its impact on health and well-being, and Social Sciences, which are where the most research has been done as well [100].

In particular, the following topics have become relevant in FL given their impact on governments, companies, families, and citizens: retirement [55], microfinance [6,36], women [52,54], entrepreneurship [63], investment [76], household finance [26], multidimensional poverty [98], credit scoring [18], credit use [27], numeracy and wealth [23], home ownership [97], education programs for children and adolescents [4], among many others.

To mention a few relevant systematic literature reviews, the work of Lusardi and Mitchell [57] reviewed the economics research on FL, highlighting its implications on welfare, the policies to reach a larger population, the effects and consequences of financial illiteracy, as well as dimensions of FL to be explored or understood. This is a relevant work because it surfaces the connections and relationships with many other research areas significant to our well-being.

Moreover, Santini et al. [84] identified FL factors like educational level, financial attitude, financial knowledge, financial behaviour, gender, household income, and investments which influence the credit score, and the willingness to take investment risks. Tiwari et al. [90] reviewed online FL efforts as they argued that "offline" FL is well researched but there is a lack of studies on the former. They "establish that using online tools to impart FL, coupled with digital literacy amongst individuals has led to an increased and targeted use and subscription of financial services by consumers around the world." Thus, a digital learning experience is suggested to a broader impact on citizens and institutions.

Amagir et al. [4] employed the educational lens highlighting "experiential learning" as a promising method for designing effective FE for children and adolescents in primary and secondary schools. Birkenmaier, Maynard and Kim [10] reviewed FE and financial products and/or services interventions and their effectiveness; they argue that financial knowledge alone is insufficient for today's world so financial behaviour and financial attitudes are necessary but typically the interventions in financial education do not consider attitudes for its difficulty to measure them. Thus, the development of skills in FL becomes more relevant.

The study of Zaimovic et al. [100] points out the current trends and topics in FL research namely FL of the youth, FL from the gender perspective, financial inclusion, retirement planning, digital finance and digital FL as well as identifying that financial education is the main determinant of FL. It is likely that FL is multifactorial ranging from individuals' numeracy skills to their social context [70]. While there are many dimensions and related research areas in which FL has been systematically reviewed and studied, there is a shortage of studies reviewing design, its sub-disciplines, and FL or FE.

2.1 Financial Literacy

In the literature, different definitions of FL involve practical or general dimensions, either to facilitate their observation (operationalization), their measurement, the decision-making or planning processes involved [37,80].

For this study, OECD's FL definition [7] is utilized. This definition addresses different angles of literacy such as: acquiring knowledge, applying it and developing a behaviour toward financial well-being.

Financial Literacy vs. Financial Services vs. Financial Infrastructure. As concluded by Lusardi and Mitchell [55], high availability and accessibility of bank branches for most people and access to ATMs do not imply an increase of FL levels in its citizens. In other words, access to infrastructure, by itself, should not be seen as the solution to financial illiteracy.

Rawat, Sharma and Goyal [79] associate financial inclusion with the access to digital financial services (i.e. infrastructure). While having financial infrastructure and services are favourable, more importantly, having digital financial services designed to be accessible to a larger population, it remains critical that FL should be accompanied on how to use these services on a sustainable way. For example, having access to a digital credit card but not knowing how credit works would potentially bring a debt problem if it is not used wisely.

Financial Literacy Dimensions. The OECD [74] highlights three major dimensions to perform a comprehensive measurement of FL: financial knowledge, financial behaviour and financial attitudes. Each dimension is defined as follows:

> *Financial knowledge:* "A person with financial literacy will have basic knowledge of the key financial concepts and the ability to apply numerical calculation skills in financial situations." [74]

> *Financial behaviour:* "Behaviour is an essential element of financial literacy; and possibly the most important. The positive results of financial literacy are due to behaviours such as expense planning and the creation of a financial safety net; conversely, certain behaviours, such as excessive use of credit, can reduce financial well-being. There are a wide range of behaviours that can improve or reduce financial well-being." [74]

> *Financial attitudes:* "Attitudes and preferences are considered an important element of financial literacy. If people have a negative attitude towards saving for their future, for example, it follows that they will be less inclined to undertake such behaviour. Similarly, if they prefer to prioritise short-term desires over long-term security, it is unlikely that they will have emergency savings or make longer-term financial plans." [74]

For this report, these three dimensions of FL are considered.

2.2 Design

Nowadays, design is not restricted to an aesthetics dimension as it has permeated almost any activity of our daily life. Manzini [60] says design is being applied to all kinds of problems. For example, we -as a society- design policies for the regulation of our society [45], we design the environment through architecture [86] or we design messages through communication design and its related fields as advertising, branding, graphic and visual design.

There are many facets, kinds, sub-areas or sub-disciplines that pair with design. Each of these deal with a particular phenomena. For example, Information Design (ID) addresses the organisation and presentation of data: its transformation into valuable and meaningful information [87]. Communication Design (CD) focuses on the creation of visual messages -using an array of other designs such as graphic design, branding, visual identity or typography-, their structure to reach an audience for which the message is intended to [25]. Instructional Design is a set of frameworks to "systematise the design of learning experiences" [33] which Mayer [62] argues that it is a form of ID in the sense that it is also "concerned with how to present verbal and visual information to learners in ways that promote effective learning processes and outcomes". Caliskan and Wade [12] define Strategic Design as "as an evidence-based practice aimed at proposing new ways to arrange the interaction of devices, actors, representations, and networks in any given organisation or problem universe". Likewise, Colley and Häkkilä [17] define service design as a field which applies a holistic design approach to understand and design for human experience. It aims to make services more user-friendly, efficient and desirable. Moreover, user-centered design, participatory design and co-design are approaches in which potential users of the designed artefact participate in a minor or major capacity in a stage of the design process.

All in all, design -in general- allows any person to create an artefact, structure it, build it, deliver it, and even measure its impact once deployed in the context.

Design Lens. To date, to the best of my knowledge there is no formal definition of Design Lens but Toombs et al. [92] implies approaching a problem or situation in a different way, using that particular lens in this study a design's field one. By adopting a design lens I observed the use of a specific design sub-disciple, e.g. interaction design, as an enabler/facilitator for a component of the artefact being designed by the designer. In this article, any component of a literacy intervention as well as the intervention as a whole -i.e. their deployment-.

For this scoping review I focused on areas or sub-disciplines of design that facilitate the design and deployment of literacy experiences ranging from the inquiry process and the design itself -either involving final users as participants in the process- to the implementation of a literacy intervention -e.g. by employing service design-.

3   Methods

Due to the different fields, areas and topics intertwined in FL, its complexity as well as to explore the extent of the literature in FL and Design, I adopted a scoping review for this study following the JBI Manual for Evidence Synthesis [5]. Scoping reviews are suitable when the aim is to identify the types of available research output as well as the key characteristics or factors related to a field, in this case, FL and Design [5]. In the following subsections, I describe in detail the protocol followed.

3.1   Inclusion/Exclusion Criteria and Databases

Research literature as journal articles or conference papers, peer-reviewed, written in English, and digitally available in 2023 or before (i.e. they were in press but yet published online) were considered eligible. Books, book chapters, thesis, dissertations, editorials, reports or those non-peer-reviewed were excluded. During the screening process, articles focused entirely on finance, mathematics, economics, medical or clinical trials or utilised design solely coupled with research design or study design were excluded. Table 1 on page 6 shows the inclusion and exclusion criteria.

Table 1. Inclusion and exclusion criteria.

Criteria	Inclusion	Exclusion
Language	English	Non-English
Type of research	Peer-reviewed	Theoretical, Thesis/Dissertations Non Peer-reviewed
Time-frame	2023 and before	N/A
Lens	Design and related sub-disciplines	Non-design Entirely financial, economics, mathematics Clinical Trials Editorials/Opinion works Utilized design solely coupled with research design or study design

Databases. To ample the opportunity to reach as many articles as possible I selected different types of databases given the broad impact of FL in many other distinct research fields. I grouped the databases as Design-oriented, Technology-oriented, Educational and Multidisciplinary. Table 2 on page 7 shows the databases utilized for each group.

3.2   Search Strategy

Following the guidelines for search strategy [5], I performed two searches. For the first search, an initial limited search, I sourced literature from two of the most important databases: Scopus and Web of Science (WoS). Both were chosen due to their comprehensiveness and indexing rigour for scholarly research. I used the phrase "financial literacy" (with quotation marks) as I intended a broad search. During the searching process, I applied the selection criteria in both

Table 2. Groups of databases.

Group	Database/Journal
Design-oriented	Art and Design Commons™Design Research Society General Purpose Design Journals:
	– Design and Culture
	– Design Issues
	– Information Design Journal
	– International Journal of Design
	– The Design Journal
	– She Ji: The Journal of Design, Economics, and Innovation
Technology-oriented	ACM (Association for Computing Machinery), IEEE Xplore, and Springer Link
Educational	ERIC (as for literacy)
Multidisciplinary	SCOPUS Web of Science Taylor & Francis

databases retrieving exclusively peer-reviewed journal articles and conference papers written in English published during 2023 or before.

Then, I exported the results from both databases as bibliographic files to build a visualization map (one for each database) by a keywords co-occurrence analysis, with full counting as the method, and all keywords (author and index keywords) as the unit of analysis using the VOSViewer tool [96]. A minimum occurrence of a keyword of 1 was set to display all keywords in the map (all other parameters were left as their default value). Also, an extensive search was performed in the title and abstract of keywords associated with FL and those associated with design, for example, design thinking or inclusive design.

The process mentioned above helped me to identify: a) Keywords associated with FL that are relevant in the literature and were not previously acknowledged such as *financial education, money management, personal finance(s)*, and *financial decision-making* -which were incorporated in the second search-; b) Types of designs or design approaches employed in the articles such as web design, inclusive design, participatory design, design thinking, co-design or research through design, just to mention a few. Also, I searched for terms which are under the design umbrella but don't have the design term paired such as information visualization or interactive visualization. I excluded domain-specific designs namely: food design, fashion design, wayfinding (environmental design) or textile design. The keywords identified were the foundation of the second search and were part of a further analysis as design lens. Table 3 on page 8 shows the design-related keywords identified from the initial search analysis.

Next, I performed a second search across all databases previously chartered (see Table 2 on page 7) applying the selection criteria (see Table 1 on page 6) in all searches (i.e. exclusively peer-reviewed journal articles and conference papers written in English). For the design-oriented databases I solely employed *"financial literacy"* or *"financial education"* as their content is yet limited to the design field. The second search string was:

"("financial literacy" OR "financial education" OR "money management" OR "financial decision-making" OR "personal finance")

Table 3. Design related keywords identified in initial search analysis. Alphabetically ordered.

Co-Design	Communication Design	Design for Behavioral Change
Design Thinking	Experience Design	Game Design
Graphic Design	Inclusive Design	Information Design
Information Visualization	Instructional Design	Interaction Design
Interactive Design	Interactive Visualization	Interface Design
Narrative Design	Participatory Design	Persuasion Design
Policy Design	Product Design	Research through Design (RtD)
Service Design	Strategic Design	Sustainable Design
Universal Design	User-Centered Design	Visual Communication Design
Web Design		

AND
("Co-Design" OR "Communication Design" OR "Design for Behavioral Change" OR "Design Thinking" OR "Experience Design" OR "Game Design" OR "Graphic Design" OR "Inclusive Design" OR "Information Design" OR "Information Visualization" OR "Instructional Design" OR "Interaction Design" OR "Interactive Design" OR "Interactive Visualization" OR "Interface Design" OR "Narrative Design" OR "Participatory Design" OR "Persuasion Design" OR "Policy Design" OR "Product Design" OR "Research through Design" OR "RtD" OR "Service Design" OR "Strategic Design" OR "Sustainable Design" OR "Universal Design" OR "User-Centered Design" OR "Visual Communication Design" OR "Web Design")"

3.3   Screening Process

Once the second search was performed, the results were imported into Zotero reference manager software, duplicates were removed as well as applied the exclusion criteria as nine results were wrongly identified as research articles but they represented a book, a book chapter, report or an editorial. Next, they were screened for inclusion filtering by which had the term "design" or "visualization" in their title or abstract [5]. As a result I identified 186 articles for potential final inclusion, out of them 96 were kept identified as tentative as their potential inclusion would be determined during the full-text revision. The process was done assigning "yes", "no" or "tentative" tags to each article in the Zotero. Finally, I reviewed all articles' full-text to determined its final corpus inclusion for analysis. The "tentative" tagged articles were rejected or included in the final corpus after their full-text revision. The screening process is shown in Fig. 1 on page 9.

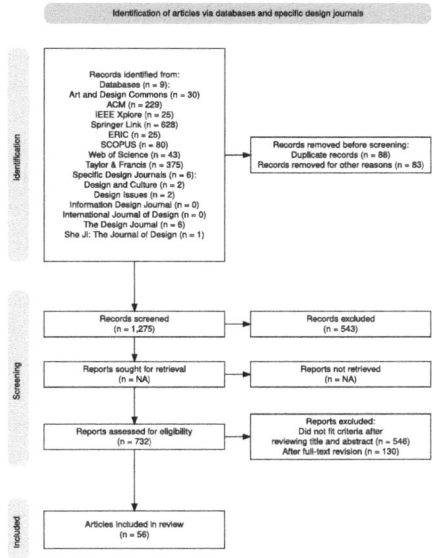

Fig. 1. Screening process workflow.

3.4   Charting

After articles' full-text revision the final corpus consisted of **56 articles**. The Google Sheet https://bit.ly/3InXfmN shows the charting summary of all 56 articles with the design lens and FL dimension(s) coded, as well as the study population and the person's stage of life where the article focused -for example: childhood, college, early adulthood, marriage, adulthood, or retirement-. Following research questions 1 and 2, I coded each article with the design lens and the FL dimension(s) -financial knowledge, behavior and/or attitudes- fostered either explicit or implicitly. I did this by assigning a tag with these titles in Zotero to each article while I carried out the article's full-text revision.

4   Results Synthesis

All **56 articles** in the final corpus were published after 2008 when FL started to become more relevant in academia as well as strategies and tools -digital or physical- were designed to find ways to address it. Majority of the studies were focused on teens, students, young adults and/or adults [34, 40, 49, 82, 88, 93] while the rest focused on families [47, 68], children [35, 42, 73, 77] and retirees [61]. Likewise, both teens and young adult's life stages are when most people are about to get into college, go through college, conclude it, or get into the job market formally which allows them to work and earn money. Hence, knowing how to manage this resource becomes critical to reach short or long-term goals namely managing an allowance or regular income, buying a house or saving for any unexpected situation like fixing a car or dealing with an accident's expenses. Research on FL for children is essential as early awareness of money management could positively impact on their future outcomes [48, 77] however it ensues some challenges such as numeracy literacy which is fundamental in FL -but is still being developed during childhood- or the role that parents play in advice or guide [51, 104]. On the other end, during or before retirement's life stage the context changes as health issues or cognitive decline arises, playing an important role in FL [16].

Most research was done in the Global North but there were examples of research done in the Global South [13, 35, 68, 69, 99, 102] which allowed to take social and cultural context into account. Additionally, it may signal that there is a shortage of research in FL and design in the Global South. Some articles [14, 69, 73, 95] took into account diverse health or individual conditions which represented the preoccupation to design inclusively towards equipping everyone with the financial knowledge necessary to interact with money.

Mobile applications were the majority of artefacts designed to address FL. Many of them used game design [8, 40, 42, 49] or employed gamification strategies [1, 83]. But not all FL efforts utilised mobile applications, some tools were designed for the web such as "Financial Web Calculators" [66] or as physical board games [48].

4.1   FL Dimensions

Majority of the designed tools or efforts for FL fall into the Financial Behavior and Financial Knowledge dimensions. Tools for budgeting [99], record expenses [34], increase savings [68], assess or manage risks [8], increase agency in financial planning [103] or change wealth management behavior [61] are examples of this kind of FL efforts for these dimensions. Zimmerman et al. [104] state that FL is a product of FE and practice in making different types of financial decisions. In this regard, financial knowledge is typically coupled with financial behavior as practicing the concepts learned is desired and convenient; for the novice as a way to understand the effects of their decisions while for the seasoned to plan ahead or envision different scenarios. Financial Attitudes are also coupled with Financial Behavior in the sense that positive attitudes foster positive behaviors [15]. Furthermore, Henchoz, Coste and Wernli [38] found that culturally shaped attitudes towards money are mostly linked with indebtedness but how to incorporate these insights in the design of FL efforts is not widely researched. Information, Persuasion and Communication Design can help in addressing this issues by carefully intertwined them into the FL efforts and strategies.

4.2   Design Lens

Several articles followed a User-Centered Design (UCD) approach to frame the design process of FL artefacts [1, 13, 82, 88] or FL intervention strategies [47]; it was the predominant approach. Human-Centered Design (HCD) surfaced as an approach in [22, 42]. Both approaches consider people and their context(s) as an essential part of the design process however in the HCD, the concept of human entails a broader understanding of people not as mere users. Several articles reported the participation of target users/people in the design process in a variety of artefacts from mobile apps [31], online tools [16], games [59] to animations [85] using Participatory Design or Co-Design methods. By following these methods, participants can collaborate with leading designers/researchers by adding a new perspectives, bring to the problem table a new unacknowledged aspect but most importantly empower them by influencing the artefacts being designed for them. Service Design was identified for mobile games [49] and the development bot-advisers [13]. Research through Design approach was identified just once [104].

Different articles reported the design of mobile or tablet apps as a platform to implement and deliver FL efforts [20, 53, 61, 64, 82, 99, 101] given the ubiquity of mobile devices to reach a broader population and utilized it while the people are in their contexts of use. For the design of these artefacts they employed Interaction Design, Information Design, Information Visualization, and Graphic Design as illustration, icons, branding, color palette, among other. However, recently an online web-based tool was designed including self-assessment quiz and instructive animations for older adults [16] which can be better perceived through a web-browser in a desktop environment. Choosing the platform to deliver FL efforts is couple with the audience its intended to.

Information Visualization and Interactive Visualization were mostly employed in the decision-making process, more importantly to assess risks and uncertainty [3, 21, 32, 81, 91]. Additionally to the support of decision-making processes, it could be relevant to apply these fields to the financial knowledge context as a way to broadly understand complex concepts such as compound interest and retirement savings.

Emotional Design [30], Information Architecture [77], Bonded Design [35], Robot Design [41], and Cognitive-Based Design [93] were identified as design methods used in the design of artefacts that are relevant in FL efforts as they can evoke emotions to users to facilitate learning or the encouragement of new behaviours, simplify the information organization, facilitate the design for groups in different life stages -e.g. childhood and retirees-, create physical robots to assist users in different tasks encouraging a behaviour, or adopting cognitive theories respectively.

5   Conclusion, Limitations, and Future Research

In this scoping review, I sought to contribute to the development of the study of FL from a design perspective. The intent was to explore and show how design and its sub-disciplines are intertwined in a panoply of FL interventions and their complexity which could inspire, guide, or ground future FL efforts. This study is part of a comprehensive project aimed at integrating design into FL strategies and efforts.

5.1 Conclusion

I have carried out a scoping review on the intersection of FL and the design field. My analysis reveals that main artefacts to address FL are digital -mobile apps, interactive web tools or videogames- but some physical -card games or board games- are also designed and utilised. Approaching both environments addresses the different and wide ranging of learning possibilities as well a people's needs and contexts. Using a design approach could help in the discovery of the suitable strategy, namely digital, physical or both. Moreover, tools for budgeting, savings and planning dominate the research efforts, this direction risks the adequate utilization of these tools which solid financial knowledge would provide; helping in cementing financial knowledge is crucial to a sustainable financial behaviour. Information Design [62] would help in explaining complex financial concepts. The results of this article are a starting point for policy makers, researchers, educators, among other stakeholders to consider design in the crafting and deployment of FL interventions.

5.2 Limitations

This paper has a several limitations. It was limited to a set of databases which did not include venues with grey literature. Future works should include this kind of databases to surface literature not properly indexed by the main scholarly databases. Search keywords variations were not considered such as "design of information" or "design of interaction" which would surface more results. FL literacy dimensions as well as design lens coding in each article was thoroughly done based on articles full-text contents and explanations, however, I acknowledge that coding could be improved, expanded or refined with more than one rater.

5.3 Future Research

Other domains where FL research and design would eventually have positive results are: a) financial robo-advisories -which advise, monitor, and assist users in their financial decision-making processes- [46] are taking momentum and the design of the information, interactions, and visualizations would be critical to the success of this kind of tools to facilitate the advisory process; b) with the availability and increasing capabilities of smart-watches and other kind of personal informatics, neuro-adaptive systems that are sensitive to users' affective and cognitive states [11] could potentially be coupled via a carefully interaction design process in spending tracking tools to convey awareness when financial decisions are about to be made under particular affective states and alert of a potential impulsive behavior.

Acknowledgments. This work is financed by national funds through FCT - Fundação para a Ciência e a Tecnologia, I.P., under the Strategic Project with the references UIDB/04008/2020 and UIDP/04008/2020.

Disclosure of Interests. The author has no competing interests to declare that are relevant to the content of this article.

References

1. Adinda, K.S., Niwanputri, G.S.: Designing for financial literacy: how adolescent learning through a mobile application. In: 2021 8th International Conference on Advanced Informatics: Concepts, Theory and Applications (ICAICTA), pp. 1–6 (2021). https://doi.org/10.1109/ICAICTA53211.2021.9640262
2. Ahmad, I., Alni, R., Arni, S., Mamduh M, H.: Financial literacy to improve sustainability: a bibliometric analysis. Stud. Bus. Econ. **18**(3), 24–43 (2023). https://doi.org/10.2478/sbe-2023-0043
3. Albrecht, S., et al.: Smarter financial life: rethinking personal financial planning. IBM J. Res. Dev. **58**(4), 1–10 (2014). https://doi.org/10.1147/JRD.2014.2329384
4. Amagir, A., Groot, W., Maassen van den Brink, H., Wilschut, A.: A review of financial-literacy education programs for children and adolescents. Citi. Soc. Econ. Educ. **17**(1), 56–80 (2018). https://doi.org/10.1177/2047173417719555
5. Aromataris, E., Munn, Z. (eds.): JBI Manual for Evidence Synthesis. Joanna Briggs Institute Adelaide, Australia (2020). https://doi.org/10.46658/JBIMES-20-01
6. Atahau, A.D.R., Sakti, I.M., Hutar, A.N.R., Huruta, A.D., Kim, M.-S.: Financial literacy and sustainability of rural microfinance: the mediating effect of governance. Cogent Econ. Finan. **11**(2), 2230725 (2023). https://doi.org/10.1080/23322039.2023.2230725
7. Atkinson, A., Messy, F.A.: Measuring financial literacy: results of the OECD/international network on financial education (INFE) pilot study. OECD Working Papers on Finance, Insurance and Private Pensions (15) (2012). https://doi.org/10.1787/5k9csfs90fr4-en
8. Bandeira Romão Tomé, N., Klarkowski, M., Gutwin, C., Phillips, C., Mandryk, R.L., Cockburn, A.: Risking treasure: testing loss aversion in an adventure game. In: Proceedings of the Annual Symposium on Computer-Human Interaction in Play, CHI PLAY 2020, pp. 306–320. Association for Computing Machinery (2020). https://doi.org/10.1145/3410404.3414250
9. Baumeister, C.: Pandemic, war, inflation: oil markets at a crossroads? (2023). https://doi.org/10.3386/w31496
10. Birkenmaier, J., Maynard, B., Kim, Y.: Interventions designed to improve financial capability: a systematic review. Campbell Syst. Rev. **18**(1), e1225 (2022). https://doi.org/10.1002/cl2.1225
11. vom Brocke, J., Hevner, A., Léger, P.M., Walla, P., Riedl, R.: Advancing a NeuroIS research agenda with four areas of societal contributions. Eur. J. Inf. Syst. **29**(1), 9–24 (2020). https://doi.org/10.1080/0960085X.2019.1708218
12. Caliskan, K., Wade, M.: DARN (part 2): an evidence-based research and prototyping method for strategic design. She Ji J. Des. Econ. Innov. **8**(3), 319–335 (2022). https://doi.org/10.1016/j.sheji.2022.11.002
13. Candello, H., Millen, D., Pinhanez, C., Bianchi, S.: Design insights and opportunities from a field study to digitally enhance microcredit practices in Brazil. In: Design as a Catalyst for Change - DRS International Conference 2018 (2018). https://doi.org/10.21606/drs.2018.339

14. Caria, S., Paternò, F., Santoro, C., Semucci, V.: The design of web games for helping young high-functioning autistics in learning how to manage money. Mob. Netw. Appl. **23**(6), 1735–1748 (2018). https://doi.org/10.1007/s11036-018-1069-0

15. Castro-González, S., Fernández-López, S., Rey-Ares, L., Rodeiro-Pazos, D.: The influence of attitude to money on individuals financial well-being. Soc. Indic. Res. **148**(3), 747–764 (2020). https://doi.org/10.1007/s11205-019-02219-4

16. Chen, K., Lou, V.: Developing an online learning tool to improve financial literacy in older adults: an intergenerational co-design case study. In: Gao, Q., Zhou, J., Duffy, V.G., Antona, M., Stephanidis, C. (eds.) HCI International 2023 – Late Breaking Papers, HCII 2023. LNCS, vol. 14055, pp. 18–27 . Springer, Cham (2023). https://doi.org/10.1007/978-3-031-48041-6_2

17. Colley, A., Häkkilä, J.: Service design methods for human computer interaction. In: Proceedings of the 17th International Conference on Mobile and Ubiquitous Multimedia, MUM 2018, pp. 563–566. Association for Computing Machinery (2018). https://doi.org/10.1145/3282894.3291046

18. Collins, J.M., Halpern-Meekin, S., Harvey, M., Hoiting, J.: "If i don't have credit, i don't have anything": perspectives on the credit scoring system among mothers with low incomes. J. Consum. Aff. **57**(4), 1605–1622 (2023). https://doi.org/10.1111/joca.12561

19. Cossa, A., Madaleno, M., Mota, J.: Financial literacy importance for entrepreneurship: a literature survey. In: Proceedings of the European Conference on Innovation and Entrepreneurship, ECIE, vol. 2018-September, pp. 909–916 (2018)

20. Cramer, M., Hayes, G.R.: The digital economy: a case study of designing for classrooms. In: ACM International Conference Proceeding Series, pp. 431 – 434 (2013). https://doi.org/10.1145/2485760.2485832

21. Daradkeh, M., Churcher, C., McKinnon, A.: Supporting informed decision-making under uncertainty and risk through interactive visualisation. In: Proceedings of the Fourteenth Australasian User Interface Conference, AUIC 2013, vol. 139, pp. 23–32. Australian Computer Society Inc. (2013)

22. De Francisco Vela, S.: Co-creating finances. a new perspective on designing for the financial world. Des. J. **20**, S444–S456 (2017). https://doi.org/10.1080/14606925.2017.1352972

23. Estrada-Mejia, C., Vries, M.d., Zeelenberg, M.: Numeracy and wealth. J. Econ. Psychol. **54**, 53–63 (2016). https://doi.org/10.1016/j.joep.2016.02.011

24. Faulkner, A.: Financial literacy around the world: what we can learn from the national strategies and contexts of the top ten most financially literate nations. Ref. Libr. **63**(1), 1–28 (2022). https://doi.org/10.1080/02763877.2021.2009955

25. Forlizzi, J., Lebbon, C.: From formalism to social significance in communication design. Des. Issues **18**(4), 3–13 (2002). https://www.jstor.org/stable/1511972

26. Gomes, F., Haliassos, M., Ramadorai, T.: Household finance. J. Econ. Lit. **59**(3), 919–1000 (2021). https://doi.org/10.1257/jel.20201461

27. Goodstein, R.M., Lloro, A., Rhine, S.L., Weinstein, J.M.: What accounts for racial and ethnic differences in credit use? J. Consum. Aff. **55**(2), 389–416 (2021). https://doi.org/10.1111/joca.12343

28. Goyal, K., Kumar, S.: Financial literacy: a systematic review and bibliometric analysis. Int. J. Consum. Stud. **45**(1), 80–105 (2021). https://doi.org/10.1111/ijcs.12605

29. Graña-Alvarez, R., Lopez-Valeiras, E., Gonzalez-Loureiro, M., Coronado, F.: Financial literacy in SMEs: a systematic literature review and a framework for

further inquiry. J. Small Bus. Manage. **62**(1), 1–50 (2022). https://doi.org/10. 1080/00472778.2022.2051176

30. Gretalita, N.W.M., Suzianti, A., Ardi, R.: Visual usability design of financial personal assistant application. In: Proceedings of the 2017 International Conference on Information Technology, ICIT 2017, pp. 142–147. Association for Computing Machinery (2017). https://doi.org/10.1145/3176653.3176700

31. Groussard, P.Y., Pigot, H., Giroux, S.: From conception to evaluation of mobile services for people with head injury: a participatory design perspective. Neuropsychol. Rehabil. **28**(5), 667–688 (2018). https://doi.org/10.1080/09602011. 2015.1117499

32. Gunaratne, J., Nov, O.: Informing and improving retirement saving performance using behavioral economics theory-driven user interfaces. In: Proceedings of the Conference on Human Factors in Computing Systems, vol. 2015-April, pp. 917–920 (2015). https://doi.org/10.1145/2702123.2702408

33. Gusukuma, L., Bart, A.C., Kafura, D., Ernst, J., Cennamo, K.: Instructional design + knowledge components: a systematic method for refining instruction. In: Proceedings of the 49th ACM Technical Symposium on Computer Science Education, SIGCSE 2018, pp. 338–343. Association for Computing Machinery (2018). https://doi.org/10.1145/3159450.3159478

34. Hahn, Y., Lee, J., Kim, M.: Envisioning personal finance and expense tracking for a sustainable future. In: DRS2022, Bilbao (2022). https://doi.org/10.21606/ drs.2022.799

35. Halloluwa, T., Vyas, D., Usoof, H., Bandara, P., Brereton, M., Hewagamage, P.: Designing for financial literacy: co-design with children in rural Sri Lanka. In: Bernhaupt, R., Dalvi, G., Joshi, A., Balkrishan, D.K., O'Neill, J., Winckler, M. (eds.) INTERACT 2017. LNCS, vol. 10513, pp. 313–334. Springer, Cham (2017). https://doi.org/10.1007/978-3-319-67744-6_21

36. Hasan, M., Le, T., Hoque, A.: How does financial literacy impact on inclusive finance? Financ. Innov. **7**(1), 40 (2021). https://doi.org/10.1186/s40854-021-00259-9

37. Hastings, J.S., Madrian, B.C., Skimmyhorn, W.L.: Financial literacy, financial education, and economic outcomes. Annu. Rev. Econ. **5**(1), 347–373 (2013). https://doi.org/10.1146/annurev-economics-082312-125807

38. Henchoz, C., Coste, T., Wernli, B.: Culture, money attitudes and economic outcomes. Swiss J. Econ. Stat. **155**(1) (2019). https://doi.org/10.1186/s41937-019-0028-4

39. Hite, N., Slocombe, T., Railsback, B., Miller, D.: Personal finance education in recessionary times. J. Edu. Bus. **86**(5), 253–257 (2011). https://doi.org/10.1080/ 08832323.2010.511304

40. Hoffmann, G., Matysiak, L.: Exploring game design for the financial education of Millenials. In: 2019 11th International Conference on Virtual Worlds and Games for Serious Applications (VS-Games), pp. 1–2 (2019). https://doi.org/10.1109/ VS-Games.2019.8864517

41. Hu, C., Chong, C., Kang, Y., Li, Y., Chen, Y.: Financial decision buddy: a decision-support tool to bridge the gaps in financial education. In: Extended Abstracts of the 2023 CHI Conference on Human Factors in Computing Systems, CHI EA 2023. Association for Computing Machinery (2023). https://doi. org/10.1145/3544549.3583835

42. Improta, V., Ferreira, A.M.: Social engagement and cultural adaptation of young refugees through gaming and playful design. In: Duarte, E., Rosa, C. (eds.) Senses

2019. SSDI, vol. 17, pp. 473–483. Springer, Cham (2022). https://doi.org/10.1007/978-3-030-86596-2_34

43. Ingale, K., Paluri, R.: Financial literacy and financial behaviour: a bibliometric analysis. Rev. Behav. Finan. **14**(1), 130–154 (2022). https://doi.org/10.1108/RBF-06-2020-0141

44. Jerrim, J., Lopez-Agudo, L., Marcenaro-Gutierrez, O.: The link between financial education and financial literacy: a cross-national analysis. J. Econ. Educ. **53**(4), 307–324 (2022). https://doi.org/10.1080/00220485.2022.2111383

45. Johnson, J., Cook, M. Policy design: a new area of design research and practice. In: Aiguier, M., Boulanger, F., Krob, D., Marchal, C. (eds.) Complex Systems Design and Management, pp. 51–62. Springer, Cham (2014). https://doi.org/10.1007/978-3-319-02812-5_4

46. Jung, D., Dorner, V., Glaser, F., Morana, S.: Robo-advisory: digitalization and automation of financial advisory. Bus. Info. Syst. Eng. **60**(1), 81–86 (2018). https://doi.org/10.1007/s12599-018-0521-9

47. Kaittila, A., et al.: A pilot randomized controlled trial of intervention for social work clients with children facing complex financial problems in Finland (FinSoc): a study protocol. J. Evid. Based Soc. Work **21**(1), 32–49 (2023). https://doi.org/10.1080/26408066.2023.2257174

48. Kalhe, A., Roy, A.: Enhanced learning experience with gamification to increase awareness of finance among young children. In: Chakrabarti, A., Singh, V. (eds.) Design in the Era of Industry 4.0, Volume 3, ICORD 2023. Smart Innovation, Systems and Technologies, vol. 346, pp. 267–287. Springer, Singapore (2023). https://doi.org/10.1007/978-981-99-0428-0_48

49. Kang, M., Yoon, S., Kang, M., Jang, J., Lee, Y.: Developing a big game for financial education using service design approach. J. Educ. Multimedia Hypermedia **27**(2), 267–287 (2018)

50. Khan, F., Siddiqui, M.A., Imtiaz, S.: Role of financial literacy in achieving financial inclusion: a review, synthesis and research agenda. Cogent Bus. Manage. **9**(1), 2034236 (2022). https://doi.org/10.1080/23311975.2022.2034236

51. Knook, D., et al.: Family valuet: a digital allowance tool for both parent and child. In: Proceedings - D and E 2016: 10th International Conference on Design and Emotion - Celebration and Contemplation, pp. 681–687 (2016)

52. Koomson, I., Villano, R., Hadley, D.: Intensifying financial inclusion through the provision of financial literacy training: a gendered perspective. Appl. Econ. **52**(4), 375–387 (2020). https://doi.org/10.1080/00036846.2019.1645943

53. Kreitmayer, S., Rogers, Y., Laney, R., Peake, S.: UniPad: orchestrating collaborative activities through shared tablets and an integrated wall display. In: Proceedings of the 2013 ACM International Joint Conference on Pervasive and Ubiquitous Computing, UbiComp 2013, pp. 801–810. Association for Computing Machinery (2013). https://doi.org/10.1145/2493432.2493506

54. Lee, C.W., Huruta, A.D.: Green microfinance and women's empowerment: why does financial literacy matter? Sustainability **14**(5), 3130 (2022). https://doi.org/10.3390/su14053130

55. Lusardi, A., Mitchell, O.S.: Financial literacy and planning: implications for retirement well-being. In: Financial Literacy: Implications for Retirement Security and the Financial Marketplace. Oxford University Press (2011). https://doi.org/10.1093/acprof:oso/9780199696819.003.0002

56. Lusardi, A., Mitchell, O.S.: Financial literacy around the world: an overview. J. Pension Econ. Finan. **10**(4), 497–508 (2011). https://doi.org/10.1017/S1474747211000448

57. Lusardi, A., Mitchell, O.S.: The economic importance of financial literacy: theory and evidence. J. Econ. Lit. **52**(1), 5–44 (2014). https://doi.org/10.1257/jel.52.1.5
58. Lusardi, A., Mitchell, O.S.: The importance of financial literacy: opening a new field. J. Econ. Perspect. **37**(4), 137–154 (2023). https://www.jstor.org/stable/27258129
59. Makri, M., Tsolaki, M.: Innovative serious games for people with dementia developed through intergenerational interventions.: the "bridge" project: a European innovative approach. In: Proceedings of the 15th International Conference on Pervasive Technologies Related to Assistive Environments, PETRA 2022, pp. 678–682. Association for Computing Machinery (2022). https://doi.org/10.1145/3529190.3534712
60. Manzini, E.: Design, When Everybody Designs: An Introduction to Design for Social Innovation. MIT Press (2015). https://doi.org/10.7551/mitpress/9873.001.0001
61. Marcus, A.: The money machine: combining information design/visualization with persuasion design to change baby boomers' wealth management behavior. In: Mobile Persuasion Design. HIS, pp. 79–161. Springer, London (2015). https://doi.org/10.1007/978-1-4471-4324-6_4
62. Mayer, R.E.: Instructional design as a form of information design. Info. Des. J. **25**(3), 258–263 (2019). https://doi.org/10.1075/idj.25.3.03may
63. Medina-Vidal, A., Buenestado-Fernández, M., Molina-Espinosa, J.M.: Financial literacy as a key to entrepreneurship education: a multi-case study exploring diversity and inclusion. Soc. Sci. **12**(11) (2023). https://doi.org/10.3390/socsci12110626
64. Mehmood, H., et al.: Towards digitization of collaborative savings among low-income groups. Proc. ACM Hum. Comput. Interact. **3** (2019). https://doi.org/10.1145/3274304
65. Mesquita, A., Peres, P., Oliveira, L.: Financial literacy in Portugal: state of the art and gap analysis. In: Proceedings of the 3rd International Conference on Technological Ecosystems for Enhancing Multiculturality, TEEM 2015, pp. 505–509. Association for Computing Machinery (2015). https://doi.org/10.1145/2808580.2808657
66. Misina, S.: Financial web calculators. In: 2019 60th International Scientific Conference on Information Technology and Management Science of Riga Technical University (ITMS), pp. 1–4 (2019). https://doi.org/10.1109/ITMS47855.2019.8940761
67. Moreno-García, E., García-Santillán, A., Gutiérrez, A.D.l.S.: Financial literacy of Telebachillerato students: a study of perception, usefulness and application of financial tools. Int. J. Educ. Pract. **7**(3), 168–183 (2019). https://doi.org/10.18488/journal.61.2019.73.168.183
68. Mukherjee, A., Winfield, C., He, S., Casalegno, F., Ruggiero, W.: Designing financial literacy and saving tools for the unbanked and under-banked in Brazil. In: Marcus, A. (ed.) DUXU 2014. LNCS, vol. 8520, pp. 71–80. Springer, Cham (2014). https://doi.org/10.1007/978-3-319-07638-6_8
69. Munoz-Soto, R., et al.: Proyect@ matemáticas: a learning object for supporting the practitioners in autism spectrum disorders. In: 2016 XI Latin American Conference on Learning Objects and Technology (LACLO), pp. 1–6 (2016). https://doi.org/10.1109/LACLO.2016.7751760
70. Méndez-Prado, S.M., Rodriguez, V., Peralta-Rizzo, K., Everaert, P., Valcke, M.: An assessment tool to identify the financial literacy level of financial education

programs participants' executed by Ecuadorian financial institutions. Sustainability **15**(2), 996 (2023). https://doi.org/10.3390/su15020996

71. Méndez Prado, S.M., Zambrano Franco, M.J., Zambrano Zapata, S.G., Chiluiza García, K.M., Everaert, P., Valcke, M.: A systematic review of financial literacy research in Latin America and the Caribbean. Sustainability **14**(7) (2022). https://doi.org/10.3390/su14073814

72. Nguyen, T.X.T., Lal, S., Abdul-Salam, S., Khan, M.S.R., Kadoya, Y.: Financial literacy, financial education, and cancer screening behavior: evidence from Japan. Int. J. Enviro. Res. Publ. Health **19**(8) (2022). https://doi.org/10.3390/ijerph19084457

73. Ntoa, S., et al.: Analysis and design of three multimodal interactive systems to support the everyday needs of children with cognitive impairments. In: Antona, M., Stephanidis, C. (eds.) UAHCI 2015. LNCS, vol. 9177, pp. 637–648. Springer, Cham (2015). https://doi.org/10.1007/978-3-319-20684-4_61

74. OECD: OECD/INFE toolkit for measuring financial literacy and financial inclusion (2018). https://www.oecd.org/daf/fin/financial-education/2018-INFE-FinLit-Measurement-Toolkit.pdf

75. OECD: OECD/INFE toolkit for measuring financial literacy and financial inclusion 2022 (2022). https://www.oecd.org/financial/education/2022-INFE-Toolkit-Measuring-Finlit-Financial-Inclusion.pdf

76. Oppong, C., Atchulo, A.S., Akwaa-Sekyi, E.K., Grant, D.D., Kpegba, Apealete, S.: Financial literacy, investment and personal financial management nexus: empirical evidence on private sector employees. Cogent Bus. Manag. **10**(2), 2229106 (2023). https://doi.org/10.1080/23311975.2023.2229106

77. Qiu, F., Zhang, Y.: Research on the payment interface design of children's watches based on user experience effect. In: 2021 IEEE International Conference on Artificial Intelligence and Industrial Design (AIID), pp. 650–653 (2021). https://doi.org/10.1109/AIID51893.2021.9456467

78. Rani, S.: The impact of financial literacy on financial well-being: the meditational role of personal finance management. In: 2023 6th International Conference on Contemporary Computing and Informatics (IC3I), vol. 6, pp. 2350–2355 (2023). https://doi.org/10.1109/IC3I59117.2023.10397970

79. Rawat, R., Sharma, S., Goyal, H.R.: Intelligent digital financial inclusion system architectures for Industry 5.0 enabled digital society. In: 2023 Winter Summit on Smart Computing and Networks (WiSSCoN), pp. 1–5 (2023). https://doi.org/10.1109/WiSSCoN56857.2023.10133858

80. Remund, D.L.: Financial literacy explicated: the case for a clearer definition in an increasingly complex economy. J. Consum. Aff. **44**(2), 276–295 (2010). http://www.jstor.org/stable/23859792

81. Rudolph, S., Savikhin, A., Ebert, D.S.: FinVis: applied visual analytics for personal financial planning. In: 2009 IEEE Symposium on Visual Analytics Science and Technology, pp. 195–202 (2009). https://doi.org/10.1109/VAST.2009.5333920

82. Ruensuk, M., Yoon, J., Park, C.: Amor: supporting emerging adult couples to manage finances for a common goal. In: Extended Abstracts of the 2019 CHI Conference on Human Factors in Computing Systems, CHI EA 2019, pp. 1–6. Association for Computing Machinery (2019). https://doi.org/10.1145/3290607.3309688

83. Samonte, M.J.C., Borja, J.M., Martin, L.N.O., Alvarez, M.L.T.: Kashing: a financial literacy microlecture app. In: Proceedings of the 3rd International Conference

on Communication and Information Processing, ICCIP 2017, pp. 214–220. Association for Computing Machinery (2017). https://doi.org/10.1145/3162957.3162964

84. Santini, F.D.O., Ladeira, W.J., Mette, F.M.B., Ponchio, M.C.: The antecedents and consequences of financial literacy: a meta-analysis. Int. J. Bank Mark. **37**(6), 1462–1479 (2019). https://doi.org/10.1108/IJBM-10-2018-0281

85. Schröder, K., Kohl, S., de Jongh, F., Putzu, M., Ziefle, M., Calero Valdez, A.: Rethinking pension communication – the role of metaphors in information visualization. In: Duffy, V.G. (eds.) Digital Human Modeling and Applications in Health, Safety, Ergonomics and Risk Management. Health, Operations Management, and Design, HCII 2022. LNCS, vol. 13320, pp. 416–429. Springer, Cham (2022). https://doi.org/10.1007/978-3-031-06018-2_29

86. Schumacher, P.: Design is communication. Philadelphia Mus. Art Bull. (4), 8–13 (2011). https://www.jstor.org/stable/41501091

87. Shedroff, N.: Information interaction design: a unified field theory of design | nathan.com (2014). https://nathan.com/information-interaction-design-a-unified-field-theory-of-design/

88. ohn, J.J., Sunil, A.: A better shopping experience through intelligent lists: mobile application and service design to improve the financial lives of young adults. In: Fui-Hoon Nah, F., Siau, K. (eds.) HCI in Business, Government and Organizations, HCII 2022, LNCS, vol. 13327. Springer, Cham (2022). https://doi.org/10.1007/978-3-031-05544-7_38

89. Storm, S.: Inflation in the time of corona and war. https://papers.ssrn.com/abstract=4138714

90. Tiwari, C.K., Gopalkrishnan, S., Kaur, D., Pal, A.: Promoting financial literacy through digital platforms: a systematic review of literature and future research agenda. J. Gen. Manag. Res. **7**(2) (2020)

91. Tomasi, S.D., Liu, J., Cheng, F., Han, C.: The role of individual characteristics: how thinking style and domain expertise affect performances on visualization. Info Vis. **22**(3), 265–276 (2023). https://doi.org/10.1177/14738716231167180

92. Toombs, A.L., et al.: Designing for everyday care in communities. In: Proceedings of the 2018 ACM Conference Companion Publication on Designing Interactive Systems, DIS 2018 Companion, pp. 391–394. Association for Computing Machinery (2018). https://doi.org/10.1145/3197391.3197394

93. Tran, D.L.: Cognitive-based design to influence structured financial planning and money management for young people. In: Zaphiris, P., et al. (eds.) HCI International 2023 – Late Breaking Papers, HCII 2023. LNCS, vol. 14060, pp. 539–549. Springer, Cham (2023). https://doi.org/10.1007/978-3-031-48060-7_41

94. European Union/OECD: Financial competence framework for adults in the European union (2022). https://web-archive.oecd.org/2022-01-11/621105-financial-competence-framework-for-adults-in-the-European-Union.pdf

95. Vallefuoco, E., Bravaccio, C., Gison, G., Pepino, A.: Design of a serious game for enhancing money use in teens with autism spectrum disorder. In: De Paolis, L.T., Arpaia, P., Bourdot, P. (eds.) AVR 2021. LNCS, vol. 12980, pp. 339–347. Springer, Cham (2021). https://doi.org/10.1007/978-3-030-87595-4_25

96. VOSViewer. www.vosviewer.com

97. Wang, S., Liu, Y.: Homeownership and financial literacy: evidence from China in the perspective of 'learning by doing'. Hous. Stud., 1–25 (2023). https://doi.org/10.1080/02673037.2023.2228238

98. Xu, S., Yang, Z., Tong, Z., Li, Y.: Knowledge changes fate: can financial literacy advance poverty reduction in rural households? Singap. Econ. Rev. **68**(4), 1147–1182 (2023). https://doi.org/10.1142/S0217590821440057

99. Yan, Y., Wei, H., Ho, J.C.F., Yap, A.: A budget setting design intervention for reducing personal expenses for Chinese young generation. In: Brooks, A., Brooks, E.I., Jonathan, D. (eds.) ArtsIT 2020. LNICST, vol. 367, pp. 409–424. Springer, Cham (2021). https://doi.org/10.1007/978-3-030-73426-8_25

100. Zaimovic, A., Torlakovic, A., Arnaut-Berilo, A., Zaimovic, T., Dedovic, L., Nuhic Meskovic, M.: Mapping financial literacy: a systematic literature review of determinants and recent trends. Sustainability **15**(12) (2023). https://doi.org/10.3390/su15129358

101. Zhang, Y.: The design of a mobile app to promote young people's digital financial literacy. In: Soares, M.M., Rosenzweig, E., Marcus, A. (eds.) HCII 2021. LNCS, vol. 12781, pp. 118–136. Springer, Cham (2021). https://doi.org/10.1007/978-3-030-78227-6_10

102. Zhu, X., Wei, Q., Yang, H., Liang, L.: Microlearning interactive teaching to enhance Chinese university students' financial literacy. In: 2022 IEEE 2nd International Conference on Educational Technology (ICET), pp. 26–30 (2022). https://doi.org/10.1109/ICET55642.2022.9944508

103. Zimmerman, J., Forlizzi, J.: Speed dating: providing a menu of possible futures. She Ji J. Des. Econ. Innov. **3**(1), 30–50 (2017). https://doi.org/10.1016/j.sheji.2017.08.003

104. Zimmerman, J., et al.: Teens, parents, and financial literacy. In: Proceedings of the 2016 ACM Conference on Designing Interactive Systems, DIS 2016, pp. 312–322. Association for Computing Machinery (2016). https://doi.org/10.1145/2901790.2901889

Enhanced User Interaction in Mobility Decision Support Using Explainable Artificial Intelligence

Luís Valina[1], Brígida Teixeira[2], Tiago Pinto[1,3(✉)], Zita Vale[2], Sonia Coelho[1], Susana Fontes[1], and Arsénio Reis[1,3]

[1] Universidade de Trás-Os-Montes e Alto Douro, Vila Real, Portugal
tiagopinto@utad.pt
[2] LASI, GECAD and Polytechnic of Porto, Porto, Portugal
[3] INESC-TEC, Vila Real Pole, Vila Real, Portugal

Abstract. Artificial Intelligence (AI) is now ubiquitous in daily life, significantly impacting society by supporting decision-making. However, in many application areas, understanding the rationale behind AI decisions is crucial, highlighting the need for explainable AI (XAI). AI algorithms often lack transparency, making it hard to understand their inner workings. This work presents an overview of XAI solutions for decision support in mobility context. It addresses the complexity of explaining decision support models by offering explanations in various formats tailored to different user profiles. By integrating language models, XAI models may generate texts with varying technical detail levels, aiding ethical AI deployment and bridging the gap between complex models and human interpretability. This work explores the need for flexible explanation formats, supporting varied user profiles with graphical, textual, and tabular explanations. By integrating natural language processing models personalized explanations that are accurate, understandable, and accessible to a diverse audience can be generated. This study ultimately aims to support the task of making XAI robust and user-friendly, boosting its widespread use and application.

Keywords: Artificial Intelligence · explainable artificial intelligence · data visualization · natural language

1 Introduction

Artificial Intelligence (AI) has become widespread in our daily lives, significantly influencing society. AI's presence is so pervasive that we routinely depend on it for decision-making in various aspects of our lives. However, for critical decisions like diagnosing diseases [1], it is crucial to understand the reasoning behind AI's conclusions. This underscores the growing importance of explainable AI (XAI). AI systems are often opaque, making it challenging to discern their internal processes [2]. The combination of neurosymbolic methods with AI technologies,

A. Coman et al. (Eds.): HCII 2024, LNCS 15375, pp. 381–390, 2025.
https://doi.org/10.1007/978-3-031-76806-4_27

such as autonomous reinforcement learning and synthetic data generation, ushers in a new era of AI capabilities. Generative adversarial networks, which drive synthetic data generation, offer an innovative solution to the ongoing problem of data scarcity in AI development. Despite these advancements, there are still limited explainable AI solutions for these emerging technologies. Most existing XAI research is focused on specific areas like healthcare and deep neural networks [3]. When faced with systems of this complexity, it is common to look for ways to facilitate the work of those who analyze them, and one of the most used means has always been to use visualization methods. In this way, the possibility of having a visual aid of the data that they generate is a direct and practical way of being able to bring together all the data in a more comprehensive way, making it possible to carry out analyses of how the systems behave throughout their execution and how, and how much the values of its variables change [4]. This type of solution can be useful in multiple application areas, including mobility. Projects such as A-MoVeR - "Mobilizing Agenda for the Development of Products and Systems towards an Intelligent and Green Mobility" can benefit from a more concrete analysis of variables to consider in the decision making process. This may ultimately lead to enabling more efficient mobility in cities, key areas to establish a mutually beneficial environment between the suggested solutions and the consumers themselves. Due to the scarcity of works covering this topic, this work studies the development of explainable AI solutions for the specific problem of decision support in a mobility context. This study addresses the complexity of explaining decision support models, including explanations, available in various formats, and tailored to diverse user profiles through integration with language models, generating texts with different technical detail levels. This research contributes to ethically deploying AI, bridging the gap between advanced model complexities and human interpretability in the dynamic landscape of artificial intelligence.

After this introductory section, Sect. 2 presents an introductory analysis of XAI where, initially, the history of AI is mentioned, followed by a brief introduction to XAI itself. In Subsect. 2.3 some models are presented, the best known and applied in representative examples. After the presentation of visualization techniques in Sect. 3, in Sect. 4 we explore the generation of natural language to describe the explanations generated as a means of transforming XAI into a reliable and transparent tool for all types of users, presenting some solutions that are already beginning to be introduced in certain situations. To conclude, we present the most relevant conclusions of this work and describe some future objectives for this project.

2   Explainable Artificial Intelligence (XAI)

2.1   Artificial Intelligence

Artificial Intelligence (AI) is a constantly evolving ecosystem, shaping the foundations of our digital reality and transcending the limitations that previously marked the horizons of innovation and an intrinsic exploration of this vast and dynamic domain, guided by a commitment to in-depth understanding and a relentless search for the next frontier of computational intelligence [6]. At its core, AI is a complex set of algorithms, mathematical models, and learning capabilities that allow machines to process information, learn patterns, and make decisions with an efficiency that defies conventional expectations.

This is not merely a technological tool; it is a catalytic force that redefines relationships between humans and machines [7]. As you continue to explore this field, an entire universe of practical applications will unveil itself, bringing together multiple sectors such as medicine, finance, transportation, security, agriculture, management, data analytics, and much more. AI not only enhances operational efficiency but also surpasses the boundaries of cognitive capabilities, prompting us to reassess how intelligence can be harnessed within lines of code. When it comes to data analysis, AI is at the forefront [8]. However, there is an even more captivating aspect to explore: the remarkable capability of generating synthetic data. This feature of AI demonstrates the innate capacity of algorithms to create, innovate, and reproduce intricate data, fundamentally reshaping both decision-making and the essence of computational creativity [9].

2.2   Introduction to XAI

In the culmination of exploring the frontiers of AI, we turn our focus to the essential facet of Explainable Artificial Intelligence (XAI) that challenges us to go beyond the raw power of machine learning, generating deep insights not just into the data, but into the data-making process itself of algorithmic decisions. At its core, XAI targets the"black box" of AI, the opaque and sometimes impenetrable stage where models make decisions without providing a transparent explanation of how, and why, they reach those conclusions. Opposing the notion of algorithms as black boxes, XAI seeks to open the curtain on the decision-making process, providing a clear and interpretable view of the internal mechanisms of models and in a way filling the gap between the inherent complexity of AI models and the human need to understand the reasons underlying the predictions and recommendations generated by these systems [10]. XAI is not limited to providing superficial explanations, it aspires to provide a deep and contextual understanding of model decisions. It involves identifying not only the "what", but also the "why", not contenting itself with highlighting only the relevant variables, but also seeking to contextualize how these variables influenced the final decision [11]. This technology catalyzes building trust between human and AI models. Understanding how a model arrives at a decision allows you to assess the legitimacy and fairness of predictions, encouraging safer adoption of AI technologies. In sectors where automated decisions impact lives, such as healthcare and justice, XAI acts as an ethical guardian.

2.3   XAI Models

The identification and mitigation of bias are critical aspects, and interpretability allows critical analysis of model decisions, contributing to equity and impartiality by offering transparent explanations and playing a fundamental role in promoting fairer results [14].

Models Applied in XAI: The challenge of interpreting complex AI models has driven the development of specific techniques in XAI and in this section, we will talk about some of the best-known. Two prominent approaches are **LIME** (Local Interpretable Model-agnostic Explanations) and **SHAP** (SHapley Additive exPlanations). These techniques play a crucial role in explaining advanced model decisions and providing interpretability at local and global levels [15].

- **LIME** is a model-agnostic technique designed to explain complex model predictions by generating approximate local interpretations and training an interpretable model in the vicinity of the instance of interest. This approach allows us to explain complex model predictions understandably, even in regions where the original model is opaque [16].
- **SHAP** is based on game theory and seeks to provide global and consistent explanations for complex model predictions where the SHAP value of a feature represents the average contribution of that feature to the difference between the model prediction and the average of all possible predictions. This approach offers a cohesive perspective on the relative importance of features in model decision-making [17].

There are also some models that are based on the previous two that appear as an alternative, but that follow slightly different approaches, such as **GraphLime**, which is applied to a specific neural network architecture, more precisely GNN [18], and **Asymmetric Shapley Values** (ASV) that allows the use of additional knowledge about the causal relationships between variables in the model explanation process [19].

Other models, such as **Meaningful Perturbation**, which are based on perturbation techniques and focus on finding variables that have negative interference on the performance of the models, can be considered as model-independent methods of explanation and where the explanation is calculated solely based on the model's reaction to a perturbed input sample These are just some of the examples of models used in XAI, there is a much greater variety and it would certainly be possible to write an article just about that [20].

3   Visualization Techniques

There are several ways to evaluate the performance of models technically applied in XAI, but over time, and with artificial intelligence increasingly present in everyday life, it is normal that not everyone can understand these processes and believe in them. Therefore intending to make the explanations provided by the XAI much more understandable, to overcome some doubts that may arise when interpreting the results, it is common to resort to different visualization techniques to facilitate the understanding of the reasoning of the models used. This need to present results in a visual way emerged as XAI moved towards a technical and machine-centered perspective which are often solutions built based on the intuition of programmers and/or experts in the field about what is a good explanation. In this sense, and more recently, a search for solutions with higher levels of usability, effectiveness, and practical understanding for common users has become of greater interest, leading to a more human-centered approach to helping them build good mental models of the system. Several visualization techniques can be used for this purpose, and, although any of them are quite viable to achieve the intended objectives, there may be situations in which a certain technique is more useful and practical to use than another. However, the choice of representation methods depends on various interrelated factors and the most contributing ones include the ease of producing the representations and overlooking the importance of the presentation method on users' comprehension

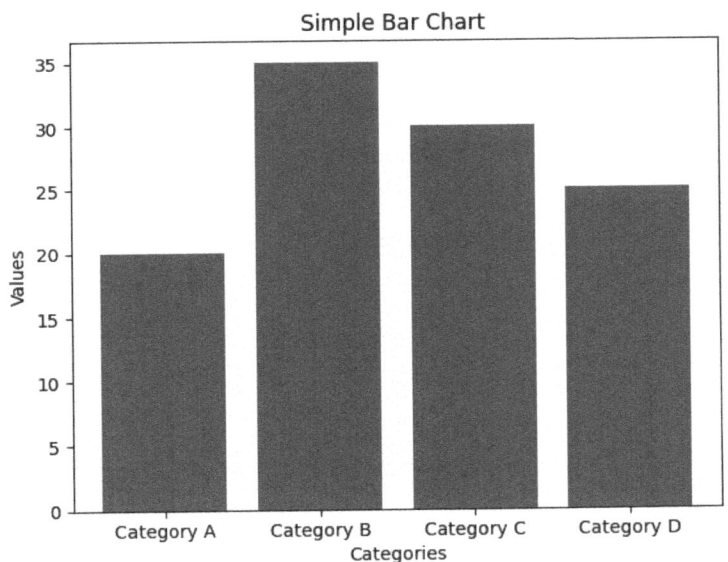

Fig. 1. Example of a Bar Chart.

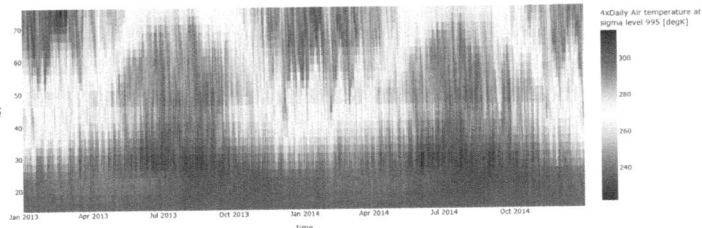

Fig. 2. Example of a Heatmap.

Fig. 3. Example of an Image Heatmap.

	XAI Models			
	SHAP	ASV	LIME	GraphLime
D	x	x	x	x
R	X	X	x	x

Fig. 4. Example of a Tabular Report.

[21]. The most popular methods are undoubtedly graphics or plots, perhaps due to the ease with which this type of visualization is generated, where representations such as bar graphs (Fig. 1), trees, heat maps(Fig. 2), histograms, etc. are included, being the chart of (vertical or horizontal) bars the most used [22]. Trees can be divided into boolean rules trees that use logical decision doors to classify records, and decision trees using boolean decisions. Heatmaps are very simple visual presentations that map a numerical value to their corresponding color and histograms are the most technical method, as their interpretation can be

complicated for users without statistical knowledge. There are also image-based presentations that are considered more sophisticated compared to the charts but also more limited as they can only be applied if the target input is an image. The main types of this category are image heatmaps (Fig. 3) which use an image as a base and add different layers of visualization, mostly coming from continuous data, the salience mask which is similar to image heatmaps in that they uses an image as a base, but instead of adding value heatmaps, they partially mask/cover the image to communicate a specific message, and image manipulation which consists of adding indicator shapes to an image to indicate a specific part of the image [23]. Although this family is close to the text category, it adopts a more structured approach to texts and is usually combined with other methods (e.g. graphics). The tabular report (Fig. 4) is the most basic in this category, conveying the desired message in a structured and direct way, as well as the decision tables, with the difference that they only have rules without any description being less flexible with the data type. As part of text explanations, the explanations in natural language, which will be deepened in the following topic, are texts written in simple English or other human languages [24].

4   Natural Language

Despite recent studies aimed at presenting explanations to the end consumer, it is still a growing phase, which, even though we are faced with strong and practical solutions from a technical point of view, does not imply that they can be used by any type of person, regardless of their technical knowledge or not, taking us to another topic, which is the communication between the system and the end consumer. The most recent research on XAI leads us to three distinct ways in which the system communicates with the user, from textual, graphic, or multimedia descriptions, using text, visual elements, and a combination of the previous ones and other representative elements, respectively [21]. Textual explanations can be expressed by rules that are simply a list of decision rules written in natural language, code, and dialogue systems, which are systems that allow the conversation between two parts even though there is no clear consensus on their definition. Nevertheless, we can generally mention the conversation agent, the conversation user interface and the chatbots are the most used or even explanations in natural language, which are an important element for interactive agents as they can provide interpretability to all types of people, with technical knowledge or not, and imitate human beings who explain their decisions verbally, becoming more efficient and enlightening than visual representations. Furthermore, as it is a more interactive solution, it allows a lay audience to have a feeling of naturalness regarding the process taking place, increasing the reliability of the explanations and helping to obtain user acceptance more easily [25]. However, this process of trying to imitate the human being, guided by mental concepts already established in human language, is not simple, and therefore, some of the most recent studies on this topic use primary language generation methods, which can, sometimes result in something not so natural due to its static nature.

Most of the approaches for generating explanations in natural language belong to the families of Natural Language Generation (NLG) and Dialogue Systems. The sentence generation task in dialogue systems is an application of NLG defined as *"The sub-field of artificial intelligence and computational linguistics that is concerned with the construction of computer systems that can produce meaningful texts in English or other human languages from some underlying non-linguistic representation of information"*. The research of NLP focusing on the transformation of computer language into natural language, having their tasks divided into "text to text" and "text to data" [21]. Some studies focus on the development of tools that seek to create an ecosystem between user and machine, where they can "dialogue" so that the machine tries to explain why certain results are achieved. There are indeed several frameworks that try to create a system that automatically provides simple, coherent, and practical explanations for a better understanding of the models to be used. Despite being a recent approach, and existing, as already mentioned, an acceptable amount of frameworks, not all are easy to access, and in this case, two Open-Source Frameworks stand out: the first one is called **RIXA**, which is an application focused on the direct interaction between the user and the machine, having a chat where the user can ask questions directly to an AI on any chart of results to his choice, for example, a Shap values chart [15], and the second one is called **OpenHEXAI** that seeks to assist humans in decision making, providing different recommendations and predictions for certain decisions to improve the transparency of assistance models and probably creating a symbiosis between human and the system so that they can make joint decisions [27]. However, another type of framework such as **INTERACTION** is divided into two crucial steps,"explanation and prediction" and "diverse evidence", consisting of four key components, the "neural end" it produces, may be highlighted. Two sequences of representations, given a pair of premise x (p) and hypothesis x (h) with an explanation Y (e) associated, the "neural infer" that is divided into "anterior network" and "outer network" where the parameters from the previous one are calculated by the previous network, only with x (p) and x (h) as inputs and the posterior parameters are determined from the inputs and outputs x (p), x (h) and y (E). Another of the components is the "neural decoder" that shapes the probability of the explanation Y (E) in a self-removed way and finally, we have the "predictor neural" where a prediction can be made only based on the premise and hypothesis, only based on explanation or, based on all previous ones [28].

5   Conclusions and Future Work Directions

Throughout this paper, we address why XAI is a very important solution for everyday life in these modern times, as it opens wings for humans and machines to work together to make supported decisions, even in high-risk areas such as medicine, economics, and mobility. Due to the transparency and efficiency of the explanations generated by XAI models, AI is more reliable. This paper has presented a study of the different types of visualization, and some visual examples of them, which can be used to represent the results of different types of models in XAI, and the use of natural language to make AI more Transparent and reliable for the user, as well as make XAI explanations comprehensive to different types of audiences regardless of their technical knowledge. This paper also briefly addresses how these models can be applied in solutions aimed at promoting comfortable, efficient and green urban mobility, providing insights to analysts so that they can determine the best way to achieve your goals.

As future work we seek to apply the explored visualization and language generation models to the enhancement of XAI solutions in the green mobility domain, especifically by making XAI adaptable to different types of users and usage contexts.

Acknowledgment. The study was developed under the project A-MoVeR - "Mobilizing Agenda for the Development of Products and Systems towards an Intelligent and Green Mobility", operation n.° 02/C05-i01.01/2022.PC646908627-00000069, approved under the terms of the call n.° 02/C05-i01/2022 - Mobilizing Agendas for Business Innovation, financed by European funds provided to Portugal by the Recovery and Resilience Plan (RRP), in the scope of the European Recovery and Resilience Facility (RRF), framed in the Next Generation UE, for the period from 2021–2026.

References

1. Lenatti, M., Paglialonga, A., Orani, V., Ferretti, M., Mongelli, M.: Characterization of synthetic health data using rule-based artificial intelligence models. IEEE J. Biomed. Health Inform. **27**(8), 3760–3769 (2023)
2. Adadi, A., Berrada, M.: Peeking inside the black-box: a survey on explainable artificial intelligence (XAI). IEEE Access **6**, 52138–52160 (2018)
3. Rayhan, S., Gross, D.: Revolutionizing intelligence: unraveling the frontiers of advanced artificial intelligence and its impact on society (2023)
4. Williams, O.: Towards human-centred explainable AI: theoretical overview and case study analysis (2021)
5. Peng, X., Li, Y., Tsang, I.W., Zhu, H., Lv, J., Tianyi Zhou, J.: XAI beyond classification: interpretable neural clustering. J. Mach. Learn. Res. **23**, 1–28 (2022)
6. Balsano, C., et al.: Artificial intelligence and liver: opportunities and barriers. Dig. Liver Dis. **55**(11), 1455–1461 (2023)
7. Harika, J., Baleeshwar, P., Navya, K., Shanmugasundaram, H.: A review on artificial intelligence with deep human reasoning. In: International Conference on Applied Artificial Intelligence and Computing, ICAAIC 2022, pp. 81–84 (2022)
8. Entezari, A., Aslani, A., Zahedi, R., Noorollahi, Y.: Artificial intelligence and machine learning in energy systems: a bibliographic perspective, **45**, 101017 (2022). https://doi.org/10.1016/j.esr.2022.1010170
9. Abraham, J., Cherian, G.J., Jayapandian, N.: Systematic review on humanizing machine intelligence and artificial intelligence. In: 2023 Second International Conference on Electronics and Renewable Systems (ICEARS), March 2023, pp. 1092–1097. IEEE (2023). https://doi.org/10.1109/ICEARS56392.2023.10084967
10. Speith, T.: A review of taxonomies of explainable artificial intelligence (XAI) methods. In: ACM International Conference Proceeding Series, pp. 2239–2250 (2022)

11. Gamoura, S. C.: Explainable AI (XAI) for AI-Acceptability: the coming age of digital management 5.0. In: 2023 IEEE International Conference on Networking, Sensing and Control (ICNSC), pp. 1–6 (2023)
12. A., S., R., S.: A systematic review of explainable artificial intelligence models and applications: recent developments and future trends. Decis. Anal. J. **7**, 100230 (2023)
13. Speith, T. : A review of taxonomies of explainable artificial intelligence (XAI) methods. In: ACM International Conference Proceeding Series, pp. 2239–2250 (2022)
14. Vilone, G., Longo, L.: Notions of explainability and evaluation approaches for explainable artificial intelligence. Info. Fus. **76**, 89–106 (2021)
15. Teixeira, B., Carvalhais, L., Pinto, T., Vale, Z.: Application of XAI-based framework for PV Energy Generation Forecasting (n.d.)
16. Ng, C.H., Abuwala, H.S., Lim, C.H : Towards more stable LIME for explainable AI. In: 2022 International Symposium on Intelligent Signal Processing and Communication Systems (ISPACS), Penang, Malaysia, 2022, pp. 1–4 (2022)
17. Oveis, A.H., Giusti, E., Meucci, G., Ghio, S., Martorella, M.: Explainability in hyperspectral image classification: a study of XAI through the Shap algorithm. In: 2023 13th Workshop on Hyperspectral Imaging and Signal Processing: Evolution in Remote Sensing (WHISPERS), Athens, Greece, pp. 1–5 (2023)
18. Huang, Q., Yamada, M., Tian, Y., Singh, D., Chang, Y.: GraphLIME: local interpretable model explanations for graph neural networks. IEEE Trans. Knowl. Data Eng. **35**(7), 6968–6972 (2023)
19. Kelen, D.M., Petreczky, M., Kersch, P., Benczúr, A.A.: Theoretical evaluation of asymmetric shapley values for root-cause analysis. In: 2023 IEEE International Conference on Data Mining (ICDM), Shanghai, China, pp. 210–219 (2023)
20. Abeyagunasekera, S. H. P., Perera, Y., Chamara, K., Kaushalya, U., Sumathipala, P., Senaweera, O.: LISA: enhance the explainability of medical images unifying current XAI techniques. In: 2022 IEEE 7th International Conference for Convergence in Technology (I2CT), pp. 1–9 (2022)
21. Cambria, E., Malandri, L., Mercorio, F., Mezzanzanica, M., Nobani, N.: A survey on XAI and natural language explanations. Inf. Process. Manage. **60**(1), 103111 (2023)
22. Sasaki, Y., Watanabe, R., Shimizu, T., Hasegawa, Y., Saitoh, F.: Visualization of evaluation viewpoints in similar customers by XAI based on review evaluation scores. In: IEEE International Conference on Industrial Engineering and Engineering Management, IEEM 2023, pp. 1052–1056 (2023)
23. Cao, K., Liu, M., Su, H., Wu, J., Zhu, J., Liu, S.: Analyzing the noise robustness of deep neural networks. IEEE Trans. Vis. Comput. Graph. **27**(7), 3289–3304 (2021)
24. Shen, L., et al.: Towards natural language interfaces for data visualization: a survey. IEEE Trans. Vis. Comput. Graph. **29**(6), 3121–3144 (2023)
25. Hu, B., Tunison, P., Vasu, B., Menon, N., Collins, R., Hoogs, A.: <scp>XAITK</scp>: The explainable AI toolkit. Appl. AI Lett. **2**(4) (2021)
26. Becker, M., Vishwesh, V., Birnstill, P., Schwall, F., Wu, S., Beyerer, J.: RIXA - explaining artificial intelligence in natural language. In: IEEE International Conference on Data Mining Workshops, ICDMW 2023, pp. 875–884 (2023)
27. Ma, J., et al.: OPENHEXAI: an open-source framework for human-centered evaluation of explainable machine learning (2024). Retrieved May 20
28. Yu, J., et al.: INTERACTION: a generative XAI framework for natural language inference explanations. In: 2022 International Joint Conference on Neural Networks (IJCNN), pp. 1–8 (2022). https://doi.org/10.1109/IJCNN55064.2022.9892336

Author Index

A. Coman et al. (Eds.): HCII 2024, LNCS 15375, pp. 391–392, 2025.
https://doi.org/10.1007/978-3-031-76806-4

GPSR Compliance

The European Union's (EU) General Product Safety Regulation (GPSR) is a set of rules that requires consumer products to be safe and our obligations to ensure this.

If you have any concerns about our products, you can contact us on ProductSafety@springernature.com

In case Publisher is established outside the EU, the EU authorized representative is:

Springer Nature Customer Service Center GmbH
Europaplatz 3
69115 Heidelberg, Germany

The manufacturer's authorised representative in the EU is Springer
Nature Customer Service Centre GmbH, Europaplatz 3, 69115 Heidelberg,
Germany. If you have any concerns regarding our products, please
contact ProductSafety@springernature.com

Printed and bound by CPI Group (UK) Ltd, Croydon, CR0 4YY
29/04/2026
02099537-0014